A Constitutional History of Secession

A Constitutional History *of* Secession

By John Remington Graham

Foreword by Donald Livingston

"What I have written I have written under a very deep sense of the responsibility imposed upon me by my position, and with an earnest desire to be guided only by the constitution. Very many will be dissatisfied with my conclusions; but I submit to the judgment of God, and also that of my fellow citizens when the present troubles shall have passed away and are felt no more."

> — Hon. Walter Lowrie, Chief Justice of Pennsylvania, November 9, 1863, upon entering an injunction to prohibit public officers from conscripting men of the Commonwealth to serve in Federal armies then invading the Confederate States.

"The most difficult task humans seem to have is approaching things in a rational way. History is replete with examples, and the Civil War is one of the them. Looking back, it is clearly evident that it could and should have been avoided."

> — Hon. John Flaherty, Chief Justice of Pennsylvania, August 26, 1997

PELICAN PUBLISHING COMPANY
Gretna 2002

Library of Congress Cataloging-in-Publication Data

Graham, John Remington, 1940-
  A constitutional history of secession / by John Remington Graham ;
foreword by Donald Livingston.
      p. cm.
Includes index.
  ISBN 1-58980-066-4 (hardcover : alk. paper)
  1. Secession—United States—History. 2. Secession—Great
Britain—History. 3. Constitutional law. 4. Constitutional history.
5. United States—Politics and government. 6. Great Britain—Politics
and government. I. Title.
  K3161 .G73 2002
  342.73'042—dc21

                                2002011343

Printed in the United States of America

Published by Pelican Publishing Company, Inc.
1000 Burmaster Street, Gretna, Louisiana 70053

*Sacred to the memory of
the Army of Northern Virginia
and the Army of Tennessee.
They fought for all of us,
of every race and nation,
in North and South America,
in Europe, Africa, and Asia,
in their time,
in the time since passing,
and in the future now approaching.*

TABLE OF CONTENTS

FOREWORD

Much time must pass in order to gain perspective on great historical events, especially those having political significance. It was over a century before David Hume's History of England was written, giving the British, for the first time, a balanced view of the English Civil War. Only recently — mainly through the work of Francois Furet — have French cultural élites dared to question the politically correct version of the French Revolution. But Americans have yet to come to terms with the barbarism of Lincoln's prosecution of the bloodiest war of the nineteenth century merely to preserve a federative union, itself founded on the right of secession.

The fundamental moral postulate of nearly all American historiography of the war is that the Union should have been preserved at all costs. A number of recent studies, however, have directly challenged this postulate: Jeffrey Hummel's *Emancipating Slaves and Enslaving Freemen;* Charles Adams' *When in the Course of Human Events, Arguing the Case for Southern Secession*; and Thomas Di Lorenzo's *The Real Lincoln, A New Look at His Agenda and an Unnecessary War*. To these we must add John Graham's *A Constitutional History of Secession*. All these authors argue, in different ways, that secession was moral, legal, and the best solution to deep conflicts confronting the American federation in 1860. All of them are Northerners.

What Graham brings to this new scholarship is an original theory of the constitutional right of secession. The right, he argues, is grounded in natural law and was first made clear, to the English-speaking world, in the principles that emerged from the Glorious Revolution of 1688 in England. This revolution has always seemed paradoxical. It was peaceful. It was carried out in the name of the rule of law; yet it involved the transfer of the Crown from James II, whose title was never in question, to William of Orange who had no legal claim to it. How could a manifestly unconstitutional act exemplify the rule of law? The answer that emerged was that a political society may confront extraordinary circumstances which require changes not possible under existing constitutional forms. Under these conditions a convention of the people — the final locus of sovereignty — or of their acknowledged leaders may lawfully institute changes not entailed by the constitution as then understood.

Graham shows that the English colonies carried this legal inheritance with them to America and how it was the animating principle of American constitutional thought up to 1860. From the first, the colonies called conventions of the people in imitation of the Convention Parliament of 1689 to petition for redress, to nullify regulations of Parliament in violation of their chartered rights, and eventually to secede. Just as the Glorious Revolution was a lawful transfer of the sovereignty of the Crown from James II to William III, through a convention of the people, so the secession of the colonies was a lawful transfer of sovereignty from the King in Parliament to the new American States.

The first written American constitution was the Articles of Confederation. In it each State is declared to be a sovereign and independent political society; the Union is perpetual; and the Articles cannot be changed without unanimous consent of all the States. Notwithstanding these constitutional restraints, the Confederation was peacefully dissolved by conventions of the people without unanimous consent of all the States, and a new Union formed. Graham argues that the States delegated limited powers to the central government, but never surrendered their sovereignty. From this Madison and Jefferson concluded that the central government could not have final say over what powers were delegated to it and what were reverved to the States. Madison held that a State had the duty to protect its citizens from illegal acts of the central government by "interposing" to declare those acts unconstitutional. Jefferson went further and said a State could "nullify" an unconstitutional act of central government. As as a final remedy, a State could call a convention of the people and vote to secede from the Union.

We have been taught to think of State "interposition," "nullification," and "secession" as renegade principles made up by Southerners to justify unworthy sectional interests. Graham makes clear that this is simply not true. They are timeless principles of natural law. And no large scale federal system that is serious about preserving both its union and the distinct cultures of its federative units can do without them. Graham shows that up to 1865 these principles were repeatedly invoked by every section of the Union. New England not only interposed and nullified what they judged to be unconstitutional acts, but considered secession in 1803, 1808, 1814, and 1843. These principles are alive in Canada today. A Canadian province may nullify certain acts of the central government in the area of civil rights. And the Supreme Court of Canada recently ruled that a Canadian province is endowed with a conditional right of secession — an opinion which Graham demonstrates to be rooted in the principles of the Glorious Revolution.

The Southern States followed these principles with legal propriety, calling conventions of the sovereign people to vote up or down an ordinance recalling all powers they had delegated to the central government. Lincoln's decision to make war was a violation of natural law. He sought to justify this action with a deeply corrupt legal theory of American Founding. Following Joseph Story and Daniel Webster, he argued that the States had never been sovereign. The States did not create the Union, he said, the Union created the States. Graham utterly destroys this absurd doctrine which has long provided a mask of legitimacy for the central government's usurpation of powers reserved to the States and the consequent destruction of local cultures and valuable ways of life those powers were designed to protect.

Lincoln's war and the ideology that justified it destroyed the federative polity of the Founders and instituted a French Revolutionary style unitary state said to be "one and indivisible." Wherever this modern unitary state has appeared in the world, it has moved in the direction of a centralizing totalitarianism. It has tended to justify acts of centralization as necessary achieving human equality and liberation. Accordingly, school children are ritualistically taught that the North's invasion was necessary to eliminate slavery. Graham has no difficulty in showing that this was not Lincoln's motive at all; that slavery was, in any case, on its way out; and that the South had ample moral resources to effect its elimination in due course.

The war was not about slavery. It was about what most wars are about: resources, territory, and revenue. Running alongside the story Graham tells about the constitutional history of secession is a story about how modern states have learned to centralize power by mortgaging future revenues. And about how the financial interests who loan the government its own credit at good interest often have a controlling voice on policy. We see how the Bank of England and the East India Company influenced government policy at the expense of the colonies, driving them to resistance. And how the American version of the same financial interests encouraged policies which heated rather than moderated the sectional conflict of the 1850s, driving the South finally into secession. While most Americans were willing to negotiate, these same interests eagerly provided the money that Lincoln illegally raised to launch an invasion.

The great merit of Graham's book is that he reminds us that interposition, nullification, and secession are timeless principles of all federative polities. In abandoning these principles for a French Revolutionary unitary state, Americans after 1865 have gradually cut themselves off from the nobler roots of their constitutional inheritance, and are thereby losing their moral and intellectual resources needed to resist the spirit-numbing centralization that is hollowing out all distinctive cultural and regional life in the United States. Americans may recall this inheritance and allow it to animate their conduct whenever they please, but it first must be shown, as Graham has eloquently done, that it is their constitutional inheritance.

DONALD LIVINGSTON

Emory University
January 8, 2002

PREFACE

The central focus of this work will be revolution, not as an armed overthrow of an established government, but as a rational and orderly process, specifically allowed by fundamental law. Far from being an absurdity contradicting itself, peaceable and lawful revolution is an indispensable principle of good government which grew out of hard necessity in human experience.

The art of government in England evolved slowly from a crude Saxon monarchy to a more elaborate constitution which was established after the Norman Conquest. It was pieced together by accommodations which matured into legal customs. In time it became the finest constitution in the world.

From ancient times established governments have been overthrown by force of arms and replaced with new regimes. Inevitably in every country situations arise in which an old system of fundamental law must give way to a new constitution, but there surely must be a better way to accomplish such a transformation than armed revolution which, in all ages, has been extremely harmful to the interests of civilization, ever portending violence, disorder, injustice, and terror. This superior alternative was perfected in a series of events in England toward the end of the 17th Century, fondly called the Glorious Revolution. It was distinguished by transfer of the Crown from James II to William and Mary.

The significance of the Glorious Revolution is that it established a particularly enlightened constitutional custom, properly so called, which gracefully accommodated natural law, then known to operate, and has since been understood to be applicable in extraordinary circumstances: — it then allowed, and still allows, in extraordinary circumstances easier to illustrate from history than to define, a peaceable and lawful transformation of government into a new legal order without ignomy or rebellion, notwithstanding the protest of the old regime, and, if necessary, contrary to charters, statutes, customs, conventions, and other provisions forming the highest law of the land.

The English historian George Trevelyan described the accession of William and Mary in his famous little treatise entitled *The English Revolution of 1688 and 1689*, first published by Cambridge University Press in 1938: — in the fifth chapter of this most standard of all standard accounts, Trevelyan spoke of the "revolutionary and extralegal basis of all that was done in 1689," because, as he rightly said, "the English Constitution cannot function legally without a King. None the less, the Revolution Settlement was first and foremost the establishment of the rule of law."

And here is the unique and curious feature of the principle of fundamental law which propelled and derives from the Glorious Revolution: — there are times when the constitution itself authorizes a revolutionary overthrow of the constitution, yet by rational and orderly means, without collapse of legal order and for the good of society, because the existing government has become oppressive, dangerous, obsolete, or ineffective. Such a transformation, as Trevelyan said, is not a deviation from, but a restoration of the rule of law.

This principle was consciously understood by the leaders of the American Revolution when they set up their republican forms of government for the several States and the Union. They knowingly allowed it to operate during their separation from the British Empire. The world knows that there was a war between the United States and Great Britain from the Battle of Lexington to the Battle of Yorktown. But little is known about the quiet and peaceful side of the of American Revolution as in Rhode Island where, before the Declaration of American Independence, the proceedings of the Convention Parliament of 1689 were perfectly reenacted and not a shot was fired.

The founding fathers of the United States consciously allowed the principle of the Glorious Revolution to operate in the demise of the old Confederation in 1788. They carefully built constitutional mechanisms for the future in the Philadelphia Convention of 1787, and such mechanisms were incorporated into the United States Constitution put into effect in 1789.

In launching their new Union in 1789, the founding fathers of the United States renewed and strengthened their confederacy of free, sovereign, and independent States. And in adapting the principle of the

Glorious Revolution to their own situation, they reserved a constitutional right of the people in each of the several States to elect a convention of delegates in extraordinary circumstances, which, notwithstanding all other forms of law, could abolish and reform their governments under the protection of the Union, or, if circumstances warranted, could withdraw or secede from the Union, and assume their place among the nations of the earth. This primordial and universal right did not suddenly appear, but evolved over the course of centuries by operation of natural law made manifest in legal tradition. While it can be misrepresented and obscured, it can never be finally extinguished by propaganda and must inevitably return in human experience.

For a long while it seemed that the right of a State to secede from the Union was destroyed in the United States by force of arms overwhelming the South in 1861-1865. It has been denied by judicial decision, and discredited in literature and politics. It has become by reputation a quaint antique gathering dust, yet it is as real as human nature itself.

The deathless legions which surrendered at Appomattox Court House and Durham Station left us a timeless legacy, waiting to be rediscovered and used for the good of mankind. Their suffering confirmed for us all a right tarnished in superficial appearances but unblemished in the profundity of truth, a right never to be used prematurely or capriciously, yet indispensable to any confederacy of nations or states, — indispensable because it serves to counterbalance and discourage excessive concentration of power in the general government, — indispensable because it induces moderation and justice which, by operation of moral causes, strengthens a federal Union with patriotic sentiment, — and indispensable because, when all else fails, it provides an escape from central authority so concentrated as to be dangerous, or so corrupted and implacable as to be irreformable by the ordinary course of the law.

This legacy, being timeless, naturally belongs to the present or a future generation of the South if they wish to claim it, but mainly it belongs to any people or nation worthy of it in any part of the world in any age in history. The truth of this proposition is proved by reviewing, as I shall attempt to do in what follows, the historical sources from which this legacy was derived and shaped, and observing how it has been spontaneously reborn on our continent in our own time under circumstances very different in particulars yet very similar in principle, thus shedding light upon the future of mankind.

ACKNOWLEDGMENTS

I wish to thank Mr. Scott Thorn, Mr. Tommy Curtis, Dr. Michael Bergeron, Mr. Chuck Rand, and other friends in the Louisiania Division of the Sons of Confederate Veterans, also Mme. Lynda Moreau and Mr. Edwin Deason at the International Headquarters of the Sons of Confederate Veterans for their assistance in making the publication of this work a reality.

My gratitude is also due to Professor Clyde Wilson of the University of South Carolina, Professor Donald Livingston of Emory University, and Dr. Michael Hill of the League of the South Institute for the Study of Southern Culture and History, for their review of my manuscript and their guidance in revisions and emendations.

I am indebted no less to Professor Maurice Arbour and Professor Henri Brun of Laval University for their generosity in teaching me Canadian constitutional law and history.

Nor can I forget my wife, Sylvie, who supported me in my labors until I finished the task, neither did she permit me to doubt that one day this book would be published.

I probably would never have produced this book had I not received encouragement from Hon. John Flaherty, recently retired as Chief Justice of Pennsylvania after a career on the bench which demonstrates that the judiciary, despite its human imperfections, can be made to work in keeping with high ideals for the good of mankind.

The views hereinafter expressed will please some and displease others, but they represent the fairest conclusions I could reach after many years of intensive study and reflection on questions delicate and difficult, and I alone take responsibility for them.   — J. R. G.

A Constitutional History of Secession

CHAPTER I

THE BRITISH CROWN

Whatever its form, whether written or customary, whether adopted on some solemn occasion or slowly developed over long ages, every civilized constitution organizes a government, and defines, vests, and limits its powers. But there is always an authority above the constitution, which creates and modifies fundamental law, and this extraordinary authority, exceeding the regular powers of the government, is the sovereign power, which has certain distinctive attributes.

At the time of the American Revolution, these attributes were identified by Sir William Blackstone, famous professor and honored scholar at Oxford University, then Justice of the King's Bench, later Justice of the Court of Common Pleas, and, in American eyes, the greatest of all commentators on the laws of England. He was the revered teacher of the lawyers, judges, and statesmen who lived during the infancy of the United States, and was considered on the western side of the Atlantic the best authority on the British Constitution.[1] The United States Constitution, as framed in the Philadelphia Convention of 1787, was an affirmation of or deviation from the British Constitution, not necessarily as it actually was at the time of the American Revolution, but as Blackstone had described it.

So it was that Americans blamed King George III in their Declaration of Independence, as if he were the real culprit behind their troubles, yet "Farmer George," as his loving subjects called him in England, "was one of the most conscientious sovereigns who ever sat upon the English throne."[2]

Americans blamed George III, in part because Blackstone, out of devotion to the Crown, did not explain that royal prerogatives were not necessarily the personal powers of the King. Nor, as among the constitutional

25

councils of the Crown, did Blackstone even mention the prime minister and his cabinet who were chosen by the party in control of the House of Commons, and governed the country by "advising" the King.

In framing the clauses on the powers of the President, the Philadelphia Convention remodeled the powers of the King,[3] as if the King were wholly free to exercise his prerogatives as he saw fit. And because most of them assumed that Blackstone was fully accurate, the framers produced by historical accident a presidential form of government in the United States, with an executive power fully independent of Congress.

So also when Blackstone wrote about the attributes of sovereign power, his remarks were noticed by Americans who in this way understood that sovereign power was something higher and grander than the regular powers of government.

The attributes of sovereign power were identified by Blackstone as preeminence, perfection, and perpetuity, which were vested in the King, and omnipotence, which came to be vested in the Commons, Lords, and King in Parliament:

— Because the King was preeminent, he was "the supreme head of the realm, in matters both civil and ecclesiastical, and of consequence inferior to no man on earth, dependent on no man, accountable to no man."[4] And so it was rhetorically asked, "Who shall command the King?"

The King was beyond the jurisdiction of every court of justice, and so could never be sued. If a subject had a private demand of the King, he could petition his Majesty in the Court of Chancery. And the Chancellor, who was styled "keeper of the King's conscience," entertained the petition and did right, but only by grace of his Majesty. If the petition was found to be just, the decree merely "recommended" that the Crown should consider making compensation in the manner proposed.

And the person of the King was sacred. However arbitrary or tyrannical the measures pursued in his reign, his Majesty could never be lawfully tried or punished for any crime or misdemeanor. Under the ancient Statute of 25 Edward III, Chapter 2 (1351), the first act condemned as high treason was to "compass or imagine the death of our Lord the King." No pretext could ever justify even the thought of taking the King's life.

Yet, if a public wrong was done in the name of the Crown, although his Majesty was untouchable, his ministers and counselors could be brought to justice on a bill of indictment, bill of impeachment, or bill of attainder, for having given bad advice or improper assistance to the King.

— Because his Majesty was perfect, it was said, "The King can do no wrong."[5] This maxim is often misunderstood. It did not mean that everything done by the government was just and lawful. On the contrary, it presupposed that the government would do wrong. But, whatever was exceptionable in public affairs, it could not be imputed to the King, nor was he ever answerable to anyone for what had been done. The Crown existed for the welfare of the people. Therefore, no power of the King could be exercised in the eyes of the law to the prejudice of his subjects or the common good.

Not only was the King incapable of doing wrong, he was incapable of even thinking wrong, for in him there was no folly, wickedness, or deceit. The principle is best illustrated by the *Case of Monopolies*, 11 Coke 84b (K. B. 1603), in which it was held that a patent of Queen Elizabeth I granting a monopoly in the manufacture and sale of playing cards ran against the common law and certain statutes; that, being perfect, her Majesty could not have intended anything illegal; and that, therefore, the patent in question was null and void.

— The King was also perpetual or immortal. Hence, it was said, "The King never dies. Henry, Edward, or George may die, but the King survives them all."[6] The moment the reigning prince closed his eyes for the last time, the Crown passed at once to his heir who then and there, without interregnum, became King. Although Charles II was not able to govern until many years later, the beginning of his reign was reckoned from the illegal execution of his father in 1649.

The sovereign attributes of the King were never meant to draw a picture of the human personalities who occupied the throne of England. They portrayed a constitutional ideal.

The Crown was a legal institution giving permanence and decency to government. His Majesty was a constitutional symbol of the whole nation, alive and human, who could be revered as a father and a prince representing everything good and right in public life.

— There remains the attribute of omnipotence, which includes the transcendent authority to institute and reform government, and to modify fundamental law. In every well-designed edifice of legal order, this supreme power should be clearly identified, and there should be an established procedure for making it active whenever necessary.

In 1085 A. D., William the Conqueror was "attended by all his nobility at Sarum, where all the principal landholders submitted their lands to the yoke of military tenure, became the King's vassals, and did homage and fealty to his person."[7] The attribute of omnipotence was then vested in the King. And thereafter, this extraordinary power of the Crown was actually used to create and write, by the King's hand and seal, a proper constitution for England.

The framing of this constitution by the omnipotence of the Crown began with Magna Carta as granted in 1215 A. D. by King John at Runnymede. In the 12th Article, the King promised, "Nullum scutagium vel auxilium ponatur in regno nostro, nisi per commune consilium regni nostri," — No scutage or aid shall be levied in our kingdom, save by consent of our Great Council, etc. A scutage was money to the Crown in lieu of knight service owed. An aid was a payment of money by a feudal tenant to his lord in time of need. These were the main taxes then levied. The 12th Article allowed reasonable aids to the Crown, without consent of the Great Council, only as needed to ransom the King when taken prisoner, and to pay for the royal feast of making the King's eldest son a knight, and the feast of marrying off the King's eldest daughter. The 14th Article identified the Great Council as the archbishops, bishops, abbots, earls, and greater barons of England.

Magna Carta as granted at Runnymede was in one form or another reissued, confirmed, or amplified on fifty-four occasions by the death of King Henry VI, but the most famous of these later versions was the Magna Carta given by King Henry III in 1225 A. D., on which an enduring commentary was written by Sir Edward Coke.[8]

The Confirmatio Cartarum, 25 Edward I, Chapter 1 (1297), republished anew the so-called Charter of the Forest and the Magna Carta of Henry III. It stated in the 6th Article that the King would not "take aids, tasks, nor prises, but by the common assent of the realm, and for the common profit thereof, saving the ancient aids and prises due and accustomed."

The 6th Article said in particular that taxes and confiscations required not only the consent of the archbishops, bishops, abbots, priors, earls, and barons, but also "all the communalty of the land." Before there had been only a House of Lords, but this Charter of King Edward I also acknowledged a House of Commons.

After the American Revolution, a learned lawyer in Virginia explained the historical origin and growth of the House of Commons in England:

> "The history of the English Parliament will show that the great degree of power which they possess was acquired from beginnings so small that nothing but the innate weight of the power of the people, when lodged in their representatives, could have effected it. In the reign of Edward I, in the year 1295, the House of Commons was first called by legal authority; they were then confined to giving their assent to supplies of the Crown. In the reign of Edward II, they first annexed petitions to the bills by which they granted subsidies. Under

Edward III, they declared they would not in future acknowledge any law to which they had not consented: in the same reign, they impeached and brought to justice some of the ministers of the Crown. Under Henry IV, they refused supplies until an answer had been given to their petitions; and they have increased their powers in succeeding reigns to such a degree that they entirely control the operation of government, even in those cases where the King's prerogative gave him nominally the sole discretion."[9]

So it was that over several centuries the omnipotence of the Crown was used to redistribute the powers of government, to concede privileges and immunities to subjects, and thereby to frame an elaborate constitution in England. The inducement of withholding money from the royal treasury was mundane, but from it evolved principles which fostered higher ideals, love of freedom, and wise legal customs.

* * * * *

An important feature of the constitutional heritage of England is the definition of the rights of a free people in charters and statutes, all of them valid because sanctioned by the King.

The 39th Article of the Magna Carta of John was restated thus in the 29th Article of the Magna Carta of Henry III: "Nullus liber homo capiatur, vel imprisonetur, aut disseisietur de libero tenemento suo, vel libertatibus, vel liberis consuetudinibus suis, aut utlagetur, aut exuletur, aut aliquo modo destruatur, nec super eum ibimus, nec super eum mittemus, nisi per legale judicium parium suorum, vel per legem terrae," — No freeman will be arrested, or imprisoned, or deprived of his freehold in land, or his liberties, or the benefit of customs allowing freedom, or be outlawed, or exiled, or in any way harmed, nor shall we sue or punish him, except by the lawful judgment of his peers, or by the law of the land.

The traditional phrasing "lawful judgment of his peers or the law of the land" was eventually rendered as "due process of law,"[10] but either phrase came over time to denote a large number of characteristic safeguards: — among others, that the King could not prosecute for a felony except on presentment or indictment,[11] or accuse anybody of a crime or misdemeanor except in writing strictly pleaded,[12] or arrest anybody who might not have the legality of his detention examined on writ of habeas corpus,[13] or punish any subject save on a finding of guilty by unanimous verdict of his peers,[14] or seize the land or chattels or money of a subject save by suit on due cause found by jury,[15] or take the property of a subject for public use unless upon payment of just compensation established by law.[16]

Again, the 40th Article of the Magna Carta of John was repeated in the nearly identical words of the 29th Article of the Magna Carta of Henry III: — "Nulli vendemus, nulli negabimus, aut differemus justiciam vel rectum," — To none shall we sell or deny or delay justice or right.[17]

The courts of common law in England acquired power to grant justice in private suits, mainly by the manufacture of original writs in chancery until further creation of such writs was limited by an act of Parliament,[18] leaving them ultimately with jurisdiction over actions of trespass, case, trover, detinue, replevin, ejectment, waste, covenant, debt, special assumpsit, general assumpsit, and account, and in proceedings for certain extraordinary writs, — mandamus, prohibition, certiorari, habeas corpus, quo warranto, and scire facias.

Such actions were called suits at common law, and were triable by jury where material facts were in dispute, excepting prohibition, certiorari, and habeas corpus. As a class of litigation, the actions on original writ were the historical basis in English law of the bulk of modern cases in tort, contract, and quasi-contract. In these the remedy was limited to money judgment, excepting detinue and replevin which allowed specific recovery of chattels, ejectment which allowed specific recovery of real estate, and waste which granted partition, forfeiture, or treble damages to redress spoilage of land.

Because the courts of common law were limited in their jurisdiction, the remedies they offered were often insufficient. Sometimes there was no writ which addressed a wrong complained of. Sometimes there was a writ but it could not meet the demands of justice. Yet because in Magna Carta the King had promised justice undenied and undelayed, the Crown was obliged to go beyond the capacity of the common law.

The Chancellor, as keeper of the King's conscience, became keeper of the King's promise. The Chancellor assumed jurisdiction where the common law could do nothing or not well enough, — in traditional phrasing, whenever there was "no adequate remedy at law." He administered a new kind of justice called equity, under a new kind of procedure which was adapted from Roman law: — the pleading and practice were different; the trials were judicial, and did not include the Anglo-Saxon jury.

In equity, there were suits for injunctions mandatory and prohibitory, and for specific performance of some contracts, most particularly those for the sale of land or some interest in land. There were proceedings enforcing express trusts, imposing constructive trusts or equitable liens, and redeeming or foreclosing mortgages. There were bills of interpleader, bills of peace, bills to quiet title, bills of discovery, and bills for account-ing. There were suits to rescind and reform contracts. This powerful sys-tem of jurisprudence, prompted by Magna Carta, both exceeded and reformed the common law.

After the House of Stuart inherited the Crown of England, the consti-tution accumulated a number of organic acts. The first of these was the Statute of Monopolies, 21 James I, Chapter 3 (1624), which declared that all royal patents of monopoly were "contrary to the fundamental law of the realm, and utterly void," excepting patents of invention granted for limited terms allowed by act of Parliament. [19]

Perhaps the greatest of such constitutional ordinances was the Petition of Right, 3 Charles I, Chapter 1 (1628), which prohibited the King from imposing any tax, any obligatory payment of money to the Crown, regard-less of names, whatever the occasion or pretext, "without common con-sent by act of Parliament," — or from arresting any subject merely on spe-cial command,[20] — or from imposing martial law, suspending the writ of habeas corpus, or quartering troops in private homes, save in times of domestic rebellion or foreign invasion when urgently necessary for the sake of public safety.

The Statute of 16 Charles I, Chapter 10 (1641) abolished the Star Chamber,[21] and the Statute of 16 Charles I, Chapter 11 (1641) abolished the Court of High Commission.[22] These acts did away with the use of administrative or summary proceedings to prosecute and punish subjects for public wrongs, so as to circumvent the rights of the accused in crimi-nal prosecutions at common law as guaranteed by Magna Carta. Gone were oaths ex officio to compel self-incrimination, confessions coerced by imprisonment or torture, and penal trials in secret without rules of evi-dence or jury of peers. Gone, at least in due course, were degenerate prac-tices such as the use of general warrants,[23] and putrid doctrines such as that which branded truth as an aggravation rather than an exoneration on a charge of criminal libel.[24]

There was also the Statute of 31 Charles II, Chapter 2 (1679), known as the Habeas Corpus Act, which forbade the detention of persons arrest-ed for crimes and misdemeanors unless reasonably bailed and seasonably charged and tried, and also liberalized the availability of habeas corpus so that every judge in every superior court at Westminster was empowered and obliged to issue the writ whenever a proper application was made,[25] and to make due inquiry of whether liberty was restrained in conformity with the law of the land. So great was this reform that it came to be known as the Second Magna Carta.

* * * * *

From the reign of William the Conqueror to the death of Charles II, and also thereafter up to the days of Blackstone, the attribute of omnipotence was gradually transferred by concessions of the Crown from the King alone to the Commons, Lords, and King in Parliament.

By the reign of George III, the House of Commons consisted of knights of the shire elected by freeholders in the counties, burgesses elected by freemen in the cities and boroughs, and members elected by the faculties and students of the universities at Oxford and Cambridge, while members themselves were required by law to own freeholds of larger size and annual revenue.[26]

It had long been established that members of Parliament enjoyed an immunity from suit or prosecution for any speech made during the course of legislative business,[27] and from arrest while attending legislative sessions except for treason, felony, or breach of the peace.[28]

And it had long been established that the House of Commons was the exclusive judge of the elections, returns, and qualifications of its members.[29] Not long after the Seven Years War, organic acts were passed to prevent abuse of this privilege: — the Statute of 10 George III, Chapter 16 (1770), amended by the Statute of 11 George III, Chapter 42 (1771), and made permanent by the Statute of 14 George III, Chapter 15 (1774), limited inquiry on the seating of members to whether a candidate had in fact received enough votes in a free and peaceable election, presented a return in proper form, and was qualified by law to sit. Under these statutes, it was no longer possible to exclude anyone otherwise entitled to be seated on the pretext that he was disreputable or that his views were wrong.[30]

From and after the reign of Charles II, the House of Commons acquired by constitutional custom certain exclusive powers, including the sole right to return of bills of impeachment, and even more important the sole right to initiate money bills or legislation for public taxation and spending.

The House of Lords consisted of bishops and archbishops,[31] called lords spiritual, and of barons, viscounts, earls, marquises, and dukes, called peers or lords temporal.

By constitutional custom, the House of Lords could initiate bills, and could approve, reject or amend bills passed by the House of Commons, except for money bills which, from and after the reign of Charles II, they could never initiate and could only approve or reject as first passed by the House of Commons.

From and after the reign of Edward III, the House of Lords sat as a special court for the trial of impeachments which, as settled in the reign of

Charles I, could originate only from the House of Commons and never from the King. The House of Lords also sat as the court of the lord high steward for the trial of peers accused on indictment or presentment of treason or felony or misprision of treason or felony. From as far back as the reign of Edward III they had been the highest court of judicature of writ of error or appeal. And for this purpose, by the reign of George III, the peers usually acted through a committee of law lords.

The House of Lords also retained a special right and duty, independent from the House of Commons, as a remnant of their ancient glory from the days before Magna Carta, to advise and counsel the Crown in times of grave crisis: — on such occasions, the House of Lords was called the Magnum Concilium.[32]

At the summit of Parliament was the King's most excellent Majesty, from whom all powers, prerogatives, rights, duties, privileges, immunities, patents, grants, titles, and honors had flowed from the time of William the Conqueror.

Even as late as the reign of George III, the King enjoyed, at least nominally, many prerogatives in his own right:[33]

The King could allow or disallow bills approved by the Commons and Lords.

He could create and confer titles of nobility — i. e., baron, viscount, earl, marquis, and duke — so as to increase or maintain the peerage, and titles of honor — i. e., knight and baronet — ; he could appoint judges to the bench, grant pardons and reprieves, receive and send ambassadors and other public ministers and consuls, make treaties, declare war and peace, establish markets, fix the standard of weights and measures, and coin money.

He was commander-in-chief of the army, navy, and militia in war and peace.

He was head of the established church, and so appointed archbishops and bishops. He was defender of the faith.

He had the power of chartering corporations, public and private.

The King's principal duty was "to govern his people according to law."[34] He could issue proclamations, admonishing obedience and warning against infractions, although by such means he could make no laws nor do anything forbidden by Magna Carta.[35] And through his privy council, he could inquire into offenses against the government, and cause proper warrants to issue for the arrest of person suspected of such offenses.[36]

The King had substantial revenues in his own right, apart from taxes. From the year 1603, he ruled England, Scotland, and Ireland by hereditary right, and he claimed even the Crown of France from concessions made to Henry V. He had many dominions, colonies, and possessions from North America to India. He was the original proprietor of all lands, and through his privy council he governed the expanses of the British Empire.

Of the tremendous power of the Commons, Lords, and King acting together in Parliament, Blackstone gave this graphic and unforgettable description:

> "It hath sovereign and uncontrollable authority in the making, confirming, enlarging, restraining, abrogating, repealing, reviving, and expounding of laws, concerning all possible denominations, ecclesiastical or temporal, civil, military, maritime, or criminal, this being the place where that absolute despotic power, which must in all governments reside somewhere, is entrusted by the constitution of these kingdoms. All mischiefs and grievances, operations and reme-dies, that transcend the ordinary course of the laws, are within the reach of this extraordinary tribunal. It can regulate or new model the succession of the crown, as was done in the reigns of Henry VIII and William III. It can alter the established religion of the land, as was done in a variety of instances, in the reigns of Henry VIII and his three children. It can change afresh even the constitution of the king-dom and of parliaments themselves, as was done by the act of union, and the several statutes for triennial and septennial elections. It can, in short, do everything that is not naturally impossible; and, there-fore, some have not scrupled to call this power, by a figure rather too bold, the omnipotence of parliament. True it is, what parliament doth, no power on earth can undo."[37]

* * * * *

It may be taken as a first principle that the fundamental law of England emanated from the Crown. And even after authority once concentrated in royal hands had fashioned innumerable privileges and immunities of freemen, and had widely distributed the powers of government function-ing apart from royal will, the whole constitutional order of England still rested upon the Crown.

Not only did the fundamental law of England derive from the Crown, but from the time of Edward I onwards it became a constitutional custom that nobody but the King by his own writ could summon a lawful Parliament.[38] The King could by his command prorogue or dissolve Parliament, and, moreover, the death or abdication of the King also dissolved Parliament.[39] Without the Crown, there could be no Parliament. Without the rightful King there could be no lawful government in England.

The civilized progress of England, therefore, depended on peaceful and orderly succession of the Crown. And to meet this need, a constitutional custom was established to transmit title to the Crown from one prince to the next by hereditary right of royal birth in wedlock, according to the rules of primogeniture for descent of real estate as modified to suit the special requirements of royal succession:[40]

The Crown normally passed from the deceased King to the eldest son or to his heir if he predeceased his father.

If there was no surviving lineal heir male, then the Crown passed to the eldest daughter, or to her heir if she predeceased her father.

If there were no lineal heir, then and only then did the Crown pass to the most eligible member of the eldest male branch of collateral heirs nearest in kin, hence in the usual case to the eldest brother, or to his heir, otherwise to the most eligible member of the eldest female branch nearest in kin, hence in the usual case to the eldest sister, or to her heir.

A child of the King born out of wedlock could not inherit the Crown, but was usually ennobled by peerage if a son, or well cared for and married if a daughter, and, in any event, venerated and addressed as a prince or princess of royal blood.

The rules of primogeniture did not become firmly settled in passing the Crown until the accession of King Henry III in 1216 A. D. Thereafter primogeniture determined royal succession flawlessly over four succeeding reigns, — Edward I, Edward II, Edward III, and Richard II.

Primogeniture could not prevent every wickedness as, for example, the brutal slaughter of Edward II in 1327, but it did permit peaceful transmission of the Crown to Edward III who in due course of time brought his father's murderers to justice, and reigned for fifty years.

The importance of primogeniture was proved by the civil strife which invariably erupted whenever it was disregarded, as occurred after the year 1399 when Richard II was overthrown by rebellion provoked by his arbitrary rule. His abdication was extorted, and he died in the dungeon of Pontefract Castle.

Richard II had no children, and so the Crown belonged by hereditary right to Edmund Mortimer, Earl of March, who was the surviving heir male of the eldest brother of Richard II. The descendants of Edmund Mortimer eventually adopted the white rose as their symbol when they married into the House of York.

But the impeccable legal rights of Edmund Mortimer were usurped by the leader of the rebellion, Henry Bolingbroke, the eldest son of a younger brother of Richard II. This branch of the family took the red rose as their symbol, and represented the House of Lancaster. With the connivance of a Parliament which had been legally dissolved, Bolingbroke was irregularly proclaimed as Henry IV. And this venture, although at first successful, ripened by degrees into excruciating tragedy.

Mortimer and his descendants acquiesced to the usurpation of Henry IV and his heirs, but never renounced their pretensions to the Crown. And after some years a series of belligerencies, called the Wars of the Roses, erupted in fits and starts over three generations between the House of York and the House of Lancaster. The struggle was initially fought with a similitude of chivalry between knights and gentlemen, but over time casualties mounted, then followed wave after wave of bloody revenge. There was eventually a forcible seizure of the Crown by the House of York, then further armed struggle, then another prince dispatched in a dungeon.

The official register of reigns of the 15th Century has the plastic appearance of regularity, — Henry IV, Henry V, Henry VI, Edward IV, Edward V, etc. But, truth to tell, all was in chaos. The epoch was an unhappy saga of revolution, usurpation, counterrevolution, treason, combat, slaughter, beheadings, and murder until 1485. Richard III, of the House of York, had become King by having his nephews declared bastards and then suffocated. The whole kingdom knew it, although the crime was concealed and could not be proved for two centuries. There was a rebellion, and Richard III was slain on Bosworth Field, shouting, if Shakespeare is to be believed, "A horse! A horse! My kingdom for a horse!"

So ended the Wars of the Roses, which included twelve major land battles, each resulting in huge losses, often followed by mass executions. About eighty princes of royal blood had been killed. Most of the ancient nobility of England had been exterminated.

The leader of the rebellion against Richard III was Henry Tudor, Earl of Richmond, who was the most eligible heir to the Lancaster claim.

Henry Tudor was universally proclaimed King, and took the name Henry VII. The truth is that he assumed the Crown not by legal right, but urgent necessity. His title was based on force of arms, as with William the Conqueror, of whom he was a direct descendant, albeit not the heir by primogeniture. He summoned a Parliament which enacted and ordained that the Crown be vested in him and the heirs of his body forever. He married Elizabeth of York, the proper heir female of the House of York, so that at least her children might inherit indisputable title to the Crown. The constitutional fabric was thus repaired as best as circumstances permitted.

* * * * *

Henry VIII was the child of Henry Tudor and Elizabeth of York, indisputably King by natural right of primogeniture. It is well known that he had his troubles with the Catholic Church over the refusal of Pope Clement VII to grant him an annulment of his marriage to his Queen, Catherine of Aragon. Out of this contention, the Church of England was established. And in his ardent desire to produce an eligible son, Henry VIII married six wives and fathered three children.

The important papal bull from Clement VII arrived in England in the spring of 1534, after the Archbishop of Canterbury had granted Henry VIII a divorce from Catherine of Aragon on grounds much debated.[41] The Holy See found that the marriage of Henry VIII to Catherine was licit, and so determined that their daughter, Princess Mary, was legitimate, and entitled to inherit the Crown. Henry VIII was ordered to take back Catherine as his lawful wife. He refused. Therefore, in the eyes of the Holy See, he was subject to excommunication and forfeiture of his kingdom.

For centuries the Pope had been the father of princes and kings: — out of necessity and for want of a better alternative the Holy Father had become a supranational power in the affairs of Europe. The bull of Clement VII was an exercise of authority which had long been customary. Yet the fact that a foreign prince was making decisions so important to the constitutional order of the country did not then set well in England.

The bull of Clement VII meant that the intervening marriage between Henry VIII and Anne Boleyn was illicit. Yet, the appeal to Rome had been prohibited by the Statute of 24 Henry VIII, Chapter 12 (1532), so as to make the papal judgment a legal nullity in England, however differently things were viewed in Rome. And, under the Statute of 25 Henry VIII, Chapter 22 (1533), the marriage between Henry VIII and Catherine had been declared null and void, so as to make Princess Mary illegitimate, excluding her from ever inheriting the throne, while the marriage between Henry VIII and Anne Boleyn was declared licit, thus giving their daughter Princess Elizabeth the right to inherit the Crown.

Moreover, the Act of Supremacy, 26 Henry VIII, Chapter 1 (1534), abolished all papal jurisdiction whatever over England, and placed the government of the established church under the Crown: — it withdrew England from the political order of Europe then under the supervision of the Holy See.

John Fisher, Bishop of Rochester, and Sir Thomas More, Chancellor of England, refused to take the oath prescribed by the Act of Supremacy.

Both were consequently found guilty of treason and beheaded, and for this brutality Henry VIII was formally excommunicated in 1535 by Pope Paul III. Fisher and More were in due course sainted as martyrs.

Meanwhile in 1536 Catherine of Aragon died, and, although she may have been innocent — her greatest offense to the King was that she gave birth to a daughter and not a son — , Anne Boleyn was found guilty of treason for having taken lovers. Shortly after Anne was ceremoniously beheaded by the swift blow of a long sword, the King married Jane Seymour. Yet, had it not been for the Statutes of 24, 25, and 26 Henry VIII, he would not have been free to contract a proper marriage again even in England, because he had been excommunicated and so could not receive any of the seven sacraments.

Thereupon, the Statute of 28 Henry VIII, Chapter 7 (1536) again declared the marriage of Henry VIII and Catherine void, and also declared his marriage to Anne void, making both Mary and Elizabeth illegitimate. The statute then confirmed that the marriage of Henry VIII and Jane Seymour was licit, allowing only their child to inherit the Crown. From their union was born Prince Edward Tudor, legitimate in England, but not in the eyes of Rome.

At length came the Statute of 35 Henry VIII, Chapter 1 (1543), which provided for royal succession upon the death of King Henry VIII: — first to his son by Jane Seymour, who reigned from 1547 to 1553 as King Edward VI; — then, if he should die without issue, as he did, to the daughter of Henry VIII by Catherine of Aragon, who reigned from 1553 to 1558 as Queen Mary I; — then, if she should die without issue, as she did, to the daughter of Henry VIII by Anne Boleyn, who reigned from 1558 to 1603 as Queen Elizabeth I; — then, in default of issue of any of the children of Henry VIII, to such heir as he should designate by patent or will.

In light of these facts, Edward VI was King by natural right of primogeniture only if his father's excommunication by Paul III was void. And Mary I was Queen by natural right of primogeniture only if the bull of Clement VII was valid. Their respective claims by primogeniture were thus precarious. Each of them depended in important degree on the Statute of 35 Henry VIII to sustain title to the Crown.

Upon the death of Mary, the accession of her half-sister Elizabeth was proclaimed by the House of Lords as having occurred "according to the act of succession of the 35th year of Henry VIII." The same judgment was repeated by Parliament in the Statute of 1 Elizabeth I, Chapter 3 (1558). Whatever else may be said in behalf of her half-brother Edward and her half-sister Mary, "Good Queen Bess" rested her entire claim to the throne upon an act of Parliament, nor did she think a better claim was possible for her, nor did she have any other claim capable of withstanding legal scrutiny.

King Henry VIII had two sisters: — the elder, Margaret Tudor, who married King James IV of Scotland, and the younger, Mary Tudor, who first married King Louis XII of France, then, upon his death, Charles Brandon, first Duke of Suffolk. Mary Tudor married a high and mighty prince on the continent of Europe for reasons of state, as a princess may sometimes be obliged to do. But she married her dear Charlie for love, then gave up political ambitions and had "de beaux enfants."

Under the said statute of the 35th year of his reign, Henry VIII executed a valid will which devised the Crown, in the event all his children died without issue, to the heirs of the body of his younger sister Mary, not the heirs of the body of his elder sister Margaret who would have inherited under the customary law of primogeniture.

The lawful authority of the King to dispose of the Crown by patent or will with the consent of Parliament, as had been allowed by the Statute of 35 Henry VIII, was specifically reaffirmed in the Statute of 13 Elizabeth I, Chapter 1 (1571), so as to leave no doubt about the statutory right of the heirs of the body of Mary Tudor to inherit the Crown in preference to the heirs of the body of Margaret Tudor.

As the reign of Elizabeth I drew to a close, there were in fact living issue of Mary Tudor through her daughters Francis and Eleanor. And it is plain enough that William Seymour, known as Lord Beauchamp, was the heir of the body of Mary Tudor, and so heir presumptive to the Crown under the Statute of 35 Henry VIII.[42]

Even so, the son of Margaret Tudor became King James V of Scotland, and Margaret's granddaughter Mary Stuart came to the Scottish throne in 1542. Mary Queen of Scots was heir to the Crown of England according to the customary law of primogeniture, if not upon the death of King Henry VIII in 1547, then no later than the death of Queen Mary I in 1558 in any event, and so was viewed by Elizabeth Tudor with jealous eyes. In an uprising with a melodramatic plot such as might appear in grand opera, Mary Queen of Scots was imprisoned in Lockleven Castle. There she was coerced by threat on her life to sign a deed of abdication in 1567 in favor of her infant son James Stuart, who thereupon was proclaimed King James VI of Scotland.

Elizabeth Tudor had some years before sent a precious ring to her cousin Mary Stuart, as a symbol of queenly promise: — if Mary should ever need her aid, Elizabeth would willingly give it. Mary Stuart escaped from Lochleven Castle in 1568, and fled to England, and there sought the protection which had been solemnly promised in royal honor. Elizabeth disregarded her past assurances, and unlawfully held Mary under house arrest for eighteen years. Elizabeth's motto was, "Strike or be stricken."

In due course, Mary Stuart was charged and convicted according to irregular procedure on dubious evidence of conspiracy to take the life of Elizabeth I, and so she was executed for treason in 1587. The martyred Queen of Scots died with dignity on the block, and became a legend, leaving her son James Stuart as the heir of her body.

And so when Elizabeth died in 1603, the weighty question arose whether the Crown of England should pass to James Stuart, heir by primogeniture, or to William Seymour, heir by statute.

* * * * *

Learned opinion prevailing in England upon Elizabeth's death was founded on an intelligent understanding, based on experience over long ages, that physics and astronomy, yet also economics, politics, and morals are governed by an inherent order of things traditionally called natural law. Now this view of the world was an old idea, described by eminent lawyers and philosophers, including Tribonian, St. Thomas Aquinas, and Hugo Grotius, among many others. The most famous affirmation of natural law is found in the opening passages of the Declaration of American Independence, but the most magnificent and eloquent statement is found in the writing of none other than Sir William Blackstone.[43]

Natural law was understood as an inescapable physical and moral order, given by the hand and defined as the will of God. It was known to enforce itself by invisible mechanisms, causing distinctive phenomena in empirical observation, and discoverable by way of human observation and reason.

Natural law was grasped as a reality in human affairs, elaborated in legal tradition, accommodated by common law and constitutional custom, and reflected in the repetitions of history. It was known to restrain governments and markets alike, to bless mankind in reward for obedience, and to punish wickedness with calamity. It was known to establish moral absolutes and vest inalienable rights, sometimes to produce revolutions, and to cause the rise and fall of nations.

The learned men of the time were no fools. They looked back over the previous two hundred years. If only Henry Bolingbroke had acquiesced to Edmund Mortimer, if only England had accepted the heirs of Margaret Tudor, then history would have been more tranquil. So it clearly seemed, and so it surely was.

Hence, it "was gravely maintained that the Supreme Being regarded hereditary monarchy, as opposed to other forms of government with particular favor," and "that the rule of succession in order of primogeniture was a divine institution."[44]

So obvious did this notion then appear, as if by rays of sunlight illuminated, that "Queen Elizabeth too, with her dying breath, had recognized the undoubted title of her kinsman James; and the whole nation seemed to dispose themselves with joy and pleasure for the reception."[45]

William Seymour acquiesced to the accession of James Stuart, making no pretense of title to the Crown under the Statute of 35 Henry VIII, even though the act had never been challenged or repealed, had twice been solemnly reaffirmed in Parliament, and had formed an indispensable basis of government in England during three previous reigns over fifty-six years. His statutory claim was unimpeachable, but he did not press it, because he conceded, as Parliament ordained in the Statute of 1 James I, Chapter 1 (1603), that a natural hereditary right was better under the fundamental law of England, all things considered, than a statutory title to the Crown.

Primogeniture was understood as an inexorable demand of natural law as it had unraveled in the events of those days. The utility of primogeniture had been proved by historical events so painful and unforgotten that no impartial and informed observer then living could plausibly object. It was known that there could be extraordinary situations in which statutory intervention might be needed to repair injury otherwise irreparable, as upon the accession of Henry VII. Such a plea of urgency could perhaps be offered to defend the Statute of 35 Henry VIII when it was enacted. But whatever could once have been said for it, the old statute had fallen into desuetude by the end of the Elizabethan age, and primogeniture again regained natural sway as a sign from heaven of the wisdom of God, — the mark of the "divine right" of a King.

The new King understood his mission: — as a prince chosen by God to rule over his people, he must ever abide by and never disobey natural law given by the hand of God.

He gave his subjects in the year 1611 the most beautiful translation of the Holy Bible ever published in the English language. And this Holy Bible, which he reverently studied and well comprehended, described the nature of his divine right:

> "He that ruleth over men must be just, ruling in the fear of God.
> And he shall be as the light of the morning when the sun riseth, even
> a morning without clouds." — 1 Samuel 23: 3-4. And, —

"Blessed be the name of God forever and ever: for wisdom and might are his: And he changeth the times and the seasons: he removeth kings, and setteth up kings: he giveth wisdom to the wise, and knowledge to them that know understanding."   — Daniel 2: 20-21.

Although he has been ridiculed for his eccentricities, such traits often accompany human genius in literature, the arts, and the sciences. James I was literally a philosopher King.

He obliged scientists, economists, bankers, lawyers, theologians, and other learned men to obey him, lest they indulge in mischief, and fail to use their knowledge for the good of mankind, yet he did so without resort to raw oppression. Undeniably he guided England into flourishing prosperity.

James I has been widely criticized for restraining Sir Edward Coke — Lord Coke as he was known on the bench — ; yet, if the King had not restrained him, the powers of equity might have been crippled and unduly retarded.[46]

The judiciary of England was profoundly corrupt in those days. When James I created Sir Francis Bacon Viscount St. Albans and elevated him to the seat of Chancellor, bribery of judges was almost an obligatory social courtesy in litigation, — what modern lawyers have since described as "costs and disbursements." Lord Bacon felt the pressure, and tried to remedy the situation by taking "gifts of esteem" from both sides, then doing justice according to law. But men of substance who paid for perversion and got justice were outraged. Their influence was felt, probably by the same means as were so often used to flatter the judiciary in those days, and Bacon was impeached for bribery.

Bacon admitted his wrongs. The peers knew the hypocrisy behind the charges, and the standing of the accused as a lawyer, judge, scientist, and man of letters, but they at least knew enough not to condone in public a grave crime against the impartial administration of justice. They removed Bacon from office, fined him into poverty, and threw him into prison with theatrical indignation.

At this juncture, James I was his characteristic best. The King pardoned the great philosopher, granted him a pension, and ordered him to spend the rest of his days completing his work on the advancement of learning. Bacon did as he was told, and produced a literary treasure on which he was still at work when death overcame him.

James I was a wise, not an indulgent father. Out of prudent caution, not niggardly disposition, he did not allow every constitutional reform then proposed. Yet, he accomplished much in this field, and prepared the country for such changes in future years.

* * * * *

When James breathed his last in 1625, his eldest son naturally became King Charles I of England, — and of Scotland and Ireland.

The first years of the new reign in England consisted of painful clashes with Parliament. There were important constitutional reforms, but eventually the situation ripened into eleven years of personal rule by the King alone without Parliament. During this period the King had no money except from revenues already established and what could be raised by dubious or unlawful methods. He was a despot, but lacked resources to become really dangerous. An era of limited, yet sometimes bad government followed, even though the country boomed with commerce and industry. His personal rule was interrupted by rebellion in Scotland, which necessitated the calling of Parliament.

Tensions immediately arose again between King and Parliament. By 1642 the King was at his wits' end, and attempted to arrest five members of the House of Commons during their proceedings over indignant cries of "Privilege, privilege!" It was a tragic royal blunder, producing a first phase of civil war in which the "cavalier" army of Charles I was finally defeated by the "roundhead" or "ironsides" army under Oliver Cromwell at the Battle of Naseby in 1645. Royalist surrenders continued into early 1646.

The common people of the realm had generally supported Cromwell, albeit with lukewarm sentiment. The nation as a whole saw the need to shift the balance of power toward Parliament; but, apart from extremists, no Englishman of good sense ever believed in radical weakening or abolition of the Crown.

So devoted were the people to the Crown that, even as a virtual prisoner of war, Charles I had great prestige and authority in the negotiations then underway for a constitutional settlement between the King and Parliament. Difficulties were encountered over the back pay and indemnity owed to the army after it should disband as anticipated. Delays led to irritations among the troops, and the army, then unbeatable, became impatient, and threatened the constitutional order of England.

The country sensed the danger and rallied around the King as the champion of the rule of law. The army turned on all classes opposed to military rule and easily prevailed by the end of 1648. From thenceforth, the English Civil War degenerated into a "Puritan" Revolution.

Truly has it been said that the victory of the army in 1648 "was the triumph of some twenty thousand resolute, ruthless, disciplined, military fanatics over all that England has ever willed or ever wished."[47] An officer known in history as Colonel Pride marched a battalion of troops to the meeting of Parliament. On his orders, forty-five members of the House of Commons were arrested. Several hundred others were excluded from attending sessions. This petulant trooper did more harm to parliamentary democracy by his lawlessness than Charles I in his worst moments ever dreamt of. Thus did the fifth Parliament of Charles I, the "Long Parliament" as it was called, cease in any proper sense to be a lawful legislature.

A contemptible "Rump" of Puritan grandees then purported to abolish the House of Lords, and brought the King to a mock "trial" which was a tumultuous scene, filled with unruly soldiers shouting "Justice!" and "Execution!" Despite the noise and disorder, the King gave an eloquent speech. He pleaded that he had taken up arms for the defense of the constitution, and that, if he conceded legitimacy to the tribunal, he would betray his public trust to uphold the fundamental law of the realm.

Charles I was "sentenced" to death by a "court" which had no precedent and no jurisdiction. He was beheaded in front of his own banqueting house in early 1649, as thousands of his subjects groaned in horror and sorrow. London became silent with shame, unable to resist because those who had a few years before sought a fairer balance between the King and Parliament were overawed by soldiers who marched in their name. It has been said of this execution,

> "The tragical death of Charles begat a question, whether the people in any case, were entitled to judge and to punish their sovereign; and most men, regarding chiefly the atrocious usurpation of the pretended judges, and the merit of the virtuous prince who suffered, were inclined to condemn the republican principle as highly seditious and extravagant."[48]

The same writer looked back on events, and supplied just balance in his commentary:

> "From the memorable revolutions which passed in England during this period, we may naturally deduce the same useful lesson which Charles himself, in his later years, inferred: that it is dangerous for princes, even from the appearance of necessity, to assume more authority than the laws have allowed them. But it must be confessed that these events furnish us with another instruction, no less natural, and no less useful, concerning the madness of the people, the furies of fanaticism, and the danger of mercenary armies."[49]

Cromwell emerged as the "Lord Protector," a dictator of sorts, but real-ly a politician general seeking to maintain a semblance of command of unruly soldiers, restraining their excesses as much as possible. The dark-ness of military rule descended upon England. Scotland became an orphaned province. Genocide was practiced in Ireland. It was a time of sorrow and shame.

In 1657 "a group of lawyers and gentry decided to offer Cromwell the Crown. 'The title of Protector,' said one of them, 'is not limited by any rule or law; the title of King is.'"[50] Cromwell saw the meaning of the flat-tery, and declined the honor.

The country had risen against their King who was said to rule by divine right, and paid dearly. In those days, subjects of Charles II suffering under Cromwell must have picked up the famous edition of the Holy Bible given to them by the grandfather of their King, republished at Cambridge University in 1648, and read these striking words:

> "If my people, which are called by my name, shall humble them-selves, and pray, and seek my face, and turn from their wicked ways, then will I hear from heaven, and will forgive their sin, and will heal their land."   — 2 Chronicles 7: 14.

In fact, the people of England did feel deep remorse. Many of them did pray with earnest hearts, and did seek divine forgiveness for what they had allowed to happen.

* * * * *

Cromwell died in 1658. His elder son was unable to carry on. An attempt was made to revive the Long Parliament, which had been legally dissolved not later than the death of Charles I. It met anyway, at first as a body of aging grandees who had made up the Rump, then all surviving members on invitation of a general of the army. Unable to make headway, it paid off Cromwell's sons, and dissolved itself in confusion and bewil-derment.

Negotiations began with Charles II. At length, the peers, styling them-selves as "keepers of the liberty of England," summoned what has been called the "Convention" Parliament of 1660. This meeting of the Commons and Lords has been so designated, because it was called by the peers and not the King, as generally required by constitutional custom. But this meeting of parliament was called in a lawful manner, because there was then still an old act of the Long Parliament on the books, the Statute of 16 Charles I, Chapter 1 (1641), which said that if the King failed for any reason to call a

Parliament by royal writ after the last assembly thereof had been dissolved more than three years, the peers might call for elections and summon Parliament.

Charles II was welcomed home with shouts of joy. He ratified the acts of the Convention Parliament of 1660. The King called another election by royal writ. A new Parliament met and ratified the restoration of the House of Stuart in the Statutes of 13 Charles II, Chapters 7 and 13 (1661), and thereby constitutional government was reestablished in England.

The breathtaking circumstances of this restoration were interpreted as a deliverance by the mercy of God, and once again it was held that the King governed by natural right of primogeniture as the mark of his divine right. In keeping with this act of faith, the new "cavalier" Parliament enacted the Statute of 16 Charles II, Chapter 1 (1664), repealing the old law on which the peers had acted in 1660, and returning to the King unencumbered, in keeping with ancient custom, his sole right and power to summon any future Parliament.

The King was able to moderate vindictiveness unleashed against his father's murderers, of whom nearly all escaped execution. He thus carried out his father's last wish on the scaffold, addressed to a friend and bishop attending his father only moments before the ax fell. His father had spoken a short and enigmatic phrase in old French so that soldiers nearby would not understand: "NE OUBLIE," — do not forget, do not forget to teach my children to forgive those who have taken my life.

The reign of Charles II was long and tranquil, notwithstanding plots and cabals. It included legal reforms of the greatest importance, which have lasted until this day. The King loved women and pleasure more than politics, yet this trait restrained his ambition. Cynical he was, and also corrupt mainly from excessive willingness to accommodate the hard facts of public life. This disposition was a response to his father's martyrdom which he did not wish to repeat. His time on the throne proves once again how exceedingly difficult it is for any prince in any era to use great power independently for good ends and yet survive.

Charles II had a rare sense of humor, excellent taste, and gentle manners. These gifts enabled him to avoid no end of trouble and earned him forgiveness for his mistakes.

If Charles II was not particularly virtuous, neither was the age in which he lived, and he was an enormous improvement over Cromwell. All things considered, he was probably as good a ruler as England then deserved.

* * * * *

When Charles II died without legitimate heir on February 6, 1685, his brother succeeded to the Crown under the style of James II of England, James VII of Scotland. The new King had been a capable admiral, and he possessed other redeeming qualities. Yet by temperament he was probably the most ill-suited man in the country to wear the Crown.

James II had converted to the Catholic faith which then carried many legal disabilities under statutes enacted during and after the English Reformation.[51] But since he was King and these acts made no suggestion of binding the Crown, he was free to be a Catholic prince, openly practicing his religion, although he was the head of the established Church of England. He was in this respect at least "above the law," yet he was in a situation fraught with danger.

James II became King because a bill to exclude him from the throne on pretext of religion was prevented from becoming law when Charles II dissolved Parliament.[52] If he had been a wise and cunning prince, James II might perhaps have slowly guided his kingdom, then full of disreputable religious bigotry not uncommon in Europe during those years, into a new era of religious tolerance and freedom. But the greatest statesman on earth would have been obliged to move cautiously in seeking to accomplish such an objective, and may have achieved but limited success. Far from enjoying such adroitness, James II was obdurate beyond measure. He was determined yet without comprehension of politics.

His abuses of royal power included a proclamation imposing duties on commerce without legislative consent,[53] — keeping up, on his own civil list, a large body of professional troops in order to intimidate the people as in the days of Cromwell, — persistent efforts to interfere with the right of subjects to keep and bear arms,[54] — setting up by royal patent an ecclesiastical court prohibited by statute,[55] then using it to weaken the established church, — arbitrary dispensation and suspension of laws, and removal of strict legalists from the bench and replacing them with others servile enough to uphold unconstitutional use of royal prerogatives.[56] James II went so far as to interfere with academic affairs in university colleges at Oxford and Cambridge.[57] He managed by these and other obnoxious acts to antagonize parts of the country traditionally loyal to the Crown.

On June 10, 1688, the lawful wife and Queen of James II, Mary of Modena, gave birth to a son, Prince James Edward Stuart, who was the lawful heir to the Crown by right of primogeniture. He was ostentatiously baptized a Catholic, assuring a continuation of a Catholic dynasty in a ferociously Protestant kingdom.

Malicious rumors were started to the effect that the baby was spurious, and introduced into the Queen's bed in a warming pan. The royal birth was witnessed by many, and, on October 22, 1688, the reality of this event was proved by over forty credible and eminent witnesses who saw the royal birth and gave testimony under oath before the privy council. This unanswerable testimony was meticulously recorded and elaborately published, as appears in *Proceedings to Prove the Genuineness of the Child of James II and Mary of Modena*, 12 Howell's St. Tr. 123 (P. C. 1688). There never was any honest doubt of the legitimacy of the infant prince as the true and lawful heir of the Crown of England.

If James II had acted with due precaution and tact, he might have made the reality of a Catholic heir palatable. Instead, he had defied every constitutional reform since the accession of his grandfather as King, and his people, still remembering their intense suffering at the hands of the "puritan saints" of Cromwell, were not about to undergo anything remotely similar at the hands of "God's anointed." Laying aside his constitutional usurpations and the rampant bribery in his royal court, which might have been corrected and forgiven, the cynical approval shown by James II for the animalistic cruelty and gross perversion of Sir George Jeffreys on the bench[58] was alone enough to divest him of any right to govern by the favor of God.

The events finally unleashing the relentless and unstoppable forces of revolution were those which produced the *Seven Bishops Case*, 12 Howell's St. Tr. 183 (K. B. 1688).

The King issued certain declarations of indulgence expressing his royal will and pleasure that all penal laws and acts imposing disabilities for nonconformity in religion be wholly suspended in their execution. Even if not strictly legal, his first declaration had a just purpose and may have done some good if taken as royal approval of benign neglect of these statutes. But then he ordered all prelates and priests of the established church to read the second declaration in public services on days certain. This act induced political uproar and indignancy.

The primate of the established church and six suffragan bishops respectfully petitioned the King to reconsider. James II in his privy council responded by ordering the seven prelates arrested for seditious libel, and thereupon informations were returned by the attorney general. Contrary to the instructions on the law by the Chief Justice of the King's Bench, a verdict of not guilty was returned on June 30, 1688. All frustrations pent up over the previous three years were let loose, and the situation in England very rapidly deteriorated.

It so happens that James II had two daughters by an earlier marriage to Anne Hyde, deceased some years previous. The elder of these daughters was another Mary Stuart who had married Prince William of Orange, Stadtholder of the United Netherlands. William was the son of the previous Stadtholder and an elder sister of James II, and so was not only the son-in-law but also the nephew of the King of England.

The acquittal of the seven bishops at Westminster inspired prominent men of the realm, including a number of peers, to begin negotiations with William of Orange. And on November 5, 1688, William landed with an army in England at Torbay on the Devon coast. James II marched to meet the invasion, at first confident of his ability to crush his foe, but the royal army melted as his lieutenants and soldiers deserted and crossed over to the other side. William advanced effortlessly as cheering crowds turned out to greet him and his troops on their victorious march to London.

In this grave predicament, the King exercised his prerogative of calling together the House of Lords as the Magnum Concilium, which met with him at his palace in London on November 27, 1688.[59] On only two occasions during the previous three centuries had there ever been such a meeting of bishops and peers. Their Lordships conceded that only the King might summon a free Parliament, yet they urged him to call for elections, and submit to inevitable constitutional reforms by then long overdue. They spoke in language of a polite and courtly nature, yet plain enough in meaning: — if his Majesty failed to take such a course, there might in any event be a parliamentary assembly, nor could revolutionary changes in government then be avoided. It was his duty, they said, to grant pardons, come to terms with his people, and see justice done.

Meanwhile, the King sent commissioners to treat with William of Orange. On December 8, 1688, at Hungerford, historic discussions took place between the royal emissaries and the Prince of Orange.[60]

It has been said that William really wanted the negotiations to fail on the calculation that the King would blunder into downfall so that he might himself seize the Crown. But the facts contradict this notion. As a practical matter, William was free to take London as a military prize, and the King as a political prisoner, then simply to dictate whatever resolution he desired. But the Prince of Orange rose to a very high level of statesmanship, and offered terms of a kind which acquit him of any intimation of unworthy ambition.

His objective was in fact to break the alliance between England and France, and to bring the resources of the British Empire to the support of his country, the United Netherlands, then ever threatened by the designs of Louis XIV. He did not seek the Crown for himself, yet he was prepared to assume it if necessary, lest revolutionary trends get out of hand in the domains of the House of Stuart.

The Prince of Orange proposed that James II call a free Parliament, and participate in the full exercise of his prerogatives, and that the royal army be encamped forty miles to the east of London, while his army be encamped forty miles to the west of London, so that the presence of armed forces might not interfere with the freedom of parliamentary sessions. The prince proposed further that he and James II each be free to attend sessions in London with a personally chosen body guard. William went on to suggest that the garrison of royal troops at Portsmouth be set under the command of an officer mutually trusted by the King and himself. And William urged that both armies be considered in the service of England, pending a constitutional settlement between the Crown and Parliament, and be obliged by law to disperse when paid as agreed by the Commons, Lords, and King.

This offer assured the safety and dignity of James II and his family, and would have permitted Prince James Edward to inherit the Crown. There would have been a price, including concessions limiting royal prerogatives and ensuring parliamentary authority. Most likely, the House of Commons would have gained important voice in choosing the King's ministers. There would have been a new organic act, declaring the privileges and immunities of freemen against unconstitutional usurpations of the Crown. And there would have been a compromise on questions of church and state, which, though imperfect, would have promoted greater religious liberty.

James II fell short of the kind of sophistication required for the state of affairs in which he found himself. He arranged secret transportation of his wife and son to France. On December 11, 1688, he threw the Great Seal into the River Thames and ordered the royal army disbanded, leaving London in wild turmoil.

James II was captured by fishermen in his escape on the 11th of December, and delivered to William of Orange, who had him carried in royal pomp and splendor to a place where he was able to escape again on the 22nd, this time arriving in France where he became the very usable guest of Louis XIV at the Palais de St-Germain. The King of France had taken the King of England, his Queen, and the lawful heir to his Crown. But checkmate it was not to be.

The Prince of Orange called an irregular assembly of notables of the realm, including the peers and members of the parliaments of Charles II.

They met with William on December 26, 1688, and advised him to summon a convention of the estates of the realm. He summoned the peers and bishops, and the counties, boroughs, cities, and universities were summoned to elect members. The deliberations began on January 22, 1689.

After debate, the body calling itself the "House of Commons" passed a famous resolution on January 25, 1689:

> "That King James the Second, having endeavored to subvert the constitution of the kingdom by breaking the original compact between the King and the people, and by the advice of Jesuits and other wicked persons having violated the fundamental laws and withdrawn himself out of the kingdom, hath abdicated the government, and that the throne is thereby vacant."

On February 12, 1689, the House of Lords agreed. On February 13, 1689, the Crown was tendered to and accepted by William of Orange and his wife Mary Stuart, who thereby became King William III and Queen Mary II of England. The occasion was commemorated by the Act of 1 William and Mary, Session 1, Chapter 1 (1689), reenacted in substance on December 16th of the same year as the Act of 1 William and Mary, Session 2, Chapter 2 (1689).

In these resolutions, the "Lords spiritual and temporal" and "Commons" recited the misdeeds of the "late King" who was said to have "abdicated" the government and left the throne "vacant" as if there were no lawful heir, then they enacted the landmark English Bill of Rights of 1689 in thirteen Articles: — 1st and 2nd, that it is unlawful for the King to suspend or dispense with laws arbitrarily without consent of Parliament; — 3rd, that it is unlawful for the King to commission an ecclesiastical court without the consent of Parliament; — 4th, that it is unlawful for the King to levy taxes without the consent of Parliament; — 5th, that it is the right of subjects to petition the King peacefully without being prosecuted or committed; — 6th, that it is unlawful for the King to keep a standing army within the realm in time of peace without the consent of Parliament; — 7th, that subjects have a right to keep and bear arms for their personal defense according to long established customs and laws, etc.

This event commencing the reign of William and Mary, embodied in the Acts of the Convention Parliament of 1689, is fondly called the Glorious Revolution.

In this Glorious Revolution there were no mass executions, confiscations, and prosecutions. It was a profound transition in government accomplished with quiet finesse.

It was a revolution as all great commentators and historians have agreed, because the Acts of 1 William and Mary and everything done by the Convention Parliament of 1689 were in defiance of the constitution of England as it then stood.

No lawful Parliament was summoned by writ of the rightful King. James II certainly signed no deed of abdication, and claimed to be King until his death. Even if the flight of James II were taken as a constructive abdication, his son born in wedlock would instantly have been the new King. There was, consequently, no vacancy in the throne. The Crown was bestowed upon a foreign prince who had no right to it under any known principle of fundamental law. The declarations of the Convention Parliament justifying transfer of the Crown to William and Mary were, quite literally, legal fiction. In the words of one great constitutional historian, the "convention pronounced under the slight disguise of a word unusual in the language of English law, that the actual sovereign had forfeited the right to the nation's allegiance. It swept away by the same vote the reversion of his posterity and of those who could claim the inheritance of the Crown."[61]

In Scotland the documents of the revolution were more forthright. It was there said that James VII had "forfeited" the Crown. Sir John Dalrymple was most responsible for this language. He was adamant about the moral error of attempting to bastardize Prince James Edward Stuart. "To defend the revolution on a pretended supposititious birth," he said honorably, "is to affront it. It stands upon a much higher foundation, the rights of human nature. The supposititious birth was a mere lie of party."[62]

* * * * *

The Convention Parliament of 1689 stipulated that William and Mary should jointly hold the Crown; — that nevertheless during their joint lives William should exercise actual powers of Government; — that, upon the death of either William or Mary, the survivor of the two should govern; — that, in the absence of heirs of the body of either William or Mary, the Crown should pass to Princess Anne of Denmark, the younger daughter of James II and Anne Hyde. Anne, conveniently, was also Protestant.

After Mary II died in 1694 and it was obvious that William III would produce no heir, provision was made for continuity of the Crown. The Statute of 12 & 13 William III, Chapter 2 (1701), known as the Act of Settlement, adopted certain further constitutional reforms, including a provision for judicial tenure on good behavior, with compensation ascertained and established, but subject to removal on bill of address. But the main provision says that, if Princess Anne of Denmark were to die without off-spring, the Crown would pass to the "most excellent Princess Sophia and the heirs of her body, being Protestant." Sophia was a granddaughter of James I by his daughter Elizabeth. Sophia was, therefore, a cousin of Charles II and James II. She was also, by her marriage to Ernst Augustus, Elector of Hanover, a princess of the Holy Roman Empire.

Princess Anne of Denmark became Queen Anne in 1702, and died childless in 1714. The Crown passed under the Act of Settlement to George, Elector of Hanover, who became King George I. All monarchs since reigning have inherited the Crown as Protestant heirs of the body of Princess Sophia under the Act of Settlement: — George II in 1727, George III in 1760, George IV in 1820, William IV in 1830, Victoria in 1837, Edward VII in 1901, George V in 1910, Edward VIII then his broth-er George VI in 1936, then Elizabeth II Dei gratia Regina since 1952.

* * * * *

There were many who never accepted the Glorious Revolution, because it was an "unconstitutional" transformation of government in England. They were called "Jacobites" after the Latin "Jacobus" for James II and his son James Edward. They were not necessarily opposed to the idea of making William of Orange regent to act in place of James II after he fled to France. But they insisted that, after James II, only his son had a proper and lawful right to wear the Crown.

Among these Jacobites were some colorful characters, such as Sir John Graham of Claverhouse, Viscount Dundee, whose Scottish army smashed troops of the Prince of Orange at the Pass of Killiecrankie in 1689. "Bonnie Dundee," as he was called, fell gloriously on the field wearing the cross of Knight Templar, for the papal bull abolishing the ancient order in 1312 A. D. had never been published in Scotland. With his death, his warriors vanished into the highlands.

When his father died in 1701, Prince James Edward Stuart was imme-diately proclaimed King James III of England, James VIII of Scotland, at the Palais de St-Germain in France. He created a prolific number of peers, baronets, and knights. He lived a royal life on the continent of Europe until his death in 1766. He was shown the deference owed to a King, and in his heart he was a King.

By those who favored the Glorious Revolution, James III was called the "Old Pretender," which was a play on words from the French verb "pretendre" meaning to maintain or contend, not to pretend as in English. His contemporaries in France naturally said of him, "Il pretend qu'il est le roi d'Angleterre." And by the fundamental law of the country of his birth as it stood when he was born, he most certainly was the King of England, and also the King of Scotland and the King of Ireland. When he wed Princess Clementina Sobieska of Poland, his three Crowns were laid on satin pillows before the alter at the High Mass.

James III was of generous mind and gracious character,[63] and might really have been "the best of Kings." He may well have saved his people from many calamities, as has been speculated in erudition.[64] Most likely, he would have kept England out of wasteful involvement in the wars on the continent of Europe, which in turn would have avoided or weakened dangerous currents leading to the American Revolution.

In 1715 and 1716, a highland rebellion known as "the Fifteen" was mounted in Scotland by Prince James Edward Stuart who, in anticipation of this expedition, had been created the Chevalier de St-Georges by Louis XIV. The rebellion was raised to a high pitch because of reaction against the Act of Union, 5 Anne, Chapters 6 and 8 (1707). The Act fused the parliaments in London and in Edinburgh into a single British Parliament in which members and peers from Scotland were greatly outnumbered by those from England, thus depriving Scotland of a constitutional shield to protect her distinct interests against exploitation by England.

At length the Fifteen was beaten down. James Edward left a large treasure behind him to pay weary soldiers and to relieve the distressed in burned villages. He bade farewell to his people from Montrose: — "It was with the view of delivering this my kingdom from hardships it lies under and restoring it to its former happiness and independency," he said, "that brought me to this country."[65] A few weeks later, one of the chiefs of the beaten army of James III delivered an oration from the scaffold on which he was about to die. James Earl of Derwentwater declared,

> "I only wish now that the laying down of my life might contribute to the service of my King and country, and the reestablishment of the ancient and fundamental constitution of these kingdoms, without which no lasting peace or true happiness can attend them; then I should indeed part with my life even with pleasure. As it is, I can only pray that these blessings may be bestowed upon my dear country; and since I can do no more, I beseech God to accept of my life as a small sacrifice towards it."[66]

Six other English peers were sentenced to death. Two escaped. Three were amnestied. But William Viscount Kenmure also perished by the headman's ax for the cause of James III.

Thereafter the House of Stuart found protection in the Papal States.

In 1745 and 1746 Prince Charles Edward Stuart, elder son of the Chevalier de St-Georges, raised another highland rebellion which was called "the Forty-Five." The Jacobite heir, fondly called "Bonnie Prince Charlie," became the most romantic of the many romantic characters in Scottish history. He had a brilliant personality, an electrifying presence, an irresistible charm.

In July 1745, he landed on the Isle of Eriskay, in August he stood on the mainland at Borrodale, in September he raised his royal standard at Glenfinnan, then entered Edinburgh in triumph: — before cheering crowds and magistrates in robes, his father was proclaimed King James VIII of Scotland. That evening Charles Edward held a state ball at Holyrood Palace, the traditional home of the Royal Stuarts. His great great great grandmother Mary Queen of Scots had resided there. The white rose, as it had been the symbol of the legitimate heir of the House of York, became also the emblem of the Jacobite cause, and ever since has stood for courage in the face of oppression. Two days later, the prince routed troops of George II at Pestonpans. Soon thereafter he was master of Scotland.

The Jacobite regiments marched into England as far as Derby. If as he ardently wished, Bonnie Prince Charlie had tried to enter London, he might have died with his troops, for his little army was heavily outnumbered, — or he might have been received with open arms by the people as in Edinburgh, and King James III might have been proclaimed by natural right as the true sovereign of England. There was a council of war. The military chiefs insisted upon retreat, and Charles Edward acceded only because he could not persuade his commanding officers to take an heroic risk. Sober military and political assessments, since made with all the advantages of hindsight, are inclined to concur with the prince, because the House of Hanover was unpopular, and George II was involved in a foreign war more important to his duchy in Germany than to the liking of the people of England.

The retreat was militarily successful, but the advantage from the momentum of success was lost. Bonnie Prince Charlie marched far to the north, and encamped near Inverness. Large bodies of infantry, cavalry, and artillery under the Duke of Cumberland, a son of George II, moved from several directions upon the weaker Jacobite formations. In the hope of reversing the tide by a quick and stunning blow before Cumberland's forces were concentrated, the prince gave battle at Culloden Moor. The highland charges were smashed by overwhelming firepower. Wanton slaughter of defeated soldiers followed upon the field. There were seventy-seven vindictive executions in the aftermath.

Bonnie Prince Charlie made a narrow escape by the Isle of Skye with the help of gallant Flora McDonald. Some of his followers escaped with him, including James Johnstone, the aide-de-camp to the Jacobite lieutenant general, Lord George Murray. After the Forty-Five, Johnstone joined the French Army, and ended his career as the aide-de-camp to the Marquis de Montcalm on the Plains of Abraham in Canada. The British general on the Plains of Abraham, James Wolfe, had earlier fought against Johnstone as a brigade major at Culloden. In retirement, this old Jacobite soldier of the Forty-Five and the Seven Years War, still loyal to King James VIII of Scotland, was granted a pension and created the Chevalier de Johnstone by King Louis XV of France.

Charles Edward was celebrated in Paris after his return from the Forty-Five, but he was a broken man. Thereafter his life, once so full of dash and charm, degenerated aimlessly as it became painfully clear that the Jacobite cause was dead in law as administered, dead in political hope, and alive only in sentimental memory. He was prone to nurse his melancholy with Scotch whiskey. In 1788 he died in Rome an alcoholic in the care of his daughter by an old lover, — outcast, destitute, bored with life, without child born in wedlock, in Jacobite eyes King Charles III of England, surviving in historical memory as perhaps the most beloved of all the royal Stuarts.

Thereupon his younger brother, Prince Henry Benedict Stuart, who was a cardinal in the Catholic Church, assumed the title and style of King Henry IX of England. He struck a silver medal upon his accession, on the reverse side of which was found his motto: "Non desideriis hominum sed voluntate Dei," — Chosen not by men but by the will of God.

The "Cardinal King," as he was called, enjoyed a very cordial relationship with the House of Hanover. While the Duke of Sussex, a son of George III, was once visiting Italy, his carriage met the carriage of Prince Henry Benedict Stuart. The younger man got out of his carriage and paid homage to his elder quarter cousin, who thereupon invited the Hanover prince to dinner at his villa. George III treasured one of the medals struck by Henry Benedict at the time of his accession in Jacobite eyes, and paid the old cardinal a pension from his civil list to assist him with financial difficulties in later life.

The Cardinal King was camerlingo upon the death of Pope Pius VI in 1800. In defiance of Napoleon, he organized the conclave which elected Pope Pius VII. In humbly accepting the fate imposed on him by circumstances, he quietly prevented the collapse of the Catholic Church. In fitting tribute, the mortal remains of James III, Charles III, and Henry IX were interred in a monument at the Vatican.

When he died in 1807, the claim of Prince Henry Benedict Stuart was inherited by King Charles Emmanuel IV of Sardinia, next in line by right of primogeniture through Henrietta, Duchesse d'Orléans and daughter of King Charles I of England. The old Stuart claim has since been passed down from generation to generation. Those who have since inherited the honor have cherished it, but politely acquiesced to the present British royal family.

There was once an Italian princess who was heir of the body of Henrietta, Duchesse d'Orléans. When her uncle the Duke of Modena died in 1875, she inherited his titles, and was socially honored as Queen Mary III of England. She married a prince of the House of Wittelsbach in Bavaria. Since her death in 1919, the heirs of her body in Bavaria have each in turn inherited a natural right to the British Crown. It so happens that during the last years of Adolf Hitler's Third Reich, a group of students in Bavaria rose up against Nazi tyranny. They were hunted down, found guilty, and guillotined. Their symbol was the white rose.

* * * * *

Looking back upon events, there was a grand attempt by Pope Leo III to revive the West Roman Empire by the coronation of Charlemagne. Although this effort later floundered, it did succeed in reestablishing a beneficial degree of viable political order in Europe during the Dark Ages. A commonwealth of princes and kings grew up under the Holy See.

The English Reformation was really a formal secession of England from this papal commonwealth in keeping with the fundamental law of the kingdom.

The change of dynasty from the House of Tudor to the House of Stuart was, again, a constitutional transformation in the government of England.

The Puritan Revolution was nothing but the unlawful imprisonment of the English nation by an army utterly out of control, not unlike the murder of the Emperor Pertinax by the pretorian guard of Rome, and the sale of the purple to the highest bidder at public auction.[67]

Constitutional order was after all restored by the return of Charles II according to a process which was, again, impeccably regular and legal.

But nothing in the previous history of England was quite like the Glorious Revolution.

There is no honest way to justify what happened upon then existing principles of fundamental law, yet it has become a true and proper basis for the rule of law.

The event happened at a time when the practical choices were greatly limited: — either submission to grave menace against vital interests which the nation was absolutely unwilling to surrender or negotiate, or else building a new legal order, even if upon an irregular basis, yet as far as possible according to legal tradition.

It happened after James II had left unused or actively destroyed opportunities to promote moderation, justice, and reconciliation, as were made possible by the advice of the House of Lords sitting as the Magnum Concilium and the proposals of William of Orange at Hungerford.

The revolution in England happened peacefully. There was no extorted abdication, no murder in a dungeon, no brutal usurpation, no ceremonial beheading. Troops went through the motions of advances and retreats. At one point there was a mock encounter, but no real battle. The first Act of the Convention Parliament in 1689 began the reign of William and Mary. When this event occurred, it was contrary to the forms of established law. Yet it developed into a new constitutional reality, and eventually it became a venerable principle of fundamental law.

Upon the accession of William and Mary, the revolution rested upon a principle which, in due course, was acknowledged as a constitutional custom, capable of abstract formulation so as to apply in the future under certain but exceptional circumstances, not as an event requiring force of arms, least of all justifying violence or injustice, but as allowing a perfectly rational and lawful occurrence.

It is true that the Jacobite movement was led by characters brave and virtuous. And it is a fact which many prefer to overlook, but a fact not unworthy of notice that in 1696 William III proposed that James III should become his successor.[68] It is unfortunate that James III did not become King, because he would have been in a stronger position to prevent injustice against Scotland, Ireland, and the colonies in North America. His would have been the longest, and surely the most beneficial reign in the history of England.

But James III did not become King, nor did Charles III produce an heir. And in the words of the poet, "The moving finger writes, and having writ, moves on: Nor all they piety nor wit shall lure it back to cancel half a line, nor all thy tears wash out a word of it."

The misfortunes following the death of William III may be lamented, but can never be used to discredit the Glorious Revolution which contained within itself an indispensable principle of fundamental law: — it allows a revolutionary but lawful and peaceful transformation of government in extraordinary circumstances, by the dignified means of a convention of the people and estates of the kingdom, assembled in as orderly a way as possible by a distinguished prince or the natural leaders of the realm for the purpose of reassuming the attributes of sovereign power, repairing the constitution so as to make it operable once again, and resettling the government of the land.

The idea was thus expressed by Blackstone:

> "Indeed, it is found by experience that, whenever the unconstitutional oppressions even of the sovereign power advance with gigantic strides, and threaten dissolution to a state, mankind will not be reasoned out of the feelings of humanity, nor will sacrifice their liberty by a scrupulous adherence to these political maxims, which were originally established to preserve it. And, therefore, though the positive laws are silent, experience will furnish us with a very remarkable case, wherein nature and reason prevailed. When King James the Second invaded the fundamental constitution of the realm, the Convention declared an abdication, whereby the throne was vacant, which induced a new settlement of the Crown. As so far as this precedent leads and no farther, we may now be allowed to lay down the law of redress of public oppression. If, therefore, any future prince should endeavor to subvert the constitution by breaking the original compact between King and people, should violate the fundamental laws, and should withdraw himself from the kingdom, we are now authorized to declare that this juncture of circumstances would amount to an abdication, and the throne would thereby be vacant. But it is not for us to say that any one or two of these ingredients would amount to such a situation, for there our precedent would fail us. In these, therefore, or other circumstances which a fertile imagination may furnish, since both law and history are silent, it behooves us to be silent too, leaving for future generations, whenever necessity and the safety of the whole require it, the exertion of those inherent but latent powers of society which no climate, no time, no constitution, no contract can ever destroy or diminish."[69]

NOTES

CHAPTER I

1 - From numerous references to Blackstone in the processes of framing and adopting the United States Constitution a few examples may be given: — on ex post facto laws in 1 Blackstone's Commentaries 45-46, discussed by John Dickenson in the Philadelphia Convention, 5 Elliot's Debates 488, Tansill's Documents 633, 2 Ferrand's Records 448-449 (Madison's Notes, August 29, 1787); on the power of the King to make treaties in 1 Blackstone's Commentaires 257, discussed by James Madison, 3 Elliot's Debates 500-501 (Virginia Convention, June 18, 1788), George Nicholas, 3 Elliot's Debates 506 (Virginia Convention, June 18, 1788), and Charles Cotesworth Pinckney, 4 Elliot's Debates 277-278 (South Carolina House of Representatives, January 17, 1788); on the right to trial by jury in 3 Blackstone's Commentaries 349-350, discussed by Patrick Henry, 3 Elliot's Debates 544 (Virginia Convention, June 20, 1788); and on the writ of habeas corpus in 1 Blackstone's Commentaries 438, discussed by Alexander Hamilton in the 84th Federalist, Mentor Edition at 513.

2 - 3 Churchill's History 172.

3 - The most striking instance of framing constitutional provisions on the President of the United States by reference to the King of England is found in the Philadelphia Convention on June 4, 1787, as appears in 5 Elliot's Debates 150-155, Tansill's Documents 145-153, 1 Ferrand's Records 96-105 (Madison's Notes): — attention was there given to the questions of whether the executive power should consist of one officer or several, and whether the executive power should include a power to veto legislative bills. The most systematic discussion of the principal powers of the President by reference to corresponding preroga-tives of the King was written by Alexander Hamilton in the 69th Federalist, Mentor Edition 415-423.

4 - 1 Blackstone's Commentaries 242.

5 - 1 Blackstone's Commentaries 246.

6 - 1 Blackstone's Commentaries 248.

7 - 2 Blackstone's Commentaries 49.

8 - Sir Edward Coke served as solicitor general and attorney general for the Crown, then as Chief Justice of the Court of Common Pleas and Chief Justice of the King's Bench. Most associated with his name was the Case of Commendams pending before the King's Bench in 1616. During argument in this private litigation, counsel questioned the right of the King to grant a benefice in commendam to a certain bishop, — i. e., counsel maintained that James I had no authority to name a bishop with the stipulation that the prelate should continue in the enjoyment of his previous stipend as a clergyman even after taking episcopal office. When the question was raised, the King demanded an opportunity to intervene by his attorney general, because his prerogative was challenged. This request of the King to be heard was altogether reasonable, and, in most jurisdictions today, when public rights are questioned in private litigation, the attorney general must be notified, and given an opportunity for hearing. Lord Coke, however, refused to allow a hearing of the attorney general, and in support of his intransigence cited the second clause 29th Article of the Magna Carta of Henry III, which forbids delay of justice. Most students overlook the fact that the first clause of the 29th Article of the Magna Carta of Henry III demands due process of law, including the right of a person to be heard whenever the court might decide adversely to his interests, and that the King had a right to be heard, the same as any freeman. In the face of Coke's bold affront, the King called the judges together and admonished them. While the rest begged the King's pardon, Coke stood firm. Instead of promising that, in the future, he would heard from the Crown whenever the King's prerogative was questioned in private litigation, Coke petulantly stated that he would do whatever was fit for a judge to do, meaning that he would do whatever he wished. For his defiant behavior, Coke was removed from the bench by the King. Whether on that celebrated occasion Coke was brave or foolish, law-abiding or lawless, is highly debatable. In any event, Coke became a member of Parliament in 1620. He framed the Petition of Right, and had witnessed the assent of Charles I in 1628. He was the author of famous institutes in four books, the first on tenures in land, the second on the Magna Carta of Henry III, the third on criminal law, and the fourth on courts of justice and their jurisdiction. His thirteen volumes of case reports are legal classics to this day. He was no doubt a great lawyer and scholar, and he enjoys historical fame. A convenient and standard account of his career is found in Maitland's History 268-271.

9 - Wilson Nicholas, 3 Elliot's Debates 16 (Virginia Convention, June 4, 1788).

10 - The Statute of 28 Edward III, Chapter 3 (1354), first substituted the phrase "due process of law" for "lawful judgment of his peers or the law of the land."

11 - As expressed in 2 Coke's Institutes 50 and 4 Blackstone's Commentaries 309-310, both based mainly on the Statute of 25 Edward III, Chapter 4 (1451), which was one of many acts elaborating Magna Carta.

12 - As expressed in 4 Blackstone's Commentaries 306-307, based mainly on the Statute of 1 Henry V, Chapter 5 (1413), which was one of many acts elaborating Magna Carta.

13 - As expressed in 2 Coke's Institutes 51-52, and in 1 Blackstone's Commentaries 134-139, 3 Blackstone's Commentaries 131-138, and 4 Blackstone's Commentaries 438-439.

14 - As expressed in 2 Coke's Institutes 48-49, and in 4 Blackstone's Commentaries 348-364. Both of these references discuss jury trial in criminal prosecutions in light of legal customs given reference in Magna Carta. Both mention in particular the right of a peer accused of a felony by indictment or presentment to be tried before the House of Lords, in such case known as the Court of the Lord High Steward, and the right of any subject accused by indictment, presentment, or information to be tried by jury before the King's Bench.

15 - The right of trial by jury in suits at common law, as developed by legal customs given reference in Magna Carta, is extensively discussed in 3 Blackstone's Commentaries 349-385. It was on the basis of Magna Carta that, in those suits of a civil nature brought at common law by or in the name of the King, the right of trial by jury was preserved. So it was in a suit on writ of scire facias on the common law side of the Court of Chancery to recover anything granted by patent of the Crown contrary to law or subject to forfeiture on condition broken, as appears in 3 Blackstone's Commentaries 48-49 and 260-261, or suit at common law in behalf of the Crown in the Court of the Exchequer to recover money including taxes due and unpaid, land, or chattels, or to redress a private wrong against the King, as appears in 3 Blackstone's Commentaries 261-262, or a suit at common law on information in the nature of quo warranto to oust a usurper wrongfully holding a public office or to terminate a corporate charter or other public franchise for misuser or nonuser, as appears in 3 Blackstone's Commentaries 262-264.

16 - The right, deriving from Magna Carta, not to be deprived of private property for public use, except upon payment of full indemnification pursuant to an act of Parliament, is described in 3 Blackstone's Commentaries 148-141.

17 - The right, deriving from Magna Carta, to sue for adequate remedy to redress every injustice in the courts of the King is described in 2 Coke's Institutes 55-56 and 1 Blackstone's Commentaries 141-142.

18 - The principal act was part of the comprehensive procedural reform call the Second Statute of Westminister, viz., the the Statute of 13 Edward I, Chapter 24 (1285). Technically, suits at common law were brought on original writ only before the Court of Common Pleas. Suits at common law before the King's Bench on bill of Middlesex, and before the Court of the Exchequer on writ of quo minis in behalf of private subjects, and on information in behalf of the Crown, yet these suits could not exceed the scope of writs and actions over which the Court of Common Pleas had jurisdiction.

19 - A perpetual copyright at common law in the writings of a private author, good at least in the absence of modified statutory interpretation, was recognized in *Miller v. Taylor*, 4 Burrow 2303 (K. B. 1769), and also Donaldson v. Becket, 4 Burrow 2408 (H. L. 1774). A copyright has always been legally different from a patent of invention, because unlike a patent it does not protect an idea, but only a particular literary expression of an idea. A classic discussion of copyright at common law is found in the majority and dissenting opinions in *Wheaton v. Peters*, 8 Peters 591 (U. S. 1834).

20 - In the *Five Knights Case*, 3 Howell's St. Tr. 1 (K. B. 1627), five gentlemen refused to loan money to the King as demanded, then were thrown into prison so they might reflect on their lack of generosity to his Majesty. They sued out writs of habeas corpus, and the Crown answered that the five gentlemen were confined to the King's "special command," which the court found to be sufficient reason for the confinement. This judgment did not set well with the country, and more than almost any other event prompted the Petition of Right.

21 - The Star Chamber was formally instituted by the Statute of 3 Henry VII, Chapter 1 (1488), in which a kind of summary justice was dispensed against corrupt or lawless sheriffs and other officers in the administration of justice. This court originally brought about important reforms, but over 150 years it grossly exceeded all limits on its jurisdiction, allowed proceedings against private individuals, and adopted uncivilized procedures. By the reign of Charles I, the court became an engine of oppression, remaining to this day a symbol of judicial atrocity.

22 - The Court of High Commission was established by royal proclamation in 1583 under the Statute of 1 Elizabeth I, Chapter 1 (1559), to deal with ecclesiastical discipline and other affairs of the church of England. Like the Star Chamber, this administrative tribunal exceeded its jurisdiction and indulged in practices which made the court odious in political memory.

23 - The main judicial decision against the use of general warrants — i. e., warrants for arrest or search not limited to certain persons or places or evidence — was given by Lord Camden in *Entick v. Carrington*, 19 Howell's St. Tr. 1030 (K. B. 1765). Lord Camden's opinion was quoted in extenso and given great praise in *Boyd v. United States*, 116 U. S. 616 at 625-630 (1886).

24 - The last case in which this judicial doctrine was pronounced was *The King v. Shipley*, 4 Douglas 73 (K. B. 1784), informally known as the Dean of St. Asaph's Case. In this prosecution for criminal libel, the great barrister Thomas Erskine argued that truth is a defense in a case of criminal libel, as maintained by Sir John Powell in the *Seven Bishops Case*, 12 Howell's St. Tr. 183 (K. B. 1688), and that the jury in a criminal case may always find the accused not guilty, regardless of the law and the facts, as sustained by Lord Vaughn in *Bushell's Case*, 6 Howell's St. Tr. 999 (C. P. 1670). In the Dean of St. Asaph's Case, the jury was brow-beaten by the court into a finding of guilty, but the accused was relieved of punishment on motion in arrest of judgment on account of a techni-

cal flaw in the indictment. The doctrine that truth is no defense in a case of criminal libel was abolished by Fox's Libel Act, 32 George III, Chapter 60 (1792).

25 - Prior to 1679 the justices of Common Pleas and the barons of the Exchequer issued writs of habeas corpus on the basis of certain legal fictions, but the Statute of 31 Charles II gave them and the Chancellor express authority equal to the justices of the King's Bench, removing all doubt, as appears in 3 Blackstone's Commentaries 131-138.

26 - The requirement that electors of knights of the shire own freeholds yielding annual revenue of at least 40 shillings was originally instituted by the Statute of 8 Henry VI, Chapter 7 (1430), and was amended by the Statutes of 10 Henry VI, Chapter 2 (1432), and 14 George III, Chapter 58 (1774). Qualifications of burgesses were generally regulated by local custom until the Statute of 3 George III, Chapter 15 (1763), which required that electors be admitted to freedom for at least twelve months. The Statute of 9 Anne, Chapter 5 (1711) required that members of the House of Commons own a freehold or copyhold yielding an annual revenue of at least £600, except for burgesses who were each required to own a freehold or copyhold yielding an annual revenue of at least £300. The qualifications of electors and members of the House of Commons are discussed respectively in 1 Blackstone's Commentaries at 170-174 and 175-177.

27 - Finally sustained in the judgment of the House of Lords in 1667 on writ of error, reversing the King's Bench in the Case of Sir John Eliot, Denzil Holles, and Benjamin Valentine in 1630, and upholding as a general law the Statute of 4 Henry VIII, Chapter 8 (1512). Freedom of parliamentary speech was further vindicated in the 9th Article of the Bill of Rights adopted by the Convention Parliament in 1689. Abuse of freedom of speech in Parliament could be redressed by censure or expulsion for misbehavior, but not by prosecution or suit brought outside of Parliament.

28 - The history of this privilege against arrest of legislators during sessions grew out of controversies arising during the reigns of James I and Charles I. The privilege excluded arrest of a member of Parliament during sessions for criminal libel, since the offence, though a misdemeanor, was not a breach of peace, as held by Lord Camden in *The King v. Wilkes*, 2 Wilson 251 (C. P. 1763).

29 - The history of this development, especially from and after the reign of James I, was prolonged, but the right of the House of Commons to admit its members, without interference from the King or any others outside of Parliament, was vindicated by the guarantee of free elections in the 8th Article of the Bill of Rights adopted by the Convention Parliament in 1689, and was confirmed again by the Statute of 7 William III, Chapter 7 (1695).

30 - These Statutes of 10, 11, and 14 George III were adopted to correct the refusal of the House of Commons to seat John Wilkes who had been elected after he had been driven into foreign exile on account of his denunciation of certain policies of the Crown: — he had been tried in absentia while abroad and found

guilty on a charge of sedition, then sentenced upon his return hom, as appears in *The King v. Wilkes*, 4 Burrow 2527 at 2574 (K. B. 1770). The proceedings to exclude Wilkes from the House of Commons, notwithstanding his lawful election, were expunged from legislative records in 1782 as subversive of free elections guaranteed by the 8th Article of the Bill of the Rights adopted by the Convention Parliament in 1689. Wilkes became a brilliant reformer, and his efforts ultimately matured after he died in the abolition of rotten boroughs by the Statute of 2 & 3 William IV, Chapter 45 (1832).

31 - Abbots and priors were excluded from the House of Lords during the English Reformation by the seizure of the monasteries under the Statutes of 27 Henry VIII, Chapter 28 (1537), and 31 Henry VIII, Chapter 13 (1539). The redistribution of theses assets among the nobility consolidated the King's power against the Catholic Church.

32 - The origins and proceedings of the House of Lords as the Magnum Concilium of the King are discussed in 1 Blackstone's Commentaries 227-229.

33 - The prerogatives of the Crown as they stood at the end of the Seven Years War were discussed in 1 Blackstone's Commentaries 250-280. These pages give no hint whatever that the powers of the King were to be exercised by anybody other than the King himself according to his personal discretion.

34 - 1 Blackstone's Commentaries 233.

35 - As was held by Sir Edward Coke and three other judges in their formal advice to the privy council in the *Case of Proclamations*, 12 Coke 74 (1611).

36 - In 1 Blackstone's Commentaries 231-232, it was said that an arrest on warrant issued by the privy council was subject to examination on writ of habeas corpus, the same as for a warrent issued by a mere justice of the peace, in keeping with the Statute of 16 Charles I, Chapter 10 (1641), abolishing the Star Chamber.

37 - 1 Blackstone's Commentaries 160. The sweeping and irresistible power of Parliament was the constitutional basis in England for bills of attainder, i. e., legislation convicting and ordering execution of individuals for capital crimes, and bills of pains and penalties, i. e., legislation convicting and punishing individuals for lesser public offenses. These devices of Tudor autocracy were, not formally abolished, but largely discontinued and radically changed in usage to accommodate the demands of due process, after bills of attainder, loaded with political hatred, were forced through the Long Parliament in 1641 by stirring up mobs in order to bring about the execution of Thomas Wentworth, Earl of Strafford, and William Laud, Archbishop of Canterbury.

38 - As explained in 1 Blackstone's Commentaries 150-152, which, however, contains a remarkable claim, — that the Convention Parliament in 1689 met on the full conviction that James II had abdicated the government, which has absolutely no

relationship to the operative political facts which were known and understood by everybody involved. The 13th Article of the Bill of Rights adopted by the Convention Parliament in 1689 declared that the King, who then had the sole power, also had a solemn duty to call Parliament frequently. It was specifically enacted in the Statute of 6 William and Mary, Chapter 2 (1694), that the King should call a new Parliament within three years of the termination of the previous Parliament.

39 - As explained in 1 Blackstone's Commentaries 188-189. It should be noted that, after the Glorious Revolution, the Statutes of 7 & 8 William III, Chapter 15 (1696), and 6 Anne, Chapter 7 (1708) were enacted to continue the life of Parliament for an extra six months, notwithstanding demise of the King or Queen. The prerogative of dissolving Parliament came in time to be used less and less, and, therefore, it was ordained in the Statute of 6 William and Mary, Chapter 2 (1696) that Parliament should be automatically dissolved after three years, but this limit was found to be impracticable, and so was extended to seven years by the Act of 1 George I, Statute 2, Chapter 38 (1715).

40 - The principles of succession to the Crown by right of primogeniture were restated in 1 Blackstone's Commentaries 193-195, although these passages contain some legal fiction to make the explanation plausible. This body of customary law for the succession of the Crown was taken from the principles of primogeniture for the inheritance of land under the feudal system in England, these described in 2 Blackstone's Commentaries 208-240. The main difference was that, if there were no heir male, land went to the heirs female together; but, if there were no heir male, the Crown went exclusively to the eldest heir female.

41 - Catherine of Aragon first married Arthur Tudor, an elder son of Henry VII and Elizabeth of York. But Prince Arthur predeceased his father, and so the Crown went to the next son as Henry VIII. When it became obvious that Catherine would bear no son, Henry VIII feared that the accession of his daughter might raise questions about whether Elizabeth of York should have inherited the Crown rather than Henry VII. In this situation, Henry VIII resolved to sue Catherine for a divorce — i. e., an decree annulling his marriage to her as avoid ab initio to satisfy the canon law — , and the pretext cooked up for this occasion was a stretching of the natural meaning of Leviticus 18:16, which says, "Thou shalt not uncover the nakedness of thy brother's wife: it is thy brother's nakedness." This verse prohibits sexual relations between a man and his brother's wife, naturally while his brother is living, because, when his brother dies, her marriage with him has ended, she is no longer is wife, and she is free remarry any eligible male. Clement VII was, therefore, perfectly correct in refusing an annulment on such spurious grounds, and that appears to be the simplest and fairest view of the case It has been maintained nevertheless that the whole episode had nothing to do with Leviticus 18:16, and that events were driven by a grand imbroglio of global politics: — the theory is that Clement VII was under the control of the Holy Roman Emperor Charles V, nephew of Catherine, and absolutely opposed for reasons of state to the designs of Henry VIII. Insight into this theory can be

found in 2 Fears' Acton 259-311 and 2 Churchill's History 47-65.

42 - The royal heir under the Statute of 35 Henry VIII was the eldest male descendant of Lady Catherine Grey and Edward Seymour, Earl of Hertford and nephew of Queen Jane Seymour. Lady Catherine was the second daughter of Henry Grey, created second Duke of Suffolk by Edward VI, and Francis Brandon, elder daughter of Mary Tudor by Charles Brandon. After the death of her elder sister Lady Jane Grey in 1554, Lady Catherine Grey was certainly the heir presumptive to the Crown under the Statute of 35 Henry VIII, and so also was her eldest legitimate son after her. The marriage between Edward Seymour and Lady Catherine was presumed valid at common law, and, during their lives, both of them gave testimony under oath as to the ceremony and consummation of their marriage, nor was their testimony ever disproved or even disputed in any satisfactory way whatever. The minister of religion who witnessed their vows was available at one point to testify. Edward Seymour, Lord Hertford, lived to an advanced age, and upon the monument of his grave was an epitaph in Latin, attesting to his undying love for his wife Lady Catherine. The elder son of Edward Seymour and Lady Catherine, born about 1561, was William Seymour, known as Lord Beauchamp in recognition of the barony he held. Because of his legitimate and gentle birth, he was heir to the Crown upon the death of Queen Elizabeth under the Statute of 35 Henry VIII. During the reign of Charles II, the title of Duke of Somerset, which once belonged to the Seymours, was restored to the son of Lord Beauchamp. The patent restoring the title conceded that this son of Lord Beauchamp was the "heir male of the body of the first duke," i. e., the brother of Queen Jane Symour and the father of the Edward Seymour who sired Lord Beauchamp by Lady Catherine Grey. By necessary implication, the marriage of Lord Beauchamp's parents was lawful. The grandson of Lord Beauchamp was the Charles Seymour, Duke of Somerset, who made the famous remark to James II, "Your Majesty may be above the law, but I am not." The essential facts can be gathered in standard accounts, including Hallam's History 98-103 and 209-212, 2 Macauley's History 247-248, and 2 Churchill's History 82-87, 397.

43 - 1 Blackstone's Commentaries 38-43.

44 - 1 Macauley's History 73-74. Gloating with whiggish bias, Lord Macauley expanded this description into a sarcastic caricature. Wiser men have thought better of it.

45 - 5 Hume's History at 4.

46 - As Chief Justice of the King's Bench, Lord Coke twice attempted to assert the superiority of jurisdiction at common law over jurisdiction in equity. In *Courtney v. Glanville*, Croke Jacobus 343 (K. B. 1615), he released on writ of habeas an individual incarcerated by the Chancellor, Lord Ellesmere, for contempt of court, consisting of disobedience of a decree setting aside a judgment entered at common law which had been secured by fraud. He held that, in questioning a judgment of the King's Bench, the Chancellor had committed a species of crime called praemunire. In *Bromage v. Gunning*, 1 Rolle 368 (K. B. 1615), Coke held that the common law

had exclusive jurisdiction over all covenants under seal, and issued a writ of prohibition enjoining the Court of Chancery from entertaining a suit for specific performance of such a covenant for the sale of land. Both judgments were extravagant, both were against natural justice, and both savored more of politics than anything else. Acting upon the advice of Sir Francis Bacon recorded in the first volume of *Reports in Chancery*, King James I intervened by judgment of the Crown, acting on the advice of Sir Francis Bacon, on July 14, 1616: — "We in our princely judgment do will and command that our Chancellor, or Keeper of the Great Seal for the time being, shall not desist to give unto our subjects, upon their several complaints now and hereafter to be made, such relief in equity, notwithstanding any proceedings at common law against them, as shall stand with the merit and justice of the cause and with the former, ancient, and continued practice and presidency of our Chancery." While Coke enjoys historical fame, his character was not all good, as illustrated by his unworthy conduct as attorney general in the trial of the Earl of Essex and the trial of Sir Walter Raleigh, respectively described in 4 Hume's History at 325 and 5 Hume's History at 10.

47 - 2 Churchill's History at 275.

48 - 5 Hume's History at 544.

49 - 5 Hume's History at 545-546

50 - 2 Churchill's History at 310.

51 - These many oppressive laws on religious conformity are restated in 4 Blackstone's Commentaries 41-65. A few examples may here be given: — the Statute of 1 Elizabeth I, Chapter 2 (1559) forbade celebration of the Catholic Mass; — the Statute of 27 Elizabeth I, Chapter 2 (1585) made it an act of treason for a Catholic priest born within the dominions of the Crown to visit England for more than three days without submission to public authority; — and the Statute of 1 James I, Chapter 4 (1603) and subsequent acts imposed heavy fines, forfeitures, and other disabilities upon parents who had their children sent abroad for education in the Catholic faith. The Corporation Act, 13 Charles II, Chapter 1 (1662) ordained that no person could hold public office, unless within the year previous he had received communion according to the rite of the Church of England and took an oath of allegiance to the King. The Test Act, 25 Charles II, Chapter 2 (1673) required all public officers, civil and military, to take oaths and declare against the doctrine of transubstantiation. Catholics were unaided by the Act of Toleration, 1 William and Mary, Session 1, Chapter 18 (1689), which granted religious toleration to those dissenting against the Church of England only if they took oaths or affirmations against the Pope. Charles II feigned indifference to religion, but was secretly a Catholic during his life, as explained in 2 Fears' Acton 132-162, and was reconciled when he received the Holy Eucharist and the Last Rites from a Catholic priest on his deathbed, as related in 1 Macauley's History 387-397. By contrast, James II was obtuse in professing the Catholic faith to the point that he needlessly offended the sensitivities of his

20

Protestant subjects: — e. g., contrary to diplomatic convention for a King receiving a foreign diplomat, James II knelt before the papal nuncio from Innocent XI, then dismissed the Duke of Somerset for refusing his order to swell the pomp of the occasion, as related in 2 Macauley's History at 247-248.

52 - There is a touching story about Charles II who, though cynical about many things, remembered his restoration in 1660, which he considered an act of God. He therefore upheld the divine right of a natural heir to be King. He was aware that his brother "Jimmy" was unfit by temperament to be King, and would have considered legislation to make him King in name only. Yet, when in 1681 he was faced with a bill to exclude the Duke of York from the throne altogether, Charles II answered Anthony Cooper, Earl of Shaftsbury, "Let there be no delusion. I will not yield, nor will I be bullied. Men usually become more timid as they become older; it is the opposite with me, and for what may remain of my life, I am determined that nothing shall tarnish my reputation. I have the law and reason and all right-thinking men on my side." — 2 Churchill's History 374. A few days later, Charles II dissolved Parliament.

53 - In *Bates' Case*, 2 Howell's St. Tr. 271 (Exch. 1606), it was held by servile judges that, notwithstanding Confirmatio Chartarum and other such sources of fundamental law, the King could by proclamation impose duties on commerce. This decision was certainly superseded and reversed by the Petition of Right in 1628. The claimed right of the King to impose by proclamation a land tax called ship money, notwithstanding the Petition of Right, was upheld by seven of twelve judges in *The King v. Hampden*, 3 Howell's St. Tr. 825 (Exch. Ch. 1637), informally called the Case of Ship Money, but this judgment was manifestly wrong, and was annulled by the Statute of 16 Charles I, Chapter 14 (1641). The judges who voted to uphold the royal levy were impeached by the House of Commons for the high misdemeanor of rendering a lawless judgment, tried and convicted before the House of Lords, the removed from the bench and sent to prison, as appears in the *Case of Sir Robert Berkeley*, 3 Howell's St. Tr. 1263 (H. L. 1641).

54 - Here involved was the right of subjects under the Statute of Northampton, 2 Edward III, Chapter 3 (1328), on which discussion is found in 3 Coke's Institutes 160-161 and 1 Blackstone's Commentaries 144-145. This statute made reference, not to the duty of freemen to bear arms for the King in the posse comitatus or the militia, but to the right of freemen to keep and bear arms for the defense of themselves and their property: — the statute made it unlawful for subjects not the King's servants to "come before the King's justices or other of the King's ministers doing their office with force of arms," or to bring "force in affray of peace," or to go or "ride armed by night" or "day in fairs or markets," etc. The scope of this right was defined in the old landmark reported as *Sir John Knight's Case*, 3 Modern 117 (K. B. 1686), in which a gentleman was charged by information with going armed to a church during holy service. The jury was instructed that that the statute was confirmatory of the common law, and was meant "to punish people who go armed to terrify the King's subjects." The verdict was not guilty.

James II tried to abridge this right by oppressive application of militia and game laws then on the books, especially the Statute of 13 & 14 Charles II, Chapter 2 (1662), and the Statute of 22 Charles II, Chapter 25 (1670).

55 - When the Court of High Commission was abolished by the Statute of 16 Charles I, Chapter 11 (1641), it was conjectured that perhaps the King could reestablished the tribunal by proclamation, owing to the fact that he was the supreme head of the Church of England. In order to put an end to such speculations, the Statute of 13 Charles II, Chapter 12 (1661) expressly prohibited the King from ever setting up the court again by proclamation. James II simply ignored the statute and reestablished the court by exercise of claimed prerogative.

56 - James II wanted Catholic officers in his army, because he feared betrayal by Protestant soldiers. Therefore, he dispensed with the Test Act (discribed in note 51) at will. No doubt, there was then and always has been a prerogative inherent in executive authority, in extreme situations, to dispense with or suspend execution of laws according to the maxim, "Salus populi est suprema lex." Nor can this principle ever be abolished, because it is natural law, as appears in Book XXVI, Chapter 23 of the Baron de Montesquieu's *Ésprit des Lois*, published in 1748, and in a letter from Thomas Jefferson to J. B. Colvin on September 20, 1810, reprinted in Koch and Peden's Jefferson 606-607. But in *Godden v. Hales*, 11 Howell's St. Tr. 1165 (Exch. Ch. 1685), informally known as Hales' Case, it was held by eleven of twelve judges that James II had an unlimited prerogative to dispense with the Test Act. Even though the King might have had some discretion so far as his personal safety was concerned, the language of the judgment was far too broad, and suggested the right of the King to dispense with and suspend any and all laws under almost any circumstances. Worse still, James II secured this result by visiting with the judges before the case arose, and discharging those whose views were not to his liking. This abuse of power was addressed by the provision on judicial service during good behavior in the Act of Settlement, 12 & 13 William III, Chapter 2 (1701).

57 - Aside from the accounts of Hume, Macauley, and other such historians, the case of Magdalene College at Oxford University was given an eloquent description by Daniel Webster in his argument in *Dartmouth Colleged v. Woodward*, 4 Wheaton 518 at 584-586 (U. S. 1819).

58 - During the "bloody assizes" of 1685 in the wake of Monmouth's Rebellion, Lord Jeffreys was Chief Justice of the King's Bench. His depravity during this period dis described in lurid detail in 2 Macauley's History 571-599. He ordered Lady Alice Lisle burned alive for giving food and comfort to rebel soldiers. He ordered a lad named Tutchin whipped every two weeks for the rest of his life as punishment for seditious words. The boy begged to be hanged instead, but Jeffreys refused to remit the sentence until he was paid a large bribe. James II rewarded this beast by making him Chancellor of England. Largely in reference to the abject indecency of Lord Jeffreys that cruel and unusual punishments were prohibited by the 10th Article of the Bill of Rights adopted by the Convention Parliament in 1689.

59 - Most accounts of the Glorious Revolution omit reference to this important event, establishing a constitutional custom which requires that the Crown or the government acting in the name of the Crown, whenever possible, to seek justice, moderation, and reconciliation so as to prevent revolution in times of urgent politicial crisis. This meeting of the Magnum Concilium is described in 2 Macauley's History 467-472. Cf. 6 Hume's History 514.

60 - Most accounts of the Glorious Revolution omit reference to these negotiations, which are important because they so plainly illustrate why sabotage of peace-seeking efforts at a time of urgent political crisis makes revolution inevitable. A respected description of these transactions, and the failure of James II to react properly, is found in 2 Macauley's History 483-495.

61 - Hallam's History at 675.

62 - *Proceedings to Prove the Genuineness of the Child of James II and Mary of Modena*, 12 Howell's St. Tr. at 157.

63 - It was truly said of James III in 2 Petrie's Jacobite Movement at 166-167, "Never, during all the long period when he knew nothing but adversity, was he guilty of a single unkingly act." And, — "The ill-fortune that pursued him from cradle to grave drove James neither to the bottle nor to brothel, and by his behavior in the hour of defeat it is easy to see how he would have comported himself in that of victory." Further, — "One has only to reflect upon the men who wore his crown to realize how the whole moral tone of eighteenth century England might have been raised by the presence over, not by boorish German princelings, but James III."

64 - E. g., it was said in 2 Petrie's Jacobite Movement at 98-99 that James III "might have bridged the gulf that divided the two religions in Ireland, and, having profited by the blunders of James II, might have changed for the better the whole course of that country's unhappy history. Above all, James would have restroed to the monarchy the dignity that it had lost, and was not allowed to know again until the reign of Victoria, together with the influence which George III had tried to asset in vain because of the fundamental weakness of his position as King by act of Parliament."

65 - 1 Petrie's Jacobite Movement at 197

66 - 1 Petrie's Jaccobite Movement at 202-203.

67 - The standard account, from the accession of Commodus through the murder of Petinax and the sale of the imperial purple to Didius Julianus, is in 1 Gibbon's Rome 101-128 (Chapter IV, and the beginning of Chapter V).

68 - 1 Petrie's Jacobite Movement at 112 and 116.

69 - 1 Blackstone's Commentaries at 245

CHAPTER II

THE AMERICAN UNION

Under the fundamental law of England as established from the time of William the Conqueror, the King was the universal lord and original proprietor of all lands, and no one acquired title or interest in any lands which could not ultimately be traced back to an enfoeffment or patent from the Crown. The King was the source of title to the territories which were discovered in the new world by exploration and claimed for England,[1] and his title was the basis of his power to establish and govern colonies peopled by his subjects in North America.

On April 10, 1606, King James I granted a charter to Sir Thomas Gates and other adventurers.[2] This charter authorized these adventurers to settle two colonies on a huge stretch of continent in the new world, including the Atlantic seacoast and mainland from 34 to 45 degrees north latitude.

On May 24, 1607, the first of these colonies was founded by debarkation of colonists from England at Jamestown on the southerly side of the peninsula between the James and York Rivers flowing eastward into Chesapeake Bay.

On July 24, 1624, an ordinance or constitution was granted in Virginia,[3] whereby a general assembly and a council of state were established, and the royal governor was recommissioned. Laws were passed, taxes were levied, and courts of justice were set up in the name of the King.

The Charter of James I established two companies to govern these two colonies. The southern settlement came to be known as Virginia, and the northern settlement came to be known as Massachusetts Bay.

There were eventually thirteen colonies of England in North America between Spanish Florida along the southerly extremity and New France or Canada which, after the Seven Years War, fell under the control of the British Crown.

These thirteen colonies of England in North America fell under the supervisory jurisdiction of the privy council of the King, and were regulated by Parliament as the sovereign power of the British Empire.

The Charter of James I contained a 15th Article which was never superseded and was confirmed and reconfirmed on various occasions. In order to induce his subjects to become colonists in North America, the King promised solemnly,

> "Also we do, for us, our heirs and successors, declare, by these presents, that all and every persons, being our subjects, which shall dwell and inhabit within every or any of the said several colonies and plantations, and every and any of their children, which shall happen to be born within any of the limits and precincts of the said several colonies and plantations, shall have and enjoy all liberties, franchises, and immunities, within any of our other dominions, to all intents and purposes, as if they had been abiding and born, within this our realm of England, or any of our said dominions."

The Charter of James I was thus the Magna Carta of all the King's subjects in North America, promising them the constitutional rights of Englishmen, not only as defined in the year 1606, but as augmented in later constitutional embellishments, including the essential privileges and immunities declared or implied in the Statute of Monopolies, the Petition of Right, the Statute abolishing the Star Chamber, the Habeas Corpus Act, the Acts transferring the Crown to William and Mary, the Bill of Rights promulgated in the Glorious Revolution, and the Act of Settlement.

* * * * *

It is not possible to understand the American Revolution merely from an enumeration of the overt acts of misgovernment associated with the disillusionment of English colonists against their King and the British Empire.

The conventional view says that the war was fought over taxes levied by the British Parliament upon the colonies of England in North America. Generations have been taught that these taxes and a few related abuses of imperial power were the root cause of the conflict. But this quibble was not the real issue at all.

It is true that the Charter of James I imposed the principles of the Petition of Right as constitutional restraints upon the British Parliament. Hence, no taxes of any description could be properly imposed on the colonies of England in North America without the consent of the King's subjects through their legislative assemblies.

The Statute of 5 George III, Chapter 12 (1765), known as the Stamp Act, was unconstitutional for the reasons given in the speech of William Pitt the Elder, later created the Earl of Chatham, in the British House of Commons on January 14, 1766, especially where he so memorably said,

> "In ancient days, the Crown, the barons, and the clergy possessed the lands. In those days, the barons and the clergy gave and granted to the Crown. They gave and granted what was their own. At present, since the discovery of America, and other circumstances permitting, the Commons are become the proprietors of the land. The Church (God bless it!) has but a pittance. The property of the Lords, compared with that of the Commons, is as a drop of water in the ocean; and this House represents those Commons, the proprietors of the land; and those proprietors virtually represent the rest of the inhabitants. When, therefore, in this House we give and grant, we give and grant what is our own. But in an American tax, what do we do? 'We, your Majesty's Commons for Great Britain, give and grant to your Majesty' — what? Our own roperty? No! 'We give and grant to your Majesty' the property of your Majesty's Commons of America! It is an absurdity in terms."[4]

But as soon as its flaws were laid bare in public debate in the British Parliament, the Stamp Act was promptly repealed,[5] and it was repealed in response to formal written memorials, not only from the colonies of England in North America,[6] but from the hard-working merchants of London.[7]

It is true that additional duties were imposed on the commerce of the colonies in the Statutes of 7 George III, Chapters 41 and 46 (1767), usually called the Townshend Acts. These duties were mainly taxes on imports of glass, lead, paper, and tea, and were meant to defray some of the cost of providing military defense, the administration of justice, and the support of civil government in and for the American colonies, which needed and wanted the protection and tutelage of the British Empire.

Such a guiding and maternal hand was a thing of great worth, because the British Empire was centered in England, which had over some centuries developed the most advanced constitution in the world. No other power in Europe then had anything approaching the constitution of England.

The duties imposed by the Townshend Acts, like the duties imposed by the Stamp Act, were unconstitutional. The revenues sought to be raised by these imperial duties should have been granted by colonial assemblies, and voices of moderation in better circumstances might easily enough have persuaded these legislatures to grant necessary supplies to the Crown. And, as a matter of fact, the Townshend Acts were repealed by Parliament, except for an impost on tea of three pence on the pound.[8]

A revolution is not fought over a three-penny tax on tea, nor was all the growing agitation against England based on such a triviality. Had it not been for another problem of incomparably greater magnitude, a problem generally overlooked or ignored, there would have been no revolution.

The political explosion which triggered events was not ignited by an imperial statute which imposed a tax, but by an imperial statute which, on the contrary, exempted certain subjects from the payment of a tax.

At the time most of the duties imposed by the Townshend Acts were repealed, there was a merchantile corporation in London called the East India Company, which had been in existence and become fabulously rich over the reigns of eight Kings and three Queens of England.[9] The enormous but hidden financial interests behind this enterprise were so powerful that they could dictate to the Crown and Parliament of Great Britain. The governors of the East India Company commanded a wide-ranging network of businesses, possessions, and enterprises, and these characters were the culprits behind the American Revolution and other destructive mischief throughout the British Empire.[10]

These financial interests had for many years demanded policies and statutes dishonorable to the Crown and disloyal to their countrymen in England. And they got what they wanted. The Commons, the Lords, and the King had become puppets of high finance, sometimes by means of bribes under the table,[11] but also by other more compelling inducements which seemed more respectable but were not less depraved.

The East India Company had at the time a surplus of tea and a shortage of cash, and so procured in their usual quiet way the Statute of 13 George III, Chapter 64 (1773), known as the Tea Act, which was a scheme to bail out the company at public expense. The company had previously been obliged by law to sell their tea from India at public auction to domestic merchants in England, who shipped it to colonial vendors in North America, paying thereon an export tax. The colonial vendors in turn sold to the public at prices which absorbed wholesale costs and export taxes levied in England, and the impost of three pence on the pound levied in North America. The Statute of 13 George III allowed the East India Company to ship tea from England directly to their selected agents in North America, without using domestic wholesalers and payment of export duties. And these agents were able to undersell colonial vendors who had to buy tea from unprivileged interests in England. The Act gave the East India Company an effective monopoly in the colonies, a profitable way to dump excess tea, and a cure for their shortage of cash. The plan supplied a much sought-after excuse for "patriots" in the colonies to stir up trouble against the British Crown.

The Boston tea party followed on December 16, 1773, staged by rowdy "sons of liberty" dressed as Indians who dumped duty-free cargo into the harbor, whereupon the board of governors of the East India Company retaliated by demanding unconstitutional and oppressive legislation which was obediently passed by the British Parliament in early 1774.

These "Intolerable Acts" included several Statutes of 14 George III: Chapter 6, which closed the port of Boston; Chapter 39, which allowed the governor at discretion to transfer for trial in England any person indicted in Massachusetts Bay of murder and other felony while resisting officers of the Crown; Chapter 45, which suspended important provisions in the charter of government, and prohibited town meetings in Massachusetts Bay; Chapter 54, which quartered troops and kept up a standing army to overawe the people in Massachusetts Bay; and Chapter 83, which abrogated the claims of Virginia, Connecticut, and Massachusetts Bay to western lands beyond the Appalachian Mountains.

The thinking behind the Tea Act and the Intolerable Acts was not distinguished by genius and cunning. The program was simply the product of greed and revenge stupefied by power founded upon means sufficient to pervert and debase even the ultimate authority of the British Empire. A good constitution may lessen the harm done by rampant corruption in public life, but no government is improved, nor are statesmanship and intelligence fostered by actively rewarding it.[12]

These statutes electrified the American colonies which united in the Resolves of the First Continental Congress.[13] They were denounced no less by hard-working merchants in London.[14] But no matter, there was by then an unstoppable momentum which quickly matured in the Battle of Lexington on April 19, 1775.

War was soon declared by the Second Continental Congress against the King,[15] and war was shortly thereafter declared by the King against his American subjects.[16]

The people of England did not want this war, neither did the people in the colonies of England in North America. It was a war agitated, ignited, and perpetuated by the bungling avarice of monied interests in London.

It remains to consider how those responsible for this calamity became so inordinately powerful, yet have been able to hide in the shadows of history, escaping all blame for their enormous wrongs against humanity and civilization, while King George III became an unlucky scapegoat.

* * * * *

These financial interests became powerful by subversion of the King's all-important prerogative of coining money.

The prerogative of fixing the standard of weights and measures was the power of the King to establish by proclamation all units or criteria necessary for reducing anything bought and sold in commerce to the same or equivalent value in all markets, be it weight, time, distance, or whatever.

The King's power to coin money was a special branch of his power to fix the standard of weights and measures.[17] Money in this sense was thought of as a common standard of value for all commodities, products, goods, land, chattels, intangibles, capital, labor, service, talent, entrepreneurship, literally anything offered for sale or desired for purchase in this world.

In fixing this common standard three things were essential in England at the time of the American Revolution, and had been essential over long ages from time immemorial. Laying aside any and all alternative systems of money which might have been established by act of Parliament, the money coined by prerogative of the King could only be gold or silver,[18] although alloy was mixed with precious metal to make it more durable in passing from hand to hand. Money minted by the King had to be fabricated into coin bearing an image approved by his Majesty. And once produced, such coin had to represent a denomination or number of monetary units called its value.

The King's impression, as defined by his proclamation, served to certify the purity and weight of the gold or silver used, so as to make possible a determination of the intrinsic worth of the coins upon visual inspection, and also to transform the gold or silver from a metallic commodity into legal tender or money proper, passing current as payment which all creditors were obliged to accept in satisfaction of debts, lest they forfeit their right to collect amounts due and payable.

The Statute of 25 Edward III, Chapter 13 (1351) established the sterling standard for all money coined by the King. A troy pound of sterling gold consisted of 22 carats gold to 2 carats alloy (a ratio of 11 to 1, about .917 fine), and was divided up into 44.5 guineas of 21 shillings each, while a troy pound of sterling silver consisted of 11 ounces and two pennyweights silver to 18 pennyweights alloy (a ratio of about 12.33 to 1, .925 fine), and was divided up into 62 shillings. The sterling standard remained in effect for centuries after it was established by law, and it still prevailed in the British Empire at the time of the American Revolution.

Anybody who wanted to transform gold or silver into legal tender coin of the realm took his metal to the royal mint, and paid a charge called seigniorage to the King. The amount of cash obtainable was usually the full amount desired, and the seigniorage, if not always the same, was less than the enhanced value of coin over bullion, — low enough to diminish the incentive to counterfeit, yet high enough to discourage minting down or exportation, and high enough to yield a reasonable margin of profit or revenue for the Crown.

The King could also decry outstanding pieces, or annul their character as legal tender. And he could regulate foreign coin by proclaiming how many units thereof were equivalent to corresponding units of domestic money.

By constitutional custom, then, the King possessed the immense prerogative, which in the absence statutory changes was exclusively his Majesty's power, to expand and contract the supply of money in the economy. Under the constitution of England, unperverted by statutory innovations or runaway corruption, the creation and annulling of money, and thereby control of the supply of money, were exclusively acts of sovereign power and public authority.

There were also paper bills and notes which were governed by the law merchant and floated around in lieu of gold and silver. Banks held coin or bullion convertible to coin, and issued currency upon cash payable when presentment was made. These bills and notes were not legal tender but they were highly convenient, and they were safe to accept so long as their aggregate face value did not exceed the amount of cash on deposit plus the face value of such paper needed for current transactions in the economy served.

Gold and silver coin did not necessarily prevent an elastic supply of currency, because the same amount of cash might accommodate more or less circulating bills and notes as needed for business in the economy.

If circulating bills and notes exceeded the amount required for current transactions and the amount on deposit to redeem in cash on demand, there could be a run on the banks or financial panic. More paper might be presented than could be paid off. Banks might then be forced to close. Debts might remain unsatisfied for inconveniently long periods. Judgments could not be collected. Business would be seriously injured or crippled until public confidence in paper was at last reestablished.

Gold and silver coin thus served as a natural monetary discipline, because they limited the amount of paper currency issued, assuring that circulating bills and notes were "sound" or readily convertible into cash as and when needed. The system prevented inflation by exacting a painful price of irresponsible emission of paper currency.

Gold and silver coin also limited the amount of money which the Crown or Parliament or anybody else could spend without borrowing from willing lenders at acceptable interest. This ancient regime forced everybody, even the King himself, to spend no more than so much in his generation.

Gold or silver coin was always acceptable, because these precious metals have universally passed well, and have always been desired. Because of their unique qualities, gold and silver have always been natural money. Governments may rise and fall, but gold or silver still passes as a medium of exchange in commerce.

Money based on gold and silver had certain advantages, yet was not necessarily the best of all possible worlds. Whatever its strengths and weaknesses, it was undeniably in historical fact the system which prevailed over many centuries in England, and it existed in pure form upon the accession of James I as King of England.

It so happens that, due to retardation of technical knowledge on how to extract silver from the earth in countries of the Far East, the mint price of pure silver to pure gold in India at the end of the 16th Century was about 9 to 1, making the value of silver much higher in India than in England where, under the sterling standard, the ratio of pure silver to pure gold in circulating coins was about 15.2 to 1. Consequently, if silver could be shipped from England to India and there converted to gold, then shipped back to England, a very handsome profit could be made.

The difficulty for those who had an eye on this gain was that money had only one lawful purpose, which was to pass current for payment of debts. A merchant abroad might demand English pounds as payment for goods shipped by him to Great Britain. The sum paid to him might be either in gold and silver coin, or in drawing rights represented by bills of exchange or bank notes presentable in London. This much was legal, but it was not legal to destroy the measure of value, extract the metal as a commodity, sell the commodity for private gain, and thereby deplete the supply of money required for the business of the nation.

Going back at least to the Statute of 9 Edward III, Chapter 1 (1336), which was renewed again in many acts up through the Statute of [19] Henry VII, Chapter 5 (1504), and thereafter, it was unlawful to efface, melt down, or export wholesale the coin of the realm.

Even so, the Crown was occasionally tempted to abuse royal prerogatives to fill up the treasury whenever it was deemed impolitic to ask for
money from Parliament. Such evidently was the situation when, on
December 31, 1600, Queen Elizabeth I granted two hundred fifteen capitalists or "billoneurs" a charter to the East India Company, including a
monopoly in transoceanic trade with India. Under the charter the company enjoyed an exclusive privilege of exporting to India each year up to
30,000 pounds worth of silver in the form of coin or bullion, provided that
a like amount in such silver were imported into England within six
months.

Because it granted exclusive privileges, the charter was unlawful under
the judgment of the King's Bench on monopolies in the first year of James
I, as reaffirmed by Parliament some years later in the Statute of
Monopolies.

Yet by stealth of the cosmopolitan band in the East India Company,
their charter went unchallenged, then after expiration was renewed by
Oliver Cromwell, and was shortly thereafter renewed again by Charles II.

Later the monopoly granted by the company's charter was upheld in a
shockingly lawless judgment by Lord Jeffreys, the most depraved judge in
the history of England. The case is reported as *East India Company v.
Sandys*, 10 Howell's St. Tr. 371 (K. B. 1684). The company continued to
defy the whole legal order of the kingdom, obtusely flaunting its ill-gotten
privileges through and after the Glorious Revolution. The company then
bribed its way to a confirmation of its rights through the Statute of 9
William III, Chapter 44 (1698).19

The East India Company made unbelievable profits from importing silver into England and exporting it to India, then bringing back mounds of
shining gold from the Far East. Silver greatly diminished as a medium of
exchange, and gold became the predominant money in England.

Next came the Navigation Acts, first the Statute of 12 Charles II,
Chapter 18 (1660), and then the Statute of 15 Charles II, Chapter 7
(1663), both providing that cargo imported into or exported from the
colonies overseas, especially those in North America, had to be carried on
ships whose owners, masters, and crews were mainly natural-born
Englishmen.

The ostensible purpose of these regulations of imperial commerce
were "the increase of shiping and encouragement of the navigation" of the
nation with which, "under the good providence and protection of God, the
wealth, safety, and strength" of the kingdom were concerned, and "maintaining a greater correspondence and kindnesse" between England and

other parts of the British Empire. The real objectives were to enrich the entrepreneurs behind the East India Company who owned the shipping to which navigation was limited, and to keep the colonies, not so much loyal to the King, as obliged to do business exclusively with and on terms dictated by associated commercial interests in London.

The second of these Navigation Acts contained another intriguing feature. The twelfth section of the Statute of 15 Charles II allowed exportation of all foreign coins or bullion of gold or silver, free of interdict, regulation, or duties of any kind. The ostensible purpose was to enhance the freedom and vigor of commerce. The real objective was to increase the profits of the monopoly which alone could benefit from such exportation.

The billoneurs behind the East India Company became wealthier still. Their capacity to buy the King and Parliament greatly increased. And buy they did. The dowry of Catherine of Braganza was the City of Bombay in India, previously a possession of her father Alphonso VI, King of Portugal. In 1668, for an infusion of ill-gotten cash, Charles II transferred to the East India Company most rights of his Crown to the City of Bombay. The company became an empire within an empire, with an army, a navy, valuable territory, and actual powers of government.

There was also the Statute of 18 Charles II, Chapter 5 (1666) which was continued in succeeding laws until made perpetual by the Statute of 9 George III, Chapter 25 (1769). This act abolished seigniorage at the royal mint. The ostensible purposes of "free coinage" were to bring bullion into the royal mint and to increase the money supply. The real objectives were to give the capitalists enjoying privileged control of bullion greater freedom to transform gold and silver into cash, and to remove the disincentive against melting down and exportation which seigniorage imposed. The sop to the King was the revenue from certain duties on imported spirits, wines, beer, cider, and vinegar, paltry compensation for the power to coin money.

From their illicit monopolies in transoceanic commerce, their illicit privileges to export gold and silver, their illicit advantages from statutory limits on colonial trade, and their illicit access to the royal mint, the financial interests behind the East India Company acquired virtually exclusive means of expanding and contracting the supply of money to suit their convenience without regard to the public good.

Whenever they wished, the governors of the East India Company could arrange for the free coinage of their gold and silver, and, through lending institutions under their control, they could mount loans of bank notes, on good security, in such parts of the economy as they wished. Nobody dared breathe against their will, because their discretion was virtually the sole factor in determining the extension of credit which to business and trade was then, as it is now, like the smile of sunshine upon flowers of the field.

When the supply of money was expanded, the economy was stimulated, and prices rose. In order to achieve the opposite effect at the right moment, new policies were established, of tightening credit, recalling as many loans as possible, and transforming coin back into bullion for export abroad, whereupon commerce slowed down, prices fell again, foreclosures gobbled up the property mortgaged as collateral, a few merchants and producers were ruined, bankers took their windfall profits, and the whole process could then be started all over again.

Business cycles were carefully planned and executed by private interests which had undermined the public authority of coining money, mainly through the Statutes of 15 and 18 Charles II. Such cycles were not the wonders of nature correcting unwholesome excesses in the free market, but man-made fluctuations. They were not invented by the East India Company, but the institution certainly increased the sophistication of this worldly art, so as to achieve capacity for truly massive devastation and aggrandizement.

The British Empire appeared to be governed by the Crown and Parliament, but by the end of the 17th Century the British Empire was run by the East India Company. This subversion was aggressively expanded after the Glorious Revolution.

In a less thoughtful moment, a noted historian once said, "On the day of the accession of James the First, England descended from the rank she had hitherto held, and began to be regarded as a power hardly of the second order. During many years the great British monarchy, under four successive princes of the House of Stuart, England was scarcely a more important member of the European system than the little kingdom of Scotland had previously been."[20]

The truth is that the House of Stuart was generally successful in keeping England out of war on the continent of Europe. Peace, it is true, has generally been less exciting than war, and those who have enjoyed it have often been regarded by superficial observers as less important than those who have led grand armies, set huge fleets of warships upon the seas, and launched magnificent military campaigns. Even so, peace has ever had certain homely virtues.

James I gave England a graceful union with Scotland, elementary restraints on monopoly, colonies in the new world, and best of all peace at home and abroad. He understood that peace kept royal prerogatives intact, that peace was very good for civilized progress, and that peace was much less expensive. His son and grandsons were not as successful as he was in maintaining peace, but in this respect they all surpassed William III who in this art was a failure.

William III threw the British Empire against the massed power of France, which for almost two centuries had been no real threat to or enemy of England. Since war costs money, the King dealt with those enterprising fellows in London who had practical command over the supply and flow of money in the British Empire, and from his dark negotiations with them emerged the Bank of England, chartered in the Statute of 5 & 6 William and Mary, Chapter 20 (1694).

A large amount of capital, initially about 1.2 million pounds sterling, was privately subscribed. It was enough money in values of the day to put regiments onto the field with ample support. This amount could only have been raised by those who dominated the East India Company. The bank then made loans to the King, advanced mainly as paper currency or bank notes, and the King then went off to fight wars on a grand scale.

In consideration of loans received, the King gave bonds to the bank. The bonds called for repayment over a term of years, and were "funded" by statutory dedication upon specified duties, excises, and imposts on commerce. These bonds then served as security for the issuance of bank notes which could be lent to private parties at interest.

The bank also earned interest on the bonds held, paid annually in specie by the government, and was granted a monopoly as the corporate banker for the Crown. With revenues from double interest and from banking services to the richest elements in the kingdom, the returns to stockholders were fabulous.

The notes of the Bank of England, like the notes of other banking houses, were technically not legal tender in general commerce. They could in theory be presented for good coin, and so the face amount of this circulating paper was kept at a safe ratio to specie in the vaults.

Yet the notes of the Bank of England were better than other currency, because they were receivable in payment of taxes and other debts owed to the government, and also because they represented national debt which was payable from every taxable source in the kingdom. These bank notes were not easily convertible to coin, because they were held and passed between parties who, for the most part, owed money to the bank. They were thus said to be "good as gold" and used as if cash for satisfaction of debts private as well as public, and even as reserves in other banks to support loans.

Thus developed an arrangement whereby the Crown borrowed from financiers by giving paper in exchange for paper. The Bank of England became an enormous parasite, bloated with wealth and power by lending the government its own credit.

If confined within reasonable limits, this franchise might have offered consolations, because it supplied useful currency in business. But reasonable limits were not maintained, since making war has never been a particularly reasonable activity. From the reign of William and Mary through the 18th Century, Great Britain became involved in endless wars on the continent of Europe, defending the Dutch frontier, reducing the French monarchy, disputing the Spanish succession, protecting the imperial house of Austria, safeguarding the King's dutchy in Germany, and both opposing and supporting the kingdom of Prussia. The result was a stupendous national debt, monetized by the Bank of England, at least two hundred times the amount first borrowed by the end of the Seven Years War, — three hundred times that amount by the end of the American Revolution.

The British people groaned under heavy taxes to pay the interest on the national debt without ever touching the principal due.[21] Each war nudged the King and Parliament into an increasingly servile condition, ever more obliged to the huge financial network behind the East India Company and the Bank of England. So it was that these interests were able to demand and obtain the legislation which ignited the American Revolution.

* * * * *

In the colonies of England in North America, more was involved than the baneful Statutes of 13 and 14 George III.

The Resolves of the First Continental Congress were a respectable petition to George III, who, in fact, received it as a father would hear the pleas of his children. And if the King had been free to react as a father, he would have restored peace to the British Empire.

But the King was not free to do right, because he, his prime minister, the cabinet of his ministers, his privy council, his commons, his lords, his judges, and his church were in no position to refuse the indignant demands of the financiers who had settled down so comfortably in London.

For many years there had been mounting tensions in the American colonies, which were naturally underdeveloped, yet were bound by the Navigation Acts to trade only with England. The result was that these colonies were caught in an unending cycle of dependency and indebtedness.

There was a Statute of 6 Anne, Chapter 30 (1708), which made the gold and silver coin of England legal tender in the American colonies. The difficulty was that there were no known deposits of gold and silver in the American colonies. Whenever the King's money came into the hands of merchants in Boston, New York, Philadelphia, or Charleston, it had to be used in paying off firms in London.

In the latter part of the 17th Century, "pine tree" shillings were minted in Massachusetts Bay, but much of the silver used in the fabrication of these pieces probably came from buccaneers who paid high seigniorage to launder their pirated loot. In any event, not enough of this coinage actually circulated in the markets of New England.

About the only way to find and retain good coin was in trade on the black market with Spanish possessions in the Caribbean Sea. Spanish milled dollars, made of excellent silver, were eagerly sought in the English Colonies. Because of the shortage of precious metal, these dollars were prized and valuable. It was unthinkable to refuse or melt down such pieces, yet they could not readily be used in trade with England, because mere possession of any sizeable quantity of such coin was suggestive evidence of commerce prohibited by the Navigation Acts.

Therefore, the American colonies were obliged to use or create substitutes of the King's money. There were make-shift systems of tobacco, wampum, and country pay, but these attempts were not very important in the long run. More interesting were American experiments during the colonial era with paper currency.

In 1690 and 1691, in an effort to offset the scarcity of money, the provincial legislature of Massachusetts Bay issued bills of credit which were nothing but promissory notes of the colonial government to pay specie, to be raised by taxation, at a future day. Such paper was not legal tender except in payment of dues to the public treasury. The bills were spent into circulation to pay public obligations, and passed with pretty good results in the economy.

Beginning in 1692, the colony of Massachusetts Bay issued bills of credit which were by statute ordained legal tender for all debts public and private, except for special contracts which called for payment in designated coin or currency. The new currency was good only in domestic commerce, because the bills were not accepted in London. But the effect on domestic commerce was astonishing. Business boomed. Immigration was encouraged. The population quickly grew.

Up through 1712, taxes assured a sufficient reflux of currency to make increases in the amount outstanding reasonably proportionate to increases in economic activity. There was some inflation, but it was moderate, and proved actually wholesome insofar as it eased payment of debts. These paper shillings were fairly stable, and certainly better than silver shillings which virtually did not exist.

As time went on, the provincial legislature was obliged to postpone payment in specie of bills not absorbed by taxes and other public dues, and old issues were sometimes paid with new issues. As paper was paid off with paper, gold and silver coin became more theoretical, and fiat currency became de facto the money of the day. Massachusetts Bay had a public monetary authority, but the system was crude, since it had no intrinsic discipline. The amount of currency outstanding depended on nothing but human discretion which was too readily warped to meet political demands of the moment. By 1728 inflation became excessive in the eyes of all parties. Immoderate inflation made anticipation of the future too difficult and so discouraged investment and production: — it made credit in business too hazardous, raised interest rates in excess, weakened currency as a medium of exchange, and induced breakdowns in commerce.

Meanwhile, the colony was rechartered so as to provide for a royal governor who took orders from the privy council in London, which in turn took orders from the East India Company and the Bank of England. The problem of inflation in Massachusetts Bay might have been contained by the gradual and steady hands of informed and impartial governors, but the governors actually in office were marionettes of those who sought to maximize their profits by domination and control of the business of the colony. The legislature was ferociously brow beaten and bullied into drastic contractions of paper money, which caused a harsh depression full of misery.

Pennsylvania came up with a superior kind of paper money, a regime so remarkably successful that the powers behind the East India Company and the Bank of England had to exert themselves very strenuously to destroy it.

In 1723 the colonial legislature of Pennsylvania began to emit bills of credit which were made payable in specie at a future day, and were made legal tender for all debts public and private within the colony. A portion was spent into circulation to pay for operations of the government, and was funded by dedicated taxes and other public revenues. But the bulk of these bills were lent out to borrowers who gave mortgages on land as security and promised repayment with moderate interest over ten years. The interest paid on these loans served to reduce taxes.

The system contemplated future issues to assure a continuing influx of currency sufficient to facilitate adequate reflux from taxes and repayment of loans.

The program expanded currency to fill the void of sound circulating media. It pumped money into the hands of entrepreneurs whose spending primed business, employed workers, enhanced production, and created income. It erected intrinsic discipline of currency in place of human whim and caprice. If the government created excessive currency, the anticipated return from the repayment of loans decreased. The regime sustained a fully public monetary authority. It inclined toward an optimum supply of currency, and in this sense was better than gold and silver coin which tended more in the direction of keeping circulating paper "safe" even at the expense of activity in business.

Benjamin Franklin published a defense of this monetary system in a classic monograph entitled *A Modest Inquiry on the Nature and Necessity of a Paper Currency*.[22] This little treatise was very advanced in its day, but has been energetically caricatured, misrepresented, and discredited ever since.

Franklin's central precept was, "There is a certain proportionate quantity of money requisite to carry on the trade of a country freely and currently, more than which can be of no advantage in trade, and less, if much less, exceedingly detrimental to it." An undersupply of money, he taught, was likely to promote high rates of interest which could not be effectively curbed by laws on usury. An undersupply of money was sure to depress production and commerce. An adequate supply of money in Pennsylvania lowered rates of interest, made liquidity more affordable, and promoted investment, industry, agriculture, employment, profit, and exportation, — the very opposite of what was desired by the monied interests in London.

The real measure of wealth, said Franklin, has never been gold and silver, which could fluxuate on the market as any other commodity. The key to wealth, Franklin continued, has always been labor, which he defined as any human work capable of producing or acquiring whatever may be needed to survive and prosper in the material world. The value of corn, land, gold, silver, or anything else is ultimately based on the labor or work required to fetch it. The essence of commerce has always been the exchange of labor or work, the true measure of wealth.

In order to facilitate such exchanges of labor without becoming redundant, Franklin maintained that money must be disciplined by something with value dependent on labor. Because gold and silver rose or fell in price from forces of supply and demand which were largely independent of value measured by labor, Franklin thought that something else should be found to regulate the supply of money. And this, said Franklin, was land, because the value of land was known to vary mainly with commerce and population which together serve as a good index of labor.

As gold and silver could generate and discipline bills and notes in circulation, land could do likewise, and more reasonably, said Franklin, because the market value of land has ever been closely linked to the totality of productive work in the economy. As gold and silver were placed on deposit to support paper, land could be appraised and mortgaged. Franklin called the paper circulating in Pennsylvania "coined land," because it was disciplined by the value of real estate.

Pennsylvania became an important part of the British Empire. Philadelphia became a great and prosperous city in the English-speaking world, full of culture, learning, trade, and business. The powers of high finance in London moved hard to crush this promising upsurge of development independent of their control.

They engineered the Currency Acts. First came the Statute of 24 George II, Chapter 53 (1751), which prohibited the colonies in New England from reissuing, postponing, or depreciating bills of credit purporting to pass as legal tender for any purpose whatever. Then followed the more drastic Statute of 4 George III, Chapter 34 (1764), which prohibited all bills of credit purporting to be legal tender, even for payment of taxes, in all colonies of England in North America.

These acts, particularly the Statute of 4 George III, destroyed viable domestic currency in the colonies of England of North America. Prosperity was dried up all along the Atlantic coast, even in Pennsylvania.

With this economic injury it was easier for voices of dissent to use the trivia of taxes and tea as inflammatory pretexts to foment public sentiment against the King and Parliament.[23]

These inflammatory protests have since diverted attention from a painful reality: — it was the monied interests behind the East India Company and the Bank of England which subverted the fundamental law of England, undermined the utility of the British Empire, weakened the currency of the colonies from New Hampshire to Georgia, unleashed the injustice of the Intolerable Acts, and created a real and urgent need for these colonies to form an alliance among themselves as new nations, an alliance which they called the United States of America.

* * * * *

The colonies of England in North America did not break away in one movement or in one block, but initially acted one by one in attaining self-government. Before the Declaration of American Independence, five colonies separately declared independence and set up republican constitutions,[24] and all of them had established provisional governments, apart from the British Crown, but also apart from the Second Continental Congress.

There was a significant phase of the American Revolution in Rhode Island which was so quiet, peaceful, and orderly that it has gone unnoticed.[25]

Under the liberal Charter of Charles II, the people elected a governor and a legislature which enacted a statute on May 4, 1776: "Whereas, in all states existing by compact, protection and allegiance are reciprocal," the preamble began, "And whereas" George III "forgetting his dignity, regardless of the compact," had acted contrary to the "duties and character of a good king," — so the recitations went, unmistakably taken from the formalities in the Act of the Convention Parliament on February 13, 1689, which began the reign of William and Mary. The statute then repealed the act which prescribed oaths of allegiance to George III, and ordained that, from thenceforth, all commissions, writs, and processes should go out under the name and authority of the governor and company of Rhode Island.

Judge William Staples, the most eminent constitutional lawyer in the history of the State, remarked that this statute, not a declaration of the Second Continental Congress, "severed the connection between Rhode Island and the British Crown."

Not a shot was fired. No battle was fought. British troops occupied Newport temporarily during the war, but otherwise life continued as if nothing extraordinary had occurred until some years later when, in the Treaty of Paris, George III conceded that Rhode Island, specifically mentioned by his Majesty, was not subject to the British Crown.

The revolution in Rhode Island was an irregular but lawful transformation according to the constitutional customs which propelled the Glorious Revolution. In England, the original compact between the King and his people was Magna Carta and the Petition of Right. In Rhode Island, the compact was the Charter of Charles II, which was deemed to have been established by competent authority of the King in 1663, and not in need of repair or improvement beyond what might be prescribed by revolutionary statutes. In Rhode Island, the transformation was from monarchy to the governor and company.

The revolution in Virginia was more important in establishing distinctive formalities of constitutional government in the United States.

In the passionate days after war broke out in New England, the Virginia House of Burgesses clashed with the royal governor, who seized the powder and dismantled the weapons in the arsenal of the colonial militia, then went aboard a warship of the royal navy. Angry correspondence went back and forth between him and the colonial legislature. The governor left Virginia in June 1775 as James II fled England in December 1688.

The Virginia House of Burgesses dissolved itself in Williamsburg, then moved to Richmond and formed the Virginia Convention of 1775, which was a provisional legislature and government, entirely revolutionary. Troops were raised, rules of discipline were adopted, and a committee of public safety was established. An ordinance was passed, calling for the election of the Virginia Convention of 1776 in striking language:

> "By the unhappy differences subsisting between Great Britain and this colony, the usual meetings of the general assembly, deliberations on the situations of the country, and making provision for the exigencies of government in a constitutional way are altogether obstructed: For these reasons, it has become indispensably necessary for the oppressed people of this country, at a crisis so alarming, to adopt such other modes of consulting and providing for the general safety as may seem condusive to that great end."[26]

It was conscious reenactment of the call by William of Orange for the Convention Parliament of 1689.

The delegates attending the Virginia Convention of 1776 were elected by the same freeholders as had elected the Virginia House of Burgesses. When it met on May 15, 1776, the People of Virginia in Convention assumed all the constitutional attributes of the King and Parliament of Great Britain. The convention was above the jurisdiction of every power on earth, could neither do nor intend wrong, represented undying permanence behind all government, and could do anything in law not naturally impossible.[27]

The convention established the new fundamental law of Virginia, a famous prototype of what became known as a "republican form of government," the unique and enduring invention which characterized the American Revolution.[28]

On June 12, 1776, the convention adopted the Virginia Bill of Rights,[29] which ordained primordial rules of a new constitutional order: — that the people in convention possess sovereign power, and may change the constitution or form of government; — that all men enjoy certain inherent rights by natural law, which no temporal government may take away; — that the proper objects of government are the safety and happiness of the people; — that no public office may be hereditary; — that legislative, executive, and judicial powers must be kept separate and distinct; — that there should be frequent and free elections; — that suffrage belongs to anyone with a permanent attachment to and interest in the community; — that the people may not be taxed or otherwise charged or deprived of their property without consent of their elected representatives in the legislature; — that no person may be deprived of his property for public use without just compensation; — that the people may never be subjected to laws not enacted by their elected representatives in the legislature for the common good; — that necessary and proper laws may not be suspended except by consent of the legislature; — that, in all criminal prosecutions, the accused shall be informed of the cause and nature of the charge or charges against him, shall be entitled to a speedy and public trial by impartial jury of the vicinage, nor shall he be found guilty without unanimous verdict, nor shall he be denied liberty except by lawful judgment of his peers or by the law of the land; — that bail shall not be excessive, or punishments cruel and unusual; — that general warrants shall never be allowed; — that in private disputes over property, the right of trial by jury shall be preserved; — that freedom of the press shall not be denied; — that the militia, composed of the great body of the people, is the proper and natural defense of a free country; — that standing armies shall be avoided as far as possible in time of peace; — that the military establishment shall always be held in strict subordination to civil power; — that the people have a right to uniform laws throughout the commonwealth; — that no free government can be preserved without frequent recourse to fundamental principles; — and that free, equal, and peaceable exercise of all religions, according to the dictates of conscience and Christian love, shall ever be respected.

On June 29, 1776, the convention framed and adopted the Virginia Constitution.[30] The preamble enumerated grievances in language reminiscent of the Acts of the Convention Parliament which denounced James II and welcomed William and Mary. After enumeration of grievances, the important legal language appeared, "By which several acts of misrule, the government of this country, as formerly exercised under the Crown of Great Britain, is totally dissolved." This declaration was promulgated for Virginia only, and did not even mention the United States.

The new constitution of Virginia established a House of Delegates, elected annually by freeholders of the counties and cities, and subject to a provision against rotten boroughs, with exclusive power to originate all legislation, and also a Senate, elected by freeholders for terms of four years, with power to negative or amend bills from the House, except for money bills which could only be approved or negatived as originally passed.

The Governor, subject to the advice of a privy council, both elected annually by joint ballot of the General Assembly, was vested with power to execute laws, and to grant reprieves and pardons except in cases of impeachment or cases otherwise excluded by statute, but no power implied from kingly office, and no power to veto legislation or to prorogue or dissolve the General Assembly.

There was to be a general court of law, courts of chancery and admiralty, and a Supreme Court whose judges were appointed by joint ballot of the General Assembly to serve during good behavior.

There were to be an attorney general and a secretary of state appointed to serve during good behavior, and a treasurer appointed annually, by joint ballot of the General Assembly.

The House of Delegates was to have a general power of impeachment against the Governor when out of office and against all others offending against the Commonwealth, to be prosecuted by the attorney general before the general court of law, unless a judge of the general court were impeached in which case the attorney general was to prosecute before the Supreme Court.

The Virginia Convention of 1776 introduced the new government by appointing the first Governor and privy council, then acted as a temporary legislature until the first General Assembly could be elected, whereupon it adjourned sine die.

A republican form of government, illustrated by the Virginia Bill of Rights and Constitution of 1776, was thought of as a characteristic body of fundamental law, expressed in a document framed by the People of Convention who possessed the sovereign attributes of the King and Parliament and were called into session according to the legal customs of the Glorious Revolution and the American Revolution. A republican form of government was adopted either by the convention or in a popular referendum authorized by the convention. Such a constitution presupposed the reality of natural law elaborated by legal tradition. It incorporated a regular government which was subject to dissolution and resettlement by the People in Convention. It was a constitution which prohibited hereditary office and titles of nobility,[31] ordained separation of powers,[32] liberally conferred the right to vote, required popular election at least of the lower house of the legislature where taxation had to originate, defined terms of office as so many years or good behavior, made all public officers accountable for misconduct in the exercise of power, and subordinated military power to civil authority. It was a constitution under which, either by a bill of rights or by necessary implication, citizens were to enjoy the privileges and immunities of freemen at common law and all inalienable rights under natural law.

A republican form of government was not a mere political idea, but a definite principle of constitutional order which judges understood and expounded.

There was, for example, an old case in England reported as *Dr. Bonham's Case*, 8 Coke 114a (C. P. 1610), wherein Lord Coke laid down a remarkable doctrine of jurisprudence. A statute authorized the royal college of physicians to summon, adjudge, fine, and keep part of the fine assessed against anyone who practiced medicine without a proper license. Coke held that the law was null and void, because it was against Magna Carta for a judge to sit a matter involving his own interests.

But Lord Coke's doctrine, that no statute could defy the constitution, died in England for reasons later explained by Sir William Blackstone.[33] The fundamental law of England was that the Commons, Lords, and King in Parliament together possessed supreme legal authority, power so irresistible that not even Magna Carta was beyond its legal omnipotence. No act of Parliament, therefore, could be null and void because it ran against Magna Carta.

The superior courts at Westminster nevertheless came up with powerful means to combat legislative oppression. If the general language of a statute, as applied to particular facts, yielded a result contrary to legal tradition or natural law, or a result wholly unreasonable in the circumstances, then the judiciary was "at liberty to expound the statute by equity, and only quoad hoc to disregard it," it being supposed that Parliament intended no such bad result. And so, if a statute generally conferred upon a certain lord jurisdiction in his court baron to hear causes arising upon his manor, the law would be read, if at all possible, not to give the lord power to decide even a case in which he were a party to the suit. Republican constitutions retained this judicial authority.[34]

But republican forms of government also restored to jurisprudence in the United States the idea of Lord Coke that, where a statute could not be saved by strict construction and unavoidably demanded an unconstitutional act or omission, the judiciary was duty-bound to find the statute null and void as if it had never been enacted at all. American statesmen understood this idea from the beginning.[35] And American judges used this new power very early.[36] In *Calder v. Bull*, 3 Dallas 386 at 388 (U. S. 1798), Justice Samuel Chase observed:

> "The nature and ends of legislative power limit the exercise of it.
> This fundamental principle flows from the very nature of our free

Republican governments, that no man should be compelled to do what the laws do not require; nor to refrain from acts which the laws permit. There are acts which the federal, or state, Legislature cannot do, without exceeding their authority. There are certain vital principles in our free Republican governments, which will determine and overrule an apparent and flagrant abuse of legislative power, as to authorize manifest injustice by positive law; or take away that security for personal liberty, or private property for the protection whereof the government was established."

The same idea of a republican form of government was given another rich expression in the venerable case of *Vanhorne's Lessee v. Dorrance*, 2 Dallas 304 at 308 (U. S. Cir. Ct. Pa. 1795), in which Justice William Patterson instructed the jury:

"What is the constitution? It is the form of government delineated by the mighty hand of the people, in which certain first principles of fundamental law are established. The constitution is certain and fixed: it contains the permanent will of the people, and is the supreme law of the land; it is paramount to the will of the legislature, and can be revoked or altered only by the authority that made it. The life-giving principle and the death-doing stroke must proceed from the same hand. What are legislatures? Creatures of the constitution; they owe their existence to the constitution; they derive their powers from the constitution. It is their commission; and, therefore, all their acts must be conformable to it, or else they will be void. The constitution is the work of the people themselves, in their original, sovereign, and unlimited capacity. Law is the work of the legislature in their derivative and subordinate capacity. The one is the work of the creator, and the other of the creature. In short, gentlemen, the constitution is the sun of the political system, around which all legislative, executive, and judicial bodies must revolve."

This statement of principle excels over all other attempts, because it is the most literate, and most plainly declares the roots of the underlying idea. It makes lucid that the primacy of fundamental law is not a judicial power,[37] but a duty of legislative, executive, and judicial officers.[38]

* * * * *

When the Second Continental Congress went into session on May 10, 1775, delegations were received from all thirteen United Colonies of North America. This Congress had no independent powers. And when it emitted bills of credit, commissioned officers of the army and navy, directed military operations, granted letters of marque and reprisal, declared war and independence, and concluded a treaty of alliance with France, it acted upon authority delegated by the several States.

The Virginia Convention of 1776 authorized its delegates in the Congress at Philadelphia to approve a declaration that the United Colonies were "free and independent States, absolved of all allegiance to, and dependence upon the Crown and Parliament of Great Britain."[39]

In the Declaration of American Independence, the Second Continental Congress, having received delegated power from the several States, declared on July 4, 1776, that "these United Colonies are, and of right ought to be free and independent States," and that "as free and independent States, they have full power to levy war, conclude peace, contract alliances, establish commerce, and to do all other acts and things which independent States may of right do."[40]

One of the signers of the Declaration of American Independence was Samuel Chase of Maryland. He later stated as a Justice of the United States Supreme Court in *Ware v. Hylton*, 3 Dallas 199 at 224 (U. S. 1798),

> "In June, 1776, the convention of Virginia formally declared that Virginia was a free, sovereign, and independent State, and on the 4th of July, 1776, following, the United States in Congress assembled declared [that] the thirteen united colonies [were] free and independent States; and that as such they had full power to levy war, conclude peace, etc. I consider this as a declaration, not that the United States jointly in a collective capacity were independent States, etc., but that each of them was a sovereign and independent State, that is, that each of them had a right to govern itself by its own authority and its own law, without any control from any other power on earth."

After military operations were brought to a conclusion, negotiations produced the Treaty of Paris which was formally approved by King George III on September 3, 1783. "In the Name of the most Holy and undivided Trinity," it began, then followed the soothing language of consolation and forgiveness, then the first article:

> "His Britannic Majesty acknowledges the United States, viz., New Hampshire, Massachusetts Bay, Rhode Island and Providence Plantations, Connecticut, New York, New Jersey, Pennsylvania, Delaware, Maryland, Virginia, North Carolina, South Carolina, and Georgia, to be free, sovereign, and independent States."[41]

And so, from every authentic point of view, the name "United States of America" was understood to designate, not a "new nation conceived in liberty," but thirteen new nations, each free, sovereign, and independent, each under a republican form of government, united in a confederacy.

* * * * *

On July 9, 1778, the United States in Congress assembled, approved and proposed the Articles of Confederation, inviting adoption by the legislatures of the several States. This first written constitution of the United States was a statutory pact, the charter of a public corporation which was designed to formalize previous practice under the Second Continental Congress, to coordinate the war against the British Empire, and to supervise the American Revolution.

Congress was entrusted with certain powers in dealing with foreign nations, — to make war and peace, to conclude treaties, to grant letters of marque and reprisal, etc. Congress was also granted certain important domestic powers, — to fix the standard of weights and measures, to coin money, to emit bills of credit, to run a post office, to commission generals of the land forces and all officers of the navy, and to direct military operations. Congress could make requisitions of the several States of money, supplies, troops, and ships, yet had no power to correct any delinquency in meeting requisitions. Congress had almost no power to regulate commerce, or even to make useful treaties of commerce. And it could set up a court for the trial of piracies, a court of appeals for cases of prize and capture, and certain courts authorized on occasion to settle disputes over territory and jurisdiction between two or more States.

Each State undertook to refrain from certain international and warlike acts, and to guarantee citizens of the other States the constitutional privileges and immunities enjoyed by its own citizens, also free ingress and egress, and no less the privileges of trade and commerce enjoyed by its own citizens.

The second article ordained, "Each State retains its sovereignty, freedom, and independence, and every power, jurisdiction, and right, which is not by this Confederation expressly delegated to the United States in Congress assembled."

The thirteenth article ordained, "Every State shall abide by the determinations of the United States in Congress assembled on all questions which by this Confederation are entrusted to them. And the articles of this Confederation shall be inviolably observed by every State, and the Union shall be perpetual; nor shall alteration at any time be made in any of them, unless such alteration be agreed to in a Congress of the United States, and be afterwards confirmed by the legislature of every State."

Congress had almost no power to enact laws touching upon the people of the United States. In this respect, the Confederation vaguely resembled the Holy Roman Empire, which then languished in a debilitated and ghostlike existence in Europe.[42] It has been said that the Confederation floundered because it was afflicted with the fatal weakness as the Holy Roman Empire, — i. e., that it was a pure league, a mere government for governments.[43]

But the Holy Roman Empire lasted a thousand years. There has hardly ever been in history a more enduring political institution, which, therefore, should be considered a resilient success. A government for governments it was, but it worked very well for centuries in Germany.

The final decline of the Holy Roman Empire was produced by the Thirty Years War, and it is more instructive to understand the basic cause of that prolonged conflict, than to focus on the painful effects as if the symptoms were the disease.

The imperial scepter passed to the Emperor Ferdinand II in 1619. Determined and implacable, this Habsburg prince set out to convert what had become a workable confederacy of Germanic states into an Austrian military monarchy. Ferdinand II worked energetically to bring Italy back into the imperial domain, and to restore all ancient and sweeping prerogatives of his diadem over all is vassals. His alliances were formed. With his armies he marched. On his own authority he outlawed those who resisted him with the ban of the Empire. Protestant princes were helpless before him. Catholic princes complained, but dared not oppose his lawlessness.

In four campaigns, King Gustavus Adolphus of Sweden destroyed the forces and prestige of the Emperor, devastated his lands, emptied his treasury, and left him at last so enfeebled that he could never recover and again be formidable.

The Thirty Years War was concluded in 1648 by the Peace of Westphalia, which broke the power and spirit of the Holy Roman Empire, causing it to pass into gradual irrelevancy until it collapsed in 1806 on mere demand of Napoleon Bonaparte.

Viewing events from a larger perspective, the Holy Roman Empire did not fall from internal weakness. It fell from an obnoxious attempt to consolidate imperial power. So much for the argument that the Confederation had the same flaws of the Holy Roman Empire.

Attempts to exaggerate the flaws in the constitutional structure of the Confederation are answered by the fact that this league of fledgling States in North America did, after all, defeat the overwhelming might of the British Empire.

After the surrender of Lord Cornwallis at Yorktown on October 19, 1781, the Confederation began to sink because the danger had passed, and with it expired the sentiment which had excited voluntary cooperation among the several States. As its original purpose vanished, the Confederation floundered, and requisitions became massively delinquent. Congress could not so much as pay the interest on foreign and domestic loans which had saved the United States from defeat. Western lands conceded by the British Crown in the Treaty of Paris were left unprotected.

There was, consequently, a need to renew, remodel, and strengthen the Union. Sufficient changes might well have been accomplished by prudent amendments. But attempts in this direction failed, because the concurring voices of all thirteen States were required. It appears plainly from official records that Rhode Island irresponsibly held all progress hostage, notwithstanding ardent wishes for improvement of the Union by the leaders and governments in and of all the other States.[44]

The old Union, by its express terms, was perpetual. But this feature did not prevent breaking up the Confederation by secession of the several States so they might be free to form a new Union. Commenting on the Confederation, Alexander Hamilton lamented,

> "Resting on no better foundation than the consent of several legislatures, it has been exposed to frequent and intricate questions concerning the validity of its powers, and has in some instances given birth to the enormous doctrine of legislative repeal. Owing its ratification to the law of a State, it has been contended that the same authority might repeal the law by which it was ratified. However gross a heresy it may be that a party to a compact has a right to revoke that compact, the doctrine itself has respectable advocates."[45]

These advocates were respectable, and they were right. If a contract has been materially breached, the injured party may elect to rescind. The Articles of Confederation had been breached again and again by failure of several States to meet lawful requisitions of Congress as and when due. In the Philadelphia Convention, James Madison explained,

> "If we consider the federal Union as analogous, not to the social compacts among individual men, but to the conventions among individual states, what is the doctrine resulting from these conventions? Clearly, according to the expositors of the law of nations, that breach of any one article, by any one party, leaves all other parties at liberty to consider the whole convention dissolved, unless they choose rather to compel the delinquent party to repair the breach. In some treaties,

indeed, it is expressly stipulated that a violation of particular articles shall not have this consequence, and even that particular articles shall remain in force during war, which in general is understood to dissolve all subsisting treaties. But are there exceptions of this sort in the Articles of Confederation? So far from it that there is not even an express stipulation that force shall be used to compel an offending member of the Union to discharge its duty."[46]

A roll call vote of States was taken in the Congress of the Confederation on July 2, 1788, on whether the Confederation should be dissolved. New York, Delaware, Maryland, North Carolina, and Rhode Island did not then and there give assent.[47]

North Carolina and Rhode Island never gave consent to dissolution of the old Confederation, and were independent nations when George Washington was sworn as President under the United States Constitution on April 30, 1789. The old Confederation, a "perpetual" Union, was lawfully dissolved without constitutional amendment, and without consent of all the States.

* * * * *

In the Philadelphia Convention, there were three main plans for a new Union of American States.

There was a plan, offered by William Patterson of New Jersey, to keep the old Confederation, but to enhance the powers of Congress, while adding some permanent executive and judicial authority, yet retaining the essential features of a pure league of confederacy among free, sovereign, and independent States. It was to be a government for governments not unlike the Holy Roman Empire. There was a very thorough and learned debate over several days. The main burden of argument against the proposition, exceedingly polished, was carried by James Madison. At length the plan was politely rejected.[48]

There was a plan, offered by Alexander Hamilton of New York, to create a powerful and consolidated Nation, reducing the several States to mere administrative provinces. Congress was to be transformed into a National Legislature with authority to enact any laws on any subject. There was to be a National Judiciary, with judges appointed to serve during good behavior, and with plenary jurisdiction in cases of national and international concern. An imperial Governor, chosen for life, was to possess and wield very large and ample executive powers. Hamilton's speech was heard with distress and shock, then died on the table without a vote taken it. [49]

What was wrong with such a grand and glorious American Empire? A timeless answer was given by George Mason:

"Is it to be supposed that one national government will suit so extensive a country, embracing so many climates and containing inhabitants so very different in manners, habits and customs? It is ascertained by history that there never was a government over a very extensive country without destroying the liberties of the people. History also, supported by the best writers, shows us that monarchy may suit a large territory, and despotic governments ever so extensive a country, but that popular governments can only exist in small territories. Is there a single example on the face of the earth to support a contrary opinion? Where is there an exception to this rule? Was there ever a general national government extending over so extensive a country, about in such a variety of climates, etc., where the people retained their liberty?"[50]

And Patrick Henry added,

"I will submit to your recollection whether liberty has been destroyed most often by the licentiousness of the people or the tyranny of rulers. I imagine, sir, you will find the balance on the side of tyranny. Happy you will be if you miss the fate of those nations, who, omitting to resist their oppressors, or negligently suffering their liberty to be wrested from them, have groaned under intolerable despotism! Most of the human race are now in this deplorable condition; and those nations who have gone in search of grandeur, power, and splendor have also fallen sacrifice, and been victims of their own folly. While they acquired those visionary blessings, they lost their freedom."[51]

In any event, there were two propositions diametrically opposed to each other. For the sake of convenience, the plan proposed by Judge Patterson was said to call for a "federal" government, and the plan urged by Colonel Hamilton was said to call for a "national" government.

In order to balance between the extremes, the framers endorsed intermediate principles laid down by Edmund Randolph of Virginia. These principles became the basic framework of the new Union.[52] Of the ultimate result James Madison said,

"The [United States Constitution] is in strictness neither a national nor a federal Constitution, but a combination of both. In its foundation it is federal, not national; in the sources from which the ordinary powers of the government are drawn, it is partly federal and partly national; in the operation of these powers, it is national, not federal; in the extent of them, again, it is federal, not national; and, finally, in the authoritative mode of introducing amendments, it is neither wholly federal nor wholly national."[53]

The new Union was a sophisticated invention, in some ways like, yet in other ways unlike the Holy Roman Empire, — in some ways like, yet in other ways unlike France during the reign of Louis XIV.

* * * * *

An enduring question has always been and still remains whether the several States retained a constitutional right to secede from the new Union as under the old Confederation.

It is needful to direct attention to the Preamble of the United States Constitution, which begins, "We the People of the United States, in Order to form a more perfect Union," etc. The history of this Preamble in the Philadelphia Convention removes all confusion over these words.[54]

On August 6, 1787, the committee on detail reported a preamble which began, "We the People of the States of New Hampshire, Massachusetts, Rhode Island," etc., mentioning each and every one of the thirteen States which had fought together in the American Revolution, and which, it was hoped, would belong to the new Union.

On August 7, 1787, the convention quickly adopted this preamble without dissent, then it was sent over to the committee on style which had no task other than to render provisions approved by the convention in more graceful language.

On September 12, 1787, the committee on style made a masterful report, in which the Preamble appears as it was finally approved and as it now stands, substituting "United States'" in place of "New Hampshire, Massachusetts, Rhode Island," etc., in keeping with the definition of King George III in the first article of the Treaty of Paris.

It follows that the "People of the United States" in the Preamble were considered, not as one people of one nation, but the people in each and every one of the "free, sovereign, and independent States" mentioned by his Britannic Majesty in 1783.

The Preamble announced that the people in and of each of the several States were to "ordain and establish" the constitution of the new Union. Article VII then explained how the new Constitution was to be ordained and established: — "The Ratifications of the Conventions of nine States shall be sufficient," etc. Again, the history of Article VII in the Philadelphia Convention makes lucid exactly what was meant by this provision, and why it was considered so important.[55]

On June 13, 1787, it was reported by the committee of the whole, that the new constitution should be submitted to special conventions in each of the several States, consisting of delegates chosen by qualified voters, in public elections called by the legislatures solely and expressly to consider setting up a new Union under a revised body of fundamental law.

On July 23, 1787, the main debate on this proposition occurred in the Philadelphia Convention. The proposition called upon each of the several States to adopt the United States Constitution by her People in Convention, as the ultimate legal power of society with all the attributes vested in the King and Parliament in England upon the restoration of Charles II, — all the attributes of the Virginia Convention of 1776 and of like conventions throughout the several States at the time of the American Revolution. There were various practical reasons for this item, but the major justifications were of a substantive nature.

The power to create is the power to destroy. Judge Patterson expressed the idea when he said that a constitution "can be altered or revoked only by the authority that made it." Under the old Confederation, the power to adopt the fundamental law of the Union was vested in the legislatures of these several States, and for this reason any State could for good cause secede from the Union by act of her legislature repealing the earlier act of adoption. And these several States did for good cause dissolve the old Union.

But a session of a legislature of the conduct of ordinary business was not deemed to be a sufficiently solemn occasion for the critically important decision of whether a State should adhere to or secede from the Union. In order to deprive the legislatures of the several States of the power of secession from the Union, the task of adopting the United States Constitution was given to the People in each State, from New Hampshire to Georgia, each meeting by the customary mode of an extraordinary Convention, called and elected for the announced purpose of exercising sovereign power.

The fundamental law of the new Union was intended to modify the constitutions of the several States, which in each case had been adopted by the People of Convention. The only legal way to accomplish necessary constitutional changes in each of the several States was by the People in Convention.

It was with these objectives in mind that the proposition later appearing as Article VII was approved by vote of nine out of ten States on July 23, 1787, then effortlessly thereafter passed through the Philadelphia Convention.

The use of the People in Convention in each and every one of the several States, as required by Article VII, perfect the republican form of the United States Constitution. In the 39th Federalist, James Madison said,

"It appears, on the one hand, that the [United States] Constitution is to be founded on the assent and ratification of the people of America, given by deputies elected for a special purpose; but, on the other, that this assent and ratification is to be given by the people, not as individuals composing the entire nation, but as composing the distinct and independent States to which they respectively belong. It is to be the assent and ratification of the several States, derived from the supreme authority in each State, — the authority of the people themselves."[56]

The ultimate authority of the society was distributed, in all its attributes, among each and every one of the several States: — as such, it could make and unmake any constitution, and create or destroy any Union. And this authority continued to exist after it was exercised, as it still exists to this very day, because sovereign power in and of itself represents the undying permanence which underlies all civilized government. The right of a State to secede from the Union, therefore, was not abolished but transferred from the legislatures to the people in convention, — from the limited and ordinary power of enacting statutes, to the supreme and irresistible power of doing anything in law not naturally impossible in each and every one of the several States. The right of secession was in this way made more difficult to exercise, and, consequently, there was "a more perfect Union."

The people in convention of each and every State retained the lawful discretion to ordain secession from the Union launched in 1789. This power was never meant to be exercised for light and transient causes. The gravity of the circumstances which might justify such exercise of sovereign power had been illustrated in history: — the obnoxious and unlawful usurpations of James II, the cunning subversion of the British Empire and deliberate wreckage of the prosperity of the American colonies by the powers of high finance behind the East India Company and the Bank of England, and the obtuse refusal of Rhode Island to permit urgently needed amendments of the old Confederation.

Nor was this constitutional, albeit revolutionary right of secession merely a theoretical inference. It was consciously understood by the political leaders of the time when the United States Constitution was framed and adopted.

The framers did not believe that the new Union was legally indissoluble. On August 8, 1787, in the Philadelphia Convention, Nathaniel Gorham rose to speak. He was highly respected as a statesman from Massachusetts, having been chairman of the committee of the whole in the Convention, and had been a president of Congress. "Can it be sup-posed," he asked rhetorically, "that this vast country, including the west-ern territory, will one hundred and fifty years hence, be one nation?"[57]

Alexander Hamilton had previously entertained very different wishes, yet he conceded the right of States to secede from the Union designed in the Philadelphia Convention. In the 9th Federalist, he quoted at length from a translation of the Baron de Montesquieu in order to describe the United States Constitution. The French philosopher defined a "confeder-ate republic" as a "convention by which smaller states agree to become members of a larger one which they intend to form." Of such an institu-tion Hamilton said, quoting Montesquieu, "The confederacy may be dis-solved, and the confederates preserve their sovereignty."[58]

Judge Edmund Pendleton, President of the Virginia Convention of 1788, energetically propounded the right of a State to secede from the new Union:

> "We the people, possessing all power, form a government, such as we think will secure our happiness. And suppose, in adopting this plan, we should be mistaken in the end. Where is the cause of alarm in that quarter? In the same plan we point out an easy and peaceable method of reforming what may be found amiss. No but, say gentlemen, we have put the introduction of that system in the hands of our servants, who will interrupt it for motives of self-interest. What then? We will resist, did my friend say, conveying the idea of force? Who shall dare resist the people? No, we will assem-ble in Convention, wholly recall our delegated powers, or reform them to prevent such abuse, and punish those servants who have perverted powers and designed for our happiness to their own emolument."[59]

Again in the Virginia Convention of 1788, John Marshall forthrightly added,

> "We are threatened with the loss of our liberties by possible abuse of power, notwithstanding the maxim that those who give power may take it away. It is the people who give power, and can take it back. Who shall restrain them? They are the masters who give it, and of whom their servants hold it."[60]

In the same Virginia Convention of 1788, James Madison conceded the right of secession. Answering critics of the proposed constitution, he said, "If we be dissatisfied with the national government, if we choose to renounce it, this is an additional safeguard to our defence."[61]

All of the foregoing assurances of the right of secession were made by friends of the new Union. In the ordinance adopting the United States Constitution, the Virginia Convention of 1788 assured the people in unforgettable words:

> "We the delegates of the people of Virginia, duly elected in pursuance of a recommendation of the General Assembly and now met in Convention, having fully and freely investigated and discussed the proceedings of the Federal Convention and being prepared as well as the most mature deliberation hath enabled us to decide thereon, do in the name and in behalf of the People of Virginia declare and make known that the powers granted under the Constitution, being derived from the People of the United States, may be resumed by them whensoever the same shall be perverted to their injury and oppression, and that every power not granted thereby remains with them and at their will."[62]

The phrase "people of the United States" in the ordinance of the Virginia Convention of 1788 was taken directly from the Preamble of the United States Constitution. But, as understood by the Philadelphia Convention, this Preamble was drawn from the concessions of King George III in the Treaty of Paris. Therefore, the powers delegated to the government of the Union could be resumed by the people of each and every one of the "free, sovereign, and independent States" of the Union.

Nor was Virginia alone in declaring the right of secession from the Union. When New York and Rhode Island ratified the United States Constitution, their conventions ordained the root principles on which the right was founded: — "That all power is naturally vested in, and consequently derived from the people," — and "That the powers of government may be reassumed by the people whensover it shall become necessary to their happiness."[63]

* * * * *

The first clause in Article I, Section 8 of the United States Constitution says, "The Congress shall have the Power to lay and collect Taxes, Duties, Imposts, and Excises, to pay the Debts, and provide for the Common Defence and general Welfare of the United States."[64]

This broad language caused uneasiness. Yet, there was a rule of the common law for the interpretation of constitutions, statutes, charters, deeds, and other written documents that provisions interrelated by subject matter should be read together so as to avoid, if possible, contradiction, redundancy, or surplusage, allowing each clause to serve a useful end, and all classes to complement each other in a harmonious whole.[65]

The powers of Congress were each distinctly enumerated. And if the power of Congress to provide for the common defense and general welfare were taken as a power to legislate in all cases whatsoever, the enumeration of the other powers would have been pointless and unnecessary. On this basis, James Madison and Alexander Hamilton agreed that the power of Congress to promote the general welfare was only a power to spend money, and did not confer a general authority to enact regulatory statutes.[66]

Even so, in the Virginia Convention of 1788, George Mason warned that forced constructions of the new articles of Union could pave the way to tyranny. And as an antidote, Mason made a proposal:

> "That Congress should have power to provide for the general welfare, I grant. But I wish a clause in the Constitution, with respect to all powers, which are not granted, that they are retained by the States. Otherwise, the power of providing for the general welfare may be perverted to its destruction. Many gentlemen, whom I respect, take different sides on this question. We wish [an] amendment to be introduced to remove our apprehensions. There was a clause in Confederation reserving to the States every power, jurisdiction, and right not expressly delegated to the United States. This clause has never been complained of, but approved by all. Why not then have a similar clause in this Constitution, in which it is more indispensably necessary than in the Confederation, because of the great augmentation of power vested in the former?"[67]

Everybody knew that Colonel Mason was right. And so when the Virginia Convention of 1788 adopted the United States Constitution, it was declared, "That all power is naturally vested in, and consequently derived from the people," — meaning, that sovereign power is vested in the people in convention. And it was proposed as a constitutional amendment, "That each State in the Union shall respectively retain every power, jurisdiction, and right which is not by this Constitution delegated" to the government of the United States.[68]

James Madison was elected to Congress. On June 8, 1789, he introduced a bill in the House of Representatives to amend the United States Constitution according to Article V by adding a Federal Bill of Rights.[69] Drawing from the Virginia Convention of 1788, he framed one clause in his proposal to say "that all power is originally vested in, and consequently derived from the people," — and another clause to say that the "powers not delegated by this constitution, nor prohibited by it to the States, are reserved to the States respectively."

On August 18, 1789, Congressman Thomas Tucker made a motion to combine and clarify these two clauses into a single proposition: — "All powers being derived from the people, the powers not expressly delegated by this constitution, nor prohibited by it to the States, are reserved to the States respectively." His objectives were to deny implied power to the government of the Union, and to reaffirm sovereign power n the people of each State. The motion was defeated because it was believed impractical to deny any and all implied power. Roger Sherman on the floor of the House gave an illustration. "Corporate bodies," he said, "are supposed to possess all powers incident to a corporate capacity, without being absolutely expressed." A new motion was then made by Daniel Carroll to retain the unobjectionable features of Tucker's motion by striking "expressly" and annexing the phrase "or to the people" to the proposition on the floor. The idea was quickly approved by all.

On August 21, 1789, the text was settled in what now appears as Amendment X of the United States Constitution: — "The powers not delegated to the United States by this Constitution, nor prohibited by it to the States, are reserved to the States respectively, or to the people."

Amendment X added nothing new, but was meant to stress again that the regular governments of the several States and of the Union were but public corporations, not vessels but creatures of sovereign power; that, as between these regular governments, what was not granted to the Union was reserved to the several States;[70] and that sovereign power, including the prerogative to make or unmake the constitution and the Union, was vested in the people, not of one nation, but of the several States.

* * * * *

Tied to the right of secession was the twin right of nullification, which was a cautious and gradual kind of secession actually understood at the time of the formation of the United States Constitution, as an extraordinary mode of redress against unconstitutional acts within or of the Union in a case of unusual magnitude where, due to the passions of the day, or the very nature of the question, normal modes of redress by petition or litigation could not be effective and beneficial. It was a process known to have three distinct stages:

— First, there might be an act of interposition, — i. e., a resolution of formal protest adopted by the legislature of an offended State, promulgating a solemn declaration identifying the offensive acts of the government of the Union or of sister States as unconstitutional and injurious, and concluding with an appropriate demand for redress, lest further measures become necessary;

— Secondly, if interposition should fail to induce justice, the legislature of the offended State might then issue a summons for the election and assembly of the People in Convention, which could then meet, and, by command of supreme and irresistible authority, adopt an ordinance of nullification, declaring the unconstitutional acts null and void, and authorizing or directing the government of the State to proceed with concrete measures to obstruct any further implementation of the wrongful acts within her territory; and

— Thirdly, if the ordinance of nullification should fail to restore proper balance between the Union and the State, the People in Convention could then, by act of sovereign power, as the means of enforcing the nullification, adopt an ordinance of secession, lawfully withdrawing the State from the Union.

Interposition as a precursor to nullification was well illustrated by the resolutions of the Virginia House of Burgesses on May 30, 1765, denouncing the unconstitutionality of the Stamp Act.[71] Due to the wisdom and eloquence of William Pitt, the crisis passed, and interposition did the not mature by stages into secession from the British Empire. Secession occurred only a decade later on another occasion, upon fresh and aggravated wrongs, inducing Rhode Island, Virginia, and other colonies of England in North America to withdraw from the British Empire.

Interposition was also mentioned by James Madison in the First Congress under the United States Constitution where he said, "The state legislatures will jealously and closely watch the operations of this government, and will be able to resist with more effect every assumption of power."[72]

The formal use of nullification by the ultimate legal powers of the several States was foreseen in the Virginia Convention of 1788 where George Nicholas noted worry over abuse of the power of Congress, then asked, "Who is to determine the extent of such powers? I say, the same power which, in all well-regulated communities, determines the extent of legislative powers. If they exceeded these powers, the judiciary will declare it void, or else the people will have the right to declare it void."[73]

After George Washington began his second term as President, relations began to cool with France. These relations cooled because Louis XVI was a martyred King, beloved in the United States, and the ugly spirit of the French Revolution was widely viewed with deep suspicion.[74]

Events deteriorated with increasing strides until a war of the high seas broke out between the United States and the French Republic,[75] following revelation by President John Adams on April 3, 1798, of a diplomatic rupture known as the XYZ Affair. Congress passed the Alien Act,[76] which authorized the President, in his unrestrained discretion, to deport any foreigner without due process of law, and the Sedition Act,[77] which broadly criminalized libel against public officers of the United States,[78] and was vindictively enforced by the party in power against the party out of power. As if freedom of press had not become part of constitutional heritage in the United States, Congressman Matthew Lyon of Vermont was convicted under the Sedition Act for writing a letter to the editor of a newspaper under loaded jury instructions of an outraged Federal judge. Lyons was reelected to Congress as he sat in prison. There were many such abuses.

At the time, James Madison had retired from Congress, but he had good friends in the General Assembly of Virginia. Thomas Jefferson was then Vice President of the United States. Together they set a nullification movement in motion.

Jefferson went to Kentucky, which had recently been admitted to the Union. He authored a resplendent set of resolutions which were passed by the House and Senate, then signed by the Governor on November 19, 1798. The first of these resolutions deserves particular notice:

> "Resolved, That the several States composing the United States of America are not united on the principle of unlimited submission to their general government; but that, by compact, under the style and title of a Constitution for the United States, and of amendments thereto, they constituted a government for special purposes, delegated to that government certain definite powers, reserving each State to itself the residuary mass of right to their own self-government; and that, whensoever the general government assumes undelegated powers, its acts are unauthoritative, void, and of no force; that to this compact each State acceded as a State, and is an integral party; that the government created by this compact was not made the exclusive or final judge of the powers delegated to itself, since that would have made its discretion, and not the Constitution, the measure of its powers; but that, as in cases of compact among powers having no common judge, each party has an equal right to judge for itself, as well as of infractions as of the mode of redress."[79]

Madison went to work in Virginia. He authored a similar set of resolutions, likewise expressed in memorable prose, and introduced by John Taylor of Caroline in the General Assembly sitting in Richmond. The resolutions were passed by the House, then approved by the Senate on December 24, 1798. The third of these resolutions read:

"Resolved, That the General Assembly doth explicitly and peremptorily declare that it views the powers of the federal government as resulting from a compact to which the States are parties, as limited by the plain sense and intention of the instrument constituting that compact, and as no further valid than they are authorized by the grants enumerated in that compact; and that, in case of a deliberate, palpable, and dangerous exercise of other powers not granted by the said compact, the States, who are parties thereto, have the right, and are in duty bound, to interpose for arresting the progress of the evil, and maintaining within the respective limits the authorities, rights and liberties appertaining to them."[80]

Upon the principles of these resolutions, the legislatures of Kentucky and Virginia declared the Alien and Sedition Acts unconstitutional, and urged their sister States in the Union to join them in petitioning Congress for repeal.

It is important to appreciate what the Kentucky Resolutions meant in saying that the United States Constitution is a "compact" between several "States" as parties, in which there is "no common judge" to determine infractions and to give redress, leaving each of the several States to "judge for itself."

In Article III, Section 2 of the United States Constitution, the judicial power of the Union was granted jurisdiction to decide controversies between two or more States, and on this basis it might be supposed that there was meant to be a common judge between the several States. Yet it is clear from the debates of the Philadelphia Convention that the jurisdiction there conferred was over disputes between the incorporated governments of two or more States of the Union.[81]

James Madison addressed this question in a replication to the resolutions of other States, styled a Report on the Virginia Resolutions of 1798, a timeless and masterful exposition which supplied clarity for the record of history:

The term "State," said Madison in his Report, is used in different ways to designate the territory occupied by a political society, or the established government of a political society, or the population or people at large of a political society, or, finally, the people of a political society in their highest sovereign capacity. The old Confederation was a compact between the regular governments of the several States, but the new Union, as Madison asserted, was a compact between the people of the several States, each acting in their highest sovereign capacity.[82]

No tribunal could be given jurisdiction over the People of a State in

Convention, who, possessing sovereign power, retained the attribute of preeminence no less than the King of England, and so have ever been above the jurisdiction of every court on earth. In this sense, that there was no common judge between the several States.

But there were those who insisted that only the judiciary could declare statutes unconstitutional. Madison made a particularly striking answer in his Report:

> "The resolution presupposes that dangerous powers may not only be usurped and executed by the other departments, but that the judicial department also may exercise or sanction dangerous powers beyond the grant of the Constitution; and, consequently, that the ultimate right of the parties to the Constitution, to judge whether the compact has been dangerously violated as well as by another, — by the judiciary as well as the executive or by the legislature."[83]

The Kentucky and Virginia Resolutions of 1798 were not pronouncements of sovereign power, but the warnings of legislative bodies that, unless the situation were corrected, it might be necessary to summon sovereign power to deal with the constitutional crisis within the Union.

On November 22, 1799, the General Assembly of Kentucky passed a second set of resolutions which concluded that the States, "being sovereign and independent, have an unquestionable right to judge" infractions of the United States Constitution, and that "a nullification by those sovereignties, of all unauthorized acts done under color of that instrument, is the rightful remedy."[84]

On January 7, 1800, the General Assembly of Virginia renewed its "protest against the Alien and Sedition Acts as palpable and dangerous infractions against the Constitution."[85]

It was not necessary to press further, for these protests bore fruit. Negotiations were opened and peace was concluded with France in the Treaty of Morfontaine, which became effective on December 21, 1800. The Alien and Sedition Acts remained on the books but were held in disgrace, then expired. The crisis passed, and the Union waxed strong.

* * * * *

The United States Constitution established a more perfect Union of free, sovereign, and independent States to manage the business of a great continent and provide security in foreign affairs.

The fundamental law of this Confederacy reserved rights of interposition, nullification, and secession which, in the event of dire need, could be exercised by acts of sovereign power in each of the several States.

These rights were founded upon the anticipation that the mere existence of these extraordinary remedies would restrain the government of the Union from excess, and promote accommodations among the several States.

The idea was wise, sane, and right. Yet as the idea was set in motion, unhappy prophecies were heard:

Answering Judge Edmund Pendleton who had spoken so hopefully and earnestly of the constitutional right of the people of Virginia to withdraw their Commonwealth from the Union in time of great extremity, Patrick Henry said,

> "A standing army we shall have, also, to execute the execrable commands of tyranny. And how will you punish them? Will you order them to be punished? Who shall obey these orders? Will your mace-bearer be a match for a disciplined regiment?"[86]

Later answering James Madison, master architect of the United States Constitution, Patrick Henry spoke of the future:

> "He tells you of the important blessings which he imagines will result to us and mankind in general from the adoption of this system. I see the awful immensity with which it is pregnant. I see it! I feel it! I see beings of a higher order anxious concerning our decision! When I see beyond the horizon that bounds human eyes, and look at the final consummation of all human things, and see those intelligent beings which inhabit the ethereal mansions reviewing the political decisions and revolutions which, in the progress of time, will happen in America, and the consequent happiness or misery of mankind, I am led to believe that much of the account, on one side or the other, will depend on what we now decide. Our happiness alone is not affected by the event. All nations are interested in our determination. We have it in our power to secure the happiness of half the human race. Its adoption may involve the misery of the other hemisphere."

Then the reporter's notes indicate, "Here a violent storm arose, which put the house in such disorder that Mr. Henry was obliged to conclude."[87]

NOTES

CHAPTER II

1 - The title of the King of England over certain parts of North America, based on the discoveries and claims of explorers by him sent and commissioned, consisted of a franchise, exclusive of other powers of Europe by virtue of conventions under the law of nations, to acquire land by war and conquest or by purchase and treaty from the Indian tribes living on the stretches of continent thus procured, and any rights of possession secured in the enjoyment of such franchise. This title of the British Crown, no more and no less, was later ceded by George III under the first and second articles of the Treaty of Paris in 1783. Chief Justice John Marshall so described the nature of such title in *Worchester v. Georgia*, 6 Peters 515 at 536-564 (U. S. 1832), drawing upon the principles in the opinion of Justice Smith Thompson in *Cherokee Nation v. Georgia*, 5 Peters 1 at 50-89 (U. S. 1831). In these judicial pronouncements, it was recognized that the aboriginal peoples of North America were nations proper, because they were distinct and independent political communities which governed themselves by their own laws and customs, and did not surrender their right to govern themselves when they placed themselves under the protection of more powerful white nations. As such, Chief Justice Marshall, drawing upon the views of Justice Thompson, held that Indian tribes were competent to make treaties, or in other words agreements between nations. The status of the Indian tribes as nations proper, capable of making treaties, was confirmed when, on the urging of President George Washington, the United States Senate gave advice and consent to a treaty with the Six Nations Confederacy in conformity with the second clause of Article II, Section 2 of the United States Constitution, as recorded in 1 Annals of Congress 80-82 and 84 (September 17 and 24, 1789).

2 - 1 Hening's Statutes at Large 57-66, the first of many such charters granted by the Kings of England. These various charters authorized numerous settlements and governments. A good illustration is the Charter of Charles I granted on March 4, 1629, reprinted in 1 Commager's Documents 16-18, which established Massachusetts Bay, and cured technical irregularities in the founding of the

colony at Plymouth upon the Mayflower Compact on November 11, 1620, reprinted in 1 Commager's Documents 15-16.

3 - This ordinance or constitution was granted by the company exercising authority delegated by the King, as appears in 1 Hening's Statutes at Large 110-113

4 - Peterson's Speeches at 120-121.

5 - By the Statute of 6 George III, Chapter 11 (1766), was followed nevertheless by the Statute of 6 George III, Chapter 12 (1766), which declared "That the said colonies and plantations of America have been, are, and of right out to be subordinate unto, and dependent upon the imperial Crown and Parliament of Great Britain; and that the King's Majesty, by and with the advice and consent of the lords spiritual and temporal and the Commons of Great Britain in Parliament assembled, had, hath, and of right ought to have full power and authority to make laws and statutes of sufficient force and validity to bind the colonies and people of America, subjects of the Crown of Great Britain, in all cases whatsoever." The meaning of this Declaratory act has often been misunderstood, but it is easier to grasp in light of remarks by William Pitt during his argument for repeal of the Stamp Act: — "The distinction between legislation and taxation is essentially necessary to liberty. The Crown and the peers are equally legislative powers with the Commons. If taxation be a part of simple legislation, the Crown and the peers have rights in taxation as well as yourselves, rights which they will claim, which they will exercise whenever the principle can be supported by power." And, "The Commons in America, represented in their several assemblies, have ever been in possession of the exercise of this their constitutional right of giving and granting their own money. They would have been slaves if they had not enjoyed it! At the same time, this kingdom, as the supreme governing and legislative power, had always bound the colonies by her laws, by her regulations, and restrictions in trade, in navigation, in manufactures in everything except that of taking their money out of their pockets without their consent." — Peterson's Speeches 121. Pitt conceded and the Declaratory Act confirmed that the Parliament at Westminster had sovereign power, including authority to establish fundamental law for colonies and dominions of the British Empire. Even so, by his charter of April 10, 1606, the King solemnly promised his subjects in North America the constitutional privileges and immunities of Englishmen, which eventually included those declared in the Petition of Right. Therefore, in keeping with the *Case of Monopolies*, 11 Coke 84b (K. B. 1603), the King could not properly give assent to any statute imposing on such subjects, without consent of their legislative assemblies, any tax of whatever description or on whatever pretext.

6 - Most importantly in the resolutions of the Stamp Act Congress on October 19, 1765, reprinted in 1 Marshall's Washington 487-488 and 1 Commager's Documents 57-59.

7 - Their petition of merchants in London to the British House of Commons dated January 17, 1766, is reprinted in 1 Commager's Documents 59-60.

8 - In the Statute of 10 George III, Chapter 30 (1770), and with it also went nearly all vice admiralty jurisdiction within the body of counties or for the collection of taxes, as had been allowed by the Stamp Act contrary to the ancient customs and statutes, and denounced by the Stamp Act Congress in 1765. There was one case in which the superior court of Massachusetts issued a general warrant styled writ of assistance, reported as *Praxton's Case*, Quincy 51 (1761), but the argument of James Otis against the writ was upheld a few years later in England, e. g., in the opinion of Lord Mansfield in *Leach v. Money*, 19 Howell's St. Tr. 1001 (K. B. 1765). There were also the Quartering Acts, mainly the Statute of 5 George III, Chapter 33 (1765), which housed royal troops among the people of the colonies of England in North America, again contrary to the Petition of Right. But these statutes lapsed with most of the duties imposed by the Townshend Acts.

9 - A good introductory account of how the financial interests behind the East India Company acquired their inordinate power over the British Empire, and helped foment the American Revolution, is found in Del Mar's Monetary Crimes at 7-59 and Del Mar's Money in America at 91-116.

10 - In the 6th Federalist, Mentor Edition at 54, Alexander Hamilton mentioned those antagonisms between nations and within empires which "take their origin entirely in private passions; in the attachments, enmities, interests, hopes, and fears of leading individuals in the communities of which they are members. Men of this class, whether the favorites of a king or of a people, have in too many instances abused the confidence they possessed; and assuming the pretext of some public motive, have not scrupled to sacrifice the national tranquillity to personal advantage or personal gratification." Hamilton had in mind the outwardly respectable monied interests in London which fomented the American Revolution.

11 - A few preliminary illustrations of the gross corruption then and long previously infecting the British government may here be given. During the reign of James II, Charles Spencer, Earl of Sunderland, was president of the privy council. It has been said of him, "What sums he made of selling places, titles, and pardons can only be conjectured, but must have been enormous." Then continuing, "All fines, all forfeitures went to Sunderland. On every grant toll went to him. If any suitor ventured to ask any favor directly of the King, the answer was 'Have you spoken to my Lord President?' Once a bold man ventured to say that the Lord President got all the money in the court. 'Well,' replied his Majesty, 'he deserves it all.'" 2 Macauley's History 400. In the Philadelphia Convention, Benjamin Franklin commented on the situation in Parliament during the reign of George III: "It is true, the King of Great Britain had not, as was said, exerted his negative since the revolution [of 1688-1689]; but that matter is easily explained. The bribes and emoluments now given to the members of Parliament rendered it unnecessary, everything now being done

according to the will of the ministers." — 5 Elliot's Debates 152, Tansill's Documents 148, 1 Ferrand's Records 99 (Madison's Notes, June 4, 1787). Again, in the Philadelphia Convention, Gouverneur Morris made reference to the secret treaty of Dover in 1670, in which Charles II received a "subsidy" from Louis XIV, enabling the King of England, in exchange for initiatives in foreign policy favorable to France, to hire his own troops without asking Parliament for money. Accounts of this royal intrigue are found in 1 Macauley's History 196 and 2 Churchill's History 352-353. And so Morris argued that the President of the United States should be impeachable for bribery. He said, "one would think the King of England well secured against bribery. He has, as it were, a fee simple in the whole kingdom. Yet Charles II was bribed by Louis XIV." — 5 Elliot's Debates 343, 2 Ferrand's Records 68-69, Tansill's Documents 421 (Madison's Notes, July 20, 1787).

12 - There have always been a few interesting fellows, who have thought the contrary, or least in an unguarded moment spoke the contrary. In a letter to Benjamin Rush on January 16, 1811, Thomas Jefferson related an incident at Monticello during the presidency of George Washington, involving a "collision of opinion between [Vice President John] Adams and [Secretary of the Treasury Alexander] Hamilton on the merits of the British constitution, Mr. Adams giving it as his opinion that, if some of its defects and abuses were corrected, it would be the most perfect constitution of government ever devised by man. Colonel Hamilton, on the contrary, asserted that, with its existing vices, it was the most perfect model of government that could be formed, and that correction of its vices would render it an impractical government." Koch & Peden's Jefferson 608.

13 - The resolutions were promulgated and sent to the King on October 14, 1774, detailing the rights of English men in North America and enumerating the unconstitutional features of the taxes and legislation imposed by the British Parliament after the Seven Years War, as well as the obnoxious Statutes of 14 George III. These resolutions are reprinted in 1 Marshall's Washington 496-500, Tansill's Documents 105, and 1 Commager's Documents 82-84.

14 - The petition of merchants in London to the British House of Commons, dated January 12, 1775, explained why the war would ruin their business, and urged reconciliation with the American colonies. It is reprinted in 1 Commager's Documents 87-89. Upon presentation to the House of Commons, the petition was disregarded on demand of the East India Company and the Bank of England.

15 - The Declaration of the Causes and Necessity of Taking Up Arms, adopted on July 5, 1775, is reprinted in Tansill's Documents 10-17 and 1 Commager's Documents 92-95.

16 - The proclamation of King George III, declaring a state of rebellion in the colonies of England in North America, and authorizing war to put down the insurgency, was dated August 23, 1775. It is reprinted in 1 Commager's Documents 95-96.

17 - The power to coin money as an adjunct to the prerogative of the King to fix the standard of weights and measures is described in 1 Blackstone's Commentaries 274-277.

18 - Sir Edward Coke was emphatic on the legal necessity of using gold or silver as an inherent limitation on the prerogative of the King to coin money, as is explained with utmost clarity in 1 Blackstone's Commentaries 277-279. The phrase "coin money" was a legal term of art, meaning striking usable pieces of gold or silver to circulate as legal tender or money properly so called. Any system of money other than gold or silver had to be authorized by an act of Parliament.

19 - The principal agent of the East India Company was Thomas Osborne, who raised corruption to sublime artistry in England. As the Earl of Danby, he arranged the bribe paid to Charles II by Louis XIV through the secret Treaty of Dover. In 1679 he was impeached for his complicity in the treaty, but was pardoned by the King. Osborne then pleaded the pardon at the bar of the House of Lords, whereupon the House of Commons protested that the plea was not good in law against an impeachment. Charles II then prorogued Parliament to suspend the impeachment which was not taken up again. In the third section of the Act of Settlement in 1701, it was ordained that a pardon could not be pleaded against an impeachment. Osborne thus had the distinction of corruption so incorrigible that a constitutional amendment was necessary to stop it. At the Glorious Revolution, Osborne adroitly feathered his nest by opening negotiations with the William of Orange immediately after the acquittal of the seven bishops, and, as a reward, was created the Marquis of Carmarthen, then the Duke of Leeds. He was advanced further when he became president of the privy council: — in this position in consideration of a bribe, he secured renewal of the charter of the East India Company. He was again impeached, as appears in the *Case of the Duke of Leeds*, 13 Howell's St. Tr. 1263 (H. C. 1695), but was saved again when William III prorogued Parliament to suspend the impeachment which was not renewed. He was exceedingly rich when he died in 1712.

20 - 1 Macauley's History 72.

21 - The gravity and weight of this national debt, all out of proportion to any advantage deriving from the currency it generated, was bemoaned in 1 Blackstone's Commentaries 327-330.

22 - This essay is reprinted in 1 Labaree's Franklin 139-157 (April 3, 1729).

23 - As a colonial agent in London, Franklin proposed a uniform system of paper currency throughout the colonies form New Hampshire to Georgia, based on the ideas of his *Modest Inquiry*. The particulars are fond in Franklin's outline of the proposed legislation, reprinted in 11 Labaree's Franklin 205-207 (March 31-April 5, 1766), and Franklin's report from London, reprinted in 12 Labaree's Franklin 76-87 (March 11, 1767). A motion for leave to bring in a bill incorporating Franklin's proposal came up in the British House of Commons on May 14,

1766, but was quickly negatived on voice vote, whereupon the eventual outbreak of the American Revolution was almost sealed. Two later Currency Acts were passed with a view of appeasing the colonies, but these laws offered too little too late. The Statute of 10 George III, Chapter 35 (1770) allowed the colony of New York to issue 120,000 pounds in bills of credit, payable in fourteen years, and receivable in payment of public dues to the provincial government. The Statute of 13 George III, Chapter 57 (1773) allowed the American colonies outside New England to emit bills of credit receivable in payment of public dues to the governments issuing them.

24 - Judge Joseph Story was noted for his fixation that the American people, as one nation and in one voice, withdrew from the British Empire, and formed one indivisible republic called the United States of America. This notion is stated in Story's own words in 1 Elliot's Debates 63-67. Yet, Story conceded that New Hampshire set up her own independent government in December 1775, that South Carolina did likewise in March 1776, that Virginia did likewise in June 1776, and that New Jersey did likewise in July 1776, all apart from the Declaration of American Independence. And he overlooked the independence of Rhode Island in May 1776. These facts alone destroy Story's argument.

25 - The official account is Staple's Rhode Island 65-67.

26 - Reprinted in 9 Hening's Statutes at Large at 53-54 (July 1775, Chapter 4).

27 - In Query XIII of *Notes on Virginia*, published in 1782, Thomas Jefferson claimed that the Virginia Convention of 1776 did not have sovereign power, but was only a temporary legislature, and, consequently, lacked power to frame a constitution which could not be changed by a subsequent assembly, as appears in Koch & Peden's Jefferson 239-240. A similar view was expressed by Edmond Randolph, as appears in 3 Elliot's Debates 70 (Virginia Convention, June 16, 1788). But Judge St. George Tucker, the most respected constitutional lawyer in Virginia during the era of the American Revolution, demonstrated clearly that the Virginia Convention of 1776 did possess sovereign attributes, and framed a bill of rights and constitution which the general assembly could not modify, as was held by the judiciary of the Commonwealth. It so appears in 1 Tucker's Blackstone, Appendix C at 79-95.

28 - In the Philadelphia Convention, the delegates had all undergone the experience of the revolution, and all understood the idea so well that nobody there saw a need to define it, as is clear from the framing of the part of Article IV, Section 4 of the United States Constitution which guarantees a republican form of government to every State of the Union, recorded in 5 Elliot's Debates 128, 182, 190, 332-333, 376, 381, 497-498, 536, 564, — Tansill's Documents 118, 155, 203, 406-408, 470, 481, 645-646, 711, — 1 Ferrand's Records 22, 121, 202, 237, 2 Ferrand's Records 47-48, 128, 188, 466-467, 578, 602, 662 (Madison's Notes, May 29, June 5, 11, and 13, July 18 and 26, August 6 and 30, September 10, 12 and 17, 1787). Rhode Island

was the only State in which constitution was not adopted by a special convention apart from the legislature as in Virginia, but the method there used was in keeping with the Glorious Revolution in England, and the legislature under the Charter of Charles II was in the circumstances a convention of the people. In the 39th Federalist, Mentor Edition 240-241, James Madison held that a republican form of government was alone "reconcilable with the genius of the people of America" and the "fundamental principles of the Revolution" and could be defined as "a government which derives all its powers directly or indirectly from the great body of the people, and is administered by persons holding their offices during pleasure for a limited period or during good behavior."

29 - Reprinted in 9 Hening's Statutes at Large 109 (May 1776, Chapter 1).

30 - Reprinted in 9 Hening's Statutes at Large 112 (May 1776, Chapter 2).

31 - James Monroe observed, "The revolution, in having emancipated us from the shackles of Great Britain, has put the government in the hands of one order of people only, — freemen, not freemen and nobles. This is a particular trait in the character of the revolution." - 3 Elliot's Debates 208-209 (Virginia Convention, June 10, 1788). This reality was rooted in the fact that there was no historical basis for a class of titled peers in North America. In explaining why the United States Senate could not be modeled after the British House of Lords, Charles Pinckney said, "The genius of the [American] people, their mediocrity of situation, and the prospects which are afforded their industry, in a country which must be a new one for centuries, are unfavorable to the rapid distinction of ranks." - 5 Elliot's Debates 235, Tansill's Documents 269-270, 1 Ferrand's Records 400 (Madison's Notes, June 25, 1787).

32 - The American idea of separation of powers came from the observations of the Baron de Montesquieu in Book IX, Chapter 6 of his celebrated treatise l'Ésprit des Lois, published in 1748. The American idea was given a classical expression in the third article of the Virginia Constitution of 1776, which, subject only to minor exceptions, required three distinct branches of government, viz., legislative, executive, and judicial, and prohibited anybody from holding or exercising the powers of more than one branch of government at the same time. The principle was far more strict than separation of powers in the British Constitution, under which, for example, the House of Lords was both the upper chamber of the legislature and the highest court of judicature. James Madison's views on separation of powers are found in the 47th and 48th Federalist, Mentor Edition 301-313. Because of separation of powers, a legislature cannot delegate law-making authority to executive officers, as brought out in debates leading to Section 2 of the Post Office Act of 1792 (1 U. S. Statutes at Large 232 and 233): 3 Annals of Congress 229-241, 303-310 (House, December 6 and 7, 1791, and January 3 and 5, 1792).

33 - In 1 Blackstone's Commentaries at 91.

34 - In the famous case of *Marbury v Madison*, 1 Cranch 137 (U. S. 1803), it was held that Section 13 of the Judiciary Act of 1789 (1 U. S. Statutes at 80-81), construed in light of the second clause of Article III, Section 2 of the United States Constitution, did not confer upon the United States Supreme Court original jurisdiction to issue a writ of mandamus against the secretary of state. Notwithstanding the rhetoric in the opinion of Chief Justice John Marshall, neither Section 13 of the Judiciary Act of 1789, nor any clause in Section 13 was ever found unconstitutional, and, therefore, null and void. This point becomes clearer from Marshall's opinion in *Ex Parte Crane*, 5 Peters 190 (U. S. 1831), in which a writ of mandamus was allowed within the appellate jurisdiction of the United States Supreme Court under Section 13 of the Judiciary Act of 1789 then and there deemed to be fully operative for any proper use.

35 - In the Philadelphia Convention, there were many speeches in which the power of judges to declare statutes unconstitutional was acknowledged: — e. g., Elbridge Gerry, 5 Elliot's Debates 151, Tansill's Documents 147, 1 Ferrand's Records 97-98 (Madison's Notes, June 4, 1787); Roger Sherman and James Madison, 5 Elliot's Debates 321, Tansill's Documents 390-391, 2 Ferrand's Records 27-28 (Madison's Notes, July 17, 1787); James Wilson, 5 Elliot's Debates 344, Tansill's Documents 422-423, 2 Ferrand's Records 73 (Madison's Notes, July 23, 1787); John Mercer and John Dickenson 5 Elliot's Debates 428-429, Tansill's Documents 547-549, 2 Ferrand's Records 298-299 (Madison's Notes, August 15, 1787). So also in the 78th Federalist, Mentor Edition 468, Alexander Hamilton conceded the power of judges to declare statutes unconstitutional.

36 - This feature of republican forms of government became dominant even in Rhode Island. In *Trevett v. Weeden*, 10 Rec. R. I. 218 (1786), the superior court of the State found a statute unconstitutional, which directed trial without jury of anybody accused by information of the misdemeanor of refusing to take paper currency as legal tender. The chief justice held that the American Revolution had restored the doctrine of Lord Coke that an unconstitutional statute is null and void.. The Charter of Charles II received the Statute abolishing the Star Chamber. In the often misunderstood case of *Luther v. Borden*, 7 Howard 1 (U. S. 1849), the majority and the minority agreed that it was a practical impossibility to decide the question, which of two competing governments of Rhode Island was legitimate at the time of the mild civil war within the State in 1842. That question was found to be nonjusticiable. Even so, both the majority and the minority agreed that it was a proper legal question fit for judicial determination whether a statute of the general assembly imposing martial law was in keeping with the Federal guarantee of a republican form of government; further, that the government under the Charter of Charles II, as adapted to the circumstances of the American Revolution, was republican in form; and that, as such, the government was subject to the principles inherent in the Petition of Right insofar as it limited the power to impose martial law. Using this standard, the majority held that the

statute was constitutional, while the dissenter thought that the statute was unconstitutional.

37 - E. g., in the Philadelphia Convention, when it was conceded that Federal courts should have jurisdiction over questions arising under the United States Constitution, it was understood, as carefully indicated in Madison's Notes for Augsut 27, 1787, "that the jurisdiction given was constructively limited to cases of a judiciary nature." — 5 Elliot's Debates 382-483, Tansill's Documents 624-625, and 2 Ferrand's Records 430.

38 - A prominent illustration of this principle is found in the pardons granted by President Thomas Jefferson to those who were convicted before circuit courts of the United States under the Sedition Act of 1798. Brushing aside the opinions of the judges who presided over the trials, Jefferson found the statute was unconstitutional. In a letter to Abigail Adams, dated September 4, 1801, he answered the objection that only the judiciary had the power to declare statutes unconstitutional. "The opinion which gives to the judges the right to decide what laws are constitutional, and what not, not only for themselves in their own sphere of action, but for the legislative and executive also, in their own spheres, would make the judiciary a despotic branch." — 8 Ford's Jefferson 311. It was later conceded in New York Times v. Sullivan, 376 U. S. 254 at 276-277 (1964), that Jefferson had the power to grant these pardons on constitutional grounds.

39 - Tansill's Documents at 20 (May 20, 1776).

40 - 1 Elliot's Debates at 62-63, Tansill's Documents at 25, 1 Commager's Documents at 102.

41 - Commager's Documents at 117. The treaty was approved by Congress on January 14, 1784.

42 - The best account in English on the final decline and fall of this ancient institution is Bryce's Holy Roman Empire at 384-417.

43 - As maintained in the 15th, 16th, and 17th Federalist by Hamilton, and the 18th, 19th and 20th Federalist by Hamilton and Madison, and the 20th and 21st Federalist by Hamilton, Mentor Edition 105-152.

44 - The public record of transactions from 1781-1786 speaks for itself, and appears in Elliot's Debates at 92-120.

45 - 22nd Federalist, Mentor Edition at 152.

46 - 5 Elliot's Debates 207, Tansill's Documents 227, 1 Ferrand's Records 315 (Madison's Notes, June 19, 1787).

47 - As appears in 1 Elliot's Debates 332, Tansill's Documents 1060-1061. Delegations from Rhode Island, Delaware, and North Carolina were not present. The delegation from New York was equally divided. Only one delegate appears

for Maryland, but the second article of the Confederation stipulated that a State must be represented by at least two delegates. The ratification of the United States Constitution by New York, the eleventh State, occurred on July 26, 1788, as appears in 1 Elliot's Debates 327-331, Tansill's Documents 1034-1044. On September 13, 1788, the Congress of the Confederation called for elections of the new Congress and of the President under the United States Constitution, as appears in Tansill's Documents 1062. The new government officially commenced on March 2, 1789. when the First Congress initially met. Discussion of this point is found in *Owings v. Speed*, 5 Wheaton 420 (U. S. 1820). The United States Constitution was not adopted by North Carolina until November 21, 1789, as appears in 1 Elliot's Debates 333, Tansill's Documents 1051, and was not adopted by Rhode Island until May 29, 1790, as appears in 1 Elliot's Debates 333-337, Tansill's Documents 1052-1059, Staple's Rhode Island 674-680.

48 - The proceedings on Patterson's plan are recorded in 5 Elliot's Debates 191-198 and 206-212, — Tansill's Documents 203-215 - and 226-234, — 1 Ferrand's Records 240, 242-245, 249-256, 282, 313-322, 2 Ferrand's Records 126 (Madison's Notes, June 14, 15, 18, and 19, 1787).

49 - Hamilton's presentation appears in 5 Elliot's Debates 198-205, — Tansill's Documents 215-225, — 1 Ferrand's Records 282-293 (Madison's Notes, June 18, 1787).

50 - 3 Elliot's Debates at 30 (Virginia Convention, June 4, 1788).

51 - 3 Elliot's Debates at 47 (Virginia Convention, June 5, 1788).

52 - The plan, actually written by James Madison, was introduced on the first day of debates. It was considered over two weeks by the convention sitting as a committee of the whole, then adopted, then reconfirmed after the Patterson's plan was finally voted down by vote of seven against three States, with one State divided, as appears in 5 Elliot's Debates 126-128, 132-190, 211-212, — Tansill's Documents 114-119, 120-225, 234-237, — and 1 Ferrand's Records 18-23, 33-38, 47-55, 64-69, 78-89, 96-105, 119-126, 132-140, 150-156, 14-169, 175-180, 196-204, 214-220, 232-237, 322 (Madison's Notes, May 29, 30, and 31, June 1, 2, 4, 5, 6, 7, 8, 9, 11, 12, 13, and 19, 1787).

53 - 39th Federalist, Mentor Edition at 246. Madison made a speech to the same effect, as appears in 3 Elliot's Debates at 94-95 (Virginia Convention, June 6, 1788).

54 - The framing of the Preamble of the United States Constitution, is traced in 5 Elliot's Debates 127, 129, 132, 135, 189, 214-223, 357-358, 375, 382-383, 536, 558, — Tansill's Documents 116, 119, 124-125, 201, 234, 241-252, 441, 465, 471-472, 482-483, 702, — 1 Ferrand's Records 95-96, 128, 177, 196-197, 565, 590, 651 (Madison's Notes, May 29 and 31, June 13, 20, and 21, July 23 and 26, August 6 and 7, September 10, 12, and 17, 1787).

55 - The framing of Article VII of the United States Constitution is traced in 5 Elliot's Debates 128, 157-158, 183, 190, 352-356, 376, 381, 498-499, 512, 532-535, 536, 541, — Tansill's Documents 119, 156-157, 192, 203, 237, 434-439, 470, 481-482, 647-648, 648-653, 668, 697-701, 712-713, 720, — 1 Ferrand's Records 22, 122-123, 214, 237, 2 Ferrand's Records 88-94, 128, 189, 467-469, 475-480, 511, 559-564, 579-580, 603, 608-609, 663, and 665-667 (Madison's Notes, May 28, June 5, 12, 13, and 19, July 23 and 26, August 6, 30 and 31, September 5, 10, 12, 13, and 17, 1787).

56 - Mentor Edition at 243.

57 - 5 Elliot's Debates 554, Tansill's Documents 496, 2 Ferrand's Records 221 (Madison's Notes, August 8, 1787).

58 - Mentor Edition at 74-75, quoting from Book IX, Chapter 1 of *L'Ésprit des Lois*. Hamilton also conceded the "fundamental principle which admits the right of the people to alter or abolish the established constitution whenever they find it inconsistent with their happiness." — 78th Federalist, Mentor Edition at 469.

59 - 3 Elliot's Debates 37 (June 4, 1788).

60 - 3 Elliot's Debates 233 (June 10, 1788). Marshall was not so forthright in his opinion as Chief Justice in *Cohen's v. Virginia*, 6 Wheaton 264 at 389 (U. S. 1821), where he said by way of obiter dictum having not the remotest connection with the technical point of appellate jurisdiction under consideration, "The people made this constitution, and the people can unmake it. It is the creature of their own will, and lives only by their will. But this supreme and irresistible power to make or unmake resides only with the whole body of the people, not in any subdivision of them." Marshall knew better, and, if he had made such a comment in the Virginia Convention of 1788, his State would never have joined the new Union, as becomes obvious from reading the full proceedings in volume 3 of Elliot's Debates. A full and ample rebuttal to Marshall's remark is found in the debates of the Philadelphia Convention on July 23, 1787, as shown in Madison's Notes. A proposition to refer adoption to the legislatures of the several States was voted down. Thereupon, Gouverneur Morris, who wanted a "national," and not a "federal" government, "moved that the reference of the plan be made to one general convention chosen and authorized by the people" from all parts of the United States so as to create one sovereign power for the entire country, as opposed to a convention chosen and authorized by the people of all the States. The idea was heard in disbelief. Madison recorded simply, "Not seconded." The convention then voted to refer the new constitution to special conventions in each and every State, as appears in 5 Elliot's Debates 356, Tansill's Documents 439, 2 Ferrand's Records 93-94.

61 - 3 Elliot's Debates 414-415 (June 14, 1788). It has been alleged, on the basis of a letter he wrote to Daniel Webster on March 15, 1833, that in old age James Madison abandoned the idea that the several States retained a constitutional right to secede from the Union. In the said letter, Madison warned Webster not to confound

"the claim to secede at will with the right of seceding from intolerable oppression. The former answers itself, being a violation without cause of a faith solemnly pledged. The latter is another name only for revolution about which there is not theoretic controversy." No doubt, as Madison held, secession is an act of revolution, but an act of peaceable and lawful revolution, such as occurred in the transition from James II to William and Mary in 1688 ad 1689. Thus in his letter Madison added that the constitution of the Union inaugerated in 1789 was always "subject to the revolutionary rights of the people in extreme cases." - 9 Hunt's Madison 604-605.

62 - 1 Elliot's Debates 327, 3 Elliot's Debates 656, Tansill's Documents 1027 (June 27, 1788).

63 - As appears in 1 Elliot's Debates at 327, Tansill's Documents at 1034 (New York Convention, July 26, 1788); and in 1 Elliot's Debates at 334, Tansill's Documents at 1052, Staples' Rhode Island at 675 (Rhode Island Convention, May 29, 1790).

64 - The framing of the first clause of Article I, Section 8 of the United States Constitution is traced in 5 Elliot's Debates 378, 432-434, 440-441, 451-452, 463-464, 469, 471, 475-477, 479, 506, 507, 536, 543, 560, — Tansill's Documents 475, 552-555, 564-565, 580-581, 597-598, 605, 608, 614-616, 619, 659-660, 661, 706, — 2 Ferrand's Records 181, 305-308, 325-326, 355-356, 376-377, 392, 400, 412-414, 418, 497, 499, 569, 594, 614, 655 (Madison's Notes, August 6, 16, 21, 22, 23, 24, and 25, September 4, 10, 12, 14, and 17, 1787). The key part of this history is that on August 25, 1787, the convention was asked to consider a clause giving Congress the power of spending for "defraying the expenses that shall be incurred for the common defence and general welfare." The problem was referred to a special committee which, on September 4, 1787, reported the clause, intended to have the same meaning, giving Congress the power to "provide for the common defence and general welfare."

65 - James Madison's statement of this principle and its corollary was as follows: "There are two rules of construction, dictated by plain reason as well as founded on legal maxims. The one is that every part of an expression ought, if possible, to be allowed some meaning, and to be made to conspire to some common end. The other is that, where several parts cannot be made to coincide, the less important part should give way to the more important part; the means should be sacrificed to the end, rather than the end to the means." — 40th Federalist, Mentor Edition 248.

66 - Madison so held in the 41st Federalist, Mentor Edition 263. And Hamilton so held in the 83rd Federalist, Mentor Edition 497.

67 - 3 Elliot's Debates 442 (June 14, 1788).

68 - Following the ordinance of the Virginia Convention dated June 26, 1788, were declarations and proposed amendments dated June 27, 1788. The second

declaration is reprinted in 3 Ellliot's Debates 657, Tansill's Documents 1028, and the first proposal for amendment is reprinted 3 Elliot's Debates 659, Tansill's Documents 1031.

69 - The most important episodes in the framing of Amendment X of the United States Constitution are found in 1 Annals of Congress 424-450, 761-768 (House, June 8, August 18 and 21, 1789).

70 - Those who regard Amendment X as a mere truism, as suggested in *United States v. Darby*, 312 U. S. 100 at 124 (1941), have not understood that the phrase "or the people" reserved sovereign power, and thus the power to secede from the Union was reserved to the several States. Those who think of Amendment X as a mere truism are inclined to assign a bloated meaning to the second clause of Article VI of the United States Constitution, which says, "This Constitution, and the Laws of the United States which shall be made in Pursuance thereof, and all Treaties made, which shall be made, under the Authority of the United States, shall be the supreme Law of the Land." In fact, this "supremacy clause" is a mere truism, so much so that it was offered by Luther Martin, the strongest advocate of the rights of the several States in the Philadelphia Convention, in order to give added emphasis to the principle that the Federal government must not transgress the limits imposed by the Constitution. It so appears in 5 Elliot's Debates 190, 321-322, 375, 377, 379, 467, 478, 536, 564, — Tansill's Documents 203, 237, 390-392, 467, 476, 603, 618, 712, — 1 Ferrand's 237, 2 Ferrand's Record 27-29, 128, 183, 389, 417, 572, 603, 663 (Madison's Notes, June 13 and 19, July 17 and 26, August 23 and 25, September 10, 12, and 17, 1787). Of this same provision, Alexander Hamilton said, "If a number of political societies enter into a larger political society, the laws which the latter may enact, pursuant to the powers intrusted to its constitution, must necessarily be supreme above those societies and the individuals of whom they are composed. It would otherwise be a mere treaty, dependent on the good faith of the parties, and not a government, which is only another word for political power and supremacy. But it will not follow from this doctrine that the acts of the larger society which are not pursuant to this constitutional powers, but which are invasions of the residual authorities of the smaller societies will be the supreme law of the land. These will be merely acts of usurpation, and will deserve to be treated as such." — 33rd Federalist, Mentor Edition 204.

71 - Reprinted in 1 Marshall's Washington 486 and 1 Commager's Documents 55-56.

72 - 1 Annals of Congress 439-440 (House, June 8, 1789). In the 46th Federalist, Mentor Edition 297-298, Madison also acknowledged the propriety of using interposition by legislative protest to arrest excesses of the government of the Union.

73 - 3 Elliot's Debates 443 (June 14, 1788).

74 - George Washington revered King Louis XVI who saved American independence by faithful adherence to the treaty between the United States and France, concluded on May 4, 1778, reprinted in 1 Commager's Documents 105-107. After framing the Federal Bill of Rights, and proposing the articles as constitutional amendments for adoption by the several States, Congress asked President Washington to proclaim a day of Thanksgiving, which he did on October 3, 1789, establishing the last Thursday in November "to be devoted by the People of these States to the service of that great and glorious Being who is the beneficent Author of all the good that was, that is, or that will be." The proclamation urged prayers asking God "to protect and guide all Sovereigns and Nations, especially such as have shown kindness to us." — Commins' Washington 565-566. He meant above all others, Louis XVI. It is not to be expected that a man of such pious temperament should endorse such an anti-religious and murderous event as the French Revolution, and certainly, as President, Washington stiffly rebuffed all efforts to import its baneful spirit into the United States, as appears in 5 Marshall's Washington 7-70.

75 - Declared by Congress as a limited or imperfect war, as appears in *Bas v. Tingey*, 4 Dallas 37 (U. S. 1800).

76 - 1 U. S. Statutes 577 (June 256, 1798).

77 - 1 U. S. Statutes 596 (July 14, 1798).

78 - The Sedition Act of 1798 is remarkable because the third section provided that "it shall be lawful for the defendant upon the trial of the cause to give in his defence the truth of the matter contained in the publication charged as a libel. And the jury who shall try the cause shall have a right to determine the law and the fact, under the direction of the court, as in other cases. The guarantee of freedom of speech and press in Amendment I of the United States Constitution was certainly intended to include in a prosecution for sedition or criminal libel not only the defense of truth, but also the defense of good faith, as maintained by Sir John Powell, dissenting Justice in the *Seven Bishops Case*, 12 Howell's St. Tr. 183 at 415 (K. B. 1688), and as later held in *Garrison v. Louisiana*, 379 U. S. 64 (1964).

79 - These Kentucky Resolutions of 1798 are reprinted in 4 Elliot's Debates 540-544, 1 Commager's Documents 178-182, 1 Stephens' View 570-576.

80 - These Virginia Resolutions of 1798 are reprinted in 4 Elliot's Debates 528-529, 1 Commager's Documents 182-183, 1 Stephens' View 576-578.

81 - Under the ninth article of the Confederation, Congress had power to establish a special court on occasion to settle disputes over territory and jurisdiction between two or more States, which, in the nature of things, could only have been disputes between incorporated governments of different States holding title to land or exercising certain powers. In the Philadelphia Convention, the committee

on detail proposed to give the Senate power of resolving disputes over territory and jurisdiction between two or more States, and the Supreme Court authority to adjudicate all other disputes between two or more States. Thereafter, the proposed jurisdiction of the Senate was transferred to the Supreme Court, which then had power to resolve all kinds of disputes between two or more States, — i. e., between incorporated governments of two or more States. These phases of framing can be traced in 5 Elliot's Debates 379-380, 380, 471, 484, 536, — Tansill's Documents 477-478, 479, 608-609, 626, 710, — 2 Ferrand's Records 183-187, 400-401, 437, 576, 600-601 (Madison's Notes, August 6, 24, and 28, September 10, 12, and 17, 1787).

82 -The important discussion to this effect in Madison's Report is found in 4 Elliot's Debates 547, 1 Stephens' View 580.

83 - 4 Elliot's Debates 549, 1 Stephens' View 582. On many occasions, Madison opposed the idea that the judiciary alone should have the power to declare statutes unconstitutional. At several points during the Philadelphia Convention, he proposed that the Supreme Court and the President should sit together with as a council of revision to pass on the constitutionality and wisdom of legislation passed by the House and the Senate. When this proposal was finally defeated, the President was left with a power to veto bills on any proper basis, including constitutional grounds, as appears in 5 Elliot's Debates 428-429, Tansill's Documents 547-549, 2 Ferrand's Records 298-300 (Madison's Notes, August 15, 1787). And on several occasions as President, Madison vetoed legislation which he believed to be unconstitutional, — e. g., where he vetoed a bill to incorporate a church in the District of Columbia, because the legislation minutely regulated the internal affairs of the congregation, contrary to the prohibition of laws establishing a religion in the 1st Amendment, as appears in 22 Annals of Congress 982-985, 995, and 997 (House, February 21 and 23, 1811).

84 - 4 Elliot's Debates at 545.

85 - 4 Elliot's Debates at 580.

86 - 3 Elliot's Debates at 51 (Virginia Convention, June 5, 1788).

87 - 3 Elliot's Debates at 625 (Virginia Convention, June 24, 1788).

CHAPTER III

THE NORTHERN SECESSIONISTS

The constitution framed by the Philadelphia Convention includes exceedingly interesting provisions on the armed forces of the Union. The face of these provisions, read together as clauses dealing with the same subject matter, clarifies their intended meaning, and, lest there be any question about the evident significance of these clauses, legal history supplies reinforcement for the conclusions which may be drawn from the language interpreted according to the rules of the common law.[1]

Article I, Section 8 of the United States Constitution provides that Congress shall have certain enumerated powers: — in the twelfth clause, to "raise and support Armies, but no Appropriation of Money to that Use shall be for a longer Term than two Years;"[2] — in the fifteenth clause, to "provide for calling forth the Militia to execute the Laws of the Union, suppress Insurrections, and repel Invasions;" — and in the sixteenth clause, to "provide for organizing, arming, and disciplining the Militia, and for governing such part of them as may be employed in the Service of the United States, reserving to the States respectively the Appointment of the Officers and the Authority of training the Militia according to the Discipline prescribed by Congress."[3] Amendment II then says, "A well regulated Militia being necessary to a free State, the right of the people to keep and bear Arms shall not be infringed."[4]

It is plain from the text of Amendment II that the militia was understood to be a force made up of the people. It so appears because the purpose of the right of the people to keep and bear arms is to strengthen the militia. Seen in this light, the evident meaning of Amendment II is that Congress may not disarm the people, but may regulate them for service in the militia.

And it is also clear that the power of Congress in the twelfth clause of Article I, Section 8 to raise and support armies, was intended to authorize the voluntary enlistment of professional soldiers, and was not meant to include conscription of citizens to fill the ranks. Were it otherwise, the elaborate limitations on the powers of Congress to train and employ the militia could be circumvented at will, and the fifteenth and sixteenth clauses of Article I, Section 8 would serve no useful purpose. As the power of Congress to provide for the common defense and general welfare was confined to spending, lest enumeration of other powers of Congress be unnecessary, so the power of Congress to raise armies was limited to hiring troops for pay, lest enumeration of other powers of Congress over the militia be redundant.

The distinction between armies and militia can be traced back to the hus carls of Canute the Dane and the fyrd of Alfred the Great. The hus carls were stipendiary troops. The fyrd was the great body of the people bearing arms to assure domestic peace and defend the kingdom.

After the Norman Conquest, the old fyrd of the Saxon monarchy became dormant, leaving the new King unable to defend England except by the use of troops who made war a profession. A later invasion from Denmark made it necessary for the King to defend England with hired soldiers brought over from Normandy and Brittany. The invasion caused deep injury to the kingdom, and this injury was aggravated by the necessity of quartering troops among the people until the invasion was finally repelled.

These were the circumstances in which the earls and barons of England met with William the Conqueror at Sarum in the year 1085 A. D., there conceded all their lands to the Crown, and then received their lands back by enfeoffment from the King on condition that they serve his Majesty with service as knights forty days every year. The lands or fiefs so granted and held as payment for military service were called "fees" to signify that the knights were soldiers for hire upon terms agreed, and thus part of the King's armies, which could be used for war as needed at home or abroad. So it remained until the abolition of military tenures in the Statute of 12 Charles II, Chapter 24 (1660).

The old fyrd or militia was defined as "tota communa liberorum hominum," or the whole body of freemen, by King Henry II in the First Assize of Arms in 1181.

The freeman of England were obliged by the Statute of Winchester, 13 Edward I, Chapter 6 (1285), to keep and bear arms as and when required by immemorial custom to maintain domestic law and order, to put down armed uprisings at home, and to resist foreign invasions of the kingdom, and thereafter like laws requiring service in the militia were adopted, revised, and renewed as necessary up to the time of the American Revolution.[5]

In the 13th and 14th Centuries, the Crown indulged in the practice for conscripting freemen into royal armies to fight foreign wars, but the people rose up against this presumption of the King. The result was the Statute of 1 Edward III, Chapter 5 (1327), which provided, "That no man shall henceforth be charged to arm himself otherwise than he was wont to do in the time of the King's progenitors, and that no man be compelled to go out of his shire but where necessity requireth, and [there be] sudden coming of strange enemies into the realm, and then it shall be used as in times past for the defence of the realm." This ancient statute abolished all conscription of freemen as a means of raising armies by prerogative of the Crown, and was confirmed on several occasions.[6] It was the prerogative of the King to raise armies, but, from and after the reign of Edward III, he exercised this prerogative by hiring soldiers.[7]

During the American Revolution conscription was frequently practiced by the several States to bring up troops in support of the Continental army against an impending invasion of the United States by armed forces of the British Empire, but this conscription was always by calling forth the militia in keeping with legal custom since the days of Alfred the Great.[8]

There is nothing mysterious about the original understanding of the clauses in the United States Constitution on raising armies and calling forth the militia.

In the Philadelphia Convention, on September 14, 1787, George Mason proposed that the fifteenth and sixteenth clauses of Article I, Section 8 of the United States Constitution be prefaced with language explaining why the people should always be happy to do their duty in the militia: — "and that the liberties of the people may be better secured against the danger of standing armies in time of peace."[9] There was immediate and enthusiastic support for the idea.

But Gouverneur Morris "opposed the motion as setting a dishonorable mark of distinction on the military class of citizens." Morris feared that too firm a warning against standing armies might discourage citizens from entering the profession of arms, which has always been necessary, and has included, as one of the paradoxes in life, some of the most virtuous characters ever to have walked on earth. Everybody knew the type of men whom Morris had in mind. General George Washington then presided over the Philadelphia Convention, acknowledged even in those days as the father of his country, awesome in his presence, saying not a word, his manly face full of quiet dignity, listening attentively.

Mason's proposal of September 14, 1787, was voted down. The motion was meant to clarify what was already though clear enough in the report of the committee on style. It was meant to remind future generations of Americans that compulsory military service was a duty of citizenship as it had been since the Statute of Winchester, but that this service was authorized only in the militia, as had been the established law since the ancient Statute of 1 Edward III. The proposal was meant to express of the necessity of service in the militia as a bulwark against the danger of standing armies which were understood to consist of the "military class," — i.e., troops for hire or soldiers by profession.

The motion was defeated because of fear that adoption might offend General Washington, who was held in almost fearful reverence. Everybody present agreed with the substance, which, unbeknownst to most members of the convention, had been approved with extraordinary language in the papers of none other than General Washington himself.

For Washington had already explained in an old military report[10] that it is important for citizens to be active in the militia and thereby to lessen the need for armies or enlisted troops. His language was particularly impressive:

> "Were it not totally unnecessary and superfluous to adduce arguments to prove what is conceded on all hands, the policy and expediency of resting the protection of the country on a respectable and well established militia, we might not only shew the propriety of the measure from our particular situation, but might have recourse to the histories of Greece and Rome in their most virtuous and patriotic ages to demonstrate the utility of such establishments. Then passing by the mercenary armies, which have at one time or another subverted the liberties of almost all the countries they have been raised to defend, we might see with admiration the freedom and independence of Switzerland, supported in the midst of powerful and jealous neighbors by a hardy and well organized militia. We might also derive useful lessons from other nations of Europe; but, I believe it will be found, the people of this continent are too well acquainted with the merits of the subject to require information or example."

General Washington had added,

> " It may be laid down as a primary position, and the basis of our system, that every citizen who enjoys the protection of a free government, owes not only a proportion of his property, but even of his

personal service to the defence of it, and consequently that citizens of America (with a few legal and official exceptions) from 18 to 50 years of age should be borne on the militia rolls, provided with uniform arms, and so far accustomed to the use of them, that the total strength of the country might be called forth at short notice on any very interesting emergency."

Lest there remain any doubt over whether armies were thought of as enlisted troops, attention may be given to the records of the Maryland Convention of 1788. As a restraint against "the unlimited power of raising and regulating standing armies, the natural enemies of freedom," it was proposed that the United States Constitution should be amended to include a prohibition that "no soldier be enlisted for a longer time than four years, except in time of war, and then only during the war."[11]

And lest there be any doubt about whether compulsory military service was understood as militia duty, the proceedings of the First Congress on August 17, 1789, on the framing of Amendment II will set the record straight.[12]

One of the amendments offered by James Madison read, "The right of the people to keep and bear arms shall not be infringed, a well armed and regulated militia being the best security of a free country, but no person religiously scrupulous of bearing arms shall be compelled to render service in person." Since "exceptions from a power mark its extent,"[13] it is clear enough that the power to compel military service was understood in the First Congress as limited to organizing, arming, disciplining, and calling forth the militia. If military service could have compelled also in the armies of the Union, the provision for conscientious objectors would have been proposed also as a limitation on the power of Congress to raise armies.

Elbridge Gerry then in Congress argued against this clause to exempt conscientious objectors from compulsory military service for fear that it might be used as a pretext to weaken the militia and to raise armies, — which indicated his understanding of raising armies as enlisting troops.

Historical evidence of this kind is abundant. It is obvious that compulsory military service was understood as a high duty of citizenship, but always in the militia, and never in the armies of the United States. The power to regulate firearms was the power to regulate the militia.

* * * * *

The framers of the United States Constitution were not worried about the ability of future generations of Americans to build great armies for adventures of war. They feared that the country might actually be rash enough to make such an attempt when there was no just necessity for it. Not much time passed before such folly occurred in the War of 1812.

It is possible to trace a long course of diplomatic errors which led to the message of President James Madison on June 1, 1812, asking for a declaration of war against Great Britain. The main pretext for this request was that the British navy had on various occasions boarded American ships, and impressed from their crews seamen believed but not proved to be subjects of the King, when in fact many were citizens of the United States. The British navy had engaged in this practice as a war measure against Napoleon.

Thomas Jefferson was legendary as a statesman and philosopher, yet he had a fatal attachment to revolutionary France and an irrational aversion to the British Crown. And during his presidency, he failed to resolve outstanding differences by beneficial treaties with the British government, which might have eliminated irksome questions and lingering irritations one by one as opportunity offered. He failed to renew Jay's Treaty of 1794, which had consolidated independence conceded by King George III in 1783, and been the diplomatic triumph of George Washington's administration. Another advantageous treaty with the British government, negotiated in 1806, he did not submit to the United States Senate for advice and consent. If Jefferson had had not been misled by ideological distractions and had better understood Washington's warnings against undue foreign entanglements, the problem of impressment could have been more easily isolated, given proper focus, and resolved in a fair-minded, timely, and peaceful manner. And it was most unfortunate that, upon becoming President, James Madison too closely imitated his predecessor in attitudes and foreign policy toward Great Britain and France.

Impressment as practiced was an affront to the rights of a neutral power, and his Majesty's government, knowing the importance of resolving the issue, had repeatedly expressed a desire to adjust differences with the United States, giving ample assurances in good faith as a basis for further negotiations. Standing alone, therefore, impressment could not have justified a general war between the United States and the Great Britain.

But there were other considerations which motivated the United States to take the ill-fated step of renewed warfare with the British Empire. Napoleon had begun his invasion of Russia. Great Britain was heavily engaged in Europe. Canada was a rich territory, vast and underpopulated, dangling like a succulent apple waiting to be picked. Politicians from the Southern States were in aggressive mood, anxious for expansion of the

United States throughout North America They included John Calhoun and Henry Clay later renowned for sagacity and moderation, but then taken up by the unbounded energy of youth. They exaggerated every grievance with Great Britain as a casus belli. They indulged in delusions that the British could not defend Canada, and that the French population there would welcome liberating regiments from the United States.

War was declared over the protest of New York and New England which wanted peaceful and beneficial commerce with Great Britain and Canada.

Napoleon learned the lessons of the Russian winter. Militia from Connecticut and Massachusetts refused to march on orders of the President, because there was no invasion of the United States from Canada.[14] Enlistments fell off, because most people of the United States had no wish to invade Canada. American armies were soundly defeated in their thrusts against Montreal, along the Niagara River, and beyond Detroit. Only very meager success in arms on land and sea prevented military humiliation of the United States. The British navy blockaded the Atlantic coast, which dried up commerce with Europe, and tax revenues from it.

The summer and fall of 1814 brought still greater disaster. A British army ceremoniously marched into Washington D. C. to the crisp music of a military band. The King's troops set fire to the capitol, the white house, and other government buildings. A British fleet bombed Ft. McHenry near Baltimore. Veterans from Europe landed in Canada. It was then learned that the Federal treasury was almost empty. Pandemonium reigned as President James Madison called an early meeting of Congress in September, delivering a speech full of fighting bravado, yet by then he had secretly instructed American diplomats to negotiate peace as quickly as possible, if necessary without any satisfaction on impressment.

In October, the secretary of war, James Monroe, proposed a plan which he submitted to the House Committee on Military Affairs in Congress, to conscript private citizens into the army of the United States. The men of the country were to be divided into classes of a hundred, each class was to supply a certain quota for the army, and, if the quota was not met by volunteers at agreed compensation and bounties, the deficiency was to be made up by draft. Any citizen so drafted was entitled to the same compensation and bounties as a volunteer. "The men are not to be drawn from the militia," said Monroe, "but from the population of the country." The measure was plainly unconstitutional, and did not reach the floors of Congress.

Meanwhile, Senator William Giles introduced a bill which would have authorized formation of the militia of the several States into new classes, each of which was to provide one man for two years' service by contact or draft. The President was then to organize the militia so requisitioned into battalions which were to march with the regular army but under officers appointed by the several States, yet they could never be used outside the boundaries of their respective or contiguous States. The bill had cosmetic features to make it appear as a measure for calling forth the militia. Even so, there were a number of speakers in the Senate who condemned the Giles Bill as unconstitutional, because it circumvented the processes for calling forth the militia and raised armies by conscription.[15]

On November 22, 1814, the Giles Bill passed the Senate on vote of 19 to 12, and was sent over to the House of Representatives. There was no more advocacy of Monroe's wild ideas which fell in such great disrepute that Congressmen from New England had a field day characterizing the Giles Bill as a measure for drafting armies, thus obviously unconstitutional. This maneuver proved to be highly effective, putting supporters on the defensive, and forcing them to maintain that it was really intended to call forth the militia. The most powerful speech in the House was made on December 9, 1814, by Congressman Daniel Webster.[16] First, he exposed the legal infirmity:

> "This, then, sir, is a bill for calling out the militia, not according to its existing organization, but by draft from new created classes, — not merely for the purpose of repelling invasion, suppressing insurrection, or executing the laws, but for the general objects of war, for defending ourselves or invading others, as may be thought expedient, — not for a sudden emergency, or for a short time, but for long stated periods, for two years if the proposition from the Senate should finally prevail, for one year if the amendment from the House should be adopted. What is this, sir, but raising a standing army out of the militia by draft?"

The orator from New Hampshire glared at the Southern politicians who had dragged the country into an unjust and unnecessary war, at the great cost of blood and treasure, and sought to prevert the fundamental law of the Union:

> "Is this, sir, consistent with the character of a free government? Is this civil liberty? Is this the character of our Constitution? No, sir, indeed it is not. The Constitution is libeled, foully libeled! The people of this country have not established for themselves such a fabric of despotism. They have not purchased at a vast expense of their own treasure and their own blood a Magna Carta to be slaves. Where is it written in the Constitution, in what article or section is it contained,

that you can take children from their parents, and parents from their children, and compel them to fight the battles of any war in which the folly or the wickedness of the government may engage it? Under what concealment has this power lain hidden, which now for the first time comes forth with a tremendous and baleful aspect, to trample down and destroy the dearest rights of personal liberty? Who will show me any constitutional injunction which makes it the duty of the American people to surrender everything valuable in life and even life itself, not when the safety to the country and its liberties may demand the sacrifice, but whenever the purposes of an ambitious and mischievous government may require it?"

Webster's speech crippled the onslaught. The Giles Bill was diluted by amendments, then passed the House by vote of 83 to 73 on December 14, 1814. A joint conference of the House and Senate was convened.

About that time there was a meeting in the making in New England. It had been organized by the legislature of Massachusetts, a perfect replica of the First Continental Congress. It met on December 15, 1814, in reaction to the proposal by the secretary of war to draft armies for continuing war with Great Britain.

Delegates from Massachusetts, Connecticut, Rhode Island, Vermont, and New Hampshire met in a deliberative assembly which came to be known as the Hartford Convention, named after the capital of Connecticut where the meeting took place. They were merchants, lawyers, soldiers, and statesmen, true in love of their country, sober in judgment, devoted in their sense of duty, firm in resolve, and brave in their deeds.

On January 5, 1815, the labors of the Hartford Convention were crowned by a report which, after a simple prayer, was signed and published by the delegates.[17]

Yankee statesmen laid the groundwork for secession of New England from the Union over a war which had been provoked and mismanaged by a faction of politicians from the Southern States. Northern States felt the pressing need to form a new alliance among themselves for their own safety. The report of the convention drew focus upon ultimate constitutional remedies:

"If the Union be destined to dissolution, by reason of multiplied abuses of bad administrations, it should, if possible, be the work of peaceable times, and deliberate consent. Some new form of confederacy should be substituted among those States which shall intend to maintain a federal relation to each other. Events may prove that the causes of our calamities are deep and permanent. They may be found to proceed, not merely from the blindness of prejudice, pride of opinion, violence of party spirit, or the confusion of the times; but, they may be traced to implacable combinations of individuals, or of States, to monopolize power and office, and to trample without remorse upon the rights and interests of the commercial sections of the Union. Whenever it shall appear that these causes are radical and permanent, a separation, by equitable arrangement, will be preferable to an alliance by constraint, among nominal friends, but real enemies, inflamed by mutual hatred and jealousy, and inviting by intestine divisions contempt and aggression."

The report then focused upon the real and impending constitutional grievance which justified secession unless the situation were quickly moderated by the government of the Union:

"The power of compelling the militia and other citizens of the United States by forcible draft or conscription to serve in the regular armies, as proposed in a late official letter of the secretary of war, is not delegated to Congress by the Constitution, and the exercise of it would not be less dangerous to their liberties than hostile to the sovereignty of the States. The effort to deduce this power from the right of raising armies is a flagrant attempt to pervert the sense of the clause in the Constitution which confers that right, and it is incompatible with other provisions in that instrument. The armies of the United States have always been raised by contract, never by conscription, and nothing more can be wanting to a government possessing the power thus claimed to enable it to usurp the entire control of the militia, in derogation of the authority of the States, and to convert it by impressment into a standing army."

The report then echoed the warning which President Madison had himself made in another crisis sixteen years before:

"That acts of Congress in violation of the Constitution are absolutely void is an undeniable position. It does not, however, consist with respect and forbearance due from a confederate State towards the general government to fly in open resistance upon any infraction of the Constitution. The mode and energy of the opposition should always conform to the nature of the violation, the intention of its authors, the extent of the injury inflicted, the determination to persist in it, and the danger of delay. But in cases of deliberate, dangerous, and palpable infractions of the Constitution, affecting the sovereignty of a State, and the liberties of the people, it is not only the right but the duty of such a State to interpose its authority for their protection, in a manner best calculated to secure that end. When emergencies occur which are either beyond the reach of judicial tribunals, or too pressing to admit of delay incident to their forms, States which have no common umpire, must be their own judges, and execute their own decisions. It will thus be proper for the several States to await the ultimate disposal of the obnoxious measures recommended by the secretary of war, or pending before Congress, and so to use their power according to the character these measures shall finally assume, as effectually to protect their own sovereignty and the rights and liberties of their citizens."

It so happens that, while the Hartford Convention was in session, the House and the Senate in Congress agreed upon a compromise version of the Giles Bill, which, on December 27, 1814, was passed by the House by vote of 73 to 64, but on December 28, 1814, was postponed in the Senate on a vote of 14 to 13 to the second Monday in March, 1815. The bill thus died for all practical intents and purposes.

On January 8, 1815, a British infantry attack was repulsed at New Orleans.

On February 15, 1815, the Senate gave advice and consent to the Treaty of Ghent, an accommodation between the United States and Great Britain which brought the war to an end, without territorial concessions to Great Britain because the Duke of Wellington recommended against any further attempts to invade the United States. The Treaty of Ghent brought peace without a word about impressment of American sailors into the British navy, which shows that it never was the real cause for going to war. The British navy stopped impressing American seamen, but only because of voluntary orders from the prince regent and the admiralty in London.

It is a fact overlooked by many that, by November 14, 1814, as plans were laid for the Hartford Convention, President Madison had come to recognize that the war was a military and moral failure, for on that day he issued a proclamation in which he recommended to the people of the United States a solemn day of "humble adoration to the Great Sovereign of the Universe, of confessing their sins and transgressions, and of strengthening their vows of repentance and amendment."[18] The people took the President's urging to heart. Within weeks the situation radically changed and the danger evaporated. What later was billed as a second war of independence had in reality been adversity teaching wisdom to the country. Peace as then restored has since matured into a practical, beneficial, and lasting friendship between the United States, Great Britain, and Canada.

NOTES

CHAPTER III

1 - This historical background, which illuminates the debates in the Philadelphia Convention concerning raising armies and calling forth the militia, is described in 1 Blackstone's Commentaries 408-421.

2 - The framing of the twelfth clause of Article I, Section 8 of the United States Constitution, during the proceedings of the Philadelphia Convention, can be traced in 5 Elliot's Debates 379, 440-441, 442-443, 445, 503, 510-511, 536, 544-545, 561, — Tansill's Documents 475, 564-565, 567-568, 572, 655, 666, 706, 725-726, — 2 Ferrand's; Records 182, 325-327, 329, 341, 481, 508-509, 570, 595, 616-617, 656 (Madison's Notes, August 6, 18, 20 and 31, September 5, 10, 12, 14, and 17, 1787). Important discussion of this clause is found in the 24th, 25th, 26th, 27th and 28th Federalist, Mentor Edition 157-182, by Alexander Hamilton, and also in the 41st Federalist, Mentor Edition 256-260, by James Madison.

3 - The framing of the fifteenth and sixteenth clauses of Article I, Section 8 of the United States Constitution, during the proceedings of the Philadelphia Convention, can be traced in 5 Elliot's Debates 379, 440, 441, 443-445, 447, 451, 464, 464-467, 536, 544-545, 561, — Tansill's Documents 475, 564, 565, 569-571, 574, 580-581, 598, 598-602, 706, 725-726, — 2 Ferrand's Records 812, 326, 327, 330-333, 344, 377, 384-388, 570, 595, 616-617, 656 (Madison's Notes, August 6, 18, 20, 21, 22, and 23, September 10, 12, 14, and 17, 1787). Important discussion of these clauses is found in the 29th Federalist, Mentor Edition 182-187, by Alexander Hamilton, and in the 46th Federalist, Mentor Edition at 298-300, by James Madison.

4 - The most important episodes in the framing of Amendment II of the United States Constitution are found in 1 Annals of Congress 424-450, 749-752, 766-767 (House, June 8, August 17 and 20, 1789).

5 - Laws were frequently enacted and renewed to assure that the militia was

ready, following the pattern of the Statute of Winchester, but these acts always limited the use of the militia to keeping domestic peace, never allowing their use outside their respective counties, except to repel invasion, as illustrated by the Statutes of 13 Charles II, Chapter 6 (1661), 30 George II, Chapter 25 (1757), and 16 George III, Chapter 3 (1776).

6 - By the Statutes of 4 Henry IV, Chapter 13 (1403), and 16 Charles I, Chapter 28 (1641). These and all laws enacted in England up to the American Revolution for organizing, arming, disciplining, and calling forth the militia, including even the Statute of 16 George III, Chapter 3 (1776), maintained the limits on the use of freemen in the militia which were imposed by the ancient Statute of 1 Edward III. During the American Revolution, the British Parliament enacted the Statutes of 18 George III, Chapter 53 (1778), and 19 George III, Chapter 10 (1779), which authorized impressment of beggars and paupers into the King's armies to fight abroad, but the acts were strictly contrary to established custom and organic statutes in England. They were of short duration and regarded with abhorrence. Judge St. George Tucker inserted an annotation in 1 Blackstone's Commentaries at 418, "There is nothing in the constitution of the United States which warrants a supposition that such a power as that of impressment can ever be authorised or exercised under the government of the United States. On the contrary, the principles of the constitution and the nature of our government strongly militate against the assumption or countenancing of such a power." — 2 Tucker's Blackstone 420.

7 - Hence, Alexander Hamilton recounted, "As incident to the undefined power of making war, an acknowledged preprogative of the Crown, Charles II had, by his own authority, kept on foot in time of peace a body of 5,000 regular troops. And this number James II increased to 30,000, who were paid out of his own civil list. At the revolution, it became an article of the Bill of Rights then framed that 'the raising or keeping of a standing army within the kingdom in time of peace, unless with the consent of Parliament, was against the law.'" — 26th Federalist, Mentor Edition at 169.

8 - A fair illustration of acts authorizing compulsory military service to repel British military operations against the United States is found in 10 Hening's Statutes at Large 309 (May 1780, Chapter 35), which authorized the governor of Virginia to send any number of militia outside the boundaries of the State to support the Continental army. There were a few acts which allowed drafts from the militia, if enlistments failed to fill the quotas levied by Congress for the Continental army, as appears in 9 Hening's Statutes at Large 275 (May 1777, Chapter 2); such drafts were seldom used, because enlistments were nearly always sufficient, but the practice was, in any event, drafting from the militia to repel an invasion as had been allowed even under the Statute of 1 Edward III, nor was it contrary to any provision for calling forth the militia in the Virginia Constitution of 1776.

9 - 5 Elliot's Debates 544-545, Tansill's Documents 725-726, 2 Ferrand's Records 616-617.

10 - The report, dated May 2, 1783, was entitled "Sentitments on a Peace Establishment," and was addressed to Colonel Alexander Hamilton. It is .reprinted in Commins' Washington 467-487. The passages quoted are found in Commins at 479-480. General Henry Knox, chief of artillery in the Continental army, became secretary of war in the administration of President George Washington. In keeping with Washington's ideas, Knox proposed a sweeping plan for compulsory military service, reprinted in 1 Annals of Congress at 1076 ff., and 2 Annals of Congress at 2087 ff. "General Knox's Militia Plan" called for aggressive exercise of the powers of Congress under the fifteenth and sixteenth clauses of Article I, Section 8 of the United States Constitution. Able-bodied men across the country at 18-19 years of age were to train thirty days each year, at 20 years of age ten days each year, at 21-46 years of age four days each year, and at 47-60 years of age two days each year. Congress rejected Knox's ideas, and established a small peacetime army by enlistment, as appears in 1 U. S. Statutes at Large 119 (April 30, 1790), and adopted more modest plans for preparation of the militia, as appears in 1 U. S. Statutes at Large 264 (May 2, 1792), and 424 (February 28, 1795).

11 - 2 Elliot's Debates 552 (Address to the People, April 21, 1788). Exactly the same limit on enlistment as a check on the power of Congress to raise armies was proposed by the conventions of other States, as appears in 3 Elliot's Debates 660 and Tansill's Doucments 1032 (Virginia Convention, June 27, 1788), and 4 Elliot's Debates 245, Tansill's Documents 1049 (North Carolina Convention, August 1, 1788).

12 - 1 Annals of Congress 749-752.

13 - Gibbons v. Ogden, 9 Wheaton 1 at 191 (U. S. 1824).

14 - In Massachusetts, the governor in council requested an advisory opinion from the supreme court as permitted by the constitution of the Commonwealth on whether, as commander-in-chief of the militia, the governor could refuse a requisition by the President under the Act of February 28, 1795 (1 U. S. Statutes at Large 264). The governor was advised that he could refuse the President, if it was obvious that no invasion threatened the country, as appears in Opinion of the Supreme Court upon Questions of Governor Caleb Strong, 8 Mass. 648 (1812). Governor Strong refused to send the militia of Massachusetts upon demand of the President, because there was no invasion of the United States from Canada. The truth is that Canada was then invaded by the United States. Some years later, however, the President's judgment was sustained in Martin v. Mott, 12 Wheaton 19 (U. S. 1827).

15 - Particularly important were the speeches of Senator David Dagget of

Connecticut and Senator Jeremiah Mason of New Hampshire on November 16, 1814, reprinted in 28 Annals of Congress 70-80.

16 - Reprinted in Van Tyne's Webster 56-68.

17 - The entire report has been reprinted in the account of the meeting by the secretary of the convention: Dwight's History 352-379.

18 - 1 Richardson's Messages at 558. Notwithstanding the magnificent heritage of the Hartford Convention, the practice of drafting private citizens to raise armies was instituted on both sides during the American Civil War, although subject to the protests of eminent judges, as appears in *Ex Parte Coupland*, 26 Tex. 387 at 405-430 (1862), and *Kneedler v. Lane*, 45 Pa. St. 238 at 240-274 and 323-338 (1863-1864). Drafting armies was upheld in the *Selective Draft Law Cases*, 245 U. S. 366 (1918). But serious doubt of the constitutionality of drafting armies, without regard to the processes for calling forth the militia, was judicially acknowledged during the Vietnam War in *United States v. Crocker*, 420 F. 2d 307 (8 Cir. 1970).

CHAPTER IV

THE SOUTHERN ABOLITIONISTS

Under the Articles of Confederation, each of the several States, regardless of territory, population, or wealth, had one vote in the unicameral Congress. This type of arrangement was possible for a government of very limited powers acting as a domestic and international agent for the several States.

But the new Union was given far more extensive powers, including regulation commerce, and taxation upon the people at large and the wealth of the country. And these powers were to be exercised without intervention of the several States.

Under these circumstances, it was necessary to remodel the Congress of the United States, but it was a difficult question how this objective should be accomplished. And this question was addressed in prolonged and interesting debates which occupied most of the proceedings of the Philadelphia Convention, concluding in what historians like to call the Great Compromise.

The principal elements of this accord are found in three clauses of the United States Constitution, which were amplified and supported by several other provisions. The main building blocks of this accord deserve closer focus:

— The third clause of Article I, Section 2, provides, "Representatives and direct Taxes shall be apportioned among the several States which may be included within this Union, according to their respective Numbers, which shall be determined by adding to the whole Number of free Persons, including those bound to Service for a Term of Years, and excluding Indians not taxed, three-fifths of all other Persons."[1]

Engraved by H.B.Hall from an original Portrait by G. Stuart

THOMAS JEFFERSON.

— The first clause of Article I, Section 3 says, "The Senate of the United States shall be composed of two Senators from each State, chosen by the Legislature thereof, for six Years, and each Senator shall have one vote."[2]

— And the first clause of Article I, Section 7 ordains, "All Bills for raising Revenue shall originate in the House of Representatives; but the Senate may propose or concur with Amendments as on other Bills."[3]

Of particular interest here is the index for distribution of representatives and direct taxes throughout the several States of the Union, set forth in the third clause of Article I, Section 2.

Under the eighth article of the old Confederation, Congress had to requisition money from the several States by an index difficult to use:

> "All charges of war and all other expenses that shall be incurred for the common defence and general welfare, and allowed by the United States in Congress assembled, shall be defrayed out of a common treasury, which shall be supplied by the several States in proportion to the value of all land within each State, granted to or surveyed for any person, as such land and buildings and improvements thereon shall be estimated according to such mode as the United States in Congress assembled shall from time to time direct and appoint."

The idea of using the assessed value of land came from Benjamin Franklin, who favored this measure of value to discipline the paper currency of Pennsylvania. This measure was suitable to float loans secured by mortgages on specific parcels, and in this way to pump money into circulation, as Franklin proposed, yet it was not practical to assess the value of all land in every State.[4] Therefore, on April 18, 1783, Congress proposed several amendments to the Articles of Confederation. These amendments would have given independent taxing authority to Congress, by allowing the levying of import duties at various rates for rum, other liquors, wine, tea, paper, sugar, molasses, cocoa, and coffee, and at 5% ad valorem on all other imported goods, and by apportionment of the public debt of the Union among the several States. Yet requisitions from the several States would still have been permitted. One amendment in particular would have modified the eighth article of the old Confederation to provide for a more convenient measure of such requisitions:

> "All charges of war and all other that have been or shall be incurred for the common defence and general welfare, and allowed by the United States in Congress assembled, except so far as shall be

otherwise provided for, shall be defrayed out of a common treasury, which shall be supplied by the several States in proportion to the whole number of white and other free citizens and inhabitants of every age, sex, and condition, including those bound to servitude for a term of years, and three-fifths of all other persons not comprehended in the foregoing description, except Indians not taxed, in each State, which number shall be triennially taken and transmitted to the United States in Congress assembled."[5]

In historical fact, this index proposed by Congress on April 18, 1783, was the basis of the formula set forth in the third clause of Article I, Section 2 of the United States Constitution, as becomes clear enough from the records of the Philadelphia Convention.

The phrase "those bound to servitude for a term of years" referred to those who gained passage from Europe by promising to work as servants for a term of years upon indentures which were enforceable by actions in covenant at common law. These individuals were freemen, and counted as such in the index proposed by Congress on April 18, 1783, nor could any suit be brought in trespass, trover, detinue or replevin to recover the benefit of their services as if they were chattels.

When the Europeans first arrived in North America, they found native inhabitants with reddish skins, enjoying various civilizations and speaking numerous languages. They were called Indians, it is said because of the initial belief of Europeans that they had come upon India, and this usage persisted even after the truth was learned that a new continent had been discovered. These peoples consisted of many distinctive tribes, which occupied territories, established governments, held councils, made laws, lived by their own customs, were led by chiefs or princes, appointed magistrates, contracted alliances, formed confederacies, carried on commerce, entered into treaties, waged war, and concluded peace. Such tribes conducted themselves, were considered, and deserved to be regarded as sovereign nations in and of themselves.

In due course of time, some Indians chose by marriage or otherwise to live among the white population of the English colonies and the several States. When they did so, they were deemed to be free citizens and inhabitants, enjoyed all the privileges and immunities of free citzens and inhabitants, were taxed by white governments, and were included in the index proposed by Congress on April 18, 1783, as "other free citizens and inhabitants."

Those Indians who remained apart with their own tribes were beyond the jurisdiction of any white government; therefore, they were "Indians not taxed" and were excluded by the index proposed by Congress on April 18, 1783.

The phrase "three-fifths of all other persons" represented persons held in bondage or slavery in North America. This provision recalls an institution now long gone, but the memory reverberates even to this day as if it were an unhappy memory of childhood, exciting sensitivities, creating enormous social resentments, distorting priorities, and confounding understanding. Many years must yet pass before the people of the United States feel a sense of equanimity about this phase of their history.

And the healing balm must be the truth, not part of the truth, not truth caricatured or highlighted to achieve dramatic effects, but the whole truth plainly laid out, or at least as much of it as can be pieced together to achieve a fairly balanced perspective. What of slavery? How did it come about?

As an institution found in civilized nations in past ages, it was "not an ownership of the servant's moral personality, soul, religious destiny, or conscience, but a property in his involuntary labor. And this right to his labor [implied] just so much control over his person as [enabled] his master to possess his labor."[6] Unlike an indentured servant, a slave was the chattel of his master. Wherever the institution was allowed in the British Empire, if a slave was injured or taken, the master might recover by suit at common law for injury to his tangible property.[7]

In the code of the law given by Moses, slavery was expressly mentioned, tolerated if not approved, regulated, and moderated. Interesting passages are found in the 25th chapter of Leviticus, where it is said that slaves could be purchased from foreign nations, and as such could be inherited by one generation from another, but that in the year of jubilee slaves were to be granted their freedom, as debts were to be forgiven and mortgaged lands were to be restored to their original owners.

While the code of Moses did not prohibit slavery, it did prohibit racial prejudices and attitudes, as appears in the 12th chapter of Numbers: — there it is said that Moses himself married a black Ethiopian wife; the account goes on to say that, when Aaron and Miriam protested this union, they were rebuked by God.[8] And so, if the perennial problem of slavery ought to be tolerated in some circumstances out of deference to the teachings of holy scripture, race has never had anything to do with the justification.

This lesson from Mosaic law establishes the right frame of mind for appreciation of the historical epoch in which white Anglo-Saxon people of England were held in a state of feudal bondage every bit as difficult, only more prolonged than the experience of black African people in North America.[9]

It is not certain exactly when the feudal system in England really began. There were traces of it in the days before the Norman Conquest, nor was it implanted universally at once after the defeat of King Harold II at the Battle of Hastings in 1066 A. D. It was widely entrenched when the landed barons of England submitted to military tenures under William the Conqueror at Sarum in 1085 A. D. By the death of that prince, the feudal system flourished. It was well-nigh universal by the time King John granted Magna Carta in 1215 A. D. And this system continued over some centuries, although it became weaker and weaker, ever more a matter of form and ever less a matter of substance, until it was sweepingly uprooted in all but a few ceremonial and formal incidents by the abolition of military tenures in the Statute of 12 Charles II, Chapter 24 (1660). It is not unjust to reckon this period as over six hundred years.

A feudal tenure resulted when a conveyance was made by enfoeffment, whereby the lord or foeffor granted land to his tenant, vassal, or foeffee. At the time of such investiture, in a ceremony called livery of seisin, the tenant gave an oath of fealty and paid homage to his lord, thereby promising in consideration of the parcel, called a feud or fee, to answer suit and act as a juror in the lord's court baron, and to render unto his lord the service of a knight in war, which was called chivalry, or to tender rent in money or peaceable service to the lord, such as plowing a field, harvesting crops, or repairing the manor, which was called socage. And there were a few rarer forms of feudal tenure: — grand serjeantry, petit serjeantry, burgage and gavelkind.

Feudal tenures were subject to various other burdens or incidents, particularly aids and scutage which were mentioned in the Magna Carta granted at Runnymede, and still others, including relief, premier seisin, wardship, fines for alienation, and escheat. The nature and extent of these burdens or incidents varied according to the nature and terms of tenure.

The law of feudal tenures is the true basis of our modern law of real estate. Learning it requires attention to the intricacies of the Statute De Donis Conditionalibus, 13 Edward I, Chapter 1 (1285), which strengthened the estate in fee tail for the sake of social stability in medieval times; the Statute Quia Emptores, 18 Edward I, Chapter 1 (1290), which limited subinfeudation and eventually produced the estate in fee simple; and the Statute of Uses, 27 Henry VIII, Chapter 10 (1535), which was intended to preserve the King's feudal revenues by limiting innovations drawn from the civil law of Rome, but in the end induced modern forms of conveyancing.

Behind this medieval labyrinth is found the institution of villeinage which, in its lowest form, was unadulterated slavery, yet also included several forms of "privileged" bondage. In order to come upon this institution, it is necessary to look beyond the charming indentures, the ceremony at livery of seisin, the ancient real actions of mort d'ancestor and novel disseisin, and other such historical curiosities.

A manor included the castle or great house of a lord, who might be a baron, typically holding as a tenant in chivalry of a mesne lord, say a viscount or earl, who stood in the middle of the system, himself holding usually in chivalry of a yet higher lord, perhaps a marquis or even a duke, holding in capite from the King himself. The lord of the manor held certain land called his demesne, unencumbered by feudal grants to his tenants, for the use of himself and his family. The manor also included lands which were granted by the lord to his tenants, often in what was called "free" socage, for services of a certain and honorable nature, these suitable for a freeman yet required for keeping the manor thriving as a community.

An estate in free socage was coveted more than an estate in chivalry. It is true that a knight, even if not a peer, was an honorable sir who enjoyed social prestige. But a knight had feudal burdens so heavy that, during his personal rule, Charles I rather twisted the arms of wealthy gentlemen so they too might become knights. Over their protests these fellows were honored anyway, and thus obliged to pay more dearly to the Crown, which thereby acquired money without calling Parliament. A tenant in free socage, on the other hand, was a gentleman farmer who paid rent or rendered service or delivered produce from his surplus. In time, an estate in free socage was considered "privileged" tenure.

Then at last, a manor included folk land which was home to the lowest strata of society, — several degrees of villeins, who lived on their parcels initially at the pleasure of the lord, were each in some sense the property of the lord under the common law, and were each assigned such base or menial services as the lord in his discretion might see fit to impose unless over time such services were defined by concession and agreement.

There were villeins in gross, who were simply personal chattels of the lord, also villeins regardant who were property of the lord but attached to the land as if fixtures upon real estate, and then those who actually enjoyed land of right but subject to base or menial services usually of a certain and specified nature, such as carrying out so many wagons of dung in the course of a year, which was called "villein" socage.

The institution of villeinage flourished vigorously in England until the "black death" or bubonic plague struck the country with a vengeance during the 14th Century. As the country recovered, there was an uprising of peasants in 1381, including demands for the abolition of villeinage, and Richard II promised reforms. The reforms were either delayed or annulled, but nothing could reverse the trend toward gradual extinction of villeinage.

Villeins eventually acquired permanent rights to their parcels of land by legal custom of the manor, no longer subject to ouster at the discretion of the lord. Their resulting estates were called copyholds, which finally became very valuable, and were treated in due course with the legal and social respect due to estates in fee simple or other freeholds. The Statute of 12 Charles II in 1660 abolished estates in chivalry, but left copyholds intact, together with estates in free socage and the coveted duties of attending the person of the King in grand serjeantry. Long after the last villeins became freemen, even as late as the American Revolution, their descendants enjoyed copyholds by inheritance.

Over time manumissions became increasingly frequent by operation of the common law. The liberating principle had roots as ancient as the 29th Article of the Magna Carta granted by King Henry III, which stipulated that no freeman could be denied "de liberis consuetudinibus suis," — in other words, the benefit of legal customs promoting his freedom. In obedience to these customs, the common law actively searched for reasons to make a man free. If, for example, a lord granted his villein a life estate in land, the villein became a freeholder, and thus a freeman. And if, without pleading disability from villeinage, a lord answered his villein squarely on the merits in a suit at common law, the lord made the villein a freeman, for by thus answering the lord conceded the standing of is adversary to sue in the King's courts, which was the right of a freeman.

It is not known exactly when the last villein was freed in England. The institution became so evanescent after the death of Henry VIII that a man of substance might live out his whole life during the three succeeding reigns, traveling all through the kingdom, yet never once encounter a villein. The last known case in which villeinage was pleaded in a court of common law was *Pigg v. Caley*, Noy 27 (K. B. 1618).

Pigg was the plaintiff. The name of his family suggested the duty with which his ancestors were charged as villeins. He sued Caley in trespass for taking a horse. The defendant Caley pleaded that Pigg was a villein regardant, attached to the manor of which he was seised, and that, being lord of the manor, he was free to take the horse. Pigg traversed de injuria, — i. e., he broadly denied that he was a villein regardant as alleged. The jury found for Pigg, and Caley made a motion in arrest of judgment, testing the legal sufficiency of Pigg's traverse.

The argument on the motion was hypertechnical, as was not infrequent in those days on fine points of pleading in suits at common law. Caley's lawyer was boldly creative: — it was necessary, he said, for Pigg to aver specifically that he was not in Caley's actual possession in order to counteract the defense pleaded. Yet, Caley's lawyer gravely maintained, Pigg merely denied being attached to the manor, and so his replication was legally insufficient.

The Chief Justice denied the motion, and ordered judgment for Pigg as a freeman in the amount found by the jury to be his damages. It would have been necessary for Pigg to aver specifically that he was not in the possession of Caley, only if Caley had pleaded that Pigg was a villein in gross, which was not disclosed on the record. Hence, the Chief Justice held, Pigg's traverse was legally sufficient.

Most important was the general rationale of the Chief Justice. The common law, he said, always favored liberty. The common law was established legal custom, built upon and consistent with natural law and right reason. Long usage going back over centuries, probably even before the death of Edward the Confessor, had given England a state of bondage called villeinage, whereby human beings were owned as chattels. The common law could not undo such an old and undeniable custom, but natural law always conceded liberty as the proper condition of mankind, and, therefore, it was the duty of the bench to practice strict scrutiny of existing restraints on liberty, and thus to encourage emancipation of villeins as soon and as often as honestly possible in the administration of justice. When Pigg became free by judgment, villeinage felt the frowns of the common law for the last time and died in legal history.

Barely a year after this last judicial decision in England on villeinage, the first black slaves from Africa were transported to and sold in Virginia. The colonists were faced with a desperate shortage of labor. They did not think it was wrong to purchase slaves from foreign nations as allowed in the law given by Moses, and to make them work as villeins had been obliged to work for centuries in England.

In Africa, nations of the black race engaged in brutal warfare. It was not seldom in these conflicts for whole populations to be slaughtered or sold into slavery. Black merchants in Africa sold their black prisoners of war to white merchants from Europe, who transported their human merchandise to the colonies of England in North America where the survivors, who had not died of malnutrition or disease in coming over, were unloaded and resold as slaves in all of the colonies from New Hampshire to Georgia.

After some years, white merchants from New England got involved in this unhappy but profitable trade. Due to climate and geography, the utility of slavery was less in the several States above the Mason-Dixon Line, yet slavery was more lucrative and extensive in the South, where the institution became more domesticated as a fact of life.

It is important to spread the blame fairly. It is true that white traders transported black cargo, which historians have reprobated; even so, if these white merchants had not indulged in such traffic, many if not most of these black prisoners would have been slaughtered by their black captors in Africa, and their descendants would not be with us today, nor would the contributions of those descendants have enhanced human progress.

Who, after all, financed and undertook this great and immoral traffic between Africa and North America? None other than those enterprising fellows who hid behind the East India Company and associated enterprises. Naturally for due consideration which eased strains on the King's treasury, they first acted through the Royal African Company chartered by Charles II. But their pretended rights of monopoly expired not long before the death of William III.

Not so much of this trade had been undertaken up through the reign of Queen Anne. By the year 1708, there were only about 12,000 slaves in Virginia.[10] Allowing for a natural increase in this population, the total number of slaves in Virginia would not have exceeded 40,000 or 50,000 by the time of American independence. Gradual but effective manumission of this number would not have been excessively difficult.

But as the new princes from Hanover acquired the Crown and involved Great Britain in extended and expensive warfare on the continent of Europe, the King learned that he was not able to carry on these adventures without substantial cooperation from the friendly Bank of England, which financed the unhappy traffic out of Africa. In these circumstances, his Majesty's government was expected to do a few good turns for the financial interests which had so cheerfully lent to the Crown. These favors were considerable, and included systematic royal vetos of all colonial legislation of the English colonies in North America to limit or prohibit the slave trade.

And this cynical deal triggered a huge leap in the slave trade, profitable especially to the same entrepreneurs and bankers who had secured these royal vetos, supposedly for the good of the British Empire. Because of the steady throb of importations from Africa, the number of slaves in Virginia was about 42,000 by 1743, about 120,000 by 1756, about 259,000 by 1782, and about 292,000 by 1790 at which time the white population of the whole

State, including what is now West Virginia, was not much above 442,000. In every census thereafter, the ratio of blacks to whites in Virginia increased. East of the Blue Ridge, the number of blacks exceeded the number of whites by 1800, and thereafter the proportion of blacks over whites further increased. In this way, the institution of slavery assumed stupefying proportions in Virginia, and in other parts of the South.

The rule is not without exceptions, but the people of the South have generally been more traditional in their outlook than the people of the North. And so it should not be surprising that, when confronted with such a giant problem as slavery had become for them, the people of the South should have consulted the same King James Bible which had given the people of England guidance when they were oppressed by Cromwell's protectorate.

Slavery has ancient roots in history, and in one form or another it has been a part of many civilizations, including the Roman Empire at the time of Christ. And sure enough, the New Testament has some interesting things to say about slavery.

In the 6th chapter of his Epistle to the Ephesians, St. Paul enjoined masters and slaves to love each other tenderly, — to care for and honor each other! He repeated the same message in the 3rd and 4th chapters of his Epistle to the Colossians. In some circumstances, it is deeper wisdom, as was true of villeinage in England, to tolerate an entrenched social fault, allowing it to be phased out gradually, lest by sudden uprooting greater harm result. And in keeping with this homely view of things, as appears in the 6th chapter of his 1st Epistle to Timothy — in the same venerable teaching where he said that "the love of money is the root of all evil" —, St. Paul rebuked those who were of a mind to stir up slaves against their masters as "proud, knowing nothing, but doting about questions and stifes of words, whereof cometh envy, strife, railings, and evil surmisings."

It so happens that the slaves to whom St. Paul made specific reference were mainly of white stock, but the people of the South were discerning enough to understand that St. Paul would not have changed his message merely because their slaves were of another race.

This teaching of St. Paul is paralleled in the story of the centurion's servant as recounted in the 7th chapter of the Gospel of St. Luke. With the aid of a good concordance tracing back to the original Greek, it is plain enough that the centurion's servant was a slave sick unto death and much beloved by his master, who in tears went to Jesus, and asked for the favor of miraculous healing. Jesus praised the master, not because he owned, but because he loved his slave. Jesus then but said the word, and the "servant" was healed.

The ideas of St. Paul were preached from pulpits, and taught to masters, slaves, and others in the South. The people listened and reflected. The words of the apostle had a great moderating effect, producing an astonishing situation which was thus described by a scholar in Virginia:

> "Notwithstanding the furious and ill-omened outcry which has been made in recent years against the continuance of slavery, the communities where it prevails exhibit the only existing instance of a modern civilized society in which the interests of the labourer and the employer of the labourer are absolutely identical, and in which reciprocal sympathies of both are assured. The consequence is that both interest and inclination, the desire of profit and the sense or sentiment of duty concur to render the slaveowner considerate and kind toward his slave. So general is the feeling, so habitual is the consciousness of this intimate harmony of interests and duties of both, that it has formed an efficient public sentiment in the South which brands with utter reprobation the slaveholder who is either negligent of his slaves or harsh in his treatment of them. It goes even further than this; it makes every man in the South the protector of the slave against injury by whomsoever offered, thus establishing an efficient and voluntary police, of which everyone is a member, for the defence of the slave against either force, fraud, or outrage. Such habitual regard for the rights of a subordinate class generates in its members a kindliness of feeling and a deference of bearing to the slave holder in general, which no severity could produce and no rigor maintain. It is this intercommunion of good offices and good will, of interest and obligations, which renders the realities of slavery so entirely different from what they are imagined to be by those who have no intimate familiarity with its operation."[11]

Slavery thus became a paradoxical condition, nestled into the refinement of the South, which displayed abundant hospitality, gracious manners, and peaceful contentment in society. Travelers could cross great distances on horseback, even whole States, passed from family to family, without fear of molestation, in the assurance of help if ever needed. The people, white and black, were sober and quiet. Cities and towns were generally small. The population was mainly spread out across the land.

Aside from the mitigations of slavery from humane practices in the South, important legal developments should be given close attention.

There were a number of statutes which allowed slavery in the British Empire,[12] yet, because they restrained human freedom, these acts were read strictly and were deemed inapplicable in England. And because slavery was deemed contrary to natural law, the common law was deemed incapable of supporting title to slaves. Villeinage had been imposed by usage so old that the common law could do no more than nudge gently until the institution died, but slavery arising from the ignominious traffic out of Africa had no such basis in custom older than Magna Carta, and so was never properly recognized at common law.

The record in *Sommersett's Case*, 20 Howell's St. Tr. 1 at 80-82 (K. B. 1771), discloses that James Sommersett, a slave from Jamaica, was taken by his master as a body servant on a business trip to England. The slave escaped, was recaptured, then sued out a writ of habeas corpus. It was the day when Lord Mansfield gloried as Chief Justice of the King's Bench. He concluded his opinion,

> "The state of slavery is of such a nature that it is incapable of being introduced on any reasons, moral or political, but only by positive law, which preserves its force long after the reasons, occasions, and time itself from which it was created, are erased from memory. It is so odious that nothing can be suffered to support it but positive law. Whatever inconveniences, therefore, may follow from the decision, I cannot say this case is allowed or approved by the law of England; and, therefore, the black must be discharged."

The American Revolution likewise accelerated the process of emancipation in the South, as may be illustrated by various statutes enacted by the General Assembly of Virginia:

— The first of these was founded on the recognized contradiction between republican governments and the institution of slavery.[13] In order to pave the way for eventual liberation of all slaves, the legislature prohibited further importation and ordained that a violation of this interdiction would result in forfeiture of title and and grant freedom to slaves so imported.[14]

— There was another type of law illustrated by a special act which granted freedom to three slaves, viz., John Hope, William Beck, and a mulatto girl named Pegg, on petitions of their masters.[15]

— At length the number of such petitions became so frequent that provision was made for emancipation by deed or will, without special act of the legislature, subject always to the duty of the master to care for the aged and infirm.[16]

— Another example can be found in a special act which recited that a slave named Kitt had discovered a band of counterfeiters of paper money, and reported them to public authorities, leading to their apprehension. As a reward for his exemplary services, the statute granted Kitt his freedom.[17]

— And there was a statute which recited that, during the revolutionary war, a number of slaves enlisted in the army on appointment of their masters who tendered them as freemen in order to induce their acceptance into the ranks. The attorney general was ordered to bring suit in behalf of such black men for title to their freedom. The same act emancipated a slave by the name of Aberdeen as a reward for his services in lead mines to support the war effort.[18]

In reading and pondering the teachings of St. Paul on slavery, the people of the South naturally came upon the two verses in the 7th chapter in 1st Corinthians which say plainly enough that, notwithstanding all other admonitions, a slave had a right, even a duty to seek freedom by peaceable and lawful means if it could be thus secured. And so slaves of the South, who were taught from St. Paul, sued for their freedom whenever possible, and the judges of the South, who had read the law as it was handed down by such grand characters as Lord Mansfield,[19] liberally accorded them favorable judgments. There are a good many reports revealing the authentic character of Southern jurisprudence on the liberation of slaves.

A statute of the Old Dominion was enacted to stabilize the slave population and thus facilitate anticipated emancipations in future years.[20] It provided that "slaves which shall hereinafter be brought into this Commonwealth, and kept therein one whole year, or so long, at different times, as shall amount to one year, shall be free." There was another provision which stated that the rule did not apply to a slaveholder from another State who settled in and became a citizen of Virginia, if after his arrival he took a prescribed oath within a certain time.

Because the common law always favored freedom, it strictly construed the exception to the liberating provision, as illustrated in the case of *Murray v. McCarty*, 2 Munford 393 (Va. 1811). A citizen of Virginia moved to Maryland, and declared himself a citizen of that State. The record showed nevertheless that he left property behind him and voted in a public election in Virginia while he sojourned in Maryland. He bought a female slave in Maryland by the name of Nancy Murray, returned with her to Virginia, then took the oath prescribed for slaveholding immigrants from other States. Following the teaching of St. Paul, the slave sued for title to her freedom, and she prevailed. "I shall, in considering McCarty's citizenship," said Justice Joseph Cabell of the Virginia Supreme Court, "confine myself to the principles of general and universal law: and I am clearly of the opinion that, even according to those principles, his removal from this State, under the particular circumstances, would not amount to an expatriation." The slaveholder was thus deemed to be a citizen of Virginia, importing a slave into the State, and so, by operation of the statute, once the slave had remained one year on the soil of Virginia, it was to her as if she had stepped onto free soil. Nancy Murray then and there became free.

Because the number of emancipations in the South became considerable, there was a substantial population of freed black people in that part of the country. Whatever theories may have been concocted by a few politicians,[21] the true legal status of these individuals was described by Chief Justice William Gaston of the North Carolina Supreme Court in *State v. Manuel*, 4 Devereux & Battle 20 at 24-25 (N. C. 1838):

> "According to the laws of this State, all human beings within it who are not slaves, fall within one or two classes. Whatever distinctions may have existed in the Roman law between citizens and free inhabitants, they are unknown to our institutions. Before our revolution all free persons born within the dominions of the king of Great Britain, whatever their color or complexion, were native born British subjects. Those born out of his allegiance were aliens. Slavery did not exist in England, but it did exist in the British colonies. Slaves were not in legal parlance persons, but property. The moment the incapacity of disqualification of slavery was removed, they became persons, and were then either British subjects or not British subjects, accordingly as they either were or were not born within the allegiance of the British king. Upon the revolution, no other change took place in the law of North Carolina than was consequent upon the transition from a colony dependent on a European king to a free and sovereign State. Slaves remained slaves. British subjects in North Carolina became North Carolina freemen. Foreigners, until made members of the State, continued aliens. Slaves manumitted here become freemen — and therefore, if born within North Carolina, are citizens of North Carolina — and all free persons born within the State are born citizens of the State."

Judge Gaston was greatly beloved in North Carolina, and his words express the authentic character of Southern jurisprudence, favoring emancipation of slaves and conferring upon the new freemen proper standing as citizens of their respective States.

And in this light, it is easier to understand the mystery of the third clause of Article I, Section 2 of the United States Constitution, insofar as it says that only three-fifths of "all other persons," meaning slaves, would be counted for apportioning direct taxes and representatives in Congress among the several States of the Union.

It was known in the Philadelphia Convention that direct taxes would seldom if ever be imposed for many years following the formation of the new Union. And in fact, duties, imposts, and excises, not subject to apportionment, supplied nearly all tax revenues of the United States before 1860. It was known that the clause counting slaves at three-fifths of their number would, therefore, have no serious tax consequences; but the hope was that the clause would help phase out slavery by rewarding States which increased the proportion of their free citizens who would be counted five of five, thus giving them more representatives in the House, and enhancing their power and influence in Congress. While the clause was disliked by Southern abolitionists in the Philadelphia Convention, led by George Mason[22] and Luther Martin,[23] they tolerated it in the end because it served to promote emancipation of slaves.

* * * * *

In the Dixie States at the time George Washington was President, slavery had become so congested and entrenched into the fabric of society that the institution could not be quickly uprooted. The revolution had terminated the slave trade and inspired numerous manumissions in Virginia and other parts of the South. But then progress stalled, and an increasing number of men in public life grew anxious as they watched events.

Slavery was not a subject excluded from polite conversation in Virginia. Abolitionists were among the greatest sons of the Commonwealth, many in public office, many distinguished in education, agriculture, industry, and commerce. The most famous of them all was Thomas Jefferson,[24] whose basic idea was to establish a future date, and to free slaves born thereafter, first training them in the arts of survival until reaching majority, then sending them out with ample supplies to such places as became available for settlement, offering them the alliance and protection of the United States. Judge St. George Tucker lectured from his chair in law at the College of William and Mary, demanding of his students that they, as future lawyers, must assist in getting rid of this system of involuntary servitude.[25]

He spoke with animation to the sons of planters,

> "That a people who have declared, 'That all men are by nature equally free and independent,' and have made this declaration the first article in the foundation of their government, should in defiance of so sacred a truth, recognized by themselves in so solemn a manner, and on so important an occasion, tolerate a practice incompatible therewith, is such an evidence of the weakness and inconsistency

of human nature, as every man who hath a spark of patriotic fire in his bosom must wish to see removed from his own country. If ever there was a cause, if ever an occasion, in which all hearts should be united, every nerve strained, and every power exerted, surely the restoration of human nature to its unalienable right is such. Whatever obstacles, therefore, may hitherto have retarded the attempt, he that can appreciate the honor and happiness of his country, will think it time that we should attempt to surmount them."

The system of exploiting labor in the South, called Negro slavery, was a vehicle of transition, and, if it had not long persisted, it would have been easy enough to overlook as a passing oddity of historical experience. Going back one step further, if the slave trade had been terminated even as late as the death of King William III, the system it fed could easily have been phased into natural extinction throughout the United States. But the slave trade was not so quickly and mercifully ended, and the peculiar institution became a bloated monster beneath the Mason-Dixon Line and the River Ohio.

The leaders of the American Revolution were confounded by it. Patrick Henry said, "Slavery is detested. We feel its fatal effects. We deplore it with all the pity of our humanity." And he went on, "I would rejoice my very soul if every one of my fellow human beings was emancipated. As we ought with gratitude to admire that decree of heaven which has numbered us among the free, we ought to lament the necessity of holding our fellow men in bondage. But is it practicable, by any human means, to liberate them without producing the most dreadful and ruinous consequences?"[26]

The problem was how to take a race captured and carried away in an uncivilized condition from the wilds of a faraway continent, a race making gradual progress but still not fully adapted to their new circumstances, and suddenly turn its members loose on an advanced society. The brightest men of that day, the flower of the South, pondered this tremendous quandary.[27]

Over time the burdens of slavery became visibly lighter. The South became a happier place, the masters kinder, and the slaves more content. A remarkable insight is found in a description, written by the Duc de la Rochefoucault-Liancourt during the summer of 1796 while visiting Monticello, on the way Thomas Jefferson managed his slaves. The Frenchman said,

> "I found him in the midst of the harvest, from which the scorching heat of the sun does not prevent his attendance. His Negroes are clothed and treated as well as white servants could be. Every article is made on his farm. His Negroes are cabinet makers, carpenters, masons, bricklayers, smiths, etc. The children he employs in a nail

factory which yields already a considerable profit. The young and old Negresses spin for the clothing of the rest. He animates them by rewards and distinctions."[28]

Not only did the practice of slavery become gentler, but the emancipation legislation of the revolutionary era soon had noticeable effects. By the early 19th Century certain trends became evident in the course of manumissions.[29] The freeing of slaves moved at a fairly rapid pace. Some freed blacks adapted very well, becoming prosperous freemen of color, enjoying the encouragement of whites and forming a kind of natural aristocracy among blacks. But many were simply unable to cope, and floundered in poverty or idleness.

The causes of this phenomenon included insufficient education of freed blacks and prejudices of whites, yet there were undeniably deeper causes which have always been hard to identify, and always controversial. Whatever the exact nature of these deeper causes, the effects were empirical facts, nor were these facts ignored by Jefferson, Tucker, and others anxious to get rid of slavery.

It was important to consider not only the South where slavery was still vigorously practiced, but also the situation in the North where the institution was not quite but almost dead by the time John Quincy Adams was elected President. Wherever the black population was much smaller in relation to the white population, slavery grew quickly more nominal. In such circumstances the institution was more easily phased out, even though the adaptation from bondage to freedom was sometimes precarious and difficult. Yet wherever the black population was very large in relation to white society as was typical in the South, emancipations invariably slowed down as assimilation of freed blacks ran into complications.

In New Hampshire, general emancipation of a mere 158 slaves was feasibly begun before Thomas Jefferson became President,[30] but this hopeful effort did not mean that at the same time hundreds of thousands of slaves could be instantly freed and worked into the social and economic fabric of Virginia. It was simply a fact of life in those days that, if there was a heavy density of slaves in a given community, progress in abolition tended to reach a maximum number which could not be exceeded without pitiful inability of freed blacks to adjust and adamant refusal of whites to tolerate more. Despite all such problems, the number of emancipations in the South dwarfed those in the North during the antebellum period

James Madison well understood the conundrum in Virginia where slavery was robust, particularly in the eastern counties. In his political youth, slavery troubled Madison but did not occupy much of his time. As he grew older he began to see the enormity of the problem. He probably got out his notes of the Philadelphia Convention to read the speeches of George Mason. He must have marveled over the old patriot's wisdom. He must have felt some regrets for not having seen the danger more clearly in his earlier years.

Never did any man of the old South wish more eagerly to abolish slavery than the elder Madison. He speculated, calculated, wrote, and wrung his hands as he felt the effects of age creep up on him. He suggested a plan not unlike Jefferson had proposed only with more precision and detail, with appropriations to compensate masters who voluntarily emancipated their slaves, together with ample procurement of lands in the western territories held by the Union, in the islands of the West Indies, and on the continent of Africa. His idea, drawing upon Jefferson, was to provide asylum for blacks whenever possible as they were gradually freed.[31] Resettlement of freed blacks was essential in Madison's eyes. Yet, he knew that a substantial part of the population of freed blacks would probably settle in other States including those in the North, and in the territories of the Union. And he knew that a substantial part would inevitably remain in Virginia.

Sometimes he became depressed by the baffling complexity against which he pitted his wits. He refused to give up. He knew he could not quit. But every now and then he wondered whether the problem had a rational solution.

* * * * *

And so the people of the South was filled with bewilderment, improving the lot of slaves wherever possible, freeing as many as they dared, disappointed in the incapacity of freed blacks and white society to blend easily, pondering the question quietly, and resenting the situation imposed on their civilization by events in history past. But the clock could not be turned back, and things floated al long, until a serious trouble arose at the end of the third week in August 1831, in Southampton County, in the Tidewater region of Virginia.

The man who stirred the pot was Nat Turner, a black preacher and prophet who interpreted a strange blue cast of the sun as a heavenly sign that he should begin his mission of leading about 75 slaves in a strike of vengeance against the owners of plantations. If the confessions attributed to him are believed, he and his so-called "army" did not react against physical mistreatment or excessive work. The rebellion seems to have been meant as a holy war. The attack was mounted. There was killing and arson, but in a few days the affair was under control. Most of the insurgents were shot down by units of militia. Turner was hunted down, captured, tried, convicted, and hanged.

Whatever he failed to accomplish, Turner did inspire earnest discussion among the white folks of Virginia. In his message on December 6, 1831, Governor John Floyd advised legislators in Richmond that something had to be done about slavery. The proceedings following upon this message, held in the Virginia House of Delegates from January 11 through 25, 1832, attracted attention throughout the United States. The event was of transcendent importance as an expression of the troubled heart and mind of the South. Nowhere in any public meeting in the United States was there ever such a gallant and honest effort to abolish the institution by law.

As the General Assembly of Virginia began its work in the session of December 1831, scores of petitions calling for amelioration of the problem of slavery poured into the House of Delegates where all bills had to originate. An editorial in the *Richmond Enquirer* trumpeted, "And though we speak almost without a hope that the legislature will do anything in the present session to meet this question, yet we say now, in the utmost sincerity of our hearts, that our wisest men cannot give too much of their attention to this subject, nor can they give it too soon."[32]

The petitions were all referred by the speaker to a select committee, which, however, was weighted in favor of the eastern part of the Commonwealth, where the slave population was most congested, and where, therefore, the problems of abolition appeared more perplexing to all and insurmountable to many.

William Goode, who was against any program of abolition, made a motion on January 11, 1832, to dismiss the select committee. Rising in opposition was none other than Thomas Jefferson Randolph, favorite grandson of his famous namesake. Randolph proposed that the committee should consider and report a bill to effectuate a specific measure, which was not unlike thinking of his grandfather fifty years earlier: — the children of all female slaves born on or after July 4, 1840, unless taken by their masters elsewhere, should become the property of the Commonwealth, the young men at age 21, the young women at age 18, and thereupon hired out until the amount earned should be sufficient to defray the cost of their resettlement upon available territory as a free people.

The proposal was incomplete by itself, and would surely have required the cooperation of the United States in acquiring sufficient lands for settlement of liberated blacks. Federal participation was mentioned as a likely necessity by Thomas Marshall, son of the Chief Justice of the United

States, in a speech he gave a few days later, when he said that "many masters cannot afford to give away their slaves, who would be content to sell their slaves at a very reduced rate, perhaps at half price, for the benefit of the slaves themselves. But where again it will be asked, in what way shall the money be obtained for making these purchases? Sir, the proceeds of the public lands are at the disposal of Congress."[33] Those public lands included the Northwest Territory which had already yielded to the Union several new States without the blight of slavery. And so William Brodnax observed, "Of the public lands held by the general government, a large portion, it will be recollected, was ceded by Virginia, a portion too which was exceedingly valuable."[34]

Randolph and Marshall, who both owned many slaves in the Piedmont region of Virginia, were certainly aware that removal of the entire slave population of the State born on or after some set date in the future would be unfeasible and undesirable: — they knew that a proportion of freed blacks would remain in Virginia, and they knew that relocation of liberated blacks could not be wrought entirely outside the United States.

They knew it, because James Madison, aged and weary at Montpelier, was the hierophant of the anti-slavery movement in Virginia. He was already thinking of 200 million acres of western lands belonging to the Union. He was already thinking of Federal appropriations to assist in purchasing slaves at $400 each from masters willing to deed their freedom. He saw the need to reduce the proportion of blacks to whites in some places, and to even out that proportion across the country as much as possible, in order to facilitate workable abolition. He had told young Randolph and Marshall that they must face facts, which they did, because their teacher was somewhat more than venerable.

The evil of slavery was not only the wayward error of the South, but also the wayward error of the North: — it was an accumulated enormity, caused mainly in generations past by Africans, Europeans, and Americans. Fair or not, the descendants of only a few of these perpetrators on three continents were called upon to cure this insidious disease. Still it was so, and Randolph and Marshall, under the guidance of Madison, were doing their best to lead their countrymen out of the circumstances closing upon them.

The opposing motions of Goode and Randolph on January 11, 1832, triggered debate. On January 16, 1832, the select committee returned a report which concluded, "That it is inexpedient for the present legislature to make any legislative enactment for the abolition of slavery."[35]

William Preston then and there sought an amendment to reverse the report by substituting the word, "expedient" for the word, "inexpedient," so as to require some concrete measure in that session of the General Assembly of Virginia, whereupon the debate raged on as the public watched and listened in amazement. There were flights of superlative oratory. George Summers proclaimed,

> "There is a continual and abiding danger of insubordination from the natural love of liberty, which the great Author of our being has imparted to all his creatures. It belongs to every thing which breathes the breath of life. The imprisoned songster pants to plume his wings and wanton in his native air. The caged lion seeks to rend the bars which confine him, and to range again the lord of the dark forest. It is a portion of the divine essence which can never be wholly destroyed. Oppression cannot eradicate it. Amid the profoundest mental darkness, its feeble ray will sometimes light up the gloom within. It is a scintillation struck from the eternal rock of being, which can be extinguished only by the tomb."[36]

George Williams sailed high in the eloquence of his spectacular plea,

> "The poorest tattered Negro, who tills the planter's field under his task master, and labors to produce those fruits which he may never call his own, feels within him that spark which emanates from the deity, the innate longing for liberty, and hears the inmost recesses of the soul, the secret whisperings of nature that tell him he should be free. The love of freedom is a universal animal principle. It is concomitant with vitality. No human being was ever born without the wish for liberty implanted in his breast. God never made a slave, for slavery is the work of man alone. The imprisoned bird flutters against the bars of his narrow cage, and pants for the shades of his native wild wood and the breath of his native sky."[37]

Continuing this terrific moral bombardment, James McDowell thundered majestically,

> "Sir, you may place the slave where you please. You may dry up, to your utmost, the fountains of his feeling, the springs of his thought. You may close his mind to every avenue of knowledge and cloud it over with artificial night. You may yoke him to your labors as the ox which liveth only to work and worketh only to live. You may put him under any process which, without destroying his value as a slave, will debase and crush him as a rational being. You may do all this, and the idea that he was born to be free will survive it all. It is allied to his hope of immortality. It is the ethereal part of his nature which oppression

cannot reach. It is a torch lit up in his soul by the hand of deity. It was never meant to be extinguished by the hand of man."[38]

In such masterful rhetoric, the Virginia reformers of 1832 propounded their central premise, which was set forth in bold relief in the 1st Article of the Virginia Bill of Rights of 1776. Slavery was a violation of natural law, because it sought to take away freedom which cannot be purloined or alienated.

But here it is critical to understand in what respect slavery in Virginia was not wrong, and did not run against the natural order of the world. In the interests of justice, it is important to refute a persistent libel against the South which was later circulated by irresponsible voices in the North.

George Summers had condemned slavery because the natural love of liberty is struck from the eternal rock of being, but he observed,

> "I believe that, at the present day, the situation of Virginia Negroes, so far as regards mere animal comfort, may be well compared with that of a large portion of the laboring classes in other countries, particularly in the severer governments of Europe. I know that many of them, perhaps the greater portion of them, are content with their destiny, and have furnished, in frequent instances, rare example of undying friendship, of grateful devotion and fidelity to those under whose control circumstances have placed them."[39]

James McDowell had damned slavery because the urge to be free is tie to the hope of immortality, yet he conceded,

> "It is true, sir, to the letter, what gentlemen have frequently declared, that there is no laboring peasantry in any other part of the world, who, in all external respects, are better situated than our slave, — who suffers less from want, who suffers less from hardship, who struggles less under the toils of life, or who has a fuller supply of the comforts which mere physical nature demands. In all these respects he shares the equalizing and benignant spirit of our institutions and our age. He is not the victim of cruelty. He is rarely, if ever, harmed by oppression. He is governed by an authority which year after year is abating of its harshness, and is admitted to every privilege which the deprivation of his liberty can allow."[40]

But if slavery was against natural law, yet was not unkind to those held in bondage, how did it harm in society? It was in expounding this question that the abolitionists of the Virginia spoke with painful candor.

"I think I may safely assert," said Samuel Moore, "that ignorance is the inseparable companion of slavery," nor can it be contended that "where so large a mass of the population of the country is corrupt, the other classes can entirely escape the contagion." The Southerner continued his indictment: — slavery promotes a "prevalent and almost universal indisposition of the free population to engage in cultivation of the soil, that species of labor upon which the prosperity of the country chiefly depends."[41]

"A slave population exercises the most pernicious influence upon the manners, habits, and character of those among whom it exists," explained George Summers. He complained of "miserable notions of self-importance" which infected the mentality of many whites who were served by slaves. "Habits of idleness and dissipation are seldom avoided in a slaveholding community," this native of eastern Virginia warned, then added, "Men seldom labor when they can avoid it. Labor becomes dishonorable, because it is the business of a slave, — and when industry is made dishonorable or unfashionable, virtue is attacked in her strongest citadel." Moreover, he implored, "Where slavery prevails, the spirit of free inquiry and adventurous enterprise is much repressed."[42]

Once more, said Philip Bolling, slavery was uneconomic. "Why, sir, is slavery labor more expensive, and consequently less profitable than the labor of the white man? The answer is to be found in the operation of moral causes. Slaves have no immediate self-interest to act upon them."[43]

It is an odd yet beautiful the way that natural law works, for when its lofty commands are ignored or disobeyed, the priorities and directions of society become twisted or warped.

Charles Faulkner stated in exasperation,

> "Slavery, it is admitted to be an evil. It is an institution which presses heavily against the best interests of the State. It banishes free white labor. It exterminates the mechanic, the artisan, the manufacturer. It deprives them of occupation. It deprives them of bread. It converts the energy of a community into indolence, its power into imbecility, its efficacy into weakness. Sir, being thus injurious, have we not a right to demand its extermination? Shall society suffer that the slaveholder may gather his crop of flesh? What is mere pecuniary gain, compared to the interests of the common weal? Must the country languish, droop and die that the slaveholder may flourish? Shall all interests be subservient to one? Shall all rights be subordinate to those of the slaveholder?"[44]

James McDowell later summarized these appalling effects of slavery when he made the elegant observation "that the slaveholding interest of the country will and can coalesce with no other interest" and "must be hostile to all others."[45] He meant that the institution tended to dominate any community where it flourished, to reduce all other civilized activities into relative insignificance, and to pull society away from its own best interests into servility.

Then came perhaps the greatest orator of all. Henry Berry represented a county in which his constituents owned about 4,000 slaves. This Southern gentleman held a large estate to the east of the Blue Ridge, consisting of land and slaves. He slowly rose, politely thanked the speaker, then begged the pardon of his "eastern brethren for saying a few words on this important and deeply interesting subject." And that he did, stirring up warmth in the breasts of his fellow Virginians. He spoke of the problems which freed blacks were having in making transitions.

> "Pass as severe laws as you will to keep these unfortunate creatures in ignorance. It is in vain, unless you can extinguish that spark which God has given them. Let any man who advocates slavery examine the system of laws that we have adopted, from stern necessity it has been said, towards these creatures, and he may shed a tear upon that, and would to God, sir, the memory of it might thus be blotted out forever. Sir, we have as far as possible closed every avenue by which light might enter their minds. We have only to go one step further, — to extinguish the capacity to see the light. Then our work will be completed. They would then be reduced to the level of beasts of the field, and we should be safe. And I am not certain we would not do it, if we could find out the necessary process, and that also on the plea of necessity."[46]

Berry here spoke of laws in Virginia and other Southern States which limited the teaching of reading and writing to slaves. Such laws were meant to counteract the danger of incendiary literature which was sometimes circulated by Yankee fanatics to incite slave insurrections. There were actually very few slave insurrections, perhaps one every fifty years across the Southern States. The British army had attempted to excite a slave insurrection during the American Revolution, but had utterly failed.

Later generations have been tempted to justify literature designed to incite such insurrections by reference to the supposed cruelty of slavery. Those advancing this notion overlook the reports of Southern abolitionists and many others who, living in the midst of or otherwise viewing Southern reality, denied that such cruelty was practiced. They overlook also the majestic teachings of St. Paul who forbade stirring up slaves against their masters. They overlook no less the gentler remedies, favored by Southern abolitionists, of nudging slavery gradually into extinction. And they overlook the pending death of the institution by natural causes then inexorably operative.

In fact, these statutes did not impose absolute prohibitions, but merely required the consent of masters before slaves could be taught to read and write.[47] They were analogous to laws reserving to parents the right to control the education of their children, for such, after all, was the nature of the legal relation between masters and slaves.

These acts were mostly ignored, and, when enforced on rare occasions, the penalties were lenient. Some planters, it is true, neglected the duty; but most masters saw to it that their slaves were taught to read and write. The King James Bible was often the main text used for this purpose — it was not different for Abraham Lincoln and Jefferson Davis —, and this fact helps to account for characteristic features of traditional black Christianity in the South.

Henry Berry's objection was that it was not enough merely to allow education of slaves by consent of their masters. He saw the need to encourage such teaching actively, or even to make it obligatory in preparing the way for abolition.

There was another favorite bugaboo of slavocrats. They insisted on their right to just compensation, full value as they reckoned it. Property, they said, was one of the chief ends of society, and slaves were their property. Then some of them went further, insisting that the taking was not for public use, because the title expropriated was not thus employed but extinguished, and that, therefore, the power of eminent domain could not take their property without their consent. A few became even more extravagant, saying they were entitled not only to their slaves, but the offspring of their slaves in perpetuity. And so they rattled on, as if Lord Mansfield had not long ago spoken unambiguously on this unnatural species of property in the case of James Sommersett. Henry Berry had a short answer for these characters, with knowledge which could be found in Blackstone, read by every lawyer in Virginia:

> "Sir, I am sick with the clamor in this debate about this property, this wealth. I consider it all as mere trash when weighed against the public safety. The right of property in slaves is entirely the creature of the positive law. All our rules of property are under the control of the legislature. Our law of descents, distribution, and so forth, can be altered by the legislature whenever it shall seem expedient. And a fortiori can the legislature alter the rule with regard to property in slaves, because the right is purely the creature of the legislature."[48]

Viewing the situation most favorably to slaveholders, the General Assembly had power at least to set a future date after which slaves would cease to be chattels by statutory law. Once this protection was removed, there remained no right under the common law, nothing to take, and nothing to pay for. This idea appears to have been already settled by the Virginia Supreme Court in the case of Nancy Murray.

The post-nati projects of Jefferson, Tucker, and Madison were founded on principles parallel in humanity and law. In the form African servitude existed in the South, if all slaves were freed without preparation or training, most of them would be tossed out from the security of plantation life as helpless creatures in a society with which they could not cope; moreover, statutory property at one time vested in anticipation of a lifetime of work would be divested. On the other hand, if a future date was set, and a generation to be emancipated was carefully prepared and trained until the strongest years of adulthood, and then released from bondage, the new freemen and freewomen would not be helpless; then also the legal objection would be circumvented, because there would be no retroactive divestiture of preexisting rights.

The case had thus been ably argued by the Virginia reformers of 1832. Slavery ran against the natural law, for it ignored the spark of freedom implanted in human nature. As practiced in the old South, slavery was not a system of physical cruelty to blacks. But the peculiar institution debilitated the whole of society, for it becalmed trends toward economic diversity, and it undermined virtuous industry by making hard work appear as the fate of an inferior class. It promoted ignorance in blacks, retarding their capacity to become free, a form of ignorance incapable of producing bliss. It promoted general dissipation of society. Slavery could lawfully and practically be abolished by acts having gradual operation in futuro. And it was important to start the process in motion by concrete, even if modest first steps.

As of January 25, 1832, the slavery debates had run their natural course, whereupon Vincent Witcher made a motion to postpone indefinitely both the report of the select committee and the pending motion to reverse its recommendation. Witcher was an avowed slavocrat. He was worried that the tide had turned against the slaveholding class.

The arguments in defense or in mitigation of slavery had not been very impressive. An answer of James Gholson to the abolitionists of Virginia was that they were "better poets than planters."[49] Then there was the discourse of William Roane, who said,

> "I am not one of those who have ever revolted at the idea or practice of slavery, as many do. It has existed and will ever exist in all ages, in some form and to some degree. I think slavery as much a correlative of liberty as cold is of heat. History, experience, observation, and reason have taught me that the torch of liberty has ever burnt brightest when

surrounded by the dark and filthy, yet nutritious atmosphere of slavery. Nor do I believe in that fanfaronade about the natural equality of man."[50]

Alexander Knox argued that slavery, far from being an evil, was responsible for the "high and elevated character" of society in Virginia, and "indispensably requisite to preserve the forms of a republican government."[51] There was even the play to the gallery by John Chandler that slavery presented no danger to society, for he said, "Look, sir, at the females who grace this auditory. The dimples of joy on their cheeks, and the expressions of mirth and happiness in their eyes attest there is no cause of alarm."[52]

Witcher explained his motion as seeking a test vote: those who were against legislation toward abolition should vote, "aye" so as to assure postponement, and those in favor of such legislation should vote "nay" so as to prevent postponement. His objective was to sound out the extent of opposition against slavery. There were 60 ayes and 71 nays. The postponement was defeated. Interested citizens in the capitol reacted audibly in excitement after the roll call vote was taken and the speaker announced the result. It appeared that Southern whites were about to set slavery on a path of ultimate extinction. Despite all the confusion of subsequent history, this vote captured the true and timeless dreams of Virginia, — that this curse, arising from a century of whoredom engineered by financiers in London, would in cautious and gradual steps be expelled from the future of the South.

Of the seventy-one legislators voting against general postponement and for progress toward abolition, the main body saw the need to seize the historic moment. Thomas Jefferson Randolph, William Preston, George Summers, George Williams, James McDowell, Samuel Moore, Philip Bolling, Charles Faulkner, Henry Berry, and many other great sons of Virginia must have pondered the sentiments of Brutus, "There comes a tide in the affairs of men, which taken at the flood leads on to fortune. Omitted, all the voyage of their life is bound in shallows and in miseries. On such a full sea we are now afloat, and we must take the current when it serves, or lose our ventures."

Thirteen legislators trembled in doubt, not of the need for eventual abolition, but of belief in the ripeness of the moment, as if the occasion might easily be recreated in the future. They felt a mortal hesitation which they mistook for prudence. Thomas Marshall, even he was among them!

Their thinking was exemplified by Robert Powell. "Mr. Speaker," he said, "I do not deem this an appropriate occasion to discuss the abstract question of slavery, although certainly the very fundamental principles upon which our free institutions are based, so highly prized and so justly boasted of, all go to repudiate it." He continued in perfect sincerity, "I am not at this session prepared to vote for any scheme of general emancipation. But while I am not now willing to legislate definitely on this subject, I am willing that the committee to whom this question was referred shall go on with their investigations, that they shall make their report to this house, that that report may go before the public, that the people may be brought to reflect upon it, and that a future legislature may come here to act definitively."[53]

The vote was taken on Preston's motion for an amendment to reverse the report of the select committee, so as to require in the current session a bill requiring some progress toward abolition There were 58 ayes and 73 nays. In their hesitation and uncertainty, the thirteen compromisers withheld critical momentum from the Southern movement to free the slaves.

This reality becomes clearer in subsequent events. Archibald Bryce proposed a preamble to the report of the select committee, which was added on vote of 65 ayes to 58 nays. It can be seen from the reduced number voting that, after the defeat of Preston's amendment on January 25, 1832, the critical point had already passed, for eight legislators had left the floor in disappointment or disgust. The report, as altered in the committee of the whole, was approved so as to read substantially, "Profoundly sensible of the great evils arising from the condition of the colored population of this Commonwealth, but believing there should be further development of public opinion, it is resolved as the opinion of this committee that it is inexpedient for the present legislature to make any legislative enactment of the abolition of slavery."[54]

There was no standing committee to continue investigations, as had been suggested by Robert Powell. Somehow or other that detail was overlooked. Public opinion did not develop in Virginia, because the people were given nothing concrete to consider, and because there were no easy solutions. The debates left a natural impression across the Southern States that slavery should be abolished, but that there was no obvious way out of the thicket.

*　*　*　*　*

After this great upsurge, progressive thought was sedated by an essay from the literate pen of Professor Thomas Dew who taught history, metaphysics, and political economy in the College of William and Mary. His *Review of the Debate in the Virginia Legislature of 1831 and 1832.*[55] was widely distributed throughout the Dixie States.

Dew's work had enormous hypnotic power over budding intellectuals of the South. For more than a generation leading up to the spring of 1861, many very fine young men, decent characters full of bright ideals, brave and noble fellows who later marched into battle wearing gray and butternut uniforms to defend the land and people they dearly loved — certainly not all but perhaps most educated Southerners, innocent of any wrong intent — saw considerable merit in Dew's argument, which, in a nutshell, was this:

— "The historical review, which we have given of the origin and progress as slavery, shows most conclusively that something else is required to convert slavery into freedom than mere enunciation of abstract truths;" and

— "It is, in truth, the slave labor in Virginia which gives the value to her soil and her habitations;" and

— Little or nothing can now be done to terminate slavery. We must make the system as humane as possible, allowing society to mature naturally and slowly, then maybe someday these black folks can be set free, for we must "learn wisdom from experience, and know that the relations of society, generated by the lapse of ages, cannot be altered in a day."

The power of Dew's argument at that time in history was what then fairly appeared from hard experience, — that sudden liberation en masse would cause adverse consequences to both races. Society as a whole could not gracefully and effectively accommodate more than a certain limited number of freed blacks each year. Resettlement of freed blacks appeared to be a possible way to speed up the rate of emancipations, yet sudden resettlement en masse was unthinkable to most whites and blacks alike. Oddly enough, it was unthinkable largely because of the tender sentimental ties between the races. In the end, the only feasible and humane solution appeared to be a gradual nudging of slavery into natural extinction at every opportunity, as suitable new territory for expansion of the institution became less available, and as the quasi-feudal society of the old South gave way by degrees to modernization. Patient and persistent effort over time could accomplish much, but the relatively slower pace of such progress was displeasing to those who, having no personal familiarity with slavery, understood only its glaring philosophical absurdities.

As the Southern abolitionists tried to devise moderate and workable remedies, the Northern abolition movement became radicalized. The likes of James McDowell and Henry Berry knew what they were doing, and they loved the South. Harriet Beecher Stowe, on the other hand, replaced the honest humanitarians of the North, such as Lydia Maria Child.[56] To put it mildly, Mrs. Stowe was a blatant propagandist. If she was sincere, she was misguided. If she was motivated by altruism, she found it lucrative, for she earned fabulous royalties.

Her book, *Uncle Tom's Cabin*, first published in 1852, was not a work of scholarship, but a novel in which she attempted to portray very rare exceptions of abusing slaves as the normal, approved, and routine practice of the South. She did not live or travel in the South. But she felt an intestinal hatred for the people and culture of the Dixie States. Her thunderstruck readers in the North were effectively told that slavery was a system of whipping, selling out families, cruel murder, heinous brutality, impotent virtue, triumphant evil, — in short, an unending hell which was suffered by poor blacks at the hands of sadistic whites.

No falsehood can be harmful, unless there is at least a tiny morsel of truth which may be used to win initial credulity, and only then twisted and exaggerated so wildly as to inspire enmity. Mrs. Stowe's merciless and evocative pen told such an exceedingly damaging falsehood. Naturally, her readers in the North were outraged against the South. And naturally, the South was outraged at being unfairly accused. Once the whirlwind of animosity was sown between the North and the South, slavery almost ceased to be an issue. In the dark storm clouds generated by Mrs. Stowe's powerful sensationalism, the contenders all but forgot Uncle Tom.

As estrangement grew between the North and the South, each moral inconsistency spurred deeper disaffection, as may be instanced. The people of Minnesota framed a state constitution in 1858, using an odd process of two simultaneous partisan conventions, which produced two drafts reconciled into a single instrument by conference, whereupon this instrument was adopted by referendum. This state constitution prohibited slavery, but allowed only white freemen to vote. The debates in the two conventions show that the limitation on the electoral franchise was consciously meant to exclude blacks, because they were regarded as an undesirable element of any population.[57] The intense hostility against blacks in Minnesota, it should be added, was typical throughout the North. In view of attitudes of this kind above the Mason-Dixon Line, pharisaical sermons of Yankees on the subject of slavery, very often founded on the preposterous writing of Mrs. Stowe, were received with revulsion in the South where the two races, although certainly not on equal terms, manifested a genuine friendship for each other on a continuing and familiar basis day by day.

The unhappy dénouement was an unleashing of grave insults between the two civilizations of the United States. The hatred was let loose, and once that happened, questions such as slavery or secession, which were then and are still extremely important in themselves, became mixed up in passions too large, and rational interaction became too difficult.

NOTES

CHAPTER IV

1 - The framing of the third clause of Article 1, Section 2 of the United States Constitution, during the proceedings of the Philadelphia Convention, can be traced in 5 Elliot's Debates 127, 134-135, 175-178, 178-181, 190, 248-249, 249-255, 255-260, 273, 273-279, 280-282, 287-290, 290-294, 294-302, 302-306, 306-309, 310-316, 316-317, 320, 362-363, 375, 377, 379, 391-394, 433, 451, 452-453, 512, 530, 536, 540, 541, 547, 555-556, 559, — Tansill's Documents 116, 123-124, 181-184, 184-189, 202, 235-236, 287-289, 289-297, 297-304, 342-346, 346-352, 352-362, 362-368, 383-384, 389, 448, 467-468, 472, 476, 494-499, 554, 580, 581-588, 591-597, 600-606, 2 Ferrand's Records 2-11, 15-16, 106, 128, 178, 183, 219-223, 300, 350, 357-359, 511, 553, 566, 571, 590-591, 607, 612, 623-624, 643-644, 651-652, (Madison's Notes, May 29 and 31, June 9, 11, 12, 13, 19, 27, 28, and 29, July 2, 5, 6, 9, 10, 11, 12, 13, 14, 16, 24, and 26, August 6, 8, 16, 20, and 21, September 5, 8, 10, 12, 13, 14, 15, and 17, 1787). Important discussion on this clause is found in the 54th Federalist, Mentor Edition 336-341, by James Madison.

2 - The framing of the first clause of Article I, Section 3 of the United States Constitution, during the proceedings of the Philadelphia Convention, can be traced in 5 Elliot's Debates 127, 137-139, 166-170, 186-187, 189, 190, 233-241, 241-245, 260-261, 261-269, 269-273, 273-279, 285-287, 310-316, 316-317, 318-319, 356-357, 375, 376, 377, 396-397, 536, 559, — Tansill's Documents 116, 117, 127-129, 168-174, 196-198, 201, 202, 235, 236, 267-278, 279-284, 304-305, 317-323, 323-331, 339, 341, 374-383, 383-384, 385-388, 439-440, 466, 468, 470, 473, 502-504, 703, — 1 Ferrand's Records 2-11, 15, 17, 17-20, 94-95, 128, 179, 232-234, 566, 591, 652 (Madison's Notes, May 29 and 31, June 7, 12, 13, 19, 25, 26, 29, and 30, July 2, 5, 7, 14, 16, 23, and 26, August 6 and 9, September 12 and 17, 1787). Important discussion of this clause is found in the 62nd and 63rd Federalist, Mentor Edition 377-390, by James Madison.

3 - The framing of the first clause of Article I, Section 7 of the United States Constitution, during the proceedings of the Philadelphia Convention, can be traced in 5 Elliot's Debates 127, 139, 188-189, 190, 273-279, 282-285, 316-317, 375, 377, 378, 394-395, 395, 396-397, 410-411, 414-420, 427-428, 452, 453, 503, 510, 511, 514, 529, 536, 560, — Tansill's Documents 116, 117, 129, 199-200, 201, 235, 323-331, 335-339, 383-384, 466, 472, 474, 499-500, 502-503, 522-523, 528-536, 546-547, 582, 583, 655, 666, 667, 671, 692-693, 705, — 1 Ferrand's Records 21, 52-53, 233-234, 236, 526-534, 542-547, 2 Ferrand's Records, 15-16, 128, 178, 181, 223-2235, 230, 232-233, 262-263, 273-280, 296-298, 357, 358-359, 481, 508-509, 509-510, 514, 552-568, 593, 654 (Madison's Notes, May 29 and 31, June 13 and 19, July 5, 6, 16, and 26, August 6, 8, 9, 11, 13, 15, 21, and 31, September 5, 8, 12, and 17, 1787). Some light is shed on the political reasons for this clause in the exchange between William Grayson and James Madison in the Virginia Convention on June 14, 1788, as appears in 3 Elliot's Debates 375-378.

4 - Alexander Hamilton disapproved of the assessed value of land as a universal index for the imposition of direct taxes. In the 21st Federalist, Mentor Edition at 141, he argued, "The wealth of nations depends upon an infinite variety of causes. Situation, soil, climate, the nature of productions, the nature of the government, the genius of the citizens, the degree of information they possess, the state of commerce, of arts, of industry, — these circumstances and many more, too complex, minute, or adventitious to admit of a particular specification, occasion differences hardly conceivable in the relative opulence and riches of different countries." Benjamin Franklin's answer would have been that, even so, gold and silver are less satisfactory as a measure of wealth, and that the assessed value of land is a better basis of monetary discipline.

5 - The entire proposal for amendment, which was never adopted, is reprinted in 1 Elliot's Debates 93-95.

6 - Dabney's Defence of Virginia at 214. R. L. Dabney was on the staff of General T. J. "Stonewall" Jackson during the War Between the States. He wrote after the defeat of the South, not in order to justify slavery, certainly not to revive it, but in order to defend his generation and his culture from the infamy of abolitionist propaganda, and to preserve a record for historians of a future day. His account is an indispensable aid in understanding slavery as a phase American history

7 - E. g., in *Barwick v. Barwick*, 11 Iredell Law 80 (N. C. 1850), the plaintiff sued in trover to recover for conversion of slaves. The court there held that, in trover, (and, by implication, detinue, or replevin), the plaintiff must have more than mere possession, which would be sufficient for trespass, for he must prove title as well. The decision was governed by a principle equally applicable to a horse, a plow, or any chattel whatever. In *Jack v. Martin*, 14 Wendell 507 (N. Y. 1835), it was observed that a slave could be recovered bodily by suit in replevin, and that the writ of homine replegiando would be available in such case.

8 - The code of Moses thus anticipated by over three thousand years *Loving v. Virginia*, 388 U. S. 1 (1967), where it was held that a statute forbidding miscegenation, especially any marriage between male and female, one white and the other black, is unconstitutional.

9 - A standard discussion of feudal tenures, including an ample description of the institution of villeinage, is found in 2 Blackstone's Commentaries 59-102.

10 - Demographic figures on the black and white populations in Virginia during the 18th Century, up through the early 19th Century, are set forth in 2 Morris' History at 442 and 512-514, and Robert's Monticello at 11. Related demographic information, especially as it concerns distribution of slave populations up to the year 1860, is found in 2 Morris' History at 514-516. The distribution of free whites, free persons of color, and slaves throughout the several States after the first census in 1790 is conveniently set forth in tabular form in Ellis' Founding Brothers at 102.

11 - The author of these words was Professor George Frederick Holmes in his classic Review of Uncle Tom's Cabin, 18 Southern Literary Messenger 721-731 (1852), reprinted in important part in McKitrick's Slavery Defended 99-110. After teaching at the College of William and Mary and the University of Mississippi, Holmes held a chair in history and literature at the University of Virginia from 1857 through 1897. He was one of the most famous and honored literary figures in the South during the 19th Century.

12 - E. g., the Statutes of 10 William III, Chapter 26 (1699); — 5 George II, Chapter 7 (1732); — and 32 George II, Chapter 31 (1759).

13 - Luther Martin of Maryland attended the Philadelphia Convention as the attorney general of his State in which slavery was widely practiced. His labors in the convention were prolific, but in the end he opposed adoption of the United States Constitution because it did not "authorize the general government from time to time to make such regulations should be thought most advantageous for the gradual abolition of slavery, and the emancipation of slaves which are already in the States." He said in justification, "Slavery is inconsistent with the genius of republicanism, and has a tendency to destroy those principles on which it is supported, as it lessens the sense of the equal rights of mankind, and habituates us to tyranny and oppression." — 1 Elliot's Debates 374, 3 Ferrand's Records 212 (Joint session of the Maryland House and Senate, January 17, 1788).

14 - Reprinted in 9 Hening's Statutes at Large 471 (October 1778, Chapter 1).

15 - Reprinted in 10 Hening's Statutes at Large 211 (October 1779, Chapter 47).

16 - Reprinted in 11 Hening's Statutes at Large 39 (May 1782, Chapter 21).

17 - Reprinted in 10 Hening's Statutes at Large 115 (May 1779, Chapter 44).

18 - Reprinted in 11 Hening's Statutes at Large 308 (October 1783, Chapter 3).

19 - The principles of common law regarding slavery, as handed down by Lord Mansfield in 1771, were fully anticipated in 1 Blackstone's Commentaries at 127 and 423-425. The rule was that the instant a slave landed in England or wherever slavery was not allowed by positive law, he became free.

20 - Reprinted in 12 Hening's Statues at Large 182 (October 1785, Chapter 77), as amended by acts reprinted in 13 Hening's Statutes at Large 62 (October 1789, Chapter 45) and 121 (October 1790, Chapter 9).

21- The most deplorable of these political frauds appeared in a speech in the United States House of Representatives on February 13, 1821, by Congressman Charles Pinckney of South Carolina, who had been a delegate to the Philadelphia Convention. The debate then pending in Congress concerned the admission of Missouri to the Union, and turned on the meaning of the first clause of Article IV, Section 2 of the United States Constitution. Congressman Pinckney said, "It appears by the Journal of the Convention that formed the Constitution of the United States, that I was the only member of that body who ever submitted the plan of a constitution completely drawn in articles and sections. And this, having been done at a very early state of their proceedings, the article on which now so much stress is laid, and on the meaning of which the whole of this question is made to turn, and which is in these words, 'The citizens of each State shall be entitled to all privileges and immunities of citizens in every State,' having been made by me, it is supposed I must know and perfectly recollect what I meant by it. In answer I say that, at the time I drew that constitution, I perfectly knew that there did not exist in the Union a black or colored citizen, nor could I then have conceived it possible such a thing could ever have existed in it; nor, notwithstanding all that has been said on the subject, do I now believe one does exist in it." — 37 Annals of Congress at 1134. The journal of the Philadelphia Convention shows that Pinckney submitted a draft on the first day of debates, but that it was never considered on the floor. It was worked into the report of the committee on detail with useful effect, as appears in 1 Elliot's Debates 145-149 and 224-230, and 1 Ferrand's Records 16, 2 Ferrand's Records 176-189, 3 Ferrand's Records 595-609 (Journal, May 29 and August 6, 1787). The clause on privileges and immunities in Article IV, Section 2 of the United States Constitution evidently was taken from Pinckney's plan. But the deception in Pinckney's speech in Congress on February 13, 1821, was that he did not originate the clause on privileges and immunities: — he drew it from the corresponding clause in the fourth article of the old Confederation, which was probably drafted by Benjamin Franklin. There can be no doubt that, Franklin, who was an abolitionist, believed that freed slaves became citizens. And at the time, there were many black freemen, citizens, and soldiers in the United States.

22 - In the Philadelphia Convention, George Mason of Virginia opposed the counting of slaves the same as freemen for purposes of representation in Congress, as appears in 5 Elliot's Debates 296, Tansill's Documents 354-355, 1 Ferrand's Records 581 (Madison's Notes, July 11, 1787). Colonel Mason was an

ardent abolitionist, as appears in his speeches during the framing and adoption of the United States Constitution, — e.g., in 5 Elliot's Debates 458, Tansill's Documents 589-590, 2 Ferrand's Records 370-371 (Madison's Notes, August 22, 1787), and 3 Elliot's Debates 452-453 (Virginia Convention, June 15, 1788).

23 - Luther Martin, attorney general of Maryland, tolerated the counting of slaves as three-fifths their number, because it encouraged the emancipation of slaves; but, like George Mason, he wanted an absolute prohibition on importation of slaves. Even so, he argued that counting them as three-fifths of their number might encourage further importations as appears in 5 Elliot's Debates 457, Tansill's Documents 588, 2 Ferrand's Records 364 (Madison's Notes, August 21, 1787). He was an ardent abolitionist, as appears in his public speeches, e. g., in 1 Elliot's Debates 373-374 (Maryland House of Delegates, January 27, 1788).

24 - The views of Thomas Jefferson on slavery are found expressed most clearly in Query XIV and Query XVIII of his Notes on Virginia, published in 1782, reprinted in Koch & Peden's Jefferson at 255-262 and 277-279 respectively.

25 - An exhaustive discourse on slavery by Judge St. George Tucker, published in 1803, is laid out in 2 Tucker's Blackstone, Appendix H at 31-85. After a tough-minded assessment of the great obstacles general liberation which few students have understood, he proposed a blueprint, drawing both from the thinking of Thomas Jefferson whose views were well known in Virginia, and of Benjamin Franklin who developed a plan of gradual abolition then already operating in Pennsylvania. It may be noted as an aside that, in 1790, according to 2 Morris' History at 513, there were less than 4,000 slaves in Pennsylvania as compared to about 292,000 in Virginia. Tucker's program called for liberation of children born of female slaves on or after a certain future date, upon reaching the age of 28. He proposed that such persons should be taught marketable skills before becoming free, and that, when released from further servitude, they should be provided with a prescribed quantity of money, clothing, and other necessities. He thought that freed blacks should be subject to various civil disabilities in Virginia so as to induce the emigration of as many of them as possible into other States and western territories of the Union, thus spreading them out and easing their assimilation into society. He hoped that, as natural adjustments were made over time, both in the condition of freed blacks and in the attitudes of free whites, these various civil disabilities could be removed in stages until all traces of legal inequality between the races were completely removed.

26 - 3 Elliot's Debates 590-591 (Virginia Convention, June 24, 1788).

27 - On January 25, 1830, in the United States Senate, Robert Hayne of South Carolina described the situation as he and many learned people in the South actually saw it at their time in history: "If slavery, as it now exists in this country, be an evil, we of the present day found it ready made to our hands. Finding our lot cast among a people, whom God had manifestly committed to our care, we did not sit down to speculate on abstract questions of theoretical liberty. We met it as

a practical question of obligation and duty. We resolved to make the best of the situation in which Providence had placed us, and to fulfill the high trust which had developed upon us as the owners of slaves, in the only way in which such a trust could be fulfilled without spreading misery and ruin throughout the land. We found that we had to deal with a people whose moral, physical, and intellectual habits and character totally disqualified them from the enjoyment of the blessings of freedom. We could not send them back to the shores from whence their fathers had been taken; their numbers forbade the thought, even if we did not know that their condition here is infinitely preferable to what it possibly could be among the barren sands and savage tribes of Africa; and it was wholly irreconcilable with all our notions of humanity to tear asunder the tender ties which they had formed among us, to gratify the feelings of a false philanthropy." After lamenting the situation of freed blacks lured by Northern abolitionists to live in Philadelphia, New York, and Boston, Hayne went on, "Liberty has been to them the greatest of calamities, the heaviest of curses. Sir, I have had some opportunities of making comparisons between the condition of free negroes in the North and the slaves of the South, and the comparison has left not only an indelible impression of the superior advantages of the latter, but has gone far to reconcile me to slavery itself." - Belz' Webster-Hayne Debate at 45-46.

28 - Quoted in Mellon's Early Views at 113 (translated from the original French).

29 - The best source of information, as balanced and objective as any available, is found in the answers of James Madison, made on March 14, 1832, to various inquiries of an abolition society in Liverpool, England, together with certain supplemental observations, all reproduced in Mellon's Early Views at 143-147.

30 - The emancipation legislation in the Northern States is summarized in Dabney's Defence of Virginia at 79-87.

31 - Madison's projections and ideas appear in certain correspondence with the Marquis de Lafayette and others, and in his answer to Professor Thomas Dew, all written after his retirement from public life when he could study in depth, as appears in Mellon's Early Views 133-142.

32 - Quoted in Robert's Monticello at 18, published in Richmond on January 7, 1832.

33 - Robert's Monticello at 80 (Appendix A, House of Delegates, General Assembly of Virginia January 17, 1832).

34 - Robert's Monticello at 72 (Appendix A, House of Delegates, General Assembly of Virginia, January 13, 1832).

35 - Quoted in Robert's Monticello at 19.

36 - Robert's Monticello at 87 (Appendix A. House of Delegates, General Assembly of Virginia, January 17, 1832).

37 - Robert's Monticello at 94 (Appendix A, House of Delegates, General Assembly of Virginia, January 18, 1832).

38 - Robert's Monticello at 103 (Appendix A, House of Delegates, General Assembly of Virginia, January 21, 1832).

39 - Robert's Monticello at 85 (Appendix A., House of Delegates, General Assembly of Virginia, January 13, 1832).

40 - Robert's Monticello at 103 (Appendix A., House of Delegates, General Assembly of Virginia, January 21, 1832).

41 - Robert's Monticello at 62-63 (Appendix A, House of Delegates, General Assembly of Virginia, January 11, 1832).

42 - Robert's Monticello at 86 (Appendix A, House of Delegates, General Assembly of Virginia, January 17, 1832).

43 - Robert's Monticello at 109 (Appendix A., House of Delegates, General Assembly of Virginia, January 25, 1832).

44 - Robert's Monticello at 77 (Appendix A, House of Delegates, General Assembly of Virginia, January 14, 1832).

45 - Robert's Monticello at 103 (Appendix A, House of Delegates, General Assembly of Virginia, January 21, 1832).

46 - Robert's Monticello at 99 (Appendix A, House of Delegates, General Assembly of Virginia, January 20, 1832).

47 - The actual state of the law as it then stood is described in Dabney's Defence of Virginia at 216-217. "The only enactment which touches the subject is the following sentence in the statute defining what were 'unlawful assemblages' of negroes, 'And every assemblage of negroes for the purpose of instruction in reading or writing, or in the night time for any purpose, shall be an unlawful assembly.' Statutes 1830-1831, p. 107. The previous section, commencing the definition of these unlawful assemblies, expressly states that they are unlawful if held without the master's consent."

48 - Robert's Monticello at 99-100 (Appendix A, House of Delegates, General Assembly of Virginia, Jnauary 20, 1832).

49 - Robert's Monticello at 67 (Appendix A, House of Delegates, General Assembly of Virginia, January 12, 1832).

50 - Robert's Monticello at 80-81 (Appendix A, House of Delegates, General Assembly of Virginia, January 16, 1832).

51 - Robert's Monticello at 84 (Appendix A, House of Delegates, General Assembly of Virginia, January 17, 1832).

52 - Robert's Monticello at 87 (Appendix A, House of Delegates, General Assembly of Virginia, January 17, 1832).

53 - Robert's Monticello at 73 (Appendix A, House of Delegates, General Assembly of Virginia, January 14, 1832).

54 - Quoted in Robert's Monticello at 32.

55 - Published in Richmond in 1832, republished in Charleston in 1852, and reprinted in important part in McKitrick's Slavery Defended 20-53.

56 - Her Anti-Slavery Catechism, published in 1839, was free of the sophomoric theorizing and hysterical exaggeration which characterized most abolitionist literature in the North. She confronted uinderstandable fears with reasoned argument and available facts, stating her case tactfully and fairly. Her work is reprinted in important part in Thomas' Slavery Attacked at 63-69. Child was respected by many activists in the large abolition movement which flourished in the antebellum South, as she was detested by radical abolitionists in the North.

57 - The referenced developments in Minnesota are discussed and documented in 2 Thorpe's History at 533-534.

Engraved by H.B. Hall, from a Daguerreotype by Brady.

JOHN CALDWELL CALHOUN.

CHAPTER V

THE NULLIFICATION CRISIS

The true founder of the school of strict construction of the United States Constitution was Thomas Jefferson. The precepts of this school were worked into the early agenda of his "democratic republican" party, later called the "democratic" or even the "democrat" party, which however has undergone various mutations in ideology over many generations, swaying back and forth so as to make the party label at any one time in history an unreliable sign of principles held. Yet regardless of all affiliations of a partisan nature, if a statesman or judge firmly believes in and lives by the philosophy of strict construction of laws, as taught by our third President, he deserves the honorable cognomen of "Jeffersonian democrat."

In his judicious observations and studious endeavors, Thomas Jefferson came upon a universal principle: — if prudently limited and wisely directed, almost any government can be a blessing; yet, unless firmly constrained, any government of whatever form will tend to augment its powers in excess, going beyond even the plainest legal limits on its just authority, and will sooner or later become dangerous.

History has included occasional epochs, such as the marvelous age from the accession of Nerva to the death of Marcus Aurelius,[1] or the brilliant but short and tragic reign of Majorian,[2] or the fabulous reign of John Comnenus,[3] in which nations have enjoyed extraordinarily virtuous and skillful leaders, who from the discipline of well-formed character have restrained the energies of government from almost every act of immoderation and injustice, allowing civilization to flourish. Unfortunately, these periods have been infrequent, and usually brief in duration. In the absence of truly great spirits at the helm of power, governments have invariably tended to become obnoxious and oppressive in a thousand ways. And

185

against this melancholy proclivity, constitutional barriers must be carefully designed and erected. The formula for such safeguards was thus stated by James Madison:

> "Ambition must be made to counteract ambition. The interest of the man must be connected with the constitutional rights of the place. It may be a reflection on human nature that such devices should be necessary to control abuses of government. But what is government itself but the greatest of all reflections on human nature? If men were angels, no government would be necessary. If angels were to govern men, neither external nor internal controls on government would be necessary. In framing a government which is to be administered by men over men, the greatest difficulty lies in this: you must first enable the government to control the governed; and in the next place, oblige it to control itself."[4]

This insight, which shaped the republican forms of government erected in the era of the American Revolution, also supplied the guiding impulse which animated the school of strict construction. For as long as they could do so with respectability in pubic life, and for as long as it was at all practical to make the attempt, those inspired by Thomas Jefferson sought to give clauses granting powers to the government of the Union a rigorous and restricted interpretation.

Jefferson and his disciples knew that this approach was only a breaking mechanism which might wear out before very many years had passed. The brightest of them knew that strict construction was only a first line of defense against usurpations of the government, and might eventually have to give way to more ultimate devices for counteracting abuses of power. Jefferson himself was the first American statesman to use the word "nullification," as appears in the Kentucky Resolutions of 1799, indicative of what such more ultimate mechanisms should be.

What remains of this school of thought is not its original positions, which have long since been overwhelmed, but the spirit which first moved its adherents to act. This spirit was an unaffected willingness to expound the powers of the government by giving life and reality to the limits of its powers, based on a philosophical understanding of the need to do so as a duty to fellow citizens for the protection of their liberties, lest the government become wasteful, inefficient, corrupt, overbearing, and tyrannical. No less was this spirit an ardent willingness to persist, if possible and necessary, in using second, third, and further lines of defense against such encroachments on the rights of the people given by natural law and protected in legal tradition.

* * * * *

On December 13, 1790, a report was sent from the treasury department to Congress, recommending incorporation of a Bank of the United States. A bill was accordingly introduced and passed in the Senate, then sent over to the House of Representatives, setting up a banking institution which, aside from enjoying usual corporate powers, was authorized to generate bank notes redeemable in gold or silver coin, and receivable in payment of all taxes and other dues owed to the United States. These notes could be lent at interest, given in exchange for deposits, or used in public expenditures, and thereby this valuable currency was to be put into circulation.

The bill allowed private subscription of four-fifths of the total capital stock of $10 million, which was an immense sum of money in those days: — $2 million in stock was to be privately subscribed with gold and silver, and $6 million was to be privately subscribed with tax-funded bonds of the United States. Subscription of the remaining $2 million in stock was reserved to the United States in consideration of money raised by the sale of tax-funded bonds to private subscribers of stock in the bank, whereupon $2 million was to be loaned back to the United States.

The government of the Union was to elect five of twenty-five directors. The other twenty were to be elected by private interests, including major financiers domestic and foreign who purchased fourth-fifths of the stock.

The new bank was to be incomparably larger than all then-existing financial institutions. It was to enjoy substantial holdings of specie, and was meant to be the depository of all funds of the Federal government. It was to have the capacity of lending to smaller banks when they were confronted with heavy drains of cash on hand, and of regulating their soundness and condition by presenting their notes for redemption in specie on a systematic basis. It was meant to have a discretion of making, withholding, or recalling loans on a large scale so as to stimulate and diminish activity in the economy.

The chartered duration of the corporation was not perpetual, but limited to twenty years, unless the term should be extended by further act of Congress.

This Bank of the United States was remarkably similar to the Bank of England. The institution earned double interest from tax-funded bonds of the Federal government and from loans, mainly in the form of bank notes and drawing rights, to private borrowers. Its currency was receivable in payment of all dues owed to the United States. And the corporation enjoyed the valuable franchise of lending the Federal government its own credit.

The bill was passed by the First Congress which included sixteen of the framers of the United States Constitution, divided among themselves of over whether the bank could be lawfully established.[5] The question was difficult, because the United States Constitution does not mention a power of Congress to establish a Federal bank, nor do the records of the Philadelphia Convention resolve the question of whether the framers intended to vest an implied power in Congress to incorporate such an institution.[6]

After passing the Senate, then the House, the bill was sent to President George Washington who, before acting on this historic legislation, requested opinions in writing from the attorney general Edmund Randolph, the secretary of state Thomas Jefferson, and the secretary of the treasury Alexander Hamilton. These opinions are classic papers in American legal thought.

Jefferson's Opinion on the Bank[7] was submitted on February 15, 1791, and was reinforced by the very similar views of the attorney general. It was the first formal argument of the school of strict construction.

Jefferson's anxiety was excited, not because he was necessarily opposed to a well-designed Federal bank, for he knew that such an institution might be an important and beneficial, perhaps an indispensable means of assuring a reliable, steady, and optimum supply and flow of good currency throughout the several States. Yet, if Congress possessed power to set up such an institution, the legal authority had to be found lurking behind broad language, leaving the awesome dynamo of high finance largely undefined and unguarded. The prospect was ominous, because it was an invitation carte blanche for subversion of the government of the Union by interests alien to the public good, followed by tremendous abuse of economic and political power with the most appalling effects.[8] Jefferson was unwilling to trust bare legal inference on a question of such magnitude. Therefore, he rendered his opinion on a very frugal and cautious reading of several constitutional provisions drawn into question.

The first clause of Article I, Section 8 says that Congress shall have power of levying taxes, duties, imposts, and excises to pay the debts and to provide for the common defense and general welfare of the United States. The second clause of Article I, Section 8 allows Congress to borrow money on the credit of the United States. The third clause of Article I, Section 8 grants Congress the power to regulate commerce among the several States. The eighteenth clause of Article I, Section 8 gives Congress authorized to enact laws necessary and proper for carrying into execution its express powers. And Amendment X reserves to the several States all powers not granted to the Union.

Jefferson noted that the bank bill levied no tax, and insisted that, in any event, no tax could be authorized for any purpose other than raising funds for paying debts, and providing for the common defense or general welfare. Therefore, on the basis of a very literal reading of words, Jefferson excluded all use of the taxing power for regulatory purposes.

The bill, Jefferson claimed, borrowed no money, but merely allowed the Federal government to borrow back what it had paid into the bank, which, he insisted, was not authentic borrowing, but a deceptive subterfuge.

The bill was not a regulation of commerce, Jefferson argued, because, in setting up a bank, it regulated nothing, but merely created an object in commerce which might be regulated.

And the bill was not designed to enact a law necessary and proper for carrying other powers into execution, Jefferson held, because a means was not necessary merely because convenient or expedient for some such purpose. Jefferson interpreted "necessary" in contrast to "reasonable" and more akin to "indispensable" and thus held that a means should be considered necessary in a constitutional sense, only if without it an express power "would be nugatory."

Hamilton's Opinion on the Bank[9] was submitted on February 23, 1791. It represents the contrasting school of "liberal interpretation" of the United States Constitution, — i. e., an expansive reading of clauses granting power to the government of the Union, exploiting ambiguity in the words used and drawing the aid of external sources as required, with a view to encouraging an aggressive program of blending the disparate parts of the country into a unified nation and major power in world affairs, both in commerce and in war.

Patrick Henry had said,

> "Consider our situation, sir: go to the poor man, and ask him what he does. He will inform you that he enjoys the fruits of his labor, under his own fig tree, with his wife and children about him in peace and security. Go to every member of society, — you will find the same tranquil ease and content, you will find no alarms or disturbances. Why, then, tell of us danger, to terrify us into an adoption of this new form of government?"[10]

Alexander Hamilton answered such dreamy eloquence by pointing to the harsh competition among the nations of the earth, and demanded ample power for the American government. He added,

"Reflections of this kind may have trifling weight with men who hope to see realized in America the halcyon scenes of the poetic or fabulous age, but to those who believe we are likely to experience a common portion of the vicissitudes and calamities which have fallen to the lot of other nations, they must be entitled to serious consideration. Such men must behold the actual situation of their country with painful solicitude, and deprecate the evils which ambition or revenge might, with too much facility, inflict upon it."[11]

From this tough-minded outlook, Hamilton demonstrated the constitutionality of the bank with military precision:

His central idea was that "necessary" ought not be read as if "absolutely" or "indispensably" were prefixed, for such a reading would often draw into question important powers of the Union, and so run contrary to the evident purpose of the clause giving Congress the power to enact necessary and proper laws. And for this reason, Hamilton held that a means chosen by Congress should be considered "necessary" if it were merely "needful, requisite, useful, or conducive to" the accomplishment of some authorized and lawful end.

There was no express mention of a Federal bank in the work of the Philadelphia Convention. Whatever may have been the thoughts and speeches of individual members of the convention, and whatever propositions may have been offered but not adopted during the debates, Hamilton insisted that the legal intent and true meaning of the United States Constitution should be determined solely "according to the usual and established rules of construction."[12] He had in mind rules then well identified and understood, — rules from the common law of England, used specifically for the interpretation of legislative will by signs natural and probable.[13]

Those rules clearly ordained that, unless there were obvious indications to the contrary, the words and phrases of a statute or constitution should be assigned their usual and unstrained meaning and coalesce with legal customs and practices at the time of enactment or adoption.

Hamilton pointed out that establishing corporations was a necessary and proper method of exercising the powers of government, as in setting up institutions for the government of the territories of the Union. He then contended that the bank was a necessary and proper means to facilitate the levying of taxes, because it provided currency with which taxes could be paid, exactly as was common practice in England. Hamilton maintained that the bank was a necessary and proper means of borrowing, because it attracted and organized capital in a lending institution from which money or rights redeemable or transferable in lieu of money could more readily be borrowed by the Federal government on good security. This practice had long been a known and accepted way of borrowing by the government in England. And, he said, the institution was a necessary and proper means of regulating commerce, because providing viable currency to lubricate business had been thought of as a regulation of trade, as had certainly been true in England. In his discussion he mentioned the fact that the levying of otherwise lawful duties, excises, and imposts on business transactions had long been a customary mode of regulating commerce, no less than prescribing rules for the conduct and avenues of trade, as surely was true in England.

Hamilton's argument was thorough, tenacious, and irresistible. On February 25, 1791, the bill to incorporate the bank was approved by the President.[14] Washington himself was known to have felt some doubt. And each in his turn as President, Jefferson and Madison reluctantly approved like legislation.[15] The gnawing uncertainty which troubled Washington, Jefferson, and Madison remained an embarrassment over many years.

Jeffersonian democrats continued even after Jefferson's death to deny that an implied power to establish a Federal bank was ever vested in Congress. They stood firm, notwithstanding that an act authorizing a "second" Bank of the United States was judicially upheld as constitutional in the famous case of *M'Collough v. Maryland*, 4 Wheaton 316 (U. S. 1816). The court found that the institution was a necessary and proper means of exercising public powers of the United States. The opinion of the Chief Justice John Marshall was in practical effect a judicial restatement of Hamilton's Opinion on the Bank.

The second bank lacked adequate statutory controls to prevent abuse of power. It bought and sold politicians with impunity. It engineered expansions and contractions of credit to benefit stockholders. The institution performed so badly that, if it had not influenced Congress in the manner customary for the Bank of England in the British Parliament, the bill to extend the duration of its charter would never have passed the Senate and the House. The bill was vetoed by President Andrew Jackson on July 10, 1832. The message returned with the bill to the Senate was masterfully written by Jackson's attorney general.[16] The message said that the United States Supreme Court cannot bind the President, who, no less than Congress, has an independent right and duty to assess the constitutionality of legislation. The President found the bank to be unconstitutional. His main premise, utterly unanswerable and overlooked by Hamilton, was that "Congress cannot establish a bank for purposes of private speculation and gain, but only as a means of exercising delegated powers of the General Government."

The second bank expired. A vacuum was left in an era of free banking. There were an infinite variety of bank notes, some sound, some not. The ratio of bank paper to specie became distorted to great excess, and was controlled by private interests not in tune with the public good, whereupon the greatest Jeffersonian democrat of them all, John Calhoun of South Carolina, labored in the United States Senate to describe a remedy. He delivered two powerful speeches seeking to bring order to disorder, proposing careful interim measures, and conceding at least a practical, if not legal need for a constitutional amendment which would grant Congress an express power to establish a Federal bank.[17] He spoke of the need of a "bank to unbank the banks."

Calhoun's ideas as then stated were still forming in his powerful mind, but the seeds of a grander plan can be discerned in his words. The express power, foreseen by Calhoun as eventually necessary in the future, would have been qualified so as to assure as far as possible an identified, regulated, limited, and supervised instrumentality to maintain optimum supply and flow of good currency, impartially directed so as to enhance production, employment, learning, and culture throughout the several States, — a central banking institution unlike the Bank of England which, in satisfying private greed, had induced war and disorder in the British Empire. This new bank of the Union would be wholly public in ownership and control, yet legally restrained from abuse of power, in any event insolated from private subversion, allowing the Federal government to benefit from disciplined use of its own credit without unnecessary drain to private financial parasites, and focused solely upon a mission of promoting the civilization and well-being of the United States.

* * * * *

The third article of the old Confederation, in the nature of a preamble, declared that the several States had entered a "firm league of friendship for their common defence and general welfare." The eighth article then said that "all charges and other expenses that shall be incurred for the common defence and general welfare, and allowed by the United States in Congress assembled, shall be defrayed out of a common treasury," etc. There is rule of the common law, ancient in origin, that clauses dealing with the same subject should be read side by side, and compared, so that, if possible, one might shed light on the meaning of another. And a preamble, announcing the purposes of a document, whether large or limited, is often used to elucidate language in the body of a statute or constitution.[18]

In keeping with this rule, the third article stated the grand purposes of the old Confederation, and controlled the meaning of the eighth article, not the other way around. Hence, the phrase "common defence and general welfare" was meant to be read expansively, not narrowly. Under the old Confederation, Congress was not limited in its constitutional power of spending to paying for the exercise of other powers specifically granted, but was allowed to disburse public money any purpose which might fairly be characterized in the exercise of reasonable legislative discretion as common defense and general welfare. The difficulty under the old Confederation was not want of legal power in Congress, but lack of effective means of raising money which might be spent.

In the United States Constitution, there is a parallel structure of clauses. The Preamble drew from the third article of the old Confederation, and so ordains that the new Union was established to "provide for the common Defence" and to "promote the general Welfare." And in the first clause of Article I, Section 8, the power of Congress to spend money was drawn from the eighth article of the old Confederation, and accordingly was defined by purpose of the new Union, — i. e., "to pay the Debts and provide for the common Defence and general Welfare."

It is thus plain enough that the Preamble was meant to enhance the meaning of the first clause in Article I, Section 8, which thus granted Congress wide discretion in spending, not confined to carrying out other specified powers, and allowed outlays for any objective which might fairly be considered as common defense and general welfare, — be it the building of roads and canals, support of education and the arts, or whatever. And since the new Congress was to have very ample powers of taxation, the power of spending became vastly more important than it was before.

The power of Congress to regulate commerce under the third clause of Article I, Section 8 of the United States Constitution was certainly intended and understood as a broad power to regulate trade throughout the Union, including transportation, communication, insurance, finance, negotiation, and other avenues and incidents of such trade.[19]

It seems plain enough that the framers thought of commerce, agriculture, and manufacturing as three distinct domains of activity, and so thought that the power of Congress to regulate commerce, however broad in itself, was not a power to regulate agriculture and manufacturing.[20] Yet, as can be gathered from the debates of the Philadelphia Convention, they believed that commerce could be regulated by levying duties, excises, and imposts, as in England, and that, so long as such regulatory use of taxation touched only upon commerce, Congress might seek to influence activity otherwise beyond its regulatory powers.[21]

With a firm grasp of these principles of fundamental law, Alexander Hamilton as secretary of the treasury wrote his famous Report on Manufactures,[22] and forwarded it to the United States House of Representatives on December 5, 1791. In this paper he outlined a dynamic vision of the future.

He wanted Congress to enhance production in agriculture and manufacturing by regulating and taxing commerce, and spending liberally to lubricate the economy and improve the infrastructure of the whole country. Among other things, he hoped to see the use of tariffs to protect fledgling domestic industries so they might not be undersold by foreign competition before they had an ample opportunity to mature as fully as their potential allowed. He wanted bounties to promote excellence in production. He wanted to see the United States develop into a great power which could in due course confront, defend against, or overwhelm any hostile kingdom or empire in Europe or Asia. He envisioned the interaction of the several States in all parts of the Union, forming a graceful, powerful, shining, and modern nation, fully independent and self-sufficient in war and peace.

As a Jeffersonian democrat, James Madison was alarmed by Hamilton's view of the power of Congress to spend money. In his Report on the Virginia Resolutions of 1798, he argued that the power of Congress to spend money under the first clause of Article I, Section 8 of the Untied States Constitution derived from the eighth article of the old Confederation, which, without considering the third article as a preamble, he assumed must have been limited by the enumerated powers of the old Congress. And therefore, overlooking the Preamble defining the purposes of the new Union, he argued that spending for the common defense and general welfare was limited to spending in carrying out the enumerated powers of the new Congress.[23]

Madison stuck to this position with spectacular tenacity, even until March 3, 1817, his last day as President, when he interposed a veto against the so-called Bonus Bill,[24] which would have established a permanent fund, from dividends paid on the stock owned by the Federal government in the second bank, for building and improving roads and canals throughout the United States. His thought was that, if it could spend so liberally, Congress could assume all the great and most important powers of government because the spending of money has always been an important means by which public authority exercises power. If the objects of the bill were desirable, as he thought likely, new powers might be added to the authority of Congress by constitutional amendments prudently and cautiously framed, introduced, and adopted as allowed by the fundamental law of the Union.

Firm though his position had been as President concerning limits on the power of Congress to spend money, the elder Madison in retirement began to change his mind, especially as he saw the urgent need for spending by the Federal government to assist in emancipation of slaves in Virginia and other Southern States. By the end of the presidency of James Monroe, not all but most members of Jefferson's party conceded, albeit with varying degrees of reluctance, the power of Congress to spend public money on internal improvements.[25]

Jefferson had said that taxation could never be used as a means of regulating commerce. John Randolph of Roanoke led a faction in Congress called the "teritum quids" who continued to preach this dogma for many years, and remained more Jeffersonian than Jefferson himself on every question of strict construction. Even so, in correspondence written after he had retired from public life,[26] Madison plainly conceded that Congress did, after all, have power to lay duties, excises, and imposts on commerce in order to promote agriculture and manufacturing in the United States. And he thought that Congress should use this power in a coordinated manner for the benefit of the whole Union.

The theory of free trade has been a perennial nostrum. The idea is that, if commerce between nations is left unregulated, the natural forces of competition will eventually promote the highest production at the lowest price. Aside from the fact that the highest production at the lowest price is not necessarily the most desirable objective, Madison exposed a critical flaw. The philosophy of laissez faire presupposes an unlimited freedom of commercial intercourse, universal willingness of all governments to allow it, perpetual peace among nations, and equal capacity for competition. But since these conditions have never existed in the history of mankind, free trade has generally been incapable of the wonders attributed to it, and may actually be dangerous by leaving a country underdeveloped in time of war, as was the case with the United States during the War of 1812.

Madison came to see that an unregulated market, either domestic or international, may not be a free market, but rather a market in which the stronger may more readily exploit the weaker, causing great dislocations and injustice. He knew that it has never been possible, either within a country or between countries, for smaller producers in disarray to fare well against huge concentrations of organized wealth.

And so in growing older Madison agreed with Hamilton, and urged Congress to design and adopt a just policy of taxation to promote of strong common market within the United States, enabling the country to be self-sufficient in war and peace.

Again the greatest Jeffersonian democrat of them all, John Calhoun of South Carolina, understood the constitutionality and necessity for reasonable and balanced tariffs, designed not only to raise revenue for the treasury of the Union, but to protect underdeveloped American manufacturers against underselling by manufacturers in Europe. He conceded the point in a speech on April 4, 1816, as a member of the United States House of Representatives.[27] Such tariffs were indispensable in the long run, he said, to protect the overall economic strength of the United States, in war and in peace, in the South and in the North. In his speech Calhoun said,

> "Neither agriculture, nor manufacturing, or commerce, taken separately, is the cause of wealth. It follows from the three combined, and cannot exist without each. The wealth of any single nation, or any individual, it is true, may not immediately depended on the three, but such wealth always presupposes their existence. Without commerce, industry would have no stimulus. Without manufacturers, commerce would be without the means of production. And without agriculture, neither commerce nor manufacturing can subsist. When separated entirely and permanently, they perish. War in this country produces that effect, and the great embarrassments which follow in its train. The failure of wealth and resources of a nation necessarily involves the ruin of its finances and its currency. It is admitted by the most strenuous advocates on the other side that no country ought to be dependent on another for its means of defence; that at least our musket and bayonet, our cannon and ball ought to be of domestic manufacture. But what is more necessary to the defence of a country than its currency and finance? Circumscribed as our country is, can these stand the shock of war? Behold the effects of the late war on them! When our manufacturers are grown to a certain perfection, as they soon will under the fostering care of government, we will no longer experience these evils. The farmer will find a ready market for his surplus produce, and, what is almost of equal consequence, a certain and cheap supply of his wants. His prosperity will defuse itself to every class in the community; and instead of that languor of industry and individual distress now incident to a state of war and suspended commerce, the wealth and vigor of the community will not be materially impaired."

Hamilton's view thus ultimately prevailed. Yet Jefferson's efforts had not been without beneficial effect, for the true purpose of strict construction had been to assure a cautious and wise growth of Federal power in fulfillment of the true dreams which the fundamental law of the Union had ordained: — common defense, not wasteful military spending and unnecessary wars; general welfare, not enrichment of one section of the country at the expense of another; justice, not encroachment on the legitimate rights of the people; and domestic tranquillity, not schemes to fatten a selfish few.

This task of strict construction had been admirably executed, whereupon John Quincy Adams of Massachusetts became President of the United States on March 4, 1825. He was the son of brilliant parents who had known from the beginning that he was unusually full of promise. He believed in Hamilton's Report on Manufactures. Serving under him was Vice President John Calhoun, who presided with patrician grace over the Senate.

There was on the books at the time a basic statute enacted by Congress on April 27, 1816, which was amended on April 20, 1818, and again on May 22, 1824. These three acts read together imposed tariffs, of which some were intentionally above levels required to satisfy the ordinary expenses of the Federal government, to keep up a respectable army and navy, to maintain an extensive system of necessary fortifications, and to pay interest and principal on public debt as and when due. The rates were adjusted to provide a measure of protection against foreign competition both for manufacturing in the North and for agriculture in the South.

The North and the South increased their commercial intercourse with each other. Americans traded with Europe, but the United States gradually became less dependent on foreign powers. The system was not perfectly balanced, but it was generally fair and did much good for the country. Some inequity appeared here and there, but it was known that periodic monitoring and readjustment, if carefully and expertly carried out in light of maturing experience, could achieve nearly optimum proportions of revenue and regulation.

* * * * *

Everything was progressing well until the 20th Congress met on December 3, 1827, full of characters pushing the candidacy of General Andrew Jackson for President. Jackson had gained popularity because of his victory in repelling a British infantry attack on New Orleans at the conclusion of the War of 1812. It was a battle almost impossible to lose as tight ranks of redcoats marched against American sharpshooters and artillery lodged comfortably behind cotton bales. "Elevate them guns a little lower," Jackson ordered as enemy formations advanced as if on parade. Whether "them guns" were raised or lowered may be disputed, but there can be no doubt that the volleys were lethal. And after the engagement, Jackson became a folk hero. His fortunes in politics skyrocketed year after year.

The Jackson men figured that their candidate would enjoy the support of his native South. They knew that, by posing as a military giant, Jackson could appeal to the West. New England they conceded to Adams, but they wanted the middle States on the Atlantic coast. These middle States desired some protection for their budding industries, and, in the normal course of business, they would have received fair consideration of their requests. But the conspirators proposed a new system of tariffs, adjusted so outrageously high that they supposed even New England would vote against. Upon the expected defeat of their bill of straw, they intended to raise an uproar across the country by insisting that the supporters of President John Quincy Adams had been at fault in preventing adjusted tariffs. Then "Old Hickory" would appear on the political horizon, make inflammatory speeches, mislead the people, get elected, and reward his partisans.

In any event, the plot did not pull off quite as planned. New England went along, having been induced to believe that the protection allowed by the bill must not be objectionable. The Jackson men were surprised and had to change their strategy. Knowing the bill was bad for the country and unfair even to their own constituents, they supported it solely to deprive Adams of a campaign issue. The President assumed the bill must have been honestly introduced and passed, and, therefore, he signed it. Such were the infamous origins of the Act of May 19, 1828, which became known as the "tariff of abominations."

Congressman John Randolph of Virginia summed it all up in saying, "The bill referred to manufactures of no sort or kind, but the manufacture of a President of the United States." The man from Tennessee postured, orated, and bowed. He stood by the flag and posed as a champion of the common man. The dignified gentleman from Massachusetts was too cerebral and decent to indulge in such a gutter
war. The impostor won. "Andy" Jackson was inaugurated on March 4, 1829. For days Washington D. C. was full of whiskey-soaked drunks in coon-skin caps.

Just as the country started to get over the revelry of the election contest between Adams and Jackson, merchants in the South began to feel the harsh consequences of the new imposts. The new schedule of tariffs, designed to be rejected in hopes of electing a President from Tennessee but adopted by political accident, was exceedingly unjust to the Southern States. The people had been cheated by disloyal politicians, the country had been betrayed, and, although the great mass of ordinary folks still brimmed in happiness, many began to appreciate the enormity of what had happened in the selling of "Old Hickory" to the American people. The General Assembly of South

Carolina passed a set of eight resolutions on December 19, 1828, protesting the Act of Congress passed on May 19, 1828, as an unconstitutional abuse of the power of laying and collecting taxes, duties, imposts, and excises.[28]

These South Carolina Resolutions of 1828 were of exactly the same order as the Virginia Resolutions of 1798. They were an act of interposition, the precursor to nullification, — a political suggestion that the constitutional mechanisms of the Union had failed to work properly, and that, unless the situation should improve within a reasonable time, the crisis would demand the attention of the People of the State in Convention. In his Report on the Virginia Resolutions of 1798, James Madison explained the legal meaning of such legislative resolves. "The declarations in such cases," he said, "are expressions of opinion, unaccompanied with any other effect than what they may produce on opinion, by exciting reflection."[29]

The South Carolina Resolutions of 1828 protested the "tariff of abominations" on the basis of two principles:

It was declared that Congress could regulate commerce but not production, and that, therefore, Congress had no authority to impose a tax upon any object where the primary purpose was to regulate manufacturing or agriculture.[30] Jefferson would have agreed. Hamilton would have disagreed.

It was also declared that the tariff enacted in 1828 was unconstitutional, because it was not passed to promote the common defense and general welfare, or to establish justice and ensure domestic tranquillity, as required by the Preamble of the United States Constitution. Accordingly, the South Carolina Resolutions of 1828 said, "Even admitting Congress to have a constitutional right to protect manufactures by the imposition of duties, or by regulations of commerce, designed principally for that purpose, yet a tariff of which the operation is grossly unequal and oppressive is such an abuse of power as is incompatible with the principles of a free government."

The tariff of 1828 so vastly reduced the buying power of South Carolina, the resolutions said, that "the fate of this fertile State will be poverty and utter desolation." The economic effects of the tariff of 1828 were immediate and devastating.

Moreover, this broader constitutional objection, as just as anything ever pronounced in favor of the American Revolution, could not be judicially remedied. No judicial standards existed to measure the complaint. This breach of fundamental law was portentous in its dimensions, and had to be remedied by extrajudicial means and extraordinary processes. It was, in short, a case of nullification exactly as had been threatened by the Kentucky Resolutions of 1799. Still, there could be no nullification unless the legislature of the State should call a public election of delegates for the express purpose of speaking with sovereign authority as the People of South Carolina in Convention. And the time for such a large step was still unripe when Jackson was sworn in as President.

* * * * *

The angry simmering over the "tariff of abominations" continued, without overt action one way or another, until Senator Samuel Foote of Connecticut proposed a resolution on December 29, 1829, in the United States Senate: — "Resolved, That the Committee on Public Lands be instructed to inquire into the expediency of limiting for a certain period the sales of public lands only as have heretofore been offered for sale, and are subject to entry at a minimum price. And also whether the Office of Surveyor General may not be abolished without detriment to the public interest."[31]

Senator Thomas Benton of Missouri charged that Foote's Resolution was intended by New England to inhibit settlement in the West. His statement caused a political explosion. There had been fears in New England over some years that the South might expand into the West and form a new combination of States which would dominate the Union. At the same time, the South feared that New England might use the Union to prevent expansion into the West, and to prevent repeal of unjust impositions on commerce.

Senator Robert Hayne of South Carolina leaped to his feet on January 19, 1830, likewise inveighing against Foote's Resolution. During his allocution, the question of public lands gave way to ill-feelings of the South against the North over the tariff of 1828. Because the South had been oppressed by Congress so as to benefit the North, nullification as taught by Jefferson and Madison in 1798 and 1799 became attractive to Hayne in 1830. Hayne let fly with a brilliant salvo:

> "If I could, by a mere act of my will, put at the disposal of the Federal Government any amount of treasure which I might think proper to name, I should limit the amount to the means necessary for the legitimate purposes of the Government. Sir, an immense national treasury would be a fund for corruption. It would enable Congress and the Executive to exercise control over the States, as well as over great interests in the country, nay, even over corporations and individuals — utterly destructive of their purity, and fatal to the duration of our institutions. It would be equally fatal to the sovereignty and independence of the States. Sir, I am one of those who believe that the very life of our system is the independence of the States, and that there is no evil more to be deprecated than the consolidation of this Government."[32]

This challenge struck a disagreeable note in the ears of New England, which depended on the Union for its protective tariffs. Never mind that, when the South and the West abused the power of the Union in starting the War of 1812, the North was the bastion of States' Rights. Daniel Webster, the greatest lawyer of the age, had by then become Senator from Massachusetts. He rose on January 20, 1820, and protested,

"I wish to see no new powers drawn to the General Government, but I confess I rejoice in whatever tends to strengthen the bond that unites us, and encourages the hope that our Union may be perpetual. And, therefore, I cannot but feel regret at the expression of the opinions as the gentleman has avowed; because I think their obvious tendency is to weaken the bond of our connection. I know that there are some persons in the part of the country from which the honorable member comes, who habitually speak of the Union in terms of indifference, or even of disparagement. The honorable member himself is not, I trust, and cannot ever be one of these."[33]

Thereupon Foote's Resolution was virtually forgotten, and the Senate became the forum for an exchange between Hayne and Webster, justly celebrated in American oratory. The passionate subject was States' Rights and the Union.

Hayne spoke on January 25, 1830. Webster's reply to Hayne was delivered on January 26 and 27, 1830. Rejoinder and surrejoinder were delivered on January 27, 1830.

Hayne brought up the Hartford Convention during the War of 1812. He pointedly asked how, in light of the history of this meeting, New England could denounce the cause of States' Rights. Webster answered,

"Supposing, as the gentleman seems to do, that the Hartford Convention assembled for any such purpose as breaking up the Union, because they thought unconstitutional laws had been passed, or to consult on that subject, or to calculate the value of the Union, — supposing this to be their purpose, or any part of it, then I say the meeting itself was disloyal, and was obnoxious to censure, whether held in time of peace or time of war, or under whatever circumstances. The material question is the object. Was dissolution the object? If it was, external circumstances may make it a more or less aggravated case, but cannot affect the principle. I do not hold, therefore, that the Hartford Convention was pardonable even to the extent of the gentleman's admission, if its object was really such as has been imputed to it. Sir, there never was a time, under any degree of excitement, in which the Hartford Convention, or any other convention, could have maintained itself one moment in New England, if assembled for any such purpose as the gentleman says would have been an allowable purpose. To hold conventions to decide constitutional law! To try the binding validity of statutes by votes in a convention! Sir, the Hartford Convention, I presume, would not desire that the honorable gentleman should be their defender or advocate, if he puts their case upon such untenable and extravagant grounds."[34]

It is an undeniable fact of history, as the records of the meeting show, that the Hartford Convention assembled to consider breaking up the Union, no less than the First Continental Congress met to ponder secession from the British Empire. The delegates consulted on the subject, and calculated the value of the Union. These great Americans in fact contemplated dissolution of the Union. And, far from being disloyal, they were justified in doing so. If the President of the United States had not recognized his personal error in leading the country into the War of 1812, then begged for the pardon of God, and promptly concluded peace with Great Britain, as he literally did, the Hartford Convention would have been morally right, politically wise, and legally correct in recommending that the several States of New England ought to secede from the Union.

In those days, the Hartford Convention declared a conscription bill unconstitutional, and Congressman Daniel Webster did likewise. It was because of these declarations of fundamental law that Americans at the time of the War of 1812 were spared the despotism of conscripted armies to support an invasion of Canada.

But in the United States Senate on January 26, 1830, Daniel Webster either never knew or conveniently forgot the inestimable heritage of the Hartford Convention.

It so happens that the manufacturers in New England had assumed that the Union must be wonderful, because protective tariffs were making them rich. Naturally, the entrepreneurs of Massachusetts rather expected Webster to speak up for them. Why, therefore, should anyone be astonished to find that, at this time in his career, Daniel Webster was a high priest of national consolidation, as if he had never heard of the Hartford Convention? The Union was not only useful, but holy! He concluded his reply to Hayne,

"When my eyes shall be turned to behold for the last time the sun in heaven, may I not see him shining on the broken and dishonored fragments of a once glorious Union, — on States dissevered, discordant, and belligerent, — on a land rent with civil feuds, or drenched, it may be, with fraternal blood! Let their last feeble and lingering glance rather behold the gorgeous ensign of the republic, now known and honored throughout the earth, still full high advanced, its arms and trophies streaming in their original lustre, not a stripe erased or polluted, nor a single star obscured — bearing for its motto, no much miserable interrogatory as 'What is all this worth?' Nor those other words of delusion and folly, 'Liberty first and Union afterwards' — but everywhere, spreading all over in characters of living light, blazing on all its ample folds, as they float over the sea and over the land, and in every wind, under the whole heaven, that other sentiment, dear to every true American heart — 'Liberty and Union, now and forever, one and inseparable!'"[35]

During his rejoinder on January 27, 1830, Hayne probed the surface of his antagonist's contention, then exposed the inner error:

"Sir, I will put the case home to the gentleman. Is there any violation of the constitutional rights of the States, and the liberties of citizens, which, if sanctioned by Congress and the Supreme Court, he would believe to be the right and duty of a State to resist? Does he contend for the doctrine of passive obedience and non-resistance? Would he justify an open resistance to an act of Congress, sanctioned by the courts, which would abolish trial by jury, or destroy freedom of religion, or freedom of the press? Yes, sir, he would advocate resistance in such case, and so would I, and so would all of us. But such resistance would, according to his doctrine, be revolution: it would be rebellion. According to my opinion, it would be just, legal, and constitutional resistance."[36]

The time had arrived to repair the damage, to grant Daniel Webster his wish that the gorgeous ensign would have not have a stripe erased or a star obscured. Instead, an Act of July 14, 1832, made things worse by removing or reducing some of the duties which were regarded with displeasure by manufacturing and commercial interests of the North, but leaving mostly unrepealed those duties which were oppressive to the South.

* * * * *

The political antics of Andrew Jackson served as distractions from the issue of tariffs which was understood in South Carolina, but not so well in other parts of the Union. And so Old Hickory was elected once again on December 5, 1832.

In South Carolina, the passage of the Act of July 14, 1832, was like a spur in the side of a horse. Governor James Hamilton called a special session of the legislature, which met on October 22, 1832. An election was called for a convention of the people, which met on November 19, 1832. It was here for the first time in forty-four years that there had been an assembly of the sovereign power of South Carolina. It was this convention alone which was preeminent, perfect, perpetual, and omnipotent, and which, therefore, was competent to nullify acts of Congress, or cause the State to secede from the Union. An ordinance of nullification was passed on November 24, 1832.[37] The ordinance recited the grievance of sectional abuse in laying tariffs by Congress, and then stated,

> "We, therefore, the People of the State of South Carolina, in Convention assembled, do declare and ordain, and it is hereby declared and ordained, that the several acts and parts of acts of the Congress of the United States, purporting to be laws for the imposing of duties and imposts on the importation of foreign commodities, and now having actual operation and effect within the United States, and more especially an act entitled 'an act in alteration of the several acts imposing duties on imposts,' approved on the nineteenth day of May, one thousand eight hundred and twenty-eight, and also an act entitled 'an act to alter and amend the several acts imposing duties on imports,' approved on the fourteenth day of July, one thousand eight hundred and thirty-two, are unauthorized by the Constitution of the United States, and violate the true meaning and intent thereof, and are null, void, and no law, nor binding upon this State, its officers or citizens; and all promises, contracts, and obligations made or entered into, or to be made or entered into with the purpose to secure the duties imposed by the said acts, and all judicial proceedings which shall hereafter be had in affirmance thereof, are and shall be held utterly null and void."

The ordinance directed the legislature of the State to enact statutes of implementation, to forbid any appeals from courts of the State to the supreme court of the Union in any causes wherein its validity or effect was drawn into question, to require support by oaths all officers of the government of the State, then warned that any legislation or force attempted by the Federal government to compel obedience would be considered as cause for secession of the South Carolina from the United States. The general assembly of the State passed laws to enforce the ordinance and prepare the militia.

The events leading up to this resurgence of sovereign power had stretched out over four years. Grave economic injury was felt, and no remedy was forthcoming. In order to terminate the affront, resort was had to a venerable procedure which interrupted the turbulence of politics as usual, and allowed the highest voice of society to speak with unanswerable majesty.

Andrew Jackson often posed as a disciple of Thomas Jefferson, but the deception in this stance was about to appear. The South Carolina Convention of 1832 and 1833 had followed the precise doctrine laid down by Jefferson himself in the Kentucky Resolutions of 1798 and 1799. The legal form and dignity of the ordinance of November 24, 1832, were impeccable. But by way of answer Jackson issued his proclamation to the people of South Carolina on December 10, 1832,[38] in which he systematically caricatured and misrepresented the facts of history, the provisions of the constitution, the proceedings of the convention, and the nature of the ordinance. Thus spoke the man from Tennessee:

"This ordinance is not founded on the indefeasible right of resisting acts which are plainly unconstitutional." But the tariffs of 1828 and 1832 were acts contravening the highest law of the land, and most injurious, having originated in a factious engineering of Jackson's election as President.

Jackson continued with political fiction: "We declared ourselves a nation by a joint act, not by several acts." But secession from the British Empire ordained thirteen "free and independent States," each of which had authorized Congress to speak, and several of them had previously seceded on their own authority. After the revolution, the British Crown conceded the existence of thirteen "free, sovereign, and independent States."

Attempting to buttress his untenable premise, Jackson said, "The States severally have not retained their entire sovereignty," which was the very reverse of the truth, because only conventions of the people in the several States retained sovereign attributes properly so called, nor did they mingle these attributes in one convention of the people for the whole nation, nor did they surrender these attributes to the republican governments which they set up, least of all to the government of the Union.

Jackson then sought to justify the intimidation which he was about to articulate: "The laws of the United States must be executed. I have no discretionary power on the subject. My duty is emphatically pronounced in the Constitution." He was not quite so pious about the rule of law when he refused to honor treaties of the United States with the Cherokee Nation to aid the lawlessness of his partisans in Georgia.[39]

"Be not deceived by names," Jackson warned, "Disunion by armed force is treason. Are you ready to incur its guilt?" Secession from the United States was not only lawful, but peaceable, as much so as the accession of William and Mary in England and the withdrawal of Rhode Island from the British Empire. It was Jackson who threatened use of armed force. The sovereign power had spoken with finality, but there was no armed rebellion in South Carolina.

Finally, the President set up and knocked down a straw man, because he could not honestly address the real grievance of South Carolina. "These are the alternatives that are presented by the convention: repeal of all the acts for raising revenue, leaving the government without means of support, — or an acquiescence in the dissolution of the Union by the secession of its members." Jackson knew that South Carolina did not demand repeal of all acts for raising revenue. He knew that South Carolina was anxious to supply the Union with sufficient funds to pay all expenses of the Federal government. And he knew that, over four years, South Carolina had sought reforms which were urgently necessary for the well-being, not only of the South, but of the Union.

So went Jackson's plea to the gallery. The General Assembly of South Carolina answered on December 20, 1832:

> "Resolved, That each State of the Union has the right, whenever it may deem such a course necessary for the preservation of its liberties or vital interests, to secede peaceably from the Union, and that there is no constitutional power in the general government, much less in the executive department of that government, to retain by force such State in the Union. . .

> "Resolved, That, while this legislature has witnessed with sorrow such a relaxation of the spirit of our institutions that a President of the United States dare venture upon this high handed measure, it regards with indignation the menaces which are directed against it, and the concentration of a standing army on our borders. The State will repel force with force, and, relying upon the blessings of God, will maintain our liberty at all hazards."[40]

The magnificent Union of States, which had been so carefully designed by master architects in the city of brotherly love, was on the brink of a civil war in less than five decades. Where did the fault for this pending calamity lay?

The simplistic view says that the source of trouble was the dangerous belief in the right of a State to resist the will of the Union. This view says the solution must be deployment of overwhelming military power in the Union.

When the historical facts are seen in the right light, it is clear enough why civil war threatened the United States at the end of 1832. The reason is that a bloated and torpid idea of national consolidation had become, fortunately not universal, but most respectable, and, what is as bad or worse, very presidential.

It is first necessary to understand the maximum price of avoiding civil war in such a situation. In the 16th Federalist, Alexander Hamilton philosophically observed,

> "And as to those mortal feuds which in certain conjunctures spread a conflagration through a whole nation, or through a very large part of it, proceeding from weighty causes of discontent given by the government or from the contagion of some violent popular paroxysm, they do not fall with the ordinary rules of calculation. When they happen, they commonly amount to revolutions and dismemberments of empire. No form of government can always either avoid or control them. It is in vain to hope to guard against events too much for human foresight or precaution, and it would be idle to object to a government because it could not perform impossibilities."[41]

The framers of the United States Constitution knew that empires were prone to disintegrate, that it was not necessarily a tragedy if a confederacy should fall apart, and that events of this kind have been common and unavoidable fare in history. And certainly they believed it was better that two peoples should go their separate ways in peace than that the stronger should subdue the weaker in war. The glue designed to hold the Union together was no mysterious substance, — it was nothing more than the enjoyment of prosperity, safety, life, liberty, and happiness, under the protection of a common shield, coordinated by wise statesmen, and promoting friendship among distinct societies inhabiting the face of a continent. It was a regrettable and harsh necessity which prompted the nullification and threatened secession voiced by the people of South Carolina at the end of 1832. It was most fortunate that the problem of Federal taxes on commerce had a relatively easy solution, and that there were great leaders in the United States Senate.

The presiding officer was still John Calhoun of South Carolina, whose speech in Congress sixteen years before proved that he was no enemy of a sensible regime of protective tariffs. When John Quincy Adams was defeated for reelection as President in late 1828, so high was his standing throughout the Union that Calhoun was nevertheless reelected as Vice President. Yet not long after the inauguration in early 1829, Calhoun came to see through the man from Tennessee. He bided his time. From the presiding chair in the Senate, Calhoun heard the words of Hayne and Webster in early 1830. By the time of the nullification crisis in late 1832, Calhoun and Jackson no longer spoke.

Calhoun was elected as Senator from South Carolina on December 12, 1832, and on December 28, 1832, he resigned as Vice President and took his place to defend his native State in the United States Senate. Jackson sent a message to Congress on January 16, 1833, asking for authorization to use the military power of the Union against South Carolina.

As the "hero" of New Orleans brooded in the White House over his force bill, Senator Henry Clay of Kentucky formulated a new tariff bill which was introduced in Congress on February 12, 1833, providing for gradual reduction over the next ten years of all imports down to levels calculated to raise revenues sufficient to satisfy the fiscal wants of the Union. The bill was designed to give interim protection, but at gently decreasing rates, and then to eliminate the policy protective tariffs altogether unless a revised and constructive understanding should be reached in the future. The structure of this legislation was acceptable to the new Senator from South Carolina.

While a fierce contest was underway between those who desired to use military means to reduce a protesting State, and those who desired to restore harmony to the Union, Daniel Webster and John Calhoun clashed in the United States Senate. It was another great debate in American history. As it was splendid in rhetoric, it was timeless in law.

Calhoun offered a set of resolutions in the Senate on January 22, 1833, of which the first two read,

> "Resolved, That the people of the several States, composing these United States, are united as parties to a constitutional compact, to which the people of each State acceded as a separate sovereign community, each binding itself by its own particular ratification, and that the Union, of which the said compact is the bond, is between the States ratifying the same; and

> "Resolved, That the people of the several States, thus united by the constitutional compact, in forming that instrument, and in creating a general government to carry into effect the objects for which they were formed, delegated to that government, for that purpose, certain definite powers, to be exercised jointly, reserving, at the same time, each State to itself, the residuary mass of powers to be exercised by it own separate government; and that, whenever the general government assumes the exercise of powers not delegated by the compact, its acts are unauthorized, and are of no effect; and that the same government is not made the final judge of the powers delegated to it, since that would make its discretion, and not the constitution, the measure of its powers; but that, as in all other cases of compact among sovereign parties, without any common judge, each has an equal right to judge for itself, as well of the infraction as of the mode and measure of redress."[42]

Here laid out was classical Jeffersonian theory in the Kentucky Resolutions of 1798 and 1799, which gave legitimacy to the ordinance of nullification passed by the South Carolina Convention on November 24, 1832. In the sense of these resolutions, a State was to be understood as the people thereof in convention, being its sovereign power.

It is in respect to sovereignty, consisting of the power to make and unmake constitutions and governments, as distinguished from the distribution of the powers of regular governance from day to day, that the Union was built to rest entirely upon a constitutional compact between the several States, that the several States had the right to adjudge infractions of fundamental law by the Union, and that the several States were not subject to the authority of the legislative, executive, or judicial power of the Union.

It was not the legislatures of the several States which had a right to nullify acts of, and secede from the Union. The public corporations and public officers of the republican governments in the several States were in substantial degree subject to the legislative, judicial, and executive power of the Union.

Be it so, yet the people in convention in and of each of the several States remained ever sovereign, and, therefore, could not be commanded by the Federal government or any department thereof on any pretext whatever. This Federal government was only a public corporation with a republican form of government, a mere creature of the sovereign powers of the several States. The Federal government embodied and had power over the Union, but was a mere instrument of the people in each of the several States. And such was John Calhoun's message to the President of the United States. Daniel Webster answered in the Senate on February 16, 1833:

> "The constitution does not provide for events which must be preceded by its own destruction. Secession, therefore, since it must bring these consequences with it, is revolutionary, and nullification is equally revolutionary. What is revolution? Why, sir, that is revolution which overturns or controls or successfully resists the existing public authority, that which arrests the exercise of the supreme power, that which introduces a new paramount authority."[43]

The Senator from Massachusetts was awakening to the meaning of events. The constitution of England certainly provided for revolution, and the principles were put into action in 1688 and 1689 when James II was pushed off the throne, and as William and Mary were invited to sit upon it. Yes, the occasion was revolutionary, and it was also lawful, peaceable, bloodless, orderly, necessary, beneficial, and glorious.

And likewise the United States Constitution, as it was given to posterity by its framers, certainly provided for such revolution, taking the forms of nullification and secession. The underlying principles were put into action in 1832 and 1833, as Calhoun and Clay restored proper order to the Union.

Meanwhile, in the Senate, Webster answered Calhoun with his own thesis:

> "1. That the constitution is not a league, confederacy, or compact, between the people of the several States in their sovereign capacities, but a government proper, founded on the adoption of the people, and creating direct relations between itself and individuals.

> "2. That no State authority has power to dissolve these relations; that nothing can dissolve them but revolution; and that, consequently, there can be no such thing as secession without revolution.

> "3. That there is a supreme law, consisting of one constitution of the United States, and acts of Congress, passed in pursuance of it, and treaties; and that, in cases not capable of assuming the character of a suit in law or equity, Congress must judge of, and finally interpret the supreme law, so often as it has occasion to pass acts of legislation; and, in cases capable of assuming and actually assuming the character of a suit, the supreme court of the United States is the final interpreter.

> "4. That an attempt by a State to abrogate, annul, or nullify an act of Congress, or to arrest its operation within her limits, on the ground that, in her opinion, such law is unconstitutional, is a direct usurpation on the just powers of the general government, and on the equal rights of other States, a plain violation of the constitution, and a proceeding essentially revolutionary in its character and tendency."[44]

Webster stipulated that the whole dispute, with its many minute ramifications, reduced in the end to but one question: — whether, as his adversary maintained, the constitution of the Union was a compact between the peoples of the several States, each acting in her sovereign capacity, and retaining her sovereign attributes, or, on the other hand, as he maintained, an irrevocable charter of permanent government for a single and unified whole consisting of one people of the United States and considered as an indivisible Nation. Calhoun agreed that the whole debate revolved around this sole issue.

Webster stipulated that the constitution of the Union was ratified by conventions of the people in the several States, the same as the constitution in each State was framed by a convention of the people such State in convention. He had no choice but to acknowledge this much, for this fact is not only known to everyone who has personally studied the details, but is expressly announced in Article VII of the United States Constitution.

Webster then grounded and rested his entire case by saying, "The constitution, sir, is not a contract, but the result of a contract." He went on to explain,

> "We say habitually that one house proposes a bill, and the other agrees to it, but the result of this agreement is not a compact but a law. The law, the statute, is not the agreement, but something created by the agreement, — something which, when created, has a new character, and acts by its own authority. So the constitution of the United States, founded in or on the consent of the people, may be said to rest on compact or consent, even if it is not itself the compact, but its result. When the people agree to erect a government, and actually erect it, the thing is done, and the agreement is at an end. The compact is executed, and the end designated by it attained. Henceforth, the fruit of the agreement exists, but the agreement itself is merged in its own accomplishment. There can be no longer a subsisting agreement or compact to form a constitution or government, after that constitution or government has been actually formed or established."[45]

If this notion held for the Union, it held even more for every State. Webster's principle was that the people gave their assent, whereupon the government delineated in the constitution was established: the agreement was consummated and merged into the resulting work of fundamental law, which continued thereafter, and could not be changed save as expressly provided in clauses for working amendments, nor could it be dissolved except by extralegal means. On this theory Webster's whole case against South Carolina was founded. Was his principle an authentic portrait of the republican ideals of the American Revolution?

Rather than retrace again the whole tedious course of constitutional formation in the early days of the United States, or review any part of the many historical facts and legal authorities which were diligently canvassed by Calhoun in his reply, it is sufficient to look at the seventh article in the first part of the Massachusetts Constitution as adopted on October 25, 1780, where it was ordained by the sovereign power of Webster's own State, that "the people alone have an incontestable, unalienable, and indefeasible right to institute government, and to reform, alter, or totally change the same when their protection, safety, prosperity, and happiness require it." And so also, in adopting the third article of their Bill of Rights on June 12, 1776, the sovereign power of Virginia said that the people have "an indubitable, unalienable, and indefeasible right to reform, alter, or abolish" their government "in such manner as shall be most conducive to the public weal." Such phrasing has always been as American as the 4th of July.

The people of Massachusetts retained their attributes of sovereignty, never alienated them to any government on earth, and nearly exercised their omnipotence in 1815 in exactly the same way the people of South Carolina had used their supreme authority in 1832. The Union was created by a compact made by the sovereign powers of the several States, And each of those sovereign powers retained the means to unmake the Union for good cause, as they had used their authority to make the Union for good cause.

Webster's house, therefore, was built on a foundation of sand. But he had one exceedingly powerful argument. Suppose in abstract theory that Jefferson and Calhoun were technically right. Would not their theory be hopelessly impractical? Webster drove home this point like a general throwing an attack and rolling up the flank of the enemy:

> "Nullification, if successful, arrests the power of the law, absolves citizens from their duty, subverts the foundation of both protection and obedience, dispenses with oaths and obligations of allegiance, and elevates another authority to supreme command. Is not this revolution? And it raises to supreme command four and twenty distinct powers, each professing to be under a general government yet each setting its law at defiance at pleasure. Is not this anarchy as well as revolution? Sir, the constitution of the United States was received as a whole, and for the whole country. If it cannot stand together, it cannot stand in parts; and, if the laws cannot be executed everywhere, they cannot be executed anywhere. The gentleman very well knows that all duties and imposts must be uniform throughout the country. He knows that we cannot have one rule or one law for South Carolina, and another for other States. He must see, therefore, and does see, and every man sees that the only alternative is a repeal of the laws throughout the whole Union, or their execution in South Carolina as well as everywhere. And this repeal is demanded because a single State interposes her veto, and threatens her resistance!"[46]

Webster thus painted a picture of inane debility in the government of the Union, if nullification were deemed reserved to the several States. But his thinking did not calculate the grievous extremity of agitation which must exist before it should be politically possible even to contemplate, much less to form, through a special election on call by the legislature of a State a convention of the people, including enough delegates who would actually vote for an ordinance of nullification. Such an event may hardly ever be anticipated in a well-run confederacy.

The temptations of ambition are considerable, and those temptations, if allowed to run wild without fear of reprisal, are likely to produce the warped laws and policies which nullification was designed to address. Such ambitions caused the tariff of abominations in 1828, made worse in 1832. And, if the real possibility of nullification had then been remembered as a lawful response for corruption and usurpation in the Federal government, there never would have been such sectional abuse of protective imposts, nor would there ever have been a need to call the people of South Carolina in convention in 1832.

But now suppose that the attempt of South Carolina to nullify the tariff of abominations should not have induced the repeal thereof by Congress. Would there be, as Webster proposed, one rule for South Carolina and another rule for the other twenty-three States then within the Union? No, not at all, because then South Carolina would have seceded from the United States. The primary legal sanction for nullification was thought to be secession, as was plainly stated in the ordinance of the South Carolina Convention on November 24, 1832.

It was supposed from the beginning of the new Union that secession was constitutionally secure, and, therefore, would not produce a civil war. Indeed, well-directed reflection will reveal that, in a properly built system such as the American framers set up, such a separation may fairly be supposed to have a contrary and sanguine effect, for events of this kind, when consummated, must surely induce sobriety of thought which, as all experience shows, encourages reconciliation, since Union enhances capacity for survival, and survival is among the strongest of all drives in human nature.

Why, then, were nullification and secession, as inherent in the work of the Philadelphia Convention, not destabilizing? The answer to this quandary is simply that there were too many heavy counterweights built into the system set up by the founding fathers of the United States.

Answering Webster on February 26, 1833, Calhoun noted the objection that, if the will of the Union did not prevail, "the peace of the country should be destroyed." He asked, "But what if it should prevail? Would there be peace? Yes," he answered, "the peace of despotism: that peace which is enforced by the bayonet and the sword, the peace of death, where all vital functions of liberty have ceased." But he went on to say, "For my part, I have no fear of any dangerous conflict, under the fullest acknowledgment of state sovereignty: the very fact that the States may interpose will produce moderation and justice." He added, "Moderation and justice will produce confidence, attachment, and patriotism; and these, in turn, will offer most powerful barriers against the excess of conflicts between the States and the Union."[47]

Calhoun then noted the "objection that the doctrine" of nullification "will be a source of weakness." He answered,

> "If we look to mere organization and physical power as the only source of strength, without taking into the estimate the operation of moral causes, such would appear to be the fact; but, if we take into the estimate the latter, we shall find that those governments have the greatest strength in which power has been most efficiently checked. The government of Rome furnishes a memorable example. There, two independent and distinct powers existed, — the people acting by tribes, in which the plebeians prevailed, and by centuries, in which the patricians ruled. The tribunes were the appointed representatives of the one power, and the senate of the other; each possessed of the authority of checking and overruling one another, not as departments of the government, as supposed by the Senator from Massachusetts, but as independent powers, — as much so as the state and general governments of this country. A shallow observer would perceive, in such an organization, nothing but the perpetual source of anarchy, discord, and weakness; and yet experience has proved that it was the most powerful government that ever existed. This power was derived from the very circumstances which hasty reflection would consider the cause of weakness."[48]

Calhoun proceeded to deliver his crushing blow:

> "I am not surprised that, with the idea of a perfect government which the Senator from Massachusetts has formed, a government of an absolute majority, unchecked and unrestrained, operating through a representative body, he should be so much shocked with what he is pleased to call the absurdity of the state veto. But let me tell him that his scheme of a perfect government, as beautiful as he conceives it to be, though often tried, has invariably failed, — has always run, whenever tried, through the same uniform process of faction, corruption, anarchy, and despotism. He considers the representative principle as the great modern improvement in legislation, and of itself sufficient to secure liberty. I cannot regard it in the light he does. Instead of modern, it is of remote origin, and has existed, in greater or lesser perfection, in every free state, from the remotest antiquity. Nor do I consider it as of itself sufficient to secure liberty, though I regard it as one of the indispensable means, — the means of securing the people against the tyranny and oppression of their rulers. To secure liberty, another means is still

necessary, — the means of securing the different portions of society against the injustice and oppressions of each other, which can only be effected by veto, interposition, or nullification, or by whatever name the restraining or negative power of government may be called."[49]

Well, then, was this sterling performance of oratory in the face of the amassed wealth and power of the Union unavailing? Let the facts of the matter be consulted.

The new tariff bill passed the House on February 26, 1833 and the Senate on March 1, 1833. This bill was meant and understood as an effective repealer of that which had been declared unconstitutional by the people of South Carolina. The force bill, it is true, passed the Senate on February 20, 1833, and the House on March 1, 1833, and would have given Jackson a chance to use his sword. But, with a new schedule of imposts, there was no longer a tariff of abominations to enforce. The two bills were placed on the presidential desk at the same time. Grudgingly, Jackson signed both bills on March 2, 1833. His second inauguration was only two days away. It was no time for marching off to war.

The People of South Carolina in Convention resumed their business on March 11, 1833. An ordinance was passed on March 15,1833, reciting the new tariff law, and repeal of the obnoxious acts, then repealed the ordinance of nullification.[50] And another ordinance was passed on March 18,1833, reciting the force bill, and, even though it was a law with nothing to enforce, the convention adopted an ordinance nullifying the act.[51] Thereupon, the proud convention adjourned. The Union waxed strong. And, in due course, with the aid of the South, a more moderate and balanced system of protective tariffs was enacted by Congress.

As a study of human character, it is interesting to observe the reactions of personalities in the drama during its aftermath. August Fitch, one of the President's men, wrote from Columbia, on March 16,1833, informing Jackson of the repeal of the nullification against the tariff of abominations. Old Hickory got out his pen and scribbled across the bottom of Fitche's letter, not a description of others as he thought, but a gauge by which history might judge the calibre of his own mind: — "The ordinance and all law under it repealed. So ends the wicked and disgraceful conduct of Calhoun, McDuffie, and their co-nullies. They will only be held up to scorn by everyone who loves freedom, our glorious constitution, and government of laws."[52]

As one might expect, Webster and Calhoun long served in the public life of the Union. They were ever on cordial terms. They held each other in highest respect. It so happens that, on December 28, 1837, Calhoun introduced, and on January 3, 1838, the Senate passed a resolution which proclaimed, "That, in the adoption of the Federal Constitution, the States adopting the same acted severally as free, sovereign, and independent States,"[53] — from whence it follows, if due attention is paid to the full meaning of this premise, that everything Calhoun said in reply to Webster on February 26, 1833, was correct.

It is no surprise that the Senator from Massachusetts did not vote for this resolution, but some years later Congressman Alexander Stephens of Georgia said of him, "One of the highest exhibitions of moral sublime the world ever witnessed was that of Daniel Webster."[54] Which shows how well he was regarded by the South.

NOTES

CHAPTER V

1 - This age of five virtuous emperors (98-180 A. D.) is described in 1 Gibbon's Rome 91-96 (Chapter III).

2 - The story of this bright light in an age of feebleness and decadence (457-461 A. D.) is described in 3 Gibbon's Rome 473-483 (Chapter XXXVI).

3 - The reign of this great prince (1118-1143 A. D.) is described in 4 Gibbon's Rome 620-622 (Chapter XLVIII).

4 - 51st Federalist, Mentor Edition at 322.

5 - E. g., James Madison plainly declared his opinion that Congress had no constitutional authority to incorporate a Federal bank, as appears in 4 Elliot's Debates 412-413 and 417-418, 3 Ferrand's Records 362 (United States House of Representatives, February 2, 1791). Elbridge Gerry made an elaborate argument in support of such power, as appears in 4 Elliot's Debates 419-422, 3 Ferrand's Records 362-363 (United States House of Representatives, February 7, 1791).

6 - The eighteenth clause of Article I, Section 8 of the United States Constitution contains the broad language that Congress has power to enact laws "necessary and proper" for carrying into the execution the other powers vested in the government of the Union. The proceedings in the Philadelphia Convention on the framing of this clause were routine and uneventful, as appears in 5 Elliot's Debates 379, 447, 536, 561, — Tansill's Documents 476, 575, 707, — 2 Ferrand's Records 182, 345, 570, 596, 656 (Madison's Notes, August 6 and 20, September 10, 12, and 17, 1787). Alexander Hamilton commented on this clause in the 33rd Federalist, Mentor Edition 201-204, as did James Madison in the 44th Federalist, Mentor Edition 283-286. Their views were very similar and to the effect that the clause was adopted to remove false pretexts for denying essential powers of the Union by adopting expressly the rule of common law, otherwise implied, that the grant of a power automatically included the discretion to adopt means necessary and proper for carrying such power into execution, — i. e., reasonable means,

consistent in principle with some lawful end, not prohibited, and in keeping with legal tradition. Toward the end of the convention, Benjamin Franklin suggested that Congress be granted a power to provide for the cutting canals as needed. James Madison sought to enlarge the motion, so that Congress should be allowed a general power of granting charters of incorporation whenever the interests of the United States might require. Rufus King argued that the power to charter was "unnecessary." King evidently meant only that there was no need to make such a power express, because an implied power already existed. It so appears in light of events happening on the same day, very shortly after King spoke. A motion was made to confer upon Congress an express power to establish a university, which would have included authority to incorporate the institution. But this proposition was rejected, likewise as "unnecessary," since, as stated on the floor of the convention, Congress would have an exclusive and comprehensive power over the seat of the new Federal government where a university would be set up. King stated that an express power to establish corporations might excite premature political contention over a Federal bank, as between, say, the cities of New York and Philadelphia. After further debate, Franklin's motion on canals was defeated for reasons not clear, and Madison's attempted enlargement automatically went down with it These proceedings appear in 5 Elliot's Debates 543-544, — Tansill's Documents 724-725, 2 Ferrand's Records 615-616 (Madison's Notes, September 14, 1787).

7 - 4 Elliot's Debates 609-611, 3 Ferrand's Records 363 (abridged), and 1 Commager's Documents 158-160.

8 - These effects were described with beautiful and timeless precision in a speech of John Calhoun in the United States Senate on October 3, 1837, as reprinted in Wilson's Calhoun at 255-256."Place the money power in the hands of a single individual or combination of individuals," he warned, "and by expanding or contracting the currency, they may raise or sink prices at pleasure; and by purchasing when at the greatest depression, and selling at the greatest elevation, [they] may command the whole property and industry of the community, and control its fiscal operations. The banking system concentrates and places this power in the hands of those who control it, and its force increases just in proportion as it dispenses with a metallic basis. Never was an engine invented, better calculated to place the destiny of the many in the hands of the few, or less favorable to that equality and independence which lie at the bottom of all free institutions." Cahoun thus further described the resulting injury from capricious fluxuations in the supply of currency by hidden and private interests: "None but those in the secret know what to do. All are pausing and looking out to ascertain whether an expansion or contraction is next to follow, and what will be its extent and duration; and if, perchance, an error be committed — if it expands when a contraction is expected, or the reverse —, the most prudent may lose by the miscalculation the fruits of a life of toil and care. The effects are to discourage industry, and to convert the whole

community into stockjobbers and speculators." And he amplified on the evil in saying, "I object to the banking system because it allots the honors and rewards to the community, in a very undue proportion, to a pursuit the least of all favorable to the development of the higher mental qualities, intellectual and moral, to the decay of the learned professions, and the more noble pursuits of science, literature, philosophy, and statesmanship, and the great and more useful pursuits of business and industry."

9 - 4 Elliot's Debates 617-620, 3 Ferrand's Records 363-364, 1 Commager's Documents 156-158 (all abridged), and Cooke's Reports 83-114 (complete version in the records of the Historical Society of Pennsylvania.)

10 - 3 Elliot's Debates at 54 (Virginia Convention, June 5, 1788).

11 - 30th Federalist, Mentor Edition 192-193.

12 - Cooke's Reports at 94-95 in answer to Jefferson's speculations (recorded in 4 Elliot's Debates at 610, 3 Ferrand's Records at 363, and 1 Commager's Documents at 160) on the defeat of the proposals by Franklin and Madison in the Philadelphia Convention on September 14, 1787.

13 - Hamilton's reference was to the rules set forth in 1 Blackstone's Commentaries 59-61, — that clauses are to be construed according to the ordinary meaning of words, except for terms of art which should be assigned their technical meaning; or by reference to context, subject matter, consequences, or historical purpose. Hamilton also had in mind certain other rules: — e. g., that an enumeration of exceptions or limitations implies and defines a power, as stated in the 32nd Federalist, Mentor Edition at 199-200; that clauses dealing with the same subject or question must be construed together so as to give each clause a distinct and useful meaning which is consistent with the others, and so all clauses under consideration will harmoniously serve the same general objective, as stated in the 40th Federalist, Mentor Edition at 248; and that the enumeration of specific powers excludes a general power, as stated in the 41st Federalist, Mentor Edition at 263, and in the 83rd Federalist, Mentor Edition at 497. These several rules, correctly applied, will yield the "intended meaning" of the United States Constitution.

14 - Reprinted in 1 U. S. Statutes at Large 191. The institution thereby incorporated came to be known as the "first" Bank of the United States.

15 - In his Opinion on the Bank, Jefferson advised Washington, "[Unless] the President's mind, on a view of everything which is used for and against this bill is tolerably clear that it is unauthorized by the Constitution, if the pro and con hang so even as to balance his judgment, a just respect for the wisdom of the legislature would naturally balance in favor of their opinion. It is chiefly for cases where they are clearly misled by error, ambition or interest that the Constitution has placed a check in the negative of the President." - 4 Elliot's Debates at 611,

1 Commager's Documents at 160. As President, Jefferson siged into law a bill authorizing the first Bank of the United States to open branches in the federal territories as appears in 2 U. S. Statutes at Large 274 (March 24, 1804). And as President, James Madison assented to the Act of April 16, 1816 which set up the second Bank of the United States. In a letter of June 25, 1831, to Charles Ingersoll, reprinted in 4 Elliot's Debates at 615-617, Madison explained his reason, which, simply put, was respect for the views of others.

16 - This attorney general was Roger B. Taney, who was rewarded by an appointment as Chief Justice of the United States. The veto message is reprinted in 1 Commager's Documents 269-274.

17 - These speeches were delivered on March 21, 1834, and October 3, 1837, and are reprinted in Wilson's Calhoun at 220-271.

18 - Hence, Lord Coke maintained in the third of his Institutes that the scope of the prohibition in the Statute of Monopolies, 21 James I, Chapter 3 (1624), should be ascertained from its preamble. The point is nicely covered in *United States v. E. C. Knight & Co.*, 156 U. S. 1 at 9-10 (1895).

19 - The definition of commerce as trade and the avenues and incidents of trade was set forth in Hamilton's Opinion on the Bank, Cooke's Reports at 98-99, especially as read in light of the 17th Federalist, Mentor Edition at 118, and the 22nd Federalist, Mentor Edition at 143-144. This comprehensive view of the power to regulate commerce, at least if it physically crossed the lines of two or more States, was adopted in the opinion of Chief Justice John Marshall inf *Gibbons v. Ogden*, 9 Wheaton 1 (U. S. 1824). But the power was surely intended to be even more sweeping in its reach, as is tolerably clear from the main stages in framing of the power to regulate commerce, especially in light of the sixth resolution of the report of the convention on July 26, 1787. The general purposes of the power to regulate commerce were to promote the general interests of the Union and the harmony of the United States, as appears in 5 Elliot's Debates 375, 378, 434, 536, 560, — Tansill's Documents 466, 475, 555, 706, — 2 Ferrand's Records 128, 182, 308, 569, 595, and 655 (July 26, August 6 and 16, September 10, 12, and 17, 1787). It was an important rule of the common law for ascertaining legislative will that ambiguity in the language of a statute or constitution may be clarified by the object to be accomplished, and given larger or narrower significance depending on the nature of the end sought to be accomplished. The principle was stated with particular lucidity in *Prigg v. Pennsylvania*, 16 Peters 539 at 610-611 (U. S. 1842). In this light, the power of Congress to regulate commerce "among the several States" was not necessarily limited to commerce physically crossing the lines of two or more States, but was meant to embrace commerce in all parts of the Union in need of regulation for the benefit of the whole country.

20 - Numerous instances can be found in the debates of framing or adopting the

United States Constitution in which a distinction was made between commerce on the one hand, and agriculture or manufacturing on the other, — e. g., in the 17th Federalist, Mentor Edition 118, where Alexander Hamilton distinguished between "commerce, finance, [and] negotiation" which, he thought, ought to be "lodged in the national depository" and "supervision of agriculture and of other concerns of a similar nature" which, he thought, were "proper to be provided for by local legislation,." — and in the proposal by Gouverneur Morris during the Philadelphia Convention for explicit constitutional recognition of one cabinet officer for "commerce" and another cabinet officer for "agriculture and manufacturing" as appears in 5 Elliot's Debates 446, Tansill's Documents 573, and 2 Ferrand's Records 343 (Madison's Notes, August 20, 1787). Likewise, in a speech on June 26, 1788, in the New York Convention, Melancton Smith spoke of "agriculture, commerce, and manufactuers" as three distinct activities, as appears in 2 Elliot's Debates 336-337. Such illustrations can be greatly multiplied.

21 - E. g., George Mason proposed that Congress should have a power to enact sumptuary laws, which he thought would be important in promoting domestic frugality and simplicity of manners. He thought that regulations of and excises upon commerce, which were within the power of Congress, might significantly limit undue consumption of luxuries, but he wanted to give Congress a direct power to regulate such consumption, which otherwise, as Mason and all present knew, was reserved to the several States. It was generally argued against Mason's motion that Congress would have sufficient means to restrain such consumption by use of the power to impose taxes upon commerce in such items. Mason's motion was defeated by a large margin. The proceedings on this motion are recorded in 5 Elliot's Debates 447, Tansill's Documents 574-575, 2 Ferrand's Records 344 (Madison's Notes, August 20, 1787).

22 - Reprinted in Cooke's Reports 115-205.

23 - 4 Elliot's Debates at 551-552, 1 Stephen's View at 584-585.

24 - Madison's veto message, dated March 3, 1817, is reprinted in 4 Elliot's Debates 468-470, 1 Commager's Documents 211-212

25 - The position James Monroe was noted by Andrew Jackson in a veto message of May 27, 1830. At first Monroe adopted the view, upheld by James Madison until his last day in office, that Congress has "no right to expend money, except in the performance of acts authorized by the other specifi grants of power, according to a strict construction of them. but later, upon reflection, revised his thinking: — Upon reflection, Monroe said, "Congress have an unlimited power to raise money, and that, in its appropriation, they have a discretionary power, restricted only in the duty to appropriate it to purposes of the common defence and of general, national, not local or state benefit." Jackson believed that, if such was a desired direction for the government of the Union to take, a constitutional

amendment should be adopted to that effect, lest dangerous constructions be impossible to resist in future years — 4 Elliot's Debates at 525-527, 1 Commager's Documents at 254.

26 - 4 Elliot's Debates 600-605, 3 Ferrand's Records 477 (Letter to Joseph Cabell, September 28, 1828); 4 Elliot's Debates 605-606 (Letter to Joseph Calbell, Ocrtober 20, 1828).

27 - Reprinted in Anderson's Calhoun 125-133.

28 - Reprinted in 4 Elliot's Debates 580-582.

29- 4 Elliot's Debates at 578, 1 Stephens' View at 618.

30 - This particular theory has enjoyed considerable respectability in American jurisprudence. In 1919 Congress imposed a penal tax of 10% on profits of manufacturers who hired child labor. Since tax was imposed solely as a regulation of manufacturing, it was declared unconstitutional in *Bailey v. Drexel Furniture Co.*, 259 U. S. 20 (1922). In *Hammer v. Dagenhart*, 247 U. S. 251 (1918), an earlier act of Congress prohibiting the shipping of goods manufactored by child labor in interstate commernce was struck down as unconstitutional. In *United States v. Butler*, 297 U. S. 1 (1936), a tax imposed by Congress on processors of agricultural products to raise funds earmarked for farmers reducing their agricultural production was declared unconstitutional. And in *Carter v. Carter Coal Co.*, 298 U. S. 238 (1936), a tax imposed by Congress on the sale price or market value of coal not produced according to certain regulations was declared unconstitutional. These cases were later repudiated in *N. L. R. B. v. Jones & Laughlin Steel Corp.*, 301 U. S. 1 (1937), *United States v. Darby*, 312 U. S. 494 (1941), and *Wickard v. Filburn*, 317 U. S. 111 (1942), which blurred and did away with the classical distinction between commerce and production, and also by *United States v. Kahriger*, 345 U. S. 22 (1953), which allowed wider use of the power to tax as a means of regulating activities outside the regulatory powers of Congress. Even so, there is now a reverse trend evident in *United States v. Lopez*, 514 U. S. 549 (1995), and *United States v. Morrison*, 529 U. S. —- (2000), which have have reinvigorated the distinction between commerce which Congress may regulate, and activities apart from commerce, which Congress may not regulate under the third clause of Article I, Section 8 of the United States Constitution.

31 - Quoted in Belz' Webster-Hayne Debate at 3.

32 - Belz' Webster-Hayne Debate at 10.

33 - Belz' Webster-Hayne Debate at 24.

34 - Belz' Webster-Hayne Debate at 120.

35 - Belz' Webster-Hayne at 143-144.

36 - 4 Elliot's Debates at 516, Belz' Webster Hayne Debate at 182.

37 - Reprinted in 1 Commager's Documents 261-262 and State Papers 28-33.

38 - Reprinted in 4 Eliiot's Debates 582-592, 1 Commager's Documents 262-268, and State Papers 75-97.

39 - In *Worcester v. Georgia*, 6 Peters 515 (U. S. 1832), Chief Justice John Marshall held that certain statutes enacted by the legislature of Georgia, expropriating lands vested in the Cherokee Nation by certain treaties with the United States, were null and void under the supremacy clause in Article VI of the United States Constitution. The prisoner convicted under these statutes was released, but partisans of Andrew Jackson in the government of the State continued to take tribal lands under the same statutes and new statutes continuing the same obnoxious interference with treaties between the Cherokee Nation and the United States. Jackston supported these politicians with the swaggering remark, "John Marshall has made his decision, now let him enforce it." So much for Jackson's devotion to the rule of law.

40 - 1 Commager's Documents at 269.

41 - Mentor Edition at 118.

42 - 1 Stephens' View at 299.

43 - 1 Stephens' View at 312.

44 - 1 Stephens' View at 313-314.

45 - 1 Stephens' View at 323.

46 - 1 Stephens' View at 313-314.

47 - 1 Stephens' View at 383-384.

48 - 1 Stephens' View at 385.

49 - 1 Stephens' View at 386-387. The founding fathers of the United States identified and reprobated the evils of democracy which inevitably lead to the ruin of society. In the Philadelphia Convention, George Mason spoke of the mischief of demagogues and the tyranny of the majority, as appears in 5 Elliot's Debates 415, Tansill's Documents 529, 2 Ferrand's Records 273 (Madison's Notes, August 13, 1787), while James Madison warned against the influence of factions, as appears in 5 Elliot's Debates 417, Tansill's Documents 531, 2 Ferrand's Records 276 (Madison's Notes, August 13, 1787), and Alexander Hamilton inveighed against the ignorance, fickleness, and passions of the people, as appears in 5 Elliot's Debates 422, Tansill's Documents 781, 1 Farrand's Records 209 (Yates' Minutes, June 18, 1787). Patrick Henry warned that the people too easily surrender their freedom for security, as appears in 3 Elliot's Debates 411 (Virginia Convention, June 14, 1788). John Calhoun affirmed that the remedy for democracy, or government by absolute majority, is constitutional government. Calhoun generalized the nature of constitutional government, as an antidote to the evils of democracy,

in his last great work completed in 1849 not long before his death, the same entitled *A Disquisition on Government*, reproduced in Anderson's Calhoun 29-97. He said that constitutional government acknowledges each interest contributing to survival and prosperity of society, and gives each, regardless of numbers, an absolute or qualified negative, so that little or nothing can be done by the government unless every such interest concurs. Only by requiring such a "concurrent majority" of interests, Calhoun maintained, is it possible to assure justice and stability. Such a system works, because mankind always seeks to survive and to become prosperous, and, since cooperation is essential to achieve those ends, cooperation is invariably achieved.

50 - Reprinted in State Papers 352.

51 - Reprinted in 1 Commager's Documents 269-270 and State Papers 373-374.

52 - Quoted in 2 Thorpe's History at 405.

53 - 1 Stephens' View at 399.

54 - 1 Stephens' View at 407.

CHAPTER VI

THE MISSOURI COMPROMISE

In the Treaty of Paris in 1783, King George III ceded the title of his Crown to a vast landed empire lying west of the Appalachian Mountains out to the Mississippi River, above Spanish Florida and 31 degrees north latitude, and beneath Canada and the Great Lakes.

This huge domain was largely unsettled and subject to the claims of different States, originally derived from old royal charters. To the north of the Ohio River there were claims, to some extent conflicting, of Virginia, Connecticut, and Massachusetts. To the south of the Ohio River there were claims, again in some degree conflicting, of Virginia, North Carolina, South Carolina, and Georgia. The treaty of 1783 served as a deed of conveyance to these several States, not to the government of the Union.[1]

During the war of the revolution, these claims spelled trouble unless settled among the several States. Maryland refused to adopt the Articles of Confederation. In a remonstrance to Congress on December 15, 1778, the State pledged full support to the war against Great Britain, but demanded adjustments to resolve the problem of the western lands before she would ratify. Her argument was that royal charters granted some but not all of the colonies land to the west of the mountains, and, on this historical accident only, the claims of Virginia and a few other States were founded. British cession of these lands depended on success in the war for independence through the common effort of all thirteen States. Therefore, Maryland proposed in the interests of justice that the western lands should become the common property of all the several States, and be used to retire the war debt and open up the area for settlement so as to benefit the entire Union.[2]

Daguerreotype by Root   Engraved by A. Sealey

HENRY CLAY.

H. Clay

Congress passed a resolution on September 6, 1780, calling upon the several States to quitclaim their respective interests in the western territory to the United States, so as to assure final adoption of the Articles of Confederation.[3]

Responding to this appeal on January 2, 1781, the General Assembly of Virginia passed a resolution which recited the importance of adopting the Articles of Confederation, and promised to cede the claims of the Commonwealth to the territory northwest of the Ohio River, provided that several new States be formed from these lands and brought within the Union.[4]

The General Assembly of Maryland reacted quickly to this sign of good faith, and ratified the Articles of Confederation on March 1, 1781, as the thirteenth State.

In fulfillment of its promise, the General Assembly of Virginia passed enabling legislation which authorized execution of a deed conveying title to the United States. The deed was delivered on March 22, 1784, to the President of Congress.[5] Within two years, Massachusetts and Connecticut also ceded their claims to the Northwest Territory.

The government of the Union was a public corporation, and one of the attributes of every corporation under the common law, even if not expressed in its charter, has always been capacity to receive conveyance of and hold title to land,[6] and title to land, especially when held by a prince or public body, has always be understood to include the power of governing it, as the King had done in North America from the founding of Jamestown.

On July 13, 1787, while the Philadelphia Convention was in session, Congress passed the Northwest Ordinance which provided for a government of the lands of the United States above the Ohio River.[7] The ordinance grew out of a plan first submitted by Thomas Jefferson, and was finally drafted by Nathan Dane. In keeping with Jefferson's original idea, the sixth article of Section 14 of the Northwest Ordinance provided, "There shall be neither slavery or involuntary servitude in the said territory, save as punishment for crimes whereof the party shall have been duly convicted," etc. As the King had proprietary power to grant charters and establish colonies, Congress had the power deriving from title conveyed from Virginia, Connecticut, and Massachusetts to prohibit slavery upon lands held in fee simple by the United States.

But since this power to regulate territory did not derive from an express grant of power in the Articles of Confederation, and want of such express authority had caused some uneasiness, the Philadelphia Convention framed Article IV, Section 3 of the United States Constitution, which in the first clause provides, "New States may be admitted by the Congress into this Union," etc., and the second clause which provides, "The Congress shall have Power to dispose of and make all needful Rules and Regulations respecting the Territory or other Property belonging to the United States."[8] As quickly as possible after the inauguration of George Washington, the Northwest Ordinance was reenacted by Congress, and slavery was forever prohibited in these lands, this time by express constitutional authority.

At the time the Northwest Ordinance was framed, it was well known that Lord Mansfield had decided *Sommersett's Case*, 20 Howell's St. Tr. 1 at 80-82 (K. B. 1771), which became the universal law throughout the British Empire. Slavery was held to be contrary to natural law, and as such tolerable only during periods of transition under statutes allowing it to exist, provided in any event that such statutes were ever to be strictly construed in favor of liberty.

Jefferson's original idea was a straightforward prohibition of slavery and involuntary servitude, and did not include qualifying language inserted in the Northwest Ordinance by Congress to the effect that, if a runaway slave escaped onto the free soil, his master retained title could recover him by judicial process.[9] This "fugitive slave clause," on the contrary, was understood as a limited exception to the liberal rule given by Lord Mansfield that slavery could exist only where clearly allowed by positive law, yet outside the restricted limits of the exception, it was understood that the rule would hold sway. And so, if a master took his slave into the Northwest Territory, the slave automatically became free, exactly as was held by Lord Mansfield.

In the Philadelphia Convention, a similar provision of the recovery of runaway slaves was inserted as the third clause of Article IV, Section 2 of the United States Constitution,[10] but this fugitive slave clause should be taken as further proof that the framers assumed the liberal rule of freedom as given by Lord Mansfield. Unless the fugitive slave clause were an exception, it would be redundant. And the exception proved the existence of the rule.[11]

* * * * *

There was an alternative source of power vested in Congress to prohibit slavery in the territories of the Union.

The third clause of Article I, Section 8 of the United States Constitution granted to Congress the power of regulating commerce with foreign nations, among the several States, and with the Indian tribes. A related provision is the first clause of Article I, Section 9, which provides, "The Migration or Importation of such Persons as any of the States now existing shall think proper to admit shall not be prohibited by the Congress prior to the Year one thousand eight hundred and eight, but a tax or duty may be imposed on such Importation, not exceeding ten dollars for each Person."[12]

This infamous "1808 clause" was meant to allow the slave trade another twenty years. It had a sordid origin in the Philadelphia Convention. The scenario featured three principal characters:

Oliver Ellsworth of Connecticut was mainly interested in securing for New England a power of Congress to regulate commerce with as few limitations as possible, knowing that the Northern States would eventually be able to use this authority in gaining dominance within the Union. He was capable of manipulation and intrigue disguised as statesmanship. Judge Ellsworth made his gambit on August 21 and 22, 1787, giving sugarcoated speeches in which he minimized slavery as a social problem.

Ellsworth's adversary was George Mason of Virginia, a Southern abolitionist astonishingly farsighted and noble of heart. On August 22, 1787, Colonel Mason made a majestic speech on the need to extinguish the slave trade immediately so as to prepare the country for eventual abolition of slavery, lest failure to act with diligence produce eventual calamity. He concluded his remarks by warning his listeners that, through the wonderful operations of natural law, God punishes nations in this world for their sins.

Judge Ellsworth's easy prey was Charles Cotesworth Pinckney of South Carolina who, on account of his military valor during the War for American Independence, was highly respected in his State. He was, nonetheless, an effusive propagandist for slavery. Judge Ellsworth and General Pinckney spent much time in private conversation, probably over dinner with brandy and cigars.

On August 25, 1787, Judge Ellsworth supported General Pinckney's ardent wish for the 1808 clause. All of the States present from New England voted for it. Virginia, the largest of the slaveholding States, led by Colonel Mason, voted against it.

Then on August 29, 1787, General Pinckney arose to say how grateful he was to those "liberal and candid" gentlemen from New England, meaning especially his friend Judge Ellsworth. He then said that there was no need for additional "fetters" on the power to regulate commerce. General Pinckney then spoke mainly of a proposal then on the floor to prohibit navigation acts and other regulations of commerce without the approval of two-thirds of both the House and the Senate. And, with the support of South Carolina, but over the objection of the other Southern States, New England and all Northern States voted to defeat the proposal then under consideration, and to reject any similar safeguards against sectional exploitation by unjust legislation on trade.

Mason foresaw the forthcoming historical result as the debate continued on August 29, 1787. He exclaimed on the floor of the convention that, with the rejection of all such protections, the South would be delivered into the hands of the North. With sight clairvoyant, Mason proclaimed that the fall of the South would be as it was when the King's army was defeated as Naseby and Cromwell gloated, "The Lord hath delivered them into our hands." As the eyes of his soul looked into the future he knew that, when the South fell, the North would stink with hyprocrisy: — Yankees would proclaim that the subjugation of the South was the will of God!

It is plain enough from its history that the 1808 clause was intended as an exception to the power of Congress to regulate commerce. And it was a rule of common law that exceptions mark the extent and nature of an express power.[13] In correspondence following his retirement as the first Chief Justice of the Untied States, John Jay used this principle to expound the meaning of the 1808 clause in relation to the power of Congress to regulate commerce:

> "I understand the sense and meaning of this clause to be that the power of Congress, although competent to prohibit such migration and importation, was not to be exercised with respect to the then existing States (and them only) until the year 1808; but that the Congress were at liberty to make such prohibition as to any new State, and further, that from and after that period, they were at liberty to make such prohibition as to all the States, whether new or old."[14]

It follows also that, by regulating the commerce and the lands of the United States, Congress could prohibit the importation of slaves into the territories of the Union.

* * * * *

From the enactment of the Northwest Ordinance in 1787, there was hope that the westward expansion of slavery could sooner or later be arrested within defined limits, because especially as years rolled by, it was foreseen with increasing clarity that, when those limits were finally established, the institution would slowly begin to pass away. It was sure that slavery would naturally disappear as cheap rich lands near navigable waters ceased to be readily available, and as the South were gradually transformed from a quasi-feudal society into a modern age. Slavery was destined to extinction from irreversible demands of natural law, the same as villeinage was certain to slip away from visible history in England after the accession of Henry VII.

The great planters in the South were themselves aware that their system of capitalized labor was growing obsolete, and they wondered whether there was a way to perpetrate it. Thus in the spring of 1860, Congressman Otho Singleton of Mississippi frankly admitted, "If slavery be confined to its present limits, the institution will necessarily be overthrown. It is only a question of time." And he asked,

> "If we sever the connection which binds us and the North together, how are we to preserve the institution of slavery? There is but one mode by which, in my humble judgment, it can be perpetuated for any considerable number of years. We may fail in that, but certainly it is the surest chance offered us to preserve it. That mode is by expansion, and that expansion must be in the direction of Mexico."[15]

There was an opposite extreme made up of ideological abolitionists in the North, such as William Lloyd Garrison, who were abstractionists with no political influence to speak of. For them the fundamental law of the Union was a covenant with hell. They felt antagonisms so profound that they did not desire to have further constitutional relationships with the South, and so they stated at the 12th Annual Meeting of the Massachusetts Anti-Slavery Society in 1844,

> "We now publicly abjure our allegiance to the Constitution of the United States and the Union, and place the broad seal of our reprobation on this unnatural and unholy alliance between liberty and slavery. The Union, in our judgment, is not only at war with the law and government of God, and destructive of the peace, the honor, and the prosperity of the North, but of no real benefit to the South, since it serves to delay the day of her visitation, only to plunge her the deeper into infamy and ruin. We therefore declare its obligations, so far as they relate to ourselves, utterly null and void; and we now publicly pledge ourselves to seek, in all suitable ways, its peaceable dissolution."[16]

These ideological abolitionists echoed the traditions of New England, because Nathan Dane of Massachusetts not only helped draft the prohibition of slavery in the Northwest Ordinance, but also wrote much of the Report of the Hartford Convention, which reasoned that, if sectional antagonisms were rooted in deep and permanent causes, better that there be an honest separation in peace than continuation of a nominal alliance between real enemies.

But the real driving power in the North against the South consisted of capitalists, centered mainly in New England, who desired to gain control over the vital organs of the Federal government, and to exploit the situation by high protective tariffs and internal improvements which served their commercial convenience. Their excesses were checked by the South Carolina Convention of 1832 and 1833, but they never ceased in their subsequent efforts.

They were not the only Northern capitalists creating mischief, but they were exceedingly formidable. This class of entrepreneurs wanted to exclude slavery from the Federal territories. Eminently good and moral reasons existed for doing so, but the motive of these commercial interests was to prevent the formation of new States under the control of great planters of the South, for such new States would block their designs of domination. And here, in the competition of economic powers, an increasingly passionate struggle was pitched.

When the contest heated up, these capitalists financed agitation against slavery, — not the rational arguments of Lydia Maria Child, but the vulgar appeals of Harriet Beecher Stowe, for they wished to excite the passions of the crowd and carry Federal elections. And they went further to support a new political combination whose avowed purpose was to bar slavery from the Federal territories. There were sincere adherents of this cause, but as many or more were ambitious opportunists, and the pistons of the great machine moved on steam generated mainly by the lucre of industrialists.

And since the instruments they sought to control were lodged in the Union, these entrepreneurs promoted the idea that the Union is altogether sublime and indissoluble. They glorified this perversion, even after Daniel Webster had seen the light, and said in defense of the constitutional rights of the Southern States, "How absurd it is to suppose that, when different parties enter into a compact for certain purposes, either can disregard any one provision, and expect, nevertheless, the other to observe the rest."[17]

In the spring of 1860, Senator Jefferson Davis of Mississippi lunged at the soft underbelly of the new partisan voice in the North:

> "What do you propose, gentlemen of the free soil party? Do you propose to better the condition of the slave? Not at all. What then do you propose? You say you are opposed to the expansion of slavery. Is

the slave to be benefited by it? Not at all. What then do you propose? It is not humanity that influences you in the position which you now occupy before the country. It is that you may have an opportunity of cheating us that you want to limit slave territory within circumscribed bounds. It is that you may have a majority in the Congress of the United States and convert the government into an engine of Northern aggrandizement. It is that your section may grow in power and prosperity upon treasures unjustly taken from the South, like the vampire bloated and gorged with the blood which it has secretly sucked from its victim. You desire to weaken the political power of the Southern States, — and why? Because you want, by an unjust system of legislation, to promote the industry of the New England States, at the expense of the people of the South and their industry."[18]

As the 19th Century matured, the States beneath the Mason-Dixon Line and the Ohio River became increasingly vulnerable to unjust regulations of commerce by Congress. Their position within the Union steadily declined, because, over the protest of George Mason in the Philadelphia Convention, proper constitutional protections needed by the South had been conceded in exchange for the right to continue the slave trade until 1808.

As they viewed their weakening position, Southerners dug cautiously like archeologists around the foundations of the Union, and there they rediscovered the amazing root principles underlying nullification and secession. The people of the South became conditioned and habituated to the credo of free, sovereign, and independent States united in a Confederacy. As long as possible, they meant to defend their rights within the Union, but they conscientiously nursed the final option of withdrawing from the United States.

* * * * *

By the middle of the 19th Century, despite the disparity of economic interests between the North and the South, the government of the Union had proved capable of effective mediation. The question of tariffs had been fairly readjusted by several acts after the nullification crisis so as to provide moderate protection for both the North and the South, yet to yield sufficient revenues for the Union. And the extent of slavery had been settled by two legislative compromises.

A workable equilibrium was achieved, opening vast and ample territories as so-called "free soil" for settlement by citizens seeking new lives in new country without fear of the social and economic orientations which were associated with slavery. Yet, as a concession to the South, some expansion of slavery was permitted on western lands up to certain limits which were marked not only by statutes but geography. If this precious equilibrium had been maintained, then slavery would have quietly entered into its final phase, and it would have been possible for the Federal government to move further by assisting with organic changes in the South. It is a sad tale how this equilibrium was upset, causing poisonous reactions and counterreactions which finally brought about irreparable damage to the United States.

The first territorial accommodation between the North and the South was known as the Compromise of 1820, or the Missouri Compromise, which was developed to deal with the Louisiana Purchase.

The huge expanse of French Louisiana included New Orleans near the Gulf of Mexico, and then widened in extent as it reached 49 degrees north latitude, the boundary with Canada established by treaty with Great Britain in 1818, so as to occupy the rich center of the continent to the west of the Mississippi River. When this land was purchased from the Emperor Napoleon in 1803, the treaty with France stipulated that "the inhabitants of the ceded territory shall be incorporated into the Union of the United States, and they shall be maintained and protected in the free enjoyment of their liberty, property, and the religion which they profess."[19] When the agreement was concluded, there were some thousands of slaves held by Spanish and French planters in the territory, and the treaty was read to guarantee their title.

The State of Louisiana, embracing all land purchased from France beneath 33 degrees north latitude, was admitted to the Union in 1812, and no objection was made over the fact that slavery was there allowed by law. The new State was soon full of planters, and became culturally similar to every other State to the east of the Mississippi River but to the south of the Mason-Dixon Line and the Ohio River.

The trouble began in 1819 when both Maine and Missouri petitioned Congress for admission to the Union. The North then held an advantage over the South of 105 to 81 votes in the House, and, given the course of immigrations from Europe, everyone knew that this growing imbalance would become increasingly acute.

There were two civilizations in the Union. The North and the South had opposing interests. There had to be a way by which either section could block, delay, or inhibit obtuse designs or unjust measures of the other. The sagacious, ageless, and universal principles articulated by John Calhoun required such functioning mechanisms in order to prevent aggrandizement by one region over the other, and to promote accommodations for mutual benefit which in turn would strengthen the Union.

Since the House was irretrievably lost to the North, the Senate became increasingly important to the South. In 1819 there were eleven States in the North, and eleven States in the South. Each section had twenty-two senators. And, because of their longer terms and greater insolation from popular opinion, there was a better collegiality among members of the Senate. Quiet understandings of political necessity transcending the demands of the greatest number of the people across the country could and did develop.

The problem was that the distribution of power in the Senate was founded solely on the several States. The question which became nearly overheated in Philadelphia was how to protect the smaller States from exploitation by the greater States.

Even so, during the debates leading to the Great Compromise, James Madison had warned that more serious competition would be felt between the North and the South. And George Mason had sought to require safe-guards against abuse of specific powers of the Union as between the North and the South: — his idea was that, as to those powers which were obviously tempting to abuse in sectional exploitation, especially the power to regulate commerce, more than a simple majority of votes should be necessary to carry measures in Congress.

Although the formula adopted by the Philadelphia Convention for dis-tribution of senators was right in giving special weight to the several States as political institutions, it did not take enough into account. The arrangement did not permit the North to protect itself against the South, or the South to protect itself against the North, — not unless each had at least a rough equality in the number of States.

The situation produced the most shocking anomalies, as when represen-tatives and senators from New England opposed the fabulous purchase of French Louisiana out of fear, which was not unjustified, that an alliance of the South and the West would put them at a disadvantage in Congress. And it animated leaders of the South to expand slavery, detested by the patriots of the American Revolution, lest their wealth should be rendered valueless by political manipulations which were attempted by capitalists in the North.

In any event, when at the end of 1819 Congress was called upon to admit Maine as a free State and Missouri as a slave State, the constitu-tional provisions on the Senate were not suited to give the right balance, protection, and incentives to the North and the South.

If the great planters gained the upper hand, society became quasi-feudal and more agrarian, and culture became quiet and sentimental. Where great industrialists gained control, society flourished with business, industry, activity, and sound. Each way of life had a certain charm, but absolutely could not be mixed with the other. Those attuned to one culture assumed they enjoyed the blessings of a superior civilization. The music of the North was noise in the ears of the South. The serenity of the South was decadence in the eyes of the North.

The problem before Congress in 1819 and 1820 could not be solved without vision of the future. It was fortunate that, in 1819 and 1820, an exceptionally farsighted character served as Speaker of the House. He was a Congressman from Kentucky by the name Henry Clay. With the wisdom of a serpent, seizing political circumstances, he conceived and engineered the Missouri Compromise.

The main element of the program was to draw a line through the Louisiana Purchase, prohibiting slavery in the main part, and inviting people to settle down, build homes, raise families, farm land, start businesses, and set up towns, free of any planter influence, but leaving the lesser part open to slavery, permitting Southern planters to come in and continue their way of life. Naturally, immigrants and Northerners would in time fill up the free soil. But it was politically unthinkable to deny the South a share of the new territorial acquisition, which is why they had to be granted a right to occupy some of the public domain.

It was necessary to divide the empire in order to assure that the two civilizations were in different parts of the country. Intermingled upon the same land, they would fight it out until one prevailed and took over.

This arrangement would buy time, but it would weight the odds against the institution of slavery, because, over the then-approaching decades, there would be more petitions for the admission of free States than slave States. Meanwhile, as slave soil filled up, the institution would start to become less profitable, then it would start to decline. Up to a certain point, the South would be able to block or delay the admission of new free States which would favor the North, but finally the economic and political pressures would become excessive, and the South would be compelled to make a deal with the North.

The precise details of the expected settlement were not foreseeable, but the essential features could be imagined: — in exchange for the admission of new free States, which would weaken or undo the constitutional defense of the South in the Senate, the fundamental law of the Union might have to be amended to provide alternative guarantees, or perhaps statutory or political arrangements could be worked out for this purpose;

moreover, the powers and wealth of the Union would most likely be needed to compensate masters willing to emancipate, thereby helping in the transformation of Southern capital, and assisting freed blacks in making adjustments, thereby easing the restructuring of the labor force.

Under the skillful probing and guidance of Speaker Henry Clay, three principal legislative elements were put into place.

The first statute was a precursor, an Act of March 2, 1819, which organized the Arkansas Territory, including all but a small fragment of the lands of the Louisiana Purchase above 33 degrees but below 36 degrees 30 minutes north latitude. The western stretches of this territory included the body of what later became Oklahoma, which was relatively arid and less suited for cotton production by slave labor. The eastern portion, however, included fertile cotton lands, and was attractive to the planters of the South.

During the debates on the bill for organizing the Arkansas Territory, it was proposed that the language of the Northwest Ordinance prohibiting slavery and involuntary servitude be inserted, but this idea was voted down even in the House. It was plain as day that this territory would eventually yield one slave State to the South.

Next, Maine was admitted to the Union as a free State by an Act of March 3, 1820.

Finally came the question of Missouri, which was by far the most difficult transaction. The proposed State was to lie above 36 degrees 30 minutes north latitude, and to the west of the Mississippi River across from the free State of Illinois which had been forged out of the Northwest Territory. The Senate first passed a bill which called for unconditional admission of Missouri as a slave State.

In the House, Congressman James Tallmadge of New York secured an amendment which inserted the language of the Northwest Ordinance prohibiting slavery and involuntary servitude. The rationale was that the southerly boundary of the new State was really a statutory continuation of the natural line which separated free and slave States on the other side of the Mississippi.

The bill then went back to the Senate, where this amendment was rejected, but as a substitute Senator Jesse Thomas of Illinois proposed a critical clause, which was adopted by the Senate, and then by the House, whereupon President James Monroe approved. The resulting language was the main provision in the Missouri Compromise, appearing as Section 8 of an Act of March 6, 1820. The new State of Missouri was to be admitted with no restriction on slavery, which would maintain temporary sectional equilibrium in the Senate. Still, it was further enacted,

"That in all Territory ceded by France to the United States, under the name of Louisiana, which lies north of thirty-six degrees and thirty minutes north latitude, not included within the limits of the State contemplated by this act, slavery and involuntary servitude, otherwise than in the punishment of crimes, whereof the parties shall have been duly convicted, shall be and is hereby forever prohibited: Provided always, That any person escaping into the same, from whom labor or service is lawfully claimed, in any State or Territory of the United States, such fugitive may be lawfully reclaimed and conveyed to the person claiming his or her labor or service as aforesaid."[20]

The language was a close paraphrasing of the words of sixth article of Section 14 of the Northwest Ordinance. The prohibition of slavery and involuntary servitude was another exercise of the express power of Congress under the second clause of Article IV, Section 3 of the United States Constitution. The fugitive slave clause was a limited exception to the liberal rule given by Lord Mansfield, which, outside the contours of this exception, remained fully intact.

Section 8 of the Act of March 6, 1820, forever outlawed slavery in all of the Louisiana Purchase to the north and west of the new State of Missouri. This vast region was by far the greatest part of what had been acquired from France, and was left for the time being as Unorganized Territory. These lands were destined to yield in time a good many new free States. Here was the lever which was designed to nudge the South toward abolition of slavery as the institution became more antiquated even in the eyes of planters.

* * * * *

The program envisioned by the Missouri Compromise did not have a chance to work to its full extent, because historical and political circumstances combined to give another huge acquisition to the United States, and this new land reagitated the slavery question.

In 1820 Moses Austin secured land grants from the dying colonial government of New Spain, authorizing Americans to settle in the wilderness later known as Texas, lying to the northeast of the Rio Grande and to the west of Louisiana. A few years later his son, Stephen Austin, was able to secure a confirmation of these land grants from the new government of Mexico. Various troubles developed between the settlers and the Mexican government. The United States proposed to buy Texas, but Mexico refused the offers. After many years of irresolution, the people of Texas declared and won a war of independence in 1836, set up a republican form of government, and elected Sam Houston as their President. Congress declined to grant the petition of Texas for annexation to the Union in 1837, because it was then important in the foreign policy of the United States to have good diplomatic relations with Mexico.

Henry Clay dreaded the thoughst of annexing Texas. He and other principled men of the country knew that, even if Mexico had an unstable government and an infirm army, the United States were not yet prepared to absorb more territory, lest the settled question of slavery fester all over again. It was certain that for the time being Texas would be capable of maintaining her independence. And it was clear enough to anyone studying the situation carefully that, given time, the independent republic would inevitably become a State of the Union.

That was not all. The territorial claims of Mexico above the Rio Grande and, say, 31 degrees north latitude rested on its supposed inheritance of the legal authority of New Spain. But when that old world vice-royalty disintegrated after flourishing over three hundred years, Mexico replaced only a sizable fraction of the immense colonial empire, for many nations grew up from its ruins. The claims of Mexico over the territory of what later became Arizona, for example, were no better than its claims over what later became Guatemala. The trends of immigration already moving in North America at the fall of New Spain could never be halted by statutes of the feeble government then existing in Mexico. And those trends made inevitable that this territory would become independent of Mexico, and probable that it would eventually become part of the United States.

Yet it was one thing for men of foresight to note demographic trends and draw inferences, and entirely another to give jingoistic speeches about taking land under the nominal jurisdiction of Mexico. In due course, a peaceful and beneficial adjustment to demographic and political reality could have been accomplished by treaty and purchase. Such was the moderation favored by Henry Clay. In 1844, he was certain to be the Whig candidate for President, as former President Martin Van Buren seemed to be the likely democratic candidate. The two gentlemen met and agreed that the question of Texas should, in the public interest, be kept out of the forthcoming presidential election. Afterwards, they both made pubic statements against immediate annexation. Clay said,

> "Annexation and war with Mexico are identical. Now, for one, I certainly am not willing to involve this country in a foreign war for the object of acquiring Texas. I know there are those who regard such a war with indifference and as a trifling affair, on account of the weakness of Mexico, and her inability of inflict serious injury upon this country. But

I do not look upon it thus lightly. I regard all wars as great calamities to be avoided, if possible, and honorable peace as the wisest and truest policy of this country. What the United States most need are union, peace, and patience. Nor do I think that weakness of a power should form a motive, in any case, for inducing us to engage in or to depreciate the evils of war. — Honor and good faith and justice are equally due from this country towards the weak as toward the strong."[21]

But there was already hardy talk about so-called "manifest destiny" floating around the United States, and this rhetoric was taken, not as an admonition for prudence, but as a war cry against Mexico. Van Buren lost the nomination of his party in favor of an almost unknown politician who was willing to appeal for immediate annexation of Texas. Clay was nominated by the Whigs, but was defeated in the general election.

Actually, the returns were close. James Polk, who pleased the crowds by urging annexation of Texas, received a popular vote of 1,337,000, — Henry Clay, perhaps the greatest American statesman of the 19th Century, 1,299,000, — and James Birney, a Southern abolitionist, 62,000. It so happens that Birney, who ordinarily would have been an inconsequential candidate, and did not intend to be more than a standard bearer in that election, had a particularly strong showing of 16,000 popular votes in the western counties of New York, which caused Clay to lose the State, with 36 electoral votes, to Polk by only 5,000 popular votes. The electoral college cast 170 votes for Polk and 105 votes for Clay. If New York had gone for Clay, he would have been elected President.

Birney was a most admirable character. He had been a slaveholder in Alabama, and, through strength of heart, mind, and will, he was able to see through the social flaws in the peculiar institution of the South. Three-fourths of all Southerners had nothing to do with slavery. Of those who owned slaves, there had always been many who saw something wrong with slavery. But the remedy was in such doubt that most Southerners did not know which way to turn. It took moral courage for a man like Birney to renounce his way of life, free his slaves, and then seek unity between the North and the South in working for emancipation of all slaves wherever found in the United States. He went to New York, because the abolitionist movement in that part of the country had been discredited by eccentrics like Garrison. It is ironic that the abolitionist movement in the North was in such desperate condition that a son of Alabama had to assume the duty of leading it. And it is tragic that he managed to prevent the election of Clay who was the master architect of the policy which, left alone, doomed slavery to natural extinction.

Two days before Polk's inauguration, Texas was annexed by joint resolution of Congress. Within a year, Polk stationed Federal troops immediately above the Rio Grande. In the flicker of an eye, war broke out against Mexico, and that led to acquisition by treaty of peace in 1848 of all of the territory which had been New Spain above the Rio Grande, — everything west of the Louisiana Purchase to the Pacific coast up to the Oregon country.

The situation reopened wounds which had been closed almost three decades before by the Missouri Compromise. There had not been many slaves brought into Texas before the Mexican War. But with annexation, the cotton of Texas had a tariff-free market within the United States and with Europe. The new political stability in Texas made title to slaves more secure. There were cheap rich lands on or near rivers or coasts in the easterly part of the new State. About this time the price of cotton improved. Therefore, planters moved into eastern Texas.

In early 1848, just as peace with Mexico was negotiated, news broke of the discovery of gold in California. Whatever explains the timing, there was a great influx of adventurers from all over the world. One year's find in gold would have paid off the public debt of the United States as calculated by Alexander Hamilton in 1790.[22]

So dynamic was the growth and energy of this population that, by the end of 1849, as if Congress did not exist, the people there set up a republican form of government. They prohibited slavery and involuntary servitude by fundamental law, because obviously the peculiar institution of the old South had no place in the brightness of their culture.

In early 1850, the republic of California applied for admission to the United States. In fact, it was an offer which could not be refused, because, if Congress had spurned the petition, there would have been a new nation on the Pacific coast, — wealthy and prosperous, full of natural resources, grand in extent, indescribably beautiful, rendered impregnable by mountains and oceans, and filled with a strong and free-spirited people. California did not need the protection of the United States. By principles of the American Revolution, California had no duty to be a colony of the United States. The point is fairly debatable, but at least through the end of the 19th Century, California might actually have been better off remaining independent of the United States.

There were those who complained that California had acted unlawfully in forming her own constitution before being allowed to do so by Congress. Aside from wanting the slightest hope of legitimate foundation in a country which began with the Declaration of American Independence, all such suggestions, in the circumstances of the case, were politically delusional. And any proposal of military conquest of California, if pressed in Congress, would have been the plea of a veritable lunatic.

When the petition of California reached Congress, there were still an equal number of free States and slave States. Since the Missouri Compromise, which gave each side twelve States, Michigan, Iowa, and Wisconsin had been added to the North, while Arkansas, Texas, and Florida had been added to the South. Thus, each section had thirty members in the Senate. Even so, all possibilities of the South for adding new States had been exhausted. In fact, the anticipated tightening effect of the Missouri Compromise was being felt. The admission of California as a free State was a foregone conclusion, and soon afterwards Oregon and Minnesota would tip the scales more heavily in favor of the North.

In the summer of 1846, a bill had been introduced in the United States House of Representatives for an appropriation to facilitate negotiations leading to territorial adjustments, it having then been anticipated that there would be a large cession in favor of American interests. Congressman David Wilmot of Pennsylvania had succeeded in inserting a proviso which stated as an express condition to the acquisition of any territory by the United States from Mexico "by virtue of any treaty which may be negotiated between them, and to the use by the executive of moneys herein appropriated, that neither slavery nor involuntary servitude shall ever exist in any part of said territory, except for crime, whereof the party shall first be duly convicted." The bill was lost in the Senate. And the following year another bill was passed, but without this far-famed Wilmot Proviso.

Popular historians have sought to attribute monumental significance to the Wilmot Proviso, which was an attempt to exercise, in territories ultimately ceded by Mexico, the power of Congress which had first been employed in the reenactment of the Northwest Ordinance in 1789. But failure of the attempt, on the contrary, did not have the slightest importance.[23]

In Texas, slavery never really got beyond the Nueces River, which flowed as an arch considerably to the north and east of the Rio Grande into the Gulf of Mexico at Corpus Christi. Slave labor was expensive to maintain, because masters were obliged to provide comprehensive care of the wants and needs of their workers from cradle to grave. This feature acquitted slavery, as it was called, of most charges of inhumanity lodged against it, and simultaneously made the system unable to compete whenever cheap seasonal labor was readily available. Between the Nueces River and the Rio Grande, free Mexican labor has always been found in abundance, and for this reason slavery never was or could be established there.

The land belt separating the two rivers served as a buffer zone, because slavery was prohibited in Mexico. Aside from its incapacity to compete successfully with free Mexican labor, slavery could not flourish beyond the Nueces River for the further reason that escape across the Rio Grande brought freedom forever, and so slave property was there unsafe to hold. Nor were the wildest dreams of expanding slavery into Mexico or other parts of Latin American anything but delusions, because, aside from the impossibility of not only conquering but keeping hold of those regions, the huge supply of cheap native labor eager to be hired made slavery entirely out of the question.

Likewise out of the question for the expansion of slavery was western Texas, New Mexico, the Indian lands, Utah, and any part of the Louisiana Purchase north of the line drawn by the Missouri Compromise. In all these regions, the land was largely semi-arid and unforested, or too far from navigable rivers and other means of transportation, or otherwise unfit to implant slavery in any meaningful degree. And coming technology was a further death knell to the future of the institution.

Most politicians in the United States may not yet have come around to the reality, but at the time California petitioned for admission to the Union, neither the Federal territories nor any other lands within reach could absorb any significant expansion of the planter way of life in the old South. The unmistakable trends of immigration, an impossible and moribund system of capitalization of labor, the forthcoming creation of new free States, and generally the beckoning call of the future all weighed irreversibly toward the natural extinction of slavery.

The moment had arrived for the South to negotiate while time remained, exacting a price while a price could still be fetched, and making advantageous transactions for the future. There was one man in the South who could see the future clearly, as before Henry Clay, then representing Kentucky in the Senate. But he was getting on in years. The best the old master could do was get some breathing space for the South, and then hope that someone with sense might take his place before it was too late.

The Senator from Kentucky introduced eight resolutions in the Senate for resolving the conflicting interests of the country, as occasioned by the petition of California for admission to the Union.[24] And out of these resolutions grew the basic statutory elements of the Compromise of 1850:[25]

— California was admitted to the Union as a free State.

— The western boundary of Texas was adjusted. Land was taken from the State, with its consent, and fitted into Federal territory, in consideration of $10,000,000 in bonds of the United States.

— All territory acquired from Mexico, aside from Texas and California, was organized into the New Mexico Territory, just to the west of Texas and to the east of California, beneath 37 degrees north latitude, and also the Utah Territory, which was the remainder above 37 degrees north latitude. Each of these territories was made subject to the provision, "That when admitted as a State, the said territory, or any portion of the same, shall be received into the Union, with or without slavery, as its constitution may prescribe at the time of admission."

— There had been an old fugitive slave law, enacted by Congress when George Washington was President.[26] This old act was amended to give the courts of the Union exclusive jurisdiction, thereby relieving the courts of unwilling States of any duty to participate in this unpleasant business. Criminal penalties were prescribed for obstructing the execution of the act.

— And the slave trade, but not slavery, was abolished in the District of Columbia.

The legislative engineering of this compromise took many months. In the United States Senate, three famous speeches were delivered, the first by John Calhoun of South Carolina on March 4, 1850, — the next by Daniel Webster of Massachusetts on March 7, 1850, — and the last by William Seward of New York on March 11, 1850.

Calhoun delivered his message twenty-seven days before his death, and at the time he was so weak and wan that a colleague from Virginia was obliged to read the text for him. "The North has only to will it to accomplish it," he concluded, "to do justice by conceding to the South an equal right in the acquired territory, and to do her duty by causing the stipulation relative to fugitive slaves to be faithfully fulfilled, to cease the agitation of the slave question, and to provide for the insertion of a provision into the constitution, by an amendment, which would restore to the South in substance the power she possessed of protecting herself before the equilibrium was destroyed by the action of the government."[27]

In 1860, a full decade after Calhoun had been laid to rest, there were probably less than a hundred slaves within the boundaries of Texas beyond the Nueces River, nor did the territories to the north and west of Texas offer any attraction to planters. Slavery had expanded to its furthest natural extremity in those directions.

The new fugitive slave law was of little practical significance, because there were so few runaways, and those slaves who managed to escape were nearly always impossible to find. It was seldom worth the cost and effort even to make an attempt at recovery.

And the act abolishing the slave trade in the District of Columbia was likewise cosmetic. The whole slave population in the city of Washington and its immediate surroundings could not much have exceeded a few hundred domestic servants. The slave market there had almost ceased to exist by the middle of the century.

Agitation for the abolition of slavery never appeared on the platform of any major political party during the coming decade, but there was endless agitation on the question of slavery in the Federal territories, and this prospect troubled Calhoun, because the irritation constantly expressed by the North created a hostile atmosphere which caused the South to fear for its safety within the Union. Here was the tender spot which needed to be treated with soothing balm. The South was diffident, and unless the South was assured by the North, he warned, there would be a fissure in the Union. The remedy was formation and execution of a good settlement.

Calhoun's great precept of the need for constitutional safeguards against exploitation of minority interests was still sound, but the winds of change were bringing about new alignments within the country, and for this reason the old equilibrium Calhoun spoke of was no longer a serviceable balance for this purpose. There was instead a need to calm the sea of agitation over slavery, let the institution die naturally, and accommodate new alliances of power which were sure to arise.

Daniel Webster was damned in Boston for his "seventh of March" speech. "I speak today for the preservation of the Union. Hear me for my cause!" were his famous opening words as he supported the resolutions of Henry Clay. The thrust of his discourse was an answer to the declamations of the North against the peculiar institution of the South. He did not defend slavery so much as expose hypocrisy, for he had approved of the Wilmot Proviso, but for him the real concern was to avoid further division within the United States. And for this he was lambasted mercilessly. Webster, it was said, had sold his soul to the devil.

Webster was shrewd enough to see what Clay had in mind by his stipulation on New Mexico and Utah: the object was to let the South enjoy a nominal concession which posed no real threat whatever for the expansion of slavery into the West. The need was to build strength of the whole on a foundation of peace among the several States to terminate the cultural insults against the South, and to work on solid progress within the Union. And he was eminently correct.

William Seward opposed Clay's resolutions. He rested his case with grandiloquence: "And now, the simple, bold, and awful question which presents itself is this: — Shall we, who are founding institutions, social and political, for countless millions, — shall we, who know by experience the wise and the just, and are free to choose them, and to reject the erroneous and unjust, — shall we establish human bondage, or permit it by our sufferance to be established?"[28] It sounded glorious, but it was one of the most meaningless political speeches in American history. For never was a single slave held in all the vast stretches of the New Mexico Territory or the Utah Territory.

The triumvirate of Clay, Calhoun, and Webster provided an arrangement made up of legal symbols designed to keep the country cool and occupied, while two political niceties were gracefully addressed: California was admitted to the Union, and the South was reassured of its safety within the Union.

Slavery was set on the path of ultimate extinction by the Compromises of 1820 and 1850. And the people of the South were generally satisfied with the results, as appears from the defeat of secessionists in the Southern elections in 1851. If a little moderation and patience had been shown there would have been a natural and beneficial transformation within the Dixie States and throughout the Union.

* * * * *

By the end of 1852, Clay, Calhoun, and Webster all slept in their graves. And, unfortunately, there were meddlesome politicians, power-brokers, and judges who could not leave well enough alone. Not much time had to pass before the trouble began.

Senator Stephen Douglas of Illinois had ambitions of becoming President. Given the realities of popular election, which have usually been more a matter of financial backing than anything else, Douglas became indebted to a group of financiers whose offices were mainly in New York and Philadelphia. They wanted to build a transcontinental railroad along a central route cutting across Federal territories somewhat above the line of the Missouri Compromise. And, in order to obtain necessary support for the favorite project of these financiers, Douglas used his power as Chairman of the Senate Committee on the Territories to engineer a bill containing an element which was deceptively attractive to the South.

The bill established the Kansas Territory, lying to the west of the State of Missouri, from 37 to 40 degrees north latitude, and also the Nebraska Territory consisting of all portions of the Louisiana Purchase then still unorganized and above 40 degrees north latitude. Under Section 8 of the Act of March 6, 1820, slavery was excluded from these territories, but Douglas agreed to repeal this provision in exchange for temporary relinquishment by senators and representatives in the Southern States of their demands that a transcontinental railroad should be built through Louisiana and Texas. This bait secured enough political support for the central route.[29]

The Kansas-Nebraska Act was signed on May 30, 1854.[30] Section 14 stated that "the true intent and meaning of this Act is not to legislate slavery into any State or Territory, or to exclude it therefrom, but to leave the people thereof perfectly free to form and regulate their domestic institutions in their own way." This idea was called "popular sovereignty." It had a pious ring, but it was a certain recipe for civil war, as was foreseen by Senator Sam Houston of Texas, who pleaded on March 4, 1854, "I adjure you to regard the contract once made to harmonize and preserve the Union. Maintain the Missouri Compromise! Stir not up agitation! Give us peace!"[31] He was the sanest man in the United States when he spoke those words, but he was unheard.

In the great cession from Mexico between Texas and California, there was nary a square mile which settlers from both the North and the South would compete to acquire, and for this reason it was not so important to draw a line between free soil and slave soil in the Federal territories covered by the Compromise of 1850.

But in the lands other than the State of Missouri lying above 36 degrees 30 minutes north latitude in the Louisiana Purchase, there was a limited region along the Missouri and Kansas Rivers, in which a few crops other than cotton, such as hemp and tobacco, might profitably be grown by slave labor. And so, for the sake of domestic peace, a line was established by the Compromise of 1820. The region in question was not very large, and could hardly be expected to support more than a sparse population in bondage. Moreover, as between competing streams of immigrants from the North and from the South, it was a foregone conclusion, dictated by the offerings of geography and the weight of numbers, that Kansas would eventually become a free State.

In fact, this small domain was so minor in value to planters that it was unworthy of any strenuous exertions of the South. Yet there lay a segment of land in eastern Kansas, which Douglas opened up to Dixie squatters for the sake of a railroad. The consequences were disastrous. It caused an explosion of ill-feeling and misunderstanding which had mercifully been laid to rest by Henry Clay's last triumphant act of statesmanship in 1850.

The explosion happened just as Harriet Beecher Stowe's tale of estrange-ment was published, causing the deepest revulsion to magnify exponen-tially as between the two cultures of the United States.

The wanton destruction of the Missouri Compromise so inflamed the North that the republican party was formed in the summer of 1854 on an ideology which was announced by Senators Salmon P. Chase of Ohio and Charles Sumner of Massachusetts, joined by other members of Congress, in a political manifesto to the United States: "We appeal to the people. We warn you that the dearest interests of freedom and the Union are in immi-nent peril," they said, then continued, "Demagogues may tell you that the Union can be maintained only by submitting to the demands of slavery. We tell you that the Union can only be maintained by the full recognition of the just claims of freedom and man." They argued further, "Whatever apologies may be offered for the toleration of slavery in the States, none can be offered for its extension into the territories where it does not exist, and where that extension involves the repeal of ancient law and the viola-tion of solemn compact."[32]

This ideology missed the point, because the ancient line drawn in 1820 was repealed in 1854, not so much on demand of Southern capitalists seeking to extend slavery, as on demand of Northern capitalists seeking to build a railroad. The line drawn in 1820 should never have been erased, but the reason had nothing to do with dangers to freedom, for freedom would have unavoidably crowned the black race in forthcoming decades: — this process would not have been diminished or retarded, but would have been more natural and ample, if good will had been maintained between the North and the South during the 1850s, and if no blood had been spilled on battlefields of the United States from 1861 to 1865.

It is understandable that many in the North should be alarmed by the repeal of the Missouri Compromise. And once there was a reaction in the North, it is understandable that there was a counterreaction in the South. It is unjust to blame the panic-stricken irrationality of the two sections which followed the repeal, for it followed as naturally as night follows day.

The responsibility falls on other shoulders. James Madison defined a faction as "a number of citizens, whether amounting to a majority or minority of the whole, who are united and actuated by some common impulse of passion, or of interest, adverse to the rights of other citizens, or to the permanent and aggregate interests of the community."[33]

In England, such a faction, comfortably nestled behind the East India Company, virtually bought statutes allowing free exportation of silver in 1663, abolition of seigniorage on royal coinage in 1666, and a money-lending monopoly in 1694. They secured a corrupt judicial confirmation of an illegal royal charter over certain trade routes on the high seas in 1684, then bribed their way into renewal of their royal charter in 1695, and, for the sake of appearances, purchased a statute legalizing their ill-gotten privileges in 1698. They secured passage of currency acts against the colonies in 1751 and 1764, and destroyed their domestic money supply. They basically owned and exercised the right to interpose a royal negative on all colonial bills to prohibit the slave trade from 1714 through 1775. They excited needless wars, stimulated barbaric commerce, induced a depression, fomented a revolution, and desecrated an empire.

In comparison to these machinations, there was nothing new or unusual in the cheap sale of the Compromise of 1820 by a faction of railroad magnates who wanted to get track laid along a central route across the United States where they anticipated the largest gains. Even so, the focus of attention has never been on the question of whether slavery should be allowed or could be prohibited in the Federal territories.

That such was not the trouble at all is made plain from a few undeniable facts which put everything into perspective: — in 1860, after the legality and wisdom of the old compromise line had been argued and litigated ad nauseam, and after slavery was acknowledged by all as lawful above 36 degrees 30 minutes north latitude, there were exactly two slaves in the whole expanse of the Kansas Territory, and only fifteen slaves in the great land mass of the Nebraska Territory. The question of slavery in the Federal territories was a ridiculous pretext. This triviality was no great sin which justified the grapes of wrath.

And it is fair to venture that, again in 1860, there were in any single county of the Dixie States more decent altruists, untainted by any motives of personal ambition, and desiring for the purest reasons of humanity to get rid of slavery, than could be found in all the conclaves of power in the republican party throughout all of the States in the North. The activity of these Southerners can easily be illustrated without the aid of letters and diaries:

As all concede, there was an institution known as the underground railroad, consisting of a secret network which enabled slaves to escape onto free soil. This informal system always included many whites, and existed from the days of the revolution: at the peak of its activity during the 1850s, the underground railroad must have aided and abetted about 500 to 1,000 escapes every year.[34] The greater risk in running the operation was naturally felt in the South. Obviously, this share of the burden was born by men and women of the South.

There were distinctive traits of the abolitionists in the Dixie States, which contrasted them sharply with their counterparts in the North. They were by 1860 more numerous than abolitionists in the North, both in absolute numbers and as a percentage of society. But the abolitionists of the South lived in the real world, not a world of ideological caricature. Because of their characteristic moderation they were often unnoticed by firebrands in the North. Abolitionists in the South grasped the difficulty of the task before them, and they were bewildered by it. A striking example is found in John Randolph of Roanoke. In keeping with the teachings of St. Paul, Randolph tenderly loved his slaves, and they tenderly loved him, but he dared not free them during his life. When he died in 1833, his slaves were emancipated by will under which lands were purchased for them in Ohio. Ironically, the people of Ohio drove these freed blacks from the farms which their Southern champion had procured for them.[35]

On October 16, 1854, the most legendary American of the 19th Century made a speech in Peoria, Illinois. Abraham Lincoln had served eight years in the legislature of his State, then one inauspicious term in Congress during the Mexican War. While in the House he voted for the Wilmot Proviso, whereupon he quit politics to practice law, until Senator Stephen Douglas engineered repeal of the Missouri Compromise. He then stepped forward again in public life.

Lincoln's Peoria speech was a forthright statement, by the most famous of all abolitionists, on conditions of that day which made slavery very difficult to eradicate. It is instructive to all whom the simplistic view of our modern times has blinded in ignorance and prejudice. For these were the true and unadulterated sentiments of "Honest Abe" of Illinois:

> "When Southern people tell us they are no more responsible for the origin of slavery than we are, I acknowledge the fact. When it is said that the institution exists, and that it is very difficult to get rid of it in any satisfactory way, I can understand and appreciate the saying. I surely will not blame them for not doing what I should not know how to do myself.

> "If all earthly power were given me, I should not know what to do as to the existing institution. My first impulse would be to free all the slaves, and send them to Liberia, to their own native land. But a moment's reflection would convince me that, whatever of high hope there may be in this in the long run, its sudden execution is impossible. If they all landed there in a day, they would all perish in the next ten days, and there are not surplus shipping and surplus money enough to carry them there in many times ten days. What then? Free them all, and keep them among us as underlings. Is it quite certain that this betters their condition?

"I think I would not hold one in slavery, at any rate; yet, the point is not clear enough for me to denounce people upon. What next? Free them, and make them politically and socially our equals? My own feelings will not admit this; and, if mine would, we well know that those of the great mass of white people will not. Whether this feeling accords with justice and sound judgment, is not the sole question, if indeed it is any part of it. A universal feeling, whether well or ill-founded, cannot be safely disregarded. We cannot, then, make them equals. It does seem to me that systems of gradual emancipation might be adopted; but, for their tardiness in this, I will not undertake to judge our brethren of the South.

"When they remind us of their constitutional rights, I acknowledge them, not grudgingly, but fully and fairly; and I would give them any legislation for the reclaiming of their fugitives, which should not in its stringency be more likely to carry a freeman into slavery than our ordinary criminal laws are to hang an innocent one.

"But all this, to my judgment, furnishes no more excuse for permitting slavery to go into our free territory, than it would for reviving the African slave trade by law. The law which forbids the bringing of slaves from Africa, and that which has so long forbidden the taking of them to Nebraska, can hardly be distinguished on any moral principle, and the repeal of the former could find quite as plausible excuses as that of the latter."[36]

Lincoln's objectives were to quiet the agitations in the North against the South, and to remove the cause of the discontent by restoration of the Missouri Compromise, which should never have been repealed at all. He sought to restore the political calm which had been carefully secured in 1850, hoping that the hard feelings by then severely exacerbated could be dressed again as would an old wound reopened by accident.

This explains Lincoln's tolerant, understanding, and conciliatory tone toward the South. It explains why he did not preach morality, but described reality. He was taking a course which a sensible and humane statesman should have taken. There was nothing of the vindictiveness of Mrs. Stowe in his speaking. He dreaded what she wrote, and detested the bigotry it promoted. Some years after his Peoria Speech, as slaughter and agony of previously unknown proportions ripped the North and the South, Lincoln greeted the author of *Uncle Tom's Cabin* as "the little lady who made this big war." His words were hardly prompted by gratitude, for the military operations then underway hurt him inside. At the time of his Peoria Speech, Lincoln evidently did not know that the repeal of the

Missouri Compromise had been consideration given for what later became the Union Pacific Railroad. And supposing he and others of like mind had known as much and then gained access to the inner sanctum where this deal was made, it is difficult even to imagine how they could have undone the understanding.

The upshot was, in any event, that all the passions released by the Kansas-Nebraska Act were irreversibly unleashed, whereupon the fate of the Union was sealed.

* * * * *

Lay aside all the speeches, discourses, books, opinions, debates, proceedings, exertions, and proposals of that day on slavery and secession. These had no beneficial influence whatever, for the age became gripped in a destructive and unstoppable inertia. The historical facts highlight how this calamity came to pass, as the government and constitution of the country failed to contain the driving force of potent faction.

The architects of the Missouri Compromise knew that it was important, for the sake of domestic peace, to keep Northern people and Southern people and their respective ways of life separate in those parts of the Federal territories which were likely to attract settlers from both sections of the country. Therefore, unavoidable trouble loomed when Kansas was opened up to immigration from both parts of the country.

In late 1854 and early 1855, elections were held in the territory as prescribed by Congress. A private army of 5,000 so-called "border ruffians" came in from Missouri to work fraud and violence, and this intrusion created the pretense of the election of a pro-slavery territorial delegate to Congress, and a pro-slavery territorial legislature of Kansas. And under armed intimidation, the territorial governor failed to exercise his power of declaring these elections void.

It is impossible to believe that these huge crimes were committed spontaneously. An army of 5,000 mercenary troops, carrying out systematic operations, cannot be raised and activated without extensive organization and capital. It is preposterous to say that this organization and capital could have originated solely among the planters of Missouri.

A theory often taught to uncritical students of the period is that the invasion was part of a giant "slave power conspiracy" in the South. This story emanates from the same polluted well of falsehood which says that the great sin of slavery justified military rape and political exploitation of the South. It is time that such fabrications be transpierced, and that a fresh new look be taken.

Specific evidence does not exist to trace the funds to their source. It is impossible to prove by direct evidence exactly what combination hired the mercenary troops who brought corruption and confusion into the elections of late 1854 and early 1855 in Kansas. Those who claim that there was a slave power conspiracy have drawn their inferences from historical circumstances to suit their outlook.

It is alright to draw inferences from circumstantial evidence, which every good trial lawyer knows is not inherently inferior, but is often superior to direct evidence. Yet, when relying on circumstantial evidence, it is important to draw upon as many facts as can be gathered, lest incomplete or misleading indications suggest erroneous inferences. Those who have preached the slave power conspiracy have ignored basic particulars which may be illustrated.

When trouble broke out in Kansas, the North produced greater wealth than the South. While in the real necessities of life the South was richer per capita, the North had twelve miles of railroad track for every five in the South, nine tons of shipping for every one in the South, three acres tilled for every one in the South, and twenty-two free white males from 18 to 60 years for every five in the South. The North produced fourteen times the textile goods, fifteen times the iron, thirty-eight times the coal, thirty-two times the firearms, four or five times the wheat, and twice the corn.[37]

Planters in the South had no motive to mount a military expedition into Kansas, and surely they had no giant surplus to wage such a wild gamble. The greatest source of wealth in the South during that era was King Cotton. The South then produced virtually all the cotton in the United States. But Kansas has never produced any significant quantity of cotton. Nor did it appear, when the old compromise line was removed, that Kansas held any promise for large yields of cotton.

Planters in the South might well have gone to great lengths for the sake of expanding into any rich new cotton lands as might have become readily available, because this crop would have offered them safe returns of a kind which they appreciated. Yet, it is hard to imagine that they as businessmen were really excited about the abstract possibility of a new but nominal slave State, which could have done but little to stem the growing tide in favor of the North in the Senate. Given what was then at stake, this being exceedingly speculative, they certainly would not have been willing to go so far as to pool the large sums needed to arm, equip, and organize whole brigades of cavalry, then put them into action on the field for an invasion of Kansas.

The direction and cash had to come from headquarters which were at the center of real power, — not mere power of the law, but the kind of power which could engineer huge projects over the long term, could afford to risk and lose vast capital yet survive, could make deals of continental magnitude, and could practically write legislation and elect presidents. And in those days, such resources were actually possessed by financial interests which had anchored plans for a transcontinental railroad across Nebraska.

It was their needs, after all, which were impressively served when Stephen Douglas sold out the Missouri Compromise. They had a motive to deliver Kansas to the South as payment for support of the railway route they favored across the middle of the United States. They easily had access to extra cash in amounts sufficient to hire 5,000 armed men to fix territorial elections in Kansas.

It would be helpful if more details were available to elaborate upon this theory: — even so, it is far more solid and coherent than the claim of a slave power conspiracy, because it supplies a more meaningful picture of motive and means for what happened. And, if the evidence be not enough against railroad magnates in the North, then neither should anyone accuse planters of the South. There must be no double standard of evidence.

There are additional reasons for inferring that the border ruffians were mercenaries of railroad magnates in the North. The railroad magnates were capable of picking and choosing the transcontinental route they preferred, and dictating terms which others might accept. They actually did as much, and Southern interests were virtually forced to take the bare pittance of a chance to settle Kansas.

Given the extensive liquidity in their great banking houses, the railroad magnates were in a position of command. A president of the Union might be rendered so dependent on their resources that he could be forced to obey their will. By contrast, given the awkward form of their wealth, Southern planters as a class could never enjoy more than a position of influence. A president of the Union might hear them and feel sympathy for their pleas, but never could they order him about.

As to the situation in Kansas during the 1850s, the occupants of the White House were not merely helpful to the bogus government, but positively servile. They did not try to wade through political turbulence, but plainly did what they were told. And the voices who spoke must have had their offices in Philadelphia or New York, not Atlanta or New Orleans.

It is noteworthy also that the most distinguished efforts to prevent the forceful imposition of a pro-slavery government and constitution upon

Kansas were made by statesmen of the South. While these statesmen thus did their duty to the Union, republican politicians in the North bleated and groaned about the "crime against Kansas," which they blamed on the South.

In the summer of 1855, the pro-slavery legislature of Kansas convened at Pawnee, then at Shawnee Mission. They enacted statutes prohibiting anti-slavery agitation and demanding test oaths. By the autumn of 1855, the free State party of Kansas had been importuned enough, and settlers not wishing slavery elected a convention to meet at Topeka. There they framed a constitution, and, by the end of the year, they elected a territorial legislature and governor of Kansas. There were two governments, and civil war broke out along the Wakarusa River.

President Franklin Pierce delivered a special message to Congress early in 1856, denouncing the Topeka government as an act of rebellion. Not surprisingly, he supported the financial interests which set up the pro-slavery government of Kansas. His position was indefensible, and it strongly indicates his status of a pawn. The territory became known as "bleeding Kansas." The civil war continued until late that year, when John Geary, the territorial governor appointed by the President, managed to mediate peace.

Notwithstanding Pierce's denunciations, the Topeka government petitioned Congress in the spring of 1856 for the admission of Kansas to the Union as a free State. Senator Robert Toombs of Georgia introduced a bill for a free and open election of a new constitutional convention in Kansas. His plans conformed exactly to a recommendation of James Madison in the 43rd Federalist.[38] If a civil war should break out between two regimes, each claiming to be legitimate, Madison had urged Congress to intervene, as by calling a new convention to settle the government. Toombs was an ardent voice for Southern planters. If the huge effort to impose a pro-slavery government and constitution upon Kansas had been a slave power conspiracy, Toombs would have made no proposal which, as he certainly knew, would lead to the admission of Kansas as a free State. His bill passed the Senate but was not acted upon in the House. Kansas was left in anarchy, because the republican party, which already had impressive strength in the North, chose to make political hay in the elections of 1856.

In early 1857, the pro-slavery legislature met at Lecompton, and called for a constitutional convention to be elected according to statutes which excluded the participation of anyone who had supported the Topeka government, and disallowed a popular referendum on the final work. To this injustice Governor Geary interposed a veto, which, however, was promptly overridden. In the closing days of his administration, President Pierce gave no support or encouragement to the embattled territorial executive, who then saw the situation as hopeless, and resigned. In the summer of 1857, a pro-slavery constitutional convention met at Lecompton.

Meanwhile, President James Buchanan appointed Robert Walker as territorial governor of Kansas. Governor Walker was from Mississippi. He was no enemy of slavery, and favored the interests of the South. But far from supporting a slave power conspiracy, Walker called for election of a new territorial legislature. He went to Topeka, and promised free State men that their rights would be protected. In the territorial elections in the fall of 1857, there was a massive block of fraudulent pro-slavery votes. Walker threw out all the bad ballots. Because of the fairness and integrity of a statesmen of the South, the free State party won a decisive victory in both the house and the senate of the territorial legislature set up by Congress.

Nevertheless, the pro-slavery convention in Lecompton still remained in session, and at length they succeeded in framing a constitution. The delegates knew their cause was almost finished, but they made a last desperate attempt to create Kansas as a slave State. They proclaimed the constitution, but submitted only two options to the people by referendum: — shall the constitution thus framed in convention be accepted with or without the clauses allowing slavery? If the vote was negative, slavery was to be abolished in futuro, but title to slaves then living would remain secure. The free State party denounced the proposition as a public fraud. Governor Walker agreed, and he went to see President James Buchanan. So unable was Buchanan to act independently that he rejected the plea of the Southern governor whom he had appointed, and upheld the absurdity at Lecompton, whereupon Walker resigned in despair.

In the referendum called by the Lecompton Convention in the fall of 1857, the free State people generally refused to participate. The vote was 6,200 for the constitution with slavery, of which 2,700 ballots were thrown out as fraudulent, and 560 for the constitution without slavery. The new territorial governor was Frederick Stanton of Tennessee. He was no abolitionist, and he favored planter interests. But neither did he support a slave power conspiracy. Governor Stanton convened the new territorial legislature, which promptly called a new referendum on the constitution framed at Lecompton, subject to three options: — for the constitution with the slavery, for the constitution without slavery, or against the constitution. The result was decisive, 10,200 votes were cast against the constitution, and less than 200 votes were cast in favor, these split over the question of slavery.

In spite of the best efforts of statesmen from Georgia, Mississippi, and Tennessee to guarantee the right of the people of Kansas to enter the Union without slavery, President Buchanan recommended to Congress in early 1858 that Kansas be admitted to the Union as a slave State under the constitution framed at Lecompton. Congress rebelled by authorizing another referendum. The constitution framed at Lecompton was again overwhelmingly defeated, and in early 1861 Kansas was admitted to the Union as a free State.

* * * * *

As troubles brewed in Kansas, a fateful case arose before the United States Supreme Court. The matter seemed to turn on important legal questions concerning slavery. Yet on the record, there was no real need to decide anything at all. It was inexcusable that any extended opinion should have been entered in the cause. Still, the justices imagined that, if they spoke, using their grand authority as the highest court of the land, the country would acquiesce, satisfied that the problem had been settled with august finality.

Uncle Tom's Cabin had been a social and moral disaster. The repeal of the Missouri Compromise had been an economic and political calamity. The Kansas Civil War threatened the ruin of the United States. The case of *Dred Scott v. Sandford*, 19 Howard 391 (U.S. 1857), enhanced antagonisms beyond any reasonable hope of reconciliation.

Dred Scott was a Negro slave of Dr. John Emerson, a citizen of Missouri, and a surgeon in the United States Army. In 1834, Emerson took Scott to the army post at Rock Island, in the State of Illinois, where slavery had been prohibited since the Northwest Ordinance. In 1836, Emerson took Scott on another tour of duty at Fort Snelling in what was then the Wisconsin Territory and, in any event, within the Louisiana Purchase above 36 degrees 30 minutes north latitude, where slavery had been prohibited by the Missouri Compromise. There Emerson purchased, from an army officer, a female slave by the name of Harriet, whom Scott married, and in due course two daughters, Eliza and Lizzie, were born of this union. In 1838, Emerson returned with Scott and his family to Missouri.

Dred Scott had learned to read the King James Bible. In keeping with the 6th chapter of Ephesians, he had served his master well, as his master had treated him well; but, in keeping with the 7th chapter of 1st Corinthians, he lawfully and peaceably sought freedom when the opportunity arose. In 1846, Scott sued Emerson's widow and heir in the circuit

court of Missouri, seeking title to his freedom and the freedom of his wife
and daughters. In 1850, because Dred and Harriet had been voluntarily
taken by their masters onto free soil, a circuit judge granted freedom to
Scott and his family, relying on the views of Lord Mansfield, the
Northwest Ordinance, and the Missouri Compromise. The cause was really a routine affair, since the applicable law had been laid down in repeated and unequivocal decisions of the Missouri Supreme Court.[39] The
decree of the circuit court of Missouri was merely another illustration of
the established and authentic jurisprudence of the old South.

It was astonishing, therefore, when in 1852 the Missouri Supreme
Court held that the question was governed, not by the law prevailing in
Illinois or Wisconsin, but the law of Missouri, under which Scott and his
family were slaves.

There had long been a principle governing conflict off laws, designed
to deal with cases of title and incidents of title to ordinary personal property. The rule was that, if a chattel had been acquired under the laws of a
certain place where the owner was domiciled, those proprietary charac-
teristics remained, even after the thing had been moved to another jurisdiction which might otherwise have established title or distributed rights.
A majority of two to one on the Missouri Supreme Court held that this
rule applied even to the unique case of slave property.[40] It was said that
Dr. Emerson had lawfully acquired title to Dred Scott in Missouri, and
that his title was not impeached in the slightest when he took his slave to
the State of Illinois and the Wisconsin Territory. As for Harriet, Eliza, and
Lizzie, the rule trapping husband and father was generalized to them also:
— the status of bond or free for anyone alleged to be slave depended on
the law of the domicile of the person alleged to be his or her master. Chief
Justice Hamilton Gamble wrote a powerful dissent in which he cited
numerous decisions of judges across the Southern States, and said of the
law as it then stood in Missouri, "In this State, it has been recognized
from the beginning of the government as a correct position in law that a
master who takes his slave reside in a State or territory where slavery is
prohibited, thereby emancipates his slave."

The rule for choice of laws used by the Missouri Supreme Court presupposed that a slave was like a horse, an ox, or any other species of
moveable property. But it had been assumed in the Philadelphia
Convention that, save where otherwise stipulated in the fugitive slave
clause in Article IV, Section 2 of the United States Constitution, the rule
given by Lord Mansfield was the universal law throughout the Union. It
was, therefore, understood generally that ordinary rules of property did

not apply to the special case of slavery. And this history had been fully acknowledged by the United States Supreme Court.[41]

Bad as this decision was, the judgment was final. There has long been a rule of common law, known as res judicata, based on the practical necessity of bringing litigation to an end, however imperfect human justice. The rule was and remains that, when parties have litigated a case between them to final judgment, all issues connected with the suit in light of the pleadings and record are forever settled as between them or their successors in interest, nor can either side challenge the final result in any subsequent litigation between them. The rule of res judicata applied to Dred Scott and his family, and should have ended the litigation on title to their freedom.

On the record of the circuit court of Missouri, defending counsel evidently made a motion for nonsuit, whereupon the parties stipulated the facts, and further proceedings turned solely on questions of law. Therefore, the technical effect of the reversal by the Missouri Supreme Court was a judgment of nonsuit against the plaintiff as well as his wife and children. But this technicality should have made no difference, because at common law the effect of a final judgment on the merits has always been the same, whether based on a jury verdict, a demurrer, or any of several types of motions addressing the merits.

Yet, whether by design or fluke, not long after the decision of the Missouri Supreme Court, the United States Supreme Court handed down a decision which suggested that, if a cause had been fully litigated between certain parties in the courts of a particular State, and the plaintiff was dismissed on a judgment of nonsuit, whatever the circumstances, the final judgment there entered did not bar the plaintiff from bringing the same suit against the same defendant or his successor in interest, in a circuit court of the United States, so long as he could fit the case into the subject matter jurisdiction of the Federal judiciary.[42] It is somewhat of a mystery where this exception to the rule of res judicata came from, neither was any cogent judicial explanation ever given for it.

Yet here was a judicial pronouncement, which was almost a greeting card asking Dred Scott to relitigate his cause. If Dred Scott was a freeman, as Judge Gamble of Missouri had said he was indeed, then he was a citizen of Missouri, according to the unambiguous exposition of Judge Gaston of North Carolina.

By curious coincidence, Dred, Harriet, Eliza, and Lizzie were sold to John Sandford, who was supposed to be a citizen of New York. This transaction did not ring true, because Sandford could not take his property to

New York without losing his title. Indeed, if the domicile of the owner determined title to a slave, and if Sandford were a citizen of New York, he would technically have been domiciled in New York where slavery was forbidden, and he could never have acquired title to Scott and his family.

In any event, this dubious transaction was used as a pretext by Scott to claim that he, as a freed black, was a citizen of Missouri and that Sandford was a citizen of New York, and thus to bring suit against Sandford in a circuit court of the United States in Missouri under Section 11 of the Judiciary Act of 1789.[43] On the other hand, if Sandford had really been interested in keeping Scott and his family as slaves, he could easily have pleaded that he was a citizen domiciled in Missouri where he had lived for many years, and that would have led to dismissal for want of jurisdiction, and not word would have had to be said about slavery, or he could have pleaded the judgment of the Missouri Supreme Court confirming the title of Dr. Emerson from whom his title derived. But Sandford entered no such pleas in his behalf, which deepens the mystery about this case.

Neither Scott nor Sandford could finance such high-powered litigation as was then fought out before the Federal judiciary. Scott had no significant resources. If he and his wife and children were slaves, their fair market value could not have exceeded a few thousand dollars in money of the day. His legal fees must have been paid by somebody posing as a philanthropist; but if the freedom of Scott and his family had really been the desired objective, their manumission could have been bought for a mere pittance compared to the cost of bringing a suit of this kind. Even after a century and a half, the record stinks with collusion, which has always been cause for dismissal of litigation. The case, handled by expensive lawyers of high calibre, must have been staged and bankrolled by big money from behind the scenes.

The suit was brought before the Federal circuit court in St. Louis in 1854 about the same time as the Missouri Compromise was destroyed in Congress.

Scott's declaration alleged the circumstances of his transportation to Illinois and Wisconsin, his marriage, and the birth of his children, and thereupon demanded his freedom.

Sandford pleaded in abatement that Scott and his family were not and could not be citizens of Missouri, as required to bring the cause within the jurisdiction of the Federal circuit court, because they were Negroes whose ancestors were imported from Africa and sold as slaves, and as such could not become citizens of any State of the Union. To this plea there was a demurrer, which was sustained, and Sandford answered over. The cause went to trial on the merits, but the Federal circuit judge directed a verdict for Sandford, following the earlier holding of the Missouri Supreme Court. On Scott's demand, a writ of error issued from the United States Supreme Court under Section 22 of the Judiciary Act of 1789.

Chief Justice Roger B. Taney wrote the "opinion of the court," but all other members of the court wrote separate opinions. The nine opinions together made up 239 closely printed pages of text prolix enough to make any seasoned lawyer bleary-eyed.

The plea in abatement, attacking jurisdiction, was not before the United States Supreme Court, because neither side challenged the holding of the Federal circuit court that it had jurisdiction to decide whether Scott was free or slave. It is true that the Federal judiciary enjoyed only a limited jurisdiction over subject matter, and the circumstances thereof in any case had to appear on the face of the pleadings of a case whenever the question was raised on demurrer or motion, otherwise there was no power to adjudicate. And from the days of Chief Justice John Jay, Federal courts had taken a fairly strict view of their constitutional and statutory powers.

This curiosity had given rise to odd situations. If, for example, a plaintiff sued in a circuit court of the United States, but failed to allege diversity of citizenship or some other basis of jurisdiction over subject matter, and suffered adverse judgment on the merits, he might sue out a writ of error and secure reversal of the judgment against himself.[44] Such a plaintiff could obtain such an odd result, notwithstanding the ageless rule of appellate litigation that a party might not take advantage of his own mistake in the court of first instance, all because of the restricted powers of the Federal judiciary. But never had jurisdiction sustained in a Federal circuit court been reexamined where it had been left unchallenged by either side in a cause brought before the United States Supreme Court. Dred Scott did not object to the holding of the Federal circuit court that it had jurisdiction to entertain the suit. And if Sandford had been dissatisfied with the adjudication of the Federal circuit court on his plea in abatement, he was free to sue out a writ of error, but he chose not to do so.[45]

Therefore, it was stretching things to a fatuous extent when Chief Justice Taney held that the question of jurisdiction over the subject matter had to be addressed. His insistence on confronting this question, on the record as it stood, shows that he was doing everything imaginable to decide a question which did not have to be passed upon at all.

The plea in abatement assumed, for the sake of discussion only, that Scott and his family had been legally emancipated, and proposed that, even if they had been freed, they were not citizens of Missouri as they had to be in order to bring their suit within the jurisdiction of the Federal circuit court in St. Louis. And the reason they were not citizens, the plea maintained, was that all members of the black race sold as slaves, and their descendants, even if freed by means impeccably lawful, were incapable of becoming citizens by any process, even by act of Congress.

This dogma presupposed that Benjamin Franklin, John Adams, and Thomas Jefferson did not mean to include black Africans sold as slaves, or their descendants, even if lawfully freed, as among "all men" who, according to the Declaration of American Independence which they had co-authored, were "endowed by their Creator with certain unalienable rights." The Chief Justice approved of this mendacious idea, in justification of which he said,

> "Yet the men who framed this declaration were great men, — high in literary acquirements, — high in their sense of honor, and incapable of asserting principles inconsistent with those on which they were acting. They perfectly understood the meaning of the language which they used, and how it would be understood by others; and they knew that it would not in any part of the civilized world be supposed to embrace the Negro race, which, by common consent, had been excluded from civilized governments and the family of nations, and doomed to slavery. They spoke and acted according to the then established doctrines and principles, and in the ordinary language of the day, and no one misunderstood them. The unhappy black race were separated from the white by indelible marks, and laws long before established, and were never thought of or spoken of except as property, and when the claims of the owner or the profit of the trader were supposed to need protection."[46]

But Taney well knew that Franklin, Adams, and Jefferson were aware of the inconsistency between the words they used and the condition of slavery, and that, for this very reason, they were all ardent in their desire to bring freedom to the black race as soon as practical means could be developed and implemented. Taney knew that Adams was an outspoken abolitionist in Massachusetts. He knew that Franklin had drawn up a much admired plan of emancipation in Pennsylvania. And he knew that Jefferson had been foremost among the fathers of the Southern abolition movement in Virginia. All of them were famous throughout the land because of their pioneering work to eradicate slavery.

Plainly, therefore, the plea in abatement had no merit, and the Federal circuit court was right in sustaining Scott's demurrer. Even so, Taney reversed the Federal circuit court, and held that it had no jurisdiction over the subject matter of the cause. Supposing Taney to have been correct, the proper result on writ of error would have been reversal with directions to quash the original writ. The merits would then have been beyond judicial cognizance, and nothing further would have been in need of decision. But deciding nothing about the merits of the case was not the agenda of the court, and so Taney trudged ahead, saying that even though the question was outside the original jurisdiction of the Federal circuit court, it was within the appellate jurisdiction of the United States Supreme Court.

When Dred and Harriet met and married at Fort Snelling, where they had been voluntarily brought by their masters. Under the second clause of Article IV, Section 3 of the United States Constitution, Congress was empowered to enact statutes such as the Northwest Ordinance, from which it follows that Congress had power abolish slavery in all Federal territories. By the Missouri Compromise, Congress had prohibited slavery at Fort Snelling. Given the holding of Lord Mansfield in the case of James Sommersett, assumed by the Philadelphia Convention and the First Congress, it was clear that Scott and his family were entitled to a judgment on the merits, granting their freedom.

Yet, in a protracted discourse, Taney held that the second clause in Article IV, Section 3 was restricted to the lands to the west of the Appalachian Mountains and to the east of the Mississippi River, which had been ceded by King George III in 1783. His premise presupposed that the Philadelphia Convention did not expect that the United States should ever acquire new territory by treaty or conquest or annexation. And it assumed that there was no normal anticipation of the future in the minds of James Wilson, George Washington, or Alexander Hamilton.

This notion was untenable, and so the Chief Justice was obliged to say that, yes, Congress could acquire and govern new territory, not from an express power to regulate territory belonging to the United States, but as an inevitable consequence of some unquestionable but unspecified power. The strain was too much for an unbiased and learned citizen to accept, but Taney went on. In exercising this mysterious authority, he held, Congress was bound by the guarantee of due process of law of Amendment V of the United States Constitution, which, he said, forbade the sudden cessation of legal protection of title to slaves when a planter took his property into any part of the Louisiana Purchase. Therefore, he held, Section 8 of the Act of March 6, 1820, was a nullity, and the events at Fort Snelling did not free Dred Scott, his wife, and his children.

The guarantee of due process of law derived from Magna Carta. Lord

Mansfield, drawing from Magna Carta and earlier decisions of the King's Bench on the liberation of villeins, made it too plain to be misunderstood that the liberation of a slave voluntarily taken by his master onto free soil was certainly not a violation of, but was rather obedience to Magna Carta. And, if it was no violation of Magna Carta for Congress to enact the Northwest Ordinance, then it was no violation of Magna Carta for Congress to enact the Missouri Compromise. The analysis of the Chief Justice was again too distended for belief.

Taney had one last corner to cover. In Rock Island, Illinois, he said, nothing happened to free Dred Scott, because that question was governed by the law of Missouri, which was the law of the domicile of Emerson under whom Sandford held title. This argument ran against nearly all the reported decisions of the judges in the Southern States.

But, no matter, Taney held that the judgment of the Federal circuit court in St. Louis, already found to be without jurisdiction, should be affirmed on the merits. Lawlessness ran riot.

Justice Benjamin Curtis wrote a dissent particularly admired, holding that, if the plea in abatement was before the court, the principles set forth by Judge Gaston of North Carolina governed. And as to the merits, he maintained, the principles laid down by Judge Gamble of Missouri were correct. The experience of sitting on the case so disquieted him that he finished his pending work, resigned his seat, and returned to Boston, there to take up the private practice of law. Justice John McLean wrote a dissent based on similar authority and reasoning.

Shortly before his inauguration as President in the spring of 1857, two justices on the majority siding with Taney in the case of Dred Scott informed James Buchanan of the forthcoming decision. The new President said in his first address that he would cheerfully abide by the result, whatever it should be, pretending he had no idea what was coming, then he urged the people to let the question of slavery in the Federal territories be settled by the United States Supreme Court. Two days later, the decision was announced by the Chief Justice. Less than a year later, Buchanan recommended the admission of Kansas as a slave State.

There was an anticlimax in the case. After ten years of litigation, in which it was finally decided that Dred Scott and his family were slaves, the four of them were emancipated by Sandford. Father, mother, and daughters had been used like pieces of furniture on a stage. All the signs of collusion and bankrolling from behind the scenes were confirmed as the whole country exploded with passions which could never thereafter be contained by peaceable and lawful means.

When citizens read the perverse language of Chief Justice Taney, there was widespread loathing against the United States Supreme Court. Taney's words were interpreted as portraying the thinking of most people in the South, which was not so. The decision excited the strongest feelings of extremists, — of those who wished to raise slave insurrections, and of those who wanted to reopen the slave trade. The case illustrates why in general courts should not decide questions which they have no need to decide. The very wish to decide in such situations may produce tragedy and mischief beyond what ambition can foresee.

* * * * *

There had been a string of events, obviously moved by the same interests and tending in the same direction, starting with the mass marketing of *Uncle Tom's Cabin*, then the Kansas-Nebraska Act in 1854, which was followed by the Kansas Civil War in 1855 and 1856, and then the case of Dred Scott in 1856 and 1857, then Buchanan's recommendation of the Lecompton Constitution in 1858. It is an insult to human intelligence to insist that these events occurred because of broad forces in history, and were not the planned results of a factious conspiracy.

Abraham Lincoln became the republican candidate for the office of United States Senator from Illinois in 1858, running against Stephen Douglas. In accepting the nomination of his party, Lincoln delivered a famous speech in which he said,

> "A house divided against itself cannot stand. I believe this government cannot endure permanently half slave and half free. I do not expect the union to be dissolved, — I do not expect the house to fall, but I do expect it will cease to be divided. It will become all one thing, or all the other. Either the opponents of slavery will arrest the further spread of it, and place it where the public mind shall rest in the belief that it is in the course of ultimate extinction, or its advocates will push it forward till it shall become alike lawful in all the States, old as well as new, North as well as South."[47]

Lincoln reviewed the circumstantial evidence, and deduced that there had been a factious conspiracy which must have been bound up in some way with Douglas, and which had as its object the legalization of slavery everywhere throughout the United States. He was barely touching the surface. Douglas was involved, but as an advocate of railroads backed by great banking houses. The particulars were not yet fully evident, but they would become clearer in years not far distant.

In the ensuing months, the two contenders debated the issues of the day, including the case of Dred Scott. Douglas dutifully stated, "I intend to yield obedience to the decisions of the highest tribunal in the land in all cases, whether their opinions are in conformity with my views as a lawyer or not."[48]

But Lincoln complained that Douglas "would have the citizen conform his vote to that decision; the member of Congress, his; the President, his use of the veto power. He would make it a rule of political action for the people and all the departments of the government. I would not."[49]

Douglas had learned the law by reading Blackstone who, in the introductory passages of his great work, had written about the rule of common law called stare decisis. Blackstone said that it was the rule to abide by former precedents so as to keep the scale of justice steady: even so, there was an "exception, where the former determination is most evidently contrary to reason, much more if it is contrary to divine law. But even in such cases, the subsequent judges do not pretend to make new law, but to vindicate the old one from misrepresentation. For if it be found that the former decision is manifestly absurd or unjust, it is declared, not that such sentence was bad law, but that it was not law."[50]

The case of Dred Scott decided the issues before the United States Supreme Court, but was not binding precedent because it contradicted natural law, legal tradition which elaborated natural law, and the intended meaning of the United States Constitution which was built upon them both. The bitter truth is that Taney and those concurring with him had managed in one destructive thrust to wreck a consistent and large body of jurisprudence going back at least three centuries. Taney misrepresented the established law. His judgment was not bad law, but not law at all.

Great was the injustice to Dred Scott and his family, yet they were at least liberated in the end, and their innocence was made known to the world. Even greater was the injustice done to the South, for the region had fostered a large body of jurisprudence under which Scott and his family were entitled to their freedom. And a Southern judge, acting upon this jurisprudence, did grant Scott and his family their freedom. But the South suffered the infamy for this hideous decision. And the South was punished by a brutal military and political rape which cruelly inflicted injury to the black race even more awful, if possible, than was visited upon the white population.

NOTES

CHAPTER VI

1 - Under the law of nations, a treaty has always served to convey territory, as if it were a deed of title. The legal sufficiency of the King's grant of lands in North America to the United States in the Treaty of Paris, notwithstanding objections in the British House of Commons, was discussed by Charles Cotesworth Pinckney before the South Carolina House of Representatives on January 17, 1788, in 4 Elliot's Debates at 277-278. The first and second articles of the treaty must be read together, as they appear in 1 Commager's Documents 117-118. In the first article, George III conceded the independence of the "United States, viz., New Hampshire, Massachusetts Bay, Rhode Island," etc. The King then relinquished "all proprietary and territorial rights to the same," meaning the several States, each named individually. The second article then gave an exact legal description of the territory in question so as to avoid "all disputes which might arise in the future on the subject of the boundaries." Nobody at the time construed this grant as a conveyance of territory to the government of the Union.

2 - The remonstrance of the General Assembly of Maryland and its instructions to the delegates of the State in Congress, both dated December 15, 1778, are reprinted in 10 Hening's Statutes at Large at 549-556.

3 - This resolution is reprinted in 10 Hening's Statutes at Large at 562-563.

4 - This resolution is reprinted in 10 Hening's Statutes at Large at 564-567.

5 - The enabling legislation is found in 11 Hening's Statutes at Large 326 (October 1783, Chapter 18), and the deed of cession to the United States is displayed in 11 Hening's Statutes at Large at 571-575.

6 - The powers, rights, and capacities necessarily and inseparably incident to every corporation at common law are stated in 1 Blackstone's Commentaries at 475.

7 - Reprinted in Tansill's Documents 47-54, 1 Commager's Documents 128-132.

The Northwest Ordinance was reenacted word for word by the First Congress on August 7, 1789, 1 U. S. Statutes at Large 50-53.

8 - The framing of Article IV, Section 3 of the United States Constitution can be traced in 5 Elliot's Debates 128, 156-157, 190, 332, 381, 439, 492-497, 536, 550, 564, — Tansill's Documents 118, 155, 203, 236-237, 406, 470, 480-481, 648-645, 711, 734, — 1 Ferrand's Records 22, 121, 237, and 2 Ferrand's Records 46, 128, 188, 455-466, 578, 602, 628, 662 (Madison's Notes May 29, June 5, 13, and 19, July 18 and 26, August 6, 29, and 30, Sepember 10, 12, 15, and 17, 1787). The purposes of these clauses are discussed in the 38th Federalist by James Madison, Mentor Edition at 239, and the 43rd Federalist, also by James Madison, Mentor Edition at 273-274. It is plain from these sources that the first clause of Article IV, Section 3 was intended to authorize the admission of new States, regardless of whether the territory in question were part of the United States in 1787 or subsequently acquired, and that the second clause was intended to give Congress a constitutional power of regulating territory after the manner of the Northwest Ordinance. It was well known in the convention at the time these clauses came up for debate that Congress had passed the Northwest Ordinance, and that the ordinance included a prohibition of slavery. Nor did any of the known advocates of slavery, such as Charles Cotesworth Pinckney, express any objection.

9 - Jefferson's original plan appears in his Report of Government for the Western Territory dated March 22, 1784, while he was a member of Congress, and is reprinted in Koch & Peden's Jefferson at 313-319. Jefferson's hope was that slaves willing to run away from their masters into the western lands of the Union should become free, according to the principle on which Lord Mansfield handed down the judgment in *Sommersett's Case*, 20 Howell's St. Tr. 1 at 80-82 (K. B. 1771).

10 - The fugitive slave clause in Article IV, Section 2 of the United States Constitution was inserted during the Philadelphia Convention on the demand of Charles Cotesworth Pinckney, as appears in 5 Elliot's Debates 487, 492, 536, 550, 564, — Tansill's Documents 631-632, 638, 711, 734, — 2 Ferrand's Records 443, 453-454, 577, 601-602, 628, 662 (Madison's Notes, August 28 and 29, September 10, 12, 15, 17, 1787). In his address to the South Carolina House of Representatives on January 17, 1788, General Pinckney expressed awareness that, without this clause, a slave who escaped into free territory automatically became free. He said, "We have obtained a right to recover our slaves in whatever part of America they may take refuge, which is a right we had not before." — 4 Elliot's Debates at 286.

11 - In the 32nd Federalist, Mentor Edition at 199-200, Alexander Hamilton made reference to "what lawyers call a NEGATIVE PREGNANT — that is, a *negation* of one thing, and an *affirmance* of another." He meant a provision which

constitutes an exception implies a power of legislation or a rule which governs outside the perameters of the exception. There he explained that the clause in Article I, Section 10 of the United States Constitution restraining the several States from laying duties on imports, exports, and tonnage establish that the several States otherwise may impose taxes. Likewise, the constitutional right to recover runaway slaves on free territory implies that the slaves would otherwise be free men.

12 - The framing of the 1808 clause in Article I, Section 9 of the United States Constitution, and the related proposals for a two-thirds majority in both the House and the Senate for regulations of commerce in general or at least for navigation acts in particular, can be traced in 5 Elliot's Debates 357, 378, 457-461, 470-471, 477-478, 488-492, 536, 552, and 561, — Tansill's Documents 476, 589-594, 608, 616-618, 633-638, 707, 736, — 2 Ferrand's Records 95, 183, 364-365, 369-374, 400, 414-417, 449-453, 571, 596, 631, 656, 657 (Madison's Notes, July 23, August 6, 21, 22, 24, 25, and 29, September 10, 12, 15, and 17, 1787).

13 - Such reasoning appears in *Gibbons v. Ogden*, 9 Wheaton 1 at 190-191 (U. S. 1824), where Chief Justice John Marshall noted an exception to the power of Congress over navigation in commerce in the sixth clause of Article I, Section 9 of the United States Constitution, and from thence inferred that the power of Congress to regulate commerce must include, save as limited, a power to regulate navigation.

14 - 4 Johnson's Jay at 431 (in a letter to Elias Boudinot, November 17, 1819).

15 - Singleton's speech is reprinted in Rozwenc's Slavery as a Cause 20-23.

16 - Quoted in Thomas's Slavery Attacked at 91.

17 - 1 Stephen's View at 404 (speech at Capon Springs, Virginia, June 28, 1851).

18 - Quoted in Rozwenc's Slavery as a Cause at 48.

19 - The text of the treaty, signed on April 30, 1803, and given the advice and consent of the United States Senate on October 20, 1803, is reprinted in 1 Commager's Documents 190-191.

20 - 3 U. S. Statutes at Large 545 at 548 (March 6, 1820). The most important motions, statutes, and resolutions related to the Missouri Compromise are collected in 1 Commager's Documents 224-227.

21 - 1 Commager's Documents at 304-305 (Clay's Raleigh Letter, April 17, 1844).

22 - According to 1 Morris' History at 207, the annual output in gold in California by 1851 was about $55,000,000. On Janauary 9, 1790, Alexander Hamilton estimated the public debt of the United States, as measured in gold and silver coin, to be $11,710,379 owed as principal and interest to the governments

of France and Spain and to Dutch lenders, together with $40,414,086 owed as principal and interest on domestic loans and on "new tenor" continental currency issued after March 18, 1780, and also $2,000,000.00 to retire "old tenor" continental currency. Altogether, therefore, the public debt of the United States, as calculated by Hamilton, was $54,124,465, as appears in his First Report on Public Credit, Cooke's Reports at 19-22 and 32. It may be observed that the old tenor currency consisted of bills of credit emitted by Congress from June 22, 1775, through November 29, 1779, in an aggregate amount of $236,501,920. See e. g., 1 Thorpe's History 124-125 and Del Mar's Money in America 112-113. In an effort to curb the inflation produced by this redundant currency, Congress passed a resolution of March 18, 1780, to retire all outstanding bills over the course of one year in satisfaction of requisitions of Congress at 40 to 1 in good coin, as appears in Del Mar's Money in America at 106. About $80,000,000 in old tenor currency was not retired according to the terms of the resolution of Congress on March 18, 1780, and so remained in circulation, as may be inferred from footnote 10 in Cooke's Reports at 21, and the corresponding text. In the thirty-eight emissions of "old tenor" currency, all approved by signers of the Declaration of American Independence, redemption was promised in the face amount in spanish milled dollars or the equivalent in gold or silver, nor did the resolution of March 18, 1780, have any further effect after a year had passed. The entire amount of this $80,000,000 was part of the public debt of the United States under the twelfth article of the old Confederation and the first clause of Article VI of the United States Constitution. Yet it was sweepingly repudiated by Congress on Hamilton's recommendation to the extent of $78,000,000. The episode illustrates the inherent prerogative of Congress to discount and thereby to repudiate public debt for just cause in exercising its power to "pay the debts of he United States" as set forth in the first clause of Article I, Section 8 of the United States Constitution. When it is remembered that, at the time, western lands were valued by Hamilton at about 20 cents per acre in good coin (Cooke's Reports at 26), and that the price of the the Louisiana purchase was $15,000,000, this particular repudiation of public debt was truly astronomical.

23 - One of the most insightful discussions of slavery in the territories before the outbreak of the American Civil War is the classic article by Charles Ramsdell, *The Natural Limits of Slavery Expansion*, 16 Mississippi Valley Historical Review 151-171 (1929), reprinted in Rozwenc's Slavery as a Cause 59-71 and Roawnc's Civil War 150-162. The article debunks the "Battle Hymn of the Republic" theory of the Ameican Civil War that, of moral necessity, the evil of slavery had to be extirpated by political domination and military conquest of the Southern States. This propaganda was used to justify the war crimes of William Tecumseh Sherman against the people of Georgia and South Carolina, and is expressed in the florid rhetoric of Abraham Lincoln in his second inaugural address on March 4, 1865, where he said, "Fondly do we hope, fervently do we pray, that this mighty scourge of war may speedily pass away. Yet, if God wills

that it continue until wealth piled by the bondman's two hundred fifty years of unrequited toil shall be sunk, and until every drop of blood drawn by the lash shall be paid with another drawn by the sword, as was said three thousand years ago, so still it must be said, 'The judgments of the Lord are true and righteous altogether.'" — 1 Commager's Documents at 443, Speeches and Debates at 541. Ramsdell showed by cold facts that the natural limits of geography had already terminated the expansion of slavery, and, consequently, that the institution was already doomed to extinction, probably by the early 20th Century, without the massive destruction of the American Civil War. Ramsdell's article contains valuable demographic and geographic information relied upon in this work. Further information on slavery in the United States, including the size of the slave population, the capital value of slaves held, and the number of runaway slaves, is found in 1 Stephens' View 539-540, and 2 Morris' History 514-516.

24 - Reprinted in 1 Commager's Documents at 319-320 (January 2, 1850).

25 - The Compromise of 1850 consisted of five acts of Congress which are found in 9 U. S. Statutes at Large 446-467: the acts admitting the State of California, adjusting the western boundary of the State of Texas, organizing the New Mexico Territory, and organizing the Utah Territory were all signed on September 9, 1850; the new fugitive slave law was signed on September 18, 1850; and the act abolishing the slave trade in the District of Columbia was signed on September 20, 1850. These several acts are conveniently reprinted in 1 Commager's Documents at 319-323.

26 - The old act is found in 1 U. S. Statutes at Large 302 (February 12, 1793). The third section provided that a slaveholder or his agent could arrest a runaway slave and bring him before any judge or magistrate of the State or the United States, and, on application founded on oral testimoy or on affidavit attesting to the material facts, could secure a certificate authorizing removal of such slave to the State where he was held in bondage. The chancellor of New York was certainly correct in his views, expressed in *Jack v. Martin*, 14 Wendell 507 (1835): that Congress had no authority to enact a law in aid of recovering runaway slaves, except a statute allowing Federal courts to take jurisdiction over some or all questions arising under the fugitive slave clause in Article IV, Section 2 of the United States Constitution; that, without any such act of Congress, the courts of the several States were duty bound to enforce the fugitive slave clause by writ of homine replegiando or other suit or writ allowable at common law, subject to trial by jury; and that, in any event, the third section of the old act of 1793 was manifestly unconstitutional as a denial of due process of law.

27 - Quoted in 2 Thorpe's History at 436.

28 - Quoted in 2 Thorpe's History at 450.

29 - Sir Winston Churchill thus explained the reason for the repeal of the

Missouri Compromise: "A fresh cause of divergence sprang from the choice of the transcontinental railway route. The rival interests of North and South were decisively involved, and in the political dispute the North and West drew together. The southern route was the shortest to the Pacific coast, and passed through organized territories from New Orleans to Texas, and thence by the Gila Valley to San Diego. The northern followed the natural trail of emigration which bound California and Oregon to the States bordering the Great Lakes. In between lay a third route through regions as yet unorganized, but in which Northern capital was invested. Senator Stephen A. Douglas of Illinois, who ardently wished to settle the West, and was heavily committed to the central line, became the champion of the Northern interests. In order to organise this central zone he proposed in January 1854 a bill establishing the territory of Nebraska. As a bait for Southern votes he included a clause embodying the conception of 'popular sovereignty.' This changed the issue and aggravated the dispute. People in the North had taken the compomise of 1850 to apply only to the former Mexican territories. Now it was propsoed to introduce it into regions where hitherto the line of the Missouri Compromise had prevailed. As these areas of the Great Plains were north of latitude 36 degrees 30 minutes, the new bill implicitly repealed the Missouri Compromise. The Southerners wished this to be done explicitly, and Douglas agreed." — 4 Churchill's History at 158.

30 - 10 U. S. Statutes at Large 277.

31 - Peterson's Speeches at 484.

32 - 1 Commager's Documents at 331 (Appeal of Independent Democrats, January 19, 1854).

33 - 10th Federalist, Mentor Edition at 78.

34 - 2 Morris' History at 514.

35 - Kirk's Randolph at 155-189.

36 - Speeches and Debates at 9-10.

37 - Pollard's Lost Cause at 131-133 discusses the figures showing that, in the real necessities of life per capita — land, livestock, agricultural productions, etc. —, the South was richer. But in Times Atlas at 222-223, the figures showing greater production of wealth in the North are given.

38 - Mentor Edition at 277, where Madison addressed the question of what Congress might do under Article IV, Section 4 of the United States Constitution in the event of a civil war between rival governments within a State, or, by implication, within a Territory. He asked, "In cases where it may be doubtful on which side justice lies, what better umpires could be desired by two violent factions, flying to arms and tearing a State to pieces, than the representatives of the confederate States, not heated by the local flame?"

39 - In the case of *Winney v. Whitsides*, 1 Mo. 473 (1822), it was held that, when a master took his slave into that part of the Louisiana Purchase which was distinct from Missouri, above 36 degrees 30 minutes north latitude, the slave became free. This holding was followed and liberalized in *Lagrange v. Choteau*, 2 Mo. 20 (1823), and the same principle was extended to States that had been formed out of the Northwest Territory, first in *Ralph v. Duncan*, 3 Mo. 194 (1826), and in *Julia v. McKinney*, 3 Mo. 270 (1826). The foregoing procedents were further sustained in Nat v. Ruddle, 3 Mo. 400 (1827), again in *Rachel v. Walker*, 4 Mo. 350 (1830), and still again in *Wilson v. Melvin*, 4 Mo. 595 (1831). In the argument of counsel found in Strader v. Graham, 10 Howard 82 at 85-89 (U. S. 1852), there is a good exposition of these cases, and at least a dozen like decisions on appeal by Southern courts in Louisiana, Maryland, Kentucky, and Virginia. All of them, like *Murray v. McCarty*, 2 Munford 393 (Va. 1811), and *State v. Manuel*, 4 Dev. & B. 20 (N. C. 1838), rested upon *Sommersett's Case*, 20 Howell's St. Tr. 1 at 80-82 (K. B. 1771), which in turn derived from ancient decisions on villeinage such as *Pigg v. Caley*, Noy 27 (K. B. 1618). These and many like decisions of Southern judges are discussed in the opinions of Justice John McLean and Justice Benjamin Curtis in *Dred Scott v. Sandford*, 19 Howard 391 at 547-564, 573, and 601-604 (U. S. 1857).

40 - The case is reported as *Dred Scott v. Emerson*, 15 Mo. 576 (1852), including the dissenting opinion (in 15. Mo. at 587-592) of Chief Justice Hamilton Gamble who entered into a good discussion of Southern jurisprudence on the liberation of slaves. The misapplication of the law of the domicile of the owner to determine the proprietary attributes of slaves as for any other chattels gained further impetus from the opinion of Chief Justice Roger B. Taney in *Strader v. Graham*, 10 Howard 82 (U. S. 1852). Certain slaves in Kentucky were allowed by their master to work as musicians in Ohio, from whence they voluntarily returned. Their master, Graham, later sued Strader in the court of chancery in Kentucky, on account of subsequent events, for loss of these slaves. Strader pleaded that, by their travel to Ohio with the permission of their master outside the protection of the fugitive slave clause in Article IV, Section 2 of the United States Constitution, these slaves became free under the Northwest Ordinance and the Ohio Constitution incorporating the Ordinance. The court of chancery and the court of appeals in Kentucky held that the common law of the State governed the case, because the master was there domiciled and that under such law the slaves remained the property of their master and did not gain their freedom by travel to Ohio. Strader sought a writ of error on the theory that the prohibition of slavery and involuntary servitude in the Northwest Ordinance was perpetual, notwithstanding the adoption of the same language in the Ohio Constitution, and that, in any event, save where the fugitive slave clause of Article IV, Section 2 applied, it was obligatory to follow the principle given by Lord Mansfield in *Sommersett's Case*, 20 Howell's St. Tr. 1 at 80-82 (K. B. 1771). But Taney held that the prohibition of slavery and involuntary servitude in the Northwest

Ordinance no longer governed because it had been merged into the Ohio Constitution, and that the United States Constitution did not oblige the courts of Kentucky to apply the law of Ohio. Having found that there was no question arising under the constitution, treaties, or laws of the United States as required by Section 25 of the Judiciary Act of 1789 (1 U. S. Statutes at Large at 85-87), Taney dismissed the writ of error.

41 - E. g., in *Prigg v. Pennsylvania*, 16 Peters 539 at 611-612 (U. S. 1842), Justice Joseph Story extensively discussed the fugitive slave clause of Article IV, Section 2 of the United States Constitution as an exception to the general rule given by Lord Mansfield in *Sommersett's Case*, 20 Howell's St. Tr. 1 at 80-82 (K. B. 1771). This commentary was particularly significant because Story was the author of a famous treatise on the conflict of laws which states that in the normal case, apart from slavery, the domicile of the owner of a chattel determines its proprietary attributes. Chief Justice Taney was fully aware of Lord Mansfield's holding and its acceptance by judges throughout the Southern States. This fact appears from Taneys own words in 16 Peters at 626 where he expressly made reference to and concurred with Story's conclusions in 16 Peters at 611-612. Under the general law as given by Judge Gaston of North Carolina in *State v. Manuel*, 4 Dev. & B. at 24-25, the moment a slave was emancipated by any lawful means, he became a free citizen of the State where he was born or domiciled: he thus became entitled to enjoy all "privileges and immunities" of citizens of the several States under the first clause of Article IV, Section 2 of the United States Constitution. This clause was drawn from the fourth article of the old Confederation and inserted into the work of the Philadelphia Convention, as appears in 5 Elliot's Debates 381, 487, 536, 563, — Tansill's Documents 480, 631, 711, — 2 Ferrand's Records 187, 443, 577, 601, 662 (Madison's Notes, August 6 and 28, September 10, 12, 17, 1787), — also the 41st Federalist by James Madison, Mentor Edition at 270-271, and the 80th Federalist by Alexander Hamilton, Mentor Edition at 478. In view of this background, the "privileges and immunities" mentioned in Article IV, Section 1 were to be contrasted with "privileges of trade and commerce" also mentioned in the fourth article of the old Confederation. Thus, in *Corfield v. Coryell*, 6 Fed. Cas. 546 (U. S. Cir. Ct. E. D. Pa. 1823), Justice Bushrod Washington held that such "privileges and immunities" were to be understood as the rights of free citizens under the constitutions of the several States. And upon becoming free by entry into the territory of a free State by consent of his master, a freed black was entitled, by operation of the fundamental law of the Union to the constitutional rights of citizens of such free State, including the right not to be held in involuntary servitude.

42 - This odd exception to the principle of res judicata was allowed by Justice James Wayne in *Homer v. Brown*, 16 Howard 352 at 365-366 (U. S. 1853).

43 - 1 U. S. Statutes at Large at 78, which gave circuit courts of the United States original jurisdiction to hear any suit at common law or suits in equity between a

plaintiff who was a citizen of the State in which such suit was brought and a the defendant who was a citizen of another State, and the amount in controversy exceeded $500.00.

44 - See, e. g., *Capron v. VanNoorden*, 2 Cranch 126 (U. S. 1804).

45 - According to the rules of common law, Sandford did not waive his objection by answering over to the declaration but he could not in a higher court challenge a decision against him on his plea to jurisdiction, unless he sued out a writ of error. Taney attempted to justify his right to address the decision of the Federal circuit court on the plea in abatement, even though neither party challenged that decision by writ of error, by distinguishing the Federal judiciary as courts of "limited" jurisdiction from the courts of common law, as if they were courts of "general" jurisdiction. But all courts of common law were courts of limited jurisdiction, with authority confined to certain writs or bills and none other. Under Section 22 of the Judiciary Act of 1789 (1 U. S. Statutes at 84-85), there were specific exceptions to the appeallate jurisdiction of the United States Supreme Court as allowed by the second clause of Article III, Section 2 of the United States Constitution. One of these exceptions was that there could be no reversal on writ of error for any decision on "any plea in abatement other than a plea to the jurisdiction of the court." In light of the common law, it was impossible under Section 22 to challenge a ruling upon a plea to jurisdiction before the United States Supreme Court, except on writ of error sued out by the party aggrieved.

46 - 19 Howard at 410. These infamous words are proved fraudulent by well-known language of Thomas Jefferson, the principal author of the Declaration of Independence, in Query XVIII of his *Notes on Virginia*, published in 1782, where he said in condemnation of slavery, "And can the liberties of a nation be thought secure when we have removed their only firm basis, a conviction in the minds of the people that these liberties are the gift of God? That they are not to be violated but with His wrath? Indeed, I tremble for my country when I reflect that God is just; that his justice cannot sleep forever," etc. — Koch & Peden's Jefferson at 278-279.

47 - Speeches and Debates at 52 (Springfield, Illinois, June 16, 1858).

48 - Speeches and Debates at 134 (Springfield, Illinois, July 17, 1858).

49 - Speeches and Debates at 155 (Springfield, Illinois, July 17, 1858). Lincoln echoed this view in a particularly elegant way in his first inaugural address: — "I do not forget the position assumed by some that constitutional questions are to be decided by the supreme court, nor do I deny that such decisions are binding in any case upon the parties to a suit, as to the object of that suit, while they are also entitled to a very high respect and consideration in all parallel cases by all other departments of the government. And while it is obviously possible that such a decision may be erroneous in any given case, still the evil effect of following

it, being limited to that particular case, with the chance that it may be overruled and never become precedent for other cases, can better be borne than could the evils of a different practice. At the same time, the candid citizen must confess that, if the policy of the government, upon vital questions affecting the whole people, is to be irrevocably fixed by decisions of the supreme court, the instant they made in ordinary litigation between parties in personal actions, the people will have ceased to be their own rulers, having to that extent practically resigned their government into the hands of that eminent tribunal." — Speeches and Debates at 535-536 (Washington, D. C., March 4, 1861).

50 - 1 Blackstone's Commentaries 69-70.

CHAPTER VII

THE SOUTHERN CONFEDERACY

A few days before his death on March 31, 1850, John Calhoun spoke of the future in conversation with a friend. "The Union is doomed to dissolution," he said, "I fix its probable occurrence within twelve years." He concluded, "It will explode in a Presidential election."[1]

Slavery was dying more rapidly in the South upon the election of Abraham Lincoln than the feudal system was dying in England upon the accession of Henry VIII. The institution was in fact dying a natural and humane death. Yet only two years before William Seward had wildly exclaimed that there was an "irrepressible conflict" over this lingering quasi-feudal anachronism, which, he claimed, was about to overwhelm the United States. Hysterically he warned that "the rye fields of Massachusetts and the wheat fields of New York must again be surrendered by their farmers to slave culture and to the production of slaves, and Boston and New York must become once more markets for trade in the bodies and souls of men!"[2]

In hearing or reading such bizarre comments by Yankee demagogues, the people of the Southern States reckoned the growing weakness of their position within the Union. Even abolitionists among them feared turbulent upheaval in their society at the hands of uncomprehending fanatics from the North. Slavery was a delicate and difficult problem to address, and, as John Randolph of Roanoke and countless others learned, freedom sometimes created more problems than it solved. Therefore, Southerners made tentative plans to escape from the Union. It was not reality, but falsehood which induced the fulfillment of Calhoun's forecast.

On May 24, 1860, the United States Senate adopted seven resolutions which had been introduced by Jefferson Davis of Mississippi.[3] The first of these resolutions read,

"Resolved, That, in the adoption of the Federal Constitution, the States adopting the same acted severally as free and independent Sovereignties, delegating a portion of their powers to be exercised by the Federal Government for the increased security of each against dangers, domestic and as well as foreign; and that any intermeddling by any one or more States, or by a combination of their citizens, with the domestic institutions of the others, on any pretext whatever, political, moral, or religious, with a view to their disturbance or subversion, is in violation of the Constitution, insulting to the States so interfered with, endangers their peace and tranquility — objects for which the Constitution was formed —, and, by necessary consequence, tends to weaken and destroy the Union itself."

This language was adopted on vote of thirty-six against nineteen in the United States Senate. Voting in favor, as might be expected, were both senators from most of the Southern States, but also both senators from California, Indiana, Minnesota, Oregon, and Pennsylvania, as well as one senator from Ohio and one from New Jersey. Both senators from Delaware and both senators from Illinois abstained.

The first resolution began with an affirmation that the Union is a confederacy of free, sovereign, and independent States. From this premise, viewed in light of constitutional history, the right of secession ineluctably follows. The vote adopting this resolution was a posthumous tribute to John Calhoun's view of the Union as expressed in his debate with Daniel Webster in 1833. It was a view that was about to be trashed by politicians resembling the crusaders who took Constantinople, and thereby caused the final decline of the Byzantine Empire, but in the end failed to reach the Holy Land.[4]

As Davis' resolutions were considered in the United States Senate, the nominating conventions of the major political parties began to meet.[5] The democratic party was then an alliance of conservatives in the North and the South. The alliance had no clear objective except to maintain stability in unsettled times. The party may have been bland and uninspiring, yet it had long controlled Congress and the White House, and it offered the only electable alternative to unrest and calamity within the Union, which was a humble but inestimable virtue in politics.

The leading candidate for nomination by the democratic party as President was Stephen Douglas of Illinois. By this time, many informed Southern politicians were wise to Douglas. They knew that he had sold out the transcontinental railroad route through Louisiana and Texas for worthless concessions in the Kansas-Nebraska Act. They knew that

Douglas preached a program desired by financiers in Philadelphia and New York. Such was the main bone of contention which this faction of Southern politicians had with Douglas.

It was increasingly obvious to thinking men in the South that geography barred their peculiar institution in the Federal territories. No amount of argument can change the unanswerable reality that, outside of Kansas where they were doomed before they started, planters from the Dixie States had made no serious effort to import slaves into the huge land mass affected by Compromise of 1850 and the repeal of the Missouri Compromise in 1854. They made no serious effort, because there was nothing attractive to them in those vast stretches. And the proof of this stubborn fact is that in 1860 there were no slaves at all in the New Mexico, Utah, and Washington Territories, none in the Indian or Oklahoma Territory, none in the Dakota Territory, virtually none in the Kansas Territory which entered the Union as a free State in 1861, and barely more than a dozen in the Nebraska Territory, nor was there a prospect that more would ever arrive.

The burning issue for Southern democrats was the transcontinental railroad, because it would have been of great value to their region of the United States as a stimulus to modernize their economy and society, and thereby to help phase out slavery.

The old party met in Charleston on April 23, 1860, to nominate candidates for President and Vice President. Compromised by railroad and allied financial interests Douglas was. But he was the front runner. And he was a practical man: — he would pick a Southerner to run with him for Vice President; moreover, he would be indebted to the South for his election, and so would be obliged to repay with a political quid pro quo. The lesson on the nature of politics to be learned from this episode is augmented by an additional fact: — nobody knew it at the time, but Douglas had only months to live, for he died on June 3, 1861. Which means that, if he had been elected, Douglas would not have been President very long, and the new President would have been a Southerner.

The anti-Douglas faction had a grievance, but they lacked vision. At the convention in Charleston, they prevented the nomination of Douglas after fifty-seven ballots, and thereby produced an irreparable split in the party on whose unity their best available option depended. Eight Southern delegations staged a walkout, using as their pretext the failure of a meaningless resolution denying the right of a territorial legislature to prohibit slavery. In the midst of this senseless political wreckage, the convention adjourned on May 3, 1860.

The stronger wing of the old party reconvened in Baltimore, and, on June 18, 1860, while calling themselves "union" democrats, they nominated Stephen Douglas of Illinois as President and Hershel Johnson of Georgia as Vice President. Their platform stipulated that, as to "the institution of slavery within the territories, the democratic party will abide by the decision of the Supreme Court of the United States," which sounded safe and respectable enough to limit controversy. And their platform stated further that the democratic party "will pledge such constitutional government aid as will assure the construction of a railroad to the Pacific coast at the earliest practicable period." And that was a real question, because the railroad given reference had already been planned for the central route through the Nebraska Territory.

The Southern wing of the democratic party later met, first in Richmond then in Baltimore, and calling themselves "national" democrats, they voted their nominations on June 28, 1860: — John Breckenridge of Kentucky for President and Joseph Lane of Oregon for Vice President. Breckenridge was then Vice President of the United States, undoubtedly qualified by character, temperament, and experience to be President. His heroic career as a patriot and statesman is a story in itself.6 In reluctantly accepting the nomination, he hoped that he might persuade Douglas to step aside or make concessions, and thereby to help reunify the party and win the election.

The platform of the "national" democrats pledged that any territory with sufficient population should be freely admitted as a State of the Union "whether its constitution prohibits or recognizes slavery," — an obligatory platitude without real significance, since none of the existing territories would under any circumstances seek to become a State allowing slavery. Their platform then promised support of legislation "to the extent of the constitutional authority of Congress, for the construction of a railroad from the Mississippi River to the Pacific Ocean, at the earliest practicable moment." But this railroad was understood by the "national" democrats to be along the shorter route through Louisiana and Texas, or a least a route selected as part of a compromise in which the Southern States had a real voice.

And if the split between the democrats was not bad enough, the rump of old whigs formed a constitutional union party which met in Baltimore and on May 9, 1860, nominated John Bell of Tennessee for President and Edward Everett of Massachusetts for Vice President with an empty slogan for a platform, — "the Constitution of the country, the Union of the States, and the enforcement of the laws."

It is common belief that this splintering of conservative and moderate votes happened by misfortune or accident. But a situation characterized by two democratic tickets with seemingly identical platforms, and a similar third ticket running on a mere shibboleth, is simply too pronounced and absurd not to be suspicious. Sophisticated politicians were involved in this scenario. They foresaw the obvious consequences of their splintering, and they would not have permitted it unless they had been skillfully manipulated by the kind of money men who perennially supply the life blood of political campaigns. Three parties were manipulated, not to win, but to lose the election, because those pulling the strings had their eyes on the republican party, then the epicenter of radical politics in the United States.

Breckenridge was not able to make a deal with Douglas. Those controlling Douglas did not give him enough latitude. They had invested their capital in a central route for a transcontinental railroad, and none other was acceptable to them. It may be fairly surmised that these capitalists were in the circle of financiers who had secured repeal of the Missouri Compromise, and paid the "border ruffians" who started the Kansas Civil War.

And the money men who had induced the splintering between the two wings of the democratic party, also worked hand in glove with the money men behind the republican party. In order to swing the election their way, they weakened the conservative and moderate vote by splintering it, then supported the radical vote as a united front. The coordinated interaction between the two groups may be inferred insofar as men generally intend the foreseeable consequences of their acts, and the foreseeable consequences of events then operated to produce a crisis likely to induce the secession of Southern States.

The final element, absolutely crucial to the larger plan then unhatching, was to assure that secession, when it occurred, would erupt in a civil war. On May 16, 1860, the republican convention met in Chicago, and two days later nominated Abraham Lincoln of Illinois for President and Hannibal Hamlin of Maine for Vice President. Their platform announced, "We hold in abhorrence all schemes of Disunion, come from whatever source they may," thus assuring that, when the republicans took over the direction of the Union and the anticipated secession of Southern States occurred, military force would be used to prevent it. That would guarantee a bloody and expensive conflict.

And in order to excite passions against the people of the South — a necessary ingredient in inducing fellow Americans to kill each other in battle —, the republican platform stated that "the new dogma that the Constitution of its own force carries slavery into any or all of the territories is a dangerous political heresy." This new dogma was a political heresy, indeed worse than a political heresy: — it was made respectable by a judicial heresy of the United States Supreme Court which rejected the jurisprudence of the South on the emancipation of slaves. It was particularly dangerous, not because Southern planters had any realistic hope of implanting slavery in the territories, but because impassioned debate about this unreal possibility created an inflammatory atmosphere of misunderstanding and hatred.

The election of Abraham Lincoln as President was thereby assured, — "rigged" would be a more accurate and realistic word. He carried eighteen States in the North, one county in Missouri, and one county in Kentucky, but not a single State in the South.[7] So certain in advance was the outcome that Lincoln could afford the luxury of not giving even one campaign speech. He simply sat at home and waited for his election victory on November 6, 1860.

As was anticipated by all informed observers, there was an explosion in the Southern States when the election results became known. Forthwith a resolution was passed at a public meeting in Floyd County, Georgia:

> "That Georgia is and ought to be a free, independent, and sovereign State. She came into the Union as a sovereignty, and by virtue of that sovereignty has the right to secede whenever, in her sovereign capacity, she shall adjudge such a step necessary. In our opinion, she ought not to submit to the inauguration of Abraham Lincoln and Hanibal Hamlin as her President and Vice President, but should leave them to rule over those by whom they were elected. We request the legislature to announce this opinion, and to cooperate with the governor in calling a convention of the people to determine the mode and measure of redress."[8]

The legislature of South Carolina called for the election of a convention to speak as the sovereign power of the State. On December 20, 1860, the people in convention adopted an ordinance:

> "We, the People of the State of South Carolina, in Convention assembled, do declare and ordain, and it is hereby declared and ordained, that the Ordinance adopted by us in Convention on the 23rd day of May in the year of our Lord 1788, whereby the Constitution of the United States of America was ratified, and also all Acts of the General Assembly of this State ratifying amendments to the said Constitution, are hereby repealed, and that the Union now subsisting between South Carolina and other States, under the name of the United States of America, is hereby dissolved."[9]

A few days later the South Carolina Convention of 1860 promulgated a Declaration of the Causes of Secession,[10] which, as anticipated, expounded the constitutional basis of the right asserted. It was a restatement of the classical theory of the Virginia and Kentucky Resolutions of 1798, the Report of the Hartford Convention in 1815, and the addresses to the people promulgated by the South Carolina Convention in 1832. The text was sonorous and beautiful.

The declaration then proceeded to set forth the supposed justification for South Carolina's exercise of the right to secede from the Union, but here the case faltered badly. It was said that Northern States had enacted statutes which frustrated the rights of slaveholders under the fugitive slave clause in Article IV, Section 2 of the United States Constitution. For the most part, these statutes were but attempts to guarantee due process of law for the benefit of persons alleged to be slaves but claiming to be freemen.

The fugitive slave clause in Article IV, Section 2 was adopted in the Philadelphia Convention on the assumption that slavery was a quickly dying institution, and that, therefore, its language would soon be inoperative from desuetude. Progress in freeing slaves initially went apace, then later slowed down in the South. Even so, in absolute numbers there were far more manumissions in the South than in the North, and as slavery lingered but weakened in the Dixie States, the number of runaway slaves was astonishingly small.[11] There were about 4,000,000 slaves in the Southern States in 1860, and over the previous decade never more than a thousand runways fled in any year into the North, and in some years it was half that figure.[12]

Breach of the fugitive slave clause was still more unconvincing as a pretext for secession, because withdrawal from the United States abrogated the constitutional obligation of the Northern States and the Union to assist in the retrieval of runaways. If the provision was of dubious value before secession, it was utterly worthless thereafter.

Moreover, the United States Supreme Court had always been extremely solicitous of the rights of slaveholders in the Southern States in retrieving their runaways.[13] And, under Section 13 of the Judiciary Act of 1789, South Carolina could bring suit in the highest court of the Union to enjoin the operation of the law of any other State, which unduly interfered with the rights of planters in recovering their runaways.[14]

In any event, Abraham Lincoln expressly conceded and never disavowed the executive duty to aid in the recovery of fugitive slaves under the laws of the Union. It was, in any event, a problem ever diminishing and destined to become extinct in the foreseeable future, because slavery was a moribund institution, visibly dissolving.

The convention in South Carolina railed at the politics of the President-Elect, mainly his desire to prohibit slavery by law in the Federal territories where slavery was already prohibited by geography. In Congress, there might be an attempted renewal and extension of the Missouri Compromise which had already been declared unconstitutional by the United States Supreme Court. The judgment of the United States Supreme Court might be reversed or reaffirmed in a subsequent case. By act of Congress, slavery might be completely prohibited or sweepingly permitted in all the territories. But, regardless of what might happen, the result would be exactly the same: — slavery would not be established in the territories of the Union.

The legal contentions and political effusions in the declaration of the convention in South Carolina were obligatory, but flat, unfelt, and unconvincing. What, then, was the problem? It was not so much Lincoln, for he had a moderate and practical side, but his party overflowed with bombastic Yankee orators who detested, because they did not understand the people and culture of the Dixie States. And that terrified the South, as it would have terrified any people or culture in a like situation.

The greatest statesman then living in the South was Alexander Stephens whose defense of the constitutional right of any State to secede from the Union, written later in his life, stands yet unexcelled in American literature.[15] While Stephens defended the right, he urged the people of his time not to exercise it. His political wisdom was expressed in his "Union" speech, which he delivered before the legislature of his native Georgia shortly after Lincoln prevailed in the popular vote.[16] He proposed a conference of Southern States to explore avenues of united action, and to search for reconciliation within the Union. Stephens knew that secession, as a constitutional right existing but not exercised, had brought peace with France in 1800, peace with Great Britain in 1815, and reconciliation with South Carolina in 1833. "Should Georgia determine to leave the Union," he said to his countrymen, "I shall bow to the will of her people. Their cause is my cause, and their destiny is my destiny." But he added, "I am for exhausting all that patriotism demands before taking this last step."

There had been an intense quarrel. A venomous dispute had been cynically orchestrated over the previous decade. Outrage and weariness prevailed. South Carolina wanted to leave the Union, and to unite with her sister States who understood their common culture and civilization. The most exacting portrait of Southern feeling was given by Edward Pollard, editor of the *Richmond Examiner:*

> "Foreigners have made a curious and unpleasant observation of a
> certain exaggeration of American mind, an absurd conceit that was

never done asserting the unapproachable excellence of its country in all things. The Washington affair was the paragon of governments; the demagogical institutions of America were the best under the sun; the slip-shod literature of the country, the smattered education of the people were the foci of enlightenment; and, in short, Americans were the lords of creation. DeTocqueville observed: 'the Americans are not very far from believing themselves to belong to a distinct race of mankind.'

"But it is to be remarked that this boastful disposition of mind, this exaggerated conceit, was particularly Yankee. It belonged to the garish civilization of the North. It was Daniel Webster who wrote in a diplomatic paper that America was 'the only great republican power.' It was Yankee orators who established the Fourth-of-July school of rhetoric, exalted the American eagle, and spoke of the Union as the last best gift to man. This afflatus had but little place among the people of the South. Their civilization was a quiet one, and their character as a people has always been that sober estimate of the value of men and things, which, as in England, appears to be the best evidence of a substantial civilization and a real enlightenment."[17]

* * * * *

On December 3, 1860, President James Buchanan delivered an address to a joint session of Congress.[18] Buchanan knew that Southern States were preparing to withdraw from the Union. He pleaded with them:

"In order to justify secession as a constitutional remedy, it must be on the principle that the Federal Government is a mere voluntary association of States, to be dissolved at pleasure by any one of the contracting parties. If this be so, the confederacy is a rope of sand, to be penetrated and dissolved by the first wave of public opinion in any of the States."

But speaking of the Northern States twenty-one days later in language as historically accurate as can be found in any text on the formation of the Union, the people of South Carolina in convention said,

"In separating from them we invade no right, no interests of theirs. We violate no obligation or duty to them. As separate, independent States in convention, we made the Constitution of the United States with them, and, as separate, independent States in convention, each acting for himself, we adopted it. South Carolina, acting in her sovereign capacity, now thinks it proper to secede from the Union. She did not part with her sovereignty in adopting the Constitution. The last thing a State can be presumed to have surrendered is her sovereignty. Her sovereignty is her life. Nothing but a clear, express grant can alienate it."[19]

And seventy-two years before, Edmund Pendleton and James Madison had openly conceded the right of a State to secede from the Union, and the Virginia Convention of 1788 had expressly ordained that the right of secession was reserved to each State. This invaluable constitutional right, far from being a rope of sand, had on repeated occasions be used as an instrument of reconciliation among the several States, and had brought strength to the Union.

In his address to Congress, Buchanan asked,

> "The question fairly stated is, Has the Constitution delegated to Congress the power to coerce a State into submission, which is attempting to withdraw or has actually withdrawn from the Confederacy? If answered in the affirmative, it must be on the principle that the power has been conferred upon Congress to declare war and to make war against a State. After much serious reflection I have arrived at the conclusion that no such power has been delegated to Congress, or to any other department of the Federal Government. It is manifest upon an inspection of the Constitution that this is not among the specific and enumerated powers granted to Congress, and it is equally apparent that its exercise is not necessary and proper for carrying into execution any one of these powers. So far from this power having been delegated to Congress, it was expressly refused by the Convention which framed the Constitution."

It is an historical fact that, on two occasions during their deliberations, the framers in the Philadelphia Convention voted to deny Congress the power of calling forth military forces of the Union to compel obedience of a State, and on two further occasions they voted to deny Congress the power of sending the Federal army or navy into the territory of any State, except, as allowed Article IV, Section 4 of the United States Constitution, — to repel a foreign invasion or at the request of its legislature or governor to deal with domestic violence.[20]

Buchanan was right, there was no constitutional power vested in the government of the United States to prevent the secession of any State from the Union. What he did not understand was that this deliberate omission of power was intended to accommodate the right of secession which was consciously reserved by the founding fathers of the United States.

Buchanan had not been a great President. Yet in the final months of his term, after his ambitions in public life had died, he was transformed into a bona fide statesman. Of the supposed power to use force of arms against secession, He stated to Congress,

> "But if we possessed this power, would it be wise to exercise it in existing circumstances? The object would doubtless be to preserve the Union. War would not only present the most effectual means of destroying it, but would vanish all hope of its peaceable reconstruction. Besides, in the fraternal conflict a vast amount of blood and treasure would be expended, rendering future reconciliation between the States impossible. In the meantime, who can foretell what would be the sufferings and privations of the people during its existence?
>
> "The fact is that our Union rests upon public opinion, and can never be cemented by the blood of its citizens shed in civil war. If it cannot live in the affections of the people, it must one day perish. Congress possesses many means of preserving it by conciliation, but the sword was not placed in their hand to preserve it by force."

Buchanan's speech should be carved on the stone of a conspicuous monument for the guidance of every leader who might in the future guide the destiny of a federal Union. Children should be obliged to memorize this speech, not the better known allocution by Buchanan's successor at the dedication of a military cemetery near a little college town in Pennsylvania.

* * * * *

Within a few weeks after Buchanan spoke those timeless words, the United States went through deepening crisis which proved how right he was.

Faced with pending secession of one or more Southern States, a powerful and respectable movement for reconciliation was activated. The chief architect of peace was Senator John Crittenden of Kentucky. On December 18, 1860, he came forward with a set of resolutions, including proposed amendments to the United States Constitution.[21]

Crittenden suggested several constitutional amendments which would limit the power of Congress to regulate or abolish slavery, but these were intended to be sacrificed as concessions in exchange for a principal object. And that principal object was a constitutional amendment which would have reestablished the old line of 36 degrees 30 minutes north latitude, and extended it through the Federal territories from the southwestern boundary of Missouri to the eastern boundary of California: — slavery was to be forever forbidden above the line, and States carved from territory beneath the line could be admitted with slavery if their constitutions allowed the institution. In other words, the Missouri Compromise was to be resurrected as a permanent monument of reconciliation between the North and South in the form of a constitutional amendment reversing the judgment of the majority on the merits of the case in *Dred Scott v. Sandford*, 19 Howard 391 (U. S. 1857). The proposal would have allowed slavery, if it could be established, in territories which offered no attraction for Southern planters, — territories which, in any event, would not be ready to become States until slavery were practically extinct throughout the country by operation of natural causes.

The idea had no practical significance, but neither was the controversy over a real problem. The controversy had risen to a dangerous pitch over empty abstractions and symbols of a dying age. There was a need to quiet public excitement, and the palliative was restoration of a venerable principle of an earlier era. Crittenden's proposals, unimportant in substance but urgent as a symbolic antidote to civil war, were sent to a committee of thirteen in the United States Senate. Power brokers in the republican party advised Lincoln to oppose them all, and when the views of the President-Elect became known, the committee adjourned on December 31, 1860, without coming to any agreement on what should be done.

The advice of the power brokers had the desired effect of inducing a stampede which the new administration could use as an excuse to foment a civil war: — Southern States followed South Carolina in seceding from the Union, staring with Mississippi on January 9, then continuing with Florida on January 10, next Alabama on January 11, then Georgia on January 19, then Louisiana on January 26, then Texas on February l, 1861, at which point Lincoln was still a month away from his inauguration.

A peace conference was called by the Commonwealth of Virginia. Former President John Tyler was the speaker of this assembly of highly respectable delegates from twenty-one States, meeting from February 4 though 23, 1861, in Washington D. C. A variation of Crittenden's resolutions was recommended to Congress, but nothing came of this gesture.

Congress did, however, propose a constitutional amendment on the evening of March 3, which was signed by James Buchanan in the early morning of March 4, 1861, as his last official act as President. It read, "No amendment shall be made to the Constitution which shall authorize or give to Congress the power to abolish or interfere, within any State, with the domestic institutions thereof, including that of persons held to labor or service by the laws of the said State."[22]

Nothing ever came of this proposition, and it was soon forgotten. The provision was unnecessary, because, even if adopted, the proposal would not have disallowed a constitutional amendment prohibiting slavery directly by operation of fundamental law, and, in any event, the Dixie States already had capacity to prevent adoption of a constitutional amendment abolishing slavery, nor did the people of those States necessarily want an interdiction of abolition by act of Congress, for there were then more abolitionists in the South than in the North.

The problem, after all, was not about propositions, but a flow of passion. Those confused days and weeks of American history cannot be appreciated as if the differences between the North and the South were a formal debate over slavery or some such subject. The differences between the North and the South were too irrational and too profound to be settled by compromise. They could be resolved only by a civilized parting of ways and the passing of time.

Secession was the only available constitutional remedy, not necessarily because the North was wrong and the South was right, but because it was, in the circumstances, the only way to apply healing balm, — separation, reflection, patience, and diplomacy, then perhaps reunion if the opportunity should allow in the future.

* * * * *

Many have believed that Abraham Lincoln as close to sainthood as anyone who ever served as President of the United States. To put it mildly, not a few have had their doubts. It is more instructive to remove his halo, and to judge his acts for what they really were.

In his first inaugural address on March 4, 1861, Lincoln reviewed the secessions of Southern States from the Union, then proceeded to announce the official position of his administration that the United States are an indissoluable Union.

> "I hold that, in the contemplation of universal law and of the Constitution, the Union of these States is perpetual. Perpetuity is implied, if not expressed, in the fundamental law of all national governments. It is safe to assert that no government ever had a provision in its organic law for its own termination. Continue to execute all the express provisions of our national Constitution, and the Union will endure forever, it being impossible to destroy it except by some action not provided for in the instrument itself.

> "Again, if the United States be not a government proper, but an association of States in the nature of a contract merely, can it, as a contract, be peaceably unmade by less than all the parties who made

it? One party to a contract may violate it, break it so to speak, — but does it not require all to lawfully rescind it? Descending from these general principles, we find the proposition that in legal contemplation the Union is perpetual, confirmed by the history of the Union itself.

"The Union is much older than the Constitution. It was formed in fact, by articles of association in 1774. It was matured and contained in the Declaration of Independence in 1776. It was further matured, and the faith of all the then thirteen States expressly plighted and engaged that it should be perpetual, by the Articles of Confederation in 1778; and, finally, in 1787, one of the declared objects for ordaining and establishing the Constitution was to 'form a more perfect Union.' But if the destruction of the Union by one, or by a part only, of the States be lawfully possible, the Union is less perfect than before, the Constitution having lost the vital element of perpetuity.

"It follows from these views that no State, upon its own mere motion, can lawfully get out of the Union; that resolves and ordinances to that effect are legally void; and that acts of violence within any State or States against the authority of the United States are insurrectionary or revolutionary, according to the circumstances.

"I, therefore, consider that, in view of the Constitution and the laws, the Union is unbroken, and that, to the extent of my ability, I shall take care, as the Constitution expressly enjoins upon me, that the laws of the Union shall be faithfully executed in all the States."[23]

There are so many things wrong with this dialectic that it is hard to know which point should first be decimated.

The Union is perpetual, said Lincoln, and, therefore, indissoluable. Not so, for the Union set into motion in 1789 was but a public corporation as are all governments in republican form, yet even a perpetual corporation may be lawfully dissolved. Such corporations are frequently dissolved. The attribute of perpetuity in a legal sense means only that the corporation is not limited in duration by a term of years, and so will last, not necessarily forever, but until lawfully dissolved.

The Union existing at independence in 1776 was perpetual, yet it was a Union of thirteen free and independent States, and at least five of them declared their separation from the British Empire before the Declaration of American Independence. The first Union, while perpetual, was dissolved when a second Union was established by final ratification of the Articles of Confederation in 1781, and its existence apart from the British Empire was acknowledged by King George III in 1783. As such, this second Union consisted of thirteen free, sovereign, and independent States, each distinctly mentioned by his Majesty in the Treaty of Paris. Although this second Union was expressly made perpetual, and could not be amended except by consent of all thirteen States, it was nevertheless dissolved in a lawful manner without the consent of every State. The old Congress met for the last time in 1788. In the Philadelphia Convention, a third Union was designed, and during deliberations it was stated by delegates on the floor that the Union would not last forever. In joining the third Union, several States expressly stipulated the right to resume powers delegated to the Federal government. After the third Union was finally launched in 1789, two States continued to exist as independent Nations.

And it is wrong to say that no government ever had a provision in its organic law for its own termination. For every government is ultimately founded by sovereign power, which can do anything in law not naturally impossible, including termination of its present existence, and transformation into any shape which might be desired, as by interchange between hereditary monarchy and democratic republic, or between national consolidation and pure confederacy. Even the national government of Great Britain has always possessed the constitutional means to dissolve and transform itself by united consent of the Commons, Lords, and King in Parliament, and, by constitutional custom, such a transformation may also occur on extraordinary occasions by a Convention Parliament, even if contrary to other existing principles of fundamental law, as upon the accession of William and Mary.

The question in every case is where the locus of sovereign power is found. In the United States, as reestablished by the summer of 1790, such legal omnipotence was arrayed among thirteen focal points, — i. e., it remained vested in the people of each of the thirteen States in convention whenever summoned and elected to exercise the ultimate powers of society. By the time of Lincoln's election, the number of such focal points had increased to thirty-three.

It is true that the Union of 1789 was designed to be more perfect, and, consequently, was more difficult to dissolve than the Union of 1781. The Union of 1789 was created, and, therefore, could be dissolved only by sovereign powers in the several States, whereas the Union of 1781 was created, and, therefore, could be dissolved by legislatures of the several States. In 1860 and 1861, Southern States withdrew from the Union by ordinances of secession adopted by the people of each State in convention, each of them exercising sovereign power.

Lincoln stated that, if the United States Constitution were a compact of

Union among several States, then it would be in the nature of a contract; but a contract, he said, cannot be rescinded without mutual agreement. Secession is not like rescission of a contract by mutual agreement. Rather, the governing principle is analogous to the rule that, if one party to a contract has breached a material condition, the other may consider the contract at an end. The Union of 1789 was, in undeniable historical fact, designed as a compact among the several States, each acting by her people in convention as a sovereign power. In so acting, the people of each State in convention retained its sovereign attributes, including the right to adjudge material infractions of the compact of Union by supreme and final authority, beyond the jurisdiction of any temporal court of justice.

In 1860 and 1861, the conventions in the Southern States determined that the United States Constitution had been breached because the government of the Union had fallen into hostile hands, and that, therefore, the purposes of the Union proclaimed in the Preamble had been subverted, — essentially the same thing was said of the States of New England by the Hartford Convention in 1815. Such a judgment is of a kind which every society must be able to make for the protection of its well-being. The right to make this judgment was reserved by the United States Constitution in Article VII and Amendment X for each of the several States in the Union. And in denying the right of the Southern States to exercise this judgment in peace, Lincoln urged on by his partisans denied the most evolved principle of the American Revolution and the Glorious Revolution. The price of this error was catastrophic, and is still being paid.

* * * * *

The seven seceding States sent delegates to a convention in Montgomery, Alabama, which began deliberations on February 4, 1861, and produced a provisional constitution of the Confederate States of America on March 11, 1861. This constitution, intended to maintain only a temporary Confederate government, established a unicameral Congress with each State having one vote.

The enumerated powers of this Congress were similar to the powers of the Congress of the United States, but included authority to appoint a provisional President and Vice President.

The judiciary of the Confederate States under the provisional constitution consisted of the judges of the district courts of the United States at the time of secession. Together these judges made up a supreme court which was to meet as prescribed by Congress.

On February 22, 1862 — George Washington's birthday —, a permanent constitution of the Confederate States was formally put into operation. It was largely a word-for-word copy of the constitution framed by the Philadelphia Convention. Certain interesting alterations in either or both Confederate constitutions should be noted:

The preamble in the permanent as in the provisional constitution, beseeching the protection of almighty God, stated in unmistakable language that the Confederate States were a confederacy of free, sovereign, and independent States.

The ten articles of the Federal Bill of Rights framed in 1789 were inserted into the main body of the provisional and permanent constitutions of the Confederate States, so as to make clear that these articles should read to qualify only the powers of the general government, and not the powers of the several States.[24]

The House of Representatives in the Southern Congress was given exclusive power of impeachment, except that a judicial or other public officer of the Confederate States could be impeached by two-thirds of both chambers of the legislature of the State of his residence if he wielded power only in his own State.

And as had been proposed by James Madison in the Philadelphia Convention,[25] taxes on exports could be imposed on concurrence of two-thirds of both the House and the Senate in Congress.

The permanent constitution kept the electoral college but stipulated that the President serve one term of six years, and not be eligible to serve again.

The President was to enjoy a power to veto legislation, subject to being overridden by vote of two-thirds of the House and of the Senate, as under the Union of 1789, but this power was to be significantly increased in the Confederate States. The permanent constitution that every bill or law-making resolution should be limited to one subject expressed in the preamble. And both the provisional and the permanent constitutions granted the President a line-item veto on bills appropriating public funds.

The permanent constitution was adopted by the people of each State in convention, as under the Union of 1789. After the inauguration of Lincoln, other Dixie States joined the Southern Confederacy, — Virginia on April 17, Arkansas on May 6, Tennessee on May 7, and North Carolina on May 20, 1861. The regular government of Missouri, through its legislature, made an alliance with the Confederate States on October 31, 1861. And a convention of the people in Kentucky, called by pro-Southern troops, adopted an ordinance of secession and joined the Confederate States on November 17, 1861. Therefore, thirteen stars eventually appeared on Confederate battle flags and flags of state.

In view of the political history of the old South, it was obligatory that the provisional and permanent constitutions of the Confederate States should provide in unequivocal language the doctrine of James Madison in the Virginia Resolutions of 1789: — Congress was to have the power of spending public money only in exercising enumerated powers of the Confederate government. Moreover, public money could be appropriated only on concurrence of two-thirds of both the House and the Senate, save where needed to pay for the operations of Congress, or estimated and requested by the head of an executive department and submitted by the President, or where the amount had been found due by the judiciary of the Confederate States.

As had been suggested in Thomas Jefferson's Opinion on the Bank and reaffirmed in the South Carolina Resolutions of 1828, Congress was to have no power of levying duties, imposts, and excises as a means of promoting any branch of industry. Alexander Hamilton's Report on Manufactures was rejected outright, because the founding fathers of the Southern Confederacy were more mindful of the harm which might follow from abuse of power than the benefit which might follow from judicious government.

The provisional and permanent constitutions of the Confederate States were striking in that the existence of African slavery was expressly acknowledged. The polite phrasing of the Philadelphia Convention — "all other persons" and such like — was removed, and the noun "slaves" was substituted. Yet in seceding from the Union, the South acquitted the North of all obligation under the fugitive slave clause as framed in 1787. Moreover, the provisional and permanent constitutions eliminated the old 1808 clause and prohibited all shipping of slaves from Africa to the Confederate States, exactly as George Mason had demanded in   the Philadelphia Convention. It became the express duty of Congress to enact laws against such traffic.

It was naturally assumed that the New Mexico Territory and the Indian Territory belonged of right to the South as their share of the territories of the United States. Accordingly, there was a stipulation in the permanent constitution of the Confederate States that slaves could be taken into the territories and that property in slaves was there to be protected. It was an obligatory formality touching upon an anachronism then fading into the mists of time past.

There was a noteworthy feature of territorial relations in the Southern Confederacy, adopted to cure earlier injustices against Indian tribes then living in the main body of Oklahoma. Each Indian tribe there settled was deemed to be a free, sovereign, and independent Nation allied with the Confederate States. Accordingly, each such tribe sent a territorial delegate to the Congress meeting in Richmond from and after 1862. It was actually contemplated that in due course the Cherokee Nation, the Choctaw Nation, the Creek Nation, and the Seminole Nation would eventually associate in terms of equal dignity with the several States of the Southern Confederacy. These aboriginal Nations supplied troops which fought gallantly under military commissions granted by the Confederate States. The last organized Confederate army to surrender in the War for Southern Independence was an Indian division under the command of General Stand Watie in Oklahoma.

* * * * *

The various provisions acknowledging slavery as a lawful and protected institution in the Confederate States gave rise to a much noted speech by Alexander Stephens in Savannah, Georgia, a few weeks after his appointment as Vice President by the provisional Congress in 1861.[26] This "Cornerstone" speech has been branded as infamous, but it should be confronted in its age and context.

"The prevailing ideas entertained by Jefferson and most of the leading statesmen at the time of the formation of the old Constitution," recounted Stephens, "were that the enslavement of the African was in violation of the laws of nature, and that it was wrong in principle, socially, morally, and politically. It was an evil they knew not how to deal with, but the general opinion of the men of that day was that, somehow or other, in the order of Providence, the institution would be evanescent and pass away."

This observation was as historically accurate as anything ever said about the intended meaning of the United States Constitution. In making this observation, Stephens exploded the premise of the Chief Justice of the United States in the case of Dred Scott. The founding fathers of the United States, including key Southern delegates attending the Philadelphia Convention, did not consider slaves like any other property; they believed in the rights of slaves to citizenship upon emancipation, and accepted as law the exalted principles of Lord Mansfield in the case of James Sommersett. Stephens never ever attempted to defend the opinion of the court in the case of Dred Scott, for as a great constitutional lawyer he knew that something was there wanting. But he repeatedly applauded the carefully formed views of Justice Benjamin Curtis, another constitutional lawyer great in stature, who had cited and expounded the jurisprudence of the old South on the emancipation of slaves, and on that basis would have granted freedom to Dred Scott, his wife Harriet, and his daughters Eliza and Lizzie.

Then, however, came the remarks for which Stephens has since been mercilessly branded as an odious racist. The ideas of Jefferson, said Stephens, "were fundamentally wrong. They rested on the assumption of the equality of the races. This was an error."

With the full benefit of hindsight, this idea of black inferiority can no longer withstand impartial and enlightened scrutiny. But neither can the attitude expressed by Stephens be used to condemn the South, least of all to justify the American Civil War. And the reason is that in 1861 the same basic notion prevailed in the North. Not only was this idea expressed in Stephens' "Cornerstone" speech, but Lincoln articulated the same basic thought in his Peoria speech. Stephens and Lincoln knew each other, and held each other in high regard.

"Our new government," said Stephens, "is founded upon exactly the opposite ideas: its foundations are laid, its cornerstone rests, upon the great truth that the Negro is not the equal of the white man; that slavery, subordination to the superior race, is his natural and moral condition." Here is the sentence which has since excited so much hurt and anger. Yet these words were spoken by the one of the most gracious human beings living at that time in history.

It is unjust and unrealistic to measure a perception in one century by the standards of a later century, nor can anything useful be learned by considering history in this fashion. In the days of Edward III, writs of ship money were necessary and lawful; but by the reign of Charles I — after three hundred years of growth in parliamentary government —, these writs were held to be dangerous and lawless. The gradual passing of time and progress account for a grand measure of what appears as truth. Never has it been more so than in regard to the phenomenon of slavery in the United States.

In his famous debates with Stephen Douglas in 1858, Abraham Lincoln said at one point, "I have no purpose to introduce political and social equality between the white and black races. There is a physical difference between the two which, in my judgment, will probably forever forbid their living together upon the footing of perfect equality. And inasmuch as it becomes a necessity that there be a difference, I, as well as Judge Douglas, am in favor of the race to which I belong having the superior position."[27]

Measured by advances in years following him, Lincoln's views on race are indefensible; yet weighed in light of the age in which he spoke, his opinions were held by most learned men throughout the United States. His views were surely different, but not far and away different from the views of an eminent political leader from Virginia. "African slavery," said this gentleman, "is no relic of barbarism," — and then he spoke further:

> "Its history, when fairly written, will be its ample vindication. It has weaned a race of savages from superstition and idolatry, imparted to them a general knowledge of the precepts of the true religion, implanted in their bosom sentiments of humanity and principles of virtue, developed a taste for the arts and enjoyments of civilized life, given an unknown dignity to their type of physical, moral, and intellectual man, and for two centuries during which this humanizing process has taken place, made for their subsistence and comfort a more bountiful provision than was ever before enjoyed in any age or country of the world by a laboring class. If tried by the test which we apply to other institutions, the whole sum of its results, there is no agency of civilization which accomplished so much in the same time for the happiness and advancement of mankind."[28]

The floweriness of this rhetoric may annoy, and the meaning of these words may shock conscience in a modern reader who has the greatest difficulty in viewing things from the perspective of the gentleman who spoke those words. Yet, if a thinker in the present age could let the eyes of his soul look back in time, he would see things as they then appeared, and, no doubt, he would be astonished. He would better understand why a lawyer in Richmond, Virginia, a man of intellectual acquirements and developed refinement, said at the peace conference in Washington D. C. in 1861, "In respect to the colored race we challenge comparison with San Domingo, with the freed regions of Jamaica, with those who have been transferred to the coast of Africa. Ask travelers who have visited those distant shores to contrast the condition of the colored people there with that of those on our Southern plantations, and they will give you but one answer — they will say, we have redeemed and kept well our high and our holy trust."[29]

Such words now seem outrageous, but were fair and rational when and where spoken. The reason is that the generation now living is, not more enlightened, but literally living in a different world. The march of time has moved apace.

The black race was transported from Africa to North America in an uncivilized condition. It is no less a fact that every race was at one time or another in an uncivilized condition. Nor has there ever been a race which could quickly and effortlessly adapt to the ways of a higher civilization. Some members of a maturing race will stand out in front of others, and display amazing powers for any human being, but as a whole the differences will be observed over very many years, for such transitions take time.

Under these circumstances, it was understandable enough that decent and humane thinkers should have considered race itself as an important determinant of human ability. Thomas Jefferson honestly conjectured, "I advance it, as a suspicion only, that the blacks, whether originally a distinctive race, or made distinct by time and circumstances, are inferior to whites in the endowments of body and mind. It is not against experience to suppose that different species of the same genus, or varieties of the same species, may possess different qualifications."[30] As befitted a man of his intelligence, Jefferson offered this view merely as an hypothesis for investigation in natural science, but in his mind there seemed to be enough evidence to warrant tentative acceptance of the idea.

A traveler to Greenland may see a glacier, and suppose it to be stationary, even though it certainly is moving, and in due course, given wisdom and patience, the glacier will be seen majestically sliding into the North Atlantic. In a not dissimilar way, the progress of the black race, moved according to the rhythms of nature in gradual and steady strides, yet slower than those great leaps of change occurring noticeably within a single life span. Hence, a general consensus had developed among most whites in the United States that race was the cause of the perceived inferiority of blacks.

What then appeared as racial inferiority was an illusion created by differing patterns of social evolution. As white Anglo-Saxon people in England outgrew conditions which had earlier sustained villeinage, black African people in the Southern States were then outgrowing conditions which sustained slavery. Time has since overwhelmed theories of racial inferiority, but in 1861 the general impression was otherwise. And this perception seemed to clash with Jefferson's pronouncements on the universal equality of mankind. Thus, a philosophical enigma to which Lincoln proposed an ingenious solution. In 1858, he said,

> "I hold that there is no reason in the world why the Negro is not entitled to all the natural rights enumerated in the Declaration of Independence, — the right to life, liberty, and the pursuit of happiness. I hold that he is as much entitled to them as the white man. I agree with Judge Douglas, he is not my equal in many respects, — certainly not in color, perhaps not in moral or intellectual endowment. But in the right to eat the bread, without the leave of anybody else, which his hand earns, he is my equal, and the equal of Judge Douglas, and the equal of every living man."[31]

Since these words were spoken, it has become almost a postulate that, even though there are without doubt various levels of human capacity —

and these distinctions have innumerable causes —, everyone should be able to enjoy a reasonable share of the fruits of his own labor. And this notion was highly attractive in the North which prided itself on a system of free enterprise. Then again, there existed cultural and economic misunderstandings which were clarified in an intriguing lecture given by an important Southern leader in Boston only two years before Lincoln and Douglas debated.[32] In describing the situation of a typical slave in the antebellum South, he observed,

> "He has, by universal custom, the control of much of his own time, which is applied, at his own choice and convenience, to the mechanic arts, to agriculture, or to some other profitable pursuit, which not only gives him the power of purchase over many additional necessities of life, but also many of its luxuries, and, in numerous cases, enables him to purchase his freedom when he desires it. Besides, the nature of the relation of master and slave begets kindnesses, imposes duties, and secures their performance, which exist in no other relation of capital and labor. Thus the monster objection to our institution of slavery, that it deprives labor of its wages, cannot stand the test of truthful investigation. A slight examination of the truth theory of wages will further expose its fallacy. Under a system of free labor, wages are usually paid in money, the representative of products, — under ours in products themselves."

Expanding his point, he went on,

> "If we pay in the necessaries and comforts of life more than any given amount of pecuniary wages will buy, then our laborer is paid higher than the laborer who receives that amount in wages. The most authentic agricultural statistics of England show that wages of agricultural and unskilled labor in that kingdom not only fail to furnish the laborer with the comforts of our slave, but even with the necessaries of life, and no slaveholder could escape a conviction for cruelty to his slaves who gave them no more of the necessaries of life for his labor than the wages paid to agricultural laborers by the noblemen and gentlemen in England would buy."

In historical fact, the condition of slaves was very good in the old South. The peculiar institution of the Dixie States had been woven into a cultural fabric of gentle and quiet beauty. And the personal relations between whites and blacks were in excellent order. A civilization of high and noble bearing had evolved throughout the region. The architecture was graceful. The landscapes were magnificent. Education focused on classical knowledge. Traditions were honored. Modern innovations improved but did not dictate the style of life. The old South was a society graced by good manners, radiant with happiness.

If independence had been conceded to those States, and there had been no civil war, the elucidations of social progress, the adaptations demanded by economics, the discoveries of science, and, not the least, the benefits of peace would have produced results worthy to contemplate. In his time Jefferson noticed humane improvements in the practice of slavery. Beneficial trends continued year after year as the institution steadily became more nominal and its rigors abated. By 1861 great strides had been made, and ever more Southerners foresaw and conceded that general liberation could not be far distant.

* * * * *

When Lincoln first took office as President, he was faced with an immediate problem of what to do about the Federal military fortifications which were situated within the seceded States. The most worrisome case was Fort Sumter in the harbor of Charleston, South Carolina. The installation was defended by a small garrison, eighty-six officers and men

Evacuation was recommended by Winfield Scott, then general-in-chief of the United States Army. The old soldier had grown exceedingly wise, for age had enhanced his perspective. He knew what war meant. He understood carnage on battlefields. He knew that a military confrontation over the fort would trigger a war. He knew that the cost of a war against the then seven seceded States, if it could be prosecuted with success, would be enormous in blood and treasure. In his professional opinion, not less than three years would be consumed in such an effort. The war would greatly injure civilized values and constitutional government. In his thinking, the price far exceeded the moral and practical value of the Union formed in 1789. His recommendation to the new President, — "Let the wayward sisters depart in peace."[33] Lincoln's response, — an order to General Scott "directing him to employ every means to strengthen and hold the forts."[34] Having been fully advised of the consequences, Lincoln deliberately took a course which was certain to erupt in the most terrible war ever fought in North America.

On March 15, 1861, his heart disappointed and his ambitions gone, Stephen Douglas offered a resolution in the United States Senate, calling for withdrawal from all Federal military installations in the seceded States, except for Key West and Dry Tortugas.[35] The purpose was to defuse an explosive situation and to prevent the outbreak of war. He outlined the alternatives: — either restoration of the Union by constitutional amendments, which was the course he favored; or peaceful dissolution of the Union, followed by liberal treaties of commerce and friendship, which he was willing to consider, for he knew that most Southerners desired ultimate reunion with the United States; or a war of conquest and subjugation against the seceded States, which was a course favored by politicians blinded by hatred against the South. Douglas' motion was tabled. Fourteen senators from seven Southern States had resigned, and radical republicans were in control of the United States Senate.

Almost the day it was organized, the provisional government of the Confederate States sent commissioners to Washington D. C. for the purpose of negotiations for normalization of relations with the United States. They were rudely awakened in their mission of peace upon receiving intelligence of a naval expedition to reinforce Fort Sumter.

As a Federal naval squadron approached Charleston, the choice was between allowing a dangerous military buildup in a large commercial harbor, certain to ignite a major battle with heavy casualties, or else immediate surgical bombardment to reduce Fort Sumter. As provisional President of the Confederate States, Jefferson Davis ordered reduction of the fort. Southern artillery opened fire in the early morning hours on April 12, 1861. The garrison surrendered early in the afternoon on the next day. The operation was a success by every measure of civilized warfare. Not a man was hurt. The Federal commandant and his troops ceremoniously marched out with colors flying. So began and might have ended the War Between the States.

* * * * *

Lincoln had refused diplomacy and provoked a war. Yet still it was not too late, for the bonds of friendship still existed. There could have been a Union of Northern States and a Confederacy of Southern States, co-existing side by side in peace, each shielding a distinct civilization, — both enjoying vast continental expanse as neighbors, carrying on commerce, and exchanging ambassadors. The irritations intolerable in one union could have been manageable in two, because the new arrangement would have removed the political means by which the two civilizations threatened each other.

After the Philadelphia Convention, fears were expressed that, if the United States were broken up into two or more confederacies, the result would be frequent wars and internecine struggles.[36] But such conjectures have since been refuted by historical experience.

In only a few years after the formation of the Southern Confederacy, still another federal Union was formed under the British North America Act of 1867, 30 & 31 Victoria, Chapter 3. The uninterrupted peace since existing between Canada and the United States proves not only the feasibility, but the desirability of multiple confederacies adjacent to each other upon the same continent, each protecting unique customs and traditions.

There is an optimum size for a federal Union. If too large, it may include interests too dissimilar for successful coordination under one general government, and in such case the stronger will seek to control and exploit the weaker. In 1860 the United States had exceeded optimum size. And a more balanced and satisfactory arrangement for North America today might well be, not two, but three federal Unions above the Rio Grande, all interacting by treaties and diplomacy.

Two different questions about the American Civil War must never be confused. Laying aside the hidden causes of the eruptions on the surface of American politics in those days, the proximate cause of the breakup of the United States in 1860 and 1861 was the passion unleashed by the repeal of the Missouri Compromise.

But the catastrophe following the bombardment at Fort Sumter is a very different question. The rudimentary cause was a deluded and fatal attachment to a political fiction of "national unity" which has never had any foundation in reality, and was at the time only an effusion of war propaganda. This fixation now serves mainly to sedate and silence the conscience of Americans over the injustice produced by the war against the South. And it has produced imperial power, imperial militarism, imperial conquest, imperial oppression, and imperial ruin. It is hard to understand what necessity there has been for it, or what the compensations might be.

* * * * *

By acts of Congress then on the statute books, Lincoln as President had authority to call forth the militia of the several States to repel any foreign invasion of the United States, or to suppress insurrection against the government of any State upon application of her legislature or governor, or to act as a posse comitatus whenever needed to execute judgments of the courts of the United States enforcing revenue acts or other laws of the Union.[37]

But there was no foreign invasion of the United States, nor was there an insurrection against the government of any State of the Union or of any seceded State, nor was there any application by the legislature or governor of any State, nor was there a judgment of any court entered upon revenue acts or other laws of the Union.

Lincoln did not have power under existing acts of Congress to call forth the militia against the seceded States. But edged on by others, he began a hideous career of executive power-grabbing. On April 15, 1861, Lincoln issued a proclamation calling upon the several States for 75,000 militia over 90 days to subdue and conquer the new Southern Confederacy.[38] Not only was this proclamation contrary to existing acts of Congress, it was a Presidential declaration of war, a truly ominous subversion of constitutional government destined to plague future generations of the United States.

The eleventh clause of Article I, Section 8 of the United States Constitution states that Congress shall have power to "declare War, grant Letters of Marque and Reprisal," etc. [39] Under the first clause of Article II, Section 2 of the United States Constitution, the President is made "Commander-in-Chief of the Army and Navy of the United States, and of the Militia of the several States when called into the Service of the United States."[40] Nothing can be plainer than that the framers of the United States Constitution intended to vest the power of the King of Great Britain to declare war in the Congress, and the power of his Majesty as commander-in-chief in the President.[41]

It remains only to determine how these prerogatives of the King were defined by the British Constitution at the time of the Philadelphia Convention.[42] The King was generalissimo and lord high admiral of the realm. The classical writers laid it down that, upon entry into civilized society, men gave up the right to make war, and transferred it to public authority, — in Great Britain to the King. A declaration of war was not taken as a courtesy notifying the enemy to be on his guard, but a prerequisite for, and an ordinance commanding the nation to make war.

From these premises, the division of authority between the President and Congress, as intended by the framers in the Philadelphia Convention, is not so difficult to understand. Save in repelling sudden attacks, the President as commander-in-chief was not granted authority in his own right to use the army, navy and militia in the theatre of war, — not unless and until he should be given approval by Congress in the form of a declaration of war, either "perfect" allowing general hostilities, or else "imperfect" allowing hostilities limited to specific objectives, means, and places.[43]

Aside from larger questions of secession and the use of force to prevent it, Lincoln had no lawful authority as President to call forth the militia or to make war against the Confederate States.

The founding fathers of the United States had distinctive ideas about the abuse of power which Lincoln was about to undertake. "Whither would the militia," asked Hamilton in the 29th Federalist, "irritated at being required to undertake a distant and distressing expedition for the purpose of riveting the chains of slavery upon a part of their countrymen, direct their course, but to the seat of the tyrants who had meditated to foolish as well as so wicked a project, to crush them in their imagined intrenchments of power, and to make them an example of the just vengeance of an abused and incensed people?"[44] In this spirit, the governor of Missouri answered Lincoln's requisition for militia to invade the seven seceded States. "The requisition," he stated, "is illegal, unconstitutional, inhuman, diabolical, and cannot be complied with."[45]

Lincoln committed further unconstitutional acts of war against the Confederate States without the consent of Congress. He issued proclamations of April 19 and 27, 1861, which declared a Federal naval blockade against the seaports of the seceded States.[46]

And pursuant to these lawless proclamations of war, great ships and valuable cargoes belonging to private persons, wholly innocent of any public wrong defined by Congress, were seized as prizes. On July 4, 1861, after the seizures were made, Congress went into special session, filled with partisans intoxicated with hatred for the South. And on July 13, 1861, Congress enacted a statute retroactively "approving, legalizing, and making valid all acts, proclamations, and orders of the President, as if they had been issued and done under the previous express authority and direction of the Congress of the United States."

The proprietors of the ships and cargoes seized before the passing of the Act of July 13, 1861, sued out writs of error from the United States Supreme Court.

In the *Prize Cases*, 2 Black 635 (U. S. 1863), Justice Robert Grier, writing for a majority of five to four, upheld these seizures. And lest any unfairness be done in trying to make sense of his opinion, let his actual words be weighed.

"By the Constitution," said Grier, "Congress alone has the power to declare war against a State or any number of States," and the President, he said, "has no power to initiate or declare war either against a foreign Nation or a domestic State."

Which is why Lincoln's proclamations of April 19 and 27, 1861, were unconstitutional, the seizures were unlawful, and the property taken as prizes should have been restored to its owners with damages for wrongful detention. These inferences were unavoidable. But law and reason were no match for the irresistible power which demanded judicial approval of Presidential acts.

The Act of July 13, 1861, was said to make unlawful acts of executive war-making retroactively lawful, punishing merchants by forfeitures of valuable property for acts lawful when committed, but effectively made unlawful after the fact. "The objection made to this act of ratification, that it is ex post facto, and, therefore, unconstitutional and void, might possibly have some weight on the trial of an indictment in a criminal court,"[47] conceded Grier, "but precedents from that source cannot be received as authoritative in a tribunal administering public and international law." It is impossible to argue against such confusion. The seizures were against the first principles of Magna Carta, guaranteed in the due process clause of Amendment V, not to mention other provisions of the United States Constitution.[48]

Justice Samuel Nelson led four members of the court in dissent. His opinion prevented no injustice, but accentuated the lawlessness of the occasion for the record of history. He expressed his views with precision at the conclusion of his opinion:

> "I am compelled to the conclusion that no civil war existed between this government and the States in insurrection until the 13th of July, 1861; that the President does not possess the power under the Constitution to declare war or recognize its existence within the meaning of the law of nations, which carries with it belligerent rights, and thus changes the country and all its citizens from a state of peace to a state of war; that this power belongs exclusively to the Congress of the United States and, consequently, that the President had no power to set on foot a blockade under the law of nations, and the capture of the vessel and cargo in this case, and in all cases before us in which the capture occurred before the 13th of July 1861, for breach of blockade, or as enemies' property, are illegal and void, and that the decrees of condemnation should be reversed and the vessel and cargo restored."

* * * * *

Not only did Lincoln's militia proclamation induce the secessions of four — eventually in six — more States which might have remained with the Union and worked to encourage reconciliation with the seven States already fallen away, but his blockade proclamations caused the provisional Congress of the Southern Confederacy to adopt a resolution acknowledging a state of war with the United States. Letters of marque and repisal were authorized. The militia in the Southern States were made ready. A hundred thousand men offered to march in the armies of the Confederate States.

As regiments from Northern States marched through Maryland to Washington D. C., riots erupted in Baltimore. And these events in turn induced Lincoln to issue various proclamations, the first on May 10, 1861, or more thereafter, each purporting to delegate to his generals authority to suspend the writ of habeas corpus whenever they thought it necessary and advisable.[49] In question was the second clause of Article I, Section 9 of the United States Constitution, which provides, "The privilege of the Writ of Habeas Corpus shall not be suspended, unless when in Cases of Rebellion or Invasion the public Safety may require it."

This provision corresponds to the clauses in the Petition of Right, 3 Charles I, Chapter 1 (1628), limiting the discretion of the King to suspend the writ of habeas corpus, and on this basis it might be construed to limit the discretion of the President. Lincoln so read it, and, since in his judgment there was a rebellion underway and the public safety required it, he thought he had the power on his own to suspend the writ.

But Lincoln was wrong. A number of important prerogatives of the King — e. g., coining money, fixing the standard of weights and measures, declaring war, and raising armies — had been transferred to Congress, and the same was true for suspension of the writ of habeas corpus, as is plain from the debates of the Philadelphia Convention.[50] And the clause on suspending the writ was understood from the beginning as a limitation on the power of Congress, — not the power of the President. So obvious was this reading to the founding fathers of the United States that, on January 22, 1807, President Thomas Jefferson sent a message to Congress, asking for suspension of the writ of habeas corpus for three months with respect to persons charged on oath with treason and certain related crimes, and although there was then a seemingly dangerous rebellion underway, Congress denied the request.[51]

The first judicial test of presidential suspension of the writ of habeas corpus was the case of *Ex Parte Merryman,* 17 Fed. Cas. 144 (U. S. Cir. Ct. Md. 1861).[52] At two o'clock in the morning on May 25, 1861, John Merryman, a citizen of Maryland, was hauled out of his bed and arrested without warrant or specification of charges. He was imprisoned by Federal troops at Fort McHenry then under the command of General George Cadwalader.

Merryman petitioned Chief Justice Roger B. Taney of the United States Supreme Court, then riding circuit in Maryland, for a writ of habeas corpus under Section 14 of the Judiciary Act of 1789. Section 14 provided that all "courts of the United States shall have power to issue writs of scire facias, habeas corpus, and all other writs not specially provided for by statute, which may be necessary for the exercise of their respective jurisdictions, and agreeable to the principles and usages of law," and that any one "of the justices of the supreme court, as well as judges of the district courts, shall have the power to grant writs of habeas corpus for the purpose of inquiry into the cause of confinement. — Provided, That writs of habeas corpus shall in no case extend to prisoners in gaol, unless where they are in custody under or by color of the authority of the United States, or are committed for trial before some court of the same, or are necessary to be brought into court to testify."[53]

This provision was enacted by the First Congress, with a view to providing liberal access to the writ of habeas corpus in its various forms — ad testificandum, ad deliberandum, and so on —, but most particularly the "great writ," or the writ of habeas corpus ad subjiciendum, for determination of whether confinement under the authority of the United States were in keeping with the constitution and laws of the Union, and, if not, directing release from confinement. Such liberal access was allowed in the belief that, if jurisdiction to issue the great writ were too limited, that in itself might be regarded as a suspension prohibited by the second clause of Article I, Section 9 of the United States Constitution.

Under the first clause of Section 14 of the Judiciary Act of 1789, every Federal court could issue the great writ within the ambit of its proper jurisdiction. And in keeping with the broad reforms of the Habeas Corpus Act, 31 Charles II, Chapter 2 (1679), the second clause of Section 14 conferred upon every individual judge or justice of every Federal court the power to grant the great writ to determine, as a special court of original jurisdiction, whether a petitioner was lawfully confined under the authority of the United States. It was for this reason that Merryman was able to petition Taney directly as Chief Justice of the United States.

Taney issued the writ, but Cadwalader refused to produce Merryman in court, citing presidential delegation to him of power to suspend habeas corpus.

The Chief Justice was then eighty-four years of age. His strength had begun to fail him. He had become increasingly aware that death was not far distant. The world in all its vanity, formerly so attractive, had for him lost its allure. As his term in office drew to a close, James Buchanan had been sobered by events. He rose above mundane politics and spoke timeless truth. And now it was the turn of Roger B. Taney.

Gloriously the Chief Justice described a pageant of legal history, as he recounted the majestic story of the Five Knights, Coke's proposal of the Petition of Right, the ensuing Statute of 31 Charles II, and Jefferson's refusal to suspend the writ of habeas corpus without the consent of Congress. He decorated his graceful prose with luxurious quotations from

Blackstone. He explained that the clause on suspending the writ of habeas corpus was in the article of the United States Constitution which describes the powers of Congress, leaving the unavoidable inference that the power to suspend the writ belonged to Congress, not the President.[54] His work was perhaps the most artistically perfect opinion ever written in American jurisprudence. From all his tragic errors in the case of Dred Scott, Roger B. Taney redeemed himself forever in the case of John Merryman.

In holding Lincoln's suspension of the writ of habeas corpus unconstitutional, Taney said, "If the authority which the constitution has confided in the judiciary department and judicial officers may thus, upon any pretext or under any circumstances, be usurped by the military power at its discretion, the people of the United States are no longer living under a government of laws, but every citizen holds his life, liberty, and property at the will and pleasure of the army officer in whose military district he may happen to be found." Very true were these words, but Merryman remained in confinement, and thousands of others like him were imprisoned on mere suspicion of disloyalty measured, not by legal principles, but partisan ideology.

Taney sent his writ, his order for Merryman's release, and his opinion to the President, requesting of him to take care that the laws be faithfully executed, but Lincoln placed the papers in his desk, and went on fighting the war against the South, which the power brokers and the financiers backing his party had demanded. The evidence is convincing that Lincoln went a step further, and personally ordered the arrest of the Chief Justice. The arrest was never carried out, because it was deemed politically too risky.[55]

There can be no fair doubt that, by his lawlessness, Lincoln was guilty of high crimes and misdemeanors for which he could and should have been impeached. In the *Case of the Earl of Clarendon,* 6 Howell's St. Tr. 318 (H. C. 1667), Edward Hyde, first minister of Charles II, was impeached for infringements upon the privilege of seeking writ of habeas corpus, and these were almost trivial in comparison with the usurpations of Abraham Lincoln. Hyde fled England, and died in exile on the continent of Europe. Lincoln, by contrast, acquired a folkloric image in the vulgar eyes of popular opinion, although he has never been, nor can he ever be redeemed from what he did to Merryman, and attempted against Taney. Bad as it was, the story did not here end, but only grew worse and worse.

* * * * *

Congressman Clement Vallandigham of Ohio introduced resolutions in the United States House of Representatives to condemn Lincoln's suspension of the writ of habeas corpus. Not only were his resolutions laid on the table, but he was marked for political retaliation.

In the spring of 1863, in Knox County, Ohio, far from any theatre of war, where civilian courts were open and doing business, Congressman Vallandigham delivered a public speech in which he said, among other things, "The present war is a wicked, cruel, and unnecessary war, one not waged for the preservation of the Union, but for crushing out liberty and erecting despotism." And, "The sooner the people inform the minions of usurped power that they will not to submit to such restrictions on their liberties, the better."

The speech was not false but too true, not seditious but too patriotic, — more, in any event, than the general commanding the military district of Ohio would tolerate. The general suspended the writ of habeas corpus on the President's order allowing him to do so,[56] then directed the arrest of Vallandigham, who was tried before a military commission, and, needless to say, found guilty of expressing in public "disloyal sentiments and opinions, with the object and purpose of weakening the power of the government in its efforts to suppress an unlawful rebellion." The Congressman was thrown into a military prison. On Lincoln's order, the sentence was "commuted" by shipping Vallandigham to Tennessee and placing him beyond the lines of the Union army, — in other words, upon territory under the control of the Confederate States. Such were the infamous methods used by Lincoln to silence peace democrats — "copperheads" as they were called —, thereby preventing them from offering effective political opposition to the war .

Vallandigham's lawyers petitioned the United States Supreme Court under the first clause of Section 14 of the Judiciary Act of 1789, seeking a writ of certiorari to bring up the record of the military commission for review, and a writ of habeas corpus for determination that the confinement and exile were unlawful. And so arose the pathetic case of *Ex Parte Vallandigham,* 1 Wallace 243 (U. S. 1864).

Whereas Merryman had sought release on writ of habeas corpus issued by the Chief Justice under the second clause of Section 14 of the Judiciary Act of 1789, Vallandigham knew that no individual justice or judge could be found in the country with the intestinal fortitude of Roger B. Taney, — nor, in any event, did Taney ride circuit in Ohio, and by that time Taney was becoming too feeble for strenuous exertions. The strategy of Vallandigham's lawyers was to seek appellate review by the United States Supreme Court sitting en banc under the first clause of Section 14, thus giving the desired order for release prestige so great that Lincoln would dare not resist as he had done in the case of Merryman.

There was a case directly on point, and absolutely decisive in Vallandigham's favor. In *Ex Parte Bollman and Swartout,* 4 Cranch 75 (U. S. 1807), it was held that, if a citizen were held under the authority of the United States, so long as some tribunal had initially acted one way or another, the judgment of such tribunal could be reviewed within the appellate jurisdiction of the United States Supreme Court, under the first clause of Section 14 of the Judiciary Act of 1789, through the issuance of a writ of certiorari to bring up the record, and a writ of habeas corpus to review whether or not his confinement were lawful.

The United States Supreme Court could review the final judgments of circuit courts of the United States upon writ of error under Section 22 of the Judiciary Act of 1789, and could restrain inferior courts of the United States by writs of mandamus and prohibition under Section 13. But Section 14 was a distinct basis of appellate jurisdiction, particularly where a citizen was held in confinement under the authority of the United States, as had been held by Chief Justice John Marshall in the case of Bollman and Swarthout. Therefore, even though there was no statutory provision for appellate review of the judgment of a military commission upon appeal or writ of error, the United States Supreme Court could exercise appellate jurisdiction in such a case upon writ of certiorari and writ of habeas corpus under Section 14. It was so, because, according to the common law, certiorari had always been the writ for exercise of appellate review whenever, for any reason, an appeal or writ of error was not available, as habeas corpus had always been used to determine whether the detention of the petitioner was lawful or unlawful. It was so, no less, because Section 14 was meant to liberalize, not to restrict access to the writ of habeas corpus.

When Vallandigham's case reached the United States Supreme Court, Taney was almost dead, seldom if ever attending sessions. In those days he barely hung onto life in the hope that Lincoln might be defeated for reelection and that the new President would appoint a new Chief Justice who loved the law. The court as a whole had been intimidated into impotence. Justice James Wayne wrote as if the case of Bollman and Swartout had never been decided. He held that, since the military commission was not a court of the Union, the United States Supreme Court could not exercise appellate view of its proceedings.

The decision was nonsense, because the lawless character of the proceedings of the military commission did not immunize it from judicial scrutiny. On the contrary, the lawless character of its proceedings urgently demanded appellate review by the United States Supreme Court upon writ of certiorari and writ of habeas corpus as allowed by the first clause of Section 14 of the Judiciary Act of 1789. The decision was nonsense, because the god of war demanded nonsense. Inter armes silent leges.

* * * * *

As the civil war dragged on, the Southern Congress in Richmond passed an act suspending the writ of habeas corpus in cases of arrest ordered by the President, and certain other designated officers. But the people of the Southern States were fighting in defense of their rights under fundamental law and legal tradition. They fought a revolution as sacred and just as their ancestors ever waged, and in their valiant struggle they never lost sight of their true purposes. It is an irrefutable witness to the grandeur of Southern civilization that, as troops of the Union marched against Atlanta, the General Assembly of Georgia passed resolutions, undying in courage, and similar to the Virginia and Kentucky Resolution of 1798. These Georgia Resolutions of 1864 read,

> "That the recent Act of Congress to suspend the privilege of the writ of habeas corpus in cases of arrest ordered by the President, Secretary of War, or General Officer commanding the Trans-Mississippi Military Department, is an attempt to sustain military authority in the exercise of the Constitutional Judicial function of issuing warrants and to give validity to unconstitutional seizures of the persons of the people; and as the said Act, by its express terms, confines its operation to the upholding of this class of unconstitutional seizures, the whole suspension attempted to be authorized by it, and the whole Act itself, in the judgment of the General Assembly, are unconstitutional."[57]

No aspersions whatever were cast upon sentiments such as these. There was no idiocy which proclaimed that whatever opposed unconstitutional transgressions of central authority must be disloyal. Such crude notions were unthinkable in the South.

Under the permanent constitution instituted in 1862, no Confederate judiciary was established by Congress. Therefore all of the many petitions for writs of habeas corpus against detention by Confederate authorities were entertained by the courts of the Southern States. Chief Justice Richmond Pierson of the North Carolina Supreme Court was famous and admired, because he issued many such writs and freed dozens of citizens in the custody of the Confederate secretary of war.[58]

And so respectful was President Davis of the legal rights of his countrymen that, even as the tide of war turned mercilessly against the South, he carefully instructed his attorney general: — if any citizen detained by the Confederate government should seek a writ of habeas corpus, any claim of suspension of the writ of habeas corpus should be freely waived by the Confederate States as far as practicable, and the merits should be forthrightly argued before the judges.[59] So it was to the bitter end.

NOTES

CHAPTER VII

1 - Quoted in Anderson's Calhoun at 16.

2 - The full text of Seward's speech on October 25, 1858, in Rochester, New York, is reprinted in Rozwenc's Civil War at 11-20.

3 - Davis' seven resolutions are reprinted in 2 Stephens' View 409-411.

4 - The inglorious fourth crusade, leading to the capture and sack of Constantinople by Christians in 1204, is discussed in 6 Gibbon's Rome 48-96 (Chapter LX).

5 - The platforms of the major parties in 1860 were a striking portrait of political confusion. The moderate parties were badly splintered, as appears in 1 Commager's Documents at 365-366 for the "union" democrats, at 366 for the "national" democrats, and at 363 for the constitutional union party. The republicans were the radical party of the day, as appears in 1 Commager's Documents at 363-365.

6 - Recently given proper and unforgettable attention in Davis' Honorable Defeat.

7 - The returns in the Presidential election of 1860 are graphically represented in the Times Atlas at 225, showing a strong republican sweep in the North, and success of the other three parties mainly in various parts of the South. The raw numbers in the popular vote are set forth in 1 Morris' History at 226-227. The popular vote for Lincoln was 1,866,352. The combined popular vote for Douglas and Breckenridge was 2,224,932, while the combined vote for Douglas, Breckenridge, and Bell was 2,814, 513, which demonstrates that, if the splintering among conservative and moderate votes had not been engineered, Lincoln could have been easily enough defeated in both popular and electoral votes.

8 - Reprinted in 1 Commager's Documents at 362-363.

9 - Reprinted in 1 Commager's Documents at 372, and 2 Thorpe's History at 561.

10 - Reprinted in 1 Commager's Documents 372-372 and 2 Stephens' View 671-676 (December 24, 1860).

11 - The figures are found in 2 Morris' History at 514-516.

12 - It was not difficult for slaves to escape along the underground railroad or otherwise, because the supervision of slaves was generally relaxed, the territory of the Southern States was vast, and the land was rich in natural provisions. It would be an excellent employer who lost only one out of 4,000 to 8,000 employees in any one year from such dissatisfaction as might induce him to move from his abode. Some insight into this astonishing situation may be derived from the speech given in the Alabama Convention of 1861: — "In nine cases out of ten, in positive contentment, the Alabama slave is happier than his master. His cottage is built for him, his food provided, his meals prepared; his hearth is spread with substantial comforts, and his long nights are for those blissful dreams that are undisturbed by his knowledge of coming necessities. He has no cankering cares, no buffeting with fortune, no aspiration for expanding acres, no cares for rain or sunshine. He has neither cloth nor meat to buy; he is free from debt, he is above all civil law — and he looks forward to Christmas, not as the maturity time for his bills, but for his holidays." — Quoted in 2 Thorpe's History at 651.

13 - In Prigg v. Pennsylvania, 16 Peters 539 (U. S. 1842), Justice Joseph Story held that the power of Congress to enact statutes for the recovery of runaway slaves was exclusive, and that any laws of the several States on the subject were unconstitutional. In *Abelman v. Booth,* 21 Howard 506 (U. S. 1859), Chief Justice Roger B. Taney held that the courts of the several States had no jurisdiction to issue writs of habeas corpus for examination of the detention of any person held for violation of the fugitive slave law of 1850. Both decisions were extravagances, and departed widely from the criteria of exclusive Federal authority described by Alexander Hamilton in the 32nd Federlist, Mentor Edition at 198, and in the 82nd Federalist, Mention Edition at 142.

14 - The pertinent clause in Section 13 of the Judiciary Act of 1789 (1 U. S. Statutes at Large at 80-81) provided "That the Supreme Court shall have exclusive jurisdiction of all controversies of a civil nature, where a State is a party, except between a State and its citizens, and except also between a State and citizens of other States, or aliens, in which latter case it shall have original but not exclusive jurisdiction." And under this provision, one State could bring a suit in equity against another State within the original jurisdiction of the United States Supreme Court, as occurred in *Rhode Island v. Massachusetts,* 12 Peters 657 (U. S. 1838).

15 - Stephens' timeless and incomparable discussion of secession is found in 1 Stephens' View 17-543. The attempts of Jefferson Davis and Albert Bledsoe are grand, but nothing in comparison to the awesome precision and power of Alexander Stephens' work.

16 - Reprinted in 2 Stephens' View 279-300 (November 14, 1860). Stephens' cordial but frank exchange of letters with Lincoln as President-Elect is fully discussed

and reprinted in 2 Stephens' View 265-270. His speech against secession in the Georgia Convention of 1861 is reprinted in 2 Stephens' View 305-307.

17 - Pollard's Lost Cause at 51-52.

18 - Reprinted in 1 Commager's Documents 366-369.

19 - Quoted in 2 Thorpe's History at 579 (Address to the States of the South, December 24, 1860).

20 - The proceedings in question are found in 5 Elliot's Debates 127-128, 139-140, 437-438, 497-498, — Tansill's Documents 117, 130, 560-561, 645-646, - 1 Ferrand's Records 316-318, 416-417 (Madison's Notes, May 29 and 31, August 17 and 30, 1787).

21 - Reprinted in 1 Commager's Documents 369-371.

22 - Quoted in 2 Thorpe's History at 667.

23 - Speeches and Debates at 532-533.

24 - The debates in the First Congress are absolutely lucid in showing that the ten articles of the Federal Bill of Rights were not meant to restrain the several States, and were intended to limit only the powers of the Union, as appears in 1 Annals of Congress 434-436 and 755 (House, June 8 and August 17, 1789). This point was explained by Chief Justice John Marshall, from personal knowledge of relevant events, in *Barron v. Baltimore,* 7 Peters 243 (U. S. 1833).

25 - The fifth clause of Article I, Section 9 of the United States Constitution prohibits Congress from imposing any tax on exports. The framing of this clause in the Philadelphia Convention can be traced in 5 Elliot's Debates 357-358, 379, 432-433, 454-457, 536, 561, — Tansill's Documents 441, 476, 552-555, 584-588, 707, — 2 Ferrand's Records 95, 183, 304-308, 359-364, 571, 596, 657 (Madison's Notes July 23, August 6, 16, and 21, September 10, 12, and 17, 1787). The speeches of Madison, proposing a power to tax exports on a vote of two-thirds of the house and of the senate were delivered on August 16 and 21, 1787.

26 - Reproduced in Rozwenc's Slavery as a Cause 42-46, and is quoted and discussed at some length in 2 Thorpe's History at 652-654. There is always "the other side of the story," which on the subject of the "Cornerstone" speech is found in 1 Stephens' View at 539-543, and 2 Stephens' View at 80-86.

27 - Speeches and Debates at 179-180 (Ottawa, Illinois, August 21, 1858).

28 - From a speech by Congressman James Holcombe of Virginia to the seventh annual meeting of the Virginia State Agricultural Society on November 4, 1858, reprinted in 1 Stephens' View 621-625. Holcombe later served in the Congress of the Confederate States.

29 - From a speech by James Seddon on February 18, 1861, Chittenden's Debates

at 94. Seddon served in the Congress of the United States and the Congress of the Confederate States, and for several years was secretary of war in the cabinet of President Jefferson Davis.

30 - In Query XIV, *Notes on Virginia,* Koch & Peden's Jefferson at 262.

31 - Speeches and Debates at 180 (Ottawa, Illinois, August 21, 1858).

32 - Given by Senator Robert Tombs of Georgia at the Tremont Temple in Boston, Massachusetts, on January 24, 1856, reprinted in 1 Stephens View 625-647. After resigning his seat in the United States Senate in 1861, Toombs served as secretary of state for the Confederate States, then as a brigadier general in the Army of Northern Virginia.

33 - Quoted in 2 Stephens' View at 351.

34 - From Lincoln's letter to William Seward, April 1, 1861, reprinted in 1 Commager's Documents 392-393.

35 - Douglas' speech is quoted and discussed in 2 Stephens' View at 351-354.

36 - E. g., Alexander Hamilton said in the 6th Federalist, "A man must be far gone in Utopian speculations who can seriously doubt that, if these States should either be wholly disunited, *or only united in partial confederacies,* the subdivisions into which they might be thrown would have frequent and violent contests with each other. To presume a want of motives as an argument against their existence would be to forget that men are ambitious, vindictive and rapacious." — Mentor Edition at 54 (Emphasis added). Likewise Edmund Randolph answered those who favored a Southern Confederacy in 1789, rather than a new Union of all thirteen States: — "If there is a gentleman here who harbors in his mind the idea of a separate confederacy, I beg him to consider the consequence. Where shall we find refuge in the day of calamity? The different confederacies will be rivals in power and commerce, and therefor will soon be implacable enemies of one another." — 3 Elliot's Debates at 198 (Virginia Convention, June 10, 1788).

37 - These militia acts are set forth in 1 U. S. Statutes at Large 424 (February 24, 1795), supplemented by 2 U. S. Statutes at Large 443 (March 3, 1807), which were enacted in light of the fifteenth and sixteenth clauses of Article I, Section 8 and the guarantee clause of Article IV, Section 4 of the United States Constitution. In a speech before the United States Senate on March 15, 1861, Stephen Douglas interpreted these acts as saying that the militia could not be used as a posse comitatus "except in aid of civil process to assist the marshal to execute a writ." - Quoted in 2 Stephens View 399-401. Section 2 of the Act of February 24, 1795 actually provided that the President could call forth the militia "whenever the laws of the United States shall be opposed, or the execution thereof obstructed, in any State, by combinations too powerful to be suppressed by the ordinary course of judicial proceedings, or by the powers vested in the

marshals by this act." Douglas construed Section 2 strictly in keeping with the due process clause of Amendment V of the United States Constitution as requiring a judgment of a court of the United States, applying the laws of the Union to particular facts, before such laws could be deemed opposed or obstructed by a combination too powerful to be enforced by the ordinary course of judicial proceedings with the aid marshals. An executive determination by the President without intervening judicial proceedings, he thought, was outside the contemplation of the Act of February 24, 1795.

38 - Lincoln's proclamation is reprinted in 2 Stephen's View at 370-372.

39 - The proceedings of the Philadelphia Convention on the powers of Congress to declare war, to grant letters of marque and reprisal, and to make rules concerning captures on land and water, can be traced in 5 Elliot's Debates 378, 379, 436, 438-439, 440, 441, 510, 511, 536, 561, — Tansill's Documents 475, 558, 561-563, 564, 566, 665, 666, 706, 2 Ferrand's Records 182, 315, 318-319, 508, 509, 570, 595, 655 (Madison's Notes, August 6 and 17, September 5, 10, 12, and 17, 1787).

40 - The proceedings of the Philadelphia Convention on the power of the President as commander-in-chief of the armed forces of the Union can be traced in 5 Elliot's Debates 380, 474-475, 480, 536, 562, — Tansill's Documents 478, 612-614, 621, 709, — 2 Ferrand's Records 185, 404-406, 426-427, 575, 599, 659 (Madison's Notes, August 6, 24, and 27, September 10, 12, and 17, 1787).

41 - This division of authority between the President and Congress, by reference to prerogatives of the British Crown, was stressed by Alexander Hamilton in the 69th Federalist, Mentor Edition at 417-418.

42 - The prerogatives of the King to declare war and grant letters of marque and reprisal, and as commander-in-chief are described in 1 Blackstone's Commentaries 257-261 and 262-263.

43 - The distinction between perfect and imperfect war was judicially recognized in *Miller v. The Resolution,* 2 Dallas 19 (Conf. App. 1781), and *Bas v. Tingy,* 4 Dallas 37 (U. S. 1800).

44 - Mentor Edition at 187. Like sentiments, in language as eloquent, were expressed by George Mason, 3 Elliot's Debates 378 (Virginia Convention, June 14, 1788), and by James Madison, 3 Elliot's Debates 381-382 (Virginia Convention, June 14, 1788).

45 - Quoted in 2 Stephens' View at 375 (Governor Claiborne Jackson).

46 - Lincoln's proclamation of April 19, 1861, in reprinted in 2 Stephens' View 377-378.

47 - Grier no doubt had in the mind the narrow definition of an ex post facto law

prohibited by the third clause of Article I, Section 9 and the first clause of Article I, Section 10 of the United States Constitution, as is given in *Calder v. Bull,* 3 Dallas 386 at 390-391 (U. S. 1798). Yet that definition was rejected in favor of a much broader meaning in the Philadelphia Convention, as appears in 5 Elliot's Debates 485, Tansill's Documents 628-629, and 2 Ferrand's Records 439-440 (August 28, 1787). The Act of July 13, 1861, was an ex post facto law because it retroactively punished by forfeiture an act which at the time was perfectly lawful under existing acts of Congress.

48 - At the time Grier wrote, it had then long been established that a statute divesting an owner of property, and transferring it to another to another was a violation of due process of law, as appears in *University of North Carolina v. Fox,* 1 Murphy 58 (N. C. 1805), and contrary to the most basic principles of a republican form of government, as appears in *Calder v. Ball,* 3 Dallas 386 at 388 (U. S. 1798).

49 - The proclamation of May 10, 1861, is reprinted in 2 Stephens' View 410.

50 - It is obvious from the framing of the second clause of Article I, Section 9 of the United States Constitution that suspension of the habeas corpus was conceived to be the prerogztive of Congress. Most particularly, the clause was introduced as an express restriction upon legislative power, and in that shape adopted with immaterial changes: — it so appears in 5 Elliot's Debates 445-446, 484, 536, 561, — Tansill Documents 571-572, 627, 707, — 2 Ferrand's Records 340-342, 438, 576, 596, 656 (Madison's Notes, August 20 and 28, September l0, 12, and 17, 1787).

51 - Jefferson's request concerned the attempt by Aaron Burr to take New Orleans by force of arms. His message to Congress is reprinted in 1 Commager's Documents 195-197. The Senate approved of the President's request, but the House voted in the negative by a large majority on January 26, 1807, after a spirited debate, as appears in   16 Annals of Congress 402-422. Thereafter Burr was indicted for treason. He was morally guilty but was acquitted on a technicality, as appears in *United States v. Burr,* 25 Fed. Cas. 55 (U. S. Cir. Ct. Va. 1807).

52 - Taney's full opinion is reprinted in 2 Stephens' View 748-759.

53 - 1 U. S. Statutes at Large at 81-82.

54 - This technique of construction, whereby the meaning of a clause is determined by reference to its context or subject matter, is found among the rules for ascertaining legislative will in 1 Blackstone's Commentaries 59-61.

55 - Discussed in the account in Adams' Human Events at 45-53.

56 - Congress eventually authorized executive suspension of the writ of habeas corpus by an Act of March 3, 1863 (12 U. S. Statutes at Large 755), but this statute imposed important qualifications and conditions which Lincoln did not wish to observe. Consequently, Lincoln made no attempt to invoke his rights

under the Act, and relied on his claimed inherent authority as President until September 15, 1863. The arrest of Congressman Vallandigham was made under General Order No. 38 issued by General Ambrose Burnside who relied on nothing other than his claimed power to suspend the writ of habeas corpus at discretion, as delegated to him by the President.

57 - The full text of the Georgia Resolutions of 1864 is reprinted in 2 Stephens' View 788-790.

58 - The views of Chief Justice Pierson appear in *Gatlin v. Walton,* 1 Winston 333 at 424-441 (N. C. 1864).

59 - In *Borroughs v. Peyton,* 16 Grattan 470 at 472 (Va. 1864), a conscript sued out a writ of habeas corpus, and the attorney general of the Confederate States, as the court duly noted, expressly declined to plead that the writ of habeas corpus had been suspended pursuant to an act of Congress.

CHAPTER VIII

THE WAR BETWEEN THE STATES

The thirteen States and two territories represented in the Congress of the Southern Confederacy embraced a land mass more considerable than the original thirteen States united in the Continental Congress. But this legal jurisdiction must be pared down to political and military realities.

If, accordingly, Arizona or New Mexico and the Indian lands are excluded from calculations, as well as all of Kentucky and Missouri, a third of Virginia, and half of Tennessee and Louisiana, which were usually under occupation by the government of the Union from an early period of the American Civil War, the remaining territory under the jurisdiction of the Confederate States was still very large. In view of these adjustments, the North had effective control over a population of about 23,500,000, and the South had effective control over only about 7,700,000, of which about a third consisted of slaves.

The North enjoyed a balanced economy, with advanced industrial development, prosperous agriculture, and strong banking institutions, together with extensive railroads and shipping. The South, by contrast, had far fewer industries and railroads, few banks of large size, and very little shipping; its economy was almost entirely agricultural, producing crops such as cotton, tobacco, indigo, and rice, which were valuable mainly as exports. Yet the advantages in the means and apparatus of war enjoyed by the North, however great and obvious, were not enough to bring about the fall of the South, which, after all, had certain compensations weighing in its favor.

Unless compressed entirely into conflict on battlefields in which larger numbers and resources must finally prevail, war is often more a matter of patience and endurance than of tactics and maneuvers, as may be illustrated.

During the American Revolution, the British were capable of winning battles almost whenever engaged. At the time of the surrender of Lord

Cornwallis, their navy effectively dominated the larger part of the Atlantic coast, and their troops held Savannah, Charleston, and New York. Earlier in the war they had easily taken Boston, Philadelphia, Newport, and Richmond. They enjoyed incomparable advantages in population, resources, matériel, sophistication, and productivity. Americans had suffered defeats as or more severe than the British suffered at Yorktown.

Yet, as Lord Chatham had warned early in the war, the British could not prevail. The morale of the population in rebellion was maintained. The territory of the United States was huge. And usually the Continental army was properly led. The first imperative was to keep formations intact and supply lines open. Soldiers were kept in as good condition as possible. Their commanders knew that retreat in good order from the field or withdrawal from a city in good order was not a serious loss, whatever the score by military convention. Pitched battles were avoided, except where clearly necessary or opportune. Frontal attacks against heavy fire power were hardly ever attempted by American troops. The British gave up, not because they were beaten, but because they were exhausted.

With a few exceptions, the British government was compelled by political and fiscal realities of the day to operate within traditional restraints of fundamental law, and to pursue military objectives according to established principles of chivalrous warfare. If the war party in England had been powerful and fanatical enough to sacrifice constitutional government and civilized standards, and if they had been able to transform their country into a military despotism, the American rebellion might have been broken. But the price demanded was too much for a wise nation to pay. Statesmen in London faced facts, down came the ministry of Lord North, and the British went on to build another empire, the most stupendous and far-reaching body of dominions and colonies ever gathered under a single imperial ensign in human experience.

So stood the record of history as the Dixie States seceded in 1860 and 1861. The Southern people were animated by the just and necessary cause of defending their own homes and firesides, their sovereign rights, and their traditions and ways. At least as long as their morale could be maintained, and the war was fought according to sound military and constitutional principles, geography made conquest of the South a virtual impossibility. The country was not traversed with practical roads, but was vast, wild, and difficult, with rivers, mountains, swamps, welted with rugged mountains and landscapes, all forming an intricate and formidable system of natural military fortifications.

* * * * *

The war began with a series of minor encounters, then came the first major engagement at Manasses in Virginia on July 21, 1861. About 30,000 volunteers on each side fought it out. The battle was almost a sportive affair, — the kind of encounter at which, given their way of life, Southern boys were naturally more adept. The result was a rout of Federal troops from the field. Lincoln's cabinet and Congress soon developed a more realistic and sober idea of what they had undertaken. The estimates of General Winfield Scott, which before the reduction of Fort Sumter had been regarded as inordinate, now appeared, if anything, to be inadequate.

Preparations were begun in earnest for an ominous and prolonged war. General George McClellan was given command of all troops on the eastern theatre, and not so long thereafter supreme military command of all armies of the Union. He designed operations in the east and the west. He meticulously attended to organization, morale, and discipline. His soldiers had confidence in him, because his first concern was their safety and welfare. They knew he would not carelessly throw units into the fury of battle. McClellan's men knew that, when their general issued orders for movement, he acted with cool intelligence, comprehensively understanding the military situation, and that, therefore, they were needed, and were given objectives which they should be able to achieve. "Little Mac" was respected and admired in the ranks. He knew the conventions and gallantry of war as an art and science to be carried out with skill, humanity, and courage. He once wrote to President Lincoln,

> "This rebellion has assumed the character of a war; as such it should be regarded, and it should be conducted upon the highest principles known to a Christian civilization. It should not be a war looking to the subjugation of the people of any State, in any event. It should not be at all a war upon a population, but against armed forces and political organizations. Neither confiscation of property, political execution of persons, territorial organization of States, nor the forcible abolition of slavery should be contemplated for a moment."[1]

These exalted sentiments were his downfall, because they were utterly contrary to the views of extremists in the Federal administration, most particularly the secretary of war, Edwin Stanton. The image given by the common lot of civil war historians, preposterous in light of the facts, is that McClellan was ever afraid to fight a battle, and out of excessive caution failed to press his military advantages. For this reason, it is said, Stanton rightly removed him from command to make way for "vigorous" prosecution of the conflict.

It is very often true that accounts of the same campaign from different points of view make a student wonder whether the same or different events are under discussion.[2] The inconsistencies in reports of military actions can frequently be reconciled in terms of perspective on the field or the passions of the moment. But of all factors which distort reality in accounts of war, none is so great as the propaganda of those responsible for the suffering. The resulting distortions are often passed off as "history" in later generations.

The false myth that McClellan was to blame for his failure to take Richmond in 1862 grew out of the propaganda of Stanton's war department. So gallant was George McCellan that, when his army on the York Peninsula came upon the wife of Robert E. Lee, he placed the lady in a carriage and had her transported with military escort under flag of truce to her husband in Richmond. A character of that high standard was more than Stanton could endure. The secretary gave orders which sabotaged the campaign, a well-conceived military effort which ought to have been a success. And Stanton indulged in such treachery, because his ultimate purpose was to remove all legal and civilized restraints on the war machine of the North, and thereby to bring ruin upon the people and culture of the South. Stanton passionately wanted to get rid of McClellan, because, if the general had triumphed, he certainly would have been elected in 1864 as President of the United States. Reconciliation of all the States by diplomatic means into a renewed Union would then have become entirely possible, for the South felt the highest respect for McClellan, and Stanton's cruel and inane designs for humiliation of the South would never have been realized.

McClellan surrounded Washington D. C. with strong works and entrenchments, armed with adequate artillery, garrisoned with a respectable number of troops, secure against any assault, and capable of withstanding a long siege. Thereby his main body was freed up for offensive movement. The general carefully built a grand striking force of 155,000 men known as the Army of the Potomac, which was to land upon and march up the York Peninsula, since that route was the shortest over land for taking Richmond, capital city and rallying point of the Confederate States. His preparations were as compendious and systematic as those of the best military commanders in history.

McClellan proceeded to execute, and Stanton interfered, first taking 60,000 men from his command, depriving him of most of the numerical advantage he needed over the Southern army, which eventually amounted to about 80,000 in the vicinity of Richmond. Stanton then ordered McClellan to extend his line so as to divide his army on either side of the Chicohominy River just to the north of the city, and delayed anticipated reinforcements, leaving him in a vulnerable position which then was exploited by a Confederate attack ordered by General Joseph E. Johnston at Seven Pines on the last day of May. Johnston was wounded in the encounter. Thereupon, General Robert E. Lee assumed command, and then and there named his forces the Army of Northern Virginia. Lee ordered assaults in the Seven Days Battle Around Richmond at the end of June and the beginning of July, 1862.

Cautiously and slowly McClellan moved back during the last of the Seven Days into an impregnable position on Malvern Hill, which Lee recklessly stormed only to be repulsed at great loss. The casualties up to that point were shocking, — McClellan lost about 15,000, Lee about 20,000. Most of these losses would have been avoided if Stanton had let his general fight as he knew best, for then numerical advantage and undivided force could have been applied without tempting Southern commanders to attack. Either there would have been a long siege of Richmond, or the capital might have been abandoned to a point safer for the Confederate government to transact business, — Houston would have been ideal.

After his success at Malvern Hill, McClellan pulled back to Harrison's Landing on the James River under the protection of the Federal navy, there intending to give his soldiers well-earned repose, to fill the gaps in his formations with ample reinforcements, and then to march again on Richmond, which was only about twenty miles from where he was at the time. He wanted the 60,000 men which Stanton had taken from him. With these troops his numerical advantage would have been enough to assure success. The Southern army was in badly damaged condition and could not be as easily replenished with men and supplies.

The Army of the Potomac was still in good spirits, and they were eager to fight again for Little Mac, who praised and comforted his troops as a father would his own sons. Richmond was in grave danger, and the best military minds knew it. But Stanton ordered abandonment of the campaign as newspapers controlled by republican editors trumpeted the big lie that McClellan had been defeated.

Stanton then secured the appointment of General John Pope, whose political views were accepted by the radicals in the North, to lead a newly organized Army of Virginia, as it was called, to operate initially between Washington D. C. and the Rappahanock River. McClellan's army at Harrison's Landing was drained almost to extinction as the ranks of Pope's army swelled. In conformity with Stanton's desire, the new commander announced, "I hear constantly of lines of retreat. Let us discard such ideas, " — which was proof of his incompetence, because in real war retreat is often essential to success, while attack often produces defeat.

Lee brought his troops up from Richmond to meet Pope, and after various movements there was a Second Battle of Manassas at the end of August and the beginning of September 1862. With incoherent directives, Pope ordered his units into a badly conceived assault in open fields against withering fire. Whole regiments were mowed down, and his army was routed. Pope wired Stanton, claiming a great victory. If the evidence of utter disintegration of his forces could have been concealed, the telegram would no doubt have appeared in cheering headlines in New York. But the proofs of military disaster were too plain, and, therefore, such falsehoods of war could not be attempted. Pope's losses in killed, wounded, missing, and captured must have been on the order of 25,000 altogether. Lee's losses were perhaps half that figure.

The morale of the South had taken a beating in the spring of 1862 because of a series of grave reverses in the western theatre of the war. Large garrisons had surrendered at Island No. 10 and Fort Donelson, the thrust at Shiloh had failed, and New Orleans had fallen. If Stanton had left McClellan alone, Richmond would have been under heavy siege or may have fallen by the end of August. By his cynical manipulations, Stanton had ruined a superb general, tried to glorify a blustering fool, prevented sound military progress, and saw the tide of the war in the eastern theatre turn against the Union. Pope was expendable, and he took the blame, while Stanton escaped reproach.

Lee advanced his by then famous Army of Northern Virginia into Maryland, hoping to induce the State to join the Southern Confederacy and to invite diplomatic recognition by the powers of Europe. Stanton then turned to the ablest general in the armies of the United States. McClellan met Lee at Sharpsburg in the middle of September 1862. It was the bloodiest day of the war. Lee remained on the field, but so hurt were his ranks from casualties that he limped back into to Virginia. If Stanton had used another one of his favorites, Lee would have prevailed, the impact would have been like Yorktown, and Southern independence would have been won.

But the secretary saw to it that McClellan was not rewarded. Stanton demanded immediate movement, and Little Mac began methodical preparations to assure success. Stanton then used necessary delays as a pretext to demand the removal of McClellan, who, accordingly, was relieved of command in early November. He had been used, then was disgraced. The episode was little more than a replay of the ingratitude shown by Justinian to Belisarius.[3]

The secretary next secured the appointment of General Ambrose Burnside to command the Army of the Potomac, — another commander sufficiently hostile in his attitudes against the South, who believed that irresponsible risk of soldiers' lives in battle was bravery and energy in pressing the war. In the last month of 1862, Burnside pushed by Stanton ordered a massive frontal assault against Lee's troops positioned on the heights above Fredericksburg in Virginia. The result, perfectly foreseeable, was gross slaughter of Union soldiers for no military advantage, — casualties of about 13,000, while Lee sustained a minor fraction of that number.

Stanton then chose another political general, Joseph Hooker, whose name honors the ancient profession of ladies who entertained his troops. At the beginning of May 1863, he marched his army against the formations of Robert E. Lee near Chancellorsville. General T. J. Jackson, famous for his stand at First Manassas, his brilliant Shenandoah Valley campaign, and his maneuvers at Second Manassas, made a circling movement through the wilderness around the Army of the Potomac then struck its rear. It was another of Stanton's disasters, resulting in a loss of about 18,000 men, inflicted by a Southern army half the size of Hooker's command.

As at Second Manassas, an attempt was made to claim a great victory for the Union, but Hooker's congratulatory message to his troops was so ludicrous that the most fanatical newspapers in the North dared not indulge in the deception. Stanton's ineptitude and disloyalty should have been evident. Yet the man had connections, so the press somehow or other managed to spare him again from the fate which he deserved.

The brightness of victory at Chancellorsville was darkened by a great loss. "Stonewall" Jackson, while leading his famous attack, was mortally wounded in battle. His replacement as second in command was General James Longstreet whose temperament, style, and outlook were quite different. Jackson inspired Lee to make rapid movements and bold strikes with serene confidence of mind, and, with his guidance, Lee rose to heights of fame obscuring his humanity. Longstreet, by contrast, was a methodical, cautious, practical soldier, — the kind of general who, if well heard and allowed to lead, could continue a defensive war at minimum loss or prolong a stalemate too painful for the enemy to endure.

Longstreet was exactly what Lee needed as the summer of 1863 approached. He was what Lee needed, because, after two years of continuous fighting against a vastly more powerful adversary, the war had lost its glamour, and became a dull, hard, and awful experience.

At the time, Federal operations under General Ulysses Grant were underway against the river stronghold of Vicksburg in Mississippi, which was in danger of collapse. The situation had developed, because President Jefferson Davis in Richmond did not understand an observation of Frederick the Great: — "A defensive war is apt to betray us into too frequent attachments.

Those generals who have but little experience attempt to protect every point, while those who are better acquainted with their profession, having only the capital object in view, guard against a decisive blow, and acquiesce in smaller misfortunes to avoid greater."[4]

General Joseph E. Johnston, having recovered from wounds suffered at Seven Pines, reported for duty in November 1862. In speaking with George Randolph, then secretary of war in Davis' cabinet, General Johnston recommended that troops in Arkansas be brought over into Mississippi for the defense of Vicksburg.[5] These reinforcements would certainly have been enough to defeat Grant. They would have left the Confederate army in Tennessee at full strength, better able to deal with the invasion there. The secretary of war agreed with Johnston, but Davis countermanded Randolph's order. The secretary resigned in protest, and Johnston disavowed responsibility for the inevitable consequences. As predicted by Johnston, Vicksburg fell into the death grip of Grant's inexorable campaign and heavy siege.

As they met in conference after Chancellorsville, Lee and Longstreet discussed the various options of taking pressure off Vicksburg.[6] At length Lee decided upon an invasion of Pennsylvania, hoping in this way to draw Federal troops from various points south, or, better yet, to draw the Army of the Potomac into desperate movements on demand of frightened politicians in Washington D. C., offering the Army of Northern Virginia an opportunity for a decisive victory. Longstreet recounted:

> "I then accepted his proposition to make a campaign into Pennsylvania, provided it should be offensive in strategy but defensive in tactics, forcing the Federal army to give us battle when we were in strong position and ready to receive them. One mistake of the Confederacy was in pitting force against force. The only hope we had was to out-general the Federals. We were all hopeful and the army was in good condition, but the war had advanced far enough for us to see that a mere victory without decided fruits was a luxury we could not afford. Our numbers were less than the Federal forces, and our resources were limited while theirs were not. The time had come when it was imperative that the skill of generals and the strategy and tactics of war should take the place of muscle against muscle. Our purpose should have been to impair the morale of the Federal army and shake Northern confidence in the Federal leaders. We talked on that line from day to day, and General Lee, accepting it as a good military view, adopted it has the keynote of his campaign."

Longstreet did not mean to downplay the outstanding maneuvers of Jackson, but sought to restrain his chief from anything ever again like the assault on Malvern Hill, which cost about 4,000 casualties. Such losses were irreplaceable in the South, as months grew into years of war, and they had a devastating effect on the fighting temper of the men, even when objectives were taken.

"L'audace, l'audace, et toujours l'audace!" is a maxim attributed to Frederick the Great. But if the soldier king of Prussia ever did utter these words, he may well have been talking about fencing which battle only seldom resembles. Rapid movements can destroy an enemy if perfectly directed and timed, but are rarely possible. Generals usually must fight blind, acting on hunch and guess. And such attempts can miscarry with crippling effect. They were, in any event, too risky for rebel armies to contemplate as the war entered into maturing stages.

Longstreet pleaded with Lee to see this reality. Jackson was gone. Now, he said, it was time to use a different approach in facing the many corps and divisions which were fielded by the North. And Longstreet also stressed that, in the kind of war which the South had to fight from and after the middle of 1863, not only were hammer blows out of the question for Confederate troops, but conventional attributes of victory, such as possession of the field, were of little importance in comparison to keeping regiments and brigades intact with minimum losses and high morale. Keep the men on the march, or positioned in natural fortresses, flags unfurled and defiant in spirit.

The greater objective of keeping up the endurance and potency of Southern armies, always capable of fighting another battle on another day, was foremost in Longstreet's mind. As adapted to the circumstances then prevailing, he favored a military policy not unlike that which had been so skillfully exploited by the best Continental generals during the American Revolution. His idea of superior strategy and tactics more closely resembled Kutusov during and after Borodino than Napoleon at Austerlitz. Longstreet dreamed of placing the Army of Northern Virginia where it would be most regarded as a menace, and in safe position, tempting generals of the Union to make desperate and fool-hardy assaults as at Fredericksburg. Longstreet's formula was perfect, and, if successfully carried out, it would have won the war for the South.

There was a general in the North who might have counteracted Longstreet's plan, but McClellan had been forced into retirement.

Intellectually, Lee knew Longstreet was right, and he agreed in principle. But knowing something in the mind and believing it in the heart are entirely different. Deep inside he was hoping for another triumph such as he had engineered with Stonewall at Chancellorsville. Lee should have let

Longstreet guide him in the new way as Jackson had helped him with the old. Lee eventually did get the point, then mastered it well, but only after he learned the hard way.

On the first day in July 1863, the Army of Northern Virginia struck a detachment of Federal cavalry, then a brigade of infantry, then the whole Army of the Potomac under the command of General George Meade. The event happened a little to the west of the little college town of Gettysburg, Pennsylvania. Southern troops drove the Federal army into retreat onto a rock ribbed hill just south of the town, known as Cemetery Ridge.

As the day drew to a close, Lee and Longstreet met on Seminary Ridge just to the west of Cemetery Ridge where Union forces were grouping. The battle had erupted by accident, because Confederate cavalry was off on a raid when it should have been the eyes of the army. But once the battle began, the question was how the principles of the campaign already adopted by the commanding general and his lieutenant should be carried out. Longstreet gave an account of the critical discussion between himself and Lee:

> "I found him on the summit of Seminary Ridge watching the enemy concentrate on the opposite hill. He pointed out their position to me. I took my glasses and made as careful a survey of their position as I could from that point. After five or ten minutes, I turned to General Lee and said:

> "'If we could have chosen a point to meet our plans of operation, I do not think we could have found a better one than that upon which are now concentrating. All we have to do now is to throw our army around by their left, and we shall interpose between the Federal army and Washington. We can get a strong position and wait, and, if they fail to attack us, we shall have everything in condition to move back tomorrow night in the direction of Washington, selecting beforehand a good position into which we can place our troops to receive battle the next day. Finding our object is Washington or that army, the Federals will be sure to attack us. When they attack, we shall beat them, as we proposed to do when we first left Fredericksburg, and the probabilities are that the fruits of our success will be great.'

> "'No,' said General Lee, 'the enemy is there and I am going to attack him there.'

> "I suggested that such a move as I proposed would give us control of the roads leading to Washington and Baltimore, and reminded General Lee of our original plans. If we had fallen behind Meade and insisted on staying between him and Washington, he would have been compelled to attack, and would have been badly beaten.

General Lee answered, 'No, they are in position, and I am going to whip them or they are going to whip me.'"

After the pitched engagement on the first day, Lee felt obliged to strike the enemy again. He ordered Hood's Division, not around, but against the far left of the Union line. It was a gamble under the pressure of the circumstances, but a gamble which should never have been taken, for Longstreet was right, however much he has been criticized for trying to restrain his commanding general. It is absurd sentimentalism to imagine that Lee was right at Gettysburg, or that everything would have been different if only Jackson had been at Lee's side.

Hood's Division split in two forks. Robertson's Brigade struck Little Round Top which was defended by several units, including the 20th Maine under Colonel Joshua Chamberlain, a college professor turned soldier. Chamberlain was an excellent field commander and his courage was grand, yet his troops were on high ground, and he had support from nearby Federal units. For holding the line with magnificent fortitude, he won the Congressional Medal of Honor.

But an engagement as critical on the second day was occasioned by the attack of the other fork of Hood's division spearheaded by Wilcox's Brigade. Of this event, standard accounts of Gettyburg are often silent. The Federal Third Corps was commanded by a Tammany Hall politician general. He had disregarded orders, and placed his troops too far forward on the field. His position left an undefended part of the Union line about a half mile wide between the point where Cemetery Ridge disappeared into flat farm land and Little Round Top. At the end of the second day, Lee said to Longstreet that he could see the flags of Hood's Division moving through the Union line. Lee saw those flags alright. They were carried by the Alabama infantry of Wilcox's Brigade, followed by other Southern units, as they marched in high spirits through the gaping hole created by the forward position of the Federal Third Corps.

Nothing was standing in the way but the 1st Minnesota less three companies, 262 officers and men under Colonel William Colvill, who led his command in an attack against a rebel host ten times as numerous. The boys from Minnesota were decimated in a few minutes by the overwhelming firepower of Wilcox's Brigade. Colvill was badly wounded. Only forty-seven from those he led were able to retire from combat. A battlefield photograph shows the dead of the regiment strewn on the ground in hideous bunches. While those soldiers were cut down like wheat in harvest, reinforcements arrived to form a strong defensive line. If Wilcox's Brigade had not been slowed up for precious minutes, the

Army of Northern Virginia might have marched on the streets of Washington D. C.

On the morning of the third day, Lee ordered Longstreet to attack the west side of Cemetery Ridge. Lee had grandiose ideas of rolling up the whole Federal line. The assault as ordered was wholly unrealistic, but Lee wanted to launch the attack. Lee was a consummate master of war, and ordinarily was prudent, but the excitement of the moment, the flow of adrenaline, and the grandeur of the scene crazed his intelligence. Longstreet protested. After the war he described the conversation between himself and his venerated chief:

> "I stated to General Lee that I had been examining the ground over to the right, and was much inclined to think the best thing was to go over to the Federal left.
>
> "'No,' he said, "I am going to take them where they are on Cemetery Hill. I want you to take Pickett's Division and make the attack. I will reinforce you by two divisions of the Third Corps.'
>
> "'That will give me fifteen thousand men,' I replied. 'I have been a soldier, I may say, from the ranks up to the position I now hold. I have been in pretty much all kinds of skirmishes, from those of two or three soldiers up to those of an army corps, and I think I can safely say there never was a body of fifteen thousand men who could make that attack successfully.'"

Lee overruled his lieutenant, and directed him to make the attack. And like a good old soldier, Longstreet ordered the attack.

There was a furious cannonade. Then fifteen thousand infantry, the flower of Southern manhood, marched in long splendid ranks across an open field, officers barking commands, all heads high, bayonets glistening, banners fluttering. They shifted into double time. They climbed over fences, defying heavy clouds of bombs, grapeshot, and bullets, shouting their Celtic war cry called the rebel yell. Lee had miscalculated. The attacking columns marched into the strongest point in the Union line held by a corps under the command of General Winfield Hancock, one of the finest field commanders of the war. General Lewis Armistead, a dear friend of Hancock from antebellum days, led a Confederate brigade into the assault. At the head of a battalion Armistead reached the stone wall on Cemetery Ridge. He forced his hat over his sword and called his men forward. Over the wall he went, ordering his men to turn captured guns. Within two or three minutes he and his comrades all fell. Armistead was found by Federal troops mortally wounded on the field and taken prisoner.

He was given the best available medical attention under personal orders of Hancock, who was also wounded but recovered. The carnage was awful. Of about 250 infantry mustered in the 9th Virginia, only thirty-eight returned under the command of a sergeant. In the ordeal called Pickett's charge, half the gallant fifteen thousand were struck down, dead or wounded.

As the shattered formations came back to Seminary Ridge, Lee said quietly, "This is all my fault." Stoically he rallied and comforted the dazed men who came back. Longstreet prepared the line for a counterattack which never came. The Army of Northern Virginia, including an ambulance train stretching many miles, made it across the Potomac River. Lee offered to resign his commission, as military convention demanded for a general in his situation, but authorities in Richmond would hear nothing of it, and he was ordered back to the front.

The losses during the three days were about 25,000 on each side. The North could recover from this loss, great as it was. The South could not. And to make things worse, Vicksburg surrendered the day after the grand assault on Cemetery Ridge had failed. The catastrophe was not that enemy troops held a ridge, or that retreat was necessary, but that a battle had been fought the way Longstreet warned against, — force against force, muscle against muscle, as if the South could afford such attempts against the massed armies and huge resources of the Union.

* * * * *

The administration of Abraham Lincoln could not provide the enormous armies and fleets needed for conquest of the South without destruction of fundamental law and imposition of military dictatorship. The sacrifice was made, and at an astronomical cost, of which a minor fraction could have paid fair compensation for the emancipation of every slave in the country, and built grand transcontinental railroads along northern, central, and southern routes.[7] These facts prove the absurdity of encomiums heaped on the likes of Edwin Stanton, such as the ridiculous panegyric of a judge of that age, good in character but led down the primrose path. "I do not yield to anyone," he said, "in honoring and reverencing the noble and patriotic men who were in the councils of the nation during the terrible struggle with the rebellion. To them belong the greatest glories of history, that of having saved the Union, and that of having freed a race. For these results they will be remembered and honored as long as the English language is spoken or ready among men."[8]

As the conflict wore on, as news came home from the front, as needless casualties were reported, as the ideals of chivalry in military life were lost, as men became wise to the incompetence of most generals on the field and politicians in the cabinet, as the savagery visited upon innocent civilians could no longer be hidden, the number of volunteers began to dwindle.

Stanton's method for conquest of the South was ugly and brutal: he wanted to line up men in formations twenty to thirty deep then to march forward until advancing columns were slaughtered or a defending line was overwhelmed. His plan required that certain indispensable conditions be met. There had to be an unlimited supply of privates more fearful of dying by firing squad than of dying in battle. There also had to be an unlimited supply of money or whatever substitutes could be forced on creditors. And there had to be so-called "fighting" generals who, if artless, were willing to sacrifice the lives of their troops without excessive remorse.

The sagacious restraints on calling forth the militia, as the proper means of bringing citizen soldiers to the field, could not be tolerated. On March 3, 1863, Stanton got his wish: — Congress enacted a law for conscripting men directly into the armies of the Union.[9]

During his last illness, Chief Justice Roger B. Taney of the United States Supreme Court sketched out his ideas in an unpublished manuscript:[10]

From the face of Amendment II of the United States Constitution, Taney reasoned, it can be inferred that the powers to organize, arm, discipline, and call forth the militia fifteenth and sixteenth clauses of Article I, Section 8 are the sole powers of Congress to compel citizens to render military service in behalf of the Union. If Congress could draft citizens as a necessary and proper means for raising armies under the twelfth and eighteenth clauses of Article I, Section 8, as assumed by the Act of March 3, 1863, then, he said, "all of the clauses so elaborately prepared in relation to the militia" would be "of no practical value" and could be "set aside and annulled" whenever Congress deemed it expedient.

Taney added, "During the period when the United States were English colonies, the army of England was always raised by voluntary enlistments." And "when the power to raise and support armies was delegated to Congress, the words of grant necessarily implied that they were to be raised in the usual manner."

The old man was not alone in entertaining such thoughts. Members of the bar met to discuss the problem. Soon there was angry talk in Stanton's war department about a "lawyers' conspiracy" against the conscription act. And what lawyers they were! Their leader was Charles Ingersoll of Philadelphia who had run for Vice President with a large and respectable showing in the anti-war ticket during the election of 1812. The gentleman had known and corresponded with a number of the framers of the United States Constitution, including James Madison and Gouverneur Morris.

Supported by Ingersoll's copious research and learned advocacy, a suit in equity reported as *Kneedler v. Lane,* 45 Pa. St. 238 (1863-1864), was brought before Justice George Woodward of the Pennsylvania Supreme Court, then riding circuit in the eastern district of the Commonwealth, seeking to enjoin conscription under the statute as unconstitutional. Seeing the importance of the question raised Ingersoll's motion, Woodward called his colleagues to hear arguments en banc in the autumn of 1863. Some weeks later, a preliminary injunction was granted on vote of three against two justices.

Woodward observed that the United States Constitution was framed in reference to the fundamental law of England. Upon tracing undeniable historical experience, he concluded that the power of Congress to raise armies was a power of the King to raise troops by the traditional mode of voluntary enlistment, as had been the law since the Statute of 1 Edward III, Chapter 5 (1327). Viewed in this light, compulsory military service was confined to the processes of organizing, arming, disciplining, and calling forth the militia after the manner prescribed by the fifteenth and sixteenth clauses of Article I, Section 8 of the United States Constitution.

Woodward also recalled an important rule of common law for the interpretation of written documents that all clauses relating to the same question or subject matter should be construed read together so as to shed light on each other, to give each clause a useful purpose thus avoiding redundancy or surplusage, and to make each clause consistent with every other related clause.[11] He illustrated this rule by concrete example: Suppose that a will gave Blackacre to A and the west half of Blackacre to B. Every lawyer must concede that the devise to A would not grant him all of Blackacre, because, if it did, it would contradict or render pointless the devise to B. Instead, the devise to A must be taken as granting all of Blackacre less the west half devised to B. According to the same reasoning, Woodward held, the power of Congress to raise armies, set forth in the twelfth clause of Article I, Section 8 of the United States Constitution should be read as authorizing enlistment but not conscription. Otherwise the fifteenth and sixteenth clauses dealing with the militia could be circumvented at will, and would be, as Woodward put it, "the idlest words ever written." The power of compelling citizens to render military service, therefore, is limited to the clauses on the militia, and since the restrictions set forth these clauses were thereby exceeded, the Act of March 3, 1863, was unconstitutional. Elaborate concurring opinions, including vast historical erudition and beautiful prose, were filed by Chief Justice Walter Lowrie and Justice James Thompson.

There had been an uprising in New York City against Stanton's hated law. Troops had been sent out and fired lethal volleys into crowds exasperated by the utter wrongness of the war. Justice John Read wrote an unprofessional dissent, disgraceful to the bench. "If I had the power," he exclaimed, "I would place the New York rioters in the front ranks of the army!"

Justice William Strong had a more cunning intellect and a more flowing pen. In his dissent he observed that requisitions for the Continental army during the revolution were on occasion filled by drafting the militia. He also relied on the remark of Hamilton in the 23rd Federalist that the power to raise armies "ought to exist without limitation,"[12] together with the remark of Madison in the 41st Federalist that the power to raise armies must embrace "an indefinite power of raising troops."[13] And, he argued, conscripting citizens into the Federal army was no more inconsistent with the restrictions on the militia than enlisting them.

Strong's was the standard argument for Stanton's manpower system. And quickly its flaws could be exposed: Conscription in the American Revolution was always a process of calling forth the militia which violated neither legal tradition nor any constitutional provision. When Hamilton and Madison said that the power to raise armies should exist without limitation and be indefinite, they meant that Congress should be able to enlist or hire as many regular soldiers, even in time of peace, as might be warranted by the unforeseeable circumstances of the future. And, whereas it would not be so if citizens voluntarily enlisted in the armies of the Union, drafting them against their will for such purposes would necessarily circumvent their right, in legal tradition as ancient as the Statute of 1 Edward III, not to be drawn into military service except as militia for the limited purposes indicated particularly in the fifteenth clause in Article I, Section 8 of the United States Constitution.

Next occurred one of those quirks of fate which has many meanings in history. The term of Chief Justice Lowrie in office expired on the first Monday in December 1863. In his last days, Judge Lowrie sat in the chair of Benjamin Franklin as President of the American Philosophical Society. He was replaced by a pro-war demagogue, Daniel Agnew.

It so happens that, in the initial motion filed by Ingersoll, notice was given to the Federal district attorney so that he might have an opportunity to be heard. But the Federal district attorney refused to appear for political reasons. The thinking in his circle was that, if Lincoln could lawlessly defy the Chief Justice of the United States, Stanton could lawlessly defy the

Pennsylvania Supreme Court. Therefore, counsel for the United States did not appear for argument, nor did he interpose an answer or demurrer to the bill. Upon this state of the record, a preliminary injunction was entered in early November.

It was the law in Pennsylvania that a decree entered after notice of argument and an opportunity to be heard was entitled to the same weight as a decree entered after full argument on both sides, and that such a decree settled the law of the case for all future proceedings unless revised on appeal or writ of error. Therefore, the decree entered while Lowrie was still Chief Justice settled the law of the case, including the conclusion that Stanton's conscription act was unconstitutional.

It was also the law in the Commonwealth that, when the law of the case was settled by a majority of the Pennsylvania Supreme Court, only the facts were thereafter subject to dispute. This rule was designed to assure consistent and regular administration of justice. And since the facts were never in dispute, the judgment entered while Lowrie was Chief Justice could no longer be revised by the judiciary of Pennsylvania.

In any event, it was established practice in Pennsylvania that no final judgment or permanent decree could be entered unless papers in opposition had been filed: — it was for this reason, and only for this reason that the judgment entered while Lowrie was still Chief Justice was in technical form a preliminary injunction. But it was also established practice in Pennsylvania that no preliminary decree entered after notice of argument and an opportunity to be heard could be dissolved on motion until after an answer or demurrer had been interposed to the bill. This rule was laid down to assure a coherent and adequate record.

In order to challenge the outstanding judgment of the Pennsylvania Supreme Court in a lawful manner, therefore, the Federal district attorney would have been obliged to appear, interpose an answer or demurrer to the bill, then make a motion to dissolve the decree entered in early November. Such motion would be denied since the law of the case was settled, but then there would be a final judgment which could be reviewed on writ of error by the United States Supreme Court under Section 25 of the Judiciary Act of 1789.[14] Such was the legal penalty for his failure to intervene earlier in response to notice of argument and an opportunity to be heard. No good lawyer would have recommended his course, and he knew better than to defy the highest court of the Commonwealth.

But something other than the rule of law was at work, as the Federal district attorney was also aware. Strong learned the sentiments of the new justice. Agnew's view was that drafting armies was necessary to save the

Union, and nothing else really mattered. Strong then went out on circuit. Like lightning the Federal district attorney appeared before Strong at nisi prius, and, without interposing an answer or demurrer to the bill, he made a motion to dissolve the preliminary injunction. Ingersoll appeared, white-haired and ruffled, to argue that the motion could not be entertained at nisi prius or even en banc.

Strong allowed the motion as if the rule of law did not exist. It is hardly necessary to tell the rest of the story. The entire Pennsylvania Supreme Court reassembled en banc. And on order supported by Strong, Read, and Agnew, the suit was dismissed.

"The armies of the Union," quivered Read, "are fighting for the United States of America," and "those who have perished in this contest for the preservation of the Union, have died under the national flag, which I trust will soon wave over the whole undivided territory of our glorious and once happy Union."

Woodward, the new Chief Justice, joined by Thompson, sputtered in bewildered dissent, explaining the law which, however, had just been usurped in a coup d'état.

* * * * *

Since many lads were to die for Stanton and his generals, they had to be given a boost for their morale, as was supplied by a famous executive order which is known as the Emancipation Proclamation, the same issued by Abraham Lincoln on January 1, 1863. The instrument defined areas of the South which the President found to be in rebellion against the United States. These areas excluded Delaware and Maryland which were still part of the Union, but included all of the Confederate States except Kentucky, Missouri, and Tennessee, and parts of Virginia and Louisiana which were then under control of the Union. Invoking his powers as commander-in-chief of the armed forces of the Union, Lincoln declared that "all persons held as slaves within said designated States and parts of States are, and henceforward shall be free."[15] It brought men to enlist as they sang, "As Christ died to make men holy, let us die to make men free!"

The proclamation was widely condemned as unconstitutional.[16] It might have had meaning under the law of nations for a conquering general during invasion of foreign territory. But if this much be assumed to give the proclamation legitimacy as an executive act, it must also be assumed that there had been a lawful secession and an outbreak of war between independent countries. Jefferson Davis saw the war in that light, but Abraham Lincoln did not.

Popular belief holds that the proclamation reflects an earnest and humane desire to end slavery, and so defines the issue over which the war was fought. What are the facts?

In a letter to Horace Greeley on August 22, 1862, Abraham Lincoln was altogether forthright: — "My paramount object in this struggle is to save the Union, and is not to save or destroy slavery. If I could save the Union without freeing any slave, I would do it; and if I could save it by freeing all the slaves, I would do it; and if I could do it by freeing some, and leaving others alone, I would also do that. What I do about slavery and the colored race, I do because I believe it helps to save the Union; and what I forbear, I forbear because I do not believe it would help to save the Union"[17]

Abraham Lincoln stated that the war was not to end slavery, but to save the Union. And it was to save the Union from what Jefferson Davis, in addressing the Southern Congress on April 29, 1861, had called "the right of each State to judge and redress the wrongs of which it complains," — the prerogative of the people of the South in their conventions to "revoke their delegation of powers to the Federal Government," and to resume "all their rights as sovereign and independent States," thereby dissolving "their connection with other States of the Union."[18]

Therefore, the "official" issue over which this war was fought, as defined by the first magistrates on both sides, was whether the several States have a constitutional right to secede from the Union. The struggle was an American Civil War, because it was like the wars between Israel and Judah after the death of King Soloman. It was also a War Between the States, because it was a war between a Union of Northern States and a Confederacy of Southern States. And it was no less a War for Southern Independence, because it resembled the War for American Independence. But the French seem to have devised the best name of all, — "la guerre de sécession," because that is what it was in the eyes of both Lincoln and Davis.

From this undeniable fact derives the true meaning of the Confederate battle flag. The regulation flag was square, 51 inches by 51 inches for units of infantry, somewhat smaller for the artillery and the cavalry. It is contained within a white border on all four sides. The central feature is the diagonal cross of St. Andrew, as displayed on the flag of Scotland, only with the colors reversed as now appears in the flag of Nova Scotia. Next was the diagonal cross of St. Patrick, which is part of the current British Union Jack, and appears today as the flag of Alabama, only with the colors reversed and bars broadened so as to fit over the cross of St. Andrew, leaving a narrow white trim to distinguish the two crosses. Then over the bars of the cross of St. Andrew are thirteen States, which signify the thirteen States represented in the Congress of the Southern Confederacy.

The Confederate battle flag has been perverted in its meaning by extremists from different parts of the political spectrum, but the truth remains that it is the banner of a Christian civilization,[19] designed from hallowed Celtic symbols to signify the constitutional right of the several States to secede from the Union. The right is universal, rooted in natural law and legal tradition, — a right of peaceable and lawful revolution, illustrated by the inexorable constitutional transformation which ushered William and Mary to the throne of England. It is a right necessary in extraordinary circumstances for every free and civilized people, whatever their race or culture, wherever their location in the world, whenever they have entered into federal relations with neighboring peoples in neighboring states for mutual advantage. Without it, federal relations are too dangerous even to consider. With this right, federal relations can be a great blessing to mankind, and can assure peace and friendship among nations.

* * * * *

The war of 1861-1865 was a very great oddity in that secession as a constitutional right had been accepted by both sides before the first gun was fired upon Fort Sumter. There never was a stronger secessionist movement than in New England during the War of 1812. Secession as a right was conceded during the antebellum period by leading constitutional scholars in the United States from the North and the South.[20] And the underlying principle was reaffirmed by the United States Senate in 1861 with ample support from the North and the South. Secession was the "official" question over which the war was fought. Yet both sides had earlier agreed on this question.

Disregarding the issue of the war as defined by the leaders on both sides, many have nevertheless maintained that the war was fought of moral necessity to free the slaves. Yet the greatest Southern advocates of States' Rights were mostly abolitionists, — among them, Edmund Pendleton, Thomas Jefferson, Luther Martin, George Mason, St. George Tucker, John Randolph of Roanoke, and James Madison. Not only did their disciples succeed in condemning slavery by legislative resolution in 1832, but a new generation of their admirers were numerous and active in 1861. They were then gradually becoming an important political force in the Dixie States, more distinguished than the abolitionist movement in the North had ever been.

Why then the war? The answer is that the war was produced neither by secession nor by slavery, not even by cultural distinctness, but by a hidden cause.

The cost of the war was astronomical, something on the order of three-fourths of the assessed value of all taxable property in the United States in 1860.[21]

It was in the anticipation of a fabulous opportunity to take over the country, occasioned by a colossal public debt, that the war was planned by foreigners, and it was by cupidity and fanaticism that citizens were tempted to produce a fratricidal calamity.[22]

For the North, the problem of unending flows of money was acute, because, as the war became hideous in its proportions, with titanic casualties, death often being a merciful fate in comparison to the wounds suffered, the expenses became fantastic. A month of fighting the South cost the North more than eight years of revolution against the British Crown.

Under the second and fifth clauses of Article I, Section 8 of the United States Constitution as framed in 1787, Congress has power "to borrow money on the credit of the United States," and to "coin Money" and "regulate the Value thereof," while under the first clause of Article I, Section 10, no State shall "coin Money" or "make any Thing but gold and silver Coin a Tender in Payment of Debts." If the power of Congress to coin money were the power to emit paper currency as legal tender, the several States could not honor such currency.

The same rule of interpretation revealing the unconstitutionality of conscripting armies also shows the want of constitutional authority to emit bills and notes which might pass as legal tender in lieu of gold and silver coin. And that which is apparent from the face of the United States Constitution is made perfectly clear from the records of the Philadelphia Convention.[23] The power of Congress to coin money was understood to be the same as the prerogative of the King to coin money, and this prerogative was nothing other than the authority to strike gold and silver into circulating pieces as legal tender in payment of all debts public and private. On August 16, 1787, it was settled in the Philadelphia Convention that Congress should have no power to emit bills and notes which any private party might be obliged to accept in payment of debts. On August 28, 1787, it was determined to strengthen the limitations upon the several States so as to destroy any possibility that they should circulate or allow paper currency as legal tender for all purposes. The speeches of the framers in the debates are absolutely lucid.

Whatever its deficiencies, the monetary regime of the framers obliged Congress to restrict spending. Congress was given the means of spending only to the extent that it would be able to raise money by taxes, or borrow specie or its practical equivalent from willing lenders, — or else, as a special exercise of the power of borrowing, to pay for public necessities with promissory bills and notes receivable in payment of some or all taxes, but not legal tender for all debts public and private. The delegates attending the Philadelphia Convention knew that this system was not the most efficient means of public spending and credit, but they also knew that governments have always had a tendency to indulge in truly stupid adventures unless firmly restrained. The need for a limitation on political folly was an important reason why the framers insisted upon a system of gold and silver coin.

Because of these constitutional limits on public finance, Congress in 1861 simply did not have the financial means to prosecute a war of conquest against the Southern States. Therefore, these limits were circumvented. And when exceeding these limits proved insufficient for purposes of fighting the war, specie had to be obtained by making concessions which no comprehending patriot would ever have made. In the process, the United States lost monetary independence, and to a large extent political independence, which was the most important consequence of the war all things considered.

Not long after First Manassas, there was a deficit in the Federal budget far larger than Federal revenue. It was not possible to borrow from conventional money lenders of the world at anything but hyperbolic rates of interest. In order to overcome the shortfall, Congress enacted statutes which created "greenback" currency, legally described as United States Notes.[24] These instruments contained the formal language, "The United States of America will pay to the bearer ten dollars." But there was no indication of when, if ever, redemption in specie might ever be had, because that detail was left entirely to the discretion of Congress.

If no further significant language appeared on these notes, they could not be forced on any creditor, and would circulate like any commercial paper on the market, subject to whatever discounts from face value as might be dictated by circumstances, including supply and demand, public confidence in forthcoming redemption, and the fortune of arms.

The new currency was made receivable in payment of most dues to the Federal government. That feature was founded on venerable precedent and made this kind of paper more valuable. But the face of the new currency contained stronger language: — "This note is legal tender in its face value for all debts public and private, except duties on imports, and interest on the public debt." Since these notes were promises forever renewable, yet purported to be legal tender for most purposes, they were like the old paper shillings of New England, — in a practical sense fiat money.

The emission of legal tender currency, having no intrinsic value, to pay of public debt, without borrowing from conventional lenders at interest, may in some circumstances be a more rational proposition than a system of gold and silver coin. Such thoughts certainly had passed through the mind of Benjamin Franklin as he listened to extreme outbursts against paper money on August 16 and 28, 1787, but the good doctor did after all keep his peace. Paper money can be effectively disciplined as Franklin himself demonstrated in Pennsylvania before the outbreak of the American Revolution. And paper money is not necessarily worse than the mark of the beast in the Book of Revelations as claimed by one of the delegates in the Philadelphia Convention. Even so, paper currency made legal tender even for private debts was for cogent reasons prohibited by the United States Constitution. The system could be lawfully changed by constitutional amendment, but not on demand of power brokers in Washington D. C.

Greenbacks were as flagrantly lawless as Lincoln's suspension of the writ of habeas corpus, his acts of war on executive authority alone, and the conscripting of armies by act of Congress with no regard to the processes for calling forth the militia. The awful truth, which historians must some-day accept as a learned consensus, is that all of this lawlessness and folly leading to destruction was the work of men, some of them well-meaning, others exceedingly heartless, who acquired more power than they could wield with moral conscience and beneficial effect. They trudged ahead, and, for the sake of their uncomprehending and simplistic abstractions, hundreds of thousands died and suffered from war or starvation, their loved ones likewise felt unspeakable anguish, fire was visited upon cities and plantations, lovely countryside was laid waste, and civilized institutions fell into ruin, while constitutional government almost ceased to exist as an instrument of order in society. Upon vulgar appeals and corny music a civilian republic was transformed into a military superstate.

United States Notes were spent into circulation. By the end of 1861 most state-chartered banks had suspended redemption of their notes in specie. Coin was still to be found, but was scarce, because hoarded. Because more currency was necessary to lubricate commerce expanded by the war, and because greenbacks were receivable in payment of dues to the Federal government, and purported to receivable to payment of private debts, the new bills floated fairly well, sometimes at a premium over the paper issued by state-chartered banks, but often at a discount from face value in private transactions. If payment in gold or silver coin were demanded in commerce, the contract had to specify such expectation in express language.[25]

Up to a point greenbacks helped to activate the engines of war in the North. If the conflict had been a less serious affair, the new currency might have been sufficient, but the war was no siege of Barbary pirates. It was a gigantic attempt to subdue and humiliate a free and spirited people, numbering in the millions, enjoying an advanced civilization, well organized in units of militia, defended by a tough army, and spread out of huge stretches of continent. Therefore, more extensive financial organization was required to accomplish the conquest.

During the war, the North continued active trade with Europe, and, under Federal law, taxes on imports shipped into the ports of the so-called "loyal" States had to be paid in hard cash. The payment of such imposts gave Lincoln's administration a quantity of specie to buy the matériel of war from domestic and foreign suppliers in a position to demand money of the bright and shining variety, and to maintain the credibility of war bonds by paying interest in specie.

But in these pressing times, specie had to be amassed in ever greater amounts, as could be accomplished only by selling securities of the Federal government for gold and silver coin. And for this purpose, it was not enough to make patriotic appeals. There had to be and were large sales of Federal securities directly to great banking houses in New York, Philadelphia, London, and Paris. Eventually it was necessary to go further, and to make an offer which major financiers at home and abroad could not refuse, — in effect, it was an offer to sell them the main apparatus of banking and currency in the United States.

This expanded program of marketing securities of the United States was mounted by August Belmont in New York and Jay Cooke in Philadelphia, acting as the principal business agents for two international banking conglomerates in Europe. The larger group was headed by Jacob (also known as Jacques or James) Rothschild in Paris, who also controlled N. M. Rothschild & Co. and the Bank of England in London. The other was headed by Junius Morgan in London, then a senior partner in Peabody, Morgan & Co., soon thereafter organized as J. S. Morgan & Co., whose successors came to be known as Morgan, Grenville & Co. in London, and J. P. Morgan & Co. in New York. Their methods are noteworthy.

In 1862 a document known as the "Hazard Circular" was secretly distributed among wealthy investors in the Northern States. It explained the basic motive of a powerful combination of financiers behind the scenes, who had cunningly orchestrated every important antagonism between the North and the South in the 1850s from the mass marketing of *Uncle Tom's Cabin* to the crisis at Fort Sumter. The circular read,

> "Slavery is likely to be abolished by the war power, and all chattel slavery abolished. This I and my friends are in favor of, for slavery is but the owning of labor and carries with it the care of the laborers,

while the European plan, led on by England, is that capital shall control labor by controlling wages. The great debt that capitalists will
see to it is made out of the war must be used as means to control the
volume of money. To accomplish this the bonds must be used as a
banking basis. We are now waiting for the secretary of the treasury
to make this recommendation to Congress. It will not do to allow the
greenback, as it is called, to circulate as money any length of time, as
we cannot control that. But we can control the bonds and through the
bonds the bank issues."

Whatever the true origin of this curious document, Salmon P. Chase as
secretary of the treasury did in fact make such a "recommendation to
Congress," and this recommendation inspired the National Bank Act.[26] As
enacted on June 3, 1864, the statute made it possible for any five or more
persons with enough cash and other resources to establish a national bank.
There had to be a certain minimum of paid-in capital, of which a major
part had to consist of war bonds representing the enormous public debt of
the Union incurred in the conquest of the Southern States. These bonds,
once used to capitalize a national bank, were to be delivered to the secretary of the treasury, who received them as collateral for national bank notes
issued to the national bank in a dollar amount equal to 90% of the par
value of the bonds. Having been issued on bonds funded by dedicated tax
revenues, national bank notes were guaranteed by the Federal government.

While national bank notes were not legal tender for all purposes, they
were receivable in payment for most dues of the Federal government.
National bank notes were excellent currency, more convenient than gold
and silver coin, better secured than greenbacks, and usually superior to
the notes of state-chartered banks.

The key to gaining control of the new system of banks and their unique
currency was the purchase of war bonds in large volume as could be
accomplished only by major capitalists, especially those associated or
allied with the names of Rothschild and Morgan. These bonds could be
purchased in volume at a substantial discount, especially where the consideration was specie. The bonds earned interest paid in good coin, and
national bank notes could themselves be lent out at interest. As a practical matter, national bank notes often could be and were used in lieu of
coin or greenbacks as if legal tender for all purposes, in some circumstances even as reserves to support drawing rights. Each national bank,
therefore, became a fabulously lucrative enterprise, — a little Bank of
England it might be said, and maybe something better.

The National Bank Act was justified by a perversion of the argument made by Alexander Hamilton in favor of the first Bank of the United States. Congress, it was said, could set up such institutions as a necessary and proper means of borrowing money. But the justification overlooked the main point of Andrew Jackson's message when he vetoed the bill to extend the term of the second Bank of the United States: — Congress may establish a public bank to exercise delegated powers of the general government, but not a private bank for purposes of speculation and gain.

In any event, the private owners of the national banks had more power than the private owners of the first and second Banks of the United States. National banks had no public directors. And no business profits had to be paid to the Federal government. In lieu of all existing taxes, the new institutions paid a trivial duty of the United States on the amount of notes outstanding. Each charter, if not perpetual, was perpetually renewable without intervening legislation by Congress. There were no restrictions on ownership of multiple banks in the system. Interlocking directorates became rather usual, and the same names appeared on stock all over the country. Drawing rights and circulating notes had to be backed by defined reserves in "lawful money of the United States," — i. e., greenbacks and specie. But a substantial part of these reserves were to be held in certain large institutions in New York City serving as lender of last resort. And these institutions, as should be no surprise, were owned and controlled by interests associated or allied with the names of Rothschild and Morgan.

The country was thus mortgaged to a domestic and foreign network of high finance. The owners of this network became a real but hidden and thus unchecked power behind the government of the United States. This sale of so valuable a franchise was wholly incompatible with a nation "conceived in liberty and dedicated to the proposition that all men are created equal," because nothing can encumber or extinguish the freedom and dignity of any labor force more fully than a concealed oligarchy of high finance beyond the effective accountability of public law.

The tentacles eventually controlling the vital organs of the United States, with strings pulled by unseen hands, were extended further by another statute enacted not long before the collapse of the Southern Confederacy.[27] The act imposed a tax of 10% on the face amount of all notes issued by state-chartered banks. The tax naturally drove their notes out of circulation. Thereupon, the state-chartered banks had to maintain reserves with national banks to assure availability of adequate currency, including national bank notes, to do business. The legislation accommodated the monied interests which had financed the conquest of the Southern States by making their national banks more powerful. The pretext used to justify this act was the need for currency uniform in value and description through the country. Yet behind the sweet-sounding message was nothing but the way of all flesh.

The constitutionality of the tax imposed is still a lingering concern to legal historians. The third clause of Article I, Section 2 of the United States Constitution mentions "direct taxes" which must be apportioned among the several States according to a population index, and the first clause of Article I, Section 8 mentions "duties, imposts, and excises" which must be levied at uniform rates throughout the country. The distinction between direct and indirect taxes can be clarified by reference to constitutional history.[28] The framers thought of direct taxes as taxes, not only on land, but on any and all property or wealth, and believed that population was a convenient measure of the aggregate value of property and wealth in each State. Duties, imposts, and excises were thought of as taxes on transactions, privileges, and franchises, including sales and importation, and also on consumption of luxuries and other items.

The issuance of bank notes has always been considered as a commercial transaction, ever distinct from the underlying deposits. And so, at least for a lawyer honestly viewing the fundamental law of the Union as Alexander Hamilton had read it — Thomas Jefferson would have viewed the problem in a different light —, a 10% tax on the face amount of the circulating paper of banking institutions could be justified as a uniform duty imposed to regulate commerce.

There was a final element in the Gargantuan monetary and fiscal monolith which the North used to strangle the South, and that was a substantial Federal tax on incomes earned from business, professions, agriculture, interest on bonds and treasury notes, dividends on stock, rent on land and buildings, salaries, and gains from the sale of real estate.[29]

Never before had such an imposition been known in the United States. The tax was not levied upon commercial activity, nor upon consumption, but upon property or wealth accumulated over a defined length of time. It was, therefore, a direct tax, and it had to be apportioned. Since this levy on income was a direct tax but not apportioned, it was unconstitutional. It was collected nevertheless.

The whole machinery, including greenbacks, national banks, and income taxes, was used in the war against the seceding States without any significant challenge before the judiciary. Only after the guns ceased firing did constitutional questions reach the United States Supreme Court.

When Roger B. Taney died in the fall of 1864, Abraham Lincoln had problems with his secretary of the treasury who was notoriously ambitious for the presidency. Lincoln used the time-honored method of disposing of a political adversary by appointing him to the bench. Thereby Salmon P.

Chase became the new Chief Justice, and in that capacity he presided over the case of *Hepburn v. Griswold,* 8 Wallace 603 (U. S. 1870), in which the question was whether a private antebellum debt could be discharged in greenbacks, dollar for dollar, in lieu of gold or silver coin. To the surprise of many, but in keeping with the program described in the Hazard Circular, Chase led a majority of four to three — five to three if the vote of a justice resigning a week before the decision was announced be counted — in holding that greenbacks could not discharge, over protest of the creditor, a private debt incurred before the war in dollars then defined by Congress in terms of gold and silver coin. He held, as the framers had certainly intended, that the power of Congress to coin money is limited to striking gold and silver circulating pieces of certain purity, weight, and design as legal tender. He held further that Congress has power to emit circulating notes on the credit of the United States but cannot make such notes legal tender in payment of private debts, at least not in exercise of the power to coin money. The decision was based on the luminous argument of a lawyer by the name of Clarkson Potter, whose expositions remain today an outstanding discussion on the power of Congress to coin money as understood by the framers of the United States Constitution.

But Chase was obliged to answer the argument that the power to issue greenbacks as legal tender for all debts public and private, whenever contracted, was justified as a necessary and proper means of waging war. The Chief Justice held that making such notes legal tender for all debts could not be necessary and proper for making war. All available empirical evidence, Chase observed, showed that such notes made legal tender for debts public and private were not discounted less or accepted more readily than identical currency made receivable only in payment of public dues. Therefore, giving such notes the general quality of legal tender could not be a necessary means of making war. And, Chase observed, if such notes could over protest of the creditor discharge a debt originally payable in gold and silver coin, their use in such case would impair the obligation of contacts, take property without just compensation, and take property without due process of law. Therefore, the means chosen were not proper as applied to the situation before the court.

It may be added that the proper definition of money is legal tender, and therefore any attempt to confer the attribute of legal tender to paper currency is an attempt to create money; yet, the United States Constitution, as framed in 1787 and as Chase held, allows Congress to create money only by striking gold and silver coin for circulation in commerce. The circulation of paper currency as legal tender cannot be a proper means to wage war or to exercise any other power, because the quality of legal tender is constitutionally limited to gold and silver coin. And, if Congress could wage war by making paper currency legal tender, then Congress could establish post offices and post roads or regulate commerce or exercise any other enumerated power by making paper currency legal tender, in which case there would be no need for a distinct power to coin money.

The rationale of this decision was evidently broad enough to condemn greenbacks as legal tender even for future debts. But vacancies developed on the United States Supreme Court, and those seats were filled with good "greenback men," one of whom was none other than William Strong, the spoiler in the great conscription case before the Pennsylvania Supreme Court who had guaranteed a steady supply of Northern boys to be shot down in battles described by shocked military observers as murder not war.

No sooner was there a new and larger court than Justice Strong led a new majority of five to four in the case of *Knox v. Lee,* 12 Wallace 457 (U. S. 1872), in reversing fresh precedent and declaring greeenbacks constitutional for past, present, and future debts as a necessary and proper means of waging war. It was the same power play as had occurred in Pennsylvania after the retirement of Walter Lowrie. The repeat performance was complete with a stunned Chief Justice writing a dissent on the applicable law which the new majority had just twisted beyond recognition. Clarkson Potter was more brilliant in the second round on the greenback question than in the first, yet he was no more effective than Charles Ingersoll in the second phase of the great conscription case in Pennsylvania.

Many years later, as greenbacks were being retired and paid off, Congress tried to reverse the trend by an inexpensive expansion of currency during a period of profound peace. Retired greenbacks were reissued and pumped back into circulation, which led to the case of *Juillard v. Greenman,* 110 U. S. 421 (1884). Justice Horace Gray wrote one of those facile polemics for the majority, gracefully skating over the text of the United States Constitution, making black look white and white look black, then holding that Congress, as the legislature of a sovereign nation, may emit treasury notes or other paper currency, in that instance reissued greenbacks, and make them legal tender in any circumstances as a necessary and proper means of providing for the common defense and general welfare and exercising other powers. So unctuous were his words that it is difficult to determine what he really said.

Justice Stephen Field wrote a masterful dissent, concluding in words painfully true. "If there be anything in the history of the Constitution which can be stated with moral certainty," he said, "it is that the framers of that instrument intended to prohibit the issue of legal tender notes both by the general government and by the States." Field's admonition really conveyed another message more profound: — the conquest of the South by the government of the Union destroyed the constitution framed by the Philadelphia Convention.

The 10% tax on the face amount of state-chartered bank notes was sustained as constitutional by Chief Justice Chase in *Veazie Bank v. Fenno,* 8 Wallace 533 (U. S. 1869). Chase might have sustained the tax on circumspect grounds, but he had a larger objective in view. For it is not by mere coincidence that one of the largest banks on Wall Street was later named in his honor, or that his portrait was engraved with gratitude and adoration upon the $10,000 bill later used in central banking transactions. Chase knew that larger developments coming up required the narrowest possible definition of a direct tax.

Therefore, disregarding abundant historical evidence, Chase held that a direct tax is essentially a tax on land. Since the tax in question was not a tax on land, it had to be a duty. And, Chase held, it was a duty imposed at a uniform rate in exercise of a claimed power of Congress "to secure a sound and uniform currency for the country."

Once this narrow definition of direct taxes was established, the stage was set for the opinion of Justice Noah Swayne in *Springer v. United States,* 102 U. S. 586 (1881), who held that a tax on income is a duty, and, therefore, constitutional if imposed by Congress at uniform rates throughout the Union.[30]

* * * * *

Such was the imperial machine of war built by the North. And what did the South pit against this giant?

By an Act of April 16, 1862, the Congress in Richmond conscripted armies of the Confederate States. This statute circumvented the clauses dealing with the militia and so was unconstitutional. And it was unnecessary. Because the country was invaded, the processes of organizing, arming, disciplining, and calling forth the militia could have been fully and rigorously exploited to supply adequate manpower, both in numbers and training, subject only to a few differences.

Regiments of militia supporting the regular armies of the South could not have been used for excursions into the North. But the only major invasions of the North ended in costly reverses in Sharpsburg and Gettysburg. And regiments of militia would have been commanded by officers commissioned by the several States. Nevertheless, once called forth, all officers and men in the militia would have been subject to the orders of the President and his generals.

Army conscripts played no important part in the Southern war effort. In not a single campaign did they make any material difference. Their presence did little more than tempt commanders to believe that losses might be replenished, and thus to take rash gambles on the field.

The largest body of Southern troops ever assembled stood in defense of Richmond against McClellan. But in that campaign hardly a battalion was made up of army conscripts. Many regiments of militia were called up, and they fought well.

In January 1865, Vice President Alexander Stephens addressed the Senate of the Confederate States.[31] He then recommended that the practice of conscripting armies be discontinued and that reliance be placed again on the militia. Stephens has been ridiculed for holding firm to the principles of strict construction in the face of pending collapse. Yet he was right, because the Confederate draft law sapped the love of Southerners for their cause of constitutional liberty. Without their ardent spirit it was impossible to mount the kind of popular resistance which, apart from keeping military forces intact, was indispensable in exhausting and crippling the invading host from the North. In his speech, Stephens agreed with the views of Judge Woodward of Pennsylvania, whom he summarized as follows:

> "It exhausts the Militia of the several States, which not only existed as an institution before the formation of the Federal Government, and was not only not granted away, but was expressly reserved at the formation of the Constitution, and substitutes a new one not therein provided for; and converts into National forces as part of the Regular Army of the General Government the whole militia force of the several States, not on the contingency therein provided for, nor in the form therein prescribed, but entirely irrespective thereof."[32]

This proposition always enjoyed great respect among the judges and statesmen of the South. One very good illustration of such opinion is the deep-thinking dissent of Justice James Bell in *Ex Parte Coupeland,* 26 Texas 387 at 405-430 (1862), condemning the Act of April 16, 1862, as contrary to the fundamental law of the Confederate States.

* * * * *

Finance was a simpler affair for the South than the North.[33] The Confederate government absorbed much of the available specie by selling war bonds, and the cash was used to buy ships, guns, medicines, and other necessities of war. Otherwise, specie and the notes of private banks based on deposits in specie were hoarded by private citizens. The private banks suspended redemption of their notes in gold and silver coin early in the winter of 1861-1862 to prevent a drain of specie as a kind of insurance against future calamity.

The blockade prevented much revenue from duties on imports or exports. And borrowing specie from major banking houses by a rebel government was generally out of the question. Unlike the North, the South had no opportunity to sell its financial and political independence.

Therefore, it was necessary for the Confederate government to make ends meet by a completely artificial system of finance, based on the issuance of treasury notes promising to pay from six months to two years after a treaty of peace. These instruments were generally receivable in payment of most taxes and other public dues, but were not designated as legal tender. The permanent constitution of the Confederate States contained no clause prohibiting the several States from issuing bills of credit,[34] which meant that the several States also issued treasury notes receivable in taxes and other public dues, but not legal tender for private debts.

Confederate currency was usually accepted because it was ordinarily the best currency available. Its value depended largely on the fortune of arms. After the twin disasters of Gettysburg and Vicksburg, Confederate currency depreciated with increasing speed, and commerce depended ever more on barter. This situation was not entirely intolerable, because the South was almost exclusively an agricultural region in which considerable distribution and business had traditionally been accomplished by exchange of labor and products in lieu of cash.

There should have been taxes to assure adequate reflux and limit depreciation of Confederate treasury notes, but such taxes were very difficult to impose. It was hard enough to run a post office, let alone an elaborate system of internal revenue. Attempts were made to soak up excess currency by selling Confederate bonds, but these efforts were insufficient to contain inflation. The only levy really practicable was a tax in kind to provide food and other items for troops on the field, but this expedient was not widely used. There were also requisitions of slaves to help build fortifications and of other matériel of war, for which compensation was paid in Confederate treasury notes.

There has been much commentary to the effect that the weakness of Southern finance contributed to the loss of Southern independence. That view contains more than a grain of truth, and is favored by respectable names. Yet it is safer to say, all things considered, that the lawless usurpations of power by the Federal government, including the selling of the financial and political independence of the country to domestic and international financiers, may have won the war for the North, but at a price too high.

* * * * *

The South was unable to convert its political economy into a military superstate, and could not put more than one soldier onto the field for every three or four on the other side. For this reason, it was necessary to fight a new kind of war after Gettysburg. The hope of Southern success, if it could ever happen, depended on two great soldiers.

General Robert E. Lee was regarded as the father of his country. In military dress he was the handsomest man on earth. Disciplined self-denial was second nature to him. Although usually soft-spoken, his flashes of anger were impressive. In battle his eyes grew bright, and his face became virile. His presence was awesome, yet he had a disarming and delicious sense of humor. His greatness was his ability to inspire devotion and courage in men. His tactical and strategic judgments were usually well conceived. Nobody understood supply and other technical aspects of war better than Lee. He made a few grave errors, but generally deserved his reputation as a master of war.

By contrast, General Joseph E. Johnston is often overlooked and underrated. He grasped military situations with a characteristic clarity that enabled him to make accurate and comprehensive predictions far in advance. While others speculated, Johnston had an uncanny awareness of the strength and movements of his enemy. His plans of operation were balanced and precise. By skillful engineering and use of geography he doubled the effectiveness of the troops entrusted to his command.

There has never been a military commander more adored by all ranks than "Uncle Joe." He had restless and keen eyes which read the inmost thoughts of others. He watched after the creature needs of his men, — clothing, tobacco, furloughs, rest, shelter, comfort, and safety. His men in turn were ready to die for him. From Lee, Johnston enjoyed fond admiration. Like Lee, Johnston electrified troops with morale. And his military judgment was nearly always flawless. His Achilles' heel was that Jefferson Davis felt a blind hatred of him. The President systematically rejected his advice, and so made blunders from which the South was never able to recover. It is a sad story to tell.

The main trouble was the old game of army politics. General Braxton Bragg may have been good enough to command a brigade, but not the

Army of Tennessee. But he was a favorite of the President who habitually displayed an amazing lack of military sense. Davis and Bragg always agreed, Johnston always protested, and things always got worse.

Bragg had engaged in sanguinary conflicts, as in the two battles near Murfreesboro in Tennessee just before and after New Year's 1863. The enemy advanced against his position. He launched a surprise attack in the early morning before the Union right was formed, and Federal troops were thrown into retreat. But eventually their commander with sang-froid was able to reform his line which held against repeated attacks until an appalling number of Southern dead and wounded cluttered the fields. So badly injured was the Confederate army that Bragg had to withdraw from Tennessee.

Bragg was forced to retreat through Chattanooga near the southern boundary of Tennessee, into the valley of Chicamauga Creek in northern Georgia. There, in the autumn of 1863, he was reinforced by troops from Mississippi and Virginia, whereupon he turned on his foe, hurling another thunderbolt attack at a weak point on the enemy line. It was Murfreesboro all over again. Federal troops were thrown back, but at last they reformed a solid line on Snodgrass Hill. Instead of letting the Federal army limp back into Chattanooga as its commanders desired, Bragg attacked again, as if to seize advantage, but suffered extreme loses. Two-fifths of his command were killed, wounded, or missing in battle.

Technically, Chicamauga was a Confederate victory, inasmuch as Union forces were compelled to abandon the field and move back into southern Tennessee. But the score by military convention was meaningless, because the losses of men left Bragg's army totally demoralized. The men were as brave as any soldiers who ever fought in any war, but they had twice been ordered by Bragg to make frontal attacks which devastated their ranks for no useful purpose. No longer did they trust their commander, and, truth to tell, their commander did not deserve their trust. They simply refused to fight for him any longer, and so Bragg could do nothing.

He tried to invest Chattanooga, but failed. He positioned his men on the impregnable natural fortress of Missionary Ridge, but they were easily driven off. "Here is your commander," Bragg declared to his fleeing troops, who answered derisively, "And here is your mule!" The whole army simply went on strike.

Bragg attempted to blame others, and Davis complained about the misconduct of the troops, but in the end, much as he hated to do it, Davis had no alternative but to put Johnston in direct command of the remnants of the Army of Tennessee near Dalton, Georgia, about a hundred miles to the northwest of the important railroad center of Atlanta. Time and resources at been lost, but at last the South had the right talent in command, Lee in the east and Johnston in the west.

Davis would have done well to put Bragg in retirement, and leave Johnston alone. Instead, Davis gave Bragg a sinecure with the title of "military adviser to the President." That may have been alright as a gesture to help Bragg save face. Unfortunately, Davis was serious.

* * * * *

The campaigns in the spring, summer, and fall of 1864 were the most crucial and decisive of the whole war.

In the eastern theatre, Stanton made his choice. General Ulysses Grant whose reputation from exploits in the western campaigns had been carefully groomed by republican newspapers. Stanton liked Grant, because, upon overwhelming Fort Donelson, he demanded unconditional surrender.

If real ability in the western theatre had carried weight in the choice, another Union commander had better proved his worth, — General Don Carlos Buell. At Shiloh, Grant had been caught in the jaws of an iron trap. It was Buell who saved Grant from decimation and turned the tide. In the fall of 1862, Bragg had invaded Kentucky and struck terror in the heart of Ohio. Buell defeated Bragg at Perryville and drove him back into Tennessee. But this splendid officer had a fatal defect, which was that, like McClellan, he believed in humane principles of war and worked for reconciliation with the South. Therefore, Stanton removed Buell after Perryville on the false pretext that he did not press his advantage.

Stanton wished, not peace, but annihilation, and he had built a monster of death to accomplish his purpose. His only remaining concern was to find commanders with his outlook, whether it made military sense or not. Grant served this purpose, for he expressed the desire to "hammer continuously against the armed force of the enemy, until by mere attrition, if in no other way, there should be nothing left of him."[35]

In early May, Grant accumulated the Army of the Potomac along the Rapidan River, somewhat to the west of Chancellorsville. He had about 170,000 effectives ready to march against Lee who had barely 55,000 including cavalry and artillery. Grant moved across the river into the Wilderness where Lee met him. After three days, Grant suffered 18,000 casualties, Lee only a thousand dead, and a few thousand with wounds, most of them so light that the men were back in the field in some weeks. Grant tried to swing around Lee, who adroitly foresaw the maneuver and received him at Spottsylvania Court House, inflicting another 12,000 casualties. Grant moved to Cold Harbor where Lee was again in an impregnable position. It was madness under the circumstances, but Grant ordered a frontal attack and another 12,000 fell. Grant assaulted Petersburg, and another 8,000 fell.

It was Lee's most brilliant campaign. He had recovered from the loss of Jackson at his side, and then displayed all the dash and cunning of his days before Gettysburg, yet greater clarity of mind and more balance in judgment. He was a better soldier and a better man, beloved by his troops, worshipped by the people, and, thankfully, feared by Davis and Bragg.

By the end of June, Grant had lost 60,000 killed or wounded, more than Lee's greatest strength at the beginning of the campaign. Grant had been known to drink heavily during the siege of Vicksburg. There was a crude joke that Lincoln wanted to find out what kind of whiskey Grant drank so he could send a barrel to each of his generals. The glimmer of truth in this story was that the attacks in the campaign of 1864 might have been expected from a general full of whiskey. But the joke was only a ruse to humor folks along. Grant fought recklessly, ignoring good military judgment, on orders from the secretary of war in Washington D. C.

The people of the North began to understand that the war was a moral failure incompetently directed. The democrats put up General McClellan for President on a platform calling for "immediate cessation of hostilities and restoration of peace on the basis of the Federal Union of States."

As the prospect of an honorable settlement of differences between the North and the South became real, Stanton became frantic, for the carnage beneath the Rapidan had been his idea, and, notwithstanding all the needless sacrifice of sons and husbands, Grant in 1864 was in a less favorable position than McClellan had been in 1862 after suffering a minor fraction of the casualties and inflicting greater injury on a stronger adversary with a much smaller advantage in numbers.

* * * * *

In light of this strategic situation before Richmond, as well as the political situation in the North, the campaign against Atlanta took on heightened significance. General William Sherman was Stanton's choice to direct Federal military operations from southern Tennessee into northern Georgia, and this choice was based on Sherman's motto, "War is all hell."

Sherman knew that he faced a strong-willed people who were the backbone of the Confederate States. "No amount of poverty seems to shake their faith," he said of the citizens of Georgia, "Niggers gone, wealth and luxury gone, money worthless, starvation in view within a period of two or three years, and causes enough to make the bravest tremble. Yet, I see no sign of let up, — some few deserters, plenty tired of war, but the masses determined to fight it out."[36]

This resiliency was the mark of free people in a civilization full of exalted values. McClellan or Buell, both admired by the South, could have becalmed the effusion of spirit with an unpretentious and genuine appeal to justice. But McClellan and Buell had been disposed of, and, with Stanton's enthusiastic blessing, Sherman decided to break the sentimental heart of the South by committing war crimes.

In preparation of his campaign in the spring of 1864, Sherman amassed, according to Stanton's reports, an effective force of 139,000 men, and his first objective was to take Atlanta.

When Johnston assumed command of the Army of Tennessee near Dalton in the last month of 1863, he had less than 36,000 troops, and these were on the verge of dissolution.[37] Davis wrote him a letter from Richmond, filled with glowing ejaculations on the superb condition and great size of the army, — as reported by his "military adviser," of course.

Davis and Bragg made insensate demands. They wanted a Confederate invasion of Tennessee with troops who were to march against a well-equipped and well-supplied Federal army nearly four times the actual size of Johnston's command. "In the inspections, which were made as soon as practicable, the appearance of the army was very far from congratulation," Johnston recounted. "Instead of a reserve of muskets, there was a deficiency of six thousand, and as great a one of blankets, while the number of bare feet was painful to see. The artillery horses were too feeble to draw guns in the fields or on a march, and the mules were in similar condition, while the supplies of forage were then very irregular, and did not include hay."

With marvelous expertise, Johnston rebuilt this pitiful force. Muskets, blankets, shoes, and food were found and supplied to the troops, as horses and mules were grazed and brought back to health, no thanks to the war department in Richmond, but mainly with patriotic cooperation from the people and government of Georgia. Deserters came back in droves, ready to resume the fight. Militia were called up in support. The new chief encouraged his men, who instinctively knew they were directed by a crack soldier with a first-rate mind. His touch was like magic.

Before the start of operations in the spring of 1864, a Southern diarist recounted, "The army presented itself in the best condition that I have ever witnessed it, and thousands of hardy soldiers, marching to the shrill fife and bass drum, or the harmonious melodies of brass bands, looked grand and cheering. Everybody speaks in the highest terms of the discipline and spirit of the troops."[38]

Johnston then supervised his engineers in erecting proper works around Atlanta. Civilians, slaves, militia, and regulars made the city impregnable against any assault. "What tremendous defenses of Atlanta the Rebs had!" later exclaimed one of Sherman's staff officers. "Forts, breastworks, ditches, chevaux-de-frise, and stockade on flank, unapproachable by musketry, and protected by ground, etc., from artillery."[39]

Johnston carefully developed a strategy for his beefed up army. The landscape beneath Dalton was not rugged. It did not contain many natural obstacles which could be used to defensive advantage against Sherman's larger forces. Therefore, Johnson planned to hold available points along the way down as far as possible, and inflict maximum casualties whenever Sherman's columns were exposed, making the beast suffer, tire, and bleed, — but then to yield rather than engage in a pitched battle of any size. Slowly, slowly he would retreat, strike and withdraw, retreat more, hold firm, and retreat again, gradually reducing Sherman's size while conserving his men, guns, and resources.

After a few months, Sherman would be at the gates of Atlanta. He would be unable to surround the city. Nor could he succeed in assault. Therefore, he would be compelled to settle down for a long siege far from his base of supplies. Johnston could fill his works, and keep an extra body of troops on the move to protect his supply lines. The civilian population would bring ample provisions from the countryside, and he could hang onto Atlanta for months and months, perhaps indefinitely, in any event long enough to try the patience of the North.

Johnston executed his plans with the agility of a toreador fighting a bull, giving battle near Resaca, at Allatoona Pass, and around Marietta. Again and again from early May through early July, Sherman assaulted and was repulsed, or used his greater numbers in flanking movements, but always failed to trap or harm his adversary. Sherman suffered heavy losses. Johnston's casualties were trivial. Johnston abandoned not a single piece of artillery, not a wagon of supplies did he leave behind. His men felt their expert handling, and were proud of their general. Sherman finally crossed the Chattahoochie River about eight miles from Atlanta. All of this had been anticipated, and Johnston fell behind his comfortable and elaborate fortifications.

In Johnston's capable hands, the city could easily be held a year, and, if meanwhile skillful use of cavalry could sufficiently imperil Sherman's supply lines, which was not inconceivable, the siege might have to be lifted.

With all his numbers, Sherman had been reduced to impotency. But then he had a stroke of luck.

Bragg traveled to Atlanta, and reported to Davis that Johnston intended to retreat again. It was a jealous lie, pure and simple, and Davis could have made a proper inquiry to discover the truth. Davis knew that Johnson had settled his family in Atlanta, which the general would never have done if he had planned another retreat. But Davis wanted an "official" reason to remove Johnston, and was not interested in the facts. On July 17, 1864, Davis caused the fateful telegram to be sent. Davis knew the nature of war, for he had been educated at West Point, fought in Mexico with distinction, and served as secretary of war in the cabinet of President Franklin Pierce. His mistake was not from technical misunderstanding, but political passion, and fawning "yes" men in his administration went along.

The new chief of the Army of Tennessee was General John Bell Hood, who had served with personal fortitude as a division commander on the field. He had lost use of an arm at Gettysburg and a leg from amputation after Chicamauga. In his invalid condition, he must have sedated his pain with morphine or still taken it to deal with powerful addictive effects. The drug is known to induce mood swings and impair judgement. Hood should have been honorably retired from the service with the thanks of his countrymen. He was no longer mentally fit to direct military operations.

As Hood took command, Lincoln was in such political trouble that some republican bosses wanted him to step aside in favor of Chase as the candidate of the party. Lincoln was blamed for Stanton's mismanagement of the war, which was not unjust, because Lincoln knew what Stanton was. But Lincoln knew he had to stay, because, if he went, the rowdies in his administration would make things worse.

Lincoln had created Leviathan to defend his untutored idea of the Union. He had not understood when his predecessor had spoken on the impossibility of saving the Union except by reconciliation, and that an attempt to use force of arms would bring disaster. His life degenerated into a nightmare. He suffered from terrible depressions, and was ever weighed down by sadness.

McClellan became immensely popular. After the fruitless and bloody campaigns of Grant and Sherman, the wisdom of his cautious and methodical approach to the problems of war began to dawn. The newspaper propaganda earlier orchestrated against him began to fade. It seemed certain that McClellan would win in November.

But no sooner had Hood taken command than he put militia in the trenches around Atlanta, and ordered assaults with his regulars against Sherman's larger formations. Rebel infantry marched against superior fire power which let fly with awful effect. Hood lost over 10,000 men and barely touched his foe. This waste deprived him of infantry needed to defend the railroad south of the city and other critical points. He then sent his cavalry on a wild raid, further exposing his supply lines. Sherman made a wide sweep and took Jonesboro to the south of Atlanta. Hood made a narrow escape in early September, blowing up eighty train cars full of ammunition which he could not afford to lose.

Lincoln's political stock skyrocketed in the eyes of a fickle electorate, which, only a few days before the fall of Atlanta, was ready to turn him out, because they were fed up with the oppressions associated with his name, — secret police, martial law outside the zone of war, arrest of political opponents denied the benefit of habeas corpus, and such like. With the fall of Atlanta, Lincoln came up from behind, and was reelected. It was the signal that Sherman had waited for. He ordered civilians to leave their homes, turning women and children onto open streets and fields without food and shelter. As he set torch to Atlanta, a military band played festive music.

Davis met with Hood, and conceived another demented strategy. "Be of good cheer," Davis told the troops, "you will soon be marching on the soil of Tennessee." Instead of defending homes and population, the western army would invade territory hundreds of miles away! So pie-eyed was Davis in those days that he boasted to Congress that, although Sherman had taken Atlanta, no great loss had occurred, and that, if Richmond also fell, the South would be as defiant as ever. The national debt, he said, was manageable, and no new taxes or appropriations were needed to continue the war.[40]

The people had been abandoned, only they did not at first know it. But then Sherman marched his juggernaut through Georgia, cutting a dark swath sixty miles wide, burning and pillaging all the way to Savannah. When citizens realized in shock that there was no significant army to retard this inhuman onslaught, they became disillusioned. Their devotion to their cause was undiminished, but the cause was physically impossible to support anymore.

Hood advanced into Tennessee, ostensibly to cut Sherman's supply lines by taking Nashville. After maneuvers near Columbia and Spring Hill, Hood lunged forward. On the last day of November, at Franklin, Hood ordered a frontal attack across an open field against entrenched positions. A training exercise it was, meant to teach the boys how to fight. A brass band played martial music. Six thousand rebels fell. The wounded cried out in excruciating pain. Five brigadiers were slain, including brave John Adams of Mississippi as he tried to seize enemy colors on a parapet. General Patrick Clayburne, lawyer and abolitionist from Arkansas, was the most respected field officer in the western army. He gallantly led his division in the attack, and died sword in hand fifty yards from enemy works. The Federal garrison held, then made it across the river at night. As the horror of the carnage was felt, it was learned that a flanking movement could have dislodged the enemy. The troops then knew that Hood had lost his mind.

Soldiers came to see that further sacrifice would accomplish nothing, and that they must go home to restore a semblance of order. The desertions began. Not disloyal men, but men let down, trying to find their women and children so they could plant crops and feed hungry mouths when the end came. Facing facts and aiding helplessness became the demands of courage. Divisions melted to the size of brigades, and brigades to the size of regiments.

When Hood positioned his depleted units on heights around Nashville in the middle of December, the Federal army attacked. The men refused to fight. A brigade fled from a mere skirmish line. For why should they die in a battle for a cause good in itself but dead from hopeless leadership, when they were needed to farm the land? They disintegrated en masse. Hood lost nearly all his guns and ordnance. Very few were killed or wounded, but thousands were taken prisoner.

The Federal army at Nashville was commanded by General George Thomas, a Virginian loyal to the Union, and one of the best field officers ever to appear on either side in the American Civil War. He had an intuitive feel for the moods of fighting men. He was known to direct in person the placement of guns and regiments on the field. He rode up and down the line of battle in full dress uniform, cheering on his troops. It was Thomas who more than any other had saved the Federal army from collapse at Murfreesboro and again at Chicamauga.

It is more than curious that he did not finish the mopping up operations and compel the surrender of Hood's entire army after Nashville. Yes, he went through the obligatory motions, but made no supreme effort. Hood had no pontoon bridges to make it over the Tennessee River. There were Federal gun boats on those waters. Confederate 32-pounders were used in a feeble effort to keep the naval craft at a distance while a crossing was made. But such artillery had no serious impact on the warships. Bagging the shivering remnants in gray and butternut on the river banks should have been no problem, not for a general as outstanding as Thomas.

It is not of military record, naturally, but it is probable that Thomas deliberately sat on his hands as an act of decency. He was a Southerner at heart, and he understood the Southern way of life, which is the likely but unspoken reason why he had been left in Nashville while Sherman marched through Georgia. Thomas knew why the toughest infantry in the world had refused to fight against his assault. He knew that the war was over in the west, and that the men he had vanquished were needed to care for their people.

Stanton did not have to know, not officially anyway. In any event, Stanton could do nothing, politically speaking, to a famous commander who appeared to have destroyed a major rebel army. Hood's army actually dissolved itself, not unlike Dundee's highlanders after Killiecrankie, for they had no leader.

Shortly after New Year's 1865, the remaining fragments of the Army of Tennessee collected in northern Mississippi. Hood admitted his failure, and asked Davis to relieve him of command.

Meanwhile Sherman sent a telegram to Lincoln, offering Savannah as a Christmas present. In January, he began his march through South Carolina, intending to make a junction with Grant in Virginia and to end the war by overwhelming Lee. On the way, his troops burned homes and villages, ransacked plantations, desecrated holy places, stole money and silverware, wrecked furniture and fine art, and killed or confiscated farm animals. After the war, Sherman told a military festival in Ohio,

> "When the rebels ventured their all in their efforts to destroy our government, they pledged their lives, their fortunes, and their sacred honor to their cause. The government accepted their wager of battle. Hence, when we conquered, we by conquest gained all they had. Their property became ours by conquest. Thus, they lost their slaves, their mules, their horses, their cotton, their all; even their lives and personal liberty, thrown by them into the issue, were theirs only by our forbearance and clemency. So, soldiers, when we marched through and conquered the territory of the rebels, we became the owners of all they had, and I don't want you to be troubled in your consciences for taking, while on our great march, the property of the conquered rebels. They forfeited their rights to it, and I, being an agent for the government to which I belonged, gave you authority to keep all the quartermasters couldn't take possession of or didn't want."[41]

Columbia, South Carolina, the seat of secession, was razed to the ground; but, when public outrage was heard even in the North, Sherman attempted sophisticated deceit by blaming the arson on Confederate cavalry in retreat.[42]

* * * * *

As Sherman headed from up Savannah, the Congress in Richmond enacted a law which effectively obliged Davis to appoint Lee as supreme commander of all armies of the Confederate States. There was little that Lee could do in this position, but he did what was required.

The general-in-chief provided a realistic assessment of the military situation: — "You must not be surprised," he said, "if calamity befalls us."[43]

In order to prevent Sherman from joining Grant as long as possible, Lee placed Johnston in command of the scattered bodies of troops to the south and west of Virginia. Meanwhile, he held out brilliantly at Richmond with only about 40,000 effectives against Grant's 160,000.

When Johnston appeared on the field toward the end of February, men flocked to join him. Vanished units of Hood's old army reappeared out of nowhere to resume the fight. Battalions and companies from obscure points showed up. By early March, although Charleston, Columbia, and Wilmington had fallen, Johnston had a spirited host of 37,000 in North Carolina, which, although a new force in reality, he called with nostalgia the Army of Tennessee. He then faced 100,000 under Sherman in rapid advance, with another Federal corps on the way as further reinforcements.

In those discontented winter months, the Congress in Richmond addressed the people of the Confederate States:

> "The passage of hostile armies through our country, though productive of cruel suffering to our people, and great pecuniary loss, gives the enemy no permanent foothold. To subjugate a country, its civil government must be suppressed by a continuing military force, or supplanted by another to which the inhabitants yield a voluntary or forced obedience. The passage of hostile armies in our territory cannot produce this result. Permanent garrisons would have to be stationed at a sufficient number of points to strangle of civil government before it could be pretended, even by the United States government itself, that its authority was extended over these States. How many garrisons would it require? How many hundred thousand soldiers would suffice to suppress the civil government in all the States of the Confederacy, and to establish over them, even in name and form, the authority of the United States? In a geographical point of view, therefore, it may be asserted that the conquest of these Confederate States is impracticable."[44]

The theory was sound, because it urged proper use of geography as George Washington and his generals had illustrated during the American

Revolution. And, given the morale of the people to continue resistance, together with timely exploitation of opportunities and correct strategies on the field, the war might have continued for years. The patience and resources of the invaders might ultimately have been exhausted, and independence may have been won.

The problem was that the morale of the Southern people was broken, and it was broken, not by the atrocities of Sherman and the hammering of Grant, but by the incurable incompetence of the administration in Richmond. Stanton is said to have been a great war minister, which is an enormous falsehood, for he was only a butcher, but he had vast resources to replace whatever he lost. It was different for the South, which could afford very little waste and stupidity in this death struggle.

Davis and his inner circle had disregarded the best military advice, left Vicksburg inadequately defended, thereby created the need to take a desperate gamble by invading Pennsylvania, removed an excellent commander in front of Atlanta and replaced him with a cripple full of morphine, concurred in hopeless generalship which lost Atlanta in six weeks and destroyed the western army in six months, and allowed Sherman to march through Georgia and South Carolina virtually unopposed.

Once the people realized that their generous sacrifices were dissipated by incompetent direction of the war, only miracles could regain their confidence. The feeling grew that, since the war could no longer be successfully prosecuted, the sooner it was brought to a merciful but adverse end the better. Because such was the view of the people and nothing could be done to change it, and because by then the military situation had deteriorated too far, it was time to arrange capitulation on the best terms possible.

Lee and Johnston had armies on the field, but casualties and desertions were taking a toll. For awhile these armies could be held together and used to bargain for meaningful concessions in negotiations for peace, but time was quickly passing. And there were in Richmond characters of eminent standing, who clearly saw the inevitability of military defeat, and worked ardently to induce negotiations for a peaceable and honorable return of the Southern States back into the Union.

Due to the private intermediation of an influential politician in the North, a peace conference was held on February 3, 1865, on a steamer at Hampton Roads, Virginia, between a delegation headed by Abraham Lincoln and a delegation headed by Alexander Stephens.[45] Lee, Johnston, Stephens, and others both civilian and military understood the need to begin negotiations in earnest before it was too late, but Davis imposed the impossible demand of independence as a limitation on Stephens' negotiating authority, and thereby did his best to torpedo the meeting in advance.

Even so, Stephens was politically savvy. He knew Lincoln personally from their days together in Congress and from their cordial correspondence before the war. And, notwithstanding the attitudes of Davis, he intended to renew an old political friendship for the good of the South.

At the time of the conference, Lincoln had immense political influence in the North, because he was the President of the United States, safely reelected and on the winning side of a war. He then had significant means to block the designs of radical republicans and Stanton by alliance with democrats and moderate republicans. In exchange for termination of military hostilities, Lincoln promised liberal use of his power to grant pardons.[46]

Lincoln promised his support for the seating of Southern representatives and senators in the Congress of the Union. In other words, he would use his prestige and power as a victorious President to prevent reconstruction based on martial law, as radical republicans were known to favor out of hatred of the South.

And he wanted the Southern States to adopt a constitutional amendment abolishing slavery and involuntary servitude, proposed by the Congress of the Union only a few days before the conference. At that juncture, because of the disruptions of the war, not to mention the still-growing abolitionist sentiment in the Dixie States, the most important and thoughtful leaders of the South, including Davis himself, believed that, even if independence were won, slavery could never be successfully reestablished, and so would have to be phased out as quickly and humanely as possible.[47] A practical question, openly discussed between Lincoln and Stephens, was how former slaves could adapt practically to freedom. Both men conceded real difficulties of making this transition successful. But Lincoln assured Stephens of his support of just compensation to slaveholders. It was understood that this intervention, as a condition of peace, would be the official pretext for recapitalization and rehabilitation of the South from the ravages of war.

During the conference, Stephens understood the limitations imposed by political circumstances on Lincoln, and Lincoln understood the limitations imposed by political circumstances on Stephens. Their talk was conjectural and cryptic. As they spoke, they exchanged knowing looks. Lincoln could not promise a cease fire pending further negotiations, lest the momentum enjoyed by Federal armies be lost. Nor could he give certain guarantees of lenient treatment of the Southern States, but he did assure the Southern delegation of his best efforts, which, under the circumstances, was an exceedingly important concession. In an attempt to capitalize on Lincoln's assurances, Stephens asked Lincoln if he would reconsider on a cease fire pending further talks, — in other words, Stephens wanted to know whether, if he could bring around the Confederate government in Richmond, Lincoln would be willing to grant a cease fire pending an agreed reentry of the Southern States into Union according to the kind of terms which had been discussed.

"Well, Stephens," said Lincoln, "I will reconsider it. I do not think my mind will change, but I will reconsider," — meaning that, if after all Stephens really persuaded authorities in Richmond to promote rapid reunion of the Southern States, which seemed a doubtful prospect, well then, yes, of course, he would gladly do his part in bringing the war to an honorable end.

Stephens and his fellow commissioners reported to Davis. Obviously, it was time to negotiate termination of armed resistance on the field, pending necessary legal formalities for bringing the rebel States into normal relations with the Union. Davis rejected the possibility as unthinkable, and he sought to use the results of the conference as a platform for fanatical appeals in a speech he delivered at the African Church in Richmond.[48]

Sherman, said Davis, is "making his last march," which will lead to his ruin. "Before the summer solstice," he exclaimed, "the North will sue for peace." The military situation of the Confederate States, the President boasted, "is all I could desire." Little did Lincoln and those with him at Hampton Roads know that "they were talking to their masters!"

This swelling oratory was for Stephens the last straw. Once again Davis had recklessly tossed about the fortunes of the South. Stephens bade farewell to the President, and retired to his home in Georgia as he waited for the end, — and his arrest.

On March 19, 1865, Johnston struck Sherman at Bentonville, attempting to cripple the Federal march toward Richmond. The battle was reminiscent of Culloden, except that Johnston expertly coordinated movements on ground of his own choosing. The blood-curdling rebel yell was heard across fields and woods. The attack began to show promise, including capture of eight guns and hundreds of prisoners. The advance slowed down when Johnston cautiously ordered reinforcements to support his left wing then under mounting pressure. Sherman brought new divisions to the front, and Johnston withdrew the next day in good order.

On March 25, 1865, Lee threw a surprise assault at Fort Stedman on Grant's siege lines to the southeast of Richmond. It was an attempt to prepare an escape of Southern troops from their indefensible positions, and a subsequent juncture with Johnston in North Carolina. After initial success, the attack was thrown back. Thousands of rebel infantry were caught in enemy works and surrendered.

On April 1, 1865, the Confederate line near Five Forks collapsed, more thousands were captured, and Lee's far right was exposed.

On April 2, 1865, Grant broke through Lee's lines at Petersburg, and Richmond had to be evacuated. Thus began the last campaign of the Army of Northern Virginia.

On April 5, 1865, Davis issued an executive proclamation from Danville near the border between Virginia and North Carolina. "We have now entered upon a new phase of the struggle. Relieved of the necessity of guarding particular points, our army will be free to move from point to point, and strike the enemy in detail far from his base. Let us but will it and we are free!"[49] These words stirred nobody.

On April 6, 1865, still more thousands from Lee's army were trapped at Sayler's Creek, and forced to give up.

On April 9, 1865, Lee surrendered the rest of his men at Appomattox Court House. Grant was magnanimous and earned the respect of history. Officers were allowed to keep their side arms, men could keep their horses and mules so they could plant crops, and all troops were sent home on parole. Lee's army was hungry. Grant sent them rations. Soldiers on both sides traded stories, smoked tobacco, and struck up or renewed friendships.

On April 26, 1865, Johnston surrendered to Sherman at Durham Station on the same terms. In his final order, Johnston concluded, "Events in Virginia, which broke every hope of success in war, imposed on its generals the duty of sparing the blood of this gallant army, and of saving our country from further devastation, and our people from ruin."[50]

Meanwhile, Davis fled with the remnants of his government through the Carolinas into Georgia, rejecting the advice and assistance of all who tried to get him out of the country, lest his expected arrest and execution be used to humiliate the South. He insisted on continuing the struggle for Southern independence. He imagined that, in the darkest hour, there would be an heroic rally which would finally repel the invasion from the North.

On May 11, 1865, Davis was captured by Federal troops. He was imprisoned in chains, and charged by indictment for treason. As he suffered in confinement, he received the consolation of a crown of thorns personally woven by the hands of Pope Pius IX, sent by his Holiness from Rome. Famous lawyers volunteered to defend him. At length he was released on bail put up by prominent citizens. After further proceedings, the indictment was quietly dismissed on technical grounds,[51] and thereby Davis was denied an opportunity to argue before a court of the Union that secession is a constitutional right of the several States. It was illusory to hope for a fair hearing on such a momentous question at that time in history. It was a question which would have to wait impartial consideration in a future age.

Davis outlived the war by twenty-four years, during which he redeemed himself morally for his errors as President of the Confederate States. His life during those sad years has been described as a long anti-climax, but in reality it was a time of penance during which he undertook the noblest work of his career. For he then served as the ceremonial magistrate of the defeated Southern people, dedicating monuments, laying cornerstones, speaking at cemeteries and in churches, offering comfort to widows and orphans, and honoring veterans.

He died forgiven and beloved by his countrymen.

NOTES

CHAPTER VIII

1 - 1 Commanger's Documents at 414, Pollard's Lost Cause at 298 (Letter dated July 7, 1862).

2 - As appears in two accounts of the peninsular campaign in 1862: first, the account by the editor of the *Richmond Examiner* in Pollard's Lost Cause at 278-294, then General McClellan's account in 2 Johnson & Buel's Battles 160-187.

3 - The story of the betrayal of Belisarius by Justinian is told in 4 Gibbon's Rome at 281-286 (Chapter XLIII).

4 - Quoted in 1 Henderson's Stonewall Jackson at 173-174.

5 - General Johnston's account of the Mississippi campaign in 1863 is found in 3 Johnson & Buel's Battles 472-481.

6 - General Longstreet's observations on the Gettysburg campaign in 1863 are found in 3 Johnson & Buel's Battles 244-251 and 339-354.

7 - The total cost of the American Civil War on both sides, mounting enormous public debt, was about $8,000,000,000, as appears in 2 Stephens' View at 630. Such public spending and resulting debt were almost incomprehensible by monetary standards of the day. The public debt incurred in fighting the American Revolution was almost trivial by comparison: — even reckoning "old tenor" Continental currency dollar for dollar, it could not have much exceeded $320,000,000, as may be inferred from Hamilton's First Report on Public Credit (Cooke's Reports at 19-22), and the resolutions of the Continental Congress allowing bills of credit (1 Thorpe's History at 124-125 and Del Mar's America at 112-113). The total capital investment in slaves in the Southern States in 1860 has been fairly estimated at about $2,000,000,000, as appears in 1 Stephens' View at 539-540. The cost of building a transcontinental railroad across the United States in 1860 can be reckoned by reference to the acts of Congress which facilitated their construction, beginning with the charter of the Union Pacific Railroad, set forth in 12 U. S. Statutes at Large 489

(July 1, 1862). Such a feat would have cost about $150,000,000 in money of the day. Thus, the compensated emancipation of all slaves and the building of three transcontinental railroad would have cost less than $2,500,000,000, — a minor fraction of the cost of fighting the war in dollars, let alone the cost in human casualties, the wreckage of constitutional order, and the injury to civilization.

8 - Justice Stephen Field, dissenting, in *Knox v. Lee*, 12 Wallace 457 at 680 (U. S. 1872).

9 - 12 U. S. Statutes at Large 731.

10 - The observations of Chief Justice Roger B. Taney were cited and quoted by Justice William Douglas, dissenting, in *Holmes v. United States,* 391 U. S. 936 at 941-942, fn. 9 (1968) .

11 - Aside from many impeccable authorities supporting this rule of common law — e. g., James Madison in the 40th Federalist, Mentor Edition at 248 —, there are clear affirmations of it by members of the United States Supreme Court who were appointed to reward their support of the war against the Southern States. See, e. g., Chief Justice Salmon P. Chase in *Lane County v. Oregon,* 7 Wallace 71 at 78-79 (U. S. 1868), and Justice William Strong in *Platt v. Union Pacific Railroad,* 99 U. S. 48 at 58-59 (1878) .

12 - Mentor Edition at 153.

13 - Mentor Edition at 256.

14 - 1 U. S. Statutes at Large at 85-87.

15 - From the "emancipation proclamation" in 1 Commanger's Documents at 421, and 2 Stephens' View at 776-777.

16 - The emancipation proclamation was declared unconstitutional in a resolution of the legislature of Illinois on January 7, 1863, reprinted in 1 Commager's Documents at 421. And Judge Benjamin Curtis who had dissented in *Dred Scott v. Sandford,* 19 Howard 393 at 564-633 (U. S. 1857), protested solemnly as a lawyer in Boston against the unconstitutionality of Lincoln's proclamation, as appears in 2 Stephens' View at 551-556.

17 - 1 Commager's Documents at 418.

18 - 1 Commager's Documents at 391, Rozwenc's Civil War at 32-33.

19 - The true legal heritage of the United States is as a "religious people" and a "Christian nation," as demonstrated by Justice David Brewer with incomparable erudition in *Church of the Holy Trinity v. United States,* 143 U. S. 457 at 465-471 (1892).

20 - The right of a State to secede from the Union in keeping with the United States Constitution was reaffirmed by St. George Tucker of Virginia in his edition

of Blackstone's Commentaries, published in 1803. In 1 Tucker's Blackstone, Appendix D at 187, it says "The federal government, then, appears to be the organ through which the united republics communicate with foreign nations and with each other. Their submission to its operation is voluntary: its councils, its engagements, its authority are theirs, modified, and united. Its sovereignty is an emanation from theirs, not a flame by which they have been consumed, nor a vortex in which they are swallowed up. Each is still a perfect state, still sovereign, still independent, and still capable, should the situation require, to resume the exercise of its functions as such in the most unlimited extent." The same constitutional right of secession was expounded by William Rawle of Pennsylvania in the thirty-first chapter of the first edition, and in the thirty-second chapter of the second edition of his text, which was used for instruction on the fundamental law of the Union at West Point. He concluded a long argument, "The States, then, may wholly withdraw from the Union." — Rawle's View at 297. Both Tucker and Rawle, while conceding the right of secession, cautioned against its premature exercise. Their positions were cited, reviewed, and approved in 1 Stephens' View at 503-510.

21 - This characterization of the size of public spending on both sides appears in 2 Stephens' View at 630.

22 - Congressman Charles Lindbergh of Minnesota (1907-1917) discovered monetary politics as a basic cause of the American Civil War, although he has been overlooked or ignored by the best historians in the United States. His essential insight is found in Lindbergh's Money Trust 93-107. On pages 102-103, Lindbergh quoted and commented upon the infamous "Hazard Circular" which, never having been a document of public record, was saved by responsible citizens, later made public, then energetically suppressed or branded as a fake. The document has been mentioned in a number of works, but the most satisfactory authentication appears to be Congressman Lindbergh. The document explains the monetary legislation which followed upon it. Supporting information is found in Del Mar's Monetary Crimes 60-91 and Dean's Curse of the Funding System at 366-444. It was Lindbergh who most clearly understood that the war was planned and stirred up to generate a huge national debt represented by war bonds which were to become, and actually became by law a major and obligatory capital basis of the postbellum system of banking and currency in the United States. And it was Lindbergh, again, who pioneered in the view that, from the war grew up a cartel of high finance which settled on Wall Street in New York City, and was legalized by the Federal Reserve Act of 1913, 38 U. S. Statutes at Large 251 (December 23, 1913).

23 - The framing of the second and fifth clauses of Article I, Section 8, and key parts of the first clause of Article I, Section 10 of the United States Constitution can be traced in 5 Elliot's Debates 378, 381, 434-435, 484-485, 536, 560, 561, — Tansill's Dcouments 475, 480, 556-557, 627-629, 706, 707, — 2 Ferrand's Records 182, 187, 308-309, 448-449, 565, 577, 594, 595, 596-597, 655, 657

(Madison's Notes, August 6, 16, 28, September 10, 12, and 17, 1787).

24 - The acts authorizing greenback currency are found in 12 U. S. Statutes at Large 345 (February 25, 1862), later supplemented by 12 U. S. Statutes at Large 532 (July 11, 1862), and 709 (March 3, 1863).

25 - In *Bronson v. Rodes,* 7 Wallace 229 (U. S. 1869), it was held that, if a contract specifically called for payment in gold or silver coin, the debt could not be discharged in greenbacks over the protest of the creditor.

26 - The original National Bank Act is found in 12 U. S. Statutes at Large 670 (February 25, 1863), which was reenacted with amendments, as appears in 13 U. S. Statutes at Large 99 (June 3, 1864).

27 - The act imposing a 10% tax on the face amount of the notes of state-chartered banks is found in 13 U. S. Statutes at Large 484 (March 3, 1865), which was extended in application by the act in 14 U. S. Statutes at Large 146 (July 13, 1866).

28 - As earlier observed in this work (at the beginning of Chapter IV), the population index in the third section of Article I, Section 2 of the United States Constitution derived from a resolution of Congress on April 18, 1783, proposed an amendment to the Articles of Confederation, which would have provided a new measure for requisitions of money to be paid into the Federal treasury by the several States. When, in the Philadelphia Convention, this same population index was put to the new use of distributing representatives in Congress, Charles Cotesworth Pinckney protested, demanding that slaves be counted one for one so as to increase the power of the slaveholding States in Congress. The Southern abolitionist George Mason opposed General Pinckney's suggestion. Gouverneur Morris suggested a compromise that "direct taxes" be included in the population index, so as to reduced Pinckey's ardor for counting slaves one for one. On that occasion, Morris contrasted "direct taxes" to be included in the index, with "indirect taxes" which he defined as taxes on "exports, imports, and consumption." The compromise was accepted, although Mason was displeased, as appears in 5 Elliot's Debates 302-306, — Tansill's Documents 363-368, — 1 Ferrand's Records 591-597 (Madison's Notes, July 12, 1787). It may be further noted that John Marshall described "direct taxes" as taxes on "lands, slaves, stock of all kinds, and a few other articles of domestic property." — 3 Elliot's Debates at 229 (Virginia Convention, June 10, 1788). Alexander Hamilton gave a comprehensive definition of indirect taxes in the 21st Federalist, Mentor Edition 142-143: — he there said that duties, imposts, and excises (or indirect taxes) "may be compared to a fluid, which will in time find its level with the means of paying them," because, "if the duties are too high, they lessen the consumption, and collection is eluded," whereas direct taxes, which in those days related mainly to land and buildings, contain no such natural limit against excess and could be safely estimated in relative value by "the number of people" in each State. The reason for

apportionment in Hamilton's thinking was that it would guard against confiscation of property and wealth by taxation. Since income, whether earned by work or from property, is accumulated wealth, and an income tax cannot be avoided by reducing or eliminating consumption, such a tax is a direct tax within the intended meaning of the third clause of Article I, Section 2 of the United States Constitution. The old case of *Hylton v. United States,* 3 Dallas 171 (U. S. 1795), is not authority to the contrary, for it was there properly held that a tax on carriages, imposed at uniform rates, was not a tax on property or wealth, but a tax on consumption, and so did not have to be apportioned.

29 - 13 U. S. Statutes at Large 223 (June 30, 1864).

30 - This decision was later reversed in *Pollock v. Farmers' Loan & Trust Co.,* 157 U. S. 429 (1895), rehearing 158 U. S. 601 (1895), in which Chief Justice Melville Fuller copiously reviewed the historical evidence, and adopted the broader idea that direct taxes actually contemplated by the framers, — i. e., taxes levied on any and all property and wealth, which, he rightly held, includes taxes on income. On this basis, Fuller held that an income tax imposed by Congress at uniform rates, but not apportioned among the several States, was unconstitutional. This decision led to Amendment XVI which allows a uniform and unapportioned taxes on any and all income from whatever source Some years later, in *Bushaber v. Union Pacific Railroad,* 240 U. S. 1 (1916), Chief Justice Douglass White misrepresented Fuller's opinion as having held that only taxes on income from real or personal property — rents, dividends, capital gains, etc. — were direct taxes, as if taxes on income from work were duties valid if imposed at uniform rates throughout the Union. Contrary to White's theory, Amendment XVI was meant to allow what Fuller had found to be unconstitutional, i. e., to exempt one class of direct taxes, viz., taxes on "income from whatever source derived," from apportionment. White thus sought confirm as legitimate the income tax imposed by the Federal government during the American Civil War. It cannot go without notice that this same Chief Justice White also wrote for the court in the *Selective Draft Law Cases,* 245 U. S. 366 (1918), sustaining the constitutionality of conscripting armies, and thereby the manpower system devised by Edwin Stanton in the American Civil War, as if the Statute of 1 Edward III, Chapter 5 (1327) had never been enacted, and no legal tradition had ever been built upon it.

31 - His views expressed on this occasion are summarized in 2 Stephens' View at 570-575.

32 - 2 Stephens' View at 790.

33 - A reasonably good contemporary discussion of the Southern financial system is found in Pollard's Lost Cause at 420-428. Cf. 2 Stephens' View 569-570.

34 - James Madison believed that the prohibition of bills of credit in the first clause of Article I, Section 10 of the United States Constitution disallowed circulating

paper of the several States only if made legal tender for all debts public and private. His view appears in a letter to Charles Ingersoll on February 22, 1831, reproduced in 4 Elliot's Debates at 608. Madison's observations in his letter to Ingersoll correspond to his second speech in the Philadelphia Convention on August 16, 1787, as appears in 5 Elliot's Debates 434, Tansill's Documents 480, 2 Ferrand's Documents 308-309 (Madison's Notes). Even so, it was held over powerful dissents in *Craig v. Missouri,* 4 Peters 410 (U. S. 1830), that the prohibition of bills of credit in the first clause of Article I, Section 10 of the United States Constitution extends to promissory currency even if not made legal tender. This holding was reversed in *Briscoe v. Kentucky,* 11 Peters 257 (U. S. 1837), where it was held that the prohibition does not extend to promissory currency of a State receivable for public dues but not legal tender in payment of private debts. The prohibition of bills of credit emitted by any State was excluded from the permanent constitution of the Confederate States, partly to avoid confusion of terms, and partly because government financing by paper currency not made legal tender for all debts, even if receivable for public dues, was understood to be a dire necessity in the War for Southern Independence.

35 - Quoted in Pollard's Lost Cause at 510.

36 - Quoted in Donald's Pictorial History at 381.

37 - Johnston's professional account of his defense of Atlanta is found in 4 Johnson & Buel's Battles 260-277.

38 - Quoted in Donald's Pictorial History at 381.

39 - Quoted in Donald's Pictorial History at 389.

40 - The remarks in question are found in Davis' address to the Congress in Richmond on November 10, 1864. This address was reported from a telegraphed message in the *Citizen Extra* in Canton, Mississippi, reprinted in 2 Caren's Civil War Extra at 231.

41 - Quoted in Pollard's Lost Cause at 717-718.

42 - The unmistakable facts showing Sherman's guilt in these war crimes and crimes against humanity, contrary to then understood principles of international law and military convention — later defined as such in the resolution of the General Assembly of the United Nations on December 11, 1946, adopting the principles of the Nuremberg Tribunal —, are documented in 2 Stephens' View 510 and 766-773. In Adams' Human Events 109-127 an excellent discussion is found on the war crimes and crimes against humanity committed by the armies of the United States against the South throughout the American Civil War

43 - Quoted in Donald's Pictorial History 421. This comment was part of a report from General Lee to the secretary of war, John Breckenridge, dated March 9, 1865. Lee's report was part of an effort to reopen negotiations leading to surrender on the best terms possible for the South. Breckenridge had solicited this report in an effort

to induce renewal of such negotiations. The facts and circumstances surrounding this correspondence are well explained in Davis' Honorable Defeat at 1-35.

44 - Quoted in Pollard's Lost Cause at 645.

45 - The circumstances and proceedings of the conference at Hampton Roads are amply discussed in 2 Stephens' View 589-621, and the official papers generated on both sides in reference to the meeting are reprinted in full in 2 Stephens' View 791-803. Abraham Lincoln was accompanied by William Seward, his secretary of state, whose presence served to reinforce assurances given to the Southerners. Alexander Stephens was accompanied by R. M. T. Hunter, president pro tempore of the Confederate States Senate, who represented Davis' hard-line attitudes as if Southern independence were still a realistic possibility, and John Campbell who had served on the United States Supreme Court before the war, led a brigade and was wounded at Wincester in 1862, then became assistant secretary of war in the Confederate government, and agreed with Stephens on the urgent need to negotiate surrender on the best terms possible.

46 - In the 74th Federalist, Alexander Hamilton said, "In seasons of insurrection or rebellion, there are often critical moments when a well-timed offer of pardon to the insurgents or rebels may restore tranquillity to the commonwealth." — Mentor Edition at 449. There can be no doubt that the framers in the Philadelphia Convention intended that the power of the President to grant pardons, like the King's prerogative, should be prospective as well as retrospective, as appears in 5 Elliot's Debates at 480, Tansill's Documents at 621, and 2 Ferrand's Records at 428 (Madison's Notes, August 27, 1787), and 4 Blackstone's Commentaries 337.

47 - The attitude of Southern leaders in 1864 and 1865, as reported by the editor of the *Richmond Examiner,* is found in Pollard's Lost Cause at 572. From an early stage of the war, black troops were not infrequently found in the Confederate army, as appears in Kennedys' South Was Right at 90-96. In his private monograph *Black Confederates, Lost Historical Identity,* published in 2001, Robert E. Harrison estimates that about 65,000 black troops served in the armies of the Confederate States, and that about 13,000 saw combat. Mr. Harrison proudly traces his ancestry to one of these free black Confederate soldiers, and has pioneered in a revival of contemporary scholarship on this question. An Act of the Congress of the Confederate States passed on March 13, 1865, as implemented by General Order No. 14 of the President, allowed for enlistment of slaves in the army with freedom as a bounty, following common practice in the American Revolution. This development was widely approved by all ranks of the army, from privates to general officers, including Lee and Longstreet, and it had been recommended by the legislature of Alabama in 1863. The consensus of the Southern people was that this measure necessitated an end to slavery within a few years following hoped-for Southern independence. A commentary on this legislation is found in Winik's April 1865 at 48-62.

48 - This oration was never recorded verbatim, but the account of the editor of the *Richmond Examiner* appears in Pollard's Lost Cause at 685. Alexander Stephens' impressions of this speech, and the political context in which it was delivered, are recorded in 2 Stephens' View 622-626.

49 - Reproduced in Pollard's Lost Cause at 701. Another version of this proclamation, dated April 4, 1865, is reproduced in 1 Commager's Documents at 444-445.

50 - From General Order No. 18, Army of Tennessee, April 27, 1865, reprinted in 2 Stephens' View at 808.

51- Davis was punished by disqualification to hold public office under the third section of Amendment XIV, proclaimed by the secretary of state as part of the United States Constitution on July 28, 1868. The disqualification was an exception to the general prohibition of bills of attainder, including bills of pains and penalties, in Article I, Sections 9 and 10 of the United States Constitution. Such disqualification would have been prohibited as a bill of attainder if imposed by mere legislation, as appears in *Cummins v. Missouri,* 4 Wallace 277 (U. S. 1866), and *Ex Parte Garland,* 4 Wallace 333 (U. S. 1866). It was allowable in relation to Davis and others rebel leaders, because imposed by what was considered a constitutional amendment. Yet once punished in this way for his participation in the "rebellion," Davis could not be further prosecuted for the same acts under an indictment for treason because of the double jeopardy clause in Amendment V. Davis' counsel made a motion to dismiss on such grounds, although there was no decision upon it. President Andrew Johnson granted a general pardon or amnesty in December 1868, and thereafter the Federal prosecutor filed a nolle prosequi, whereupon the indictment against Davis was dismissed.

*Gens. Joseph E. Johnston and Robert E. Lee
in Savannah, spring 1870
(Courtesy of D. J. Ryan)*

CHAPTER IX

THE RECONSTRUCTION ACTS

On the evening of April 14, 1865, Abraham and Mary Lincoln attended Ford's Theatre in Washington, D.C., to see the last billed performance of Miss Laura Keene, a famous actress of the time, in *Our American Cousin*. During the play, the President was shot by John Wilkes Booth, who managed to penetrate security and make good his escape by means still disputed by experts on the assassination. It appears in any event that the guard was never reprimanded or punished, although soldiers falling asleep on duty were liable to be executed by firing squad in those days. The leniency shown to the guard was approved by Edwin Stanton who, it so happens, failed to close the one street and bridge over which the killer fled, although he had all other routes quickly and efficiently blocked.

Booth's diary was later recovered, but eighteen pages were missing. More than a century after the death of Stanton, it was claimed by certain "revisionist" historians that those eighteen pages were among papers held by Stanton's descendants.[1] These pages are supposed to reveal that Stanton was involved in a conspiracy which used Booth to slay Lincoln. Other conspirators said to be named in the missing text of the diary were Jay Cooke, a financier in Philadelphia, who floated most of the Federal war bonds which paid for the conquest of the South and capitalized institutions under the National Bank Act, as well as Benjamin Wade, Zachariah Chandler, and John Conness, radical republicans in the United States Senate, who, like Stanton, wanted the South divided into military districts and governed as conquered territories.

The bribes and intrigue were only a small part of the story, if the account in question may ever be accepted in polite company, for it is claimed that there was a foul cover-up. In any event, on May 1, 1865, the new President, Andrew Johnson, issued an executive proclamation, citing the opinion of his attorney general, and ordering trial by military commission of Lewis Payne, George Atzerodt, David Herold, and Mary Surratt who were arrested for having aided and abetted John Wilkes Booth in the murder at Ford's Theatre.

These unfortunate individuals were unable to escape trial before a military commission, because an Act of March 3, 1863, by its terms allowed the President to suspend the writ of habeas corpus.[2] The writ was suspended, essentially because Stanton insisted upon it. At the time of his executive proclamation, President Johnson was in almost a dazed condition as he attempted to master power which he had never expected to wield. In issuing his proclamation, he did as he was told.

It is said that someone other than Booth was shot at Garrett's farm on April 24, 1865; that Booth got away; and that years later an old man on his death bed claimed he was Booth. It is affirmed, furthermore, that Payne, Atzerhodt, Herold, and Surratt were framed because they knew of details which would have exposed Stanton, Cooke, Wade, Chandler, Conness, and others. Hired perjurers are supposed to have been brought forward under the orchestration of Stanton. The defendants were condemned in a rush to judgment. They were quickly hanged on July 7, 1865.

If only the United States Supreme Court had ordered release of Congressman Clement Vallandigham, the subsequent course of American history might have been very different. At least the trial of Payne, Atzerhodt, Herod, and Surratt would have had to be held in open court before a jury, instead of in a closed court martial. Either charges could not have been brought at all, or important particulars might have come to light. The availability of due process of law might have exposed the real culprits, which alone may have directed the country away from the furious orgy of political sadism then was about to intensify.

Within a few days of the executive proclamation on the case of Payne, Atzerhodt, Herod, and Surratt, a petition for writ of habeas corpus was filed before the circuit court of the United States in Indiana. Lamdin Milligan had earlier been arrested and tried before a military commission as directed by general commanding the military district of Indiana. On pretense of the Act of March 3, 1863, the great writ had been suspended. Milligan had been found guilty by the military commission of aiding the rebellion, and sentenced to hang. Meanwhile a Federal grand jury met in Indiana, and returned no charges against Milligan.

The two judges of the circuit court entertaining Milligan's petition disagreed on whether the writ could issue, whether Milligan was entitled to release, and whether the military commission had jurisdiction to try Milligan. Because they were divided and were asked by the petitioner to do so, the judges of the circuit court certified these questions according to an Act of April 29, 1802,[3] under which the cause went before the United States Supreme Court for determination.

A year and a half after Payne, Atzerodt, Herold, and Surrat were laid to rest, their lips sealed so the truth might be hidden, the United States Supreme Court found in *Ex Parte Milligan,* 4 Wallace 2 (U.S. 1866), that the military commission had no jurisdiction to try Milligan, and that he was entitled to release on writ of habeas corpus. The rushed trial and execution of these four individuals is thus a classic case in the annals of judicial murder.

The Act of March 3, 1863, allowed the President to suspend the writ of habeas corpus during the rebellion. But the Act provided further that, if a citizen not in the army or navy or a prisoner of war were arrested and held by authority of the President, and if a Federal grand jury subsequently met in the State where such citizen was arrested and held, and was discharged without returning an indictment or presentment against him, then such citizen could apply to the circuit court of the United States supervising the Federal grand jury and secure discharge on writ of habeas corpus.

Justice David Davis offered a lame excuse for earlier dereliction. "During the late wicked rebellion," he said, choosing his words carefully lest he offend radical republicans in Congress, "the temper of the times did not allow that calmness in deliberation and discussion so necessary to a correct conclusion of a purely judicial question." Yet, during the "wicked rebellion" as it was called, many eminent judges in the North and the South wrote memorable opinions, displayed superb erudition, acted with manly courage, and minced no words in damning lawlessness.[4]

Justice Davis held that the Act of March 3, 1863, by its terms allowed issuance of a writ of habeas corpus, and entitled the petitioner to release, and that the military commission in Indiana had no jurisdiction because Congress had not authorized it, and because "martial rule can never exist where the courts are open, and in the proper and unobstructed exercise of their jurisdiction." The power to impose martial law, including suspension of the writ of habeas corpus, was viewed as a means of waging war. As such it was held to be a power of Congress, never to be imposed in relation to citizens and civilians by authority of the President alone. And, even when allowed by Congress in relation to such citizens in time of war, it was held limited to the actual theatre of invasion or rebellion.

A minority of four, led by Chief Justice Salmon P. Chase, agreed with the majority of five in ordering the release of Milligan: — they also read the Act of March 3, 1863, strictly so as to require release in the circumstances of the case, conceding that no legislation of Congress had authorized the imposition of martial law in Indiana, and that, therefore, the military commission had no jurisdiction. But, as if Sir Edward Coke had never lived, they went on to suggest that, as a necessary and proper means of waging war, Congress could have authorized the President to impose martial law and to suspend the great writ in Indiana for all persons military and civilian, even though the courts were open and doing business. It was so, said Chase, because a rebellion was underway, and the State was threatened with invasion. Milligan was arrested some weeks after Hood's shattered army staggered to recover after the loss of Atlanta and some weeks before it was destroyed in Tennessee. Hood's army would have had to crush Sherman's army in Georgia, retake Nashville, destroy the Federal garrison there, reconquer all of Tennessee, invade Kentucky and subdue the entire State, then cross the Ohio River before an invasion of Indiana could have even begun. Indiana was then no more threatened by an invasion from the Southern States than New Hampshire or Nova Scotia. Public safety did not demand that Milligan, if he were guilty of any public wrong, should not have been charged by a Federal grand jury, and tried as a civilian in a circuit court of the United States.

Chase's dissenting speculations were about an unreal world and decided nothing. It is in any event important to note here that, in the case of Lamden Milligan, all nine members of the United States Supreme Court fully vindicated and actually exceeded the heroic pronouncements of Roger B. Taney in the case of John Merryman, yet the opinion of the late Chief Justice was not cited, for his memory was then infamous in the passions of the day.

* * * * *

And so it seemed, for a brief interlude, that things were falling back into place. But the appearance was sadly deceptive.

On December 8, 1863, President Lincoln issued an executive proclamation,[5] whereby he offered pardons freely to the people of the Southern States. When a number of citizens in any rebel State, equal to one-tenth the number of votes cast in the 1860 elections, should take a prescribed oath of loyalty to the Union, and thereupon be granted executive pardons, they could elect and form a convention to reestablish a republican constitution which Lincoln agreed to acknowledge as true and lawful.

Even before this executive proclamation, Lincoln had been able to get pro-Union regimes going in Missouri, Kentucky, Virginia, and Louisiana. And before the end of the war, he had functioning pro-Union governments in Tennessee and Arkansas. It did not matter that, in those States, there were also governments represented in the Southern Congress at Richmond. These pro-Union governments were a real thorn in the side of the rebel cause. For example, the so-called "Pierpoint government" gave assent in the name of Virginia, under the first clause of Article IV, Section 3 of the United States Constitutoin, for the admission of West Virginia as a new State of the Union in early 1863.

The prevailing circumstances were highly irregular, but in his way of thinking Lincoln was taking care that the laws be faithfully executed, particularly the guarantee that each of the several States should enjoy a republican form of government. And, there can be no doubt about it, he played a role not unlike that of William of Orange in calling the Convention Parliament. In pursuing this policy, Lincoln earned the savage and undying hatred of radical republicans in Congress, and Edwin Stanton, who passionately wanted to treat the Southern States as conquered territories, and to punish every white citizen in that part of the country as a criminal. If the missing eighteen pages of Booth's diary ever come to light, and if as claimed these papers show a plot by Stanton and others to get Lincoln out of the way, there may be questions of detail, but ther basic motives will be perfectly understandable.

While he had certainly been Stanton's patsy during his first weeks of power, President Johnson eventually gained control of his office. On May 29, 1865, he issued an executive proclamation,[6] carrying on Lincoln's policy, liberally offering pardons to former rebels, and inviting formation of new governments in the remaining seven States of the fallen Southern Confederacy. Then and there, as night follows day, he was likewise hated by radical republicans in Congress and by Stanton.

Conventions of the people in Southern States met under the authority of the executive proclamations of Lincoln and Johnson, whereupon they rescinded previous ordinances of secession, abolished slavery, repudiated public debt incurred in the war recently terminated, and reframed constitutions duly adopted in anticipation of resuming normal relations with the Union. Legislatures were elected, governors were chosen, courts were appointed, order and stability were restored.

On February 1, 1865, Congress proposed Amendment XIII of the United States Constitution, which reads in the first section, "Neither slavery nor involuntary servitude, except as a punishment for crime whereof the party shall have been duly convicted, shall exist within the United

States, or any place subject to their jurisdiction," — and in the second section, "Congress shall have power to enforce this article by appropriate legislation."

The intended meaning of Amendment XIII is not difficult to ascertain, because the text of the first section came almost word for word from the sixth article in the fourteenth section of the Northwest Ordinace of 1787.

It is plain enough that Amendment XIII was not intended to erase customary duties of citizenship.[7] It so appears, because the sixth section of the Northwest Ordinance of 1787 mentioned the militia in which citizens had a customary duty to bear arms as ancient as the Statute of Winchester. And the second article of the fourteenth section of the Northwest Ordinance of 1787 guaranteed trial by jury, which implied a customary duty to serve as jurors as ancient as Magna Carta.

And Amendment XIII did not prohibit, but allowed as a lawful alternative any contract to do work for money or other lawful compensation where the resulting obligation might be enforced by suit at common law for money damages to redress breach.

Yet it is clear that the prohibition was not limited to slavery strictly so-called, because Amendent XIII, following the Northwest Ordinance of 1787, also mentioned "involuntary servitude."

The phrase "involuntary servitude" read in juxtaposition with the reference to "slavery" according to the rule of common law called ejusdem generis or noscitur a sociis, included villeinage, peonage, any capitalization of labor, — any practice of coercing work by reason of proprietary title, right, or estate in a human being or his labor, be the form feudal, quasi-feudal, or modern, whatever the name or pretext.[8]

And involuntary servitude in the sense prohibited was contrasted with the imposition of involuntary labor which might lawfully be imposed as punishment for a crime. The inference must be that Amendment XIII was intended to prohibit any coercion of work by civil process in behalf of any private suitor, for the right to use such process would amount to a proprietary interest in the work of another human being.

The amendment was intended to give Congress the authority to enact all laws necessary and proper for preventing a resurgence, on any guise or pretext, of the antebellum system of exploiting labor in the South, or anything like it throughout the Union.

The adoption of this article was really a formality, because the abolition of slavery in many of the Southern States was accomplished at the hands of conventions of the people meeting under the executive proclamations of Lincoln and Johnson.

All moderate thinkers of that era, both in the North and in the South, including Abraham Lincoln no less than Robert E. Lee, believed that gradual or phased abolition, rather than sudden emancipation en masse, would have been best for all concerned. It takes patience and wisdom to understand this viewpoint.

James DeBow of New Orleans, editor of the nationally circulated *DeBow's Review*, recounted the situation of black freemen in his State before the abolition of slavery by the People of Louisiana in Convention:

> "There were some two or three hundred thousand free Negroes in the South, and some four or five hundred thousand of them in the country. There were a great many in Louisiana. There were in New Orleans some free Negroes among the wealthiest men we had. I made a comparison when I was superintendent of the United States census in 1850, and found that the condition of free Negroes in the South, their education, etc., was better. As a class they were immeasurably better off than the free Negroes of the North. There were free Negroes in Louisiana who owned fifty or a hundred slaves, and plantations on the coast, and there were hundreds of them who owned more or less property."[9]

For these black freemen, the abolition of slavery meant, in a few cases, a loss of capital, and, in any event, a transformation in the economic infrastructure of the South. They went through the same adjustments as white merchants and planters. But sudden liberation of the slave population in the South, accentuated by the hardship and dislocation of civil war, had devastating effects, as explained by Judge William Sharkey, who had been appointed by President Johnson in June 1865 to serve as Governor of Mississippi pending the formation of a new government of the State:

> "I believe that there are now in my State very little over half the number of freedmen that were formerly slaves, certainly not more than two-thirds. They have died off. There is no telling the mortality that has prevailed among them; they have died off in immense numbers. I should say that very little more than half the amount of land that was under cultivation before the war will be under cultivation this year."[10]

The approximate number of these deaths of former slaves may be estimated. In Mississippi, there were about 436,000 slaves in the year 1860.[11] The observation of Judge Sharkey justifies a guess that perhaps 30% of the slaves in his State, or about 130,000, died during the war.

The proportion of deaths among slaves would have been as great where the war was uninterrupted and terrible, as in Virginia, Tennessee, and Georgia, and probably less in States where the war was milder, as in Texas, Alabama, or Florida. In any event, it is not unfair to take a conservative figure for the entire South of, say, 10% of the slave population, or about 400,000 deaths from starvation and like causes.

There were about 27 million whites then in the United States in 1860, and they lost close to a million in casualties, or about 3 or 4%. The black race easily suffered two or three times the injury suffered by the white race. Why such catastrophic injury to former slaves?

In the quasi-feudal system of the old South, each plantation was a self-sustaining microcosm with a tiny service and manufacturing industry to support agricultural production. Passing from the master's house, touched with country softness and quiet elegance, a visitor could walk among the slave quarters, being rows of cabins, each with a little garden patch and a pathway leading to the main house or the fields. Every adult slave, male or female, had assigned work as a field hand, or a blacksmith, or a cook, or whatever. The master demanded fidelity between husbands and wives,[12] and supervised care of small children. He watched after physical needs and settled disputes. Slaves lived out their days, were doctored in sickness, cared for in old age, and usually had no worry. They worked to sustain interdependence, their lives simple and tranquil.

These conditions explain why so few slaves fled along the underground railroad, — why Southern planters looked upon the extreme protestations of Northern abolitionists as the raving of lunatics, — and why, even during the war, with most white freemen in the army or navy, many large plantations continued to produce under the direction of white women.

But as the scourge of Federal military expeditions was felt, a lot of these plantations were broken up, and "liberated" slaves lost the whole basis of their economic security. They became unemployed and helpless. Many were confused and broken-hearted, for they had seen the bottom fall out of their world. And so they died like flies. Such was the work of the "armies of freedom" from the North. Black people died for the same reasons that any peasant population in Europe would have died in comparable circumstances. If England had been devastated by foreign invasion, say during the reign of Henry III, manors would have been destroyed, and white villeins would have been deprived of their means of sustenance. They would have expired in shocking numbers.

After the fighting had ended, General Lee gave this testimony:

> "Q. Has the colored race generally as great a love of money and property as the white race possesses?

"A. I do not think it has. The blacks with whom I am acquainted look more to the present time than to the future.

"Q. Does the absence of lust for money and property arise more from the nature of the Negro than his former servile condition?

"A. Well, it may be, in some measure, attributable to his former condition. They are an amiable, social race. They like their ease and comfort, and, I think, look more to their present than to their future condition."[13]

Essentially, the new freemen were suddenly thrown out of a stable and familiar environment into the chaos and wreckage of a vanquished land. As General Lee suggested, they had no inculcated mentality for survival under those conditions. Consequently, as Judge Sharkey observed, former slaves "died off in immense numbers." Meanwhile, radical republicans congratulated themselves on what a wonderful thing they had accomplished for humanity.

Even if Andrew Johnson, a son of Tennessee, would have preferred a step at a time, he pressed for immediate abolition of slavery, and the South willingly assented. Nine of the thirteen States of the fallen Southern Confederacy[14] had ratified Amendment XIII when it was proclaimed adopted by the necessary majority of twenty-seven of thirty-six States as of December 18, 1865. Aside from the political impossibility of revoking the Proclamation Emancipation, the social fabric of the South had been seriously damaged by the War Between the States. Slavery had already been passing into extinction when calamity struck. Therefore, the only sane course was adaptation to irreversible changes.

The reconstructed governments of the South proceeded to enact statutes which, it was hoped, might get former slaves working again, and then to stay on the job until they had completed their tasks. Before the master's title gave him the right to enforce demands that his slaves finish their work. After slavery had been abolished, only wages and contracts could be used. In light of the previous conditioning of the enslaved race, there was cause to fear that the inducements of monetary gain and ordinary lawsuits would not be enough to make the work force reliable. James DeBow said of the new freemen in his State,

"If we can get the same amount of labor from the same persons, there is no doubt of the result in respect to economy. Whether the same amount of labor can be obtained, it is too soon yet to decide. We must allow one summer to pass first. They are now working very well on the plantations."[15]

When DeBow gave this testimony, he was probably thinking of an act earlier passed by the general assembly of Louisiana,[16] which read,

> "That all persons employed as laborers in agricultural pursuits shall be required, during the first ten days of the month of January of each year, to make contracts for labor for the then ensuing year, or for the year next ensuing the termination of their present contracts. All contracts for labor for agricultural purposes shall be made in writing, signed by the employer, and shall be made in the presence of a justice of the peace and two disinterested witnesses, in whose presence the contract shall be read to the laborer, and, when assented to and signed by the latter, shall be considered binding for the time prescribed."

The objective was to solemnize an undertaking, very much like the ritual prescribed for wills, in the hope that this much would rivet the agreement more firmly into memory. Then special provisions were inserted for the protection of the employer and the employee. The statute continued,

> "Every laborer shall have full and perfect liberty to choose his employer, but, when once chosen, he shall not be allowed to leave his place of employment until fulfillment of his contract. And if any such labor do leave, without cause or permission, he shall forfeit wages earned to the time of abandonment."

Another section provided,

> "Any employer failing to comply with his contract shall upon conviction be fined an amount double that due the laborer, to be paid to the laborer. And any inhumanity, cruelty, or neglect of duty on the part of the employer shall be summarily punished by fines to be paid to the injured party."

The statute was an attempt to replace a harness then outlawed with another believed lawful. Whereas slavery paid laborers by giving them food, shelter, goods, and privileges, the new system paid wages. Whereas slavery coerced work by the prospect of corporal or verbal punishment, the new system coerced work by the prospect of forfeited earnings. Whereas a master stingy, cruel, or negligent with his slaves met the universal reprobation and chastisement of his community, an employer not keeping his word, or cruel or negligent with his hired workers, was mulcted with double damages and monetary penalties under the new system.

There were also beneficial laws, such as an act of the legislature of Georgia, which provided,

"That persons of color shall have the right to make and enforce contracts, to sue, be sued, to be parties and give evidence, to inherit, to purchase, and to have full and equal benefit of all laws and proceedings for the security of person and estate, and shall not be subjected to any other or different punishment, pain, or penalty, for the commission of any act or offense, than such as are prescribed for white persons committing like acts or offences."[17]

Unfortunately, not all laws of the Southern States were as reasonable, for there was, as an illustration, an act of the legislature of Mississippi which stipulated,

"That all freedmen, free Negroes, and mulattos may sue and be sued, implead and be impleaded, in all the courts of law and equity of this State, and may acquire personal property, and choses in action, by descent or purchase, and may dispose of the same in the same manner and to the same extent that white persons may: Provided, That the provisions of this section shall not be so construed as to allow any freedman, free Negro, or mulatto, to rent or lease any lands or tenements except in incorporated cities or towns, in which places the corporate authorities shall control the same."[18]

The difference was that, whereas a black freeman in Georgia could hold a freehold or lease in lands, and thereby become an agricultural entrepreneur of substance, a black freeman in Mississippi he could not own a fee simple or life estate in any lands, nor could he even lease in the countryside to raise crops. The law adopted in Mississippi was frankly designed to keep the black race in a subordinate position. The pejorative term "black code" was coined to designate unfortunate statutes of this kind.

On occasion, however, this phrase was given a larger meaning in political discourse to signify laws of a kind prevailing in parts of the South such as Louisiana, which imposed transitional regulations inducing black workers to make adjustments necessary to their survival, but being severe on white employers who took advantage of former slaves. And sometimes, in an effort to smear the reformed governments of the Southern States with false propaganda, the phrase was used to designate even enlightened and farsighted statutes which wiped away most of the previous disabilities of freed black people, as enacted in Georgia.

* * * * *

As the 39th Congress of the United States met on December 3, 1865, President Andrew Johnson announced that most of the former rebel States had been restored to the Union. Not only had these States set up effective governments in republican form, but the judiciary of the Union had there been installed. Federal laws were enforced. Society and commerce had started to function more normally. The process of healing had begun.[19]

The Southern States elected representatives and senators to serve in Congress. Figures of great ability came forth. William Sharkey was chosen as a United States Senator from Mississippi. Alexander Stephens was chosen as a United States Senator from Georgia. Stephens later gave testimony which echoed the heart and mind of the whole South:

> "Q. What are the present views concerning the justice of the rebellion? Do they, at present, believe that it was a reasonable and proper undertaking, or otherwise?
>
> "A. My opinion of the sentiment of the people of Georgia upon that subject is that the exercise of the right of secession was resorted to by them from a desire to render their liberties and institutions more secure, and a belief on their part that this was absolutely necessary for that object. They were divided upon the question of the policy of the measure. There was, however, but very little division among them upon the question of the right of it. It is now their belief, in my opinion, that the surest, if not the only hope for their liberties is restoration of the Constitution of the United States and the government of the United States under the Constitution.
>
> "Q. Has there been any change of opinion as to the right of secession as a right in the people or in the States?"
>
> "A. I think there has been a very decided change of opinion as to the policy by those who favored it. I think the people generally are satisfied sufficiently with the experiment never to make resort to that measure of redress again by force, whatever may be their own abstract ideas upon that subject. They have given up all idea of the maintenance of those opinions by a resort to force. They have come to the conclusion that it is better to appeal to the forums of reason and justice, to the halls of legislation and the courts, for the preservation of the principles of constitutional liberty, than to the arena of arms. It is my settled conviction that there is not any idea cherished at all in the public mind of Georgia of ever resorting again to secession, or to the exercise of the right of secession, by force. That whole policy of the maintenance of their rights, in my opinion, is at this time totally abandoned."[20]

The founding fathers of the United States had understood that a peaceable and lawful right of secession was vested in and reserved to the people in convention in each of the several States. This right might have been exercised by Kentucky and Virginia when John Adams was President, by the States of New England when James Madison was President, and by South Carolina when Andrew Jackson was President, but in each case a better remedy was found, curing political ailments, rendering secession unnecessary and bringing renewed strength to the Union. Again this right was actually exercised by South Carolina when James Buchanan was President, and he had assured the South, in conformity with the fundamental law of the United States, that the government of the Union had no constitutional authority to use military means against a seceding State.

The unbounded evils of the American Civil war were in fact caused, as stated by James Buchanan during his retirement,[21] by the lawless arrogations of radical republicans in Washington, D.C. Abraham Lincoln was politically encumbered by his ties to these fellows, and he was pushed by them into provoking an unjust and unnecessary war. The experience brought him enormous suffering. And the intuitions of many scholars confidently sense that, when Lincoln refused to treat the South as conquered territory, his cohorts had him murdered.

No doubt, the views of Alexander Stephens and all in his school of thought were dreadful in the eyes of most members of Congress. And Stephens was prepared to lead the South in Congress, repeating these opinions so disdained by fanatics in the North.

When he surrendered his gallant army, General Joseph Johnston conceded only that the "hope of success by war" had been broken. But the principles of the South, being eternal, had not been tarnished in the slightest: — they were certain and fixed in the firmament of human intelligence, destined to be rediscovered in ages and confederacies yet unborn.

The hope of success was then to be taken to the "forums of reason and justice, to the halls of legislation and the courts." Alexander Stephens was returning to Congress. And against his massive knowledge and intellect there was nobody who could stand. Stephens had already sketched out speeches he would have made in the Senate. In the entry for June 5, 1865, in the diary he kept while in prison in Boston, Stephens had written these earnest words:

> "[The people of the South] conscientiously believed that the old Union was a compact between Sovereign Independent States; only certain powers named in the Constitution had been delegated by the States separately to the Central Government; among these was not

ultimate absolute Sovereignty, this being retained by the States separately in the reserved powers; each State had the right to withdraw
from the Central Government to powers delegated by repealing the
ordinance that conferred them and herself resuming their full exercise as a free Independent Sovereign State, such as she was when the
compact of the Union under the Constitution was formed. These
principles and doctrines the great majority cherished as sacred and as
underlying the whole framework of American constitutional liberty.
Thousands who disapproved of secession as a measure did not question it as a matter of right. The war waged by the Central Government
against the States, striking at their Sovereignty and causing as it
would, if successful, their complete subjugation, these people considered unconstitutional, monstrously aggressive, and utterly
destructive to everything dear to them as freemen."[22]

Yet, there was a Congressman from Pennsylvania, Thaddeus Stevens
by name, like Maximillien Robespierre in temperament, who cunningly
surveyed the situation, and saw that, unless he worked a drastic usurpation, democrats from the North and the South, and moderate republicans
would join together, and with the aid of President Johnson, they would
prevent him and other extremists from venting their spleens against the
South. By incredible strong-arming he seized the moment. On December
13, 1865, the House and Senate resolved,

> "That a joint committee of fifteen members shall be appointed, nine
> of whom shall be members from the House, and six of members of the
> Senate, who shall inquire into the condition of the States which formed
> the so-called Confederate States of America, and report whether they,
> or any of them, are entitled to be represented in either House of
> Congress, with leave to report at any time, by bill or otherwise."[23]

Stevens ran this Joint Committee of Fifteen on Reconstruction, which
in turn ran Congress. The committee held, in so many words, that William
Sharkey, Alexander Stephens, and other white Southerners were not
morally and politically fit to serve in Congress, even though they were
lawfully elected as prescibed by the United States Constitution and the
laws of their respective States, and presented returns or certificates in
proper form. The first clause of Article I, Section 5 of the United States
Constitution says, "Each House shall be the Judge of the Elections,
Returns, and Qualifications of its own Members."[24] It was settled before
the outbreak of the American Revolution that the exclusion of John
Wilkes from the British House of Commons on such moral and political
grounds was unconstitutional. The exclusion on such grounds of anyone

lawfully elected to Parliament was condemned in organic statutes,[25] and the same guarantees to duly elected legislators was naturally understood as having been transferred to representatives and senators in Congress.

Stevens' committee recommended and Congress concurred in exclusion of senators and representatives of eleven Southern States, not including Missouri and Kentucky, on the grounds that those States had dared to secede from the Union, and so, according to the theory used, had forfeited all civil and political rights under the United States Constitution.[26] Because these States had been deemed competent to adopt Amendment XIII, the conclusions of Stevens' committee were rank dishonesty, and the approval of those conclusions by Congress was gross lawlessness. From thenceforward the 39th Congress ceased to exist as a lawful institution. It continued only as had the "rump" of puritan grandees after the purge of Colonel Pride.

Some not unreasonable legislation was passed by the 39th Congress before things got completely out of hand, including an Act of April 9, 1866, which provided:

> "That all persons born in the United States and not subject to any foreign power, excluding Indians not taxed, are hereby declared to be citizens of the United States; and such citizens, of every race and color, without regard to any previous condition of slavery or involuntary servitude, except as a punishment for crime whereof the party shall have been convicted, shall have the same right, in every State and Territory in the United States, to make and enforce contracts, to sue, be parties, and give evidence, to inherit, purchase, lease sell, hold and convey real or personal property, and to full and equal benefit of all laws for the security of person and property, as is enjoyed by white citizens, and shall be subject to like punishment, pains, and penalties, and to none other, any law, statute, ordinance regulation, or custom to the contrary notwithstanding."[27]

The thinking behind this statute was that Amendment XIII of the United States Constitution had not only abolished slavery in express language, but by implication had removed any supposed incapacity of black people to become American citizens. And so as to remove any lingering doubts, Congress went ahead and naturalized all black freemen who had been born in the United States. Moreover, in exercise of its express power under Amendment XIII, Congress merely affirmed by statute what had already been enacted by the legislature of Georgia, on the advice and with the approbation, it may be added, of none other than Alexander Stephens.

It is true that President Johnson had interposed a veto which was overridden,[28] but his concern, even if erroneous, was understandable. "If Congress can declare by law who shall hold lands, who shall testify, who shall have capacity to make a contract in a State," he said, "then Congress can by law also declare who, without regard to color or race, shall have the right to sit as a juror, or as a judge, to hold any office, and, finally, to vote in any State or Territory of the United States."

The act, as written, addressed civil capacities and rights which had belonged to freemen at common law and under fundamental law through- out the United States since the American Revolution. It should be recalled that, even in England, every freeman, however destitute in worldly pos- sessions, was allowed to work for reasonable wages, make contracts, bring suits, and give evidence, — every freeman was immune from arrest or search on general warrant, every freeman was privileged against being compelled to witness against himself, etc. Such civil capacities and rights were addressed in the Act of April 9, 1866.

But there were a few civil capacities and rights of a higher order: — these were not conferred upon every freeman either at common law or by fundamental law; they included the capacity to vote or to sit on a jury.[29] These in particular were usually conditioned on having a freehold. Therefore, President Johnson was simply mistaken in his assumption that, if under Amendment XIII Congress could guarantee a former slave the right to sue and give evidence, so likewise Congress could give him the capacity to be a juror or the right to vote.

It is true that another amendment to the United States Constitution might have been prudent, not necessarily because the legislative power was not to be found, but to remove doubts entertained by some eminent statesmen such as Andrew Johnson over the legitimacy of statutes like the Act of April 9, 1866. But a problem arose, because the new amendment was to be framed by the Joint Committee of Fifteen on Reconstruction, and, given such a source, no end of mischief became inevitable.

* * * * *

On June 16, 1866, a resolution of Congress proposed what has since been called "Amendment XIV" of the United States Constitution. The first section is obviously of enduring interest. It contains language which has since been subjected to massive commentary and erudition, including page after page of quoted speeches and debates, attempting to show that the "framers intended" very much or almost nothing.[30] The representatives and senators swayed back and forth, contradicting themselves and each other, hopelessly confounded on occasion, sometimes giving incomplete definitions from law dictionaries, and other garbled formulations, never seeming to appreciate the meaning of the technical terms they used.

Fortunately, it is not necessary to read the journal of the Joint Committee of Fifteen on Reconstruction, nor is it necessary to read the ensuing debates in the House and Senate. The "intended meaning," as Alexander Hamilton defined it in his Opinion on the Bank, is really not so difficult to grasp. There are four main provisions in the first section, and their basic sense can be discerned easily enough by clear reasoning from known premises.

The first section began, "All persons born or naturalized in the United States, and subject to the jurisdiction thereof, are citizens of the United States and of the State wherein they reside."

It is obvious and nobody has ever denied that these words were supposed to correct Chief Justice Roger B. Taney's disposition of the plea in abatement in *Dred Scott v. Sandford*, 19 Howard 391 at 404-427 (U. S. 1857). The inference is that Chief Justice William Gaston was right in *State v. Manuel*, 4 Dev. & B. 20 at 24-25 (N. C. 1838). Every slave, however or whenever emancipated, became a citizen of the place of his birth the moment he became free. The common law of England ordained that a person was a subject of the King if born anywhere within territory subject to the jurisdiction of the Crown. It mattered not whether his parents were subjects of another prince or citizens of another nation. This rule, called the "lex soli" or law of the soil, was reaffirmed as a constitutional principle in Amendment XIV, as it had been understood at the time of the Philadelphia Convention.

The first section of Amendment XIV continued, "No State shall make or enforce any law which shall abridge the privileges and immunities of citizens of the United States."

It is generally that the phrase "privileges and immunities" in Amendment XIV was derived from the first clause of Article IV, Section 2 of the United States Constitution, and that the phrase in Article IV, Section 2 was correctly defined by Justice Bushrod Washington in *Corfleld v. Coryell*, 6 Fed. Cas. 546 (U.S. Cir. Ct. E. D. Pa. 1823). Justice Washington held that privileges and immunities protected by the first clause of Article IV, Section 2 did not include the right to take oysters for commercial purposes, because such privileges and immunities were limited to the fundamental rights which belonged to the citizens of the several States from the time of their independence under republican constitutions at the time of the American Revolution. Such fundamental rights included free exercise of religion, holding and disposing of real or personal property, enjoying the benefit of the writ of habeas corpus, and so on This construction was particularly apt, because the phrase "privileges and immunities" was drawn from the fourth article of the old Confederation, which distinguished the "privileges and immunities of free citizens" from "privileges of trade and commerce."

Lest there be any doubt, reference might be had to the 84th Federalist where Alexander Hamilton cited a passage from Blackstone's chapter on the "absolute rights of individuals." The passage referred to liberal availability of the writ of habeas corpus, which, Hamilton said, was the "bulwark of the British constitution."[31]

Again, it is generally conceded that privileges and immunities included those absolute rights of individuals described by Blackstone.[32] In expounding those absolute rights, the commentator mentioned life, liberty, reputation, property, due process of law, the writ of habeas corpus, bringing suit in courts of justice, petitioning the government for redress of grievances, even keeping and bearing arms, — in other words, the constitutional rights of freemen.

In Article IV, Section 2, the reference is to the privileges and immunities of citizens of the several States, — i. e., the rights of freemen under the constitutions of the several States. Therefore, where the first section of Amendment XIV refers to the privileges and immunities of citizens of the United States, the meaning could only have been any and all rights of freemen guaranteed by the United States Constitution, including the Federal Bill of Rights and the limitations on suspending the writ of habeas corpus in Article I, Section 9.

It was known what Chief Justice John Marshall had held in *Barron v. Baltimore*, 7 Peters 243 (U. S. 1833), — namely, that the Federal Bill of Rights framed in 1789 did not restrain the governments of the several States. Manifestly, the language concerining privileges and immunities in Amendment XIV was intended to reverse Marshall's holding, so as to "incorporate" entirely, and thus restrain the governments of the several States with all provisions in the United States Constitution which define privileges and immunities of citizens of the United States.[33]

The first section of Amendment XIV then said, "Nor shall any State deprive any person of life, liberty, or property without due process of law."

It is pretty clear what this clause was meant to cure. The framers of the United States Constitution understood the prohibition of ex post facto laws in the first clause of Article I, Section 10 of the United States Constitution as a prohibition of all retroactive legislation, whether criminal or civil, including all laws taking away rights of contract, property, or suit after they had vested.[34] Over many years, the prohibition of ex post facto laws had been misinterpreted: — outside criminal prosecution or the regulation of contracts, there was supposedly nothing in the fundamental law of the Union to prevent the several States from taking away established rights without due process of law. So stood the unfortunate opinion of Justice Washington in *Satterlee v. Matthewson*, 2 Peters 380 (U. S. 1829), which had carried this notion to the furthest extremity. The guarantee of due process of law in Amendment XIV was intended to correct this judicial mistake.

Finally, the first section of Amendment XIV provided, "Nor" shall any State "deny to any person within its jurisdiction equal protection of the laws." This renowned clause was originally designed to nullify statutes like the act of the legislature of Mississippi which denied black freemen the right to acquire freeholds or even to lease land in the countryside. The provision was designed to offset all such unjust class legislation against black people.

The question was bound to arise whether this guarantee of equal protection of the laws was meant to prohibit racial segregation of public facilities.

Such consequences most certainly were not contemplated during the session of the rump Congress which began to deliberate in December 1865. But there was one very remarkable exception in the person of Charles Sumner, who, not long before his election as Senator from Massachusetts, made an eloquent argument before the supreme court of his State that separate public schools for black children were not allowed by the fundamental law of the Commonwealth: — such institutions, he said, were inherently unequal because racially segregated.[35] Sumner did not prevail in his plea against racially segregated public schools in Boston, yet his dream continued to fluorish as an idea. In any event, there can be no doubt how Sumner read the guarantee of equal protection of the laws in Amendment XIV.

Thaddeus Stevens, on the other hand, was fanatical about punishing the South, but he had no stomach for facing the overwhelming sentiment in the North where a morbid and awful Negrophobia prevailed among whites. The very thought of racial integration in public transportation and schools would have made Stevens' blood run cold. He felt dread to his very bones when the famous black abolitionist and orator Frederick Douglass paraded arm-in-arm with white newspaper editor Thomas Tilton.

During the years following the war in all parts of the United States, the white race continued to stand in an unquestionably dominant and superior position in society over the black race. Racial integration of public facilities, it is true, was not a subject which any "proper gentleman" would in those days have brought up at the dinner table.

But in the South these two branches of humanity remained intimately familiar with each other, as they had always been. In 1865 slavery disappeared in the South, but not previous attachments between white and black people. In the South black families typically adopted their "white folks." Very often slaves remained with their old masters, and things continued almost unchanged as if emancipation had never occurred. The two races took care of each other as they had always done. When a black family and a white family became attached, the sentimental ties could last for generations. Black mammies were known to nurse white infants born of Confederate veterans. White couples visited the homes of their black people, seeing after their needs and welfare. So it was in the South, — unfathomable and curious it was, yet somehow or other it worked.

It is not easy to make legal deductions from the historical background of Amendment XIV. Certainly, at the time Amendment XIV was framed, the great preponderance of legal opinion held that equal protection of the laws did not prohibit racial segregation of public schools.[36] But this consideration is not necessarily decisive, because, while constitutional principles remain the same and are themselves timeless, they apply to human conditions as they are filled out with natural maturation of society and its component parts.[37] Of all things in human experience the interaction between races is an evolving reality.

And so, viewing history as a great panorama, Sumner's dream was destined ultimately to prevail. This perspective on things also explains why racial segregation of public schools would certainly have come to an end in the South even if independence had been conceded to the Confederate States. The pace would have been more gradual, natural, and harmonious, because it would have been adapted to the needs of both races,[38] but it would inevitably have occurred.

The fifth section of Amendment XIV, like the second section of Amendment XIII, was intended to give Congress the power of enacting "appropriate legislation" or laws necessary and proper for implementation of the substantive provisions.

Aside from these main provisions in the first and fifth sections, a number of other clauses are found in Amendment XIV, and these are mainly of historical interest.

The second section of Amendment XIV was an express repeal of the reference to "three fifths of all other persons" in the third clause of Article I, Section 2, which followed naturally from the abolition of slavery, but otherwise leaving the population index for apportionment of representatives and direct taxes in place as framed by the Philadelphia Convention. All black freemen were to be counted one for one, whereas slaves had been counted three for five. Then, however, the second section inserted a proviso in language to the effect that, if the new black freemen were as a class denied the right to vote in any given State, the number of such freemen would not be counted at all in determining the number of representatives such State should have in Congress.

The right to vote, it will be recalled, was of a higher order than usual privileges and immunities of citizens, traditionally conditioned on ownership of a freehold. This right, therefore, was left essentially untouched by the first section of Amendment XIV. The second section made clear that the several States were left with the discretion not to enfranchise black freemen, but only if such States were willing to suffer reduced representation in Congress.

Because the black population was then relatively small in the North, the second section of Amendment XIV had little meaning in those States. The effect of the second section of Amendment XIV was designed to be felt mainly in the South, which, being heavily outnumbered, needed as much representation as possible in the lower chamber of Congress. Interestingly enough, while this provision was being framed in Congress, General Lee was asked whether the South would be opposed to such inducement for enfranchising black freemen, and he answered,

> "So far as I can see, I do not think the State of Virginia would object to it. If she had the right of determining that, I do not see why she should object. If it were to her interest to admit these people to vote, that might overrule any other objection that she had to it."[39]

The fourth section of Amendment XIV was a gift to the money lenders who financed the North in its war against the South. The public debt of the Union, it said, "shall not be questioned." That kept the houses of Rothschild and Morgan happy. They could argue on the basis of this provision that they were entitled to every penny in good coin, with full interest, however excessive.

But the public debt of the South, incurred in fighting the "insurrection or rebellion" was declared "illegal and void." The said public debt of the South consisted of treasury notes and bonds of governments no longer in existence. The bankers in London, Paris, New York, and Philadelphia lost not a dime, so they cared not. And anyway, conventions of the people in the South had already repudiated that public debt. This redundancy was inserted as political window dressing.

In all corrupt legislation, there is hidden a "killer" clause, which is really the heart of the matter, and, this appeared in the third section of Amendment XIV:

> "No person shall be a Senator or Representative in Congress, or elector of President and Vice-President, or hold any office, civil or military, under the United States, or under any State, who, having previously taken an oath, as a member of Congress, or as an officer of the United States, or as a member of any State legislature, or as an executive or judicial officer of any State, to support the Constitution of the United States, shall have engaged in insurrection or rebellion against the same, or given aid and comfort to the enemies thereof. But Congress may by a vote of two-thirds of each House, remove such disability."

When Alexander Stephens had been in Congress with Abraham Lincoln, he took an oath supporting the United States Constitution, which he rightly understood to have created a confederacy of free, sovereign, and independent States. When Robert E. Lee had fought with Ulysses Grant in the Mexican War, he had taken a like oath in the same understanding. When Stephens and Lee went with their States around the time of Fort Sumter, they did so out of obedience to the people of their States in convention, which had previously established the Union.

Stephens and Lee went as patriots, wishing that there had been no secessions in Georgia and Virginia, but standing by their fellow citizens. They fought a war of independence, not an insurrection or a rebellion. Their land was conquered by those who had usurped a republic, converted it into a dictatorship, threw dissidents in prison, suspended the writ of habeas corpus, conscripted lads to be slaughtered in battles mismanaged by incompetent generals, and mortgaged the country to interests desiring only to exploit. If Stephens and Lee were wrong, then Jefferson and Washington were wrong, and Magna Carta never was.

The objective of the third section of Amendment XIV was to deprive the South of her greatest leaders, including the likes of Alexander Stephens who favored statutes removing civil disabilities of black freemen, and Robert E. Lee who was willing to see votes cast by black freemen. The third section was designed to assure the political resistance of the South against Amendment XIV, which was then to be blamed for oppressing the black race. And thereupon such resistance was to be used as a false pretext to make a penitentiary of the South. Such was the dark and awful plan of Thaddeus Stevens and his faction.

* * * * *

The ratifications of Southern States had secured the adoption of Amendment XIII. Yet eleven Southern States were illegally locked out of Congress, which, therefore, could not even propose Amendment XIV. But Congress went ahead anyway.[40]

Article V of the United States Constitution prescribes that two-thirds of the House and Senate are required to propose a constitutional amendment. Although the most respectable reasons exist for saying that this two-thirds must be two-thirds seated members in each chamber, it appears that two-thirds of a quorum present had by then been considered sufficient for this purpose ever since the presidency of George Washington.[41] In the United States House of Representatives in the 39th Congress, there were one hundred eighty-four seated members, of which all but two were present on June 13, 1866. Therefore, even disregarding the illegal exclusion of Southern representatives, and conceding the need of only two-thirds of a quorum present, one hundred twenty-two yeas were necessary. Only one hundred twenty votes were cast in favor of the resolution, thirty-two voted against, and thirty abstained.

Therefore, the measure did not pass, but the speaker ruled that only two-thirds of those present and voting yea or nay were needed. The resolution was declared passed. Out Amendment XIV illegally went to the legislatures of the several States.[42]

There were thirty-seven States then in the Union, twenty-eight States were needed for adoption, and ten States could defeat the measure. It had been understood from the days of the First Congress, through the adoption of all thirteen amendments up to that time, that each State might vote for or against, whereupon its option was exhausted.[43] By March 23, 1867, exactly twenty-one States had ratified,[44] and twelve States, all below the Mason-Dixon Line or the Ohio River, had rejected,[45] and so, by every standard then known in the fundamental law of the Union, Amendment XIV was defeated.

Nobody, least of all Thaddeus Stevens, was surprised. His plan was going like clockwork. In fact, ten States had already rejected and so defeated Amendment XIV by January 30, 1867. By this time, Stevens was "the boss" of the United States. He secured, on March 2, 1867, the first of the so-called "Reconstruction Acts."[46] The statute was enacted over the veto of President Johnson, who, although great in courage, had been reduced to a powerless functionary.[47]

The act placed the States of the fallen Southern Confederacy, excepting Missouri, Kentucky, and Tennessee, under martial law in time of profound peace. The act then stipulated that these ten States should not enjoy civilian government, until they had, by processes excluding anyone disqualified by the third section of Amendment XIV, called new conventions of the people, and established new constitutions, and until these new constitutions had been approved by Congress. The act went on to say that no such State should be entitled to representation in Congress, until its legislature had ratified Amendment XIV.

Thaddeus Stevens and his partisans knew that this statute was shockingly irregular, as immediately appears to anyone who has ever read the debates in Congress when Thomas Jefferson had asked for limited suspension of the writ of habeas corpus to deal with the treason of Aaron Burr. The United States Supreme Court had already spoken in the case of Lamdin Milligan. Even so, on July 21, 1868, Congress by joint resolution declared Amendment XIV ratified.

Attempts have been made to save Amendment XIV by saying that, since Article V of the United States Constitution speaks only of ratification, a State may reject and then ratify, but cannot ratify and then rescind.[48] The theory is a reprehensible concoction, and no pretense, however elaborate, can ever save it. But even if taken as correct, Amendment XIV cannot thereby be rescued, because necessary ratifications were coerced by the Act of March 2, 1867.[49] Congress had dared to impose martial law and suspend the writ of habeas corpus, not to deal with an armed rebellion or invasion, but to coerce States to adopt Amendment XIV. The article was never lawfully adopted, because necessary ratifications were coerced by the duress of martial law. It was a time of national shame not yet amply regretted.

* * * * *

The country was in anarchy. President Johnson made a speech at the White House on August 18, 1866, — shortly after the adjournment of the first session of the rump Congress which had excluded the South. He said with great truth,

"We have witnessed in one department of the government every endeavor to prevent the restoration of peace, harmony, and union. We see hanging upon the verge of the government, as it were, a body called, or which assumes to be the Congress of the United States, while in fact it is a Congress of only part of the States. We have seen this Congress pretend to be for the Union, when its every step has tended to perpetuate disunion and make a disruption of the States inevitable. We have seen Congress gradually encroach, step by step, upon constitutional rights, and violate, day after day and month after month, fundamental principles of the government. We have seen a Congress that has seemed to forget that there was a limit to the sphere and scope of legislation. We have seen a Congress in a minority assume to exercise power which, allowed to be consummated, would result in despotism or monarchy itself."[50]

Moreover, before so many months had passed after he became President, Andrew Johnson saw through Edwin Stanton, and decided he must go. He wanted a new secretary of war who would work to reintegrate the South back into the Union.

From the early days of the government, there had been a dispute over how, aside from impeachment, cabinet officers might lawfully be removed. The United States Constitution is silent on this point, and so the question has had to turn on legal inference. On June 16, 1789, there was an important debate on this question in the House in Congress, and prominent speakers included framers of the United States Constitution.[51]

Roger Sherman maintained that a cabinet officer could not be removed by the President without the advice and consent of the Senate, since the power of removal was, so he thought, tied to the power of appointment.

James Madison reasoned that removal of a cabinet officer is inherently an executive power, that executive power was vested by the constitution solely in the President and there it remains save where the constitution itself creates an exception, and that, whereas the executive power of appointment was qualified by the advice and consent of the Senate, the executive power of removal was not so qualified. Therefore, he held, Congress has no constitutional authority to deprive the President of the right to remove cabinet officers.

Abraham Baldwin believed that, in the exercise of its power to enact necessary and proper laws, Congress might create public offices, and define tenure as it saw fit. Baldwin thought that Congress could prescribe by law whether an executive office would expire at the pleasure of the President, or by the advice and consent of the Senate, or in some other manner.

As it was, the statutes on the books since the time of George

Washington generally made cabinet officers removable at the pleasure of the President.[52]

On the same day the first of the Reconstruction Acts was passed, Thaddeus Stevens saw to it that a Tenure of Office Act was also legislated.[53] The statute said that the President could not remove the secretary of war without the advice and consent of the Senate. Johnson had interposed a veto, relying on the opinion of Madison, and holding the bill unconstitutional.[54] But so far had the people in the Northern States degenerated into an attitude of servility and oppression that they gave Stevens the practical capacity, as long as the South was excluded, to command a majority of two-thirds either in the House, or in the Senate. He had the means at his disposal to secure the passage of any law he wished, and even to impeach anyone he pleased.

President Johnson was in danger, and he must have known it, but he went ahead for the good of his country on February 21, 1868, to order the removal of Edwin Stanton, and to appoint General Lorenzo Thomas as interim secretary of war.

With lightning speed, on February 24, 1868, the House of Representatives, urged on by Stevens, voted a resolution to impeach Johnson. The articles were displayed to the Senate in eleven counts on March 2 and 3, 1868, charging Johnson mainly with unlawful removal of Stanton, and various speeches questioning the legality and policy of the rump Congress.

A President can be impeached for culpable lawlessness, but this President was impeached for acting upon the carefully reasoned conclusions of James Madison, the principal legal architect of the United States Constitution. And Johnson's judgment in following Madison's view on the question was later expressly upheld by the United States Supreme Court.[55] Johnson got rid of Stanton, because the man was dangerous and disloyal.

The count for making speeches against the rump Congress was reminiscent of a political circus in 1628. The reverend Dr. Roger Mainwaring gave a colorful sermon in the presence of Charles I. Those who refused to pay taxes upon the command of his Majesty, said the clergyman, "did offend the law of God and the King's supreme authority." Those words were melodious to princely ears, but not to the liking of the House of Commons. The royalist parson was impeached, convicted, and punished. The comedy ended when the King pardoned Mainwaring and made him a bishop. The case was laughed out of court, and his Majesty was praised for benevolence. The practice of impeaching public men for political speeches was thus erased from the lex parliamentaria of England, and only the likes of Thaddeus Stevens could revive an abuse so obnoxious in the United States.

When Andrew Johnson was President, the times were as crazy as the days when a few burgesses and knights of the shire presumed to abolish the House of Lords and try the King. The government of the United States was flooded with notorious corruption. The so-called "trial" of Andrew Johnson was not even civilized.[56] Judge Benjamin Curtis came up from his law office in Boston to defend the President. Chief Justice Salmon P. Chase did his best to maintain order, but his efforts were not enough. Senators were bought and bullied. Senators raving with bigotry announced prejudgment.

On May 16, 1868, the roll-call vote was taken on the critical eleventh article of impeachment, an omnibus accusation which tied all counts together. There were fifty-four senators, and thirty-six votes were needed for conviction. Thirty-five votes against the President were secure. The key vote belonged to Senator Edmund Ross of Kansas. Congressman Ben Butler, a House manager on the impeachment said in exasperation of Senator Ross, "Here is a bushel of money! How much does that damned fool want?" Before the vote was taken, Ross was told in ominous tones, by Thaddeus Stevens himself, that a vote for acquittal would mean the trumped up charges and personal ruin. Ross looked down into his open grave and voted "not guilty." The vote was thirty-five to nineteen, and a judgment of acquittal was entered.

There was an adjournment for ten days, and, upon resumption of proceedings, Ross again held firm, and the vote was again thirty-five "guilty" and nineteen "not guilty" on the second and third counts, and accordingly judgments of acquittal were entered. On May 26, 1868, a motion was made for adjournment sine die, which was in effect a vote for acquittal on all remaining counts, since the rules of the Senate required a judgment of acquittal on any count on which a vote of two-thirds was not obtained. The motion passed on vote of thirty-four to sixteen. Thereupon, the Chief Justice intoned, "It is ordered and adjudged, That the said Andrew Johnson, President of the United States, be, and he is acquitted of the charges in said articles made and set forth."

The aftermath teaches something about the deeper meaning of life.

Thaddeus Stevens died within a few months.

Edwin Stanton was appointed Justice of the United States Supreme Court by President Ulysses Grant, but died before he could take his seat.

Andrew Johnson served out his term as President, then returned to the town of Washington as a Senator from Tennessee.

Edmund Ross served out his term in the Senate, shunned by his colleagues, then went home to Kansas. He was socially ostracized and never reelected to public office. He and his family were confronted with physical danger and near poverty. Only later in life was he rewarded when President Grover Cleveland appointed him as governor of the New Mexico Territory. He resembled William Colvill, the commanding officer of the 1st Minnesota who led his men in an act of superhuman bravery on the second day of Gettysburg. In the summer of 1865, Colvill was mustered out as a brevet brigadier general. As a war hero he was elected attorney general of his State. In office he endorsed the policies of Andrew Johnson for reconciliation with the South. He was promptly defeated for reelection as attorney general, and his political career was ruined. Yet Colvill was still much loved by old friends and soldiers. In advanced years, while attending a veterans' meeting, he died peacefully in his sleep.

* * * * *

It remains to consider what Salmon P. Chase was doing on the bench in those troubled times. He and his colleagues were doing their best to avoid any confrontation with the radical republicans in Congress.

In *Mississippi v. Johnson*, 4 Wallace 475 (U. S. 1867), a rebel State sued the President, invoking the original jurisdiction of the United States Supreme Court under Section 13 of the Judiciary Act of 1789, and seeking an injunction enjoining execution of the Reconstruction Acts. Previous decisions actually obliged dismissal of the suit for want of jurisdiction in the United States Supreme Court.[57] And so everything which Chief Justice Chase said in this case was technically coram non judice, — judicial opinion without authoritative meaning, worthy of no legal consideration or weight.

Chase assumed that original jurisdiction existed. He said that, if Johnson were enjoined and refused, the Supreme Court could not enforce its injunction, — but, if Johnson was enjoined and obeyed, then the House of Representatives might impeach him, yet then the Supreme Court would have been obliged to enjoin a trial in the Senate, which would be unthinkable. He did not say why it would be unthinkable, but the reason was he did not wish to be impeached himself. He dismissed the suit as nonjusticiable, — as involving a legal question of such political difficulty or magnitude that the judiciary ought not touch it.

Another suit was brought by a rebel State, seeking an injunction against the secretary of war, enjoining him from executing the Reconstruction Acts. In *Georgia v. Stanton*, 6 Wallace 50 (U.S. 1868), the opinion of the court was written by Justice Samuel Nelson. He could have held there was no original jurisdiction under Section 13 of the Judiciary Act of 1789, but preferred to say that his tribunal had no jurisdiction to enforce political as opposed to personal or proprietary rights. The distinction was only a pretext for not touching a question too explosive.

Then came *Ex Parte McCardle*, 6 Wallace 77 (U. S. 1868), 7 Wallace 506 (U. S. 1869). A newspaper editor in the South was arrested for publishing an alleged criminal libel. The charge against him was set for trial before a military commission. He petitioned a circuit court of the United States for a writ of habeas corpus under Section 14 of the Judiciary Act of 1789. The return pleaded the Reconstruction Act. Discharge was denied by the circuit court, which nevertheless released the editor on bail pending review on appeal under a certain Act of February 5, 1867,[58] with a view to testing the constitutionality of the Reconstruction Acts which could not possibly stand in light of *Ex Parte Milligan*, 4 Wallace 2 (U. S. 1866). On February 17, 1868, jurisdiction on appeal was upheld. The event was noticed by Thaddeus Stevens, as he initiated impeachment against Andrew Johnson. Stevens secured an Act of March 27, 1868,[59] which repealed the Act of February 5, 1867.

When Stevens died on August 11, 1868, there were others to take his place. In the Federal elections held on November 3, 1868, the republicans promised to pay up the national debt in gold coin, thereby assisting the beneficiaries of the fourth section of Amendment XIV. They damned Andrew Johnson and praised the Reconstruction Acts. They spoke of the "bloody shirt of the rebellion" to justify their vindictiveness, and the people of the North fell for it again. Continued dominance of the republicans in Congress demanded the continued exclusion of the South. In this dynamic situation, Salmon P. Chase understood the currents of power in the country. In behalf of the court, he could have held that the repeal of the Act of February 5, 1867, had prospective effect only, and then addressed the merits of McCardle's appeal. Instead he found that the Act of March 27, 1868, caused the jurisdiction of his court to lapse, and he dismissed the appeal.

Not long thereafter, in *Ex Parte Yerger*, 8 Wallace 85 (U. S. 1869), a Federal circuit court in Mississippi denied a writ of habeas corpus to a Southerner who was about to be tried before a military commission under the Reconstruction Acts. Chief Justice Chase held that, even though an appeal was no longer possible because of the Act of March 27, 1868, the United States Supreme Court could issue a writ of certiorari and a writ of habeas under Section 14 of the Judiciary Act of 1789 to review the judgment of the circuit court. Thereby Chase applied the very principle which had earlier been denied in the case of Congressman Vallandigham. But

Yerger was released from custody as the "reconstructed" government of Mississippi went into operation, and his case was dismissed as moot.

The most important case in this series was *Texas v. White*, 7 Wallace 700 (U. S. 1869). The military governor of Texas under the Reconstruction Acts brought suit, invoking the original jurisdiction of the United States Supreme Court. The military governor sought an injunction against the holders of Federal bonds which had been transferred to the State under the Compromise of 1850. After the beginning of hostilities in 1861, the secessionist government of the State had negotiated these bonds to the defendants as payment for medicines and other supplies needed in the war effort. A motion was made to dismiss the suit on the grounds that Texas was a conquered territory governed under the Reconstruction Acts, and as such was not a State of the Union when the suit was brought, as required by Section 13 of the Judiciary Act of 1789.

Speaking for the court, Chief Justice Chase denied the motion, and allowed the suit to proceed. Drawing from the thirteenth article of the old Confederation of 1781 and the preamble to the new Union of 1789, he held that the United States are a perpetual Union made more perfect, and therefore "an indestructible Union of indestructible States." And so Texas, according to Chase, had always been a State, and had never seceded from the Union.

Chase's sophistry is easy enough to penetrate. The old Confederation was lawfully dissolved without consent of all the States, even though the old Confederation was by its articles ordained as perpetual and could not be amended save by consent of all the States. The new Union was more perfect, because it was established by the people of each State in convention and thus could not be dissolved by mere legislative repeal as could the old Confederation. Yet the people of each State in convention retained their sovereign attributes, including ultimate power to make or unmake any constitution, government, or union. And the people of Texas had exercised this ultimate power in 1861, in lawfully seceding from the Union. These lucid and basic principles were not acknowledged by Chase, because he had served in Lincoln's cabinet, and, as secretary of the treasury, had arranged the financing of the military conquest of the Southern States. He was in no position to pronounce the law, and so he pronounced something else.

The military governor of Texas derived his authority from the Reconstruction Acts, which were unconstitutional as everybody then knew, even if nobody was prepared to admit it officially. Therefore, the military governor had no standing to bring suit. But Chase evaded this large and demanding question without explanation, because the question could not be answered without admitting that the Southern States had been unlawfully deprived of their republican forms of government and unlawfully coerced into adopting Amendment XIV.

Justice Robert Grier had a more brutal and honest view of the case, which he stated in dissent: — the question of secession had been decided by battle; the judiciary could do nothing about it, whether the result of the war were just or unjust; all legal issues raised were therefore nonjusticiable, and the suit should have been dismissed.

Chase's opinion ought to recall the bold assertion of Lord Camden when he released John Wilkes on a writ of habeas corpus to permit the legislator's attendance in Parliament.[60] Camden referred to the decrepit holding of the King's Bench in 1688 that the Seven Bishops could be denied bail when charged with the misdemeanor of criminal libel. "The case is not law," he said, "but it shows the miserable condition of the state at that time."

* * * * *

In any event, Amendment XV became a part of the United States Constitution when it was promulgated by the secretary of state on March 30, 1870. The first section says, "The right of citizens of the United States to vote shall not be denied or abridged by the United States or by any State on account of race, color, or previous condition of servitude." And the second section provides, "The Congress shall have power to enforce this article by appropriate legislation."

Black freemen were to enjoy a constitutional right to vote, which was a privilege traditionally reserved to freeholders. And enjoying such a right, they could not thereafter be lawfully denied any of the constitutional rights of freemen under any republican form of government guaranteed by Article IV, Section 4 of the United States Constitution. The entire constitutional legacy of the American Revolution lurks in the promise that every State shall enjoy a republican form of government. Everything good ever hoped for in the name of Amendment XIV, that and more can be found in an enlightened interpretation of Article IV, Section 4, — an interpretation not judicially invented, but rooted in natural law and legal tradition. With this giant thought, pregnant with hope, there is no longer a reason to fear the reality, which someday must be faced, that Amendment XIV never was lawfully adopted.

Yet there remains a lesson of even greater and deeper import. When Alexander Stephens retired to "ses chères études," as have many men ahead of their times, he wrote his magnum opus. His dedication, here shortened and reworded only slightly lest there be any misunderstanding of his powerful insight, is worth thinking about:

TO ALL FRIENDS OF CONSTITUTIONAL LIBERTY, THE WORLD OVER, NOW AND FOREVER — ESPECIALLY TO ALL, EVERYWHERE, WHO MAY NOW OR HEREAFTER LOOK TO THE FEDERATIVE SYSTEM, BETWEEN NEIGHBORING FREE DEMOCRATIC STATES, AS THE SUREST MEANS OF SAVING MANKIND FROM AN ULTIMATE UNIVERSAL CENTRALIZED GOVERNMENT —, THIS WORK IS, NOT FORMALLY, BUT SOLEMNLY AND SACREDLY DEDICATED BY THE AUTHOR

NOTES

Chapter IX

1 - This intriguing theory, not yet subjected to enough scholarly attention, but holding promise of verification in future investigation, is sketched out in Balsiger & Selier's Lincoln Conspiracy at 219-266.

2 - 12 U. S. Statutes at Large 755. Not at issue in this case was trial and punishment by court marial of enemy combatants, when in custody as prisoners of war, for war crimes or other acts of belligerency contrary to the law of nations, which has always been considered proper. Such practice was common during the American Revolution and the American Civil War. It has been held that, as a necessary and proper means of waging war, Congress may authorize such practice as appears in *Ex Parte Quirin*, 317 U. S. 1 (1942), and *In re Yamashita*, 327 U. S. 1 (1946). It goes without saying that Congress may provide for trial and punishment by court martial of military personnel in the armed forces of the United States, as expressly provided in the fourteenth clause of Article I, Section 8 of the United States Constitution.

3 - 2 U. S. Statutes at Large at 159, which provided, "That whenever any question shall occur before a circuit court, upon which the opinions of the judges shall be opposed, the point upon which the disagreement shall happen, shall during the same term, upon the request of either party, or their counsel, be stated under the direction of the judges, and certified under the seal of the court, to the supreme court, at their next session to be held thereafter, and shall, by the said court, be finally decided." A number of important cases had reached and been decided by the United States Supreme Court under this provision, including *Sturgis v. Crowninshield*, 4 Wheaton 122 (U. S. 1819). This statute was used by Lamden Milligan and his lawyers to get around the procedural difficulties encountered in *Ex Parte Vallandigham*, 1 Wallace 243 (U. S. 1864). Even so, during the course of his opinion (4 Wallace at 410), Justice Davis rediscovered *Ex Parte Bollman and Swartout*, 4 Cranch 75 (U. S. 1807), and noted jurisdiction under Section 14 of the Judiciary Act of 1789. In this way, Justice Davis admitted without mentioning the

411

injustice done to Congressman Vallandigham. Constitutional limitations on trial and punishment of civilians by court martial, as acknowledged in *Ex Parte Milligan*, 4 Wallace 2 (U. S. 1866), have since been reaffirmed in *Reid v Covert*, 354 U. S. 77 (1957).

4 - The role of honor includes Chief Roger B. Justice Taney in *Ex Parte Merryman*, 17 Fed. Cas. 144 (U. S. Cir. Ct. Md. 1861), who denounced presidential suspension of the writ of habeas corpus as unconstitutional; Justice Samual Nelson, joined by three others in the *Prize Cases*, 2 Black 635 (U. S. 1863), who found Lincoln's executive war-making unconstitutional; Chief Justice Walter Lowrie, Justice and later Chief Justice George Woodward, and Justice James Thompson in *Kneedler v. Lane*, 45 Pa. St. 238 (1863-1864), who found drafting armies unconstitutional; Chief Justice Lafayette Emmett in behalf of the whole court in *Davis v. Pierse*, 7 Gilfillan 13 (Minn. 1862), who struck down as unconstitutional under principles deriving from Magan Carta a statute which forbade citizens of rebel States from bringing suit in the state courts of Minnesota; Justice James Bell in *Ex Parte Coupland*, 26 Texas 387 (1862), who found drafting armies unconstitutional; and Chief Justice Richmond Pierson in *Gatlin v. Walton*, 60 N. C. 325 (1864), who released on writs of habeas corpus citizens unconstitutionally drafted into the armed forces after they had been exempted under contracts, based on good consideration, with the Confederate government.

5 - Reprinted in 1 Commager's Documents 429-431.

6 - Reprinted in 1 Commager's Documents 457-458.

7 - So held in *Butler v. Perry*, 240 U. S. 328 (1915).

8 - The rule of noscitur a sociis says that, in the construction of statutes, wills, deeds, and other legal instruments, the enumeration of terms must be construed in such a way that the more general are to be given a meaning analogous to the more specific. The rule of ejusdem generis is a particular application of the rule of noscitur a sociis: — whenever an enumeration of terms begins with one or several terms of limited meaning, then is concluded with a term of a more general character, the last term should not be read as broadly as possible, but on the contrary is to be read as having reference to the same restricted category as the preceeding words. These rules are very ancient, and belong to a category of rules illustrated in 1 Blackstone's Commentaries at 85-92. The underlying principle allows the use of a general term to indicate that a command or prohibition is not necessarily limited to specific terms, yet prevents use of the general term as a pretext for rendering the enumeration superfluous. In composing the language of the sixth article of the fourteenth section of the Northwest Ordinance (Tansill's Documents at 54), Thomas Jefferson no doubt added the phrase "involuntary servitude" to the term "slavery" precisely to avoid a limitation of the prohibition

to slavery strictly so called, and to include other equivalent forms of bondage, such as villeinage, which was still possible at least in theory at common law, since villeinage was not abolished with military tenures in the Statute of 12 Charles II, Chapter 24 (1660). Justice Stephen Field was surely right in the *Slaughter House Cases*, 16 Wallace 36 at 90 (U. S. 1872), where he said of the words "involuntary servitude" that they "include something more than slavery in the strict sense of the term; they include also serfage, vassalage, villenage, peonage, and all other forms of compulsory service for the mere benefit or pleasure of others." This definition was upheld in *Pollock v. Williams*, 322 U. S. 4 (1943).

9 - Trefousse's Background at 32-33 (Testimony before the Joint Committee of Fifteen on Reconstruction, 39th Congress, 1st Session, Spring 1866).

10 - Trefousse's Background at 29 (Testimony before the Joint Committee of Fifteen, 39th Congress, 1st Session, Spring 1866). Judge Sharkey was a particularly noteworthy and marvelous character. He served as Chief Justice of Mississippi from 1852 through the conclusion of the War for Southern Independence. In early autumn 1865 he led a convention of the people of Mississippi in abolishing slavery, which is why Mississippi did not see fit to adopt Amendment XIII, as appears in 2 Thorpe's History at 194. Like other Southern abolitionists, he maintained that the white people of his State were very attached to their slaves, and that slaves displayed uncommon fidelity and friendship for their masters. He insisted that such good feeling continued after the war, as appears in his testimony before the 39th Congress, recorded in Trefousse's Background at 29. Judge Sharkey was no scalawag, but a great lawyer and loyal Southerner who defended his people in time of defeat. He was elected to the United States Senate by the legislature of Mississippi in 1865, and later represented his State before the United States Supreme Court in *Mississippi v. Johnson*, 4 Wallace 475 (U. S. 1867), and in *Georgia v. Stanton*, 6 Wallace 50 (U. S. 1868).

11 - Necessary demographic information on the size of the general population of the United States, the size of the slave population in the Southern States, and the casualties suffered on both sides can be gathered from 2 Morris' History at 443 and 516, and Times Atlas at 223.

12 - The laws of the Southern States did not prohibit marriage between slaves, but statutes were often silent on the subject. Marriage between slaves was universally allowed "by custom of the manor" so to speak in the same way as marriage between villeins was allowed over some centuries in England. Masters acknowledged and regulated marriage between their slaves. An account of the situation appears in Dabneys Defence of Virginia at 228-230.

13 - Trefousse's Background at 30-31 (Testimony before the Joint Committee of Fifteen on Reconstruction, 39th Congress, 1st Session, Spring 1866).

14 - These Southern States were Virginia, Missouri, Louisiana, Tennessee, Arkansas, South Carolina, Alabama, North Carolina, and Georgia, as appears under Amendment XIII in the annotated copy of the United States Constitution in Volume I, on pages xliii-liii, of the United States Code as published by direction of Congress. Of these nine, Arkansas, Louisiana, and Tennessee slavery had been abolished by the people in convention before the adoption of Amendment XIII, as appears in 3 Thorpe's History 74-76, 83-86, and 121-123. In Mississippi and Florida slavery was abolished by the people in convention before Amendment XIII was adopted, as appears in 3 Thorpe's History 192-197 and 217-218. Shortly after Amendment XIII had been ratified by enough States, Texas also ratified, as appears in 3 Thorpe's History 226. In Kentucky, slavery was abolished by the fundamental law of the State some years later, as appears in 3 Thorpe's History 230-231.

15 - Trefousse's Background at 33 (Testimony before the Joint Committee of Fifteen on Reconstruction, 39th Congress, 1 st Session, Spring 1866)

16 - Reprinted in 1 Commager's Documents 455-456 (Extra session 1865, p. 3).

17 - An Act of March 17, 1866, quoted by Alexander Stephens, Trefousse's Background at 23 (Testimony before the Joint Committee of Fifteen on Reconstruction, 39th, 1st Session, Spring 1866).

18 - Reprinted in 1 Commager's Documents 452 (Laws 1865, p. 82).

19 - President Johnson's message to the 39 th Congress is reprinted in 1 Commager's Documents 470-476.

20 - Trefousse's Background at 64-65 (Testimoney before the Joint Committee of Fifteen on Reconstruction, 39th Congress, lst Session, Spring 1866).

21 - Buchanan's views, as expressed in his book written during the war, are set forth in Rozwenc's Civil War at 61-69.

22 - Stephens' Recollections at 265-266.

23 - Quoted in Trefousse's Background at xii.

24 - In the Philadelphia Convention, the framing of the first clause of Article I, Section 5 of the United States Constitution can be traced in 5 Elliot's Debates 378, 405-406, 536, 559, — Tansill's Documents 473, 514-517, 704, 2 Ferrand's Records 180, 251-254, 567, 592, 653 (August 6 and 10, September 10, 12, and 17, 1787).

25 - Namely, the Statutes of 10 George III, Chapter 16, (1770), 11 George III, Chapter 42 (1771), and 14 George III, Chapter 15 (1774). It has since been held in *Powell v. McCormack*, 395 U. S. 486 (1969), that a citizen lawfully elected to Congress may not be excluded on moral or political grounds, or even alleged illegal acts of which he had not been charged and convicted, and that such citizen is entitled to judicial intervention in his behalf.

26 - The formal report seeking to justify this exclusion is reprinted in 1 Commager's Documents 468-470 (Joint Committee of Fifteen on Reconstruction, 39 th Congress, lst Session, June 20, 1866).

27 - 14 U. S. Statutes at Large 27. This statute was in due course sustained as constitutional, and applicable to all private persons, under Amendment XIII in *Jones v. Mayer Co.*, 392 U. S. 409 (1968). But one hundred years beforehand, many considered this statute as not justified by Amendment XIII.

28 - Johnson's veto message is reprinted in 1 Commager's Documents 465-468 (March 27, 1868).

29 - The fundamental law of England, as established in a number of organic statutes, required that the right to vote for knights of the shire — i. e., members of the House of Commons from the counties, be freeholders enjoying certain revenue from their lands, as appears in details in 1 Blackstone's Commentaries 172-174; and that jurors likewise be freeholders or copyholders enjoying certain revenue from their lands, appears in detail in 3 Blackstone's Commentaries 362. So it was that the right to vote or be a juror was of a higher order than most other constitutional privileges and immunities of freemen, sometimes described as "absolute rights of individuals" and given reference in the venerable formulation by Justice James McReynolds in *Meyer v. Nebraska*, 262 U. S. 390 at 399-400 (1923).

30 - The most celebrated judicial commentary of this kind is the dissenting opinion of Justice Hugo Black in *Adamson v. California*, 332 U. S. 46 at 68-123 (1947). Black argued that Amendment XIV totally incorporates Amendments I through VIII as restraints on the powers of the several States. He was hotly contested by Charles Fairman in his article, *Does the Fourteenth Amendment Incorporate the Bill of Rights? The Original Understanding*, 2 Stanford Law Review 5 (1949).

31 - Mentor Edition at 512.

32 - The "absolute rights of individuals" were identified and expounded in 1 Blackstone's Commentaries 121-145.

33 - This broad view of the clause on privileges and immunities in Amendment XIV was specifically rejected by five of nine justices in the *Slaughter House Cases*, 16 Wallace 36 (U. S. 1872). Yet Justice Stephen Field (16 Wallace at 83-111), and Justice Joseph Bradley (16 Wallace at 111-124), supported by Chief Justice Salmon P. Chase and Justice Noah Swayne, wrote elaborate opinions in favor of an interpretation incorporating all guarantees of civil liberty in the United States Constitution, and applying them to the several States. Justice Bradley's formulation (16 Wallace at 118-119) was particularly striking: — he mentioned "the right of habeas corpus, the right of trial by jury, of free exercise of religious worship, the right of free speech, the right peaceably to assemble for discussion of public measures, the right to be secure against unreasonable searches and seizures, and above all, and including almost all the rest, the right of not being deprived of life, liberty, and property without due process of law. These and still others are specified in the original constitution or in early amendments of it as among the privileges and immunities of citizens of the United States." And relying on the

Statute of 21 James I, Chapter 3 (1624), Bradley and his colleagues claimed that freedom from government-created monopolies, except for copyrights and patents of invention, was among the unenumerated rights of citizens of the United States. In effect, Bradley and his colleagues favored the idea that Amendment XIV incorporated Amendment IX and applied it to the several States.

34 - The proceedings of the Philadelphia Convention on August 28, 1787, show that the term "ex post facto laws" was thought to include all "retrospective laws" and that prohibition of ex post facto laws was intended as a prohibition, not only laws which criminalized acts after they were committed, but any legislation retroactively taking away vested rights of contract, property, suit, or defense. It so appears in Madison's Notes (5 Elliot's Debates 484-485, Tansill's Documents 627-629, 2 Ferrand's Records 439), especially when read side by side with the Journal (1 Elliot's Debates 270-271, 2 Ferrands Records 435). The opinion of Justice William Johnson in *Satterlee v. Matthewson*, 2 Peters 380 at 414 and 681-688 (U. S. 1929), contains a good account of the chain of judicial errors which limited the prohibition of ex post facto law to retroactive criminal legislation, and left the States unrestrained by Article I, Section 10 of the United States Constitution from enacting statutes which took away many vested rights without due process of law. At the same time Justice Johnson wrote his opinion, the guarantee of due process of law in the constitutions of certain States had already been judicially construed as a prohibition of all laws retroactively taking away vested rights of all kinds. The pioneering case was *University of North Carolina v. Fox*, 1 Murphy 58 (N. C. 1805).

35 - Sumner's argument on December 4, 1849, before the Supreme Judicial Court of Massachusetts is reprinted in Thomas' Slavery Attacked 120-125.

36 - The decision against Sumner's classic argument appears in *Roberts v. City of Boston*, 5 Cushing 198 (Mass. 1850),. and to the same effect was *Van Camp v. Board of Education*, 9 Ohio 407 (1859). In Plessy v. Furguson, 163 U. S. 537 (1896), which turned on the equal protection clause of Amendment XIV, racial segregation in public transportation, and by inference also in public schools, was upheld on a "separate but equal" basis.

37 -This idea was particularly well expressed by Justice David Brewer in *South Carolina v. United States*, 199 U. S. 437 at 448-449 (1905).

38 - The landmark case of *Brown v. Board of Education*, 347 U. S. 483 (1954), adopted the phrasing and reasoning of Sumner's argument in 1849. The basic idea was that a child could not, on account of race, be denied the right to attend a public school in his or her neighborhood. This result in itself would not have been problematic in the South. But in applying legal principles to hard facts, practical difficulties were soon encountered, demanding greater moderation and patience, as appears, e. g., in *Stell v. Board of Education*, 220 F. Supp. 667 (S. D. Ga. 1963), rev'd. 318 F. 2d 425 (5 Cir. 1963) and 333 F. 2d 55 (5 Cir. 1964), and *Evers v. School District*, 232 F. Supp. 241 (S. D. Miss. 1964), rev'd. 357 F. 2d 654

(5 Cir. 1966). This episode in legal history was characterized by brazen disregard of human realities for the sake of ideological abstractions, causing deep injury to public education for both races. If the Southern States had won their independence, such blind judicial fanaticism and inhumanity would not have prevailed, yet in time desegregation of public schools would have been accomplished as practical difficulties were overcome.

39 -Trefousse's Background 136-137 (Testimony before the Joint Committee of Fifteen on Reconstruction, 39th Congress, 1st Session, Spring 1866).

40 - An account of the proposal, rejection, and claimed ratification of Amendment XIV may be found in 3 Thorpe's History 300-405. Another good account is found in Professor Fairman's article in 2 Stanford Law Review, pp. 81-132, summarized in the chart following p. 134. A forthright judicial discussion is found in *Dyett v. Turner*, 20 Utah 2d 403, 439 P. 2d 266 (1968), which outlines several cogent arguments against the validity of Amendment XIV as a part of the United States Constitution. These several accounts differ somewhat in minor details, but overlap and agree on all material points.

41 - In the fifth clause of Article I, Section 3 of the United States Constitution, it is stipulated that conviction on impeachment requires the votes of "two-thirds of the members present" in the Senate. Yet in Article V of the United States Constitution it is provided that proposal of a constitutional amendment requires the votes of "two thirds of both Houses." It may fairly be argued from the contrast in phrasing that the proposal of a constitutional amendment demands the votes of two-thirds, not of those present, but of all members of the House and a like two-thirds in the Senate. However, it appears from the records of the First Congress — specifically from the Journal of the Senate on September 21, 1789 — that two-thirds of a quorum in the House and the Senate has been considered sufficient to propose a constitutional amendment. And this consensus of the First Congress, including sixteen of the framers of the United States Constitution, was judicially accepted as the proper standard in *Missouri Pacific Railway v. Kansas*, 248 U. S. 276 at 281-282 (1918), and *Rhode Island v. Palmer*, 253 U. S. 350 at 386 (1919).

42 - It has been maintained that the resolution of the United States Senate was also insufficient to propose Amendment XIV. The argument says that there were fifty seated senators, including John Stockton of New Jersey, whose return was accepted on December 5, 1865. Only thirty-three votes could be garnered for Amendment XIV, one short of the required two-thirds. Stockton was known to oppose Amendment XIV, and was illegally removed from the Senate on a majority vote. Yet, under the second clause of Article I, Section 5 of the United States Constitution, two-thirds were required for expulsion, precisely to prevent removal of legislators properly seated, as appears in the proceedings of the Philadelphia Convention recorded in 5 Elliot's Debates 378, 406-407, 445, 536, 560, — Tansill's

Documents 474, 517, 571-572, 704, — 2 Ferrand's Records 180, 254, 340-341, 567-568, 592, 653 (Madison's Notes, August 6, 10, and 20, September 10, 12, and 17, 1787). Moreover, as might be inferred from the case of John Wilkes, expulsion required unparliamentary or other unlawful behavior during the session or at least unlawful behavior related to legislative business, yet no such claim was ever made against Stockton. The false pretext for removal of Stockton on majority vote, unheard of in parliamentary history, was that he was not expelled, but only removed nunc pro tunc upon reexamination of his return. The expulsion of Stockton was certainly unconstitutional. Yet, on June 8, 1866, the vote of the United States Senate to propose Amendment XIV was thirty-three yeas, eleven nays, and five not present and voting. If the rump of the 39th Congress be taken as a lawful Congress capable of any valid legislative work at all — which assumes rather too much, yet assuming this much —, the resolution was passed by two-thirds of a quorum, which has been considered since the First Congress to be necessary and sufficient for the House or the Senate to propose a constitutional amendment under Article V of the United States Constitution. It has also been contended that, because President Andrew Johnson did not sign the resolution proposing Amendment XIV, the article could not be adopted. But it has been settled since *Hollingsworth v. Virginia*, 3 Dallas 381 (U. S. 1799), that the approval of the President was not necessary for a resolution proposing a constitutional amendment. The correctness of this holding is brought out in the proceedings of the Philadelphia Convention which show that the President's power of veto, hence the necessity of his approval, was confined to bills for ordinary legislation, or resolutions serving to substitute for such bills, as appears in 5 Elliot's Debates 431, Tansill's Documents 551 and 552, and 2 Ferrand's Records 301-302 and 304-305 (Madison's Notes, August 15 and 16, 1787).

43 - The participle "ratified" appears in Article V of the United States Constitution to signify the option of a State regarding a constitutional amendment proposed by Congrress. The noun "ratification" appears in Article VII to signify the option of a State regarding adoption of the United States Constitution proposed by the Philadelphia Convention and the old Congress. The option given by Article VII was understood to be exhausted in either case by a clear ratification or rejection by a State, as appears in the adoption of the United States Constitution by North Carolina. The convention first set as a condition to ratification in behalf of North Carolina that a Federal Bill of Rights be laid before the new Congress and the several States, but meanwhile the convention expressly declared that the State neither adopted nor rejected the United States Constitution. This legalistic fence-straddling by North Carolina reflected the general understanding of those days that formal ratification or rejection exhausted the option of a State. Only after the Federal Bill of Rights was proposed by Congress did North Carolina ratify the United States Constitution. The particulars appear in 1 Elliot's Debates 333 and 4 Elliot's Debates 242 and 252-252, and Tansill's Documents 1044 and 1051 (North Carolina Convention, August 1-2, 1788, and November 21, 1789). The fairest inference is that the option given by Article V is circumscribed in the same way as the option

under Article VII. This understanding is also supported by the record of the proposal of twelve amendments by Congress on September 25, 1789, and the reactions of the several States, as set forth in 1 Elliot's Debates 338-340 and 2 Thorpe's History 259-263. There were thirteen States on September 25, 1789. Vermont became a State on February 18, 1790, as appears in 1 Elliot's Debates 337-338 and 1 U. S. Statutes at Large 191. Adoption of a constitutional amendment under Article V requires approval by three-fourths of the States in the Union. Therefore, eleven (i. e., three-fourths of fourteen) States were necessary for adoption of the Federal Bill of Rights. Nine States ratified, but two rejected the first article. Eight States ratified, but three rejected the second article. With the ratification of all twelve articles by Virginia on December 15, 1791, eleven States had ratified the ten articles which became Amendments I through X of the United States Constitution. It is not correct to say that Virginia actually rejected the proposals of Congress before adopting them. The fact is that, in Virginia, the House of Delegates at first rejected the amendments; but, since the Senate did not act one way or the other, the amendments were not formally rejected, and the option to adopt remained open. The House then passed and the Senate concurred in behalf of Virginia on December 15, 1791. Three States took no option at all. The political consensus of the day was that, after Virginia acted, nothing remained for the other three States to consider, and the first and second articles were defeated. The rule deemed applicable in those days was that every State had but one opportunity to ratify or reject whereupon her option was exhausted, and that, once enough States had formally approved or disapproved a proposed a constitutional amendment, there remains nothing further to act upon. This view of the subject was judicially upheld in *Wise v. Chandler*, 270 Ky. 1, 108 S. W. 2d 1024 (1937), cert. dism'd. 307 U. S. 474 (1939). There is no judicial consensus on this question, however, as becomes evident from reading *Coleman v. Miller*, 307 U. S. 433 (1939), and *Idaho v. Freeman*, 529 F. Supp. 1107 (D. Idaho. 1981). Most of the uneasiness over this question, never articulated but certainly understood, is that, if the view of the Kentucky Court of Appeals were ever accepted, the demise of Amendment XIV would be inevitable.

44 - In the following order, as appears under Amendment XIV in the annotated copy of the United States Constitution in Volume I of the United States Code published by direction of Congress: — Connecticut, June 25, 1866; New Hampshire, July 6, 1866; Tennessee, July 19, 1866; New Jersey, September 11, 1866; Oregon, September 19, 1866; Vermont, October 30, 1866; Ohio, January 4, 1867, New York, January 10, 1867; Illinois, January 15, 1867; West Virginia and Michigan, January 16, 1867; Kansas, January 18, 1867; Maine, January 19, 1867; Nevada, January 22, 1867; Missouri, January 26, 1867; Indiana, January 29, 1867; Minnesota, February 1, 1867; Rhode Island, February 7, 1867; Pennsylvania, February 12, 1867; Wisconsin, February 17, 1867; and Massachusetts, March 20, 1867. Professor Fairman offered slightly different dates for the ratifications of Connecticut and New Hampshire, as appears on pages 84-88 and on the chart following page 134 in his article in 2 Stanford Law Review.

45 - In the following order, as appears under Amendment XIV in the annotated copy of the United States Constitution in Volume I of the United States Code published by direction of Congress: — Texas, November 1, 1866; Georgia, November 13, 1866; Florida, December 3, 1866; North Carolina, December 4, 1866; South Carolina, December 20, 1866; Kentucky, January 10, 1867; Virginia, January 9, 1867; Delaware, February 7, 1867; and Maryland, March 23, 1867. The report by Congress does not mention the definitive rejections by near unanimous votes in the legislatures of three Southern States: — Alabama, in early December 1866, as appears in 3 Thorpe 317-318; Arkansas, December 17, 1866, as appears in 3 Thorpe 318-319, and as further amplified by Professor Fairman in his article in 2 Stanford Law Review, pp. 91-92, and on the chart following p. 134; and Mississippi, January 30, 1867, as amplified by Professor Fairman in his article in 2 Stanford Law Review, p. 106 and on the chart following p. 134.

46 - 14 U. S. Statutes at Large 428. There were three other Reconstruction Acts which implemented the Act of March 2, 1867: — 15 U. S. Statutes at Large 2 (March 23, 1867); 15 U. S. Statutes at Large 14 (July 19, 1867); 15 U. S. Statutes 41 (March ll, 1869).

47 - Johnson's veto message is reprinted in 1 Commager's Documents 481-485 (March 2, 1867). The President naturally relied on *Ex Parte Milligan*, 4 Wallace 2 (U. S. 1866). The veto was overridden by two-thirds of both chambers of the rump Congress on the very day it was returned.

48 - The classical statement of this theory is in Jameson's Conventions 624-633, which was a studied attempt to save Amendment XIV, but the effort was demolished in *Wise v. Chandler*, 270 Ky. 1, 108 S. W. 2d 1024 (1937).

49 - It appears under Amendment XIV in the annotated copy of the United States Constitution in Volume I of the United States Code published by direction of Congress that Nebraska ratified Amendment XIV on June 15, 1867, and Iowa followed on April 23, 1868, which raised to twenty-three the total number of ratifying States. Nevertheless in the same source, supplemented by 3 Thorpe's History 300-405 and Professor Fairman's article in 2 Stanford Law Review, pp. 81-132, summarized in the chart following p. 134, it appears that, in January 1868, Ohio passed a resolution to rescind her previous ratification; and that, in April 1868, New Jersey passed a resolution to rescind her previous ratification of Amendment XIV. It further appears from the same sources that seven Southern States, six earlier rejecting the amendment, were coerced by unconstitutional but irremediable imposition of martial law to ratify: — Arkansas, on April 8, 1868, after earlier rejection on December 17, 1866; Florida, June 9, 1868, after earlier rejection on December 3, 1866; Louisiana, July 9, 1868; North Carolina, July 4, 1868, after earlier rejection on December 4, 1868; South Carolina, July 9, 1868, after earlier rejection on December 20, 1866; Alabama, July 13, 1868, after previous rejection in early December, 1866; and Georgia, July 21, 1868, after earlier rejection on

November 13, 1866. By discounting two States which had rescinded their earlier ratifications, and counting seven States which had been coerced by operation of the Reconstruction Acts, Congress passed a resolution on July 21, 1868, declaring adoption of Amendment XIV by thirty States, as appears in 15 U. S. Statutes at Large 707-709. Under continuing coercion of the Reconstruction Acts, three more Southern States, which had earlier rejected, were obliged to ratify Amendment XIV: — Virginia, October 8, 1869, after earlier rejecting on January 9, 1867; Mississippi, January 17, 1870, after earlier rejecting on January 30, 1867; and Texas, February 18, 1870, after earlier rejecting on November 1, 1866. After Amendment had been proclaimed adopted, Ohio protested by passing a resolution purporting to rescind her rearlier ratification on October 15, 1868. During the 20th Century, long after the decisive events had occurred, there were three symbolic ratifications: — Delaware, February 20, 1901, after earlier rejecting on February 7, 1867; Maryland, April 1, 1959, after earlier rejecting on on March 23, 1867; and California on May 6, 1959. These symbolic ratifications are certainly invalid under the view expressed in *Dillon v. Gloss*, 256 U. S. 368 at 374-375 (1920), that a constitutional amendment is not perpetually open for consideration, but must be adopted within a period of time reasonably contemporaneous with the proposal thereof by Congress.

50 - Quoted in 1 Commager's Documents at 496 (Specification first in the tenth article of impeachment voted against President Andrew Johnson on March 3, 1868).

51 - Reprinted in 4 Elliot's Debates 350-404.

52 - The First Congress provided in express language that the secretary of state, the secretary of war, and the secretary of the treasury were respectively removable at the discretion of the President, as appears in 1 U. S. Statutes at Large 28 at 29 (July 27, 1789), 1 U. S. Statutes at Large 48 at 49 (August 7, 1789), and 1 U. S. Statutes at Large 53 at 54 (August 7, 1789). Section 35 of the Judiciary Act of 1789 created the offices of attorney general and district attorneys of the United States, but was silent on the question of removal, as appears in 1 U. S. Statutes at Large 73 at 92-93 (September 24, 1789). The power of removing the attorney general and the district attorneys was by usage under these statutes conceded to the President.

53 - 14 U. S. Statutes ar Large 430 (March 2, 1867)

54 - Johnson's veto message is reprinted in 1 Commager's Documents 486-487. The veto was overridden by the House and the Senate on the same day it was returned to the House.

55 - The lengthy opinion of Chief Justice William Howard Taft in *Myers v. United States*, 272 U. S. 52 at 106-177 (1926) fully vindicated the views of James Madison expressed in Congress on June 16, 1789. He concluded that "the Tenure of Office Act of 1867, in so far as it attempted to prevent the President from

removing executive officers who had been appointed by him by and with the advice and consent of the Senate, was invalid, and that subsequent legislation to the same effect is equally so."

56 - The full proceedings of the impeachment of Andrew Johnson were reprinted in the Congressional Globe, 40th Congress, 1st Session. A convenient abbreviated version, including the bill of impeachment and the record of the critical proceedings on May 2, 3, and 26, 1868, is reprinted in 1 Commager's Documents 493-498. A moving account of the trial appears in Kennedy's Profiles at 107-128 where special tribute was paid to Senator Edmund Ross of Kansas.

57 - Section 13 of the Judiciary Act of 1789 (1 U. S. Statutes at Large at 80-81) expressly granted the United States Supreme Court original jurisdiction in a suit in which a State was a party, save between a State and its citizens. But in *Marbury v. Madison*, 1 Cranch 137 (U. S. 1803), it was held that Section 13 of the Judiciary Act of 1789 must be read, not literally, but strictly so as to confer original jurisdiction only if allowed by the second clause of Article III, Section 2 of the United States Constitution. And in *Cohens v. Virginia*, 6 Wheaton 264 (U. S. 1821), it was held that the first clause of Article III, Section 2 defined the scope of the original jurisdiction conferred by the second clause, and that, consequently, the United States Supreme Court could assume original jurisdiction over a suit brought by a State of the Union only if such suit was brought by a State against another State or its citizens, or against a foreign State or the citizens or subjects of a foreign State.

58 - 14 U. S. Statutes at Large 385.

59 - 15 U. S. Statutes at Large 44.

60 - The opinion of Sir Charles Pratt, Chief Justice of the Court of Common Pleas, shortly before he was created the Earl of Camden by King George III, is reported as *The King v. Wilkes*, 2 Wilson 251 (1763).

EPILOGUE

As Sherman consolidated his base after the fall of Atlanta and prepared his march through Georgia, framing conventions or "conferences" were held in Charlottetown on Prince Edward Island and in the City of Quebec, which led to a later conference in London, then to the formation of a federal Union of Provinces under the British North America Act of 1867, 30 & 31 Victoria, Chapter 3, since amended on numerous occasions but still the centerpiece of fundamental law in Canada.

When these several conferences were held, it was well known that the people and government of Great Britain felt a natural sympathy for the cause of the South. And this sympathy extended far beyond the active commerce which had been conducted between the British Isles and the Dixie States.

"When in the process of time the history of Secession comes to be viewed with the same freedom of prejudice as the history of the seventeenth and eighteenth centuries, it will be clear that the fourth great Revolution of the English-speaking race differs in no essential characteristic from those which preceded it," observed Colonel G. F. R. Henderson. "In each case," he claimed, "a great principle was at stake: in 1642 the liberty of the subject; in 1688 the integrity of the Protestant faith; in 1775 taxation only with the consent of the taxed; in 1861 the sovereignty of the States."[1] Such was the perception of most people in England, Scotland, Wales, and Ireland, and for this reason they naturally favored the South.

And because the people of England, Scotland, Wales, and Ireland favored the cause of the Southern States, pro-Union politicians in Washington D. C. feigned outrage against Great Britain. Their motive was not hard to ascertain. At the time of the American Revolution, and again in the War of 1812, military expeditions from the United States had

A MARI · VSQVE · AD · MARE

The Armorial Bearings
of
THE DOMINION OF CANADA
ASSIGNED BY ROYAL PROCLAMATION
21 NOVEMBER A.D. 1921.

marched against Canada. During the American Civil War, the United States had developed the most powerful army in the world, stronger than any army in Europe. And if Stanton's army could conquer the Southern States, with a much larger population, and its huge territory and developed wealth, why should this predatory beast not be unleashed, on some concocted pretext, against the empire in North America under the British Crown?

Not long after the repulse of the last of Hood's wild sorties out of Atlanta, the La Minerve of Montreal stated the choice for Canada: "la confédération ou l'annexion."

The British North America Act of 1867 was accordingly framed and adopted. The Preamble stated that the Union was established to promote the "Welfare of the Provinces," but no less the "Interests of the British Empire." It was an organic statute of the imperial Parliament which vested broad and sweeping authority in the dominion Parliament to make all "Laws for the Peace, Order, and Good Government of Canada," subject to exclusive authority of the several Provinces over certain local affairs. In this respect, the fundamental law of Canada has always been radically different in formal structure from the confederacy of free, sovereign, and independent States which was acknowledged by George III in 1783, and continued upon the inauguration of George Washington in 1789.

The new Dominion was shaped by Sir John Macdonald who played a decisive role in the conferences in Charlottetown and Quebec in 1864, and in London in 1866. It has been observed that "Macdonald had not perhaps a high code of political ethics, and he at times raised opportunism almost to the level of a political principle."[2] As his pretext for building a strong central government for Canada, he claimed that the right of secession, or at least respectable opinion in favor of such right, was the essential cause of the American Civil War. It is an interesting question whether he actually believed what he said. In any event, he wanted to concentrate power, and he used this argument to achieve his objective.

There can be no doubt, in any event, that the British North America Act of 1867 did not create a statutory mechanism for secession. And the want of such a mechanism soon became apparent in events. A separatist government was elected in Nova Scotia in 1868, and this government sought independence in a bid which was firmly rebuffed by the colonial office in London.

Whether it was principled belief or political pretext, Macdonald's basic idea was wrong, because the American Civil War could never have been agitated if the right of secession had been freely acknowledged in 1860-1861 as it had been acknowledged by leading antebellum text writers on the United States Constitution both in the North and in the South. The right of secession would never have been exercised if Lincoln had not run on an anti-secession platform, and had pursued Buchanan's conciliatory policy. In such case Stephens' "Union" speech would have been approved by the legislature of Georgia. And the Southern States would have successfully defended their rights within the Union.

Ironically enough, it was the threatened exercise of the right of secession by New England during the War of 1812 which defeated the portentous and unconstitutional experiments then contemplated in the United States for the conquest of Canada. It was the Hartford Convention which induced the Treaty of Ghent in 1815.

The American Civil War crushed the right of secession, which in turn promoted excessive consolidation of power in Washington D. C. It was this unhappy event which made the United States a threat to Canada in 1864.

The main flaw in Macdonald's vision for Canada was that massive concentration of power in the central government of a large territory and a diverse population has, in every age, and in every country, been dangerous to human freedom.

There would have been no Jacobite uprisings in Scotland if the little northern kingdom had not been consolidated into a unitary British government by the Act of Union in 1707.

The Holy Roman Empire became a threat to civilization in Europe because Ferdinand II did not respect the rights of local princes: — for this reason it was necessary to cripple the imperial government by the Peace of Westphalia in 1648.

The French Revolution was not prompted by a spontaneous rising of oppressed people led by the goddess of liberty, her breasts partially uncovered as she carried a tricolor in one hand and a musket in the other. The old regime needed reform, which the King had acknowledged and begun. The people were not oppressed, nor were they against the King. This supreme tragedy was produced by the conspiracies of disloyal and malicious men who fomented hideous acts of political chaos and judicial murder.[3]

When in 1793 militant revolutionaries guillotined Louis XVI, the good and gracious father of France — preeminent among the founding fathers of the United States —, they set in motion a century and a half of war after war full of misery and ruin, accompanied by political turbulence and legal disorder until the last drop of innocent blood was shed during the so-called "liberation" of France in 1944-1946.[4]

Excessive concentration of power in the French Empire under Napoleon meant, not glory, but ruinous wars across the face of Europe, the wreckage of France, and the suffering of her people. Excessive concentration of power in the German Empire of the Hohenzollern princes led to the disaster of world war, the fall of the imperial government, and military defeat. Excessive concentration of power in the Soviet state led to seven decades of oppression before it collapsed. Excessive concentration of power in the German state under Hitler produced another world war, hideous despotism, painful destruction, and national humiliation. Excessive concentration of power in the government of the United States, which drew its impetus from the American Civil War, has produced an empire dangerous and unwieldy: — for the good of all concerned, it should be.

The Dominion designed by Macdonald would have failed for the same reason that every such government has failed. Canada was saved from this unhappy fate, because the formal legal order of the country was soon displaced by wiser principles.

The most important provision in the fundamental law of Canada, all things considered, is the Preamble of the British North America Act of 1867, insofar as it says in a seemingly innocuous way that the Provinces are to be "federally united into one Dominion under the Crown of the United Kingdom of Great Britain and Ireland, with a Constitution similar in principle to that of the United Kingdom."

It is through this Preamble that ambiguities in the Act itself and its amendments have been resolved, and important rules superadded to mollify the text, by reference to the British Constitution as it stood at the time of Queen Victoria. So it is, for example, that the original Act does not so much as mention the Prime Minister of Canada, and speaks as if the executive power of the Dominion, including prerogatives nominally belonging to Queen Victoria, were vested in the Governor General; yet, in fact, the Prime Minister, chosen by the political party or coalition in control of the House of Commons, has always wielded executive authority in Canada, as had long been established practice in Great Britain by the reign of Queen Victoria.

It has long been characteristic of the British Constitution that public authority be regulated not only by organic statutes, but also principles unwritten yet understood, these classed as constitutional customs and constitutional conventions. The distinction between these two kinds of unwritten law is sometimes blurred, but tolerably clear.

Constitutional customs are organic rules which activate, organize, and empower the government, and are taken as part of the common law, judicially acknowledged as such. Constitutional conventions are organic rules of political interaction between public institutions and officers, being understandings between political leaders, deemed by them to be essential for proper functioning of the government. Such conventions are identifiable from and solidified by precedent, yet they are not taken as part of the common law, even if the judiciary sometimes gives them notice.

By operation of such constitutional customs and conventions, the British North America Act of 1867, and the many organic statutes and orders in council amending and amplifying it, have taken on a legal meaning very different from what a literal reading of the text seems to say. Canada has greatly benefited from the influence of the British Constitution.

For the country has been transformed by unwritten law from a consolidated nation state, at best quasi-federal in formal structure, into a real and workable confederacy. The evolved constitutional shape of Canada is a practical alliance between diverse nations, peoples, languages, and cultures in North America. The current features of the Dominion, as they have naturally evolved over time, have made it possible to accommodate intense political frictions which otherwise would have led to grave confrontations.

As the United States were originally established to accommodate two main civilizations, one commercial and modern in the North, the other agricultural and quasi-feudal in the South, so Canada was originally established to accommodate two main civilizations, and this arrangement was perfected under the British North America Act of 1867. The older civilization was French and Catholic, historically rooted in and descended from New France which was ceded to the British Crown after the Seven Years War. The other civilization was founded by loyalist refugees of the American Revolution. Many English, Scottish, Welch, and Irish soldiers and immigrants intermarried with, settled among, and became part of the French population and culture, but the greater part of this stock settled in Ontario and elsewhere in the upper stretches of North America subject to the British Crown.

As one of several ways of accommodating the two main civilizations of Canada into the same federal Union, the British North America Act of 1867 established a bilingual country with a bilingual government. In time the French and Catholic civilization became a minority with a geopolitical center in Quebec, yet branching out into other parts of the country, while Anglo-Canada became dominant in nine Provinces on either side of Quebec. The difference between these two main civilizations cannot easily be defined. Principal language is only a more obvious distinction. It extends no less to characteristic mentality, habits, appearance, style, religion, temperament, law, customs, education, literature, and attitudes about life in general.

There has always been a tension between these two main civilizations. It has always been a tempting object for political mischief and faction. The antagonisms in one generation are forgotten, then return in some new guise in the next generation. There is a kind of friendship between the English and French in Canada, but it more resembles obligatory courtesies between competitors in business. Otherwise, the relationship is best described by the apt French phrase "deux solitudes."

The most recent of these antagonisms resulted from the imposition of a new constitution upon Quebec over her protest. The means used in this transformation are not generally well understood:

There was nothing in the original British North America Act of 1867 which provided for amendment. Therefore, the power of rewriting the fundamental law of Canada remained formally in the British Parliament, which seemingly had unlimited discretion in enacting whatever changes the Commons, Lords, and King or Queen might desire. But a constitutional convention imposed a new reality upon the old statute: — the British Parliament became a mere "legislative trustee" and could enact no amendment except upon a proper request which generated from within Canada.[5]

By operation of this constitutional convention, Canada became an independent country many years ago without any declaration of independence, without any treaty, without any enactment of positive law, without any revolution or upheaval, albeit that the country has been joined with Great Britain under one Crown, reminiscent of the independence of Scotland upon the accession of James I as King of England in 1603.

Over time, there developed a constitutional convention that there could be no amendment of any of the British North America Acts, where the object was to modify legislative powers, unless all affected legislative assemblies approved. This principle, closely tied to the constitutional convention which made Canada an independent nation, had clearly been observed by leading statesmen for the most urgent reasons of continental justice.

Passions were therefore excited to a dangerous pitch when, with the approval of nine provincial Legislatures on either side of but excluding Quebec, the dominion Parliament petitioned the British Parliament, which then enacted certain imperial legislation, known as the Canada Act of 1982, for this organic statute modified the powers of all legislative bodies in Canada.[6]

The Canada Act of 1982 abolished the old formality for securing future constitutional amendments, changed the names of the British North America Acts of 1867-1975 to the Constitution Acts of 1867-1975, and adopted a new organic statute known as the Constitution Act of 1982.

This new organic statute ordained several formulae, each depending on subject matter, for amending the fundamental law of Canada by the dominion Parliament acting alone or with some or all of the provincial

Legislatures, which was called "patriation" of the constitution, and it also imposed an "entrenched" Canadian Charter of Rights and Freedoms.[7]

The Canadian Charter restrains the dominion Parliament and all provincial Legislatures from enacting laws which contravene certain constitutional rights. Because the Canadian Charter limits the authority of all provincial Legislatures, imposing it on Quebec without consent of her provincial Legislature or "National Assembly" violated the constitutional convention requiring assent of all legislative assemblies affected.

Whereas British-style legislative supremacy had always prevailed in Canada, and civil liberties had been protected by the judiciary mainly by strict construction of statutes in light of natural law and legal tradition, the Canadian Charter introduced an American-style bill of rights, incapable of legislative modification or repeal, enabling the judiciary to strike down federal and provincial laws as unconstitutional.

Even so, Section 33 of the Constitution Act of 1982 says that the dominion Parliament or a provincial Legislature, in passing a law, may provide that it shall operate for a defined term up to five years, notwithstanding the Canadian Charter. This "notwithstanding clause" is an antidote to judicial excess, but not necessarily as ample as might be supposed, because only exceptional circumstances can justify its use as a practical matter.

Not only was the Canada Act of 1982 not approved by the National Assembly, it was imposed over the express protest of veto of Quebec.[8] The people and government of Quebec did not want "rights" and "freedoms" which might be judicially construed to undermine legislation designed to shield the Province as a bastion of the French language and culture.[9]

And since the Canada Act of 1982 was forced upon Quebec, Canada has lost much of its sense of natural law and legal tradition which once distinguished the greatest judges of the country.[10] The courts have gone on an energetic spree, in the name of the Canadian Charter, of carrying out a characteristic agenda of secular humanism and political correctness.[11]

The bitterness felt in Quebec over the imposition of the Canadian Charter rejuvenated the fires of separatism, and, therefore, certain patriots and statesmen of Canada intervened.

In 1987 a body of constitutional amendments, collectively known as the Meech Lake Accord, was proposed by the dominion Parliament after the Prime Minister of Canada and all ten provincial Premiers signified their approval in writing. The Accord contained a number of beneficial provisions, from which a few important examples may be instanced:

Section 6 of the Accord would have constitutionally entrenched or guaranteed the existence of the Supreme Court of Canada, and constitutionally assured at least three of nine justices from Quebec. This provision was not controversial, since the Supreme Court of Canada had many years before being established and reservation of three judges trained in the civil law had already been ordained by act of the dominion Parliament under an express grant of authority in the Constitution Act of 1867.

Under Section 41 of the Constitution Act of 1982, it was provided that all ten provincial Legislatures must approve any constitutional amendment which concerns the composition of the Supreme Court, but there is no limit on the number of years within which such unanimity might be achieved.

Section 1 of the Accord would have acknowledged Quebec as a distinct society within Canada, which is an undeniable political reality.[12] This section also directed that the clause recognizing Quebec as a distinct society should be employed as a rule for interpreting other provisions of fundamental law in Canada, thus helping to safeguard against the kind of judicial activism which has tended to homogenize Quebec into a trans-Canadian culture. The same provision went on to say that the provincial Legislature of Quebec has a constitutional right and duty to preserve the distinct identity of Quebec.

Some politicians and lawyers have denied it, but the clause on Quebec as a distinct society most certainly would have had the effect of enhancing the legislative power of the National Assembly under Section 92(16) of the Constitution Act of 1867, which grants every provincial Legislature the power to make laws touching matters of a local nature in the Province: — the clause would have such an effect, at very least because everything making Quebec distinct from the rest of Canada, which embraces not a little, must necessarily be a matter of a local nature within the Province.

Under Sections 38 and 39 of the Constitution Act of 1982, such a provision standing alone would require the assent of seven provincial Legislatures representing at least half the population of Canada within three years of the proposal by the dominion Parliament.

Section 2 of the Accord sought reform of the dominion Senate as originally established under the Constitution Act of 1867. The dominion Senate was an attempt to recreate for Canada a British House of Lords such as it existed in the reign of Queen Victoria, filled with a certain number of members, so many for each Province, appointed for life for each Province by the Governor General, naturally on "advice" of the Prime Minister of Canada. But the effort never succeeded, because, unlike Great Britain, Canada never has had an ancient and indigenous aristocracy from which the British House of Lords was a natural outgrowth.[13]

It was originally hoped that the dominion Senate might have some weight as an upper house of senior statesmen, thus stabilizing the country against the excesses of democracy. Instead, the institution became in time a means of paying off political debts. The stately magnificence of the speeches in the old British House of Lords before it was reformed to excess — even the United States Senate before it was weakened by popular election under Amendment XVII —, has seldom filled the dominion Senate. On the contrary, this club of old political cronies has become a redundancy needing reform.

Section 2 of the Accord proposed to remedy this fault by requiring that every new member of the dominion Senate be from a list recommended for appointment by the government of the Province which he or she should represent.

Section 42 of the Constitution Act of 1982 stipulates that constitutional amendments concerning the method of appointing members of the dominion Senate can be adopted only by the formula in Sections 38 and 39 of the Constitutional Act of 1982, and none other — in other words, only by at least seven provincial Legislatures, representing at least half the population of Canada, within three years of proposal by the dominion Parliament.

The political leaders of the era in which the Meech Lake Accord was introduced were aware that the clause on Quebec as a distinct society required the approval of seven provincial Legislatures representing half of the population of Canada within three years, and that the provision on the Supreme Court, and also another provision revising some of the formulas for constitutional amendment, required unanimous approval of all ten provincial Legislatures in any number of years. It was the consensus of these political leaders, not written but understood, that the whole Accord should rise or fall together by combing the two formulas of amendment, and hence that all articles needed assent by all ten provincial Legislatures within three years.

This consensus was certainly incorrect. If an amendment must be adopted by all ten provincial Legislatures, then of right it can be adopted in any number of years, nor can a limit of three years be imposed upon approval, nor can it be adopted by only seven provincial Legislatures even if they represent half the population and act in three years. And if an amendment can or must be adopted by seven provincial Legislatures representing half the population, it must be adopted in three years, nor can ten provincial Legislatures be required, nor can ten provincial Legislatures adopt it in more than three years. The two formulas are inescapably contradictory, and each is designed to deal with a distinct kind of changes. Approval can be by one formula or by the other, but not by both.

And there was an even more fatal flaw in the consensus. Under Section

42 of the Constitution Act of 1982, the provision in the Accord on reforming the dominion Senate could be adopted *only* by seven provincial Legislatures representing half the population in three years, and not otherwise. Yet the consensus demanded that this provision, like all others in the Accord, be approved by all ten provincial Legislatures, contrary to the express language of Section 42.

It is a mystery how the consensus on the need for unanimity within three years was reached. The legal literature is silent. Historians have supplied no insight. Political leaders and government ministers make no effort in their formal correspondence to deny the contradiction in the consensus, but merely regard as unthinkable the notion that the consensus was actually unlawful.

When the Congress of the United States proposed the Federal Bill of Rights in 1789, twelve articles were set before the country in one resolution, yet each article was treated as a separate item. Ten of the twelve articles were, but two articles were not ratified by sufficient States. The whole did not fall because two articles failed, but ten articles became constitutional amendments.[14]

The same mode of reckoning should have been used in Canada in relation to the Meech Lake Accord. Each part of the Accord should have been taken as a separate item, each subject to the amending formula particularly applicable to itself. Such reckoning should have been used, if not because of the example of adopting the Federal Bill of Rights in the United States, then because there is no other to achieve logical consistency between Sections 38, 39, 41, and 42 of the Constitution Act of 1982.[15]

If such proper reckoning had been used, the most important provisions of the Accord would have been promulgated, including the clause on Quebec as a distinct society and the clause on rejuvenation of the dominion Senate. For very soon after the Accord was proposed by the dominion Parliament, seven provincial Legislatures approved, including Ontario and Quebec which in themselves had more than half of the population of Canada, and later an eighth provincial Legislature gave assent in unanimous voice. The fires of separatism in Quebec would have been quenched by the waters of moderation and justice. Canada would have benefited from greater internal harmony and a number of technical improvements in fundamental law.

But such reckoning was not used, and the unconstitutional consensus of unanimity in three years prevailed. The situation invited treachery, and treachery followed.

The provincial Legislature of Newfoundland first granted then withdrew approval. The Premier of Newfoundland then promised renewed support of his government, solemnly and officially, then recommended against approval in the provincial Legislature.

Meanwhile, the provincial Legislature of Manitoba first did not act. Later the government again promised, solemnly and officially, to support the Accord, yet allowed a single factious deputy, by parliamentary technicality, to prevent the Accord from coming to the floor of the provincial Legislature. Nothing was done to prevent or overrule this gross abuse of privilege. The day following, the three years ran out. The Accord was "officially" pronounced dead.

Actually, the Accord was not dead. The most important provisions, including the distinct society clause in effect giving special status to Quebec and the clause reforming the dominion Senate, were constitutionally adopted by seven provincial Legislatures within three years of proposal by the dominion Parliament. The Governor General could and should then and there have promulgated those clauses as part of the Constitution of Canada. The remaining provisions of the Accord, not limited by a term of years, could be adopted whenever if ever the two remaining provincial Legislatures should deem fitting and proper.

To be more precise, Section 39 of the Constitution Act of 1982 stipulates that, when an eligible amendment has been adopted by seven provincial Legislatures representing half the population, the Governor General may not issue a proclamation making the amendment a part of the Constitution after three years from the proposal by the dominion Parliament; but, the Governor General did not act, because a constitutional convention requires the immense nominal powers of that office to be held in abeyance unless the Prime Minister "advises" the Crown to act. For the Prime Minister then in power lived in the mistaken belief that all provisions of the Accord rose or fell together depending on whether or not ten provincial Legislatures gave approval within three years, and so did not advise the Crown to act.

Many more than three years have passed since the Accord was first proposed by the dominion Parliament, and so it may be thought that Section 39 of the Constitution Act of 1982 prevents subsequent correction of the mistake. Not so.

For there is a rule of civil law and common law to deal with a situation existing when, on account of fraud or mistake or like cause, a required act has not been done as and when it should have been done. In such case, when the mistake is discovered, the act may, can, and should be done nunc pro tunc, — in other words, it should be done after the fact yet, by just fiction of the law, as if done as and when it ought to have been done.[16]

The King or Queen "can do no wrong," and so is incapable of allowing the unconstitutional denial of just rights, and, if something wrong is done by or in the name of the Crown, it is the duty of the Crown to correct the error. The failure of the Governor General to promulgate critical parts of the Accord may be considered an inadvertent mistake of the Crown, the same as an unlawful royal grant of a patent was held to be an inadvertent mistake of the Crown in the *Case of Monopolies,* 11 Coke 84b (K. B. 1603).

And, in legal contemplation, the Governor General may, can, and should be advised by the Prime Minister at any opportune moment to promulgate those parts of the Accord which were approved by sufficient provincial Legislatures, retroactively effective as of the day on which such adoption was realized.

Unfortunately, the Meech Lake Accord, although alive in legal theory, remains dead in political fact, because it is thought dead by federalists in Anglo-Canada and separatists in Quebec, and neither wants a revival of the Accord, for their motives are respectively those of the subjugation or the independence of Quebec. Only a few dreamers who believe in authentic principles of a real confederacy, such as those expounded by the Baron de Montequieu and Alexander Stephens, dare hope for an eventual revival of the Accord.

The perceived death of the Meech Lake Accord was as injurious to Canada as the repeal of the Missouri Compromise in the United States. An attempt to repair the damage by new proposals for constitutional reform, called the Charlottetown Accord, died of political mutilation, grandstanding demagoguery, irresponsible posturing, fanciful ideas, and too much exposure to the press. Tensions between the two main civilizations of Canada then greatly increased.

As night follows day, the fires of separatism again burned bright in Quebec. The people of Quebec elected a separatist government which in 1995 held a second referendum on independence. The first such referendum in 1980 was soundly defeated, but in the second referendum of 1995 the vote on secession was 49.4% "oui" and 50.6% "non", which astonished all observers. The proposition offered was that the government of Quebec would initially attempt to negotiate with the government of Canada for a new constitutional partnership, but that, if such negotiations were not productive, the government of Quebec would unilaterally declare and effect independence from Canada.

The proposition was not different in principle from the procedure used by the legislature of Rhode Island in declaring the independence of the colony from the British Empire in 1776, thereby reliving the Glorious Revolution in North America.

The vote on this proposition was close enough to warn bluntly, yet it did not set in motion processes of demanding independence. The only reason the referendum did not carry by an overwhelming vote was that French moderates were still influential, and still had hopes of reconciliation with Anglo-Canada.

In 1996, the National Assembly of Quebec passed a resolution which had a flavor of the resolutions of a number of legislatures in the Southern States before the American Civil War, reaffirming the right of the people of Quebec "de determiner, sans entrave, son statut politique," — in other words, to authorize in a lawful and peaceable manner a secession from Canada.

The government of Canada reacted by asking the Supreme Court for an advisory opinion, a lawful procedure called a "reference" — "renvoi" in French —, on whether Quebec had a right to secede under the Constitution Acts of 1867-1982.[17]

It seemed obvious, especially from the history of the framing of the British North America Act of 1867, that the answer would be without qualification in the negative. And this answer would have been technically correct, if attention were given solely to the text of the organic statutes in question.

The real objective of this reference was to give the government of Canada a pretext to adopt whatever measures it deemed necessary to prevent the secession of Quebec, whether by outlawing another referendum, or prosecuting separatist politicians for sedition, or sending troops and imposing martial law. There were many possible avenues of reconciliation, generally called "plan A" and awaited by French moderates in Quebec. But the government of Canada then in power pursued a hard line against Quebec, generally labeled "plan B." Members of the federal cabinet thundered impertinently about the rule of law. Inexorably, the country lunged toward a dangerous constitutional crisis.

The separatist Premier of Quebec stated that the reference was an abuse of judicial procedure, and that he would not send his attorney general to argue before the Supreme Court. He stated that the people of Quebec alone would decide their political status, not the judicial establishment of Canada.

The Premier was later echoed in a dramatic and eloquent statement by the Cardinal-Archbishop of Montreal. Regardless of what the Supreme Court should decide, his Eminence said, the people of Quebec are sovereign, and alone have the right to determine whether the Province should remain with or secede from Canada.

The senior federalist statesman of Quebec, who had led the opposition against an earlier separatist government of the Province, stated that, while his party favored the federal Union, he firmly believed that Quebec had the right, by decision of her people, to withdraw from Canada.

The Chief Justice of Canada sensed the gravity of the situation, but showed no outward signs of alarm. He calmly denied a motion of the attorney general of Canada for expedited hearing, appointed an amicus curiae to represent Quebec, and prepared for upcoming arguments in Ottawa.

Soon thereafter the Chief Justice delivered a striking opinion in *Reference on the Remuneration, Independence, and Impartiality of the Judges of the Provincial Court of Prince Edward Island*, [1997] 3 S. C. R. 3. The dryness of the subject matter camouflaged the significance of the case.

The question was whether it was constitutional for the provincial Legislature of Prince Edward Island, in a bona fide attempt to save public money, to reduce the salaries of the judges of the provincial courts set up under Section 92(14) of the Constitution Act of 1867.

There is nothing in any of the organic statutes of Canada which expressly addresses the problem of judicial compensation in the provincial courts. But Section 100 of the Constitution Act of 1867 which makes it unlawful to reduce the salaries of judges in the superior courts of Canada. And this provision corresponds to the third section of the Act of Settlement, 12 & 13 William III, Chapter 2 (1701): — it has protected British judges over the course of three centuries. The same provision for judicial independence, also copied from the Act of Settlement, appears in Article III, Section 1 of the United States Constitution.[18]

The underlying principle in the opinion of the Chief Justice was that, whenever the text of the Constitution Acts of 1867-1982 is silent or ambiguous on a question of fundamental law, the meaning may be supplied by the essential principles of the British Constitution as they stood in the reign of Queen Victoria, for these principles were transmitted to Canada through the Preamble of the original British North America Act of 1867.

The Chief Justice held that the provision on the judiciary in the Act of Settlement is an unwritten norm applicable Canada, and so governs the compensation of provincial judges in Prince Edward Island. He concluded that the reduction of judicial salaries by the provincial Legislature was unconstitutional.

The decision was all-important, because the first section of the Act of Settlement provides that the Crown descends to the Protestant heirs of the body of the Princess Sophia of Hanover. Without this Act, King George III could not have issued his royal Proclamation of 1763 which began British rule in Canada. Without this Act, Queen Victoria could not have approved the British North America Act of 1867, nor could Queen Elizabeth II have approved the Canada Act of 1982. The Act of Settlement, it so happens, is one of three organic statutes which confirm and presuppose the legitimacy of the Glorious Revolution.

Therefore, the principle of the Glorious Revolution, or the constitutional custom on which the Crown rests, substantially as formulated by Blackstone, is part of the fundamental law in Canada, — and this principle defines the right of Quebec to secede from the Dominion.

In the reference on secession, the amicus curiae for Quebec vigorously argued before the Supreme Court of Canada that the procedure of reference was unconstitutional, and that the constitutional question was theoretical, conjectural, political, unripe, and therefore nonjusticiable, doing all he could to prevent judicial decision, fearing that the answer on the merits would be negative, which would give the government of Canada a pretext to use heavy-handed means in retaliation against Quebec. These arguments were advanced hopefully, and supported by the views of some of the best constitutional lawyers in the United States and Canada, but they were rejected.

Thus in elegant French the amicus curiae for Quebec addressed the merits of the constitutional question, advancing the principle of the Glorious Revolution, precisely describing the irregularity yet the legitimacy of events in 1688 and 1689, citing distinguished British lawyers and historians. The argument was ironic, because William of Orange has traditionally been regarded as the ultimate ideal of statesmanship in Anglo-Canada.

The amicus curiae gave the very British idea he used a very French name, — "le principe d'effectivité" he called it. This principle of fundamental law, he said, had arrived in Canada through the Preamble of the Constitution Act of 1867, drawing attention to the recent judgment on the compensation of provincial judges in Prince Edward Island.

In extraordinary circumstances, there might be a peaceable and lawful but revolutionary change in government, taking the form of secession from Canada, leading to a new constitutional order, even though the event defied the old constitutional order. Such an event would not be legally different from what occurred when the Crown was transferred from James II to William and Mary.

Is there a lawful right of secession in Canada? In extraordinary circumstances, the amicus curiae argued, the answer is yes. The right exists, although there is no express statutory mechanism, because, as the amicus curiae argued, the Crown itself undeniably rests on events caused by "those latent powers of society which no climate, no time, no constitution, no contract, can ever destroy or diminish."[19]

In 1688 James II convened the House of Lords to sit as the Magnum Concilium. The peers and bishops urged him to grant pardons with liberality, redress legitimate grievances, and promote sound constitutional reforms. He failed to take this advice, and, of consequence, the Convention Parliament met in 1689, not in keeping with the then-existing forms of law, yet it reestablished the rule of law.

The Canadian Charter was imposed on Quebec over protest, contrary to an established constitutional convention which no judicial opinion can ever erase from the reality of history. The clause on Quebec as a distinct society in the Meech Lake Accord was designed to remedy this injustice, and was approved by all leading statesmen of Canada then in power, and it was lawfully passed, yet it was treacherously sabotaged. There was then a rebirth of separatist feeling in Quebec. The government of Canada reacted by seeking judicial license in the form of a reference to crush dissent in Quebec, which only made things worse.

There was a need for a Magnum Concilium in Canada, and this need was answered by the judgment per curiam of the Supreme Court in *Reference on certain Questions concerning the Secession of Quebec from Canada,* [1998] 2 S. C. R. 217. Thus spoke the Queen's judges:

The people of Quebec may lawfully aspire for independence. And the people of Quebec, upon call of their elected government, have a constitutional right to a free and peaceable referendum at public expense on whether they wish to secede from Canada.

While the Constitution Acts of 1867-1982 do not contemplate a formal legal right of secession, if the people of Quebec should vote in a free and peaceable referendum by a clear majority in favor of a clear proposition for independence, neither the federal government nor the other provincial governments of Canada may, in keeping with constitutional principle, be indifferent to or obstruct their wish thus expressed, but, on the contrary, they would then have a constitutional duty to negotiate comprehensively and in good faith either to redress the grievances or to accommodate the independence of Quebec. The Supreme Court admonished the government of Canada not to ask again for judicial intervention, for it is the duty of the Queen's ministers to see justice done, nor would the judicial lions under the throne reward their failure to use diplomacy and statesmanship. By judicial understatement, the court advised the federal government in Ottawa that their hard line against Quebec, or plan B, was unconstitutional.

And lest the necessity of the highest level of diplomacy and statesmanship in such a situation not be fully appreciated, the Supreme Court cautioned that, if such negotiations were to fail, especially if it were to fail because of refusal by the government of Canada to negotiate, unilateral secession of Quebec from Canada against the forms of the fundamental law still might occur, and, even if not strictly legal, such a secession might in the end become a secession de facto, recognized by other nations of the earth, and become the basis of a new constitutional order.

Generally, under the law of nations, the government of a new country is deemed legitimate, without regard to how it came into being, if it has secured effective control over the territory governed, enjoys support of the population, and has established a civilized legal order.

If not a word was said about the Glorious Revolution, the Supreme Court of Canada could not have paid higher tribute to the constitutional custom which it established.

If not a word was said about the American Civil War, the Supreme Court of Canada could not have done more to reject the legacy of *Texas v. White,* 7 Wallace 700 (U. S. 1869).

The immediate effects of this judgment were to calm antagonisms which previously had threatened the federal Union, to dampen ardor for secession in Quebec, and to encourage political reconciliation between Anglo-Canada and Quebec. In provincial elections following shortly after the judgment, the separatist party formed the government of Quebec, but was given no mandate except to govern within the federal Union, for the federalist party actually won more popular votes across the Province. It soon became evident that, in the wake of the judgment, the people of Quebec were satisfied with the vindication of their rights, were firmly against another referendum on independence, and were ready to defend the federal Union.

Unfortunately, some political leaders are made bold by capricious success in public life, created not by their political merit or skill, but lack of effective opposition, or surrender to powerful interests, or demagoguery feeding on groundless fears. After their defeat in the reference on secession before the Supreme Court, such characters in the government of Canada brushed aside judicial admonitions not to their liking, and proceeded on another unnecessary, destructive, injudicious, and bellicose offensive against Quebec.

The government then in power introduced, passed, and secured royal sanction of unconstitutional legislation against Quebec, known as the "Clarity Act" or, more formally, the Statute of 48-49 Elizabeth II, Chapter 26 (2000).

The preamble to this Act begins by saying that there is no constitutional right of secession, and that separation from Canada can be effected only by constitutional amendment, which is what the attorney general of Canada had argued before the Supreme Court, but exactly the opposite of what the Supreme Court had held.

The Act then declares that, if the government of Quebec proposed a referendum on secession, the House of Commons would decide whether the proposition for independence were clear and whether the vote for independence were clear, stating further that a proposal for negotiations between Quebec and Canada for a new continental arrangement between the two countries before proceeding for independence would render a proposition unclear. Since negotiations for a new continental arrangement are necessary to maintain peace — Abraham Lincoln's refusal to meet with commissioners from the Confederate States led to the trouble over Fort Sumter —, this declaration is a recipe for disaster and a legal absurdity.

The Act states that, unless the House of Commons determines that a proposition and vote for independence are clear, the government of Canada will not be authorized to negotiate with the government of Quebec. This provision assumes that, not the people of Quebec, but the federal government has the sole right to determine whether Quebec might ever become independent. It is not unlike saying that James II alone had the right to determine whether William and Mary should rule England, or that George III alone had the right to determine whether American independence should be granted. The pretension is too absurd for serious discussion. It serves only to suggest that the government of Quebec might well proceed forthwith to independence because of refusal of the government of Canada to negotiate in good faith as required by the judgment of the Supreme Court.

The Act also states that, if the government of Canada were to negotiate, the question of what parts of Quebec should be absorbed into Canada would be on the table for discussion. The provision is a thinly disguised threat to take territory from Quebec, if she should attempt secession. To threaten the territorial integrity of a nation or state is a casus belli under the law of nations, and justifies the use of armed force to resist it.

Such a threat is outlawed by the second article of the United Nations Charter, and armed force to resist such a menace is allowed by the fifty-first article of the United Nations Charter. Planning to seize territory under these circumstances is a crime against peace under the sixth and seventh principles of the Charter of the Nuremberg Tribunal as affirmed by the General Assembly of the United Nations in 1946. The thrust of the judgment of the Supreme Court disallows such measures by the government of Canada.

The Clarity Act is, therefore, dangerous, irresponsible, and lawless.

And it was critical for the historical record that such an affront should be answered.

In the closing days of the 20th Century — only a few days before Christmas 2000 —, by legislation commonly called Bill 99 and formally codified as Chapter 46 of Quebec Laws of 2000, the National Assembly of Quebec answered the Clarity Act in a manner reminiscent of the Kentucky Resolutions and Virginia Resolutions of 1798. Freely rendered, Quebec's historic Bill 99 declares:

— That the National Assembly never approved the Constitution Act of 1982, and opposed its adoption;

— That in the Clarity Act the federal government has threatened the legitimacy and integrity of the national and democratic institutions of Quebec;

— That Quebec claims her rights, not as declared by the Clarity Act, but as acknowledged by the Supreme Court of Canada in 1998;

— That the people of Quebec alone have the inalienable right, free of any outside interference, including any act of the government of Canada or the dominion Parliament, to determine by proper referendum, and by majority vote, their political and legal status, and thus whether to remain united with Canada or to become an independent Nation;

— That the National Assembly of Quebec, and the government it forms, are sovereign, and have a liberal right to consent to or reject any law, treaty, or convention which affects their powers;

— That, by resolution of the National Assembly in 1985, the Indian nations are guaranteed their autonomy in the territory of Quebec;

— That French is the official language of Quebec, subject to the just rights of the minority speaking English; and

— That the territorial integrity of Quebec must be protected by, and may never be modified or diminished except with the consent of the National Assembly acting in behalf of, and upon due consultation with the people of the Province.

This historic statute was enacted in the city which had been the colonial capital of New France. The symbolism found in the wonderful old city of Quebec is striking.

Above the parliament building which houses the National Assembly is the provincial banner, which is patterned after the battle flag of the personal regiment of King Louis XIV of France. For Quebec is a French country with a French culture and heritage.

This beautiful flag displays upon a background of blue a white cross to signify the death of Christ, by which mankind has been redeemed. And superimposed in white upon each of the resulting four sections in blue is the fleur de lys or Easter lily to signify the resurrection of Christ, by which the future of mankind has been promised. For in the face of contemporary folly and secular decadence across Western civilization, Quebec remains a Christian nation and a religious people.

Upon the parliament building flies no red and white maple leaf flag of Canada. For Quebec is a free and sovereign nation, now federally united with Canada, but enjoying a right of secession acknowledged even by the Supreme Court.

Not far away from the parliament building, upon the Plains of Abraham, are the headquarters of the famous 22nd Royal Canadian Infantry Regiment, which, with all the smartness and class of the guards at Buckingham Palace in London, marches in British redcoats and black bearskin busbies to orders given in French. "Le vingt-deuxième" signifies the friendship between the people of Quebec and the British Crown. All things considered, it has been a marvelous friendship, for the people of Quebec defended the British Crown in the American Revolution and the War of 1812, and the sovereignty of Quebec, including her free government and her right of secession, properly derive from the legal traditions which are embodied in the British Crown.

Quebec now enjoys the security of the Confederation, which is a thing of inestimable worth; but, if the Confederation should ever become dangerous to her future, she may become an independent Nation. If, on the other hand, her confederated neighbors understand the timeless truth which underlies her political situation, reconciliation will follow and Quebec will become finally united with them in friendship — "le bijou du Canada" as is sometimes said —, and Canada will become a light guiding all Nations in the 21st Century.

Why does the right of secession, frankly acknowledged, have the effect of strengthening and not weakening a federal Union? The answer was supplied by timeless words of Lord Acton when he spoke of the Union of Southern States formed in 1861:

> "When the Confederacy was established on the right of secession, the recognition of that right implied that there should never be occasion for its exercise. To say that particular contingencies shall be justify separation is the same thing as to say that the Confederate government is bound within certain limits, under certain conditions, and under certain laws. It is a distinct repudiation of the doctrine that the minority can enforce no rights, and the majority can commit no wrong. It is like passing from the dominion of an able despot into a constitutional kingdom."[20]

NOTES

EPILOGUE

1 - 1 Henderson's Stonewall Jackson at 94.

2 - 4 Encyclopedia of Canada at 166.

3 - The basic case for this view is well summarized in Webster's French Revolution at 3-36, and well elaborated in the pages following in this great work.

4 - A moving account of this terrible episode, in which there were five times the number of executions as occurred during the French Revolution, is given in Huddleston's France at 243-266.

5 - It is not correct to say that this limitation resulted from the Statute of Westminster 1931, 22 George V, Chapter 4. Section 4 of the Statute provided, "No Act of Parliament of the United Kingdom passed after the commencement of this Act shall extend, or be deemed to extend, to a Dominion, as part of the law of that Dominion, unless it is expressly declared in that Act that that Dominion has requested and consented to the enactment thereof." For, Section 7(1) of the Statute provided, "Nothing in this Act shall be deemed to apply to the repeal, amendment, or alteration of the British North America Acts, 1867 to 1930, or to any order, rule, or regulation thereunder." Section 7(1) was inserted to allow the operation of constitutional conventions to regulate amendments to the British North America Acts of 1867-1930. These constitutional conventions had already been established and were already operative, making Canada even then an independent nation, but united with Great Britain under one Crown.

6 - The constitutional convention prohibiting such modification was, however, denied and disregarded on highly dubious grounds in *Reference on an Objection to a Resolution to Amend the Constitution*, [1981] 1 S. C. R. 753. The constitutional convention in question had been unmistakably acknowledged by the Prime Minister of Canada on the House of Commons in 1960. As acknowledged in Parliament, an entrenched American-style bill of rights required the unanimous

consent of all provincial Legislatures, because the powers of them all were materially affected. Yet the Supreme Court of Canada, after laying out the historical facts proving the existence of the constitutional convention, and its requirement of unanimity, held that a substantial majority would be enough. The senior federalist statesman of Quebec, in a statement filed by the amicus curiae of Quebec with the Supreme Court of Canada in early 1998, truly observed that the decision was "hautement contestable" and "n'avait pas un fondement solide dans la tradition constitutionnelle du Canada." The gentlemen expressed the great weight of learned opinion in Quebec. The court lost nearly all its moral authority in Quebec, among separatists and federalists alike, as a result of that unfortunate decision.

7 - The dominion Parliament enacted an organic statute known as the Canadian Bill of Rights in 1960. This Act enumerated certain basic rights, and directed the courts to construe all acts of the dominion in Parliament so as not to abrogate, abridge, or infringe such rights, unless such acts expressly declared that they should be operative notwithstanding. In *The Queen v. Drybones,* [1970] S. C. R. 282, the Canadian Bill of Rights was read as a statutory directive to the courts that they should find laws of Canada irreconcilable with the rights enumerated to be null and void, unless the dominion Parliament had declared such laws operative notwithstanding. But the Canadian Bill of Rights was not entrenched, because it could be revised or repealed by a new act of the dominion Parliament. It is still on the books, but has fallen into disuse because it has been superseded by the Canadian Charter of Rights and Freedoms in the Constitution Act of 1982.

8 - The Supreme Court of Canada specifically held that Quebec never had a right by constitutionnal convention to veto the Canada Act of 1982, as appears in *Reference on an Objection to a Resolution to Amend the Constitution,* [1982] 2 S. C. R. 793. This judgment was really a corollary to the previous judgment which circumvented the constitutional convention requiring unity to facilitate adoption of the Canada Act of 1982: it was, therefore an unconvincing anticlimax, merely serving to confirm an illegitimate exercise of power against Quebec, and was never accepted in Quebec as a record of historical truth.

9 - The government of Quebec publishes all laws in French and English, and accepts all petitions and correspondence in French or English. Anybody may plead or testify in court, express any viewpoint, or engage in legislative or other public debate in either French or English. The rights of the English-speaking minority are even more extensive, especially in the education of children. None of these rights has ever been threatened by any legislation of the National Assembly. Yet in *Ford v. Attorney General of Quebec,* [1998] 2 S. C. R. 712, a statute enacted by the National Assembly requiring use of French in certain phases of commerce — a proper defensive measure to assure use of French — was struck down as unconstitutional on the feeble pretext that it violated "freedom of expression" guaranteed by the Canadian Charter. When the National Assembly responded to this excess of

judicial activism by invoking the notwithstanding clause in the Constitution Act of 1982, Anglo-Canada reacted with outrage, providing the opporunity used by the destructive faction which wrecked the Meech Lake Accord.

10 - An article by Michael Schneiderman, *The Positivism of Hugo Black v The Natural Law of Ivan Rand: A Study in Contrasting Judicial Philosophies,* 33 Sask. L. Rev. 267 (1968), well illustrates the kind of judicial greatness, grounded in natural law and legal tradition, which once characterized Canada.

11 - Several examples of such destructive and simplistic judicial activism under the Canadian Charter may be instanced: [1] The standing of a human fetus as a legal person in private litigation had long been recognized under the civil code of Quebec, traceable in civil law tradition to Justinian's Digest in the 6th Century, later reaffirmed by the common law, and upheld by the Supreme Court of Canada in *Montreal Tramways Co. v. Léveillé,* [1933] S. C. R. 456, then sustained in *Tremblay c. Daigle,* [1989] R. J. Q. 1735 (C. A. Quebec). Yet all of this development was judicially trashed by the Supreme Court of Canada in *Daigle v. Tremblay,* [1989] 2 S. C. R. 530, and *Winnepeg Child and Family Services v. Attorney General of Manitoba,* [1997] 3 S. C. R. 925: — these decisions deny the obvious, run against all previous legal standards, and derive from the judgment of the Supreme Court of Canada in *Morganthaler v. The Queen,* [1988] 1 S. C. R. 30, which reversed established and venerable precedent, ignoring unborn children as "an independent constitutional value," ostensibly out of deference to "liberty and security of person" in the Canadian Charter. The government of Quebec continues to discourage abortion by paying subventions to pregnant mothers who give birth. [2] Under the Quebec Charter of Human Rights and Freedoms, adopted in 1976, there is a guarantee of "freedom of religion" and of right of parents to "require that, in public educational establishments, their children receive a religious and moral education in conformity with their convictions." Accordingly, Catholic or Protestant Christianity is taught in public schools of Quebec when requested by parents. Nor can there be any doubt that, construed in light of the Preamble of the Constitution Act of 1867, the fundamental law of Canada is not characterized by a radical separation of church and state: — on the contrary, the Crown is worn by the head of the Church of England with which many Canadians are in communion. Moreover, the language in the Canadian Charter on freedom of religion was drawn from the Quebec Charter which, while protecting freedom of religion, also protects the right of parents to control the religious and moral education of their children in public schools. Yet, in *Canadian Civil Liberties Association v. Minister of Education,* 65 D. L. R. 4th 1 (C. A. Ontario 1990), "freedom of religion" in the Canadian Charter has been construed to prohibit teaching the Christian religion in the public schools of Ontario, even though dissenting parents were allowed by law to withdraw their children from such classes. [3] Another radical repudiation of legal tradition appears in *Attorney General of Ontario v. M. & H.,* [1999] 2. S. C. R. 3, which the majority, on a whimsical reading of the broad generalities of the

Canadian Charter, purported to modify the standard definition of marriage as a relationship between a man and a woman, as it has been universally accepted in all civilized countries of the world from the dawn of history.

12 - In 1995, the Canadian House of Commons passed a resolution that "Quebec is a distinct society," that "Quebec's distinct society includes its French-speaking majority, unique culture, and civil law tradition;" and that the House "undertake to be guided by this reality." This resolution probably established a constitutional convention. It serves at least to terminate the argument that it is somehow or other inappropriate that the people of Quebec should feel primary loyalty to their Province as the geopolitical center of the French Nation of North America, and should regard the Dominion merely as a useful instrument for managing continental business. In this respect, the people of Quebec have an attitude virtually identical to the attitude of the people in the Southern States before the American Civil War.

13 - In one of the most critical speeches in the Philadelphia Convention, Charles Pinckney argued that it would be an error to attempt recreation of the British House of Lords in the United States, precisely because the country did not have an ancient and indigenous aristocracy, and that, therefore, it would be necessary otherwise to construct the United States Senate, as appears in 5 Elliot's Debates 233-238, Tansill's Documents 267-274, 1 Ferrand's Records 397-404 (Madison's Notes, June 25, 1787).

14 - As appears in 1 Elliot's Debates 337-340, and 2 Thorpe's History 259-263.

15 - In Canada as in the United States, the judiciary applies the traditional rule, deriving from both the common law of England and the civil law of Rome, that clauses in pari materia must be read together so as to achieve utility for each clause and consistency between all such clauses in working toward a unified purpose. See, e. g., *Myran v. The Queen,* [1976] 2 S. C. R. 137, and *Adller v. Ontario,* [1996] 3 S. C. R. 609.

16 - The principle is traditionally expressed in the maxim, "Omnis ratihabitio retrotrahitur et mandato priori aequiparatur" — every ratification relates back and is equivalent to prior authority — which was cited in the opinion of Justice Robert Grier in the *Prize Cases,* 2 Black 635 at 671 (U. S. 1863). Grier misused the maxim to justify retroactive application of a declaration of war by Congress against seceding Southern States and thus to justify after the fact unconstitutional acts of executive war-making by President Abraham Lincoln. The maxim did not properly apply in that case, as the four dissenting justices explained, because Lincoln's blockade was unlawful when proclaimed, and, therefore, there was no inadvertent omission to be rectified by a corrective ratification done after the fact for good cause — "ratihabitio" in the proper sense embraced by the maxim.

17 - While the law is very different in the United States, this procedure is authorized by act of the dominion Parliament, and has been upheld on several occasions,

beginning with an opinion of the imperial *Privy Council in Attorney General of Ontario v. Attorney General of Canada,* [1912] A. C. 571. It is proper because, whatever the formal jurisdiction of royal courts to decide particular matters, it is characteristic of the British Constitution that the King may always ask his judges for legal opinions to guide him in governing his subjects, as appears in 1 Blackstone's Commentaries at 229.

18 - As appears in the remarks of Alexander Hamilton at the end of the 78th Federalist, Mentor Edition at 472.

19 - In the concluding pages of his "mémoire" submitted on December 29, 1997, as he detailed the events of the English Revolution of 1688-1689, the amicus curiae departed from his French, and gallantly quoted the classic English in 1 Blackstone's Commentaries at 245.

20 - From the lecture of John Dahlberg, First Baron Acton, before the Literary and Scientific Institution, Bridgenorth, England, on January 18, 1866, entitled "The Civil War in America: Its Place in History," in 1 Fears' Acton at 277.

TABLE OF SHORT TITLES

ADAMS' HUMAN EVENTS: Charles Adams, *When in the Course of Human Events: Arguing the Case for Southern Secession,* Rowman & Littlefield Publishers Inc., New York, 2000.

ANDERSON'S CALHOUN: John M. Anderson (ed), *Calhoun: Basic Documents,* Bald Eagle Press, State College, Pa., 1952.

ANNALS OF CONGRESS: *Annals of Congress,* Gales & Seaton, Washington D. C., 1834-1856, multiple volumes.

BALSIGER & SELIER'S LINCOLN CONSPIRACY: David Balsiger and Charles Selier, *The Lincoln Conspiracy,* Schick Sunn Classics, Los Angeles, 1977.

BELZ' WEBSTER-HAYNE DEBATE: Herman Belz (ed.), *The Webster-Hayne Debate on the Nature of the Union,* Selected Documents, Liberty Fund, Indianapolis, 2000.

BLACKSTONE'S COMMENTARIES: Sir William Blackstone, *Commentaries on the Laws of England,* Edward Christian, London, 1765, 4 books.

BRYCE'S HOLY ROMAN EMPIRE: James Bryce, *The Holy Roman Empire,* Macmillan Company, New York, 1911.

CAREN'S CIVIL WAR EXTRA: Eric C. Caren (ed.), *Civil War Extra: A Newspaper History of the Civil War,* Castle Books, Edison, N. J. 1999.

CHITTENDEN'S DEBATES: L. E. Chittenden (ed.), *Debates and Proceedings of the Peace Convention in Washington D. C.,* February 1861, Appelton ? Co., New York, 1864.

CHURCHILL'S HISTORY: Sir Winston Churchill, *A History of the English-Speaking Peoples*, Dodd, Mead & Co., New York, 1956, 4 volumes.

COKE'S INSTITUTES: Sir Edward Coke, *Institutes of the Laws of England,* 1797 edition published in London, 4 books.

COMMAGER'S DOCUMENTS: Henry Steele Commager (ed.), *Documents of American History,* Prentice Hall Inc., Englewood Cliffs N. J., 9th edition 1973, 2 volumes.

COMMINS' WASHINGTON: Saxe Commins (ed.), *The Basic Writings of George Washington,* Random House, New York, 1948.

COOKE'S REPORTS: Jacob Cooke (ed.). *The Reports of Alexander Hamilton,* Harper & Row, New York, 1964.

DABNEY'S DEFENCE OF VIRGINIA: R. L. Dabney, *A Defence of Virginia and the South,* E. J. Hale & Son, New York, 1867, reprinted by Sprinkle Publications, Harrisonburg, Va., 1991.

DAVIS' HONORABLE DEFEAT: William C. Davis, *An Honorable Defeat: the Last Days of the Confederate Government,* Harcourt Inc., New York, 2001.

DEAN'S CURSE OF THE FUNDING SYSTEM: Henry Clay Dean, *Crimes of the Civil War and Curse of the Funding System,* Innes & Co., Baltimore, 1868, reprinted by Crown Rights Book Co., Wiggins, Miss., 1998.

DEL MAR'S MONETARY CRIMES: Alexander Del Mar, *A History of Monetary Crimes,* 1899 edition reprinted by Omni Publications, Palmdale Calif., 1979.

DEL MAR'S MONEY IN AMERICA: Alexande Del Mar, *A History of Money in America,* 1899 edition reprinted by Omni Publications, Palmdale Calif., 1979.

DONALD'S PICTORIAL HISTORY: David Donald (ed.), *Divided We Fought: A Pictorial History of the War 1861-1865,* MacMillan & Co., New York, 1953.

DWIGHT'S HISTORY: Theodore Dwight, *History of the Hartford Convention,* Russell, Odiorne & Co., Boston, 1833, reprinted by DaCapo Press, New York, 1970. This volume includes the Journal and Report of the Hartford Convention.

ELLIOT'S DEBATES: Jonathan Elliot (ed.), *Debates on the Federal Constitution,* Lippencott & Co., Philadelphia, 2nd edition 1859, 5 volumes.

ELLIS' FOUNDING BROTHERS: Joseph J. Ellis, *Founding Brothers: the Revolutionary Generation,* Alfred A. Knopf, New York, 2000.

ENCYCLOPEDIA OF CANADA: W. Stewart Wallace (ed.), *The Encyclopedia of Canada,* University Associates of Canada, Toronto, 1940, 6 volumes.

FEARS' ACTON: J. Rufus Fears (ed.), Selected Writings of Lord Acton, *Liberty Fund, Indianapolis,* 1985, 3 volumes.

FERRAND'S RECORDS: Max Ferrand (ed.), *Records of the Federal Convention of 1787,* Yale University Press, New Haven, revised edition 1937, 4 volumes.

FORD'S JEFFERSON: Paul Leicester Ford (ed.), *The Works of Thomas Jefferson,* Putnam & Sons, New York, 1904-1905, 2 volumes.

GIBBON'S ROME: Edward Gibbon, *The History of the Decline and Fall of the Roman Empire,* the original edition of 1776-1788 with notes by H. H. Milman, Harper & Brothers, New York, 1882, 6 volumes.

HALLAM'S HISTORY: Henry Hallam, *The Constitutional History of England from the Accession of Henry VII to the Death of George II,* posthumous edition by Ward, Lock & Co., London, 1859.

HENDERSON'S STONEWALL JACKSON: G. F. R. Henderson, *Stonewall Jackson and the American Civil War,* Longmans, Green & Co., London, 1919, 2 volumes.

HENING'S STATUTES AT LARGE: William Hening (ed.), *Statutes at Large, Laws of Virginia 1619-1792,* George Cochron, Richmond, 1823, reprinted by the University Press of Virginia, 1969, 13 volumes.

HUDDLESTON'S FRANCE: Sisley Huddleston, *France: The Tragic Years, 1939-1947,* Americanist Library, Western Islands, Belmont, Mass., 1965.

HUME'S HISTORY: David Hume, *The History of England from the Invasion of Julius Caesar to the Revolution in 1688,* the revised 1778 edition republished by Liberty Fund, Indianapolis, 1983, 6 volumes.

HUNT'S MADISON: Gaillard Hunt (ed.), *The Writings of James Madison,* G. P. Putnam's Sons, 1900-1910, 9 volumes.

JAMESON'S CONVENTIONS: John Alexander Jameson, *A Treatise on Constitutional Conventions,* Callahan & Co., Chicago, 4th edition 1887.

JOHNSON & BUEL'S BATTLES: Robert Underwood Johnson and Clarence Clough Buel (eds.), *Battles and Leaders of the Civil War,* Thomas Yoseloff, New York, 1956, 4 volumes.

JOHNSON'S JAY: Henry P. Johnson (ed.), *Correspondence and Public Papers of John Jay,* G. P. Putnam's Sons, New York, 1893-1893, 4 volumes.

KENNEDY'S PROFILES: John F. Kennedy, *Profiles in Courage,* Harper & Brothers, New York, 1956, republished by Pocket Books Inc., New York, 1957-1959.

KENNEYS' SOUTH WAS RIGHT: James Ronald Kennedy and Walter Donald Kennedy, *The South Was Right,* Pelican Publishing Co., Gretna, La. 1994.

KOCH & PEDEN'S JEFFERSON: Adrienne Koch and William Peden (eds.), *The Life and Selected Writings of Thomas Jefferson,* Random House, New York, 1944.

LABAREE'S FRANKLIN: Leonard W. Labaree (ed.), *The Papers of Benjamin Franklin,* Yale University Press, New Haven, 1959 and later years, multiple volumes.

LINDBERGH'S MONEY TRUST: Charles A. Lindbergh Sr., *Banking and Currency, and the Money Trust,* National Capital Press, Washington D. C., 1913.

MACAULEY'S HISTORY: Lord Thomas Babinton Macauley, *The History of England from the Accession of James II,* Porter & Oakes, Philadelphia, 1867.

MAITLAND'S HISTORY: F. W. Maitland, *The Constitutional History of England,* Cambridge University Press, 1908 edition reprinted in 1968.

MARSHALL'S WASHINGTON: John Marshall, *The Life of George Washington,* revised edition republished by William H. Wise & Co., 1925, 5 volumes.

McKITRICK'S SLAVERY DEFENDED: Eric L. McKitrick (ed.), *Slavery Defended: the Views of the Old South,* Prentice Hall Inc., Englewood Cliffs N. J., 1963.

KIRK'S RANDOLPH: Russell Kirk, John Randolph of Roanoke, *A Study in American Politics,* Liberty Fund, Indianapolis, 4th edition 1997.

MELLON'S EARLY VIEWS: Matthew T. Mellon, *Early American Views on Negro Slavery,* New American Library, New York, 1969.

MENTOR EDITION: Clinton Rossiter (ed.), *The Federalist Papers, Alexander Hamilton,* James Madison, John Jay, New American Library, New York, 1961.

MORRIS' HISTORY: Richard B. Morris (ed.), *Encyclopedia of American History,* Harper & Brothers, New York, 1953, 2 volumes.

PETERSON'S SPEECHES: Houston Peterson (ed.), *A Treasury of the World's Great Speeches,* Simon & Schuster, New York, 1965.

PETRIE'S JACOBITE MOVEMENT: Sir Charles Petrie, *The Jacobite Movement,* Eyre & Spottiswoode, London, 1950, 2 volumes.

POLLARD'S LOST CAUSE: Edward Pollard, *The Lost Cause: A New Southern History of the War of the Confederates,* Treat & Co., New York, 1867.

RAWLE'S VIEW: William Rawle, *A View of the Constitution of the United States,* Philip Nicklin, Philadelphia, 2nd edition 1829, reprinted by DaCapo Press, New York, 1970.

RICHARD'S MESSAGES: James D. Richardson (ed.). *The Messages and Papers of the Presidents 1789-1897,* U. S. Gov't Printing Office, Washington D. C., 1896-1899, 10 Volumes.

ROBERT'S MONTICELLO: Joseph Clarke Roberts, *The Road from Monticello,* Duke University Press, Durham N. C., 1941. This volume includes an appendix containing the most important speeches in the debates of the Virginia House of Delegates on the emancipation of slaves, held in January 1832.

ROZWENC'S CIVIL WAR: Edwin C. Rozwenc (ed.), *Causes of the American Civil War,* Heath & Co., Boston, 1961.

ROZWENC'S SLAVERY AS A CAUSE: Edwin C. Rozwenc (ed.), *Slavery as a Cause of the Civil War,* Heath & Co., Boston, 1963.

STAPLE'S RHODE ISLAND: Judge William R. Staples, *Rhode Island and the Continental Congress 1765-1790,* Providence R. I., 1870, reprinted by DaCapo Press, New York, 1971.

SPEECHES AND DEBATES: *Political Speeches and Debates of Abraham Lincoln and Stephen Douglas,* Scott, Foresman & Co., Chicago, 1896.

STATE PAPERS: *State Papers on Nullification,* collected and published on order of the General Court of Massachusetts, Boston, 1833, reprinted by DaCapo Press, New York, 1970.

STEPHENS' RECOLLECTIONS: Myrtha Lockett Avary (ed.), *Recollections of Alexander H. Stephens, His Diary When a Prisoner in Fort Warren, Boston Harbor, 1865,* etc., Doubleday, Page & Co., 1910.

STEPHEN'S VIEW: Alexander H. Stephens, *A Constitutional View of the Late War Between the States,* National Publishing Co., Philadelphia 1868-1870, 2 volumes.

THOMAS' SLAVERY ATTACKED: John L. Thomas (ed.), *Slavery Attacked: the Abolitionist Crusade,* Prentice Hall Inc., Englewood Cliffs N. J., 1965.

THORPE'S HISTORY: Francis Newton Thorpe, *The Constitutional History of the United States,* Callahan & Co., 1901, reprinted by DaCapo Press 1970.

TIMES ATLAS: Geoffrey Barraclough (ed.), *The Times Atlas of World History,* Hammond Inc., Maplewood N. J., 3rd edition by Norman Stone, 1989.

TREFOUSSE'S BACKGROUND: Hans L. Trefousse (ed.), *Background for Radical Reconstruction,* Selections from Congressional Hearings, Little, Brown & Co., Boston, 1970.

TUCKER'S BLACKSTONE: St. George Tucker (ed.), *Blackstone's Commentaries,* 1803 edition, reprinted by Augustus M. Kelley 1969, 5 volumes.

VAN TYNE'S WEBSTER: C. H. Van Tyne (ed.), *Letters of Daniel Webster,* McClure, Philips & Co., New York, 1902.

U. S. STATUTES AT LARGE: Richard Peters et al. (eds), *Public Statutes at Large of the United States,* Little, Brown & Co., 1848 and subsequent years, multiple volumes.

WEBSTER'S FRENCH REVOLUTION: Nesta Webster, *The French Revolution,* 1919 edition republished by Noontide Press, Costa Mesa Calif., 1988-1992.

WILSON'S CALHOUN: Clyde N. Wilson (ed.), *The Essential Calhoun,* Transaction Publishers, New Brunswick N. J., 1993.

INDEX

Additional Civil War and Southern History Books
from Pelican Publishing Company

DOUGLAS SOUTHALL FREEMAN
By David E. Johnson
"David Johnson's even-handed biography of Douglas Southall Freeman exactly limns an extraordinary man. The Doc, as we newsmen knew him, would be pleased."
—James J. Kilpatrick
Douglas Southall Freeman (1886-1953) remains one of the greatest historians of the Civil War. His monumental biographies, including *Lee's Lieutenants* and the Pulitzer Prize-winning *R. E. Lee*, combined intellectual fervor with meticulous research and a graceful prose style. He received a second, posthumous Pulitzer Prize for his six-volume study of George Washington, still the definitive work on the first president.
480 pp. 6 x 9 20 b/w photos Appendixes Notes Biblio. Index
ISBN: 1-58980-021-4 hc

THE SOUTH WAS RIGHT!
By James Ronald Kennedy and Walter Donald Kennedy
In this best-selling history, the Kennedy brothers debunk the prevalent myth that hundreds of thousands of Southern men went to war over slavery—an issue that affected only six percent of the population. Read this book and learn the truth: there was no shining Northern force fighting a moral battle for the sake of ending slavery; there was no oppressive Southern force fighting to preserve it; and after the South declared its independence, the Union ruthlessly invaded, leaving Southerners no choice but to defend themselves.
448 pp. 6 x 9 10th ptg. Illus. Photos Notes Biblio. Index
ISBN: 1-56554-024-7 hc Over 85,000 copies sold!

THE SOUTH WAS RIGHT! AUDIOCASSETTE
Narrated by James Ronald Kennedy and Walter Donald Kennedy
Tuckend Boxed 6 cassettes Running time: 12 hours
ISBN: 1-58980-040-0

WAS JEFFERSON DAVIS RIGHT?
By James Ronald Kennedy and Walter Donald Kennedy
A Selection of the Conservative Book Club
"Every American ought to read this brilliant new book by the Kennedy brothers, not because it vindicates the South, but because it explains why we have the problems we face today. Tom Jefferson and James Madison would give this book two thumbs up."
—Charley Reese, nationally syndicated columnist
368 pp. 6 x 9 2 illus. 23 photos Appendixes Notes Biblio. Index
ISBN: 1-56554-370-X pb

WHY NOT FREEDOM! America's Revolt Against Big Government
By James Ronald Kennedy and Walter Donald Kennedy
Describes how the American middle class has been abandoned by those who control the federal government.
208 pp. 6 x 9 Index
ISBN: 1-56554-152-9 hc

THE SOUTHERN NATION: The New Rise of the Old South
By R. Gordon Thornton
The definitive primer on Southern nationalism.
224 pp. 6 x 9 Appendixes
ISBN: 1-56554-697-0 hc

For a complete list of Pelican's titles, please visit our Web site www.pelicanpub.com
Readers may order on-line or toll free at 1-800-843-1724.

Additional Civil War and Southern History Books
from Pelican Publishing Company

GLORY AT A GALLOP: Tales of the Confederate Cavalry
By William R. Brooksher and David K. Snider
    "In Glory at a Gallop, *William R. Brooksher and David K. Snider probe the real stories behind the men who became legends.*" —William C. Davis
Here, in one informative and entertaining volume, are the facts about Jeb Stuart, Nathan Bedford Forrest, Wade Hampton, and many more. A selection of the Military Book Club.
280 pp. 6 x 9 Biblio. Index
ISBN: 1-58980-058-3 pb

THE CAVALRY BATTLE THAT SAVED THE UNION: Custer vs. Stuart at Gettysburg
By Paul D. Walker
American history might have been different if Jeb Stuart's cavalry had succeeded at Gettysburg. Instead, fate intervened in the form of George Armstrong Custer. The resulting battle, pitting two of America's most gifted military heroes against each other, decided the fate of the Civil War.
160 pp. 5½ x 8½ 7 b/w photos 4 maps Appendix Biblio. Index
ISBN: 1-58980-012-5 hc

THE BOMBARDMENT OF CHARLESTON: 1863-1865
By W. Chris Phelps
Union forces began bombarding Charleston during the summer of 1863 and pounded the city continuously until it was evacuated in February 1865. This was deliberate and wanton destruction of private property and persecution of the civilian population, a Union attempt to "make Charleston pay for her sins."
176 pp. 5½ x 8½ 5 illus. 12 b/w photos 7 maps
Notes Biblio. Index 2nd ed.; First Pelican ed.
ISBN: 1-58980-028-1 pb

Michael Andrew Grissom, who has devoted his career to "the business of being Southern," writes about preserving the South's unique history and heritage.

WHEN THE SOUTH WAS SOUTHERN
By Michael Andrew Grissom
A collection of photographs, postcards, and tintypes, this book does for the lost South what Walker Evans and James Agee's book did for the Great Depression—reveal its haunting beauty undeniably.
400 pp. 6 x 9 Photos Index 2nd ptg.
ISBN: 1-56554-092-1 hc

SOUTHERN BY THE GRACE OF GOD
By Michael Andrew Grissom
The author has gathered together elements of Southern heritage and gives a short course in its splendid legacy. It could be called a "handbook for Southerners."
592 pp. 6 x 9 Photos Biblio. Index 10th ptg.
ISBN: 0-88289-761-6 hc

For a complete list of Pelican's titles, please visit our Web site www.pelicanpub.com
Readers may order on-line or toll free at 1-800-843-1724.

Additional Civil War and Southern History Books
from Pelican Publishing Company

THE SOUTH IN THE BUILDING OF THE NATION
In 1900 there was a general agreement among Southerners on the need for a comprehensive history of the Southern states. It had been and was a nation, sharing beliefs, traditions, and culture. This is a record of the South's part in the making of the American nation. It portrays the character, the genius, the achievements, and the progress in the life of the Southern people.

THE SOUTH IN THE BUILDING OF THE NATION, Volumes 1-12
ISBN: 1-58980-099-0

VOLUME I: The History of the Southern States
664 pp. 6 x 9 ISBN: 1-56554-951-1 pb

VOLUME II: The Political History
636 pp. 6 x 9 ISBN: 1-56554-952-X pb

VOLUME III: The Economic History
544 pp. 6 x 9 ISBN: 1-56554-953-8 pb

VOLUME IV: Political History of the Southern States
676 pp. 6 x 9 20 b/w photos 6 maps 3 illus. ISBN: 1-56554-954-6 pb

VOLUME V: Southern Economic History 1607-1865
592 pp. 6 x 9 17 b/w photos 1 illus. ISBN: 1-56554-955-7 pb

VOLUME VI: Southern Economic History 1865-1909
730 pp. 6 x 9 29 b/w photos 4 illus. ISBN: 1-56554-956-2 pb

VOLUME VII: History of the Literary and Intellectual Life of the Southern States
672 pp. 6 x 9 5 b/w photos 11 illus. ISBN: 1-56554-957-0 pb

VOLUME VIII: History of Southern Fiction
564 pp. 6 x 9 7 b/w photos 19 illus. ISBN: 1-56554-958-9 pb

VOLUME IX: History of Southern Oratory
586 pp. 6 x 9 31 illus. ISBN: 1-56554-959-7 pb

VOLUME X: History of the Social Life of the Southern States
826 pp. 6 x 9 13 b/w photos 13 illus. ISBN: 1-56554-960-0 pb

VOLUME XI: Biography
630 pp. 6 x 9 12 b/w photos 11 illus. ISBN: 1-56554-961-9 pb

VOLUME XII: Biography
650 pp. 6 x 9 10 b/w photos 11 illus. ISBN: 1-56554-962-7 pb

Additional Civil War and Southern History Books
from Pelican Publishing Company

PRIVATE OSBORNE, MASSACHUSETTS 23RD VOLUNTEERS
Burnside Expedition, Roanoke Island, Second Front Against Richmond
By Frederick M. Osborne
Edited by Frank B. Marcotte
In this remarkable collection of letters, sixteen-year-old Fred Osborne describes the privations and hardships of camp life, as well as its excitement and camaraderie.
304 pp. 6 x 9 15 b/w photos 37 illus. 22 maps Notes Biblio. Index
ISBN: 1-56554-965-1 pb

ANDERSONVILLE: The Southern Perspective
Edited by J. H. Segars
While there has been much written about Andersonville, this book presents seldom-seen documentation from Confederates familiar with the camp, as well as discussions by contemporary historians.
208 pp. 6 x 9 28 b/w photos 11 illus. 5 maps Notes Biblio.
ISBN: 1-56554-936-8 pb

BLACK CONFEDERATES
Compiled and edited by Charles Kelly Barrow, J. H. Segars, and R. B. Rosenburg
Modern historians cannot afford to ignore the efforts of black Americans on the side of the Confederacy, as this seemingly contradictory behavior reveals and underscores the terrible complexity of the Civil War.
208 pp. 6 x 9 34 b/w photos 4 illus. Notes Biblio. Index
ISBN: 1-56554-937-6 pb

These three novels, known as the "Trilogy of Reconstruction," inspired D. W. Griffith's cinema classic, *The Birth of a Nation*:

THE LEOPARD'S SPOTS: A Romance of the White Man's Burden—1865-1900
By Thomas Dixon, Jr.
Illustrated by C. D. Williams
Set in post-Civil War North Carolina, this novel by famed Southern author Thomas Dixon, Jr., tells of the pain of surrender and the struggle to rebuild and re-create a new identity for the South.
481 pp. 5 x 8 8 illus.
ISBN: 1-56554-981-3 pb (F)

THE TRAITOR
By Thomas Dixon, Jr.
Trapped between feuding Klan members and carpetbaggers who are out to destroy his life, Southern aristocrat John Graham must fight to keep the honor of his family and his nation.
352 pp. 5 x 8 3 illus.
ISBN: 1-56554-980-5 pb (F)

THE CLANSMAN
By Thomas Dixon, Jr.
Illustrated with scenes from *The Birth of a Nation*
Faced with a total breakdown of law and order after the Civil War, some Southern leaders called upon the spirits of their ancestors, the clansmen of Old Scotland, and formed the Ku Klux Klan.
400 pp. 5 x 8 8 photos
ISBN: 1-58980-010-9 pb (F)

For a complete list of Pelican's titles, please visit our Web site www.pelicanpub.com
Readers may order on-line or toll free at 1-800-843-1724.